379C

The Critic is Artist
The Intentionality of Art

Contemporary American Art Critics, No. 2

Donald Kuspit, Series Editor
Professor of Art History
State University of New York at Stony Brook

The Critic is Artist
The Intentionality of Art

by
Donald Kuspit

UMI RESEARCH PRESS
Ann Arbor, Michigan

Produced and distributed by
UMI Research Press
an imprint of
University Microfilms International
Ann Arbor, Michigan 48106

Library of Congress Cataloging in Publication Data

Kuspit, Donald B. (Donald Burton), 1935-
   The critic is artist.

   (Contemporary American art critics ; no. 2)
   Includes index.
   1. Art—Psychology. 2. Creation (Literary, Artistic, etc.)
3. Art, Modern—19th century. 4. Art, Modern—20th century.
I. Title. II. Series.

N71.K85 1984   701'.1'5   83-24099
ISBN 0-8357-1532-9

To my editors, the alternate critics, and to Judith and my friends who have shown me the possibility of going beyond criticism

Contents

Foreword

This series offers a selection of the writings of master art critics. It does so on the basis of a proven track record. Lawrence Alloway, Joseph Masheck, and Robert Pincus-Witten are important not only for their sophisticated treatment of complex art, but for the independence of their point of view, and their self-consciousness about it. They have all thought deeply about the nature and practice of art criticism. Working within the limiting format of journalistic articles, they have all managed to expand the conception of criticism beyond that of journalistic reporting. That may have been their model, but they transcend it through their intellectuality. One cannot help thinking of Oscar Wilde's sense of the anti-intellectualism that pervades the relationship to art, and that indeed is prevalent in society. These critics have forged a solid, non-ideological, undogmatic intellectual criticism which shames conventional reporting of "newsworthy" art, promotional reporting of the artist stars of the moment. They offer us not hagiography, but analysis, functioning to sting us into consciousness. Even though they deal with the new, and can even be said to be obsessed with it, they never give in to sensationalism and parochial partisanship. They are passionate, but they also have the reserve and caution of reason. They reason hard to prove their points, rather than give in to opinionation. They are the important critical minds of our day, and their work will last beyond it. Indeed, their conceptions have become the means by which art history assimilates the art they deal with, showing that art criticism at its best is the innovative cutting edge of art history. They show that art history can be a challenging intellectual adventure, as well as an account of documents and objects.

My prefaces were written without consultation with the critic in question. Each preface is my critical interpretation of his work, trying at once to give a conceptual overview of it as well as raise issues about it, continuing the dialogue it began. The only way to be in good faith with criticism is to continue to be critical. For what is finally at stake in all this writing is the survival of the critical spirit.

Donald Kuspit
New York, New York
October 1983

Preface

Few men have the divine grace of cosmopolitanism in its entirety; but all can acquire it in different degrees. The best endowed in this respect are those solitary wanderers who have lived for years in the heart of forests, in the midst of illimitable prairies, with no other companion but their gun—contemplating, dissecting, writing. No scholastic veil, no university paradox, no academic utopia has intervened between them and the complex truth. They know the admirable, eternal and inevitable relationship between form and function. Such people do not criticize; they contemplate, they study.

Charles Baudelaire, *The Exposition Universelle, 1855*

Like all my friends I have tried more than once to lock myself up within a system in order to preach there at my ease. But a system is a kind of damnation which forces one to a perpetual recantation; it is always necessary to be inventing a new one, and the drudgery involved is a cruel punishment.

Charles Baudelaire, *The Exposition Universelle, 1855*

As a rule, the critics ... are far more cultured than the people whose work they are called upon to review. This is, indeed, what one would expect, for criticism demands infinitely more cultivation than creation does.

Oscar Wilde, *The Critic as Artist*

It used to be that one could think of "the critic as artist," if not as an actual artist. Now it is inevitable that one acknowledge, however reluctantly—for both critic and artist—that "the critic is artist," in the fullest sense that the eroding idea of "artist" retains. All the weight of meaning in the formula of their relationship is now on the critic rather than the artist. The balance has tilted to the critic, although there may be no critic to take the opportunity it affords. It is harder to know what it is to be a critic, and to be one, than to know what it is to be an artist and to be one. The majority of artists tend towards one-dimensionality—towards a set of operations which close down the concept of art they articulate in a style. The critic separates the stylistic operations from the concept to recover the question the concept represents, the painfully uncertain meaning and use of art that the concept embodies. The critic does not accept the anodyne of style as the destiny of art, and he refuses to endorse the established modes of discourse that aim to institutionalize a dominant system of style. Unlike the artist, he does not look for a place in the sun of the existing order of art. Unlike the artist, he does not totally identify with art. He identifies also with the dialectic of ideas from which art emerges and to which it returns. Today, the meaning of criticality has become more uncertain than the meaning of artistry; but this is perhaps the discovery of what has always been the case, which is why criticism and self-criticism have been thought of as the core of art in modern times, its risky means of advance.

The true critic (not any journalistic reviewer, casual art writer, hack observer, poetic dilettante, disillusioned art historian tempted by living art as if by forbidden fruit) is as creative and imaginative as the true artist, and must be if art is to survive its own making and immediate history, its marketability and entertainment value. Baudelaire suggests why this is so. "Nothing is sweeter," he writes, "than to admire, and nothing more disagreeable than to criticize." But criticize we must because there is little to admire unconditionally. There is no art today that reduces one to dumb beholding, and, more importantly, one no longer wants to be reduced to a passive, awe-struck beholder, mired in the ineffable. One no longer wants to give up critical dialogue with the work—and one realizes there has never been any work of art that demands that one do so, contrary to conventional expectations.

As Baudelaire wrote, and this continues to be true, there are many "artists who seek to astonish the public"—to be popular, if even by being the imitators of an imitator, but few who have "a power of expression and a richness of feeling which are the inevitable results of a deep imagination." "It is imagination that decomposes all creation, and with the raw materials accumulated and disposed in accordance with rules whose origins one cannot find save in the furthest depths of the soul, it creates a new world, it produces the sensation of newness." As such, "imagination is the queen of truth and the *possible* is one of the provinces of the truth. It has a positive relationship with the infinite." Today, there is much that is superficially imaginative—that mimics the depths of the soul it does not know, that creates a world that seems new because every world of art that generates fresh interest in the world and art as popularly conceived seems new—but little that "has a positive relationship with the infinite." There is little that proposes the infinite to us in order to free us from the finite; and it is our acceptance of the finite that is the source of what was for Baudelaire the greatest vice, "the vice of banality." There are many astonishing images in today's art, but few that are visionary. There is no image that seems more than the fragment of an incomplete perspective, that has validity beyond its immediate appearance, that is able to dominate reality.

Today art is constituted by a variety of partial systems of perception and conception loosely confederated into a pluralism that masquerades as an exhaustive totality. An academic cosmopolitanism determines art-making today, the pseudo-cosmopolitanism that comes with an illusory sense of the absolute abundance of past accomplishments, a sense of *déja vu* undermining any sense of inner necessity. The art that is made today seems a recapitulation of art that was made before. It is an art so overwhelmed by information about other art that it hardly knows what it means to be itself—hardly knows what it means to pursue an independent vision. "Ontogeny recapitulates phylogeny" is a standard formula of creative evolution; today it is the preferred formula. Ontogeny does not want to be anything other than phylogeny. The individual work does not want the responsibility of being more than a member of a family of similar works. It does not want to be critical of its own kind, discovering an alien identity, for it does not believe that individual identity has much meaning or weight in the familial world. Individual identity is intrusive upon togetherness, and worst, implies an alien critical vision of the world.

There are few artists who are willing to trust their individuality as a route to the infinite. They implicitly accept some kind of totalitarianization of the finite, whether of a finite ideology, or of a tradition, and the more short-lived or finite the tradition, the more it is a "tradition of the new," the more binding it is assumed to be. It is not simply that today's art stands on the shoulders of what is unthinkingly regarded, with mannered respect, as the "giant" art of the past, but that cancerous recognition of the past has spread throughout the present to neutralize almost all but the most "technical" possibilities. It is not simply that narcissism is *the* art ideology today, but that only those ideologies that promise closure and rest to consciousness, are accepted into the inner circle of artistic self-consciousness.

Today's art has only one reliable realm of operation, one unfailing source of inspiration—popular culture. Today all art is absorbed into transcendent popularity by reason of its reduction to information. Information is not merely the raw data of knowledge but a mentality, a coercive categorization of what is the case—the undialectical display of the known as absolutely dominating the knower. Inevitably, every alien art is popularized, thereby losing its significance, its separateness from the standard version of truth, its role as an intervention in the continuum of the obvious. It loses its utopian relation to unrealized possibility and to the truth, as well as its power to actualize possibility and thereby to de-actualize reality, thus proposing its infinite significance. *In nuce,* with popularity every significant art loses the cosmopolitanism that makes it a revelation of complex truth. Totalized by popularity, it becomes simple and finite to the point of becoming summary; it gains by becoming emblematic—a logo— but it loses the power to evoke what is latent and ultimate. It becomes one more deception in the service of totalitarian popularity, one more authority in a system that trivializes in the act of making absolute.

The articles in this book were written in the seventies, when sixties heroics was waning under the impact of a change in the social character of art. Simply put, art became popular. Even the most esoteric, elitist, intellectual, and illicit art became popular, and popular art came to be regarded as unexpectedly esoteric, fraught with major meaning. Pop art, calling attention to popular imagery as an important source of concepts as well as percepts—and reminding us that from Courbet on, artists turned to popular imagery for "vital" images—is partly responsible for this, but a larger, more general phenomenon is also responsible. To use Tönnies' distinction, the art world became less of a community and more of a society. From being introverted it became totally extroverted, no doubt with the help of the technology of communication, but also because it seemed a world of opportunity, in which standards were uncertain and success seemed so relative as to be almost unspecifiable, which gave all kinds of freebooters and opportunists delusions of grandeur. The shift from community to society is succinctly recorded in Ad Reinhardt's sense of the alternatives facing artists.

> Without a true academy, high ideals, rational standards, and a formal, hieratic, grand manner, we have only our overcrowded, ignoble profession.
> We are, with Jack Paar, 'for anything that catches on,' and though some scoff, some of us, with Liberace, 'laugh all the way to the bank,' and with Lawrence Welk, and his champagne music, 'We hope you like our show, folks.'

The community of the happy few, with its argumentive intimacy and its unwilling yet inescapably artistic role, did not become the hermetic core of the "true academy," but was dissolved in the world of entertainers. Artists became— some intentionally, many no doubt unintentionally—show people. Many of their stunts were dangerous—literally—to life if not clearly to art, but all were performed over the safety net of the popular culture, documented by the all-consuming, popularizing camera eye. Andy Warhol became the new model, displacing Jackson Pollock, who seemed obsolete, the hero of a closed system of art. The new open system, which Warhol represents, makes popular culture part of the art act—that is what makes it seem "open." Art must complete a circuit to be legitimate in this system, and since all art wittingly or unwittingly completes this circuit, all art is legitimate. One must begin with a popular source—which can be information about an unpopular style—and end before a popular audience, i.e., be communicated by the media. (The only ex-communication is not being visible in the media.) Between these two states of what is essentially the same thing, one is "purely" (selfishly) artistic—archly or self-consciously "stylish," i.e., obsessed with creating a new look. But every style or look is ultimately owned by the tradition of popularity that gives it visibility and makes it fashionable.

The bottom line of the art act, then, is popular culture, which makes a mockery of high art's mantle of alienation and obscurity. High art is swallowed whole by being reproduced, its literalness becoming part of the sensuous texture of popular culture. But fewer and fewer artists are concerned to be "high," i.e., dare to be "elevated" above the randomly popular (however perversely popular it may be to be elevated). Instead, the majority of artists connect with popular culture the way Antaeus connected with the earth, falling back on it to renew their strength. They fall back on its facile, overfamiliar codes of comprehension, find succor in its pseudo-clarification of the life world. Popular culture made the provincial art community a "cosmopolitan" society by raping and ransacking it; art was grateful for the chance to act in the big time, get on the "world stage." (The broken promise of popularity is that it gives access to a world historical level of significance.) By reducing every style to a readable language or an assimilable look—overobjectifying it as information—popular culture makes the masses "literate" and the artists "cosmopolitan." Popular culture makes every style easily available and thus, apparently, equally valid. It establishes a *practical* equivalence between styles, which, however uneasy, guarantees the over-all popularity of art. Art becomes a cornucopia of possibilities (none of which departs from what is actually the case), a set of received opinions passed off as imaginative options. It becomes a constellation of visual slogans in which creative ideas dead-end, and in which over-used styles masquerade as under-used visions. Art becomes a realm of stereotypes masquerading as individuals. In other words, when popularized (uncritically or unimaginatively appropriated), art becomes a false consciousness of art, and of life, popularly conceived. Art becomes a way of disguising the hollow core of popularity, the ennui and inertia that exist at its center. Popularized, art becomes one more method for hiding the emptiness of life lived according to popular standards, the emptiness generated by the totalitarianism of popularity itself.

Into this situation comes a critical spirit that is more certain of its means than its ends. It does not intend to return art to the lost paradise of heroic intention, or to discover an art that holds out for heroic individuality, since it knows that such art, whatever its intellectual difficulty and perceptual obscurity, is condemned to popularity sooner or later. It does not think that any art is heroic and independent because it is susceptible to aristocratic analysis by apparently comprehensive, generally valid concepts. It does not expect art to be profoundly imaginative, to have "a positive relationship with the infinite." This critical spirit demands such a relationship from itself—expects itself to be profoundly imaginative. It assumes the burden of imagination—the revaluation of possibility in an "impossible" world. It assumes that the necessity of imagination has been displaced from art to criticism. For art is bound to become popular and lose its imaginative power, but criticism can never be popular, and so has a unique opportunity to be imaginative. Criticism is inherently unpopular, which is its lucky fate. The popular culture will never attempt to appropriate authentic criticism; it would be taking a snake into its bosom. Critical thinking is irreconcilable with popular understanding, the one necessarily undermines the other. Critical thinking begins by questioning popular understanding, and comes into its own when it dispenses with the assumptions and categories of such understanding and thus is inherently deconstructive. Popular understanding is superficially constructive in that it attempts to organize belief in whatever it attends to but is ultimately destructive in that it shortcircuits a dynamic relationship with the objects it holds up for belief. Thus, to become popular is, paradoxically, to become inscrutable, which correlates with the uncritical relationship one has (by definition) with what is popular. Criticism is never more than a solitary wanderer in the mediagenic world created by popularity, looking for an alternate vision of the world. This criticism first finds in the unexpected collapse of appearances in the mediagenic world, the unexpected loss of face of the popular, necessitating turnover and inadvertently allowing critical intervention in it.

My criticism accepts the idea that the root of modern art is analytic deconstruction of art as well as of the life-world. But it assumes that, because of the essentially social reasons outlined above, criticism rather than art must, and is alone able to, carry this deconstructive approach forward, making it "conclusive." This approach is still the only approach to truth—the only way of recognizing its complexity. Criticism assumes the deconstructive approach is the only way of articulating the hidden possibility within banal actuality, of making boring finitude potential infinity—of gaining a sense of inner necessity in a world (of art and life) in which so much seems "unnecessary" and completely externalized. Deconstructive criticism is the only way of escaping the inertia of existence, of avoiding the petrifaction of spontaneity as it faces the standardized world, of protecting and justifying the surprise of intensity in a neutral world of information that tries to dissipate it. Applied to art, deconstructive criticism is not simply an arbitrary way of rescuing it from its own finished materiality and formality however sensuously exhilarating these may be, but a necessary means of making it consequential in terms other than those of its own limited intention. Deconstructive criticism shows art that it can be itself only by being more than itself—primordial and visionary in a way that at first glance seems alien to being art.

In general, modernity denies any presumption of truth, regarding all imagination as an exaggeration of the given in the name of a false comprehension, all vision as a falsification of the ordinary. Deconstructive criticism is a response to the condition of modernity, arising out of its own assumptions and expectations. Imaginative deconstruction does not assume that the possibilities it finds exist in fact—that they complete the "truth." It is as doubtful of itself as it is of the ordinary—as ironical with itself as it is with the popular art it deals with. It does not think of itself as verifiable—nor does it think of itself as speculative. Rather, it sees criticality as the only means of operation in a world that thinks being popular is the end of every enterprise. Free of the consuming desire for popularity, it salvages art from its own popularity, showing it to have a power of its own, independent of its popularity, and the authority that supposedly confers on it. This, of course, is the power of the deconstruction itself.

The methods of deconstructive criticism are phenomenological and dialectical. The epoché, involving suspension of belief in art in order to recover its intentionality, and the dialectic, with its sense of the contradictoriness that structures intentionality, taken together become the cunning of critical reason, the strategies of a wandering criticism. Phenomenological reduction teaches us that one should expect nothing from art, but see what art seems to expect of one. Dialectic awareness teaches us that art is an unresolved unity of opposites that proposes a synthesis of vision but always retains an aura of self-negation and world negation. In general, while noncommittal to any particular art, dialectical phenomenology looks for art which raises critical problems, particularly those involving the relationship between form and function. That is, it looks for an art whose intentionality appears unfocused or incompletely focused—self-contradictory and thus charged with imaginative potential. The self-contradiction of such art opens a vista on infinity, i.e., opens new possibilities of art as well as of critical comprehension of the life-world. Deconstructive criticism arises when passionate, partisan criticism—once urged by Baudelaire—no longer makes sense, i.e., when no art seems absolutely convincing or generally valid, and so worth fighting for. All one can hope to find today is a popular art that is at odds with its own imaginative potential. Deconstructive criticism articulates this potential by its own imaginative methods, i.e., by its contradiction of the art to which it is tentatively committed, by its refusal to believe in even the most believable art.

The deconstructive method of criticism, utilizing phenomenological and dialectical methods of understanding in an uncertain synthesis—an uncertain vision of understanding—renews the work of art's indifference to analysis, enigmatic originality, and surprise. The existence of the work once again resists and contradicts our own existence, thereby illuminating it. There is an obvious paradox here—one that arises spontaneously in the course of imaginative deconstruction of finite art. The discovery of possible significance that might contradict or at least seriously depart from the apparent actuality of the art makes it "difficult" in a way that restricted attention to its obvious significance never could. And yet one never knows if that difficulty, evoking a sense of the limitlessness of the art, is real or not, which helps make the art surprising, and at the same time legitimate. Imaginative deconstruction sets itself the task of finding a profundity that undermines popularity—the depth that is beyond the popular appearance of the art. But since this depth is unpopular and uncertain, and thus not really actual, it remains in a kind of limbo with respect to the art, an "attribute" that is in paradoxical relationship to the art, an imaginative possibility of it.

This state of affairs serves the art well, for it restores the enchantment the art lost when it became popular and banal, acceptable and credible. This enchantment is no doubt different in kind and quality from the enchantment the work had when it was novel. Nonetheless, it shows us the work as once again intensely itself, in a way it no longer can be when it is popular. It is only by developing an unpopular consciousness of the work of art—by deliberately de-popularizing it—that one can recover it in its pre-theoretical, charged state, vital to the world yet centered in itself. Today only the exaggerations of theory can give us the originally untheoretical work of art, the innocent originality of truly imaginative art.

Baudelaire once wrote that opium, and the best art, worked "upon the senses . . . to invest the whole of nature with a supernatural intensity of interest, which gives to every object a deeper, a more willful, a more despotic meaning." Deconstructive criticism is the art which imaginatively works upon art—and as such is a "meta-art"—to invest it with a supernatural intensity of interest, giving it a deeper, more willful, more despotic meaning. Through this imaginative work the object of art loses popularity and becomes one of those "miraculous moments—veritable feast-days of the brain—when the senses are keener and sensations more ringing." Perhaps unfortunately, the way to significant sense experience these days, when every art desires to be popular and sensational, is through theory. Its deconstructive paradoxes, ironical tensions, and ominous meanings disorder our conventional sense of the work of art, changing our sense experience of it. We are sensitive to it as potentially infinite in implication, rich beyond its surface richness, so that it seems an avenue of approach to a "sense" of infinity. Today art becomes an "appetizing" opium when it is critically deconstructed, which renews its role as a critique of conventional sensing and sense. Such a deconstruction is not just a matter of interpretation, but of making everything related to the experience of art "critical" and infinite.

By subsuming art, criticism becomes not simply "a phenomenon of the will acting upon the imagination," but a phenomenon of will dominating and determining the imagination. Criticism takes more risks than art, for it subsumes art's imagination in its own deconstructive imagination, which moves even more deliberately towards an uncertain infinity. Paradoxically, this gives criticism more impact and import than art, for it indicates that criticism generates a more dynamic sense of relevance than art—extends imagination into realms of relevance unimaginable to the art it addresses.

Acknowledgments

I would like to thank the editors of *Artforum, Art in America,* and *Arts Magazine* for permission to reprint, in slightly amended form, the articles listed below which originally appeared in their magazines. The editors of *Main Currents in Modern Thought* and *Social Research* also kindly gave permission for republication.

I would particularly like to thank Julia Ballerini for her thoughtful help editing the manuscript.

Chapter	Publication
1.	*Artforum,* January 1974.
2.	*Journal of the British Society of Phenomenology,* 1973, Vol. 4, pp. 123-138.
3.	*Social Research,* Spring 1978, Vol. 45, #1.
4.	*Artforum,* September 1977.
5.	*Artforum,* October 1980.
6.	*Arts Magazine,* 53: 113-17, February 1979.
7.	*Art Criticism,* Spring 1979.
8.	*Art Journal,* 1970, Vol. 29, pp. 430-437.
9.	*Art Journal,* Winter 1974-1975.
10.	*Artforum,* June 1974.
11.	*Arts Magazine,* 53: 125-7, March 1979.

12.   *Arts Magazine,* 54: 116-19, March 1980.

13.   *Artforum,* May 1977.

14.   *Arts Magazine,* 52: 120-5, March 1978.

15.   *Artforum,* October 1979.

16.   *Art in America,* May-June 1979.

17.   *Artforum,* January 1981.

18.   *Main Currents of Modern Thought,* 1972, Vol. 29, pp. 21-27.

19.   *Arts Magazine,* 52: 118-24, April 1978.

20.   *Art in America,* January-February 1976.

21.   *Art in America,* July-August 1976.

22.   *Art in America,* September-October 1977.

23.   *Arts Magazine,* 55: 124-9, November 1980.

24.   *Artforum,* Summer 1975.

25.   *Artforum,* May 1981.

26.   *Art in America,* May 1980.

27.   *Artforum,* April 1983.

28.   *Arts Magazine,* 54: 124-6, November 1979.

29.   *Art Criticism,* Spring 1981.

Part I

A Phenomenological Approach to Artistic Intention

The approach is tripartite, each part a stage transcending its predecessor: (1) artistic intention as the matter-of-fact ground of art, in the same way in which, as Husserl describes it, the "foundation of naive-objective science" is taken for granted;[1] (2) the subjectivization of the perception of art through the deliberate introduction of a systematic doubt of the presumably self-evident objectivity of its ground resulting in a phenomenological reduction of art, which forces "the entrance" to a radical consciousness of art, to a critical consciousness of its foundation;[2] (3) the reviewing of artistic intention as "that *ultimate originality* which, once apparent, *apodictically masters* the will" to create art.[3] The naiveté of the Dadas, the frustrations of Max Kozloff in his essay on "Critical Schizophrenia and the Intentionalist Method," and the hybris of Barnett Newman will serve as exemplars of each stage.

    A brief word about phenomenology: it is premised on the intuition that all that is given is "intended," i.e., constituted, though not exclusively, by consciousness. Its aim is to uncover the constitutive consciousness of any phenomenon by transcending, through doubt, the "natural attitude" to it, which takes its experience naively and unquestioningly. Such doubt, epitomized by the epoché or phenomenological reduction, renders intuitable the characteristic constitutive consciousness as the meaning of the experience of the phenomenon.[4] Put another way, epoché grounds the transcendence which "guarantees a style of consciousness" which, in turn, guarantees a meaning to experience.[5] Ultimately, *"phenomenological disconnection"* or transcendental doubt is the self-reflexive activity of consciousness in pursuit of its own style of being, i.e., subjectivity in pursuit of its own essence.[6] The short-term justification for the phenomenological method of suspending naive involvement with things, or doubting the face value of their givenness, so as to take consciousness of them as a field of investigation in its own right, as a "region of Being" which can be formally known, is its analytic power in ontological uncovering. Such justification is, in this sense, the climax of a tradition of thinking about method formally beginning with the Platonic theory of contemplation, given new import by Cartesian doubt and the Copernican Revolution of Kant, and self-conscious sophistication and epitomization in Husserl's theory of intuition. The long-term justification for the phenomenological method is essentially humanistic: "The attempt to doubt everything has its place in the realm of our perfect freedom."[7]

Modernist art, from the time "Manet's paintings became the first Modernist ones by virtue of the frankness with which they declared the surfaces on which they were painted,"[8] i.e., from the time Manet turned our attention from the world of his art to the consciousness of his method, has an unwitting phenomenological import. Greenberg's sense of modernism as art's self-critical reduction of its medium to essentials is a first formulation of this import. It stops short of recognizing that art's attempt at self-definition—as impossible from within art as from without it[9]—implies its uncertainty about the nature of its own ground, i.e., its self-reflective awareness of its own doubtfulness. Greenberg's concentration on what is "unique to the nature of its medium" obscures the full import of this uncertainty by conceiving it to be an essentially quixotic quest for utopian purity, in the same sense in which modernist science is, from a phenomenological point of view, an impossible pursuit of precision.[10] Greenberg's quest for the grail of self-certainty fails not simply because it is false from the start, but because it is facile in its method. It handicaps the uncovering of uncertainty as a necessary if not sufficient condition for creation by giving art a historically readymade goal. In practice, purification of the medium amounts to an infinite regress of artistic form, until form becomes a tautology of the artistic object. As long as the tendency toward a tautologous self-definition of art is in force, the artistic object can be said to exist in a novel mode of natural givenness. The naiveté with which it is taken to be simply its own form amounts to a taboo to thinking about it, to reflecting on its ground rather than assuming, as Frank Stella puts it, that "what you see is what you see."[11] Thinking about it is to move from perceiving it to conceiving it, and not, as Stella thinks, categorically conceiving it in terms of the "old," "humanistic values,"[12] i.e., deliberately interpreting it in terms of an obsolete *Weltanschauung*. On the contrary, it is to reflect on it more radically. For, truly to think about the artistic object is to recognize that even to conceive it exclusively in terms of perceived forms is to put a naively a priori value on it. Thinking about the artistic object means to recognize that the immediate objectivity of its forms no more exhausts its meaning than the tendentious subjectivity which attributes values to it exhausts its experiential impact. Thinking about the artistic object means to recognize that no values can be assumed to be exclusively essential to art, i.e., to constitute it in and of themselves. Thinking about the artistic object means to take it without presuppositions, to doubt any kind of matter-of-fact meaning attributed to it, including properties without which it is thought to be incapable of existing.

Only such a thoroughgoing transcendence of conventional interpretive and formalist grounding of art can uncover the essential uncertainty with which it views itself. Modernist self-doubt, obscured as much by a humanist as a purist approach to art, is perhaps most obscured by a historical approach. For its combination of positivism with a doctrine of historical necessity precludes from the beginning, as absurd and gratuitous, any, as Duchamp puts it, "philosophical outlook" on art, any "notion of freedom" that might be found in it.[13] However, no matter how much art regards itself as "the kind of experience . . . not to be obtained from any other kind of activity," as an experience privileged to be "valuable [only] in its own right," it can never be self-validating, not only for reasons essential to its self-constitution, but because whatever it is ontologically, it is ontically constitutive of the life-world, like any other human experience. Thus Greenberg falsely defines modernist art because he ignores the issue of its world-signification. It may be that modernist art is not as conscious of its condition in the world as traditional art, nor as certain as to how it wishes to be experienced in general, let alone as a constituent of individual experience. This may explain the compulsive, not to speak of defensive, quality of its need to define itself, but such unconsciousness, or perhaps refusal of consciousness, if made into another presupposition explaining its stylistic involutedness, becomes another means of hindering the uncovering of its ultimate uncertainty.

Correlate with this immanent uncertainty, Leo Steinberg has uncovered the uncertainty—the "plight"—of art's public, much as, as will be shown, Kozloff has uncovered the uncertainty of art critics: "the shock of discomfort, or the bewilderment or the anger or the boredom which some people always feel, and all people sometimes feel, when confronted with an unfamiliar new style."[14] Steinberg mitigates this plight by showing that the implicit involvement of modernist art in the life-world can be made explicit by an investigation of values. However, in doing so Steinberg resists his own inclination to believe that the "destruction of values" he finds in modernist art is arbitrary. He acknowledges his inclination in his assertion that the reasons for the destruction are "rarely made clear," but then he all too quickly and categorically—and conventionally and fashionably—finds a reason why "modern art always projects itself into a twilight zone where no values are fixed" in "anxiety." And Steinberg takes such anxiety less as an existential structure, in the manner of Heidegger, than as a novel source of vital artistic experience. As the last pages of Steinberg's essay make clear, Cézanne's anxiety, as Picasso conceived it, is a blessing in disguise, for it energizes the viewer as well as the artist. Steinberg demonstrates that anxiety can be as useful a source of creativity for the critic as it is for the artist. How such anxiety might be constitutive of modernist self-doubt is uncertain in Steinberg, other than the fact that it makes the self-doubt self-evident.

In Greenberg and Steinberg what originate as investigatory gambits into modernist art culminate in elitist experiences of, respectively, its formal properties and its value implications. Modernist self-doubt—particularly pervasive in its avant-garde disguise of confidence[15]—is recognized but resolved, suffered but rationalized. There is a facile air about the way this is done in Greenberg and Steinberg—about the way purity and crisis of values are spoken of—which leads one to suspect that they are ritually avoiding[16] some aspect of it, in particular, the resentment, or as Max Scheler calls it, the ressentiment which is the most powerful manifestation of modernist self-doubt. It is this ressentiment, that has forced the discussion of the possibility of art in recent esthetics. Since its inception, New York art has been grounded on gesture, the fine art/popular culture continuum, information theory, and recently the photograph's view of reality. To the extent that art seems inaccessible at its root, if only through the sheer variety of grounds on which it is postulated, its existence per se becomes suspect, consciousness of it is tinged with doubt of its reality. This doubt need not have as its basis any desire to regress to an earlier sense of art, only a sense of immediate confusion as to the approach to contemporaneous art. No doubt experientially such variety and confusion indicate vitality and richness of possibilities. But from the perspective of a consciousness determined to be clear to itself, and so to be free in the face of things, including artistic objects, the variety is simply incoherence, naively pluralistic. This pluralism, which assumes that every artist, if not artistic object, has his own position, objectifies if not fetishizes uncertainty about the nature of the ground of art. From a Marxist point of view, the mutual exclusiveness of positions permeating the artistic plurality[17] indicates decadent bankruptcy, the loss of all dialectical direction. To conceive of plurality as comprehensiveness, to accept a totality without a unifying logic—and to use forced naiveté and deliberate indifference to disguise the assertion that unity is unnecessary—is for the Marxist to postulate the arbitrariness of art, an arbitrariness which is not grounded subjectively on anxiety, as for Steinberg, but objectively on bourgeois false consciousness of art, viz., its use "to flatten and harmonize (irreconcilable social) opposites."[18] In any case, the naiveté and indifference cannot be tolerated by the critic, giving way, as in Steinberg and Kozloff, to "anxiety," to an ambiguous "death wish" toward artists. The apparent arbitrariness of art, this side effect of ressentiment, increases the more art tries to be an autonomous form and is fought by a search for sincerity, in and of itself thought to be capable of transcending consciousness of uncertainty, if only by refusing to take the arbitrariness at face value, but rather as a sign of "need." The need for a self-grounding of art becomes self-evident, if not self-evidently realizable.

The problem does not stop there for the Marxist, who conceives that Alloway calls the art "network"[19] to be a system for the distribution of bourgeois art commodities, modeled on a general capitalistic system in that it is class-oriented, its goods relatively limited in number, and reproduced through the mass media, i.e., turned into an inferior product and marketed to less privileged classes in lieu of proper ownership. Thus, artistic plurality is an idealistic way of speaking of bourgeois commodities, disguising an ideology based on the principle of the "self-confirmation of the [art] commodity and its value."[20] The ontological way of approaching contemporary pluralism simply confirms the successful integration of recently produced artistic objects into the commodity market. The "plight" of the critic and public is no more than the lingering uncertainty of the consumer about the inherent value of the contemporary art commodity, an uncertainty conditioned by the fact that the supposedly inherent value which art must have if it is to be marketed successfully is usually determined by its appropriation through false consciousness, e.g., by being regarded as "universal," and achieving longevity, rather than, as in the case of most other commodities, by its immediate use and the work which made it.

Thus, from a phenomenological point of view, the art network's confirmation of the artistic object in its commodity value is another demonstration of modernist self-doubt and the modern spectator's self-doubt. So eager is he to overcome self-doubt in all its manifestations—and what better way than to give an ideological answer to it?—that he fetishizes the doubtful artistic object into a readily consumable commodity. Simply by conceiving it as a commodity he guarantees its certainty of being as well as its eventual appropriation. However, this bourgeois way of understanding the doubtful artistic object is the supremely arbitrary approach to it, and is indicative in the last analysis of a complete uncertainty about the nature of the artistic object. This uncertainty is so consummate it can as little be disguised as the creation of the art commodity for consumption can be denied. When the artistic object is explicitly declared or subtly allowed to be taken as the bourgeois commodity par excellence, then its inadequacy as art has become innate. The more completely it is taken as a commodity the less completely can it be taken as art, whatever that might mean. It has been so fetishized in compensation for the uncertainty with which it is experienced, as well as the gratuitousness on which it is thought to be grounded, that to preserve some sense of its significance a false essence is willingly if not willfully attributed to it. But this essence, its commodity value, is more easily transcended, if only because it is more obvious, than its form or its anxiety. For to conceive of art as the supreme commodity is to possess it so unequivocally, to experience it so completely as an ordinary object in a daily mode of being, that one is forced to doubt this kind of (bourgeois) experience of it, this kind of riskless taking of it, if one is to recognize its existence as art in any sense of the term.

I. The Natural Attitude to Artistic Intention

An illustration of the natural attitude to artistic intention, presupposing its self-evidence of meaning, can be found in Philip Leider's writing.

> The authority in Rosenberg's position rests on its fidelity to the intentions of the artists, and it is perhaps because so many artists felt that his essay did indeed express their intentions, and that so much of the interested public at the time felt that the essay had caught the sense of what the artists were about that it has become so much more well-known than the essay which is in many senses its antagonist, Clement Greenberg's 1955 "'American-Type' Painting." Underlying Greenberg's essay is a rather different set of assumptions. The intentions of the

artist have little enough to do with the situation in which they find themselves. Whatever their reasons for making paintings, they must begin with the state of abstract art as they find it. The future may or may not understand the "zeitgeist" of the 1940s and the '50s as Harold Rosenberg does, but it will certainly understand the main directions of 20th-century painting and the success or failure of the New York School, as any school, will depend on its relations to this direction.[21]

Apart from the issues raised by the comparison, to Leider the nature of "the intentions of the artists" is as transparent as "the situation in which they find themselves." These concepts are used in an implicitly Platonic way by Rosenberg and Greenberg, functioning formally to make given art intelligible. Both concepts are assumed a priori, and from them these critics deduce artistic objects and preform artistic experience. These concepts do not emerge from the open horizon of artistic experience, but from settled attitudes toward the artist and art history. Briefly, Rosenberg assumes that one can become an artist if one intends to be and Greenberg assumes that art history has a linear clarity which forces every artistic object into place, or discards as insignificant those that do not conform to this clarity.

Doubt about the validity of artistic intention as a source of art is exemplified by some artists themselves. Kaprow, for instance, explaining his use of the word "happenings," remarks:

It was merely a neutral word that was part of a title of one of my projected ideas in 1958-59....It conveys not only a neutral meaning of "event" or "occurrence," but it implies something unforeseen, something casual, perhaps—unintended, undirected.[22]

This unintentional intention has a narcissistic flavor, Kaprow refusing as it were to signify the meaning of his intention so that it cannot be appropriated. His intention, self-styled casualness, takes for granted his monadic insularity, and disguises not only his lack of artistic direction, but his refusal of it for the sake of his own self-sufficiency. The Dadas were expert disclaimers of artistic intention in order to appear impervious, impenetrable. Gabrielle Buffet-Picabia insists, if somewhat onesidedly, that Dada performances

were intended as nothing more than somewhat subversive amusements. I insist on the perfect gratuitousness of the "demonstrations," which learned historians have represented as conscious and meaningful—in actual fact these demonstrations issued spontaneously from the most trivial circumstances and gestures.[23]

This refusal, on ideological grounds, of consciousness and meaning makes use of a mythical spontaneity, a soi-disant irrationality, to obscure its deliberateness. There is no doubt that the Dadas made contact with a primordial irrationality, but there is some doubt that they were able to exploit its possibilities. Ostensibly, the Dada aim is to preserve vitality by remaining immediate, by intending nothing more than what can be immediately demonstrated. However, the quasi-innocence of this attitude is as unself-enlightened as the bourgeois solemnity it is designed to counteract. Its lack of seriousness is as matter-of-fact as bourgeois seriousness, which it may subvert, but which it cannot replace, for it lacks any self-knowledge on which to ground a new attitude, a presumably freer and more human intentionality.

The Dadas were not fighting the bourgeois, but the inevitable appropriation of artistic intention once it makes itself manifest in artistic objects. They refused to work at art so as to keep their artistic intention inviolate. They demonstrated spontaneously so as not to objectify deliberately, hoping thereby to preserve the experienced intensity of their intentions. But the demonstrations themselves become works, separating from the artist's experience of his own intentions, the naiveté with which he takes them, their naturalness to him. Buffet-Picabia, by insisting that others take the Dadas as they take themselves, is unwittingly insisting that others become artists, demonstrate their intentions without making them works in a world. Demonstrating with the Dadas, they will presumably discover their own spontaneity, cleansing their consciousness of its commitments to a serious, objectified world.

However, this spontaneity is self-ignorant to the extent it assumes that its manifestations can never be comprehended. The moment they appear, they acquire reality, however perplexing. However much it outruns its demonstration, the refusal to understand that artistic intention is still knowable the moment it demonstrates masks a deeper refusal to recognize the uncertainty of its ground, correlate with the uncertainty of its objectification. That is, a refusal to be pinned down to any specific intention implies that it is not certain that it has any autonomous and authentic intention. Dadaist spontaneity is simply the exteriorization of this subjective uncertainty, the objectification of the groundlessness or uncertainty of ground or simply the refusal to ground art. In Dadaism, artistic intention is unclear to itself, and so perpetually spontaneous, demonstrating, rather than working deliberately to control its inevitable objectification. However, Dadaism does not understand its own uncertainty, which is why it insists on the gratuitousness of its spontaneity and the triviality of its occasion, why it argues for an objective rather than subjective irrationality. It is also why the Dadaists succumbed to Surrealism, why Breton rather than Tzara carried the day. For the inevitable effect of unconsciousness of the ground of activity, of one's refusal to investigate one's involvements, to give them a meaning, is not only to dissipate the intention that grounded them, but to preconceive this intention. Breton dogmatically grounded Dadaist spontaneity on a Surrealist version of the unconscious, making the unconscious as autocratic as spontaneity was antiauthoritarian, as self-righteous and self-important as Dadaist spontaneity was casual and whimsical. The unconscious could be so dogmatically rigid because Dadaist spontaneity had never understood itself as a disguise of uncertainty. By ideologizing spontaneity the Dadas prepared the way for the Surrealists, who knew unconscious intention not only unequivocally but tyrannically.

The Dadas and Surrealists comprehended the nature of artistic intention only enough to keep themselves "creative," i.e., the ground, whether spontaneity or the unconscious, was taken for granted so long as it could keep them "demonstrating." As Goldwater remarks, Dadaist nihilism was more instrumental than fundamental,[24] or as Arp wrote, its spirit of negation was designed to ferment the future,[25] to gain entry into the promised land of creativity.[26] Its aim was, in a sense, conventional: to find a contemporary justification for creativity, rather than rely on traditional justifications. In this sense it cannot be said to be an investigation into the inherent nature of artistic intention, but simply another example of the anxious solipsism of artists concerned only to remain productively potent, perhaps most typified by Duchamp, whose notion that anything is art if an artist says it is[27] avoids such an investigation altogether. While Duchamp seemed intensely aware of the doubtfulness of the whole artistic experience and specifically of the uncertainty of the ground of art, as epitomized in his willingness to accept the judgment of history as to the value of given works,[28] in effect he offers an updated, more sophisticated version of a traditional conception of artistic intention, viz., creation *ex nihilo.* Much as Michelangelo's Adam awaits God's touch to be awakened to consciousness of his own life, so ordinary objects await Duchamp's attitude to them to be awakened to the fact that they are art. While substance must be given spirit by the divine artist, the conception of creation *ex nihilo* is ultimately arbitary, for it postulates no reason why the artist has spirit other than the assumption that he is divine. God seems to have created the world only to admire His handiwork, and Duchamp seems to have created art only to admire his intention to do so. But where God's creation issued in a world, Duchamp's issued narcissistically in his own attitude.

Thus, the Dadas circle back naively to artistic intention as the origin of art, postulating it as a necessary and almost sufficient condition for art. But they tell us nothing about it, simply pointing to it, to create a novel *non finito.* They "demonstrate" it but do not deliberately incarnate it, assuming thereby that it keeps its "integrity," and is never irrecoverable from its "objects." For the Dadas, artistic intention—the naive impulse to be artistic—is immortal and unconscious, while its objectification is immediate and transient. Any attempt to render it immortal, to work at it consciously, is for the Dadas to conceive art in a bourgeois way. Their desperate desire not to be bourgeois is the clue to the edge of uncertainty which taints and taunts their intentions, a clue which unfortunately they could not follow. In effect, they could not read the handwriting they themselves wrote on the wall in the temple of art.

II. The Epoché of Modernist Art

Max Kozloff, in his essay on "Critical Schizophrenia and the Intentionalist Method," attempts to follow the clue to the bitter end, to read the handwriting on the wall.[29] Unfortunately, in the end he believes its message is mistaken, and so misses the import of the fact that it exists in the first place. Unlike St. John who wrote the Apocalypse, Kozloff does not think that the message he, as an art critic, is forced to swallow by the "divine" works of art which communicate it, is finally all that bitter. Kozloff's importance to us lies in his having a more powerful grasp of artistic intention than the Dadas, although he fails to become fully conscious of it. Also, he is important because he is conscious of the uncertainty of modernist artistic intention, and because he ultimately does not know what to make of it. After attempting to formulate an intentionalist method, he regresses, as he acknowledges, to the conventional methods of formalist and evocative criticism. His failure is at the core of his value to us, but what is most important about his essay is its articulation of the experience of modernist art which led him to attempt to come to grips with its intentions.

Kozloff's experience has two aspects, on the one hand having to do with the character of contemporary criticism (mid-'60s), which, to say the least, he finds ambiguous; and another with the state of contemporary art, which he finds "provocative." As to contemporary criticism, there seem to be: "two streams: on one hand, faithfulness to the optical data, a fidelity both descriptive and analytic, and on the other, of evocative or poetic judgment, chafing to find 'content,' sometimes cued by visual fact, but not necessarily." Despite their mutual exclusiveness (an indication of their elitist or what Kozloff calls their moralistic character) they both have an "inability to see the 'otherness' of the work—that is, its distinctness as a product separate from their own systems or ideologies." This became troublesome when a "new art—Pop, and its various equivalents in abstraction," appeared, for the new style made it clear that "the then-going critical apparatus," equipped to analyze Abstract Expressionist art, was inadequate, or severely limited in its approach to the new art. But more directly to the point of Kozloff's search for an intentionalist method is his assertion:

> that the important relation in a work of art is not between two or more forms on a surface, but between itself as a complex event and the spectator. A paradox of abstractionist theory is that it imposes "apartness" on the work of art rather than allowing us to discover it personally for ourselves.

Frank Stella's work points up a further paradox of this "apartness." "But Stella demonstrates, I think, that the more reductionist the visual material, the more conceptual is its nature. Far from becoming physically provocative it becomes rhetorically provocative." However, Kozloff finds that his own rhetoric falls short of comprehending the conceptual aspects of such reductionist work, not because they are inherently difficult, but because they are protected, as it were, or almost hidden by what Kozloff calls a "Warholistic" attitude. Not only is this attitude designed to throw the critic off the scent of the art, but to invalidate any critical or conceptual approach to it, indeed, perhaps any deliberate and systematic approach to art. Warholism wishes to mute the full experiential implications of artistic experience, to prevent or at least neutralize the uncovering of any deeper implications, beyond the art itself. Above all, it insists that art be taken impersonally, in a sense trivializing the interaction between the art and the spectator. Warholism can be said to make the relationship between art and spectator as artificially naive as Dadaism made the attitude to artistic intention artificially naive. Kozloff identifies this "pervasive habit of painters and sculptors of suppressing moral values inherent in objects and sensations" with "antihumanism," and admits the inadequacy of conventional "art commentary," attuned to the artist's irrationality, to handle this new irrationalism. "If there was once a discomfort before all the immeasurable, intangible aspects of art, there is now an equal displeasure or reluctance to deal with an artistic dialectic that demands logical examination."

Kozloff comes to his abortive attempt to develop a "new (intentionalist) method in criticism" by way of response to the "antihumanist development" and "aggression by artists." The "intransigent avant-garde" can be overcome, not by an esthetically reactionary criticism which attempts to restore the traditional distinction between beauty and ugliness, long ago obscured if not obviated by modernism, but by a moralistically revolutionary criticism which attempts to restore the existential distinction between "the indifferent and committed," which has been blurred by Warholism. To recover this distinction—falsified by Kozloff from the start by being regarded as equivalent to the distinction between "good and bad," i.e., by being conceived not in terms of an existential search for an authentic artistic project but in terms of daily judgments of quality and value—Kozloff argues that: "what we are able to say about the processes and intentions of that work as they affect our experiences or change our world is more relevant, perhaps in the end more important, than our judgment of that work." This "dialectic" with artistic intention is: "the only natural (and perhaps the inevitable)—defense of the critic against the relatively amoral strategy of the artist."

Kozloff, however, has no clear way of determining "the processes and intentions," i.e., the implicit "moral" implications, of the work, and he is fully aware of the methodological objections to the search for intention, codified under the rubric "intentional fallacy," offered by Wimsatt and Beardsley in *The Verbal Icon*. He undertakes the search for intention more on emotional than intellectual grounds, partly accounting for his inability to understand the logic of intentionality: "the literary critics do not have an intransigent avant-garde and are not faced with a new kind of antihumanism in their field." Kozloff's formulation of intentionality is, to say the least, hesitant, and to say the most, totally inadequate. Kozloff acknowledges this, at the time of the reprinting of the essay in his anthology. He blames himself for disposing of "the notion of 'intention' . . . too readily . . . in view of its weighty position" in his essay but he dismisses it completely. He blames his failure on the inherent difficulties of the concept rather than on himself: "One rarely has the proper amount of 'evidence'—it is either too much or too little—to be satisfied with, or even to be at ease with, intentionalism as part of a critical method." For whatever reason,

Kozloff does well to dismiss his intentionalist method, for it amounts, as he writes, to no more than a way of "superseding formalist and evocative criticism, while feeling free to take advantage of both," and "in fact, becoming a compound of both." It is thus nothing in itself, but a bastard born of conventional methods. The furthest Kozloff goes toward a statement independent of formalist and evocative methods is the following:

> Essentially, though, what one does is to examine the physical execution of a work and all its complexities as they lead to some awareness of the organizing concept. And this in turn is based upon a visual response that constantly tests itself. The most useful way of seeing how this operates is by observing or examining perennial oppositions within works of art. How, for instance, does one determine whether what one sees are contrasts, deliberate oppositions, dramatic tensions, clever paradoxes, or just plain inconsistencies and contradictions? To ask this question—and I do not see how it can be avoided—is to inquire of intention.

Kozloff's question is to the point, but he finds no way of answering it, of determining intention, because he asks it of the work and not of himself. He expects the work to tell him whether "what one sees are contrasts, deliberate oppositions, dramatic tensions, clever paradoxes, or just plain inconsistencies and contradictions," but the import of Warholism is that the modernist work affords, in and of itself, no clues which could make such a distinction clear, and make it binding. This is because, as Kozloff notes, it is essentially a distinction between the committed and the indifferent, the deliberate and the arbitrary. The critic himself must make the distinction by determining his own commitment to the work, or more simply, because the "contrasts, deliberate oppositions, dramatic tensions, clever paradoxes, or just plain inconsistencies and contradictions" are part of "what one [he] sees." They are part of his style of seeing and his consciousness of art, signifying his intention toward it. Thus, the critic must become conscious of his own consciousness of art if he is to determine the commitment of its own consciousness of itself. Kozloff, in fact, is not searching for the work's "organizing concept" but his own, as Sontag puts it, "organizing sensibility."[30] The issue is not that the critic is threatened by Warholism as a critic, but that he is threatened, through his sensibility, as a self-identifiable integral human being. The Warhol work is amoral because it makes no appeal to a preconceived sensibility, and so to a sedimented identity—it makes no appeal to the spectator's own sense of his intentions. Kozloff is left in the lurch by Warhol works because, in fact, they have no clear "organizing concept or integrity," i.e., they exist precisely in terms of the uncertainties and ambiguities of Kozloff's question. Thus, they not only put the immediate burden of the work on the critic, but they force him back on himself, necessitate his becoming conscious of his attitude to the work, and perhaps of his fundamental attitude to art per se.

Kozloff errs in thinking Warholism amoral. It puts the spectator in the most "moral" position imaginable, one in which he can no longer take for granted that he is seeing and attending to "art" let alone that there is a unique logic—an unequivocal "organizing concept"—to its execution. It is possible that the Warhol artist is amoral toward himself in creating such a work, much as the Dadaist can be said to be amoral toward himself in insisting that he is creating no work. That is, both avoid confrontation with their own sensibility, both blind themselves to their own intentionality, perhaps their own uncertainty, by their deliberate indifference to the implications of their own "demonstrations." But the Warhol artist does the critic a moral and existential favor by radically forcing him back upon himself by forcing him back upon his intentional consciousness of art, by forcing him to determine what attitudes he brings to his seeing. Kozloff cannot sustain this radicality for long: he recommits himself to the standbys of everyday art criticism, viz., formalist and evocative methods. That is, he regresses to superficial self-consciousness and superficial consciousness of art, no longer taking either intentionally. At face value the work's form is indicative of its intention, and at face value the poetry evoked by the work adequately summarizes the dialectic between it and himself, between its "processes and intentions" and his own. In practice, historical awareness is essential to both methods, for history is the objective substitute for radical intentionality. In essence, Kozloff becomes as amoral as Warholism, because he refuses the search for his own intentionality, puts aside the self-encounter that the Warhol work provoked.

Formalist and evocative criticism can be justified, but not in any terms Kozloff offers. The formalist method of descriptive analysis is ultimately comprehensible not positivistically but in the context of an investigation of the "social physiognomy" of the work, as Adorno has shown.[31] The evocative method is ultimately comprehensible not as poetry but in the context of an investigation of the analogues which constitute the unreal object which the work is,[32] as well as in the context of an investigation of the kind of world implicitly projected by the work, as Sartre has shown.[33] Both methods investigate the work's world-signification, i.e., comprehend its intentionality as a kind of being-in-the-world. Kozloff does not touch upon this crucial intentionalist dimension to formalist and evocative criticism, which is in fact their core, but naively conceives them to be in effect the objective and subjective sides of the same artistic experience.

One reason Kozloff cannot formulate a truly intentionalist method is that he is obsessed with the artist's antihumanism; it becomes a stumbling block to any methodological originality. Kozloff does not recognize it as a form of ressentiment, nor does he realize that his own struggle with it, and eventual retreat to conventional criticism, is part of his attempt to transcend his own tendency toward ressentiment, in response to the artist's. Kozloff's avoidance of the temptation to ressentiment is successful to the extent that he does not devalue his "artistic dialectic," i.e., his consciousness of the work's effect on him. Ressentiment is the result of the apparently permanent uncertainty of the ground of personal being, individual uncertainty about raison d'être. The sufferer of such uncertainty can become perversely dependent on those who do not experience it, who possess not only self-certainty, but the clarity of values and definiteness of intention—determinate style of consciousness—which are consequent upon it. The "perversity" shows itself in the projection of antithetical values, specifically created not only to make uncertainty more tolerable but to undermine certainty, to subvert firmness and rationality, to destroy self-possession.

Ressentiment was uncovered by Nietzsche, and examined extensively by Scheler, in part to disprove Nietzsche's demonstration of Christian ressentiment. For Nietzsche, ressentiment triumphs when it produces values of its own rather than perversely attacking the values of others. It completely inverts life-values, declaring: "impotence, inability to retaliate, is to become 'goodness'; timorous lowliness becomes 'humility'; submission to those whom one hates is 'obedience' (obedience toward one of whom they say that he decrees this submission,—they call him God)."[34]

As Scheler says,

> Ressentiment is a self-poisoning of the mind which has quite definite causes and consequences. It is a lasting mental attitude, caused by the systematic repression of certain emotions and affects which, as such, are normal components of human nature. Their repression leads to the constant tendency to indulge in certain kinds of value delusions and corresponding value judgments. The emotions and affects primarily concerned are revenge, hatred, malice, envy, the impulse to detract, and spite.

Finally, Scheler remarks that "thirst for revenge is the most important source of ressentiment." There is one aspect of Scheler's analysis of ressentiment which is particularly appropriate to the antihumanism Kozloff detects in artists. Scheler notes: "Through its very origin, ressentiment is therefore chiefly confined to those who *serve* and are *dominated* at the moment, who fruitlessly resent the sting of authority." The critic, against whom Kozloff feels Warholism is specifically directed, is the authority—symbol of the art "network" the artist most tangibly encounters. He is the more or less direct agent of the authority which has the power to judge and value the artist's work. Today, he seems to have the power the patron once had—to validate the artist—and as such he becomes a symbol of social fatality. Scheler again is helpful in comprehending the artist's amoralism toward the critic:

> We must add the fact that revenge tends to be transformed into *ressentiment* the more it is directed against lasting situations which are felt to be "injurious" but beyond one's control—in other words, the more the injury is experienced as a destiny. This will be most pronounced when a person or group feels that the very fact and quality of its *existence* is a matter which calls for revenge.

Without a doubt one element in the artist's antihumanism—his inhuman attitude to the critic—is that he "feels that the very fact and quality" of his existence is determined by the critic, as the prophet, if not more, of the historian and the art "network." His revenge—Warholism—is in effect to become countercritical:

> The more a permanent social pressure is felt to be a "fatality," the less it can free forces for the practical transformation of these conditions, and the more it will lead to indiscriminate *criticism* without any positive aims. This peculiar kind of *"ressentiment* criticism" is characterized by the fact that improvements in the conditions criticized cause no satisfaction—they merely cause discontent, for they destroy the growing pleasure afforded by invective and negation.

Ressentiment criticism in art formally began with the Dadas, and, despite the increase in receptivity to and acclaim for art, despite the expansion of its public through the mass media, ressentiment criticism has accelerated violently in Warholism. Ressentiment criticism in art has two basic forms, both experienced by Kozloff: (1) the artist refuses to organize a work according to a basic concept, to allow it to clearly and distinctly manifest the concept—put simply, the artist refuses to make his work self-consistent or of a piece; and (2) the artist refuses to allow the critic to organize his sensibility with respect to the work, or "correspond" to it. More radically and ad hominem, the artist refuses to allow the critic any personal pleasure from the work, making instead the experience of it painful and discomforting, as Steinberg and Kozloff have complained. This double refusal, of principle and of pleasure, removes the most conventionally elementary objective and subjective underpinnings from artistic experience. The artist's revenge is complete to the extent that he confuses the critic about the nature of art and his (the critic's) own nature, i.e., to the extent that both become uncertain and so undermined. Thus, the artist creates invective and negation, as in Conceptual art—that is work enough. He has foiled the "fatality" of the art "network" with the fatality of his symbolic negation of it, epitomized by his "sacrifice" of the critic. In transcending it by purifying it he may have transcended—eliminated—himself, or at least any ultimate need for himself in the "network." In purging himself, apart from what might happen to the art "network," what is left of his artistic intention? Barnett Newman will give us the answer.

However, before turning to Newman, one must note that the critic's defense against Warholism and ressentiment criticism of art is: (1) to become, ironically, its reputable propagandist to the extent that he becomes its elitist censor, earning for it social acceptance as "anti-art";[35] or (2) to use it to the advantage of his own sensibility by means of a "negative dialectic" wherein the artist's negativity is assimilated by the critic as a weapon in his own struggle against false consciousness, which attempts to blur social conflict. This blends opposites into trivial contrasts, thus effecting an illusion of social harmony.[36] If the critic, like Adorno, turns to art for a marginal freedom, acknowledging that freedom begins in sensibility,[37] then the artist's negativity, which intends to unify society ironically by leveling it through the creation of a universal uncertainty, can be reconceived by the critic as a personal if last-ditch symbol of what the artist's negativity might once have been, viz., refusal of social reconciliation, of false consciousness. Sartre cited such refusal in his rejection of the Nobel Prize,[38] and Adorno has attacked Lukacs's "extorted reconciliation."[39] In attacking the critic the artist shows his naiveté, his inability to see beyond the demands of his presumably imperious creativity. He can no longer encompass the larger object of his criticism, and he no longer can use his criticism to his human—but only to his dubiously artistic—advantage. He does not comprehend his negativity as potential, if not actual, freedom, as Sartre and Adorno do, and as a truly personal critic can. He does not understand it as grounding his relationship to the world in general as well as to the art "network" in particular.

Thus, what the artist cannot do, the critic must: the modernist critic must become conscious of his intentionality in and for itself, not simply as it relates to art. He must achieve a more open horizon of life within art, and a more autonomous attitude to society. He must not, in the end, reduce Warholism to another wrinkle in the art game, another artistic strategy, as Kozloff does. Instead, he must understand that it affords an unexpected opportunity for a more telling consciousness, and that perhaps it indicates art's own call to be rescued from itself for the sake of life. The critic must explore Warholism's hermetic amoralism by appropriating its negativity for his personal freedom, using it to clear the ground of his consciousness and uncover his humanity.

III. Apodictic Artistic Intentionality

Barnett Newman was certain of the ground of his art, as is evidenced by the ontological status he gives artistic intention and the ontic character he attributes to artistic objects. Artistic intention stands to artistic objects for him as for Heidegger Being stands to the beings that reveal it. Thus, Newman can unequivocally assert that "the artist's intention is what gives a specific thing form,"[40] and again, "the question of clarity is one of intention."[41] The apodictic character of artistic intention for Newman is all the more evident in its qualification as a "feeling of exaltation,"[42] for such a feeling is for Newman an essence in and for itself, an "invariant general style" of consciousness,[43] and as such is absolute. This essence exists disguised in ordinary beauty, from which Newman believes it can be recovered by abstraction. Newman is unquestionably phenomenological in his approach to art, for he transcends to its essential intentionality by doubting its objects, he qualifies its essence by suspending involvement with its manifestations. Thus, the "sense of exaltation" which is obscured by "perfect form," can be recovered by doubting its validity, its ability to ground itself, much as, in general for Newman, the "ecstasy" of "ideal sensibility" is recoverable from the "objective rhetoric" of "perfect statement." Essential exaltation must be recovered from existing beauty and essential ecstasy from objective form in order that the formless form which is the proper object of sensibility can become manifest in and for itself, i.e., as a phenomenon, integral so far as it is intuitable, and the ultimate reality in artistic experience. Through his abstraction Newman declares its original unity of being, its unity for consciousness and its unity as consciousness. It exists as the artist's "metaphysics (his exaltation)" rather than as the artistic object's "geometry (perfection)."

This exchange of priorities, with artistic intention usurping the ultimacy traditionally reserved for the artistic object, with the facticity of art replaced in significance by the intention to art, is archetypically phenomenological. What Newman calls "the sublime" is in fact a form of epoché, the phenomenological reduction which suspends involvement with the familiar "things" of art to unmask their transcendental determination, i.e., to uncover the consciousness which for Newman constitutes their characteristic givenness, which shapes our experience of them. The characteristic "exaltation" or "ecstasy" of this consciousness, its specific existence as transcendent feeling and its power of reconceiving spontaneity as ego, conforms to Husserl's conception of the transcendental ego as projecting its self-possession into experience, which becomes meaningful or shaped to the extent it is transcendentally felt.[44] Newman is even more profoundly phenomenological: the character he attributes to the "perfect statements" of art corresponds to the character Husserl attributes to "fictions," viz., to serve as the basic method of uncovering original intentionality.[45]

Hans Hofmann makes a distinction between "form in a physical sense" and "form in an aesthetical sense" which resembles Newman's distinction between "geometry" and "metaphysics" or "statement" and "ecstasy," a distinction which in fact can be shown to dominate the thinking of many modernist artists: "We must always distinguish between form in a physical sense (nature) and form in an aesthetical sense (the form of the work itself as a creation of the mind)."[46] Newman shows a more profound penetration of artistic intention, for he understands "form in an aesthetical sense" to transcend the aesthetic and become pure exaltation of being, an ecstasy which uses "the mind" as its will. Also, Newman's sublime epoché reveals intentionality, symbolized by the formless form as separate from the form of the work, i.e., as apart from any exclusively artistic experience, or rather, artistic experience is conceived by Newman as so peculiarly exalted a state of consciousness that it discovers essential human intentionality, or at least the human tie to the infinite, in its purity, without any need to finitize itself in form.

Where Kozloff observes amoralistic artistic intention, Newman can be said to overmoralize artistic intention. Absolute artistic intention becomes a partisan position for Newman, no doubt essential if it is to lose its hermetic appeal and become the basis for experiencable art, yet at the same time it becomes so dogmatically self-revelatory that it seems to stifle its own possibilities for experiential involvement. In effect, intention tends to become inwardly dialectical. "The question that now arises is how, if we are living in a time without a legend or mythos that can be called sublime, if we refuse to admit any exaltation in pure relations, if we refuse to live in the abstract, how can we be creating a sublime art?" Abstractly, Newman's problem is how the "natural desire for the exalted," for "absolute emotions," is to be embodied in pictures which, despite the fact that their nature is self-contradictory—they are experienced facts as well as symbols of an exalted consciousness—nonetheless contain and directly communicate the "sublime message." The paradox of this position can superficially be blamed on the times, which lack "a legend or mythos that can be called sublime." But in the last analysis Newman has no deire to embody his sense of the sublime—his exaltation and ecstasy—in artistic objects, on the metaphysical ground that any such embodiment loses as much as it gains. It ultimately spoils; as Newman notes, the evocative power, the numinous communication of Renaissance, Baroque, and Impressionist forms are inevitably lost. They dutifully became beautiful and of merely historical value, losing the immediacy of the abstract, the inspiration to absolute emotion. They became, in effect, conventionally artistic, matter-of-fact in their implications to the extent they were formally appreciated as art. Newman had no wish to lose his strong sense of the sublime for the sake of inventing a beautiful artistic form, no wish to lose his possession of the infinite for the sake of an uncertain possession of form. His disbelief in the durability, let alone the adequacy, of forms does not stem from self-doubt as an artist but rather from the philosophical recognition that any experiential embodiment of absolute ecstasy is inherently self-contradictory and self-destructive. In a sense, for Newman as for any mystic, the desire to communicate his ecstasy in obvious form is a sign of its weakness, of its inability to unite with its proper object, or else, what is correlate, a sign that the familiar finite world is too much with him, so that the infinite cannot become a familiar. The world's demand for artistic objects as proof of the power of the ecstasy is a demand to abort and misuse it. The world's constant demand for explanation, rationalization, justification usurps the power of exaltation it asks after.

In a sense, Newman is closeted in his consciousness of the sublime, but not as much as Warholism is in its amoralism. Newman's consciousness of the sublime is not a subtle form of ressentiment criticism of art. Rather, he has uncovered the independent power of ecstasy, the self-validating quality of sublimity; it is not dependent, as Warholism is, on moralistic critics. It is not designed to counter their existence with the subtler existence of the artist. It does not refute their finite authority with the artist's "infinite" authority. While it is true that in some of his works, e.g., *Who's Afraid Of Red, Yellow and Blue I,* 1966, Newman is responding to the authority of other artists, in this case Mondrian, he rarely responds to the authority of critics, and in no case does his response have the peculiar involuted, self-poisoning quality of ressentiment. His artistic intention always remains pure in the sense that it is always concerned to be in terms of itself, even if superficially through the agency of another artist's style, rather than to be in terms of the other. Newman's separation of his "desire...to express his relation to the Absolute" from "the fetish of quality" takes quality not as an artistic fatality but as an obstacle to artistic intention. As such, critical attention to quality avoids coming to grips with the artist's subjectivity. If Newman thought that the fetishizing of quality was a fatality which could not be transcended, then his exaltation is a Pyrrhic victory over it. But Newman believes that objective quality is, in fact, transcended by the sublime feelings that emerge in the course of the artistic experience—if it is allowed to run its course, and is not sidetracked into poetry of perception.

In general, Newman uncovers the prereflective root of artistic intention, its existence beyond itself in a sense of the sublime. Ironically, Newman's attempt to determine the ground of his art has moved beyond art, even beyond the question of a purely artistic intention, toward the question of human intentionality in general, toward a radical consciousness of the meaning of existence. This is no failure, but an unexpected boon, for it implies that if art were to ground itself solely on other art, on "influences," if it were to be only a matter of the evolution of style, then it would never be "original" to human existence, it would never be part of human freedom. Art's paradox is that it never can be self-grounding: what it regards as self-grounding turns out to be either its reexperiencing of its history or, as with Newman, its penetration to the ground of being in general. It is either a revolutionary discovery of the authentic subject or it is a reactionary discovery of its own objectivity. Unless artistic experience implies experience of its suggested presence, as well as experience of artistic objects, then the ground and human significance of art remain uncertain. Artistic intention is most itself when it is not itself: when it can be located neither altogether in the artist nor in artistic objects, but only transcendentally, in a consummate sense of being, the origin of whatever meaning the artist and his works have. Artistic intention is always self-transcending, and as such grounding itself in the possibilities of human existence.

In a sense, the naive attitude to artistic intention represented by the Dadas, the moralistic approach to it represented by Kozloff and in a complementary way by Warholism, and the transcendental attitude represented by Newman, are all defensive. They are all approaches hoping to protect the phenomenon they wish to comprehend. They defend against "the diffusion of art in society and the greatly accelerated interest in art by the layman," for this seems a source of false consciousness of art. It can lead to the assumption that the popularity of art is a sign of reconciliation between society and individual, an end to Adorno's "wounded consciousness,"[47] for art conventionally is the sign of individuality. What Marcuse naively describes as the social utopianism of art[48] seems to be realized in its popularity, and seems to falsify the true nature of art as "the permanent antagonist." The interest in artistic intention, in the possibility of art, in the esoteric character of its self-evidence, whatever it is phenomenologically, is an effort to undermine the popularity of art, to show that it plays art false, to reassert the irreconcilability of art with society, despite its essential existence in it. Conceived as "transcendental illusion,"[49] even Newman's sense of the sublime is seen as a refusal to accept the self-evident conditions of being-in-the-world.

The esthetic interest in artistic intention, the fetishizing of intention as a value in and for itself as Newman does, the whole phenomenological approach to it, the artist's feeling that it must be carefully preserved as a precious, possibly limited reserve of creativity, are all ways out of the ironies which attend art's appearance in the world, ironies partly the result of taste and partly generated by the necessities of art's immediate situation, its need to exhibit itself to the world to complete itself. This way out can qualify itself in terms of Steinberg's anxiety or Newman's ecstasy.[50] But the essential point is that consciousness of artistic intention implies a search for a greater fundamentality and freedom than hitherto has been thought of. This necessarily involves presupposing the uncertainty of the ground of art, and thus its irreconcilability with social reality, its refusal to submit to false consciousness. The doubtfulness of art, which modernism has discovered, will always be countered by transcendental doubt of this doubt, and so long as this itself is countered by a recognition that it leads beyond art, then art's role in freedom, in the refusal of reconciliation with the self-evident naturalness of the given world, the status quo, becomes clear. Art first gives the freedom to be conscious of what is usually taken unconsciously; art first gives the freedom to make unfamiliar what is usually taken familiarly. As such, the uncertainty of its ground is a necessity of this freedom; its unclarity about its intentions will always permit it to protect itself beyond the permissibly given.

Notes

1. Edmund Husserl, *Der Krisis der europäischen Wissenschaften und die Transzendentale Phänomenologie,* The Hague, 1962, p. 202.

2. Ibid., p. 260.

3. Ibid., p. 202.

4. Edmund Husserl, *Ideas,* New York, 1952, 196.

5. Ibid., pp. 110-111. See also Donald B. Kuspit, "Parmenidean Tendencies in the Epoché," *The Review of Metaphysics,* XVIII, 1965, p. 757.

6. Ibid., p. 113.

7. Ibid., p. 107.

8. Clement Greenberg, "Modernist Painting," *The New Art,* ed. Gregory Battcock, New York, 1966, pp. 103-10. All of Greenberg's quotations are from this source.

9. The impossibility of a logically successful definition of art has been demonstrated by Morris Weitz, "The Role of Theory in Aesthetics," *Journal of Aesthetics and Art Criticism,* 15 (1956): 27-35.

10. Husserl, *Der Krisis,* sections 14, 16, and 56.

11.   Quoted in William S. Rubin, *Frank Stella,* New York, 1970, p. 42.

12.   Ibid., p. 41. In response to Stella and other antihumanists, one ought to note H.A. Enno van Gelder's distinction, in *The Two Reformations in the Sixteenth Century,* The Hague, 1961, between the humanist revolution as an unending search for self-enlightenment, and humanist reformism as a response to specific social conditions. The latter is inevitably limited to a given world, but the former is inherently human.

13.   Lucy R. Lippard, ed., *Dadas on Art,* Englewood Cliffs., N.J., 1971, p. 141. Duchamp is a primitive phenomenologist, able to understand the human and artistic need to transcend a matter-of-fact attitude to things, but not able to do so systematically and with an integral intentionality.

14.   Leo Steinberg, "Contemporary Art and the Plight of its Public," *The New Art,* ed. Gregory Battcock, New York, 1966, pp. 27-47. All of Steinberg's quotations are from this source.

15.   Renato Poggioli, *The Theory of the Avant-Garde,* New York, 1971, pp. 61-74, says as much in his discussion of avant-garde nihilism, agonism, and futurism.

16.   The concept of ritual avoidance is developed by Harry Stack Sullivan, *The Interpersonal Theory of Psychiatry,* New York, 1953, pp. 307-8.

17.   This situation is a reduction ad absurdum of the belief in the irreducible uniqueness of the artistic object. Although, as T.W. Adorno remarks in "Die Kunst und die Künste," *Ohne Leitbild; Parva Aesthetica,* Frankfurt am Main, 1967, p. 180, "Dialektik verketzern sie als sophistische Hexerei, ohne der Möglichkeit ihres fundamentum in re gern Raum zu gewähren," a plurality which insists on the irreducible facticity of the things which constitute it loses all dialectical possibility, i.e., loses its logical fundamentum.

18.   T.W. Adorno, "Ideen zur Musiksoziologie," *Klangfiguren,* Frankfurt am Main, 1959, p. 13. On the same page, Adorno describes how false consciousness operates within the artistic object itself, making it "comfortable" and "popular." The "flattering and harmonizing of opposites" operates in terms of "the leveling of the contradictions to empty parts of a reified form, which are 'filled out' by their contrasts." The bourgeois is characterized by false consciousness.

19.   Lawrence Alloway, "Network: The Art World Described as a System," *Artforum,* September, 1972, pp. 28-32.

20.   Adorno, "Ideen zur Musiksoziologie," p. 20.

21.   Philip Leider, "The New York School in Los Angeles," *Artforum,* September, 1965, pp. 5-6.

22.   Allan Kaprow, "A Statement," *Happenings, An Illustrated Anthology,* ed. Michael Kirby, New York, 1966, p. 47.

23.   Lippard, pp. 3-4.

24.   Ibid., p. 1.

25.   Ibid., p. 35.

26.   Ibid., p. 37.

27.   Ibid., p. 139.

28.   Marcel Duchamp, "The Creative Act," *The New Art,* ed. Gregory Battcock, New York, 1966, p. 24.

29.   Max Kozloff, "Critical Schizophrenia and the Intentionalist Method," *Renderings,* New York, 1969, pp. 301-12. All of Kozloff's quotations are from this source.

30. Susan Sontag. "Non-Writing and the Art Scene," *The New Art,* ed. Gregory Battcock, New York, 1966, p. 158.

31. Adorno, pp. 13-14. For a further discussion of Adorno's method "of speculative understanding, of phenomenalist ordering through provisional or even 'mimetic' conjectures about material which is not clear or—a key point—whose integral clarity can be perceived but *not clearly articulated,* which positivist criteria of meaningfulness *(Sinnkriteria)* would deny," see the anonymous discussion of Adorno's esthetics in the *Times Literary Supplement,* March 9, 1973, pp. 253-55.

32. Robert Denoon Cumming, ed., *The Philosophy of Jean-Paul Sartre,* New York, 1966, pp. 91-93.

33. Ibid., pp. 373-77.

34. Quoted by Max Scheler, *Ressentiment,* New York, 1961, p. 45. All of Scheler's quotations are from this source.

35. T.W. Adorno describes this situation well in "Kulturkritik und Gesellschaft," *Prismen,* Frankfurt am Main, 1955, pp. 8-9.

36. Adorno's attack on false reconciliation is particularly intense in "Ideen zur Musiksoziologie," pp. 30-31.

37. Freedom, as Sartre is quoted in Cumming, p. 494, "is a word that lends itself to numerous interpretations." It can mean both "abstract freedom" and "a more concrete freedom—the right to have more than one pair of shoes and to eat when hungry." Perhaps the most abstract freedom that exists is the philosopher's, "based," as Husserl says, "on the spirit of autonomy," and involving "scientific responsibility to oneself." As Husserl says, "A true philosopher cannot be other than free: the essential nature of philosophy is the most radical autonomy." (Quoted by Kuspit, pp. 749-50) Adorno locates freedom in the "mature human being," where it is connected, as Kurt Oppens notes, in "Zu den musikalischen Schriften Theodor W. Adornos," *Über Theodor W. Adorno,* Frankfurt am Main, 1968, p. 10, with "einem avancierten Humanismus," and still retains "den alten Kantisch-Hegelschen Klang," manifesting itself through a dialectical working through of existence. Sensibility becomes a method of maturity for Adorno; how this is so, and how art can combine both abstract and concrete freedom, personal autonomy and social concern, is stated perhaps most clearly by Louis Buñuel, in *The New York Times Magazine,* March 11, 1973, p. 93: "In any society, the artist has a responsibility. His effectiveness is certainly limited and a writer or painter cannot change the world. But they can keep an essential margin of nonconformity alive. Thanks to them, the powerful can never affirm that everyone agrees with their acts. That small difference is very important. When power feels itself totally justified and approved, it immediately destroys whatever freedoms we have left, and that is fascism. . . . Basically I agree with Engels: An artist describes real social relationships with the purpose of destroying the conventional ideas about those relationships, undermining bourgeois optimism and forcing the public to doubt the tenets of the established order. The final sense of my films is this: to repeat, over and over again, in case anyone forgets it or believes the contrary, that we do not live in the best of all possible worlds."

38. Cumming, pp. 493-94.

39. T.W. Adorno, "Erpresste Versöhnung," *Noten zur Literatur II,* Frankfurt am Main, 1961, pp. 152-87.

40. Quoted in *Modern Artists in America,* First Series, New York, 1951, p. 81.

41. Ibid., p. 19.

42.   Barnett B. Newman, "The Sublime is Now," *Tiger's Eye*, 1, (1948): 51-53. All subsequent Newman quotations are from this source.

43.   Husserl, *Der Krisis*, p. 29.

44.   Husserl, *Ideas*, p. 121.

45.   For a discussion of Husserl's position on the relationship between fiction and phenomenology see Donald B. Kuspit, "Fiction and Phenomenology," *Philosophy and Phenomenological Research*, 29 (1968): 16-33.

46.   Barbara Rose, ed. *Readings in American Art Since 1900*, New York, 1968, p. 148.

47.   As discussed in *Minima Moralia, Reflexionen aus dem beschädigten Leben*, Frankfurt am Main, 1964.

48.   Herbert Marcuse, *One-Dimensional Man*, London, 1964, pp. 238-39.

49.   Immanuel Kant, *Critique of Pure Reason*, B353: "We therefore take the subjective necessity of our concepts, which is to the advantage of the understanding, for an objective necessity in the determination of things in themselves."

50.   This echoes Blankenburg's contrast of Heidegger's use of anxiety and its implication of finitude with Binswanger's use of love and its implication of infinity as alternate, if not mutually exclusive existential structures. Wolfgang Blankenburg, "The Cognitive Aspects of Love," *Facets of Eros, Phenomenological Essays*, ed. F.J. Smith and Erling Eng, The Hague, 1972, pp. 27-34.

2

The Dialectic of Taste

There are some stray remarks on art in Husserl that, on the whole, show the poverty of his approach to it, yet offer some useful insights as touchstones to a "phenomenological fencing and clearing" of the area.[1] In the *Ideas* Husserl remarks:

> But it is just the same with the *object depicted*, if we take up a *purely aesthetic* attitude, and view the same again as 'mere picture,' without imparting to it the stamp of Being or non-Being, of possible Being or probable Being, and the like.[2]

Art, insofar as it is an identifiable phenomenon, i.e., strictly the consequence of the pure aesthetic attitude, is evident in objects neutral with respect to facts yet exemplary of essences.[3] Thus, Husserl notes that

> the fancy-image therefore is not a mere faded datum of sense, but in its own way a fancy *of* the corresponding sense-datum; further, that this 'of' cannot find its way in through any thinning, however drastic, of the intensity of the content, etc., of the sense-datum in question.[4]

The fancy image is qualitatively distinct from the sense-datum, irreducible in itself, rather than an afterimage of the sense-datum, in Humean terms, a weak idea of a strong impression. It is an "ideal object," implicating consciousness-of the presentational mode of being, rather than the sign of the activity of sensing. It is formal rather than informal, a determinate "knowledge" rather than an indeterminate activity. It stands to reason, then, that Husserl should find it reproducible in principle, in contrast to the sense-datum, which inevitably fades because it is grounded on the transient intensity of sensing, perishes because it is a passing phenomenon of perception.

> An ideal object, such as Raphael's Madonna can, admittedly, *actually* have a unique worldliness and actually cannot be repeated in its sufficient identity (full ideal contents). But this ideal is indeed in principle repeatable...[5]

For Husserl, the image is the consequence of the neutralization "of the 'positing' act of representation."[6] As such, it permits us to "think" about "what is performed" in representation "without 'helping to bring it about'."[7]

Imaging–imagining aims not to make facts immediate to consciousness, but to put it in a position to inquire into the nature of its own activity of representation, to disclose the "intentional implications" of the mode of being-represented.[8] The image is a kind of symbol of the security of consciousness in its own self-investigation. Its constancy is confirmed by its quotability, its ideality allowing the distinction between perception and apperception, consciousness of its depicted character allowing abstraction from its data. With the image one gathers momentum for a comprehension of a form of consciousness, suspending what Schelling has called the free functioning of unconscious perception.

For Husserl, it is through the complexity of content, the depth of consciousness implicit in the image, what he calls "the fancy that is in the fancy or the memory in a memory or a fancy,"[9] that the intentionality of the depicting consciousness is disclosed. For this "depth" is the sign that any given image, any definite "fancy," "can pass freely over into a *direct fancy*,"[10] i.e., make itself manifest aesthetically. Disclosing itself to be a matrix of implications, inextricably a part of its essential nature, it discloses itself to be an independent intentionality, for such a complexity of being, the presence of a world of interior intentions so to speak, is alien to whatever existence it might have as the embodiment of sense-data. The final "proof" of the image as a production of consciousness rather than as the consequence of unconscious sensing is its existence as a world within a world. It is not a naive reflection of the datum of being, the sheer givenness of facticity, but a creation of consciousness, not for the sake of solipsistic self-satisfaction, nor simply to know itself as a self-sufficient form in itself, but to disclose itself as directed-toward being, able to give as well as to receive, able to assert itself as well as to be stamped by being. Slowly but surely, Husserl moves from the old idea of consciousness as a semi-active wax of wonder to a view of it as an intended form of being, consciousness-of disclosing itself as a reaching-out to reality rather than its passive partner. Art is the first consciousness-of consciousness as a directed-toward. The "mere picture" is stripped of the need of arguing for or against the truth of propositions, stripped of the need for "indicating" the data referenced by the statement. Imparting nothing about "Being," it can impart something about consciousness as an attitude toward Being. It can "say" something about the state of consciousness, as well as about what it is to be conscious.

In a sense, Husserl's "fancies 'in' fancies"[11] mean no more than the themes of the picture, its abstraction from perception of the themes for thought. This content presupposes the consciousness that "constructed" it, but its main import is to turn thought about what is performed in the act of representation into theory about an isolated subject-matter. As I have noted elsewhere, it thus becomes the *prima materia* of science.[12] Husserl, however, as he insists, is not concerned with "theory" or "metaphysic," but with "essential necessities," with "Ideas, *each implying the 'and so forth'* of 'endless' possibilities."[13] Thus, there is no clear funnelling—by the image—of things into consciousness, of themes into thought, for the thing is as much an idea as it is an entity,[14] and as much implicated in a world of ideas as in a world of facts. There is no clear control by the thing over what ideas we have of it, and the image is not the instrumentality of an attempted control. For again, as we must always remind ourselves, while the image is mediate between sensing and intuition, it does not backtrack to its sensuous source, as does memory, but pushes forward to an independent intelligibility. As I have shown elsewhere, Husserl is in error to think of the image as a memory-modification of sensuousness, for he then belies his own position as to its phenomenological importance.[15] The image is a demonstration to consciousness of its own powers, which is exactly why Husserl accords it privileged status as the touchstone of phenomenological research.[16] In the aesthetic attitude is the rudiment of the pure Ego,[17] and in the image is the rudimentary meaningfulness consciousness imparts to Being.

This makes good use of the image for philosophy, but what sense does it make of it in itself, as art? Despite all that is implicit in Husserl's approach to art, his primary fancies, before they are "fancies 'in' fancies," are a kind of object. The "mere picture" is an art-object. Husserl explicates objects more than implications. "Free fancies" are the implications of the "fancy-image," but they are never explicated as fictions. For Husserl, the art-object is ultimately another kind of fact, and its implications form a schema of references to other facts of the world. Although the aesthetic attitude permits us to see the depicted object as the mere picture, there is no excursus of any characteristic experience of art once it has been established as such. The aesthetic attitude establishes the work of art as such, but it does not then make manifest what we experience when we experience this art. In essence, Husserl's aesthetic attitude accounts for the genesis of art, but it does not then explain its course in the world. It establishes the object-ivity of art as such, but not its historicity, and especially not its experience-value. Husserl's neglect of its existence as fiction is correlate with this neglect of its value for experience, for it is as a fiction that it has its specific value for experience. Husserl, at the most, establishes art as indisputably given, hence its objecthood,[18] but not the full impact of its givenness on those for whom it is given. Art's themes, presumably, are a clue to this impact, but it has been made evident that these themes, apart from their limited existence for thought, have little or no experiential value for the spectator, i.e., do little to bring him to consciousness of intentionality, for they emerge strictly as depictions of sense-data, and so as sense-activity at second remove. For no matter how much the spectator knows the depictions to be fictions, i.e., not strictly instances of sense-data, he is forced back on the conception of them as depicted objects the moment he begins to search out their themes. As a mere picture the work of art cannot begin to stimulate research into intentionality, for it is constantly alluding to the facticity of the world. To refer to it as a mere picture is to declare it a frozen depiction, one that can neither adequately renew our sense-acquaintance with the facts of the world nor competently renew our consciousness of ourselves. Only by decisively emphasizing the work of art as a fiction, as I have done in my treatment of Husserl's own elaboration of Dürer's *Knight, Death, And Devil,* demonstrating that its subject matter is not self-evidently factual,[19] can one emerge with the value of the work of art as an experience for the subject. Taking Husserl's recognition that the work of art is rich with implications to its ultimate consequences, it is possible to assert that it is so full of implications that its subject matter can never be clearly and distinctly specified, that its reference to facticity can never be fully demonstrated, that there is always, as it were, a residuum beyond the depicted subject matter, a range of implications beyond the depicted object, that cannot be accounted for by any referencing to reality, by any sense-activity, by any positing of perception. The very fact that the work of art must be interpreted, an issue ignored by Husserl, indicates that there is such a residuum of implications that cannot be explained by the theory of the work of art as a depiction, as an imitation or referencing of reality.[20] The clue to the source of explanation is afforded by the conventional Aristotelian assertion that the work of art is man-made rather than a product of nature, that it is not simply a by-product of natural perception, a kind of keepsake of consciousness, but a deliberately constructed thing showing the stamp of its maker. In effect, this means that however much the artist intends to depict reality, he ends by demonstrating his own reality. However much his point of departure may be the sensuously given, he shows himself as subjectively given. Ultimately, this acknowledgement of the human source of art shows the necessity of a Copernican Revolution in the approach to art. While Husserl's strategy is to force the subject to conform to the art-object, however much the art-object may first have indicated its presence through the aesthetic attitude, one must take seriously taste's insistence that the work of art conform, not simply to opinions about it, but to subjective attitudes toward it. In effect, the strategy is to accept the vulgar demand that the work of art have a subjective meaning as well as an objective value, that it be accessible to the personal consciousness of the spectator as well as be something in itself. When Duchamp speaks of history bringing the work of art to completion, in effect establishing it as art, he is urging that the taste of future generations will be as significant as the artist's creativity in bringing the work of art into mature being.[21] Duchamp perhaps exaggerates the sociality necessary for the acceptance of art as such, an acceptance all the more necessary in an age when there is no unequivocal conception of art,[22] but at the same time he is implicitly asserting the importance of the subject as well as the object of art. Unless the subject finds the art-object meaningful in the first place, it cannot pretend to live up to its claim that it is what it is.

For Husserl, taste, insofar as it might be mentioned, would be subsumed in the theory of predicative judgment as a case in point.[23] He would follow Kant's lead, referring the judgment of taste to "the guidance of the logical functions of judgment," i.e., the universal conditions of predication.[24] In the search for a "universal voice" in matters of taste[25] Husserl would insist that taste implicates a standard of value subject to the same criteria of intelligibility and validation as any other rule of judgment. The error in the approach to taste through logic is the assumption that taste is exclusively a matter of judgment, which bypasses the situation from which the judgment of value arises. Such an approach ignores what Heidegger calls the concern which establishes the situation of which the judgment of value is a secondary feature, a derivative quality.[26] In effect, the spectator must acquire taste before he can judge tastefully. It is this distinction which initiates the dialectic of taste. Without it, taste is conceived only as an objective judgment on art; with it, taste is conceived as a concern for the art-object which conceives its objectivity to be beside the point. What is at stake in taste is the spectator's concern that the work of art be meaningful to him personally; what is at stake in the judgment of taste is that it be objectively valuable, however difficult it is to decide on the nature of objective value in art. Scholars and connoisseurs can help the decision, but neither can create the concern for art which makes it meaningful in the first place, so as to permit inquiry into it. But again, such inquiry is secondary to the initial value conferred, a consequence of and correlate with the personal meaningfulness of the art.

The tasteful spectator, then, has no phenomenological purpose in his concern for art, no interest in pure essences or in secondary truths of perception, such as beauty. He attends to the art-object casually, with no ulterior motive of consciousness, with no interest in understanding art for its own sake. He is concerned only with art's advantage for his own subjectivity, its significance for his own existence. This attitude is customarily deplored by scholars and connoisseurs, by the objectivists in the approach to art, although we do not decry it when it is applied to other concerns of the life-world. Yet this is the first question of the consciousness of art, even prior to the question of the establishment of art as such. For it is a life-consciousness of art, not a mind-method toward it. It is a question which emerges from what Husserl called the life-world, and has nothing to do with what Plato would consider the powers of abstraction to the absolute, to the pure art-object which would be sublime truth, beauty in and for itself.

However the spectator might approach the work of art, he is forced into the situation of concern for it if he would at all find value in it, for better or for worse. Without this modicum of meaningfulness, which is existentially incommensurate with and ultimately irreconcilable to the judgment of taste, art not only has no value of any kind, but makes no sense, whether immediately or after reflection. It will eventually be indicated that the objective judgment of taste is designed to obscure the subjective concern for art, the personal situation behind the objective prerogative. At this point, it is sufficient to note that the spectator may approach the work of art with all sorts of presuppositions, ranging from acceptance of its pre-given value to a mocking notice of its effect on him. But unless he makes it part of his life-world, a consequence of his own consciousness of it, the work of art will ultimately be irrelevant to him, however much he may understand its nature in itself. In exploring the possibilities of approach to the work of art, the spectator may come to it with a modicum of aesthetic disinterestedness, the latent detachment necessary to see it as a phenomenon in itself. However, this is often no more than a consequence of the museum-situation, the awe at the suspension of the art-object in a privileged preserve. But the situation of the perception of art-objects need not be the museum. The spectator can view them in the gallery or the studio, more or less in the process of officially becoming art-objects. But in such a situation he is even less likely to take personal responsibility for his perceptions, less likely to trust his consciousness of such objects, for in the studio he is preoccupied with the becoming of the object, and in the gallery with its becoming public. In each instance, he is preoccupied with the nature of the object, not with his consciousness of it. In a sense, the museum situation is preferable, even to the home situation, where the art-object is taken too much for granted. In the museum, art's objectivity is assured, certified by fiat, and the work of art is presented as at a command performance. The spectator, not being concerned to bring the work of art into being as such, can attribute what significance he will to it. While he may be side-tracked by its novelty, struck by its contradiction of the familiar objects of the world, such dissimilarity may court a lingering attention to it, out of which will gestate the self-consciousness of his situation of consciousness of art. It is then that an authentic concern for art emerges, a concern so unashamedly personal that it forces one to re-open research into the nature of the intentionality of creativity.

In essence, then, we are not concerned with the connoisseur, for he is less spectator of art than a person who relates to art-objects as a way of life. He is the devotee attempting to acquire the presupposed fineness of fine art for his life-world. He presumes its ultimate, universal value, which he would like to make the monopoly of his life-world. Nor are we concerned with the person who identifies passionately with the presupposed passion of the artist. He adheres to the religion of the artist rather than that of the art-object, and conceives the artist's creative values as the only authentic ones in the life-world. Like the connoisseur, he usurps an abstract "meaning of life" without having become conscious of his own intentionality. The spectator we speak of is more naive, willing to have art as a constituent concern of his life-world but not as the sole source of its meaningfulness. Nor is he concerned with "good taste," as Hume puts it, "certain general principles of approbation or blame,"[27] but with the acquiring of taste as a case of his consciousness of his own intentionality in the life-world.

An exemplary account of such concern for art can be seen in the life of Henry James.[28] Young Henry finds himself encouraged by the work of art to see the world through a frame of his own making. Much has been written about the logic of the picture-limits, asserting its independence of vision and its containment of consciousness.[29] However, the young James' enthusiasm for the principle of framing was purely personal. Shy and uncertain of himself in the life-world, art imparted to him a sophisticated means of shaping it to his own purposes. Or at least the leisure to discover such purposes, for he could put the world away on a wall of consciousness by framing it. The world seen as a "mere picture" lost its immediacy. The image of the world had no absolute aesthetic value, but it made personal sense. As James notes, his reduction of the world to a picture-book, to a museum of pictures limited in scope and import yet playfully accessible, was his major source of emotional security in youth.[30] It ensured his sanity by giving him the modicum of detachment from his emotions about the world. His anxiety was stilled by treating the world as an object, where once he had been an object in it, at least to himself. Art, in other words, gave him consciousness of himself as a subject, because he could shape the world in a frame as it did, limit its appearances and impact to pictures. No longer was it a practical problem but a contemplated image, no longer a datum of sense but a fiction of feeling. In effect, through art, James discovered an attitude toward the world— discovered the possibility of having an attitude over against the world—which helped him in the life-world. Art permitted him to glimpse the power of his own consciousness, neutralizing the world-performance. Suspending the world in a picture, it need no longer be suffered, and the moment the intentional implications of the picture were brought to consciousness—almost the whole effort of James' fiction—the fiction of the world passed over into direct fancy, into a free consciousness of intentionality. That the experience of art put James in a position to explore intentionality, giving him the freedom to be conscious, the possibility of disclosing implications and not being bound by the sheer givenness of things, the indifferent facticity of the world, meant more to James than education to good taste, than learning to judge art properly. As James notes, for much of his life his taste in pictures remained poor; he preferred Gavarni to Daumier.[31] In effect, he preferred a world loosely rendered but firmly framed, i.e., clearly a fiction, clearly neutralized, to the presence of the artist's power of consciousness, to the strong subjectivity and intentionality which we call style. In effect, James realized that facts were uncanny, because they had implications, and it was this uncanniness, making demands on him, he wanted neutralized. He did not need to cope with the uncanniness of the artist's style, the uncanniness of his consciousness. Such a purely subjective concern for art as James developed, such appropriation of it purely in terms of its personal meaningfulness, formed the ground of his self hood, became the first reason for self-respect. More crucially for our purposes, he was aware of the art-object neither as art nor object but as an independent experience, a uniquely personal experience, qualitatively distinct from other experiences in the life-world. Had he been concerned for either art or objects he more likely would have found a confirmation of the world's power rather than an inkling of the power of his own consciousness. What is even more unique is that without any aesthetic attitude toward the art itself, although with the beginnings of one toward the world, so as to neutralize it, he was able to disclose an essential trait of art—its hypostasization, almost fetishizing of epoché—but without analyzing it out of the art. He had no need to do so, for he was conscious of it not as a principle in itself or of art, but as a method of existence opening the way to personal consciousness, to one's own discovery of the implications of the life-world.

Schiller was aware of the opposite. He saw the attachment to art as a possible hindrance in the life-world, the concern for art a weakness of will.

> Precisely because taste pays heed only to form and never to content, it finally gives the soul a dangerous tendency to neglect all reality entirely and to sacrifice truth and morality to an attractive facade.[32]

"Mere appearance" determines value, consciousness of the aesthetics of appearance going hand in hand with a decline in the capacity for significant action.

> It is almost superfluous to recall further the examples of the modern nations whose refinement has increased in direct proportion as their independence has declined. Wherever we turn our gaze in the ancient world, we find taste and freedom mutually avoiding each other, and Beauty establishing her sway only on the ruins of heroic virtue.[33]

For Schiller,

> This very energy of character, at whose price aesthetic culture is usually purchased, is the most powerful mainspring of all that is great and excellent in Man, the lack of which no other advantage, however great, is able to repair.[34]

It may be the case that this aesthetic culture is worthy of such energy of character, but Schiller's point is that it is a social ideal which misleads the individual in the life-world. For beauty distracts from truth and morality, which persuade to heroic action. Offered in their stead, beauty is a mute recognition of appearance that distracts attention from reality, thus crippling consciousness. But Schiller's argument makes more sense retrospectively than immediately. He tends to over-moralize history for the sake of a one-dimensional view of the life-world, as though all that was at stake in it was the sustaining of its military vitality. For in practice what Schiller is calling for is the nobility of Plato's auxiliaries in the *Republic*. Their corruption by aesthetic culture, another product of luxury for Plato, may make the ideal state impossible, but it does not lead to the destruction of the life-world. This remains to be dealt with, and in it the presupposed distinction between appearance and reality, what is valuable and what is not valuable, is not so self-evident. What seems self-evident is what has been presupposed and pre-conceived, not what is experientially the case. In effect, Schiller's subject conforms to the object as much as Hume's and Kant's, but where they offer, respectively, art objectified by a standard of taste arrived at "empirically" by consensus of opinion, and art as the objectified universal, Schiller offers the art-object as among the most significant of culture-objects, as the ideal kind of object a culture would produce. All three do not realize that morality and truth are not at stake in the existential experience of art. Nor is its definition. Weitz has demonstrated the inadequacy of existing definitions of art, and the futility of attempting to define its essence insofar as that essence is necessarily exemplified by existing art-objects, many of which contradict the essence.[35] But it has yet to be acknowledged that it is inherently unnecessary in the experience of art, that it in no way serves the search for personal significance through art. The logical contradictoriness of this assumption—how would the spectator find art personally meaningful unless he was aware that it is art?—is overcome, or at least obviated, not simply by Weitz's essentially nominalistic approach to art, but by re-conceiving art so that any logical approach to it is grounded on a pre-reflective concern for it. In the same way in which Heidegger says man cares for his seeing before it leads him to objective thought, so one can say man cares for art before he can think about it.[36] Such care can be comprehended in the context of the life-world, not in the hermetic system of definition. It is part of one's personal being-conscious, not of one's pursuit of the logic of art. Such logic, with its judgments, is an ideological superstructure superimposed on the vital experience of art's personal meaningfulness, an overlay obscuring the personal role art plays in the life-world. Ultimately, it will be shown that this vital experience implicates a special kind of anxiety, what Frankl calls "an existential neurosis" or a "frustration of the will-to-meaning".[37] It is this that the judgment of art and the whole structure of objective interest in art represses, for the subjective concern for art opens an abyss in the fluid surface of life, starts a vortex dissolving and drowning all conventional meaning of life. It is art's peculiar way of handling appearances, a displacement of their customary meanings, that must be muted by objectifying art into a thing of value or a subject of professional inquiry.

Neither the form nor content Schiller mentions—the distinction can only be made when the art-object is presumed to be an ideal object—is of concern to the casual spectator of art. Nor does he have any theory of art. He does not presuppose its constancy. Thus, his taste can never be refuted by its history or by new aesthetic standards, for he has no historical preferences and no one aesthetic outlook. In effect, he has neither prejudices of theory nor history, but is only concerned with what is accessible to his consciousness. Schiller presupposes that art necessarily raises form over content because he assumes form is the essence of art, objectifying it and serving as the measure of its permanent value. But our radically casual spectator anticipates no absolute value in art—he does not presuppose that he is dealing with the thing of beauty which is of joy forever— nor does he make any philosophical distinctions in his consciousness of art. He has no systematic approach to the work of art, but is a kind of naive savage in his attitude to it. Neither analyzing nor appreciating it, he personalizes it.

Bullough notes the neutralization of any practical value in the experience of art,[38] but he overlooks the absence of any intellectual value as well. Only the possibility of personal value is not suspended. One can still posit it, because *prima facie* art has no meaning in the life-world, and the search for such a meaning leads to the discovery that it can be arrived at only through consciousness. But not any generalized, objectifying consciousness, with such presupposed categories as Kant gives it, rather a strictly personal consciousness, not concerned to assimilate the work of art to given, prestructured, contrived consciousness, but pre-reflective consciousness concerned to orient the person in the life-world. In effect, the approach to art is part of the cleaning of the Augean stables of consciousness by existence itself. Instead of accepting pre-given meanings of life, the presence of the work of art raises the possibility of alternative, at times mutually contradictory meanings. The demand that art be moral is essentially a demand that an art reflect the *status quo* of accepted meanings of life. But, insofar as art arouses consciousness to awareness of itself, it inevitably disrupts given, predetermined meanings of life, for all such self-consciousness is self-questioning, in the sense of asking after the source of one's particular consciousness of things, one's general intentionality or attitude toward things. In his approach to art, then, the spectator is concerned to re-charge his consciousness of what is at stake in the life-world, of what is personally significant in being.

How far does he get? The work of art gives the illusion of communicating to the spectator another possibility of being, another meaning of life, another structure of importance. But it does not commit him to any given sense of significance. Rather, it leaves him suspended in his consciousness of himself and his possibilities, with no power of decision. It is this suspension which increasingly arouses anxiety, and it is the leap back to objectivity, in the form of the judgment of taste, which restores his power of decision, and more importantly, restores his old sense of the world, of the meaning of the life-world. But initially he experiences the work of art as a "comunication" of possibilities, and this illusion of communication is on a level with what Kant calls the illusions of dialectic, psychologically necessary "enrichments" of existence without which it would appear to itself incomplete.[39] It is such numinous communication which is the core of the experience of art, and without such an illusion the life-world would appear bland and purposeless, a void of naively perceived objects. For the art-object gives us the illusion that an object can be a subject, and communicate a consciousness. This is not simply animistic projection on the work of art, a desire to punish, as it were, objectivity by making it humanly familiar, but a search for the sedimented meanings of life, which seem to exist out in the world, in its objects—and so one would like some object that can communicate them. It is a condition of our being-in-the-world that our meaning is in the world, from which we must recover it to know it and ourselves. And it is the privilege of the work of art, recognized by Husserl, to create the illusion of numinous communication that gives us the possibility of such self-recovery from being-in-the-world. Yet we are never out of the world, and hence the subsequent anxiety such self-recovery initiates.

The question of the meaning of life is a difficult one to ask not because it is impossible to ask, as Wittgenstein said,[40] but because it is not so much a question as a response to a situation, an attempt at creating value in experience. Heidegger denies that consciousness is value-creating, but this is because, in positing care as the pre-reflective mode of being, all particular values are subsumed in the ontological reality of concern. Frankl's approach seems more fruitful. His distinction between creative values, experiential values, and attitudinal values, because it arises directly out of ontic activity seems more to the existential point than Heidegger's abstract concern.[41] For the artist the work of art has creative value, for the objective spectator it has experiential value, mediating the experience of beauty, as Frankl says, and for our subjective spectator it has attitudinal value, in the sense that it leads to a re-evaluation of his attitudes in the life-world, to a re-examination of the meaning of life. It does this in a painless context, not in the concentration camps in which Frankl discovered the frustration of the will-to-meaning, the collapse of consciousness due to the forced loss of objectivity, the reduction of being-in-an-objective-world to being in a world willing one's death. Here there is no question of stripping public meanings to come to existential significance, posited meanings to arrive at existential implications, for the posited, public world is taken from one and its meanings come tumbling after. One is thrust into such existential significance without having first to consciously suspend conventional sense, the ordinary performing of consciousness. The implications crowd one in, and the correlation between objectivity and subjectivity is too great to allow the meaning of life to escape. Thus there is no "room" to will meaning, for an inescapable public meaning is willed for one. Frankl notes that his therapy consisted in making the victims conscious that it was still possible to take an attitude toward the inescapable, and through this to retrieve the meaning of life. One confronted the inevitable with one's own confrontation of it. In the experience of art, the will-to-meaning is recovered by the artificial suspension of official consciousness of being, and possible new attitudes to the particulars of one's existence, to the unavoidability of one's being-in-the-world, are generated as afterthoughts, as it were, of the personal experience of suspension.

Without existing in this numinous situation, the work of art becomes so phenomenally objective as to be reducible to, as Husserl calls them, "really immanent parts".[42] Such a naturalistic analysis of art at the expense of a phenomenological analysis of its intentional implications, is in essence both the means and end of so-called art-appreciation. When Ziff writes of appreciation as an aspecting of the work of art, such an aspect emerges as a really immanent part of the work put on display for objectifying consciousness.[43] In another tact, when Dewey argues that all appreciation is a re-creation of the rhythms of the natural creation of the work of art, such rhythms emerge as the objective nature of art.[44] Only the dictum that taste cannot be disputed denies the necessity of appreciation. It, too, is a distraction from seeing art as a life-meaning in a life-world, and it is perhaps the most dangerously objectifying approach to art, since it operates within the situation of art-experience, claiming to offer a "proper" experience of art. Such propriety in approach usurps the possibility of any independent consciousness of art, with personal concern the most radically independent of any approach.

The anxiety aroused by the concern for art can be described as simultaneously benign and malignant. Both belie the ease with which personal meaning might be presumed to be achieved. Benign anxiety relieves conventional consciousness of its binding power, relaxing hardened values and meanings into a flux of feeling, easing commitment to them. Under the impact of art they seem fictional, to be studied for their implications but not to be lived for their results. Under benign anxiety opportunity is afforded for the emergence of new attitudes to life, as speculative ventures of feeling. The attitude presents itself as a noumenal limit to life, affording it security and completion, not as a phenomenal reality particularizing one's being. The work of art itself seems to project a possible world of being, or a new kind of being-in-the-world, as when Kandinsky writes of entering a work of art as casually as one enters a room,[45] or when Matisse writes of relaxing in his art as one might in an armchair.[46] Here, not simply metaphors for being-with-art are offered, but new attitudes toward being in general, a new relaxedness toward reality. Analogies are offered for new experiences of meaningfulness. A new consciousness of existence comes in under the auspices of art, implying the ease with which the will-to-meaning operates in the world of art, existence's lack of compulsion in the work of art. This absence of frustration becomes the key to the meaning of life, not its answer, but that which suggests the possibility that the life-world might indeed take on a personal meaning. Kandinsky and Matisse ask the spectator to trust the work of art, for only by doing so can he trust himself.

Malignant anxiety exposes life's emptiness, the shallowness of all life-meanings. To have discovered alternative attitudes to life is to become aware of the possibility that none might be ultimate. To claim absoluteness for any attitude is to be absurd, but it is also to make commitment difficult. It is to paralyze the possibility of commitment because there is nothing worth committing oneself to. Objectively, there is no single attitude that can claim priority over any other, no life-consciousness which has superior claims to another insofar as it is a consciousness of the life-world, except for the fact that it is one's own. Thus, as much as it reveals the life-world as the world of personal meaning, art makes it impossible for that personal meaning to arise, by making us conscious that it is limited to the person rather than universally valid. The risk of being completely personal in the life-world is not taken by consciousness. Thus, what Sartre calls the spontaneity of consciousness[47] is not an unmixed blessing, insofar as it refuses itself when it comes to determinate relations with a world, a definite mode of being-in-the-world. Art arouses this spontaneity of consciousness, this objectless self-owning, but it also makes clear that any commitment to a given attitude to being-in-the-world, a possibility which art itself posits, involves forfeiting spontaneity of being-conscious, renouncing what might be called the creativity of consciousness. Anxiety thus on the one hand affords new possibilities for authentically owning oneself, but on the other hand imparts an uncanny sense of inauthenticity of one's personal existence. Art reminds us that we suffer what has been called "dreadful freedom,"[48] necessarily willing our own meaning, acting as subjects, but at the same time that no meaning is absolute, no commitment is permanent, and that every attitude is an objectification of ourselves which immediately falsifies the subjective spontaneity of our consciousness, which negates the originality of our personal existence in the world. On the one hand, art offers numinous communication with the life-world; on the other hand, it frustrates our will-to-meaning in the subtlest way, showing us that no meaning we will is more than our own, showing objective meaning to be an abyss of possibilities, a range with infinite implications and no firm foothold, a range over which we must keep moving— one thinks of Heidegger's sense of existence as a perpetual farewell—not necessarily without a sense of our own direction, but blindly with respect to the whole of what might be possible. Art, then, works as much against existence as for it, making the personal as precarious as it makes it significant. It negates exactly what it affirms, the possibility of exclusive life-attitudes personally suited to oneself. Finally, it offers no clues to action with respect to any attitude, no sense of the worldly consequences of consciousness, of the full implications of intentionality. It gives one no way of effectively changing one's existing intentionality, insofar as it makes sense in the strictest personal terms or as a kind of generalized "philosophy of life". Thus, it creates as much self-loss as hope for a new self. It allows one to imagine oneself in another world, or as another person in the same world, but it gives one no way of effectively transcending this world with its meaning of life, which never quite becomes a philosophy of life, but remains a philosophical restraint on the spontaneity of one's consciousness. While the world is always transcendent of oneself, it is also immanent insofar as it has meaning. Art sets these two existential realities against one another. The experience of art ends in an unresolved conflict between these two intentionalities, in the self-conflict of consciousness.

This conflict is not so much resolved as suppressed by objective taste, i.e., the judgment of taste, with all its paraphernalia of appreciation of and education of art, with its categorical understanding of art. To make the art-object conform to the subject is intolerable because it reduces the subject to self-destructive tension. A qualitative change in the approach to art is made. The subject must conform to the art-object, to avoid suicidal inner conflict, self-violence of self-contradiction, if for no other reason. The turn to the objective is an existential saving device, but one which blinds existence to its own ambiguity, imposing certainty at the expense of penetration but for the sake of survival. Everyman has a right to his taste, no matter how frivolous. That is, everyman has the right to put the work of art back into place in the world, thereby ostracizing it from his life except insofar as it is objective, one more object among many. The work of art is restored to the oblivion of objecthood it had before it acquired personal meaning. Reduced to irrelevance so that ordinary life may take its course, it becomes one more thing to be located in the arena of being, this fixed place in being described by equally fixed co-ordinates of consciousness. Will-to-meaning, spontaneity of consciousness, existential anxiety or neurosis are swept away in the new positivistic approach to art, instituted by the arbitrary decision of the judgment of taste. For the issue is not whether taste approves or disapproves of a given work of art, but that it implies a matter of fact attitude to art which denies it personal meaning, significance in the life-world. The accepted arbitrariness of taste, and even desperate amusement at its relativity,[49] are indications that the judgment of taste *per se* is of no account, but rather what it tells us about the attitude to art. In this context the emotional meaning of the judgment of taste is strictly positivistic, in the sense that one or the other particular, objective emotion of the spectator is "expressed" by the judgment, its vulgarity disguised in sublime form. The emotion operates within a presupposed, unquestioned intentionality, and is not the anxiety set loose by the questioning of intentionality *per se.* The personal character of the emotion is belied by its psycho-social source, i.e., by its being a direct consequence of a naive being-in-the-world, a consciousness of the world which has not been studied for its implications, a commitment to and positing of the world which has not been bracketed by the epoché.

The special sense of significance the work of art afforded survives in the form of what is conventionally called "heightened sensibility". Heightened sensibility is no more than an attenuated self-consciousness, a truncated sense of the personal meaning of art in the life-world. All ambiguous anxiety is sublimated into sensing, almost abstract in itself because isolated from other activities of existence—certainly tautologous, since its consequence is hypersensitivity to the sensuousness of the work of art.[50] It amounts to little more than a momentary consciousness of the unity of the being of the work of art, an illuminating flash of its sensuous coherence, of its vital integrity. Such a consciousness is also numinous, like the consciousness of the communication of the work of art, in that it gives us the illusion of a latent order of being made manifest through the work of art, a microcosm of the sensuous meaning of reality. However, it is a surface event in the work of art, and in effect is no more than the sign of what the objectivists have talked about all along—the form of the work of art, its essential reality. Such sensuous awareness of the work of art's sensuous unity is the first phase of the process of the objectification of the work of art, whose final step is the regarding of the work of art as an object in itself, and of value in itself, and so to be judged by taste. The "new sensibility" may presuppose that being itself is given integrity by art, but such a presupposition is a hypothetical projection on the order of a religious commitment to the *status quo.* In effect it accepts the way things are, literally, by binding them figuratively in a new visual order. It thus justifies conventional consciousness in its conception of the world, adding some colour to the main outlines. Such a sense of the sensuous order of art mitigates the anxiety it aroused, which may not have changed one's commitment to the world but made one aware of the possibility or even the necessity of doing so, since ultimately one was not so categorically committed as one presupposed.

Initially revolutionary in its arousal of anxious awareness of existence, the work of art settles into a conservative stance. It becomes a mode of accepting the *status quo,* and even making the acceptance "stimulating". The sensuously vivid order of art seems to say that the life-world is not, after all, a chaos of possibilities, an infinite regression of implications, that one's life is not the worst if not the best, and that its meanings are not so "arbitrary" as the personal experience of art might lead one to suppose. The anxiety aroused by art is reduced to a temporary confusion of consciousness. Anxiety is reduced to aroused vitality, and consciousness to an attractive world of appearances. We are ready for Schiller's complaint.

In the judgment of taste there are two "moments". The first is, in effect, the reduction of the work of art to an eternal object, to eternal sensuousness, to what has been called the "eternal present".[51] The work of art is a permanent immediacy, the eternal verity of sensuousness, never entirely exemplified in the consciousness of its spectators but always numinously felt or appreciated by them. This new Platonism of sensuousness removes the work of art from participation in the world as effectively as Plato's intelligibles, existing in the same ambiguous relation to experienced being. Whatever beauty it might have is no more than an intoxication of consciousness, inducing what Kant called the rhapsody of consciousness. The second "moment" of objective taste is when the eternal object of art is exposed to the consensus of opinion. The work of art is expected to be accessible to all, one judgment of it is assumed to be as good as any other insofar as it is judged tastefully, rather than appreciated by the *cognoscenti.* And with patience and knowledge even the ordinary mortal, still possessed of his basic right to judgment of art, can approximate to the sensibility of the *cognoscenti.* All, then, are presumed to have the right to say whether or not they "like" the work of art. Hence the so-called universality of judgment. Historians and philosophers of art bring up the rear in this phase of judgment, completing the eternalization or perfect objectification of art by periodizing it in time, analyzing it in detail, and speculating on its essence.

Between the first and second moments of tasteful judgment an ironical relationship exists. The first raises the work of art into the cultural firmament, the second puts it into everyman's hands, and in the hands of specialists, who, by reducing it to really immanent parts, make it further accessible to everyone else. Why is the work of art considered self-evidently eternal, a thing of permanent value, when everyone has the right to pass his insubstantial judgment upon it, to have his own particular taste in art? One recalls the injunction not to take God's name in vain. Yet the work of art is on everyone's lips, and everyone's judgment of it is respected, as it would not be in the realms of science or ordinary daily practice. But this is because only consciousness is at stake in art, not truth or practicality or action. The fact that art is expected to be appreciated while science is expected to be known as truthful shows how little is thought to be at stake in it. Appreciation is an ambiguous phenomenon, for while it implies consciousness of works of art it is not conscious of them as intentionally directed, as having implications for intentionality *per se,* or more simply, of having significant influence on one's feeling of being at home in the world. Appreciation is a pause in the serious business of consciousness, knowing and acting in the world.

In effect, appreciation avoids the existential implications of art, restoring it to the conventional consciousness one has of things, "one" in the Heideggerean sense of "das Man". Through appreciation, art is neutralized into an objective possession of one's consciousness, something rationally spoken of rather than irrationally experienced. Appreciation, as such, is the final stage of the judgment of taste. It voids the essentially irrational position of art in the life-world, and in fact reduces the life-world to the world of facts. Art, making one lose one's way in the life-world, forcing one away from being oneself so that one could exist personally, is reduced to the ornament of the world of facts, the most vivid of facts. Appreciation of art restores rationality to the experience of art—a rationality destroyed by concern for art—in the sense of putting all the prerogatives of the experience in the hands of the analytic power of the everyday ego. Appreciation, then, denies that art is, as phenomenology thought, the royal road to the meaning of life, but instead makes it a comfortable way to everyday existence.

On a cultural level, taste's objective attitude to art is demonstrated by so-called changes of taste. Artists once scorned, have their works raised to prominence, thereby mocking their fates and lives. Such a change of taste is an instance of taste's subtle frivolity, the irony of its indiscriminateness. For by changing itself taste keeps consciousness from ever attending too closely to any work of art, such attention perhaps issuing in an irrational, personal experience of art. Consciousness is in subliminal fear of the devaluation of its art-objects, and so never commits itself to them personally. Instead, it is absorbed in the comparison of works of art, searching out their objective value to establish a hierarchy of worth. It is thus absorbed in the game of taste at its most objective and experientially indifferent. One is glazed at the level of objectivity, studying works of art as though they had nothing to do with one's life.

A recent form of the power of fickle taste is the so-called "happening", which cannot be judged by taste, yet which most completely destroys the possibility of any personal relationship with art by completely absorbing the person, in his dailiness, into it. Taste has here outdone itself, casting aside its judgment as too weak a repression of the existential possibilities of art by using the given immediacy of life as art itself. The happening thus allows consciousness no discovery of its powers, for it keeps it absorbed on the level of a disguised objectivity. It insists upon urgent involvement with the art-event, complete unconsciousness of one's self-commitment. By turning art into an event as well as an object it usurps life itself, for in its exact correspondence to life it forces it to stay what it is if it is to be art. If life changed, if consciousness was always at a "distance" from its objects, then it might be able to be itself, whereas to be shown unchanged in art it has no need to be itself, for then it would not be art. The happening attempts an art in which the spectator can encounter his own existence without having to confront it. Art here is no longer a consciousness confronting life with itself, but a consciousness of life as nothing but itself. The spectator's unquestioned intentionality is confirmed by being writ larger and becoming overfamiliar. Here art de-interprets existence and existence has no need to interpret art, for both are overfamiliar in their ordinariness. Thus we have artless art, art using no masterful techniques of reductive concentration, no suspension of world-positing for the sake of owning one's own meaning. Ironically, such anti-art or life-art destroys the very possibility of exploring the consciousness which created it, let alone the opportunity of exploring consciousness in general which art affords. For in overwhelming us with the immediacy of our existence it overwhelms our self-consciousness, and in overwhelming our self-consciousness it frustrates the will-to-meaning, in such a way that it cannot recover.

Notes

1.   Edmund Husserl, *Ideas* (London, 1952), p. 280.

2.   Husserl, *op. cit.,* pp. 311-312. This remark is made in the context of a discussion of "the consciousness of the 'picture' " as "the neutrality-modification of the perception."

3.   Assuming, as Husserl says, "that fancy is in fact itself a neutrality-modification" (*op. cit.,* p. 309), and that such neutralization is epoché, i.e., "completely removes and renders powerless every doxic modality to which it is related" (*op. cit.,* p. 306), then it implies a "positing of the essence" which "does not imply any positing of individual existence whatsoever" (*op. cit.,* p. 57).

4.   Husserl, *op. cit.,* pp. 312-313.

5.   Edmund Husserl, *Erfahrung Und Urteil* (Hamburg, 1954), p. 320. The remark is made in the context of a discussion of the difference between the "embodiment" of the work of art, e.g., Goethe's *Faust,* in numerous examples, e.g., books, and its "individualization" as uniquely self-identical. See also *Ideas,* p. 312, where Husserl distinguishes "the fact that the *fancy-modification* as a presentation is *repeatable*" from the fact that "the *repetition of the neutralizing*" operation "*is essentially excluded.*"

6. Husserl, *Ideas*, p. 309.

7. Husserl, *op. cit.*, p. 306.

8. Edmund Husserl, *Formal And Transcendental Logic* (The Hague, 1969), p. 245 remarks: "... every sort of intentional unity becomes a 'transcendental clue' to guide constitutional 'analyses' and these acquire a wholly unique character: They are *not analyses in the usual sense* (analyses into really immanent parts), but *uncoverings of intentional implications* (advancing, perhaps, from an experience to the system of experiences that are *predelineated* as possible."

9. Husserl, *Ideas*, p. 313.

10. Ibid.

11. Ibid., p. 312. The themes can be said to arise in terms of the "attentional backgrounds" which every "image-object or fancy-object" "necessarily" has, where 'background' is a title for potential directions of interest and 'apprehensions' " (*op. cit.*, p. 317). But it can also be said to arise as the implied substance behind the shadow-image, for "in the form of fancy" the substantial "experience" "is characterized not as being really present, but as being 'as though' it were present" (*op. cit.*, p. 315). Husserl himself uses "metaphorical speech concerning shadows, reflexion, and image," making clear that he means "no suggestion of mere illusion or deceitful intention" (*op. cit.*, p. 319). Themes arise because the "real" experience and its "modification" into the image "correspond *idealiter* with absolute precision, and *yet* have *"not the same essential nature" (ibid.),* "so that to the *primordial essence*" of the experience "there corresponds the *counter-essence*" of the theme *(ibid.).*

12. Donald B. Kuspit, "Fiction And Phenomenology," *Philosophy And Phenomenological Research*, XXIX (1968), p. 33.

13. Husserl, *Ideas*, p. 415.

14. This is a consequence of what Husserl, *ibid.*, p. 414 calls *"the regional 'Idea' of the Thing in general,"* which can serve as a "transcendental clue" or *"guiding clue* in phenomenological inquiries" (*op. cit.*, p. 416) just because of "the dimension of the infinite" which it "implicitly contains" (*op. cit.*, p. 415) or because of *"the determinately infinite multiplicities of appearances"* (*op. cit.*, pp. 418-419) it implies. This determinate infinity of implications is exactly what the work of art embodies, and although Husserl speaks of its *"correlation"* with *"the determinate appearing object as unity"* (*op. cit.*, p. 418), the unique character of the work of art is its ability to suspend the law of their conformation so that the implications can be studied in and for themselves, even without any suspicion that they imply essential generalities or typical essences.

15. Donald B. Kuspit, *op. cit.*, pp. 28-29.

16. Husserl, *op. cit.*, p. 199, remarks that "in phenomenology as in all eidetic sciences, representations, or, to speak more accurately, *free fancies*, assume, *a privileged position over against perceptions*, and that, *even in the phenomenology of perception itself, excepting of course that of the sensory data."* As Husserl says (p. 200), images afford "a freedom which opens ... for the first time an entry into the spacious realms of essential possibility with their infinite horizons of essential knowledge". Finally, Husserl asserts (p. 201) "that the *element* which *makes up the life of phenomenology as of all eidetical science* is *'fiction,'* that fiction is the source whence the knowledge of 'eternal truths' draws its sustenance". This seems to contradict Husserl's assertion (p. 280) that "there is no 'royal road' in phenomenology any more than in philosophy," but the contradiction is obviated by the context of this remark, viz., "the working out the difference between noesis and noema" where their "articulation in parallel structures" becomes difficult to comprehend and carry out (p. 279). However, fiction is present at the beginning of phenomenological inquiry, as in fact the coign of vantage which puts us in a

position to grab hold of consciousness as an independent phenomenon, and not a part of the logic of its conclusions, where its constituents are disclosed. However, there is no doubt that fiction predisposes this logic to a possible form. That is, it seems possible to assert that the constituents of consciousness are the purified implications of fiction, hypostasized and raised to essences by logical activity. It seems clear that fiction gives Husserl his model for phenomenological reduction, much as mathematics gives him his model for the intentional analysis of the constituents of consciousness. Conversely, it is possible to assert that mathematics and art are two eidectic sciences of which phenomenology is their root.

17. This becomes apparent when Husserl speaks (*op. cit.*, p. 233) of the necessary essence of "the 'being directed towards,' 'the being busied with,' 'adopting an attitude,' 'undergoing or suffering from' " as "something 'from the Ego,' or in the reverse direction 'to the Ego'; and this Ego is the *pure* Ego, and no reduction can get any grip on it," just because it is the source of all reductions. An attitude, in effect, is a form of the pure Ego's "glancing towards" (*op. cit.*, p. 121). Husserl's use of the aesthetic attitude shows it to be the most elementary glance of consciousness, i.e., a pre-logical, pre-judgmental glance at the object, not as object, i.e., as what is the case—for this would be to presuppose its truthfulness, the very possibility of its objectivity—but as its own manifestation, as a kind of clumsy self-image of consciousness itself. In the aesthetic attitude to objects consciousness sees itself in objects as through a glass darkly.

18. Husserl's use of objecthood as a springboard in the approach to art very much resembles the current critical analysis of minimal art, where, as Michael Fried says ("Art and Objecthood," *Minimal Art*, ed. Gregory Battcock (New York, 1968), p. 125), "It is as though objecthood alone can, in the present circumstances, secure something's identity, if not as non-art, at least as neither painting nor sculpture; or as though a work of art—more accurately, a work of modernist painting or sculpture—were in some essential respect *not an object*."

19. Donald B. Kuspit, *op. cit.*, pp. 30-31.

20. The whole issue of interpretation as a necessary possibility of approach to the work of art is dealt with by E.D. Hirsch, Jr., *Validity In Interpretation* (New Haven, 1967), a work which claims to be Husserlian in orientation, but is only naively so. Hirsch uses Husserl as a justification for speaking of criticism as a "subjective stance" towards the work of art, which eventually becomes "self-critical," especially insofar as it claims to approximate to the artist's (p. 241). Hirsch has no sense of epoché, or of critical interpretation as a possible epoché of the work, as a meditation on essential modes of being-in-the-world disclosed by the work under phenomenological scrutiny, nor simply as the disclosure of the independent intentionality of the work distinct from the disclosure of its author's intentionality. Instead, the work is reduced, in conventional fashion, to thematic content. Hirsch, in other words, after a fashionable Husserlian gambit, performs, as Husserl puts it, an "analysis in the usual sense".

21. Marcel Duchamp, in "The Creative Act," *The New Art*, ed. Gregory Battcock (New York, 1966), pp. 25-26, remarks: "All in all, the creative act is not performed by the artist alone; the spectator brings the work in contact with the external world by deciphering and interpreting its inner qualifications and thus adds his contribution to the creative act." Jean-Paul Sartre had an almost similar argument in *What is Literature?* (New York, 1949), pp. 41-42: "The creative act is only an incomplete and abstract moment in the production of a work. If the author existed alone he would be able to write as much as he liked; the work as *object* would never see the light of day and he would either have to put down his pen or despair. But the operation of writing implies that of reading as its dialectical correlative and these two connected acts necessitate two distinct agents. It is the conjoint effort of author and reader which brings upon the scene the concrete and imaginary object which is the work of the mind. There is no art except by and for others." Again (p. 43): "In a word, the reader is conscious of disclosing in creating, of creating by disclosing."

22.   One thinks of the arguments of Morris Weitz in "The Role of Theory In Aesthetics," *Journal of Aesthetics And Art Criticism,* XV (1956), pp. 27-35. For all their abstractness, they are symptomatic of a problem that began with modernism, i.e., that are correlate with a moment in history, *viz.,* the inability to offer a single set of properties that would define a work of art. The works historically accepted as art outstrip the definition philosophically acceptable, or the definition philosophically tenable finds no exemplifications in current production of art. As with many insoluble problems, one can take it as meaningless, or realize that one needs a novel, as yet unformulated perspective to comprehend it. See also Paul Ziff, "The Task of Defining A Work of Art," *The Philosophical Review,* LXII (1953), pp. 58-78. The fault of the so-called analytic approach to this problem is its failure to realize that one may have to introduce psycho-social considerations to bring it into focus, as well as a comprehension of past presuppositions about the nature of art. In general, a new sense of method and end is necessary which must take cognizance of the historical character of the problem, which itself is preliminary to an investigation into the new meaning of art and a new intentionality of being-conscious of art.

23.   Husserl, *Formal And Transcendental Logic, op. cit.,* p. 209, argues that any predication has its non-predicative source in experience, but such experience "makes sense" only insofar as it is evident in judgment. The experience of art, in other words, is disclosed by the judgment of taste, and there is no way of going behind, as it were, the judgment to see whether the experience makes sense prior to its logical use as the evidence for a judgment. But this, ultimately, is exactly what epoché permits us to do with the experience of art, *viz.,* to see it as meaningful apart from any judgment one might make upon it in terms of its expected role in the "natural" world. Similarly, in *Ideas, op. cit.,* p. 58 Husserl remarks that "We can be intuitively aware of essences and can apprehend them after a certain fashion without their becoming 'objects *about* which'." The same can be said about art. It is in the judgment of taste that art becomes an "object about which" we can talk, but art is also subject to disclosure prior to discourse in the sense that we can intuitively apprehend its implications.

24.   Immanuel Kant, *Critique of Judgment* (New York, 1951), p. 37.

25.   Kant, *op. cit.,* p. 50.

26.   Martin Heidegger, *Being And Time* (New York, 1962), pp. 235-241. Because "Being-in-the-world is essentially care" (p. 237), any form of being-with, such as being-with-art, is essentially prior to any positings, such as judgments, about what one is with. Being-with-art, or concern with art, is, to use Heidegger's word, "ahead of" (p. 236) being about art, or positing its nature or value.

27.   David Hume, "Of The Standard Of Taste," *Philosophy Of Art And Aesthetics,* eds. Frank A. Tillman and Steven M. Cahn (New York, 1969), p. 120.

28.   See Viola Hopkins Winner, *Henry James And The Visual Arts* (Charlottesville, Va., 1970), chapter I, "The Apprenticeship Of An Amateur." Winner speaks of James' situation as a "search for a bridge between Self and Others, his inner world and the threatening outer" (p. 11), noting that if James' "'alarm' may be understood to represent the fear of experiencing only the image of life, not life at first hand, the 'bliss' may be taken for the sense of mastering the world, of approximating experience, through art" (p. 12).

29.   E.g., Georg Simmel, "Der Bildrahmen," *Zur Philosophie Der Kunst* (Potsdam, 1922), pp. 46.-52.

30.   F.W. Dupee, the editor of James' *Autobiography* (New York, 1956), p. xii, notes that "In the almost visionary later pages of *Notes Of A Son And Brother,* James, like his younger contemporaries, seems to conceive of the literary vocation as a kind of second birth, a new soul which struggles into being out of pain and loss and humiliation." The fact of James' eventual

commitment to literary work does not mute the significance of the fact that in his youth, before he had decided on a literary vocation, the aesthetic *per se* became the only source of salvation from a troublesome world of feelings and "facts of life".

31.   Winner, *op. cit.,* p. 3.

32.   Friedrich Schiller *On The Aesthetic Education Of Man* (London, 1954), p. 57.

33.   Schiller, *op. cit.,* p. 59.

34.   Ibid.

35.   Weitz, *op. cit.*

36.   Heidegger, *op. cit.,* p. 215.

37.   Viktor E. Frankl, *The Doctor And The Soul* (New York, 1967), p. xi.

38.   Edward Bullough, "Psychical Distance As A Factor In Art And An Aesthetic Principle," *British Journal Of Psychology,* V (1912), pp. 87-98.

39.   Immanuel Kant, *Critique Of Pure Reason* (London, 1956), pp. 297-570. Kant speaks of "transcendental illusion" exerting "its influence on principles that are in no wise intended for use in experience," so that we have no criterion of their correctness (p. 298). Moreover, unlike logical illusion, it "does not cease even after it has been detected and its invalidity clearly revealed by transcendental criticism" (p. 299). It involves the taking of "the subjective necessity of a connection of our concepts, which is to the advantage of the understanding, for an objective necessity in the determination of things in themselves" (p. 299). Transcendental illusion thus gives rise to ambiguities, in the case of the work of art, that it communicates like a subject yet is essentially an object. However much the error might be "duly curbed by criticism" (p. 299), it nonetheless throws light on the way art is taken, much as the illusions Kant discusses throw light on the way man would like the world as a whole to be. In Kant's cases, the errors revolved around an expectation of the coherence of things as a whole. In art's case, the error involves the expectation of the personal meaningfulness of the work for the spectator. In both cases a unique consciousness imparts an indisputable meaningfulness to a limited object.

40.   Ludwig Wittgenstein, *Tractatus Logico-Philosophicus,* 5.621, 6.4312, 6.5, and especially 6.521.

41.   Frankl, *op. cit.,* pp. 35-37. We do not mean Frankl's attitudinal values to be taken in an exclusively psychological sense, *viz.,* as the consequence of a "response to the restraints upon (one's) potentialities" or the result of a "person's attitude toward an unalterable fate" (p. 35). The harshness—derived from Frankl's awareness of the difficult, extreme occasions on which these values made themselves evident—is mitigated by generalizing them into the consequence of an orientation to an inevitable being-in-the-world. Such an orientation to the given worldliness is not a calculated value-determined response, such as pessimistic or optimistic, but an awareness generated by the difficulty of being-oneself while being-in-the-world, *viz.,* the ambiguity of owning oneself while owning the world.

42.   Husserl, *Formal And Transcendental Logic, op. cit.,* p. 209.

43.   Paul Ziff, "Reasons In Art Criticism," *Philosophy and Education,* ed. Israel Scheffler, (Boston, 1958), pp. 219-236.

44.   John Dewey, *Art As Experience* (London, 1934), chapter VI, "The Natural History of Form" and chapter II, "Having An Experience." See also Donald B. Kuspit, "Dewey's Critique Of Art For Art's Sake," *Journal of Aesthetics And Art Criticism,* XXVII (1968), pp. 93-98.

45.   Wassily Kandinsky, "Reminiscences," *Modern Artists On Art,* ed. R.L. Herbert (Englewood Cliffs, N.J., 1965), p. 31: "I have for many years searched for the possibility of letting the viewer

'stroll' in the picture, forcing him to forget himself and dissolve into the picture." The element of casualness is of the essence here. The picture becomes the museum whose contents one casually, unself-consciously moves among. The work of art is to be experienced without any forced pursuit of its objective meaning.

46. Henri Matisse, "Notes Of A Painter," *Problems In Aesthetics,* ed. Morris Weitz (New York, 1959), p. 345: "What I dream of is an art of balance, of purity and serenity devoid of troubling or depressing subject matter, an art which might be for every mental worker, be he businessman or writer, like an appeasing influence, like a mental soother, something like a good armchair in which to rest from physical fatigue." The emphasis here is on the work of art as an experience incommensurate with worldly work, an experience taken as casually and as necessarily as rest. In both Kandinsky and Matisse the quality of ease in relation to the work of art is emphasized, and this ease allows for the work to rise up as a meaningful experience in the course of life, so meaningful that like life itself one is inescapably immersed in it.

47. Jean-Paul Sartre, *The Transcendence Of The Ego* (New York, 1957), pp. 96-97.

48. Marjorie Grene, *Dreadful Freedom* (Chicago, 1948), p. vii, discusses "existentialism as the attempt at a new 'revaluation of values'."

49. E.g., F.L. Lucas, *Literature And Psychology* (Ann Arbor, Mich., 1957), chapter XI, "The Relativity of Taste," where this becomes an ironical attitude toward the "art of interpretation," requiring the critic to describe and explain his own reactions (p. 213).

50. This is well-illustrated by Susan Sontag's essay "Against Interpretation" in the book of that title (New York, 1965), where the author calls for "an erotics of art" "in place of a hermeneutics" of art (p. 14). Such an erotics would "reveal the sensuous surface of art without mucking about in it" (p. 13). What Sontag neglects to note is that such a revelation reduces to an account of the medium of which the art-object is an instance of, the terms of sensuous description being limited either to those of the medium or quality terms which are inevitably mucky, or if not, then vague, and always implicating subjective preconceptions if not predispositions.

51. The term is used by Giedion as the title of a two volume discussion of "change and constancy" in art. Volume I *The Beginning Of Art* (New York, 1962), is especially to the point.

3

Dialectical Reasoning in Meyer Schapiro

"Intriguing opposites" could be a subtitle to signal the pervasiveness of "polarity," as Schapiro often calls it, or more simply the pursuit of "double meaning" in his thought, whether it be dealing with art, society, ideas, or, more typically, their "interplay," another favorite Schapiro word.[1] He uses it, along with "intrigue," and a number of other terms, not only to articulate poetically but to explore analytically the binding intensity between opposites or contrasts he is most—almost obsessively—interested in.[2] The awareness of "antithesis"— another term Schapiro likes—characterizes his general attitude as well as methodological approach to art, and in fact gives his empiricism its liveliness and "radicality."[3] Thus, in his analysis of the famous trumeau of the abbey church of Souillac, he concentrates on the "remarkable intrigue" that "animates the opposed predacious beasts" that constitute the trumeau.[4] It is out of his sensitivity to the vividness of their "enlacement," as he calls it at one point, that his description grows. This sensitivity is the sign of a general consciousness of contradiction—of what might be called the "integrity" of contradiction: Schapiro's conception of "engaged" opposites as an irreducible unit of form and meaning. Thus he never begins an analysis with a neutral description of simple facts—he never takes the Souillac animals as isolated phenomena—and then attempts to demonstrate their complex togetherness. Rather, he begins with the fact of the "vehemence," as he puts it—facts are always expressive physiognomies for Schapiro—of their relationship, and then, in the course of accounting for its indissolubility, moves to a discussion of its particular details. It is the relationship that "explains" the details rather than vice versa. For Schapiro, the particularity of the dynamic relationship stands out more than the particularity of its details, which are static and general without it.

For Schapiro, the unity of opposites is indisputable and primary, and while the historical detail which empirically constitutes that unity is by no means secondary, Schapiro never ventures to present it outside some characteristic structure of opposites, whose workings seem to make experience "work," that is, give it personal as well as public significance. Schapiro, then, is absorbed in both the abstract logic and expressive and social possibilities generated by opposites, which are understood to be conceptually fundamental and simultaneously functional within their empirical unity. For him, opposites bespeak what is fundamental in society and personal life, where they often remain unresolved—in conflict; and in art, where, happily, on a utopian level—for aesthetic perception—they are united to exciting effect, resolved in surprising ways, at least in the most intriguing art. Whether writing of medieval or modern art, and the psychological conflicts they reflect, Schapiro has always been interested in the way forms and means—and psychosocial facts—"interlock in alienation,"[5] in styles in which "contrast" becomes "a rule"[6] and which "multiply oppositions."[7] There is a push, almost compulsion, to reconciliation—one of the things that gives his account of medieval art its power is his use of modernist methods of formalist analysis—and to comprehensive empirical variety within the resulting unity. At the same time, Schapiro is deeply absorbed in the "restlessness"—another word that frequently recurs—of the relationship between opposites, a restlessness breaking down the superficially schematic character of their relationship, and articulating it organically rather than mechanically.[8] Because opposites haunt one another in restless interplay, they are more than a "Platonic mechanism."[9] Fleshed out by their restlessness into forces that give form its expressive energy—its persuasive, carrying power—opposites lose their abstractness, their aura of *sub specie aeternitatis,* and become, by reason of the urgency of their relationship, the driving force of concrete history, almost a *perpetuum mobile* of experience. They are the "inner necessity" of history, and while Schapiro does not directly "predict" the direction of history, he consistently uses certain opposites to qualify its dialectic, implying at least an ideal or possible direction.

The Language of Dialectic

To make my case for the dominance of dialectical reasoning in Schapiro, and to show how subtle his dialectic is, I would like to present in greater detail the language with which he articulates it, and instances of what might be regarded as "ruling" antitheses by reason of their consistent recurrence in his thought. Such dominant antitheses—particularly the contrast between authority and autonomy—in effect govern his entire exposition of art, as well as function generally as constants in his consideration of the human condition, and in fact indispensable structures for concretizing that condition. However, Schapiro rarely examines such elementary structures without focusing them through their artistic manifestation. It is not only that the art is inseparable from the structures, but that the structures, if they are truly elementary in their intensity, seem to demand artistic reification, that is, issue in a unique style, symbol of unique history.

To the language then. First we might note what can be called Schapiro's use of a principle of doubling. He rarely presents anything straightforwardly, but always as a "calculated ambiguity."[10] He speaks of Champfleury's "double attitude...to the events of 1848 and 1849,"[11] the "double character of the mousetrap...as domestic object and theological symbol" in the Mérode altarpiece of Robert Campin,[12] the "double process" whereby religious authority becomes humanized and realism spiritualized in that same altarpiece,[13] and a "double gesture...not merely designed to represent a more complex interaction, but...an element of a style which promotes contrasts and movement," and "constitutes an expressive form as well as an expressive symbol."[14] Images almost always have a "double character," particularly in Romanesque art, and particularly images of force[15]—the force suggestive of the energy necessary to integrate opposites, and generated by their integration. In such images figures from a sacred biblical context, such as Samson, are used for their secular import, or profane elements, such as the ass's jawbone that killed Abel, enliven a religious context. In such cases what seems important for Schapiro is the surprising reversal of meaning, the unexpected shift of context—a dialectical surprise, sprung by the intersection of opposites, which upsets our sense of the normative. Schapiro is fascinated with "reversing the order of interpretation,"[16] and a good deal of his work demonstrates such reversal as the consequence of the interplay between manifest and latent meaning. His sense of the way meaning works is in part derived from the psychoanalytic conception of dream interpretation, applied with fresh cunning and sense of irony, and even used against psychoanalysis, as we will see at the end of this paper. Above all, Schapiro is wittily aware of the unpredictable relationship holding between meanings and the forms that convey them, whether these be visual or verbal, as when he notes "that just as two unlike words (or syntactical forms) may have a common ancestor, so in different languages two similar words with the same meaning may be independent of each other."[17] He means this to apply to the language of art and its development, as when he speaks of the "syntax" of painting— "imageless" or abstract painting—which he regards "as complex as that of an art of representation."[18]

There is also in Schapiro a redundant interest in "counterpart elements" and "countermovements,"[19] all sorts of "counterpart patterns" including "counterpart symmetrical gestures,"[20] and all sorts of contrasts, especially the most intense kind, those of color[21] and direction,[22] as when legs vigorously cross in a stark X-form.[23] He is captivated by oppositions of the most trivial sort, such as in adossed animal form,[24] and those with the most paradoxical import, as in the way "saltimbanque" and "banker" derive from the same "bank" or bench of the fairs, while the former symbolizes the impoverished yet independent artist, in theory a man of free, deeply feeling spirit, and the latter names an authority on and priest of money.[25] Schapiro is taken with jugglers and any kind of juggling of words and visual forms,[26] with the way new art negates old art while "the old may persist beside the new in affirming an opposed or declining culture,"[27] and with Augustine's dialectical conception of beauty, that is, his discussion of it "in authentic terms...where God is an artist who employs antitheses of good and evil to form the beauty of the universe, and... where beauty is a compound of opposites, including ugliness and disorder."[28] Schapiro is painfully aware of the "counter-goals" or "competing centers" and "competing directions" that give many of Van Gogh's pictures their agonizing quality,[29] as well as of the way he uses "crossing diagonal lines to give his pictures their power,"[30] and of their general "strain" or tension, generated by such factors as his use of "self-conflicted" forms (e.g., trees crossed into X-form) and the discrepancy created by his use of hyperactivated surfaces or textures and abruptly plunging, however truncated, perspective space, a space whose violent steepness slides us away from the real world of objects to the abyss of unconscious feelings.[31] Schapiro observes Cézanne's "practice of the other pole,"[32] his attempt to overcome the "polarity" between line and color[33] and self and nature,[34] and his use of "counterpart shapes"[35] and "color contrasts"[36] to do so. Schapiro speaks of the "stress of contrasts" in Cézanne's art[37] and the "contradictions" in Van Gogh's,[38] and he attends so deliberately to both artists because of their struggle with opposites. In fact, he regards them as the epitome of the conflicted modern artist, who yet manages to resolve his conflicts,[39] fuse the numerous opposites in a novel, unexpected, unpredictable autonomous whole.[40] Cézanne is the prophet of 20th-century abstraction and Van Gogh of 20th-century expressionism, both of which have a realistic basis and point of departure. Opposites and united opposites—the weapons of analysis and the conditions of synthesis—abound in their careers, and Schapiro ends his account of Van Gogh's art and life—the opposites he most decisively and yet with the greatest difficulty fused—with a coda of opposites Van Gogh most effectively fused:

> He is caught up across the yellow fields from the chaos of the paths and the dread of the approaching birds and carried to the deep blue sky, the region of most nuanced sensibility, a pure, all-absorbing essence in which at last subject and object, part and whole, past and present, near and far, can no longer be distinguished.[41]

Similarly, Schapiro's *Words and Pictures*—written about a generation (twenty-three years) after the Van Gogh essay—dealing with their inextricability in medieval art, ends with a coda of polarities, after the nuanced interplay between words and pictures, images of states of being and actions in becoming, full-face and profile figures are discussed at length. In the grand coda he reconciles "different polar ideas,"[42] showing the "plurality of meaning"[43] which results from their dramatic intersection. Whether they be frontal and profile forms, or black and white, sky and earth, sun and moon, male and female, for Schapiro the key point is their existence as "expressive dualities" rather than static opposites, and above all that while their meaning as "polar forms" depends on the tension at once uniting yet distinguishing them, that meaning acquires its weight "within a prevailing system of (social) values."[44] For Schapiro the abstract universality of the opposites matters less than the way they are personally experienced and historically valued—than the way they are compounded by a concrete human situation. It is out of this that the variability and diversity—freedom and individuality—of their meaning emerges, and it is this kind of materialization that matters most for Schapiro.

Schapiro, then, never ceases talking of "striking contrasts, violent and astounding oppositions,... the antithetic and inverted"—he loves them as much as he says Bernard did.[45] He loves showing, as in his treatment of the Mérode altarpiece, how the marginal (secular-realistic) image acquires major meaning and the major image (religious-transcendental) becomes historically marginal,[46] or how rational form can be used to irrational, eccentric effect, as in the anamorphoses,[47] and, more crucially, in his accounts of Van Gogh and Cézanne, how "direct experience" itself seems to be dialectical, and how this innate ambiguity of experience can be confronted, and seemingly overcome, although never finally, by the willed detachment of the contemplative attitude, an intellectual construction to which Cézanne gave new form and meaning.[48] In all this involvement with dialectic, is there any mention of Hegel, the modern philosopher with whom it is most identified? Only once, and then with approval: "Hegel said very justly that in an age of piety one does not have to be religious in order to create a truly religious work of art, whereas today the most deeply pious artist is incapable of producing it."[49] This is the controlling idea behind Schapiro's treatment of Van Gogh, as he admits—and the central idea in his analysis of the secular aspect of religious art.

Hegel, then, when he appears, does so strongly, but less as a theorist than as an applied dialectician. This is typical of Schapiro, who is interested less in the theory than in the practice of dialectic. Perhaps his most sigificant formulation of it as a characteristic practice is in his notion of "discoordination," by which he means "a grouping or division such that corresponding sets of elements include parts, relations, or properties which negate that correspondence."[50] Discoordinated rather than uncoordinated elements—elements in rather than out of relationship, but not with easy, obvious harmony, and so at first glance out of relationship. (Much of Schapiro's writing corrects the superficial first glance of others. Schapiro does a "double take," in which he shows that seemingly self-evident incoherence in fact involves secret coherence: apparent disharmony is occult harmony.) Thus "contradiction" is experienced as "implied coordination," and the divergences and convergences which constitute the "discoordinate structure" issue in "a necessary balanced scheme," but one whose "balance depends on the negation of the usual order of the symmetrical... scheme."[51] In one of the major examples of discoordinate structure, Schapiro speaks of a "three-part scheme of central and flanking elements implied in the trefoil frame," which can be read as a metaphor for dialectical structure or reconciled opposites.

Growth, Change, Development

One of the reasons Schapiro introduces the idea of discoordination is to obviate any easy conception of dialectic as a mechanically superimposed scheme, as though dialectic was an entirely abstract—ahistorical and nonempirical— guarantee of universal "higher meaning." In the study of Romanesque art, this is the mistake of Jurgis Baltrusaitis. Schapiro wants as little to do with his version of an inflexible, absolute dialectic as Baudelaire wanted to do with Victor Hugo's use of "all the resources of antithesis, all the tricks of apposition" to make "eccentricity itself assume symmetrical forms."[52] Attacking Baltrusaitis's vision of a mechanical dialectic—which, as we will see, Schapiro replaces with his own organic version—he writes:

> We could not discover from this dialectic how a new style arose, or how Romanesque art ever changed at all. It is not an explanation of an active historical process, nor is it, strictly speaking, a dialectical method in the sense of Hegel or Marx. It does not expose the possible latent internal conditions of formal development as Riegl did in calling attention to oppositions within a style which rendered the style unstable and hence suggested fresh changes and solutions. Its principle of change is nowhere verified in a concrete historical sequence nor is there here an empirical consideration of social, religious, technical, or psychological sources of change in the conception or application of works of art; the factor of historical time has been eliminated. . . . A crucial weakness of B.'s dialectic lies in the inactive, neutral role of content in the formation of the work of art; it allows for no interaction between the meanings and shapes; the schemas remain primary and permanent. It is therefore an artificial or schematic dialectic which ignores the meanings of the works, the purpose of the art in Romanesque society and religion, the willed expressive aspects of the forms and meanings (which were created as wholes and not as combinations of antagonistic forms and subjects), and fails to explain the known historical development of Romanesque art. . . .
> From such a dialectic we could hardly deduce the richness and variety of Romanesque art.[53]

Much as "the church took over the dangerous critical method of dialectical reasoning for the demonstration of its dogmas,"[54] so Baltrusaitis took over dialectic to demonstrate a dogmatic conception of Romanesque art, and in the process made the dialectic itself dogmatic and used it uncritically. What above all was lost in Baltrusaitis's use of dialectic was recognition of the unique expressive physiognomy of Romanesque art. By treating dialectic as a formal logic coercing facts into fixed patterns of meaning rather than, as Schapiro thinks it is— agreeing here with such modern interpreters of dialectic as Adorno[55]—a sign of the multidirectionality of historical process, Baltrusaitis deprives us of what Schapiro thinks dialectic can most successfully do, because of its resilience: physiognomically interpret fact, explicating its inherent individuality.[56]

As Baltrusaitis is to medieval art in general and Romanesque art in particular, so for Schapiro Alfred H. Barr, Jr., is to modern art in general and cubism and abstract art in particular. In Barr's account of the emergence of abstract art, no connection is drawn between the art and the conditions of the moment. He excludes as irrelevant to its history the nature of the society in which it arose, except as an incidental obstructing or accelerating atmospheric factor. The history of modern art is presented as an internal, immanent process among the artists; abstract art arises because, as the author says, representational art has been exhausted.[57]

Schapiro then argues that Barr's "theory of exhaustion and reaction reduces history to the pattern of popular views on changes in fashion." In general,

> The theory of immanent exhaustion and reaction is inadequate not only because it reduces human activity to a simple mechanical movement, like a bouncing ball, but because in neglecting the sources of energy and the condition of the field, it does not even do justice to its own limited mechanical conception.[58]

In their conception of a mechanical, ahistorical dialectical logic, Baltrusaitis and Barr make the same fatal mistake for Schapiro: they treat content as if it were "passive,"[59] a kind of crude malleable dough which can theoretically be given any shape one wishes—rather than a real historical subject matter with a shape of its own that resists arbitrary theories. Dialectic is not such a theory because, properly understood, it does not offer "*a posteriori* extrapolated diagrams...rarely verified in our direct experience,"[60] but rather a sensitive response to the subtle process of experience itself. Dialectic articulates the "principle of growth" and change—development—that makes experience a historical process.[61] For Schapiro, growth and change, social and personal, seem to be the one historical "constant," the one ultimate given with any certainty. However, this view of nonchaotic, purposeful change never goes off the deep end by becoming a quasi-Heracleitean argument for anarchic, "arbitrary" movement—a metaphysics, that is, overgeneralization, of movement into a timeless grand flux. (Like all metaphysical theories, at once a radical reduction and overinflation of "reality"—as though historical movement were the formless ripple effect of events—until it becomes beyond the ken of experience.) For Schapiro's understanding of change as dialectical—generated by conflict and the desire to resolve conflict, in a particular historical context of events, values, and individuals—precludes any metaphysical appropriation of it, as implicitly occurs in Baltrusaitis and Barr. Instead, it is shown to be the very subtance of wordliness.

In general, Schapiro expends much effort showing that the division of history into metaphysical schemata and inexplicably singular events—into the absolute and the arbitrary—confuses rather than clarifies. It is a simplification which is unenlightening rather than a source of lucid coherence. The very conception of events as arbitrary—in effect refractory and insubordinate—is the consequence of positing a mechanical-metaphysical system of history to which they are expected to conform. When they don't they are regarded as arbitrary, and Schapiro takes particular pleasure showing how artistic events—especially the seemingly absurd extravagances of Romanesque and abstract art—are in fact far from arbitrary. Instead, they are shown to be strongly conditioned—almost overdetermined—by individual response to social reality—by the determination to be individual while at once reflecting and confronting it—so that the art is in effect a discoordinate conjunction of individual and social values. In fact, discoordination is conceived by Schapiro to show how the seemingly arbitrary is the subtly necessary, and how different kinds of values successfully if strangely—ironically—interlock. Schapiro, incidentally, repeatedly talks of values, and especially of how individual values are at once a "free" response to and utopian, idealistic projection of freedom from authoritarian social values, which overstabilize individual life by inhibiting spontaneity, expressivity, feeling.[62]

Schapiro's personal sense of dialectic is a synthesis of what he finds in Hegel and Marx, "an explanation of active historical process," and what he finds in Riegl, an exposure of "possible latent internal conditions" of development, by the analysis of the "oppositions within a style" (or society), which render it "unstable and hence suggested fresh changes and solutions." But there is also an explicit vitalism, ultimately based on biological ideas, in Schapiro's sense of dialectic: a vitalist faith in the epigenetic character of artistic and social development whatever preformations—conventions and classes—exist. This vitalist dimension to dialectic is succinctly conveyed by Schapiro's use of the word "chiasma" or "chiasm," usually in an adjectival capacity to qualify a seemingly uniform structure as discoordinate. That is, the chiasmic is a way of articulating the latent tensions within the manifest structure, the tense meanings within the harmony, making clear that it is a dynamic, expressive harmony, rather than a hypostatic form with a seemingly invulnerable, facile integrity. It is the result of a process—not self-generated, like Athena springing from Zeus's forehead—and Schapiro never wants to forget the force of that process. Schapiro most pointedly uses the concept of the chiasmic in his treatment of Romanesque art, especially at Moissac and Souillac, where the force in the figures suggests the tension of some obscure dialectical process, which Schapiro makes explicit. The chiasmic is also used to articulate the increasing secularization of society and correlate striving for individual emancipation that is the very soul of modernity for Schapiro. But apart from these reifications of it, the chiasmic comes to represent, in Schapiro's writings, the very root of secular process—the organic "justification" for historical development, indicating that it is rooted in nature.

To understand Schapiro's chiasmic dialectic one must know that "chiasm" is a word derived from anatomy meaning "intercrossing or decussation." In particular, the "optic chiasma" is "the optic commissure or decussation of the fibres of the optic nerves." In genetics "chiasmatypy" refers to "the supposed spiral twisting of homologous chromosomes about each other during parasynapsis, with fusion and possible crossing over at the points of contact."[63] Now it is significant that Schapiro shows a strong interest in natural phenomena—especially living creatures—in general. He writes a good deal about animals, whom he usually treats as emblematic of the enormous energy in nature—heraldic forms statically embodying almost uncontainable force. Most importantly, he is preoccupied with, to the extent of completely assimilating, the notion of biological individuation, as when he observes that

> individualization is rare or undeveloped in Christian architecture before the Romanesque period and is more marked in the Romanesque than in the Gothic style; it precedes by two centuries the scholastic ideas about form as a principle of individuation in living creatures.[64]

He often resorts to biological metaphors, as when he describes a picture on a medieval manuscript page as "a liquid field with swarming infusorial elements."[65] He tracks down biological lore and odd superstitions, as when he explains the visual motif of "little circles or disks marking the joints of the ass's legs" in a Syriac lectionary as perhaps due to "a widespread primitive concern for the joints and particularly the knees as the places of vital spirits and generative powers," so that "these parts received a prominent articulation."[66] His implicit insistence on the organic character of dialectic—dialectic as an articulation of the organic in general, and of the organic character of individualization in particular—is shown in his use of a quotation from the biologist Peter A. Medawar's book on *The Uniqueness of the Individual* to demonstrate the continuity, and so continued viability, of the dialectical image almost all of Schapiro's *Words and Pictures* analyzes, that of Moses seated with his hands held up by "twin supports."[67]

One might speculate that the idea of the chiasmic, as well as Schapiro's use of biologically inspired metaphor, is the contribution of his wife, Dr. Lillian Milgram. Schapiro in general speaks quite favorably of women and the feminine—the "opposite" sex[68]—and believes in the wisdom and practice of the opposite, which is perhaps why he has such sympathy for it. Women in general are perhaps more aware of their "oppositeness" and "opposition"—otherness and alienation—and Schapiro as a specialist in opposites would be expected to turn to them. Be that as it may, Schapiro borrows the idea of chiasmatypy for artistic development, whose crucial moment is the creation of a novel individuality or physiognomy—a new style. Artistic creativity occurs when a pair of styles with "homologous" yet contradictory "chromosomes" of expressively— meaningfully—charged forms "conjugate," issuing in an original style. Put another way, significant stylistic genesis results when known opposites unstably related unite, under socially and personally dynamic conditions, in a restless, risky intrigue, which stabilizes in a tense, new style charged with the contradictory meanings of its origins. Style, in other words, is for Schapiro not simply a stable pattern or convention, but a "complex" of interlocking dimensions. If there is any difference between genetic chiasmatypy and Schapiro's use of the concept, it is in his greater emphasis on the heterogeneity of the original types. Dialectical individualization is viewed more as subtle discoordination than as self-evident coordination, which is what gives it vitality. Creativity is an "off" correspondence of contradictory elements which issue in an autonomous being, with a movement and style of its own. These overlapping descriptions are meant to suggest the way in which a new art, while showing strong traces of its origins or conditions of creation, is yet an irreducible complex. For Schapiro, the spiral—simultaneously centrifugal and centripetal, extensive and intensive, movement in free play and following the laws of a universal logic—is the major symbol of the dialectical interweaving which issues in highly individualized and meaningful form, and a concrete example of such form.[69] He particularly acknowledges it in the form of the zigzag, which he treats like a two-dimensional version of the three-dimensional spiral—an incomplete spiral or one in process of formation.[70] His emphasis on asymmetry as dialectically devious symmetry serves the same purpose: a demonstration of the formative process when a style is not yet a cliché but still clearly chiasmic—like a spiral.[71]

In general, Schapiro's conception of dialectical chiasmatypy in artistic individualization is an expression of his Deweyean and Whiteheadian belief in the primacy of relationship in the determination of substance. Any substance is ontologically more the structure of its relations than its statically reduced elements.

> The relations between forms are more crucial and determinative than the form elements themselves. Hence the possible absorption of features from the most remote arts in the Romanesque, without the effect of an eclectic or unintegrated style. The judgment of unintegration is of imperfectly incorporated, not anomalous, elements.[72]

("Absorption," incidentally, is another biologically oriented word for Schapiro, having to do with the process of nourishment by osmosis. Schapiro is interested in the way old forms and meanings are absorbed by—nourish—new ones, and in the process become "trans-formed.") Schapiro is interested in the "juggling" of all kinds of elements, from "juggling phrases" such as Bernard used in his description of Romanesque art as "deformed beauty . . . beautiful deformity,"[73] to the juggling of styles, such as took place at Silos with Mozarabic and Romanesque forms. Above all, he is interested in the way worlds of meaning can be juggled together, as when otherworldly religion appropriates the worldly realism which images "the world for its own sake, as a beautiful, fascinating spectacle in which man discovers his own horizons and freedom of movement."[74] One of Schapiro's major arguments in fact—and his defense of modern and especially abstract art is the substance of that argument—is that the emancipating new vision of the world first symbolized by artistic realism (and later by abstraction) is of value in and for itself, as the source of a new individualizing of man. "Religious thought tries to appropriate all this for itself; it seeks to stamp the freshly discovered world (and man) with its own categories, to spiritualize it and incorporate it within a scheme of otherworldly values"—an effort Schapiro fights whenever he encounters it. For to him human, worldly values have a spirituality and authority of their own—they have no need to borrow any, even when spirituality is reinforced by institutional authority. Schapiro continues the battle against the effort of tradition and authority to impose and superimpose themselves on new individuality—thereby denying it any rights of its own and deliberately misreading it—into modern times. He attacks those who regard modern art as a decline from some imagined past glory, holding instead that its values more accurately reflect the "movement and life"—vital situation—of the modern world than any past art can, and in general further "movement and life" more unequivocally than has ever been the case.[75]

Two Dialectical Structures

Having shown, I think, the dominance of dialectic in Schapiro's way of thinking, I would now like to examine the two major dialectical structures framing his analysis of art: the relationship between the religious and the secular, and between institutional authority and individual autonomy. Their connection has already been suggested: the one is a symbolic exemplification of the other, standing to it as historical practice stands to philosophical values. For Schapiro, transcendence is the abstract justification for authority—institutions acquire their authority by reason of their inherent transcendental character—and personal freedom is the concrete value articulated by autonomy. The struggle of modern history is to achieve individual freedom in the face of institutional authority—initially realistic freedom of movement in the world, opening it as a personal horizon, and ultimately emotional freedom, characterized by spontaneity of expression. Against the dogmatic ultimacy of institutional authority, the value of the individual is slowly and unsteadily established as an absolute in its own right. For Schapiro, Romanesque sculpture initiates an ideal of independent individual movement—it is significant that he regards it as the first modern art[76]—and abstract art qualifies this as a sign of emotional independence. The independence and spontaneity embodied in both Romanesque sculpture and abstract painting is initially understood—by the institutional authority whose transcendental traditions it threatens—as "arbitrary." Authority feels especially threatened by the projection of a democracy of free individuals—a democracy Schapiro explicitly endorses[77]— implicit in the assertion of independence and spontaneity as traits of individuality. Authority responds to individuality by repression—Schapiro's own word[78]—which is why there is no automatic, predictable progress toward a democracy of individuals. For Schapiro, capitalism plays the repressive role in modern times that the church played in medieval times, and he sees the development toward abstract art from impressionism on as an effort to throw off that repression—it is only in "pure" painting that this is achieved, not quite fully or "realistically," since the repressed life content or feeling returns in symbolic form, that is, more as a style of art than of life.[79] Similarly, highly individualized figures show dynamic movement symbolic of intense feeling—it is just because they show this movement that they seem highly individualized—in an effort to throw off the repression of the church and realize a more personal religion, a religiosity also evident in abstract art.[80]

Secularization is the embodiment of this drive toward individuality—the proposal of an alternative to authority. As noted, Schapiro delights in demonstrating the intrusion of the secular in the religious, freewheeling autonomy with authority of its own exploiting the sacred for its own vital purposes, as it were showing the perverse independence and power of life. Thus he not only shows that "figures from secular life are extremely common in Romanesque art," but details the way the sacred can be given vital sexual import by such figures,[81] or acquire class import, that is, be interpreted ideologically or in terms of class consciousness. Thus, on the Newcastle and Ruthwell crosses certain seemingly sacred figures represent "the interests and mode of life of the native rulers and nobility,"[82] and on a manuscript page from Silos a personification of Avarice replaces the more traditional Pride as a central figure to represent "the newly formed and growing burgher class"—the class whose money and worldly curiosity gave it independence from and so made it a threat to the church, which had to accommodate itself to the new worldliness if it was to survive.[83] Schapiro's psychoanalytic and ideological analyses of medieval art, demonstrating its latent—disguised or symbolic—sexual connotations and class consciousness, are a crucial part of his effort not to debunk and undermine it but to demythologize it in the sense of showing it to be, despite its pretensions, all too human. Perhaps his single most important demonstration of the secular within and in a certain sense usurping the sacred, is his analysis of the figure of the layman Theophilus at Souillac, showing the "double nature" of the Christian,[84]

> an individual rescued from the devil, from apostasy, from material, feudal difficulties and his own corruption within the political body of the church, through the direct intervention of the mother of Christ, opposed as a woman to the loathsome male devil.[85]

In this story,

> The antitheses of rank and privation, of the devil and the Virgin, of apostasy and repentance, create a psychological depth—the counterpart of a world of developing secular activity and freedom, more complex than the closed field of Christian piety represented in the dogmatic images of the majestic Christ of Romanesque portals.

Schapiro is always concerned to demonstrate this "psychological depth"—the result of "the dramatic vicissitude of a single intriguing individual," whose fortunes "at every point depend on his relations to the feudal church" (or capitalism—any repressive authoritarian institution, which yet has the power to "redeem" the individual, that is, make good his individuality, authenticate or legitimatize it as it were by "rewarding" it with good fortune, whether that be salvation or financial success). Such psychological depth is found in the most important art, medieval or modern, and Schapiro is concerned to make explicit—much as unconscious content is brought to the surface by analytic consciousness—its role in the individual's rebellion against authority. It is the sign of the conflict that generates the energy of that rebellion, as well as a first symbolic form of the autonomy or emancipation the rebellion hopes to achieve.[86]

Already strongly suggested by Romanesque sculpture, but explicitly from impressionism on, as Schapiro has shown, subjective freedom has been at stake in art and modern society as the very embodiment of the idea of individuality.[87] Just as "the spiritual conceptions have a secular basis" in the art of Souillac,[88] so the spiritual conceptions of abstract art have a secular basis. In both cases there is a negative response to "the accumulation of wealth by the burghers," but it represents opposite things in medieval and modern times. It was emancipating in the medieval period, when it represented and gave birth to "the libertinism of the towns and the new aristocratic culture"—the new open interest in and fresh look at life, feeling, and pleasure, which the church castigated as unchastity, sister sin to avarice.[89] But in the modern period the bourgeois represents repression—the opposite of the spontaneous expression of feeling. In the medieval period religious art used its own symbols to cast the new freedom in a negative light, while in the modern period abstract art uses the materiality—in the form of the materiality of the medium—the bourgeois idolizes to find expressive release or articulate subjective freedom. That is, materiality is made to serve a purpose in art antithetical to the purpose it is meant to serve in bourgeois society: it becomes a dynamic means rather than a mute, static end—an instrument of articulation rather than an absolute to be affirmed—a symbol rather than a goal. Schapiro's belief in "the ideological value of style,"[90] or more particularly his belief that the arguments and theoretical conflicts of medieval theology symbolized sociopolitical—practical—arguments and conflicts,[91] inspires his disclosure of such dialectical reversals. Such disclosure of the material and institutional social relations governing the production of artistic and life styles is essentially Marxian. It is no accident that Schapiro ends his extended analysis of style with an approving reference to Marx's conception of ideology, namely,

> Marx's undeveloped view that the higher forms of cultural life correspond to the economic structure of a society, the latter being defined in terms of the relations of classes in the process of production and the technological level. Between the economic relationships and the styles of art intervenes the process of ideological construction, a complex imaginative transposition of class roles and needs, which affects the special field—religion, mythology, or civil life—that provides the chief themes of art.[92]

Schapiro clearly intends to "develop" this Marxist approach "in a true spirit of investigation": he means to do for art what he thinks Marx has done for economics. "Marxist writing on art," he notes, "has suffered from schematic and premature formulations and from crude judgments imposed by loyalty to a political line," a situation—similar to the way Baltrusaitis treated medieval art and Barr treated modern art—Schapiro hopes to remedy by his greater empiricism, intellectual independence, and more organic conception of dialectic.

Individuality and Individualization

I would like to deal in a little more detail with Schapiro's conception of individuality and individualization, that is, creative individual development. First, it is essential to recognize that he regards it as classbound: creativity is the individual's way of responding to the social reality of class hierarchy, and of locating himself in and orienting himself to that hierarchy. This is shown explicitly in Schapiro's treatment of Berenson—and of art historians in general[93]—and Courbet.[94] The former, like most art historians until recently, identified himself with and served the upper classes; while the latter identified with and tried to further the interests of the lower classes. The rest—Berenson's kind of art history, Courbet's kind of art—follows from this, not without irony, especially in Berenson's case, although also in Courbet's. It is an irony generated by the contrast between their stated intentions and their enormous vanity and pretensions. Schapiro pits the pretensions against the intentions, with more sympathy for the results of the contradiction in Courbet's case than in Berenson's. (With Berenson, Schapiro seems to suggest that there but for the grace of God he might go, for his superficial resemblance to Berenson—ranging from their common Jewishness, intellectual ambition, and spiritual aspiration—is great, leading Schapiro to make an implicit comparison of himself with Berenson, as suggested by the anecdote of his meeting with Berenson. Schapiro quite clearly uses himself and his gifts in a different—more democratic and humanistic—way, resolving whatever conflicts he might have had in a more subtle, discoordinate way than is evidenced by the superficial harmony between life and work in Berenson.)

Schapiro's treatment of Courbet's "sincerity" opens the way to the second major element in his sense of individuality, namely, belief in the importance of personal feelings and their spontaneous expression, so that they can be studied as vital signs of the individual's relationship with or attitude to society. Each feeling for Schapiro represents a personal possibility in the midst of a social reality—a free response, projecting life possibilities, in an unfree situation—a momentary yet creative indeterminacy in a determined world, and yet clearly not overdetermined, or it would have no room for creativity. Schapiro's concern with feeling as a latent sign of striving for autonomy—a kind of demonstration or assertion of minimum autonomy—is perhaps most evident in his treatment of Van Gogh's portraits. These use a personal technique of coloristic contrasts to achieve a novel intensity—altogether unexpected and extraordinary in terms of tradition—with symbolic import, "opening the way for a poetic searching of the personality in its varied course of feeling."[95] More generally, Schapiro's discussion of painting's "unique revolutionary" role "in the last fifty years, within the common tendency towards the more personal, intimate and free," makes the same point.[96] This tendency involves an "immensely widened" "notion of the humanity of art." This involves making the expressive values of all kinds of art emotionally accessible, creating in the process a kind of democracy of styles, all highly individual yet in human agreement as it were. Correlatively, it involves the abolition of representation, not because it is suddenly historically obsolete out of some kind of mysterious historical necessity, as Barr thought, but as a critique of "a particular standard of decorum or restraint in expression which had excluded certain domains and intensities of feeling."[97] Abstraction is thus "a criticism of the accepted contents of the preceding representations as ideal values or life interests," affirming thereby "a new liberty," "a new sense of freedom and possibility" in life—where new "spontaneity or intense feeling" emerges—and art, where the "freely made" work develops. [98] "An irreplaceable quality" is expressed: "the painting symbolizes an individual who realizes freedom and deep engagement of the self within his work."[99] This "feeling of freedom" expresses the value of "personality"[100] in an "impersonal, calculated, and controlled" world "aiming always at efficiency" and facile "communication."[101] The new abstract art does not aim at communication: "there is no clear code or fixed vocabulary, no certainty of effect in a given time of transmission or exposure," no transmission of "an already prepared and complete message to a relatively indifferent and impersonal receiver." Rather, the new painting aims "at such a quality of the whole" that it becomes "a spiritual object," affording "an experience which is not automatically given, but requires preparation and purity of spirit," and is an "equivalent of what is regarded as part of religious life."[102] Schapiro has clearly come full circle, completing the dialectic that relates medieval and modern art: the best modern art, completely secular in its origins, shows a strong religious feeling—Schapiro seems to imply that all intensity of feeling has religious connotations, a seemingly transcendental quality—and the best medieval art, completely religious in its origins, shows a strong secular feeling, which is in effect "religious" since it exists with the same intensity as religious feeling in secular art. Schapiro can make such correspondences or "crossings" because of his conception of the work of art as a spiritual as well as social product, expressing "inner freedom" as well as social control. It is simultaneously ideal and realistic, the two fusing in the energy with which it is created and which it expresses—an energy resulting both from spontaneity and control.

Freud and Schapiro

Concluding, I would like to note Schapiro's use of dialectical reasoning to generate alternatives as well as reconcile them. This can be seen in his treatment of psychoanalysis in general and Freud in particular. As noted, his repeated references to repression and his conception of manifest and latent meaning, as well as his attention to the secret sexuality in seemingly sexless art, indicate a general respect for psychoanalysis.[103] However, he is less happy with Freud, and has been sharply critical of his one-dimensional approach, especially evident for Schapiro, as one might expect from an art historian, in his treatment of Leonardo. For Schapiro, Freud becomes as dogmatic and schematic—mechanical—in his approach to Leonardo as Baltrusaitis was to Romanesque art and Barr to modern art. Such a reductionist approach precludes alternative methods, and worse yet ignores or censors—the result is the same—much of the evidence. It is exclusive and exclusionary.

> If these observations are right, they suggest another possible approach to Leonardo's character than the one followed by Freud. The father of psychoanalysis wrote as if each text and each trait had only one possible source; he reconstructed the artist's hidden life according to assumptions which allowed no alternative causes; and he assigned to the sparse documents an extraordinary significance, especially to the mistranslated fantasy of the bird on which he built an elaborate structure of inferences concerning Leonardo's childhood and the situation of his mother. In all this we recognize the method of the poet or the imaginative novelist who binds the elements of his story into a single continuous pattern, with a pervading tone of feeling.[104]

Schapiro is quite sympathetic to Freud—Freud is a kind of alternative to Berenson—as well he might be, by reason of his own ability to put extraordinary significance on Romanesque monuments and to build an elaborate structure of inferences about them—an empirically objective rather than empirically subjective structure, although with a strong subjective dimension. However, the key point is the light these remarks throw on Eissler's criticism of Schapiro's critique of Freud's psychoanalysis of Leonardo.[105] Eissler argues that Schapiro reduces Leonardo to no more than "a medium of tradition,"[106] that is, "the artist is reduced by the historian to an automaton-medium of his predecessors."[107] On the contrary, Schapiro shows that it is Freud who reduces Leonardo to an automaton-medium of his subjective experience or feelings—without even having clearly established what they are, thus violating his own proclaimed empiricism and method. Freud reduces Leonardo to a medium of sexuality, altogether ignoring the social conditions of his life and the artistic traditions he worked in response to—or else treating these in the most limited way. It is in fact Schapiro who presents the alternative approach to Leonardo, not Freud—Schapiro who counters psychological overdetermination with social and artistic determination. And it is Schapiro who is methodologically sounder in his use of well-established, trustworthy evidence.

In the last analysis the differences between Freud and Schapiro are the result of the difference in method between the psychoanalyst and the historian, or more precisely, their different conceptions of empiricism, and especially of what constitutes "radical empiricism," which they both claim to offer. The psychoanalyst's radicality is perhaps summarized by Eissler's statement that "it is in the very nature of unconscious factors that they cannot be exhibited concretely,"[108] but only inferred—reached by association with what can be exhibited concretely to consciousness. While this is a paradoxical, dialectical position like Schapiro's, its empiricism is more questionable because of the uncertainties of associational inference, and because such inference ultimately depends on an impossible exhaustive knowledge of all the variables at stake in the life in which the unconscious functions. Schapiro's position is more humble—he deals only with public knowledge, including public knowledge of unconscious factors. He thus avoids reasoning in a way which, as Eissler acknowledges, can be "considered obstinate, dogmatic, and prejudiced." This, of course, is the exact way the church, and those who know the inevitable course of history, reason. Their arguments gain their authority by reason of their monopoly on a secret source or hidden evidence. Privileged access to mysterious knowledge is a justification for the dogmatism of the church, whether it be a church of God or of reason. The assumption of such a position is a political strategy designed to grant absolute power to those holy few—the dedicated priesthood—who claim to speak in the name of the absolute, whether it be divine or unconscious, and who institutionalize themselves in its name. Schapiro questions psychoanalysis's authority and revelation of the individual much as he questions the church's. Finally, he questions their usefulness in the process of individualization: the accuracy of their accounts of human uniqueness and their ability to further it by freeing the individual from false gods. Both, he seems to imply, acknowledge psychological depth—the power of the personal—but they stereotype it by not viewing it historically and socially, and so they preclude its creativity, which for Schapiro is the key to its character. Schapiro tends to deny any conception of the immanence of individuality, even when it is understood as a structure of conflicts, for such an intrapsychic model of individuality does not regard these conflicts as the reflection of social realities. Thus, in his analyses of Van Gogh and Cézanne, for him paradigmatic of conflict-ridden modern individuality, he never fails to articulate the social pole of their psychological disturbance. In doing so, Schapiro does more to demythologize individual creativity than Freud, or for that matter the church—while at the same time articulating it as a unique response to a common social situation, a unique style of coming to grips with that situation. For Schapiro, psychoanalysis, however brilliant its insight into the workings of the individual, remains another ideology. Eissler in effect accuses Schapiro of historicism, but Schapiro can counter with an accusation of psychologism. Perhaps neither charge is true, for Freud's dialectical method expands and contradicts the traditional conception of psychology, as Schapiro's dialectical method expands and contradicts the traditional conception of art history.

Notes

1.   Some examples of Schapiro's use of "interplay," "intrigue," and "polarity." In *Words and Pictures: On the Literal and the Symbolic in the Illustration of a Text* (The Hague: Mouton, 1973), p. 17, Schapiro wants "to bring out the interplay of text, commentary, symbolism, and style of representation in the word-bound image." In "The Sculptures of Souillac," *Romanesque Art: Selected Papers,* vol. 1 (New York: Braziller, 1977), p. 127, n. 14, he talks of "the intriguing contrast of the wallet hanging from the boy's belt and the key from the old man's" in a *drôlerie* depicting their conflict. The scene has to do with the question of "submission to authority," and, Schapiro remarks, "we might even hazard the guess that the wallet and key pertain to an episodic intrigue formed like the sculptural pattern, wallet and key being complementary opposites, each incomplete in itself, like the wrestling, interlocked figures." What is startling in both these quotations is the extent of Schapiro's cross-referencing—the great number of variables he brings into play, juggles together. In *Words and Pictures,* he speaks of "polar forms" (p. 48), "polar ideas" (p. 41), "polar meanings" (p. 45), and "a polarity expressed through...contrasted positions" (p. 43). In "Style," in Morris H. Philipson, ed., *Aesthetics Today* (Cleveland: Meridian Books, 1961) he speaks of "dual polar structure" (p. 96) and "a development between two poles" (p. 97). In "'Muscipula Diaboli,' The Symbolism of the Mérode Altarpiece," *Art Bulletin* 27 (1945): 183, he speaks of "the poles of the human career of Christ," and in "From Mozarabic to Romanesque in Silos," *Romanesque Art,* p. 80, n. 66, he speaks of "the dual and polar character of this punishment...the alteration of heat and cold." This is just a limited sampling of his explicit reference to—and implicit use of—polar thinking.

2.   There is an amazing resemblance between Schapiro's way of thinking in contrasts and Whitehead's—a way extended even to Whitehead's conception of art. Thus in *Process and Reality* (New York: Humanities Press, 1955), Whitehead speaks of "Contrasts, *or* Modes of Synthesis of Entities in one Prehension" (p. 33) as one of the basic "Categories of Existence" (p. 33), and notes that "unity is a 'contrast' of entities" and "a contrast in general produces a new existential type" (p. 36). Whitehead regards the "doctrine of multiple contrast...when there are or may be more than two elements jointly contrasted, and it is desired to draw attention to that fact" as "a commonplace of art" (p. 349). He also speaks of "the organism's" creative achievement of "depth of experience" by "suppressing the mere multiplicities of things, and designing its own contrasts. The canons of art are merely the expression, in specialized forms, of the requisites for depth of experience" (p. 483). Finally, Whitehead remarks that "the universe is to be conceived as attaining the active self-expression of its own variety of opposites—of its own freedom and its own necessity, of its own multiplicity and its own unity, of its own imperfection and its own perfection. All the 'opposites' are elements in the nature of things, and are incorrigibly there." Generalized, these opposites justify "the aesthetic value of discords in art" (p. 531). That is, universal, major opposites are particularized, or as Whitehead says, given "minor exemplification," in art.

3.   Schapiro makes several passing references to "radical empiricism," particularly his characterizing as a "radically empirical standpoint" Cézanne's "wish to paint nature in complete naiveté of sensation, as if no one had painted it before" (*Paul Cézanne,* 3rd ed. [New York: Abrams, 1965], p. 19). And his assertion that, in painting as well as in philosophy and science, acknowledgement of "aesthetic choices—the immense role of hypothesis," led to "a radical empiricism," which, "criticizing a deductive, contemplative approach, gave to the experimental a programmatic value in all fields" ("Rebellion in Art," in Daniel Aaron, ed., *America in Crisis* [New York: Knopf, 1952], p. 221). In both cases radical empiricism implies a radically fresh start, a mythical—naive, sincere—new beginning (one made over and over, from Courbet on). And at the beginning one spontaneously discovers contradiction or dialectical development, the necessity of choice between opposites that yet does justice to both of them. As

Schapiro notes, Cézanne's "doubt"—his art is suffused with a sense of alternatives—is a direct consequence of his radical naiveté about experience, visual as well as in general.

4. Schapiro, "The Sculptures of Souillac," p. 115.

5. Schapiro, "The Romanesque Sculpture of Moissac II," *Romanesque Art,* p. 220.

6. Ibid., p. 249.

7. Ibid., p. 219.

8. In "The Romanesque Sculpture of Moissac I," *Romanesque Art,* Schapiro talks about the "restless effect" that results from asymmetry (p. 149), the "restless angularity" that results from "a perpetual contrast of lines and areas ... curves and straight line," a restlessness of detail that undermines the "ritual gravity" inherent in the architecture of the whole (p. 150), and the "restlessness"—shown by the use of "zigzag and diagonal movements"—in "the central portion" of a figure (p. 151). In "The Romanesque Sculpture of Moissac II" he talks of a "complex disorder" in which "the separate groups are extraordinarily restless and correspond in their zigzag and wavy movements to the asymmetrical, irregular architecture and to the highly emotional and dramatic conception of the subjects" (pp. 235-236). In remarks on a facsimile reproduction of a "Carolingian Classic," *The Lorsch Gospels, Art News* 61 (1968): 53 he notes its "unclassical profuseness, the restless details and ornaments." The "playful forms" of the restless, which turn "the canvas" into "a field of prodigious excitement, unloosed energies," is closely connected with the idea of the improvisational and fantastic for Schapiro, as in his discussion of Arshile Gorky's "improvisations" with "no predetermined sense," paintings without faces yet sometimes with "artificial faces, the masks of borrowed allusions, poets' titles" ("Introduction" to Ethel K. Schwabacher, *Arshile Gorky* [New York: Macmillan, 1959], pp. 13-14). He also talks of "the restless complexity of Pollock or de Kooning," their "art of impulse and chance," with its "remarkable ... degree of spontaneity or emphasis of effect ... energy," and "ever-changing directions" ("The Younger American Painters of Today," *The Listener* 55 [Jan. 26, 1956]: 146-47). The language of this description is remarkably similar to that used to describe Romanesque sculpture. Finally, he speaks of Cézanne's "restlessness" and "spontaneity" synonymously (*Paul Cézanne,* p. 10).

9. Schapiro, "On Geometrical Schematism in Romanesque Art," *Romanesque Art,* p. 279.

10. Schapiro, "On the Aesthetic Attitude in Romanesque Art," *Romanesque Art,* p. 22.

11. Schapiro, "Courbet and Popular Imagery, An Essay on Realism and Naiveté," *Journal of the Warburg and Courtauld Institutes* 4 (1940-41): 190.

12. Schapiro, " 'Muscipula Diaboli,' The Symbolism of the Mérode Altarpiece," p. 185.

13. Ibid., p. 186.

14. Schapiro, "The Romanesque Sculpture of Moissac I," pp. 187-88.

15. For example, writing on wresting figures at Souillac, Schapiro asserts, "Playful fantasies of force and conflict underlie the conception in Souillac, rather than a theological idea. If anything, it is a countertheological idea" ("The Sculptures of Souillac," p. 127, n. 14). In *Words and Pictures,* p. 16, Schapiro calls this theme of father-son wrestling "a secular parody with a most serious sense." In " 'Cain's Jawbone that Did the First Murder'," *Art Bulletin* 24 (1942): 212, Schapiro, dealing with a similar theme of secular violence in a religious context, remarks that "the invention of the jaw-bone as Cain's weapon in England was not only inspired by the vernacular play of words" but by "the affective connotations of both Cain and the jaw-bone for demonic and animal violence." In "The Bowman and the Bird on the Ruthwell Cross and Other Works: The Interpetation of Secular Themes in Early Medieval Religious Art," *Art Bulletin* 45 (1963): 351,

.Schapiro notes "the equivalences of the sacred and the secular with respect to themes of force," emphasizing the simultaneity or unity of both: "The alternatives are not, as is often supposed: religious meaning or no meaning, but religious or secular meanings, both laden with affect" (p. 353).

16.   Schapiro, "The Bowman and the Bird on the Ruthwell Cross and Other Works: The Interpretation of Secular Themes in Early Medieval Religious Art," p. 351.

17.   Schapiro and Seminar, "The Miniatures of the Florence Diatessaron (Laurentian Ms Or. 81): Their Place in Late Medieval Art and Supposed Connection with Early Christian and Insular Art," *Art Bulletin* 55 (1973): 518.

18.   Schapiro, "Rebellion in Art," p. 212.

19.   Schapiro, "The Sculptures of Souillac," p. 107.

20.   Ibid., pp. 113-114.

21.   He is particularly interested in the intense color contrasts of Cézanne (*Paul Cézanne,* pp. 11-12) and Van Gogh (*Vincent Van Gogh* [New York: Abrams, 1950], pp. 19-22), but also in the "intense...burning, heraldically bright...bands of contrasted color...bound to a visionary text"—"spontaneous primitive" color itself is visionary in effect—in such medieval manuscripts as "The Beatus Apocalypse of Gerona" (*Art News* 61 [1963]: 50). In "From Mozarabic to Romanesque in Silos," p. 35, he describes "Mozarabic painting as an art of color," using "constantly varied, maximum oppositions in the color through the contrasts of hue (and, to a lesser extent, of value)," and he remarks on the way in the "Beatus manuscripts color is felt as a universal force, active in every point in space and transcending objects."

22.   Note 8 remarks Schapiro's observation of "ever-changing directions" in American abstract expressionism. It remains only to note his constant reference to "contrasted directions" ("The Romanesque Sculpture of Moissac I," p. 161) in Romanesque sculpture, achieved by "an energetic asymmetry" involving the use of the "diagonal" and "zigzag." For Schapiro, contrasts of direction are a universal means of achieving dynamic expressivity.

23.   Another obsessive theme in Schapiro's analysis of the sculptural figures of Moissac and Souillac, perhaps exemplary of what he calls "chiasmic symmetry." In "An Illuminated English Psalter," *Journal of the Warburg and Courtauld Institutes* 22 (1960): 183, Schapiro observes that "the motif of the crossed legs is a general attribute of the ruler, whether good or evil; it isolates him from ordinary mankind, which sits or stands supported by both feet alike." In *Words and Pictures,* p. 21, he talks of "a type of ascetic prayer, the cross-vigil, in which the monk or hermit held his arms up for long periods in imitation of Moses on the hill."

24.   Schapiro, "From Mozarabic to Romanesque in Silos," p. 83, n. 81, and "The Sculptures of Souillac," p. 113.

25.   Schapiro, "From Mozarabic to Romanesque in Silos," p. 83, n. 87.

26.   Ibid., p. 42, where not only does he speak of "chiasmically repeated words" or "the reversal of a phrase" as a "potent device in magic song and speech," but describes such chiasmic repetition in "jongleurs, unreligious, secular figures with an accented energy of movement and vehemence of conception." Like certain Romanesque sculptors of the South, the jongleurs conceived of their art as ingenious, intricate, and woven. The terms in which they describe their poetry apply also to sculptures of the region" (p. 46). He speaks of their "autonomy" and "secularity" in the same breath (p. 46), and transposes their juggling quality to the Romanesque effort "to animate a static figure by the crossing of the legs" (p. 52), creating the "characteristic Romanesque mobility" and "independent, animating expression" (p. 55). Finally, in Romanesque sculpture the entire figure is reversed or juggled, so that Schapiro can speak of it as "self-entangled": "The

seemingly arbitrary chiasma of the legs, in violating the natural tectonic of the stable body, confers a suggestion of inwardness of the saint. The X form constitutes an inverted autonomy of action, a preventive countermovement which chastens and deforms the limbs. In some Romanesque sculptures (as in Souillac, Moissac, and Toulouse) the crossing of the legs is so pronounced that the whole body appears the more vigorous and vehement in its motion" (p. 57).

27. Schapiro, "From Mozarabic to Romanesque in Silos," p. 30.

28. Schapiro, "On the Aesthetic Attitude in Romanesque Art," p. 26, n. 10.

29. Schapiro, *Vincent Van Gogh,* pp. 29-30.

30. Ibid., p. 27.

31. Ibid., pp. 22-23.

32. Schapiro, *Paul Cézanne,* p. 27.

33. Ibid., pp. 27-28.

34. Ibid., p. 10.

35. Ibid., p. 12.

36. Ibid., p. 18.

37. Ibid., p. 26.

38. Schapiro, *Vincent Van Gogh,* p. 8.

39. Schapiro, *Paul Cézanne,* p. 19.

40. Ibid., p. 20.

41. Schapiro, *Vincent Van Gogh,* p. 34.

42. Schapiro, *Words and Pictures,* p. 41.

43. Ibid., p. 47.

44. Ibid., p. 48. Schapiro shows a consistent interest in "values" as the "ultimate" at stake in any historical determination. Thus he investigates "Mr. Berenson's Values," *Encounter* 16 (1961): 57-65, argues that "the broad reaction against an existing art is possible only on the ground of its inadequacy to artists with new values and new ways of seeing" ("Nature of Abstract Art," *Marxist Quarterly* 1 [1937]: 81), and vigorously defends and shows the pervasiveness of the value of freedom in modern art ("The Liberating Quality of Avant-Garde Art," *Art News* 56 [1957]: 36-42).

45. Schapiro, "On the Aesthetic Attitude in Romanesque Art," p. 9.

46. Schapiro, " 'Muscipula Diaboli,' The Symbolism of the Mérode Altarpiece," p. 187: "In accepting the realistic vision of nature, religious art runs the risk of receding to a marginal position, of becoming in turn the border element that secular reality has been." After showing that the mousetrap is a marginal secular-realistic image in which a major religious meaning is invested, in "A Note on the Mérode Altarpiece," *Art Bulletin* 41 (1959): 327-328, Schapiro explains how the fishtrap Joseph is making is also associated with an important religious idea, suggesting that it is a not uncommon method in medieval art to associate higher, central, major religious meanings with lower, marginal, minor objects of everyday use. The fusion of profound meaning with banal reality is perhaps Schapiro's most pointed and poignant example of the attraction of opposites, a dialectic usually unnoticed because of social expectation of the strong repulsion between its constituents.

68   Dialectical Reasoning in Meyer Schapiro

47. Schapiro, "The Fantastic Eye," review of *Le Moyen Age Fantastique* and *Anamorphoses ou Perspectives Curieuses,* both by Jurgen Baltrusaitis, *Art News* 55 (1956): 40, 51.

48. Schapiro, *Paul Cézanne,* p. 17.

49. Schapiro, "On the Aesthetic Attitude in Romanesque Art," p. 3.

50. Schapiro, "The Sculptures of Souillac," p. 104.

51. Ibid., pp. 105-06.

52. Charles Baudelaire, "The Salon of 1846," *Baudelaire as a Literary Critic,* edited by Lois and Francis E. Hyslop, Jr. (University Park, Pa.: Pennsylvania State University Press, 1964), p. 42.

53. Schapiro, "On Geometrical Schematism in Romanesque Art," pp. 267-68. See also Schapiro's critical, but on the whole positive summary of Riegl's ideas in "Style," pp. 100-102.

54. Schapiro, "'Muscipula Diaboli,' The Symbolism of the Mérode Altarpiece," p. 186.

55. See Theodor W. Adorno, *Drei Studien zu Hegel* (Frankfurt am Main, Suhrkamp, 1969), especially "Aspekte" and "Erfahrungsgehalt."

56. Schapiro makes numerous references to the physiognomy of art. His definitive position on it is perhaps in "Style," p. 85: "the general trend of research has been to look for features that can be formulated in both structural and expressive-physiognomic terms. It is assumed by many students that the expression terms are all translatable into form and quality terms, since the expression depends on particular shapes and colors and will be modified by a small change in the latter. The forms are correspondingly regarded as vehicles of a particular affect (apart from the subject matter). But the relationship here is not altogether clear. In general, the study of style tends toward an ever stronger correlation of form and expression." Schapiro himself tends to further this correlation in Romanesque sculpture and abstract art. In fact, much of the substance of his work is a demonstration of it.

57. Schapiro, "Nature of Abstract Art," p. 79.

58. Ibid., p. 80.

59. Schapiro, "On Geometrical Schematism in Romanesque Art," pp. 268, 283.

60. Ibid., p. 270.

61. Ibid., p. 280.

62. Perhaps the core of this recurrent argument in Schapiro is his acceptance, implicit in the context and explicit elsewhere, of Baudelaire's belief "that all poetry," and by extension all art, "is essentially a utopian protest against injustice, a desire for freedom and happiness" ("Courbet and Popular Imagery," p. 173). In "The Romanesque Sculpture of Moissac II" Schapiro talks a good deal about the "arbitrariness" of the architecture (p. 232), proportions of the human figure (p. 238), and detail in general (p. 241), demonstrating that such apparent arbitrariness is in fact the sign, as he puts it in "On Geometrical Schematism in Romanesque Art," of "a uniform, restless, unstable treatment" involving the use of "contradictory" forms (p. 274). Arbitrariness, in other words, is understood as a sign of dialectic: apparent incoherence is shown to be subtly— discoordinately—coherent. The same issue of arbitrariness arises in modern art, whether it has to do with the popular belief that the "impression" of impressionism was "something arbitrary" ("Rebellion in Art," p. 211), that abstraction in general was "arbitrary and private" (*ibid.,* p. 213), that "arbitrary design or convention" played "a considerable part" in "scientific law" (*ibid.,* p. 221), or that abstract expressionism involved an arbitrary and "wild discharge of feeling" ("The Younger American Painters of Today," p. 147). Schapiro consistently fields this recurrent charge of the arbitrariness of the novel—of every "advance" in art—by showing that

it represents the emergence of new values, generally new interpretations of the human and expressive, and new methods of articulating them.

63. My sources for these definitions are, respectively, the *Oxford Universal Dictionary* and the *Webster's New Collegiate Dictionary.*

64. Schapiro, "On the Aesthetic Attitude in Romanesque Art," p. 5.

65. Schapiro, "From Mozarabic to Romanesque in Silos," p. 31.

66. Schapiro and Seminar, "The Miniatures of the Florence Diatessaron (Laurentian Ms Or. 81): Their Place in Late Medieval Art and Supposed Connection with Early Christian and Insular Art," p. 503.

67. *Words and Pictures,* p. 36.

68. For example, in "Rebellion in Art," p. 228, Schapiro notes that "women...were among the chief friends of the new art, buying painting and sculpture with a generous hand.... But what is in question here is not simply the quicker disposition of American women to the fine arts, but their response to novel forms. At this moment of general stirring of ideas of emancipation, women were especially open to manifestations of freedom within the arts. A symbol of this period of insurgent modernism was the flamboyant personality of Isadora Duncan, an international figure who transformed the dance into a medium of ecstatic expression and release"—much as, Schapiro means to imply, painting was transformed into a medium of intense feeling and freedom. In "The Metropolitan Museum 1870-1970-2001: Democratize the Board of Trustees," *Art News* 68 (1970): 29, Schapiro, criticizing the board, notes: "It is remarkable, too, that the elected Board is largely male (31 to 5), in spite of the fact that the support of art in this country owes so much to the enthusiasm, generosity and tastes of women." Elsewhere, e.g., "On the Aesthetic Attitude in Romanesque Art," p. 25, n. 6, he notes how self-righteous "men of the world" tend to think that art "renders the masculine heart effeminate," enervating it, or, what amounts to the same thing, making it "superstitious" ("From Mozarabic to Romanesque in Silos," p. 39). In "Populist Realism," a review of Thomas Benton's *An Artist in America, Partisan Review* 4 (1935): 57, Schapiro, responding to Benton's contempt for "the effeminacy that he cannot tolerate in homosexuals and that he cheaply denounces...as a menace to the coming American culture," notes that Benton's "lack of delicacy, of refinement and of pathos make us regret that he is not more feminine."

69. See his remarks on spiral form in "A Relief in Rodez," *Romanesque Art,* pp. 291, 302, n. 42.

70. The zigzag or "X-scheme" is repeatedly mentioned by Schapiro as perhaps the most obvious emblematic expression of Romanesque dynamics. For example, see "The Sculptures of Souillac" pp. 107, 113; "The Romanesque Sculpture of Moissac I," pp. 149, 152, 153, 159-160 (zigzag frame), 161, 173, 192, 196; "The Romanesque Sculpture of Moissac II," pp. 206, 208 (where it is spoken of as a *contrapposto* scheme), 211, 202 (where it is connected with intensity of gesture), 221, 236 (where it is said to carry an expression independent of the meaning of the figures that show it in their limbs), and 245. Schapiro also finds the zigzag line apparent in Van Gogh's pictures (*Vincent Van Gogh,* p. 31). A particularly interesting reference is to Töpffer's *Nouveaux Voyages en Zigzag,* whose drawings illustrate a primitive, playful, childlike naiveté ("Courbet and Popular Imagery," pp. 177-178).

71. The contrast of asymmetry with uniformity is another commonplace of Schapiro's characteristic analysis of form, as in "The Romanesque Sculpture of Moissac I," pp. 149, 151, 165, 167, 169, and 171; and in "The Romanesque Sculpture of Moissac II," pp. 205, 209, and 233.

72. Schapiro, "The Romanesque Sculpture of Moissac II," p. 229.

73. Schapiro, "On the Aesthetic Attitude in Romanesque Art," p. 8.

74.   Schapiro, " 'Muscipula Diaboli,' The Symbolism of the Mérode Altarpiece," p. 186.

75.   For example, his attack on Joseph C. Sloane in his review of Sloane's *French Painting between the Past and the Present; Artists, Critics, and Traditions from 1848 to 1870, Art Bulletin* 36 (1954): 163-165. Sloane is attacked not only for not recognizing the "morality" behind the emancipation of feeling in modern art, but for not understanding the dialectic of Baudelaire's thought: his "lifelong struggle with the conflicting demands of 'imagination' and realistic 'modernity'," which "was a passionate and unresolved one" (p. 165).

76.   Schapiro, "The Romanesque Sculpture of Moissac I," pp. 197-98, where he regards it as "the very beginning of the modern tradition of sculpture," and notes that "there is already great freedom and divergence from a common method... and that the variations are not uniformly directed." In general, Schapiro attempts to suggest the "continuity"—in expressive values if not always in technical method—between medieval and modern art in a number of ways. One of the most intriguing ways in which he argues for such continuity, while seeming to argue against it, is in his note about "The Beatus Apocalypse of Gerona," p. 50, "that art of such high quality was achieved in copying, however freely, a set body of existing works.... Can one imagine a painter today copying a hundred and twenty pictures by another artist with such freshness and delight and maintaining the distinctiveness of each image beside the next? The Beatus manuscripts make us realize how limited is our present conception of the artistic process, and how much it depends on the values of art and social life today." But then, pursuing the opposite pole, in a typical pattern of dialectical attraction after repulsion, Schapiro writes: "We are able, however, precisely through our own art and point of view to appreciate these long ignored medieval works as few observers could do during the last centuries before our time. I have had occasion to look at the older Morgan Beatus with painters and I have observed with satisfaction their strong response to this art. I do not think that I am fanciful in seeing in certain of Léger's works, painted during his stay in New York in the 1940s, the effects of his enthusiasm for this Spanish manuscript. A painting of Matta's, *Siempre Maltratada*, was directly inspired by the page representing the Woman of Babylon." This theme continues in his "Introduction" to Schwabacher's *Arshile Gorky*, pp. 11-12, where, commenting on Gorky's "act of originality" in being "a disciple of Picasso in New York in the 1920's and early '30's," he in effect shows Gorky's "medieval attitude." Schapiro then develops a comparison between Gorky's attitude to and distance from the School of Paris and that of Renaissance artists to and from antiquity. Both copied their personally discovered "classic" masters, but achieved original and "unclassic" results. In "On the Aesthetic Attitude in Romanesque Art," pp. 15, 25, Schapiro argues that Romanesque artists and their contemporary appreciators valued it for the same kind of pure aestheticism as those "opposed to 'literary' or symbolic painting" value modern abstract art.

77.   Schapiro seems to share Courbet's "identification with the people" and "anti-clericalism," i.e., anti-authoritarianism ("Courbet and Popular Imagery," p. 169). This is perhaps most movingly shown in his attack on the elitism of the modern museum in general and the Metropolitan Museum in particular. In his review of *Babel's Tower: The Dilemma of the Modern Museum* by Francis H. Taylor, a former director of the Metropolitan Museum (*Art Bulletin* 27 [1945]: 272-276), Schapiro shows how "Taylor's proposals for the reform of the museum are less obviously democratic in spirit than appears," because "He ignores the immense disparity between the inherited ideals of artistic culture and the life condition of the mass of the people, which is so unfavorable to the enjoyment of good art; he does not see how the lack of inner freedom, how poverty, insecurity, ignorance and the demands of practical life today deaden the spirit and arrest the development of those who in childhood might have shown a creative impulse or some desire for art; how the commercialized culture that they absorb from the movies, the newspapers and magazines, advertising and the radio, penetrates their souls and keeps them from grasping their own world and situation." In "The Liberating Quality of Avant-Garde Art," p. 37, Schapiro argues that the "universal requirements" first fully articulated by modern

aestheticism—"that every work of art has an individual order of coherence, a quality of unity and necessity in its structure regardless of the kinds of forms used: and second, that the forms and colors chosen have a decided expressive physiognomy, that they speak to us as a feeling-charged whole, through the intrinsic power of colors and lines"—create "a greater range in the appreciation and experience of forms", "i.e., a new democracy of art." "Many kinds of drawing, painting, sculpture and architecture, formerly ignored or judged inartistic, were seen as existing on the same plane of human creativeness and expression as 'civilized' Western art." This idea is reiterated in "Nature of Abstract Art," p. 77-78, where Schapiro describes the way it "created an immense confraternity of works of art, cutting across the barriers of time and place": "The art of the whole world was now available on a single unhistorical and universal plane as a panorama of the formalized energies of man." In "Style," pp. 85-86, he makes the same argument: "the values of modern art have led to a more sympathetic and objective approach to exotic arts."

78. He particularly talks of repression with respect to *Vincent Van Gogh*, p. 28: "It is as if in his suffering, extreme condition, he found it healthier to release these feelings in the controlled forms of painting than to repress them, for they would emerge then in even more disturbing, uncontrollable fancies and hallucinations"; and *Paul Cézanne*, p. 20:"It has been said that a classic artist is a repressed romantic... it seems particularly true for Cézanne." On p. 25 he talks of Cézanne's "original vehemence"—a favorite word of Schapiro, for vehemence is unmistakably expressive—and on p. 28 he notes that Cézanne "understands the emotional root of his need for order and can speak of 'an exciting serenity'." Here repression is understood in dialectical relationship with the release of restlessness. His general belief in artistic expression as a release from emotional repression resulting from inner conflict extends to Romanesque art, where, in "On the Aesthetic Attitude in Romanesque Art," p. 10, he remarks on its "fantastic types" as "a world of projected emotions, psychologically significant images of force, play, aggressiveness, anxiety, self-torment and fear, embodied in the powerful forms of instinct-driven creatures, twisted, struggling, entangled, confronted, and superposed," and "submitted to no fixed teaching or body of doctrine."

79. Schapiro's "Nature of Abstract Art" is a study of the development of modern art from impressionism onward understood ideologically as the projection of a "domain of ideal freedom" and "integrity" in rebellious response to the humanly "stultifying" effects of "the advance of monopoly capitalism" (p. 82).

80. Schapiro, "The Liberating Quality of Avant-Garde Art," p. 41.

81. Schapiro, " 'Muscipula Diaboli,' The Symbolism of the Mérode Altarpiece," pp. 186-87. There is also an interesting remark in "Nature of Abstract Art," p. 92, where Schapiro writes that "the very choice of the motif of the peasant woman with the water pails betrays a sexual interest and the emotional context of [Malevich's] tendency toward his particular style of abstraction." This is on a par with his observation that "At the time of the Mérode panel appear also the first secular paintings of the naked female body, a clear sign of the new place of art in the contending, affective life of the individual" (p. 186).

82. Schapiro, "The Bowman and the Bird on the Ruthwell Cross and Other Works: The Interpretation of Secular Themes in Early Medieval Religious Art," p. 352.

83. Schapiro, "From Mozarabic to Romanesque in Silos," p. 37.

84. Schapiro, "The Sculptures of Souillac," p. 116.

85. Ibid., p. 119.

86. This idea is reiterated in all of Schapiro's writings on modern art. In "Rebellion in Art," p. 205, he notes: "The appeal of the new art coincided with a trend towards greater freedom in many fields."

87. Schapiro's powerful interest in individuality in art and as a value per se is usually paired with his similar interest in freedom, as in his discussion of "individual freedom" and "individual enjoyment" in "Nature of Abstract Art," p. 83. The two correlate again in "Rebellion in Art," p. 220, where he argues that for modern art "the individual, his freedom, his inner world, his dedication, had become primary." "The individual's self-realization was the central problem," and hand in hand with it went the problem of achieving a free society, for "individuality was a social fact." But for Schapiro individuality was also at stake in Romanesque art. In "On the Aesthetic Attitude in Romanesque Art," p. 5, he raises the question as to whether its spontaneity and extraordinary versatility and creativity are "inspired by an underlying Christian conception of human individuality." In "From Mozarabic to Romanesque in Silos," p. 51, he views Romanesque sculpture "under the stimulus of an advancing and more critical interest in nature, individuality, and the everyday world." In "The Sculptures of Souillac" he shows how the art reflects interest in the "contingent, unconfined activity of single individuals" (p. 120) and "presupposes the broader conception of the active, morally divided individual, at once Christian and secular" (p. 122). In "The Romanesque Sculpture of Moissac I," p. 191 he talks of "the striving to individualize" the figures.

88. Schapiro, "The Sculptures of Souillac," p. 121.

89. Schapiro, "From Mozarabic to Romanesque in Silos," p. 37.

90. Schapiro, "Rebellion in Art," p. 217.

91. Schapiro, "The Beatus Apocalypse of Gerona," p. 50.

92. Schapiro, "Style," p. 113.

93. In "Mr. Berenson's Values," p. 60, Schapiro talks of "the life-long concern with the authorship of pictures, the preparation of catalogues, the continued collecting and recording, with its excitement of discovery of the singular and precious—all this . . . may have little to do with art or the market, although its serves both; it can be found in other fields of research. . . ." However, in Berenson's case it was used for profiteering—to obtain wealth and aristocratic class—and "the worldly aims soon contaminated his intellectual goals" (p. 58). Incidentally, in ironical recognition of these worldly aims, Schapiro always, in whatever context—in other writings— he mentions Berenson, prefixes the name with "Mr." He does that with no other personage. He never even gives saints their "St." Schapiro is more general in his review of Francis H. Taylor's book on the modern museum, p. 273: "Certainly, we regret that scholars are content to devote themselves exclusively to questions of attributions and pass by the problems of criticism and interpretation." This has "resulted from . . . general conditions in the field of the arts. The character of the old painting or sculpture as a valuable commodity, the unwillingness of collectors and museum officials to trust their own taste in selecting works, and their demand for guarantees of the authenticity and historical importance of the objects they are to buy, have done more to promote the specialist in attribution. . . ." While Schapiro acknowledges that "the desire for correct classification . . . is indispensable to knowledge in any field," he is aware that in art history it is tainted by commercialism and class snobbery. In "Rebellion in Art," p. 206, he further acknowledges this class-bound, elitist character of art history, which can lead to its intellectual inadequacy as it pursues only "solemn, well certified, old European works of fabulous price." He also makes clear that, as part of this intellectual inadequacy, art history was for many art historians "a quiet succession of great masters—teachers and pupils—without conflicts or disturbing changes," a position which permitted them to shut out modern art and reward themselves with "a spiritual security that they had not earned" (p. 231).

94. In "Courbet and Popular Imagery," Schapiro studies an artist who "affirmed that he alone of the artists of his time expressed the sentiments of the people and that his art was in essence democratic" (p. 170).

95.   Schapiro, *Vincent Van Gogh,* p. 18.

96.   Schapiro, "The Liberating Quality of Avant-Garde Art," p. 37. It is interesting, however, that Schapiro's endorsement of the revolutionary character of modern art is limited by his commitment to a specifically European version of it. Thus, in "Rebellion in Art," p. 205, Schapiro insists that "The years 1910 to 1913 were the heroic period in which the most astonishing innovations had occurred; it was then that the basic types of the art of the next forty years were created. Compared to the movements of art at that time, today's modernism seems a slackening or stagnation." This was published in 1952. In 1956, in "The Younger American Painters of Today," p. 147, he writes: "If de Kooning, Pollock, and Gorky are less profound artists than the great European pioneers of the first decades of our century, I believe they are true painters whose best works, created with fresh conviction and with mastery of the canvas, will survive." To justify this critical opinion, Schapiro writes: "Where this art seems below the highest, I venture to say it is not because the painting is formless, but rather because the forms, and consequently the expressions, are limited by the spontaneity or emphasis of effect. Whether stark or effusive, there is too little growth or climax or revelation within the work itself; all is of a piece, which, though stirring in its force or purity, offers small scope to development. A single idea is pronounced and in time discloses its nature in too obvious a way. Impulse, sensation, automatism are sources here of energy and striking effects, but they have been unfertile ground for deeper qualities." This echoes his idea, from another context in "Rebellion in Art," p. 233, that many modern artists do not allow themselves to "mature slowly and ... seek depth and fullness as much as freshness and impact." I think Schapiro here has shown his limitations as critic. He is partly closed to the new expressionism because he wants it to satisfy the old ideal of a buildup to a climax rather than immediacy of effect. He prefers that power reveal itself slowly rather than rapidly or all at once. This makes one think that Schapiro is committed to the historical ideal of freedom and individuality represented by modern art, rather than to the art itself, which in fact he rarely analyzes in detail. He imposes on the art his version of the way the ideal realizes itself, rather than lets himself discover a new realization of the ideal through the art. He imposes his expectations on the thought, not because of his sense of where history may go—what might be necessary in the current art scene—but because of his sense of where it has been. This is a fundamental error in critical method.

97.   Schapiro, "The Liberating Quality of Avant-Garde Art," p. 37.

98.   Ibid., p. 38.

99.   Ibid.

100. Ibid., p. 40. The feeling of freedom manifests itself through "spontaneity" for Schapiro, another frequently referred to concept.

101. Ibid.

102. Ibid., pp. 40-41.

103. Apart from its use in " 'Muscipula Diaboli,' The Symbolism of the Mérode Altarpiece," one of Schapiro's most interesting uses of psychoanalytic sexual theory to understand medieval art occurs in "From Mozarabic to Romanesque in Silos," pp. 87-88, n. 123, where he talks of the sexual connotations of the city. In "The Sculptures of Souillac," p. 116, he in effect uses psychoanalytic methods of interpretation to understand the "supernatural vehemence" and "intensity" of the beasts in their "deforming oppositions generated by impulsive movements" as revelatory of "human complexity and inwardness ... conflicting motives." The "devaluation of absolute transcendence" which occurs in these sculptures, making way for "the contingent, the temporal, and inferior" (p. 117) is continued for Schapiro by the psychoanalytic revelation of sexuality.

104.   Schapiro, "Two Slips of Leonardo and a Slip of Freud," *Psychoanalysis* 4 (1955-56): 7. In *Words and Pictures,* p. 16, Schapiro takes a similar approach, presenting alongside one another, as though they were equally valid, a psychoanalytic and a religious interpretation of the image of wrestling young and old men. The psychoanalytic interpretation does not displace or debunk the religious one, but takes its place as another possibility—an alternative. For Schapiro, there is no precedence—no privileged means of access, because of the inherent complexity or multidimensionality of phenomena.

105.   Schapiro, "Leonardo and Freud: An Art-Historical Study," *Journal of the History of Ideas* 17 (1956): 147-178.

106.   K.R. Eissler, *Leonardo da Vinci* (New York: International Universities Press, 1961), p. 17.

107.   Ibid., p. 42.

108.   Ibid., p. 43.

4

Art Criticism: Where's the Depth?

The good critic remains what he always was, as rare, said Schopenhauer, "as the phoenix, which appears only once in five hundred years."

Henri Peyre, *The Failures of Criticism*

Tradition has it that there are two steps to criticism, namely, description and judgment, or an empirical and an evaluative step. The dilemma is, which has priority. For some it is more important to describe the actuality of a work of art accurately than to appraise its esthetic quality. For them, judgment is not a separate act because intuition of quality is inherent in perception. Perception of fact subsumes intuition of quality in the same way description subsumes judgment. Max Kozloff's view that description is "laconic interpretation"—he might also have said laconic appreciation—is perhaps the most sophisticated recent articulation of this critical strategy.[1] Others hold that one can't begin to describe a work of art cogently unless one is first certain of its value. The work is to them meaningful before it is factual, and simply to describe it, in however subtle a way, is to neutralize its value. That value, which is discovered by judgment, lies in the extent to which the work exemplifies a "universal idea of art." As Lionello Venturi wrote in the *History of Art Criticism* (1936), such an idea is "the essential condition of artistic judgment."[2] The way the work does or does not live up to the idea determines its seriousness, which in turn determines the way the critic describes it.

The two views are complementary. The one makes the work of art's facticity explicit, the other, its universal value. Both mean to be objective. The one deals with the objectively given particulars of the work of art, the other with an objective general idea of art. They would seem to go together. Yet increasingly in contemporary art criticism the description of particulars has come to seem more important than general ideas about art. This is because such ideas do not seem durable and, worse yet, seem altogether beside the point of—in fact are overwhelmed by—actual art production. Description seems better able to cope with the sheer variety and mass of art because it makes no presumptions about the general nature of art and has no fixed expectations about its quality. Description has also come to seem all-important because of the sense that past art criticism was irresponsible to the individual work of art, which is, after all, the point of departure to which all critical reflection returns. Thus, traditional idealistic criticism, geared to judgment, subsumed the particular work under a general idea of art, in effect assuming that the work was vital and viable only to the extent that it exemplifed the idea. But contemporary empirical criticism, geared to description, allows the particular work an independent life of its own, recognizing that it outlives all the general ideas that claim to give it life.

In the last analysis these reduce to a number of limited perspectives on a particular kind of art. Not only are there other kinds of art, but the art in question can survive without these perspectives. But a revitalized idealistic criticism would argue that however wrong its general idea of art—however much it is actually applicable only to a particular kind of art—the fact remains that the reason any work of art outlives the moment of its making and seems to transcend its own particularity is because it is critically mediated. In the last analysis the work's way of being present depends upon critical reflection of it, and criticism's effort to formulate general ideas is an effort to ground the particular work in such a way that it will have a durable presence. However much the work seems to be beyond the reach of any general reflection, it finds itself subject to still further reflection, without which it would not be cogently present.

From this point of view, description, however Delphic, is a limited immediate response to the work that precludes further reflection on it and forces all reflection to one level. Description not only does not deal with the work's aura,[3] but it also inhibits the capacity to create the general ideas that can. Geared to particular detail, description not only ignores general ideas, but forbids them as implicating an overinterpretation of the work's facticity. Empirical criticism, issuing in description, does not realize that, while detail cannot be transcended, the sharpness or dimness with which detail appears depends upon its unity with other detail; and this unity, with its evocative aura, can in turn be grasped only by consciously created ideas. Not to attempt to create such general ideas is to leave half the work of criticism undone. It is to forfeit critical purpose for empirical precision—which, in fact, is an illusion, since its constancy is contingent on an assumption of the way the work is known, that is, on some limited epistemology of art. Critical consciousness is not simply a passive instrument for the description of particular detail (a recorder of *fact*), but an active creator of general ideas designed to articulate the aura of the work as the whole to which the sum of its details refers—but is not equivalent to—when understood in complex, changing unity. Critical consciousness openly takes command of the work. It does not humbly submit to the work, as description implicitly does.

Neo-idealistic criticism counters the naive empiricism of descriptive criticism, with its quasi-absolutist particularism and immediatism, by arguing that whatever descriptive ideal and method is brought to bear on the work of art (whether stylistic or sociological, assimilative historical or a poetic method which displays the work's radical individuality), its "topicality" and viability depend upon the critical viewer's sense of its still undisclosed depths, its still untold pertinence, its still unmined significance: the sense that whatever method is brought to bear on the work of art, it remains an evasive, although experienced aura. In effect, the probing of the art's aura will never be completely done, for that aura (the art as operational) is itself never complete without critical probing. From this point of view, the art remains "vulnerable," and any description of it that means to be more than naive must take this vulnerability into account, openly suggesting avenues of approach to the work which the description on its own does not take. In other words, any description must imply its own contradiction, or at least openendedly emanate an aura of alternatives. Theoretically, no description is simple, unless the art's aura is itself simple and severely limited. But in "critical" practice all too many descriptions are simple, indeed simplistic, for they are implicitly concerned with eliminating the uncertainty—or at least leveling the contradictions—of the art's aura. Such seemingly "pure" description exemplifies false critical consciousness.

Very little contemporary empirical art criticism has any "idealistic" tendency, because very few empirical critics are willing to acknowledge their vulnerability, i.e. the contingency of their reflections, corresponding to the contingency of the aura of the work of art. They want closure and completeness—seeming comprehensiveness and finality—and description, pursued far enough, seems to guarantee it. But in fact it is a way of foreclosing on the work of art, a way of cutting possible future loss of meaning by gambling it away in the present by seeing the work as all fact when, indeed, it does *seem* to be all fact. Description reduces the work to a secure obviousness, abolishing the "fantasy" of what it might be. To restore contingency to the vision of it, so that it might become visionary, the critic must acknowledge the contingency of his own consciousness, and not attempt to capsulate the work in a hermetic description. This contingency is not entirely acknowledged by accepting the inadequacy, or recognizing the limitations, of critical methods. Nor is it acknowledged by admitting partisanship—the critic's willingness to defend or attack an art on the basis of his taste (whether that be the expression of a prejudiced, fixed sensibility or one which discovers itself in response to an unexpected art). The empirical critic means to be disarming by acknowledging the weakness of his methods—to abide by description alone is already to make such an acknowledgment—and his passionate partisanship (his pursuit of his sense of quality). But neither acknowledgement accounts for his inability to deal with the work's aura. The critic's contingency has less to do with the limits of rationality and the prejudices of irrationality than with a condition of consciousness itself. Consciousness is conative as well as cognitive: unless this is recognized, criticism cannot begin to comprehend either its own desire for descriptive closure or, self-contradictorily, its unhappiness with such absolutism—and its unhappiness with the work of art as given, whether in itself, in description, or in any final appraisal. Criticism is always struggling free of its bondage to its own presuppositions and knowledge, its own sense of the *given*.

Thus, critical contingency is not the same as the contingency that results from what Lawrence Alloway, in his endorsement of Apollinaire's kind of criticism, calls the "population problem."[4] That current (but not necessarily everlasting) problem creates for the critic the difficult, almost overwhelming task of responding to and sifting through immense numbers of artists and styles—the hordes in "a complex art scene" who are not pre-sorted by being associated with workshops or schools but who drift in overgeneralized, ill-defined "movements." The strain of this situation produces a kind of contingency, which, although not the kind of contingency I am driving at, is revealed in the pastiche that criticism becomes. Thus a potpourri effect, typical of the work of many critics, results not only from criticism's tendency to spread itself thin in an effort to do justice to all kinds of art, but because of, as Apollinaire suggests, the pastiche character—or else the virtuosity or mock-individuality—of much of the art itself. While Alloway argues that, given the modern situation of information density and art population expansion and modern art's own "expansionist esthetic," the critic must submit to being "hounded by topicality" and must write, like Apollinaire, from "straight journalistic motives" (hopefully speaking "in the present the words of the future") combining modest, realizable goals with immodest and ultimately unrealizable pretensions—there is no guarantee that he will do so. Indeed, the essentially descriptive journalistic approach seems to preclude doing so. For that approach wants little to do with undisclosed depths of meaning that the future might uncover, only with disclosed surfaces of meaning self-evident in the present. Alloway's approach is the best for producing the evidence itself—I know of no other critic today who so admirably produces such a wide range of evidence—but not the range of possible conclusions about it.

The fashionable, like the topical, also interferes with the development of critical consciousness, but in a different way. Where pursuit of the topical does not carry it far enough (a problem Alloway recognizes when he raises the question of the critic's "lead time"), pursuit of the fashionable in art does not allow it to get off the ground. The question of fashion seems more harrowing today than when Proust's Swann, in "his scepticism, as a finished 'man of the world'," first observed

> that the objects which we admire have no absolute value in themselves, that the whole thing is
> a matter of dates and castes, and consists in a series of fashions, the most vulgar of which are
> worth just as much as those which are regarded as the most refined.[5]

Today much art appears self-consciously fashionable, concerned as it seems with being made by a certain date, before similar art, as if that proved its originality and permitted it to acquire pre-eminent commercial and historical (use and surplus) value—and to appeal to a certain caste, if only in the art world. Or else it becomes fashionable by confirming the look of art already accepted as fashionable, much as a good deal of regional art confirms the look of cosmopolitan New York art. It can be argued that both kinds of art—the orginally fashionable and campfollower fashionable—make no attempt from the start to create the illusion of profundity or depth. They want only to create a striking, esthetic surface, or to refine known surfaces; that is, they want to deal only with what is self-evident, as regards either form or meaning. Of course art which self-consciously attempts to create such an illusion is not necessarily unfashionable. There are fashions in depth (in the art world existentialism was one and Marxism is now another) as well as in surface. The use of a readymade depth, a finished theory valued for its conclusions rather than for the reality its methods might continue to disclose, brings with it a fictional finality of eternal significance that issues in dogmatism. Whether the critic has his finger on the pulse of the topical or can readily determine profundity on the basis of a fashionable idea, the result is often the same opinionated, monodimensional description of the work of art. In such a situation the critic is forced back, in unwitting despair, on taste (Swann's seemingly implicit ability to distinguish between vulgarity and refinement); but that is itself a fashionable disguise, interfering with a depth response to art.[6]

The contingency I am asking the critic, and artist, to acknowledge involves recognition of what Robbe-Grillet scornfully called "the myth of depth." I am not only less scornful of this myth, but I think accepting it and indeed attempting to generate it constitute all that art and criticism arc about. The contingency of art and criticism lies in the difficulty of actualizing such myths, in the uncertainty or perishability of the results. Art must generate a myth of the depth of the world, even if that world is art itself (the illusion of art's autonomy is just such a myth of depth) and then criticism must generate the myth of art's depth. Both attempt to go beyond the surface of the given by charging it with implicit meaning. Indeed, to cling to the surface is to show allegiance to a greater myth than that of depth: the myth of surface is the belief that the facticity of anything manmade or deliberately exhibited for human "edification" is self-referential rather than the sign of the consciousness that made or "revealed" it. That not only falsifies it but precludes its use by another consciousness for its own purposes. And criticism is just such a use to which art can properly be put, in the name of its relevance for consciousness—for human intention in general.

Thus, criticism must not stay on the surface of the art it investigates, just as art must not stay on the surface of the reality it explores. Criticism appropriates the art, for its own sake as well as for an understanding of the art's intention, just as art appropriates and gives a "reading" of reality. Admittedly, the effort of appropriation leaves in its wake the sense of having abandoned the given for the mythical, the factual for the fictional—even the fake. For the creation of depth—

the attempt to make the given signify the relationships which make it what it is, with no sense of any absolute priority or necessary limitation on these relationships—is not only an uncertain, heuristic enterprise, but one which seems to negate rather than affirm the given. The search for depth seems to lead far afield from the given. Put another way, it seems to burden the given with an import which is neither self-evident nor inherent to it. Yet to remain on the surface of the given, always to circle back to it without having circled away from it, to mirror it tautologously, as much description does—and as that kind of esthetic exaltation which issues in a sense of the ineffable (blind recognition) does—is in the end to make the fact of the given more of a myth than any projection of its depth might do. That, in Whitehead's terms, misplaces its concreteness and treats it as an independent abstraction—a pure "fact." To abide by the facticity of the given—whether this be conceived as a matter of style, history, or fashion—is to treat it categorically and so to miss its reality as the representative of consciousness.

Art, then, finds the significance with the given—always an unfinished depth, although the art seems to complete it by embodying it—and projects this significance through its own givenness. And criticism makes explicit the implicit depth of the art, and how its facticity mediates this depth. To do this the critic must know more than both artist and scholar, those "mediums" and students of surfaces who themselves always become "academic." It is not clear that the artist necessarily knows what his work is about, or that he even understands its allure—the way it lures the critical viewer "speculatively." The artist's ignorance of his own work's import is often marked by a self-righteous assertion that his art be taken on the terms he stakes out for it and, correlatively, that it not be critically comprehended and culturally appropriated in terms other than his stated intention. Yet this demand, like a stated anticipatory intention, does not so much safeguard the meaning of the work as shrivel it. If we leave the work of art to its own arrogantly obvious appearance and to that of its artist's intent, it becomes dust. Keeping to itself behind the fence the artist builds for it, it will never become significant. So the force of criticism, which rips that fence away, is irresistible, and the work shows its power only by surviving the onslaughts of a criticism which seeks to "undermine" it—to prove to it that it is something other than it seems to be, to exhibit it in unexpected ways.

The critic must ignore the artist's protests that his art is being mangled, and he must also transcend his own tendency to exhibit it in expected ways. He must transcend his own habits of understanding, which are usually codified in descriptive purpose and enforced by the social pressures of the given art world that, insofar as it is a commercial world, wants to know art in set ways so it can be easily consumed. (Description unwittingly plays into the hands of this commerical purpose—and the general human desire for comfort and easy familiarity—by functioning as publicity for the art rather than analysis of it.) Above all, the critic must transcend his own, however laconic, empiricism, moving beyond any mediation of the work as a topic of immediate importance. And he must transcend his own will to judge, avoiding that preening of the peacock feathers of his own sensibility calling attention to the power of his own presence as on a par with that of the work of art. Not accepting the artist's efforts to control the destiny of his work, not accepting habitual ways of knowing the work used for the sake of convenience and commerce, renouncing descriptive journalism with its intellectual laziness and the mandarin posture of his own judgment and sensibility, the critic must become independent enough to begin the difficult task of descending into the depths of the work. He may use the artist, convention, description, and his own judgment as guides, but in the end he must go his own way as it cuts new paths through the work and sees new possibilities in it. And when he does not see them the work will be dead, "complete."

All methods, then, are subsumed in the attempt to determine the work's intentionality, which can only be done by the critic with the aim of determining his own intentionality through the work. It is its complex, often slowly revealed, intentionality which gives the work its staying power, and the critic can grasp that intentionality only by becoming a participant observer (participant creator, even) in the work, which requires that he become conscious of his own intentionality, seeing it as well as the work itself as a "complex." Description and judgment, to become telling, must be transfigured by this sense of the critical task as an exploration of intentionality. If they are not understood "intentionally," criticism becomes simply another form of advertising. Untransfigured, description at its best is anthropological. Historical and stylistic concerns are subsumed in a sense of the work as a social product and cultural artifact. Then judgment can become moralistic and even mystical, but neither reveals the world view or kind of consciousness, collective and individual, that the work represents. Admittedly, the anthropological sort of description puts us in a better position than the moralizing or mystical judgment (in one way or another "superior") to grasp the work's intentionality, but only if that description becomes dialectical; that is, if it shows us how the art it describes negates other art and relates to other social products and cultural artifacts in general. But to do this the critic's own intentionality must be dialectical.

The critic, then, must lead the casual viewer away from the exhibited character of the work of art, of which the critic's exhibition of his own taste is an indirect aspect, and toward its possible intended character. This may confuse the viewer, but it will free him from regarding the work of art as simply another phenomenon and product in a world already crowded with them. The critic will thereby liberate the viewer from his superficial consciousness, educating consciousness to become generally critical toward phenomena and products. Art criticism, like criticism in general, is a way of making one aware of invisible significance behind visible reality, whether in art or anything else. Criticism teaches one not to parrot the given in description nor to exult about it in quasi-religious esthetic ecstasy, which quickly creates moral hierarchies—that is, not to be raised by it, or, for that matter, lowered. The given is never to be taken on its own terms, although these are to be used to unmask it. Thus the critical revelation of the work of art's possible intended character liberates the work from its own superficial appearance. The critic must create the illusion that the work will find its own level in the context of thought he creates for it. In a sense, the critic's whole task is to construct that context, which must be deep if the work is to have the chance to prove that it—the work itself—is not shallow. The critic's "oceanic consciousness" is a cosmos in which the work of art learns whether it can swim—or sink. The critic must take on whatever art he can handle, however bizarre it may seem to his taste, and locate it in as comprehensive a climate of opinion as possible, to see how short or deep its breath is.

Notes

1.   Quoted in Lawrence Alloway, "The Use and Limits of Art Criticism," in his *Topics in American Art Since 1945,* New York, 1975, p. 251.

2.   Lionello Venturi, *History of Art Criticism,* New York, 1964, p. 31.

3.   I use "aura" in an expansion of the sense in which Walter Benjamin wrote of it in "Das Kunstwerk im Zeitalter seiner technischen Reproduzierbarkeit," *Schriften,* I (Frankfurt am Main, 1955), pp. 366-405. For Benjamin, there are two outstanding facts about the work of art's aura: (1) its "foundation in ritual," which determines its "unique worth" and guarantees its "genuine" character and (2) "its wasting away in the age of the technical reproduction of the work of art," when its foundation becomes "politics." Whether the aura of the work of art is premised on its ritual or political relationship to social reality, either is no more than the springboard of its possible depth of meaning. In other words, for me the work of art's aura does not disappear because the work of art can be technically reproduced; it only changes. The foundation of the aura of implications changes, not the fact that it has an aura.

4.   Alloway, p. 255.

5.   Marcel Proust, *Swann's Way,* New York, 1934, pp. 289-90.

6.   See Donald B. Kuspit, "The Dialectic of Taste," *Journal of the British Society for Phenomenology,* 4 (1973): 123-38.

Civil War: Artist Contra Critic

Criticism of today, when it is serious, intelligent, full of good intentions, tends to impose on us a method of thinking and dreaming which might become another bondage. Preoccupied with what concerns it particularly, its own field, literature, it will lose sight of what concerns us, painting. If that is true, I shall be impertinent enough to quote Mallarmé: "A critic is someone who meddles with something that is none of his business."
—Paul Gauguin, Letter to André Fontainas,
March 1899

Despite his lack of merit, the artist is today, and has been for many years, nothing but a spoiled child. How many honours, how much money has been showered upon men without soul and without education! ... But apart from these [Chenavard, Préault, Daumier, Ricard, Delacroix], I cannot think of any other artist who is worthy to converse with a philosopher or a poet.
—Charles Baudelaire, The Salon of 1859

In the above "observations," these mutual ventings of spleen, these profound exasperations, these positions of violent conflict, we have the issue, the horns of a dilemma. Whom are we to trust, the artist or the critic?

Initially this opposition takes a shallow form, determined by prejudice of artist against critic. Prejudice—"preunderstanding," as Hans-Georg Gadamer calls it—becomes the token of authority, dogmatic power, nonrational domination. The artist's prejudice against the critic is an expression of the desire not to be questioned. As Gadamer says, "The real power of hermeneutical consciousness is our ability to see what is questionable."[1] The artist's objection to the existence of the critic—not to any particular critic, or critical stance, but to the very fact of the critic—is intended to throw us off the scent of the art, a scent we can pick up and follow because we know that the art is questionable at its root. The artist does not want to face this fact, even though it is the only avenue to the art, the only path by which we can know it as authentic.

The structure of this premature interaction, designed to suppress critical consciousness, takes the form of a loaded question. "Why do we need the witness of the critic," the artist asks, "when we have the testimony of the artist, who is closest to the art, having labored to bring it into the world?" Frequently this opinion takes a declarative form: "The work of art speaks for itself." Both bespeak enormous vanity, the self-love of the artist, the artist's narcissistic expectation that art is self-reflective, which in an extreme form becomes solipsism—namely, the artist's godlike sense of creating a world. The critic intervenes in this narcissism, simply as a presence. The critic does not even have to ask questions to make the first relationship to the work of art one of questioning. If nothing else, the critic breaks the spell of the artist's narcissistic relationship to the art, and permanently destroys the possibility of a similar narcissistic relationship developing on the part of anyone else who might approach the art. Critical consciousness cannot begin to function until narcissistic self-consciousness is rendered ineffective—discarded as a species of false consciousness.

The first struggle between artist and critic dissolves when self-love is recognized as a poor basis for the production of art—when it is recognized that self-love will always fail to objectify itself. An unexpected by-product of this analysis is the discovery that, in rejecting the critic, the artist rejects himself: denying the necessity of the critic, he denies his own necessity. The nothingness of art and the artist without the glance of critical consciousness to make them *truly* self-conscious becomes evident. Recognition of the nihilism that the artist's objection to the critic generates is important. It is recognition that the artist's nihilistic attitude to the critic becomes suicidal, working against the artist—for criticism is necessary not simply as adjustment to the artist's view of the significance of his creation (even gods can make mistakes about the blessedness of their creations), but as the condition for creation itself. The artist must speak critically rather than narcissistically. Art is not a creation *ex nihilo,* as narcissism would have it be—a creation out of the nothingness of the undefined, inexperienced, simply "artistic" self—but rather a creation out of the reality of criticism. The creative act is a "critical" act, for it is about the nature of critical consciousness as well as an exercise of that consciousness. But this is jumping the gun, a premature conclusion—the critic's own "preunderstanding."

Looking again at the quotations from Gauguin and Baudelaire, we become aware of something more than mutual defamation and mutual narcissism— namely a competition between art and criticism. Behind all the pride of place of each, the insistence by each on its own integrity at the expense of the integrity of the other, there exists a contest for the right of expression of "the idea." This informs the anti-literature bias of Gauguin—typical of many modern artists— and Baudelaire's assumption that the "worthiness" of the philosopher and the poet is superior to that of the artist. It is an old competition, as familiar to the humanist as the correlative argument over the relative merits of word and image as means of articulating "the truth." Whatever conclusion this argument reaches does nothing to obliterate the primary elements it deals with: word and image are alternate, irreconcilable means of expression, by reason of the fact that they are radically separate mediums. This is what Gauguin and Baudelaire face up to, taking sides according to the medium each commands. But both want to express the ideas of the poet and the philosopher (we will see this later explicitly in regard to Gauguin), and both are aware that each medium shapes or embodies the ideas it expresses according to its own particular nature.

There is a history to this competition which should be noted, if only briefly, because it is indicative of the changing fortunes of word and image with respect to one another. There are at least, broadly understood, three phases of the development of their relationship: one in which the image is subsidiary to the word, primarily the case in medieval art; one in which the image and word achieve parity, primarily the case in Renaissance art; and one in which the image, if not dominant to word, seems superior to it at least as an expression of the idea. It is in effect the ideal or preferred medium for the expression of the idea, which is what Gauguin and other modern, especially modernist, artists would have us believe.

In medieval art the image is illustrative, but of the word rather than of the idea. The expressive path is from idea to word to image, the image being an easy—and ultimately inadequate—means of access to the idea for those who cannot think it themselves. (Thinking it oneself means thinking it in words.) The image, as in illuminated manuscripts, seems gratuitous, which makes it all the more distracting from ideas. It seems to call attention to itself before it calls attention to ideas, if it does at all. One can even conceive of the medieval image as a kind of decorative drain on the ideational significance or power of the word, having the effect of nullifying it as a mediator of meaning. However exaggerated or speculative this may be, the image is regarded, finally, as irrelevant to the text, at best a bad translation of it—the importance of "translation" being crucial to this argument. Much as writers rejected *visual* translation in the medieval period, so artists reject *literary* translation in the modern period. Such translation is acknowledged to occur, but is regarded as unnecessary. In the medieval period that main objection to the visual translation of the word was that such translation "profanes" the word and is in and of itself profane. The word, not the image, is sacred, for the image implicitly involves sense appeal rather than a direct appeal to the mind. And the image materially partakes of the everyday world, works in terms of experienced visibility, and, however much one needs a mind to make an image, it is not clear that it is the same mind that can use words to think an idea. In the modern period, the objection to the literary translation—assuming that is what criticism does (prima facie a mistake)—of the image is that it necessarily dismisses the "essence" of the visual medium, sometimes even ignoring the very existence of that essence. This is the crux of the modernist argument against criticism, reducing the critic to a dumb witness of and yeasayer to the artist's material exploits.

It was during the Renaissance that the image achieved parity with the word, becoming "humanistic" and "poetic." Perhaps the desire of this equality is most evident in Dürer's prints of the Apocalypse, 1496-1500, each printed on the opposite side of a page of text—as though a text in its own right, competitive with the Biblical narrative, and so in itself "Biblical." We begin to get the "word-wise" image, that is grounded in a poem or a philosophy and prides itself on its "power of speech" and knowledgeability. The ideational power of the humanistic image is acknowledged, truly accepted as a thinker's image produced by a thinking artist, rather than by one whose craft was simply illustration. It is worth noting that this development—the increase in esteem with which the image was held by reason of its power to articulate ideas—occurred, particularly in Northern Europe, against the background of a latent iconoclasm. The iconoclastic attitude—always lurking in the background when there is respect for the holy word as a pure expression of the divine idea—haunts modernism as well.

Modernism can be understood as an assertion that the image has its own divine essence, its own absolute nature, unspeakable except in its own terms, so that any charge that it is a betrayal of or distraction from the sacred is a gross mistake. Just as in the Renaissance an image could be described (as many of Dürer's were) as "subtle and ingenious,"—the language used to approve of a humanistic text—so the modernist picture is a subtle and ingenious visual text, because it explores and articulates a divine medium, a medium capable of divine effects on consciousness. With modernism, the idea of the gratuitousness of the image, as well as its accessory, secondary role in consciousness, disappears; the modernist image is understood as having as direct an effect on the mind as words. In fact, modernism moves toward a kind of reverse iconoclasm, in which the word is dismissed as ineffective, or at least less effective than the image, i.e., less able to articulate the sacred idea, and so less conceptually significant. The modernist argues that words can never do justice to an image's mental content or ideational import, which speak spontaneously through their imagery and are in no need of secondary elaboration. Words, however "critical" or cajoling, now become a poor second best, with the image the primary source of ideational faith.

From the modernist point of view the critic is in fact a closet iconoclast, who wants to destroy the artistic image with inartistic words, who implicitly argues that unless an image can be translated into words its idea is irrelevant and meaningless. This suspicion is in part what motivates Gauguin's introductory statement. And, in fact, an iconoclastic tendency, however unconscious, does seem implicit in Baudelaire's statement, for to give pride of place to the poet and philosopher is to give pride of place to words. Baudelaire can even be understood to imply that artists do not have the fundamental, creative, or as he calls it "imaginative," experience of generating ideas, "distilling the natural poetry" of things—at least not as consistently as the poet and philosopher. How, then, can the artist be expected to express ideas properly? And is it possible that the visual medium is inherently inferior to the literary medium as a process of intense, spontaneous relationship to ideas? Baudelaire's intellectual bias against artists is a form of inconoclastic doubt of and disrespect for the value of their enterprise.

The anti-literature bias of the modern artist—whether a defense against the imagined iconoclasm of the critic or a strategy for an offensive justification of personal integrity—has an important effect on the artist's writing. The writing becomes more of an apologia than an analysis, more coercive than persuasive, more pronouncement than argument, i.e., a closed rather than open system of disclosure. When Cézanne warned Emile Bernard, whom he regarded as too "intellectual," to "beware of the literary spirit which so often causes painting to deviate from its true path—the concrete study of nature—to lose itself all too long in intangible speculations," he articulated an anti-intellectualism that became the keynote of a good deal of writing by artists.[2]

While the artist's writing may pretend to intellectual virility in its rejection of the "ready-made idea—that of the man of letters," to quote Gauguin, it rarely comes up with fresh, new ideas. Instead, nihilistically and regressively, it tends to shout, also with Gauguin, "Emotion first! Understanding later," posing a false and banal dichotomy.

When one substitutes emotions for ideas, precluding the growth of new ideas as well as obliterating ready-made ones, one puts oneself in an impregnable position, beyond the reach of criticism. One has presumably appealed to the "feeling" public over the head of the critic, who "wants to make points of comparison with former ideas and other authors" before addressing a new work of art. The critic has been set up by the artist as the scapegoat of the public as well as of himself, as the thinking person who overintellectualizes ideas and so misses or obscures what is common to all people—feeling. But the artist does not realize that personal feeling—what Gauguin called "transcendental emotivity"—is not that of the public, and that the transcendental ambition of personal feeling has more in common with the critic than with the public. What one reaches is not so much that "instinct" of the public as its indifference or inertia, for the public, even more than the critic, can begin to know the new only through the old, and it needs to know the new only insofar as the new impinges on its existence. This second level of struggle between the artist and the critic, in which the artist appeals to the public rather than to the critic, must crumble in the face of the public's unresponsiveness.

The artist's prejudice against literature makes his own literary vindications of his art suspect, though, ironically, this writing opens up the horizon of the art's authenticity—for it can then begin to be seen not simply in terms of its medium, but as a highly individual phenomenon. This is one of the key uses of the artist's writing: to serve as the context for, even cornerstone of, individuality. When Cézanne says, "Do not be an art critic, but paint, therein lies salvation,"[3] "salvation" is understood to mean an "incessant and constant search for the sole and unique aim."[4] Thus what counts is to be radically unique and original—one might say, unique on the basis of a return to "origins." And whether nature is taken to be the *fons et origo,* as in Cézanne, or feeling as in Gauguin, or spirit as in Kandinsky, what counts and moves us in the best writing by artists is the sense of a return to elemental reality, to an aspect of existence taken as a primordial source of being, and the artist's introjection of this as his art's "inner necessity," to use Matisse's as well as Kandinsky's expression. This essence, grasped as inner necessity, becomes the basis for the artist's individuation of his art.

The artist's writing displays not so much an understanding of this fundamental reality as the belief in it, particularly as the spirit—the "inspiration"—of art. The artist in effect invites us to measure art against personal belief. The artist's writing thus operates on a metaphysical level, enjoining us to see how well the physical art exemplifies the metaphysical idea that inwardly sustains it. Of course, the inward is outward in the artist's writing; i.e., the "secret" of the art is revealed in it. But the writing still makes "detectives" of us all, for while we are expected to approach the art in terms of the spirit in which it was made and which it tries to make manifest, we can do so only if we have truly detected that spirit. While the artist's writing tries to lead the way, it in fact tells us simply what to expect from the art, which does not guarantee that what we are to expect is actually there. We may not experience the spirit of the work in our encounter with it, or rather, we may be visited by an unexpected spirit during our "engagement" with it. In fact, what we do experience is likely to depend upon our state of preparation, and it is questionable whether the artist's writing is always the best preparation for the work. Certainly it is not the only one we should rely on. The question of the artist's reliability as a guide to his own art is central to criticism, which trusts no guide, and which takes none as exclusive. To do so would be to forfeit the dialectical, and even adversary character of criticism.

However, through the articulation of ideas, the artist seems to get the jump on the critic, truly dispensing and reducing the critic to, at best, the chief of detectives—one who holds a mirror that does not distort the art it reflects. The artist seems to offer a general idea as well as its artistic exemplification. The artist is already in possession of the general idea the critic might bring to the analysis of the art, and is in possession of the art which particularizes the general idea and works on that idea's basis. But in the artist's writing the idea is stated rather than comprehended. It exists rhetorically rather than intellectually, and ultimately shows itself to be a new form of narcissism—a subtler narcissism, one which goes through the detour of "inner necessity"—rather than a concept in its own right, fully developed by analysis. It has ideological rather than intellectual value, a kind of innocence that makes it artistically attractive but that can also lead the art into unexpected byways of meaning, paths it did not knowingly enter and which it might have avoided had it been more critically aware.

What the critic can offer, in fact, is a sense of the consequences of unthinking obedience to the general idea. In other words, the critic sees the *concrete* generality of the idea, rather than naively proclaiming its universality, and thus is in a position to see the art as world-historically rather than only artistically significant. The critic functions as the mediator for a full-fledged artistic meaning, where such meaning is understood to make the art responsible to world history rather than simply art history. Obviously art history—the history of style—must be considered, but only as a point of departure. Just how this might work is shown in an exchange between Gauguin and the critic André Fontainas regarding Gauguin's *Where Do We Come From? What Are We? Where Are We Going?* (1897). What I want to concentrate on is not whether Fontainas's opinion about the work's lack of success in properly exemplifying its metaphysical meaning is right or wrong—and obviously Gauguin thinks it is wrong—but the fact that he bothers to question the character of that exemplification to make its method a problem. It is this questioning that is crucial, for it opens the way to the authenticity of Gauguin's art—to seeing that Gauguin has in fact found a new way of exemplifying metaphysical ideas in visual art, namely, through a musical metaphor, the music of color.

It is important to realize that Fontainas does begin with the empathetic emotion that Gaugin demanded, describing Gauguin's landscapes as existing "for the purpose, almost always achieved, of creating warm, brooding wellsprings for the surging emotions." And Fontainas is aware too that this is accomplished through color. But then the illuminating skeptical note enters, in the very act of describing the effect of color. It is this note that makes the criticism purposive more than descriptive, more than adulatory, more than a mirror regenerating and serving the artist's self-acclaim. Fontainas writes:

> If the violent oppositions of such full and vibrant tones, which do not blend and never merge into one another through intermediate values, first distract and then rivet the attention, it must also be admitted that while they are often glowing, bold, and exultant they sometimes lose their effect by monotonous repetition; by the juxtaposition, irritating in the long run, of a startling red and vibrant green, identical in value and intensity.[5]

It does not matter that Fontainas is holding out for an old way of dealing with color while acknowledging and admiring a new way—a way of violent oppositions rather than a "subdued harmony." What matters is that his skepticism creates a confrontation between the old and the new, giving neither a clear-cut victory. In other words, he generates a problem, and this does more for an understanding of the art than Gauguin's assumed resolution of "the problem of the color." The conflict Fontainas at once invents and discloses is amplified in extending the questionableness of Gauguin's art to his handling of the figure—not as a technical problem (Fontainas is skeptical, critical, enough to see that this is not the issue in Gauguin's art) but rather as an intellectual one.

> But too often the people of his dreams, dry, colorless, and rigid, vaguely represent forms poorly conceived by the imagination untrained in metaphysics, of which the meaning is doubtful and the expression is arbitrary. Such canvases leave no impression but that of deplorable error, for abstractions are not communicated through concrete images unless, in the artist's own mind, they have already taken shape in some natural allegory which gives them life.[6]

Fontainas is here again creating a confrontation between the old and the new, for he goes on to recommend that artists follow "the noble example of Puvis de Chavannes" in their attempts "to represent a philosophical ideal," i.e., to exemplify visually a metaphysical idea. In response, Gauguin acknowledges the superior "talent and experience" of Puvis, and expresses his admiration for him, "but for entirely different reasons" than those of Fontainas. More important, he continues:

> Think also of the musical role color will henceforth play in modern painting. Color, which is vibration just as music is, is able to attain what is most universal yet at the same time elusive in nature: its inner force.[7]

Speaking of his painting, he writes, quoting Mallarmé, "It is a musical poem, it needs no libretto."

Crucial to this exchange is that Gauguin needs to justify himself in a "literary" way—a way presumably repellent to him. For what he has found is a general idea—the musical model and metaphor for all the arts—large enough to contain his own art, its largeness or generality proven by the fact that it applies to another art, the symbolist poetry of Mallarmé, which also strives to be "musical." Gauguin realizes that his art is not self-justifying, and it is the critical skepticism of Fontainas, generating a comparison between Gauguin's art and other art, both contemporary and traditional, which forces him to recognize this, and appeal to the general situation or condition of "modern" art to justify his own. Fontainas forced Gauguin away from the particularity of his art into a general idea which embraced all art, articulating a new possibility for all art. This is exactly the "literary" or critical view that Gauguin was resisting, yet it did him the enormous benefit of forcing him to realize just exactly how "universal" his art was. The "literary" broke the back of his dogmatic self-justification, forcing him into a deeper recognition of his art, a consciousness of its general condition and implications.

The same happens in Gauguin's exchange with Strindberg, who repudiates Gauguin and, like Fontainas, endorses Puvis de Chavannes, only in a more complex way. At the same time Strindberg admits his own ambition, which he identifies with Gauguin's "immense need to become a savage and create a new world." Rejecting the "pitiful God who accepts blows," that Puvis depicts, in favor of the Aztec war god "*Vitsliputsli*" who in the sun devours the hearts of men," Strindberg deifies Gauguin as "a sort of Titan" who "hates a whimpering civilization."[8] This leads Gauguin to one of his more famous articulations in which he contrasts the "Eve" of Strindberg's "civilized conception [which] makes misogynists of you and almost all of us" with his own "ancient Eve," who alone "can logically remain nude before our gaze." Gauguin's Eve speaks a "rugged" language in which "everything is naked and primordial," while the European Eve speaks a "language of inflection . . . which has worn threadbare."[9] The point is that both Fontainas and Strindberg respond to him critically rather than blindly praising or dismissing him outright in a knee-jerk response, so that Gauguin is forced away from that dogmatism which permitted him to speak of one of his pieces of writing, a philosophical tract meant to accompany *Where Do We Come From? What Are We? Where Are We Going?* as "comparable to the Gospels."[10] He has been steered toward a self-awareness, and so a discovery of his own authenticity. Fontainas forces him to accept the fact that the perspective from which he viewed his art was more general than he initially cared to acknowledge, and Strindberg forces him to accept the fact that his art is not simply a gratuitous espousal of instinct but a reaction to and criticism of a presumably repressed world. In realizing that his art is a criticism of both the traditional view of nature as a realm of outer force and of a European conception of civilization, Gauguin realizes the authenticity of his art. The authenticity of art resides only in its critical generality. For this criticality brings it to a world historical level of consciousness at which it can be truly effective, i.e., at which it can test its effect and its "appeal." Here, in this interaction of two critics and an artist, we see how the critic creates a situation of awareness, and how the artist, if he is authentic—if he is to find his authenticity—is forced to justify himself.

It is important that the critic have some detachment from the artist, generating a metaphysical distance not only for itself but for the critical perspective it affords—for the way it makes criticism possible, in and of itself generates critical doubt. Oscar Wilde's assertion that the art critic's "first step" is "to realize his own impressions"[11] is very much to the point. He further describes that criticism "recognizing no position as final, and refusing to bind itself by the shallow shibboleths of any sect or school, creates that serene philosophic temper which loves truth for its own sake, and loves it not the less because it knows it to be unattainable."[12] But there is another view which sees criticism as empathy with the artist, producing what I call artist-identified critics. The ideal of such a critic is clearly Diderot, who, in the words of Sainte Beuve, had "... a great gift of semi-metamorphosis..." which not only enabled him to put himself "... in the author's place..." throw "himself into an author's mind," but also to become "... more enthusiastic on the subject than the author himself."[13] Apollinaire is another example of this kind of critic, but one who forfeits critical confrontation for enthusiastic endorsement. He is the more familiar and beloved kind of critic, who in the last analysis achieves his reputation by discovering artists who eventually become famous. In this case, the critic's enduring reputation depends upon the enduring reputation of the artists he deals with. He introduces ingenue artists, often promoting them into prominence, igniting the spark which catches fire in the minds of the general public. Thus, Sidney Geist can prefer Apollinaire's criticism to Baudelaire's criticism, because "... the artists that occupied him hold no interest for us," while Apollinaire "dealt with a period of great importance...." For Geist, the major task of the critic is "as herald of the new art—of new art," and Apollinaire's "gift for recognizing the new was equaled only by his gift for praising it."[14]

Baudelaire had the detachment and audacity to set up a frame of reference— the contradiction and confrontation between style and imagination—which permitted him to criticize such contemporary (new?) artists as Ingres and Millet. Is his criticism to be dismissed, according to Geist, as mere "literature" rather than criticism? Which critic serves the artist more? The artist-identified critic who enthusiastically praises him—and it was not clear that Diderot's enthusiasm automatically carried praise with it—or the detached critic who "blames" the artist, approaches him through the inherent skepticism of the dialectical approach, regardless of whether the artist is new or established? Which helps us understand art more, or shows it to be more useful? Apollinaire's empathetic assertion that artists are men who wish to become "superhuman,"[15] with its vulgarized Nietzschean overtones? Or Baudelaire's critical response to Ingres's "conscientious alteration of the model" by (in Ingres's words) *adding to it something which is indispensable:* that is, style"? Such style, Baudelaire argues, "is not the naturally poetic quality of the subject, which must be extracted so that it may become more visible. It is an alien poetry, usually borrowed from the past," and can only lead to artistic "disaster," as in the case of Millet's peasants, self-conscious "little pariahs" and "pedants who have too high an opinion of themselves," who are endowed by style with "a pretentiousness which is philosophic, melancholy and Raphaelesque."[16] Baudelaire opposes imagination, which extracts "natural poetry," to pretentious style, which endows a present subject with a glorious past history—a frame of reference and analysis which may not please the artists, but certainly offers more for an understanding of the art, and so for its development, than does empathy with the effort to become superhuman.

There are some artist-identified critics who argue, after denying any interest in the nature or history of criticism, that it is "just a bridge to art," presumably no more than an access route. This attitude inevitably puts one in the good graces of the artist and makes one a willing instrument of the artist. Such an approach may seem to encourage creativity, but one wonders whether creativity is better served by this attitude or that of Baudelairean skepticism, which tries to function as a "conscience" for art, in the double sense that "conscience" has in French, implying the simultaneity of conscience and consciousness. Such a position is a far cry also from that of Diderot, whose enthusiasm was always self-conscious and critical of its object. Diderot's enthusiasm, or power of "semi-metamorphosis," always linked the work to a larger generality that the artist may not have been aware determined, or at least influenced, its existence. Criticism for him was not simply a bridge to art but a clarification of intellectual and moral culture, and a clarification of art as a factor conditioning and reflecting that culture.

It may be that the artist can make this clarification in his writing as well. But too often this writing is concerned with either catalyzing or justifying artistic productivity rather than with following its consequences beyond the objecthood of the work—finding its meaning beyond the material and technical limits of the product. Or, if the artist seeks for its significance beyond its finite presence, thereby giving it a "use" beyond contemplation, he leaps to a reductivist extreme, as in the cases of Gauguin and Kandinsky. The idea of feeling in the one and of spirit in the other become reductivist extremes because they are posited as emblems or representatives of the infinite, with which no binding link can be made by any finite, thinking mind. Suprarational, they remain inaccessible, or no more accessible than gods, who appear in a revelation or, like the *deux ex machina,* appear only at the end of destiny to settle all issues. For both Gauguin and Kandinsky, their own works are epiphanies of an infinite actuality, momentary and fragmentary revelations of an absolute principle of being. This is all very well, but it is uncritical, and it implies an uncritical relationship of the work to its ground. The critic enters to make clear that such a relationship is both more and less direct than might be imagined, for it is dialectical, questionable, uncertain, in process. Only the hermeneutical critic can do this, for the artist-identified critic floats with the artist on his cloud of self-belief, which exists to be dissipated.

Notes

1.   Hans-Georg Gadamer, "The Universality of the Hermeneutical Problem," *Philsophical Hermeneutics* (Berkeley, 1977), p. 13.

2.   Paul Cézanne, Letter to Emile Bernard, May 12, 1904, in Herschel B. Chipp, ed., *Theories of Modern Art* (Berkeley, 1968), p. 19.

3.   Cézanne, Letter to Emile Bernard, July 25, 1904, ibid., p. 20.

4.   Cézanne, Letter to Emile Bernard, October 23, 1905, ibid., pp. 21-22.

5.   André Fontainas, Review of Gauguin's Exhibition, 1899, ibid., p. 73.

6.   Ibid.

7.   Paul Gauguin, Letter to André Fontainas, March 1899, ibid., p. 75.

8.   August Strindberg, Letter to Paul Gauguin, February 1895, ibid., p. 82.

9.   Paul Gauguin, Letter to August Strindberg, February 1895, ibid., p. 83.

10.   Paul Gauguin, Lettter to Daniel de Monfried, February 1898, ibid., p. 72.

11.   Oscar Wilde, "Pen, Pencil, and Poison," in *Intentions* (New York, 1912), p. 68.

12.   Wilde, "The Critic As Artist," ibid., p. 213.

13.   "Sainte Beuve on Diderot," *Diderot's Thoughts on Art and Style,* ed. Beatrix L. Tollemache (New York, 1971), p. 19.

14.   Sidney Geist, "*Salut,* Apollinaire!", *Arts Magazine* (October 1961), pp. 72-73.

15.   Guillaume Apollinaire, "The Three Plastic Virtues," *Chroniques d'Art (1902-1918),* ed. Leroy C. Breunig (Paris, 1960), p. 57.

16.   Charles Baudelaire, "The Salon of 1859," in *The Mirror of Art,* ed. Jonathan Mayne (Garden City, N.Y., 1956), pp. 276-77.

6

Modern Art's Failure of Critical Nerve

He lives only in cogent argument. Every thinker finds his own truth in criticism.
—T.W. Adorno, *Wozu noch Philosophie*

Assumption 1: the art critic is a thinker. Assumption 2: as such, he lives only in cogent argument. Assumption 3: he comes to criticism to find his own truth. The art critic is a philosopher. In a sense, his spirit is more unequivocally and profoundly philosophical—critical—than that of the professional philosopher, whose recognition of the critical nature of philosophy is compromised by traditional demands of system-building. The critic's primary intention is to criticize, openly and as his spirit moves him. He is a free spirit, uncaged by his consciousness, unbound by any belief-system. The professional philosopher does not know what his primary intention is. He thinks it is to build a system of thought rather than to criticize the given, but he comes to experience his completed system of thought as uninhabitable—or perhaps worse yet an incomplete Babel of language, with dubious perceptual and conceptual import— and so the object of criticism. He comes to the critical spirit in a roundabout way, and it is only with great reluctance that he recognizes that system-building—the notion of system itself—is absurd. This is the beginning of the wisdom of the critical spirit, and it is a hard-won wisdom for him. Yet it is something that the art critic seems born to, by the very nature of art, which shows up all systems by flouting the rules that construct them—or at least by never quite conforming to these rules, and so creating a slightly awry structure of forms. Art also seems to give the lie to system, suggesting its limited, inconclusive character, by making clear the conditions, personal and public, of its creation, and by suggesting the inadequacy of the very idea of coherence which a system tries to establish, for the idea of integrative coherence is unable to do justice to the kinds of order art creates. The unity of the work of art is not the same as that of a system of thought, and to use the latter as a model for the former is to falsify the critical spirit in which the former is conceived.

A system of thought is a fixed, dogmatic structure, not a dialectical process like the critical spirit, a process that art makes evident and that art criticism makes self-evident. A system cannot deal with any fact or idea that contradicts it;

inevitably there are such alternatives, as equivocal and indefinite as they may seem to be—and they appear "vague" or barbaric because they are outside the closed system, and in a sense are no more than attempts to open and even dissolve it—existing simultaneously with the system in history. Indeed, such unassimilated intrusions into the system—such indigestible realities—drag the system down into history, make it clear that it was always part of history. The system of thought is one kind of response to—one effort to come to terms with—history. Art, by contrast—and with it art criticism—seems never to premise, or even attempt comprehensiveness and complete coherence, and in general seems less inclusive, less orderly, and even without any singular principle of order. As such, it seems to embody the critical spirit much more directly than the system of thought, and above all seems to argue implicitly the impossibility of any absolute system, whether of thought or art—and even to encourage the dissolution of all existing systems. This seemingly anarchic, anti-dogmatic spirit in art seems to restore to credibility all that systems—of thought, of society, of past art—disenfranchised and meant to discredit, casting it in the role of "outsider," and eventually of scapegoat for the failings of the system. Of course the critical spirit of art—its protest against and threat to all systems, whether of knowledge or social systems—can be overstated, for even such a spirit and art, as its history shows, have their conventions. Nonetheless, the most original art seems to introduce, if only as a utopian gesture, an alternative to the known order of things, meant as a criticism of that order—meant to put it on an unpredictable path, with the implicit assumption that the path it is on moves the wrong way. Let us leave, art seems to say, our well-worn ways for a fresh, untried path, however slender and absurd it may seem—an implicit criticism of life that has been reduced to a system, and finally allowed, by art, to acknowledge the poor fit.

Art criticism, then, following the lead of art, seems not to start from any system, preconceived or in the process of conception, but from the free encounter with individual works of art or constellations of works of art, much as art seems to begin from the free encounter with the world, and the nuances of its condition. The art critic does not seem to have to dismantle any system of thought about art to discover his criticality, because he began with none—as little as art began with any system of thought about the world of appearances, or any presuppositions about the nature of ultimate reality (an "ultimacy" which is an intellectual illusion generated by the systematic way such presuppositions are made). But all too often such spontaneity is specious, for art criticism in practice usually begins and ends with the attempt to demonstrate a system of art, these days generally premised on a system of taste, so that the articulation of the system of art validates the system of taste. Much contemporary art criticism is a self-righteous justification—passing for a synthesizing theory—of a system of art, rather than what it ought to be once one recognizes that the mythical spontaneity of relationship with art is just that—mythical: namely, a lover's quarrel with art, in which the critical spirit of art criticism tries to articulate and unite with that of art. Art criticism which builds systems or justifies them, in a pseudo-philosophical (in the traditional sense of philosophy) way, betrays the critical spirit it pursues and which art embodies by denying the first and last necessity of such a spirit, namely, in Adorno's words, "to free itself of any suspicion of apologetics," and to remain free of such suspicion. System-building is the primary and system-justification the secondary instrument of such apologetics, with which the "life blood"—the very "nerve"—of the critical spirit has nothing to do. Its essence, as Adorno says, is "opposition or resistance to current practice and the justifications which serve it."[1]

Now in art criticism there is irony in such opposition, for significant art originates in opposition to current practice in the art world and life-world, so that significant art criticism, which originates in opposition to significant art, seems to negate its opposition, and thereby imply an affirmation of the current practice in opposition to which it originated. But the opposition of art criticism is not a generalized mechanical reflex against all art; it is an organic response to "high art," as Clement Greenberg calls it. Critical opposition to high art is an organic part of the general development of art, rescuing from high art the critical spirit in which it originated, but has forsaken in order to develop itself systematically. It preserves the critical spirit the art loses in the process of becoming respectable, reconciling itself with the world it originally opposed. It becomes a codification of this world rather than a resistance to it: high art articulates the principle of autonomy this world embodies in its own presumed autonomy—but when an art becomes high it gives up the autonomy it articulated with its own opposition. Freshly and falsely conceived as *sui generis* and so self-validating, it acquires the autonomy of what it originally opposed. The model is the divine right of kings: the kings—who originally opposed the gods, and by opposing became kings over other men who did not dare to oppose the gods—become, as they are accepted by other men as kings, surrogates for the gods, institutionalized signs of them, as it were, their priests rather than their enemies. One may say that institutionalized opposition—permanent revolution—is self-contradictory. But one may also say that when opposition too willingly identifies with what it opposes, the quality of its opposition is suspect. One assumes it wanted entry into a system, and was asserting its "independence" and strength to show its worthiness for entry—to show that it would be a powerful defender and propagator of the system, given a chance. Criticism's job is to show it the quality of its original opposition—to show it the ambiguity, even dubiousness of its own motives and thereby to allow art to grow in and for itself. The task of criticism becomes the development of critical consciousness, not the exposition of art. It exposes the art's critical spirit of opposition, to articulate that critical spirit as an end in itself, a permanent safeguard against dogmatic closure of consciousness, premature emptying of wakefulness. Art criticism, then, is not the sycophantic courier of art, extending the arena of its exhibition beyond the gallery and museum to some ideal universal public—in a sense, announcing the absolute and universal presence and dominance of art through its possession of the critic's parasitic person. Rather, it is an instrument for the protection and articulation of the critical spirit per se. Art criticism thus necessarily transcends art, becoming "critical" not only of art but of its sources—of the society and history in which it originated. It becomes an investigation of the spirit of opposition in human history, however principled or unprincipled, artistic or non-artistic that spirit may show itself to be.

Is there anything in the current situation of art production that makes this conception of art criticism especially important today? I think so: it has to do with the renewed debate, and the new crisis in art production which this debate signals, about the old question as to whether art is, in Baudelaire's words, "inseparable from utility," or exists only for its own sake—the debate between an art of social and personal sincerity, and an art of taste. This 19th-century question, suggesting the self-contradictoriness of art—and corresponding uncertainty about its status and significance—is the typical question of capitalist art production, and has never really been answered one way or another, for capitalist production in general does not know whether it exists for human welfare or for the edification of the commodity. Capitalism does not know whether it exists to be humanly useful or whether it is production for production's sake. Obviously and self-contradictorily, it means to be both, only half-heartedly realizing that one may get in the way of the other, and not acting on this inarticulate realization—not acting to resolve the contradiction, as little as art does. What matters, of course, is the display of the disjunction, not its resolution—not any decision in favor of one or the other of its terms. There may be momentary reconciliations, in an art of life—or an art of arts—but these are transient and self-dissolving, as long as social production remains equivocal about its intentions. Only when the society itself disintegrates, either in utopian self-transcendence or demonic self-destruction—either by cutting the Gordian knot with one revolutionary gesture of self-transformation or strangling helplessly in its coils, worn out by irresolution—will the problem of the nature of artistic production disappear. Until then, there will be perpetual uncertainty about the nature and purpose of art.

Now the question of whether art is sincere in its intentions toward society and selfhood, or true only to its own ideal self and the society of other works of art returns today with renewed urgency and cogency because of the recognition— perhaps still more implicit than explicit but certainly obvious from a non-academic history of post-Abstract Expressionist art—that taste and novelty are no longer viable as the basis of artistic production, because they produce an art which comes across neither as sincere nor insincere, neither as for itself or for others. The system of taste and the pursuit of novelty have produced an art, whether realistic or abstract, which is increasingly "nondescript," in the sense that its differentiation from and transformation of its sources, whether of form or meaning, is nominal—a matter of qualifying nuance rather than of urgent, persistent reconsideration and re-cognition. Since Pop and Minimal-Systemic art, art as a whole has not significantly opposed its point of departure, its social and aesthetic sources, its ideological and formal roots. (Happenings and performance art, including the Fluxus movement, and so-called protest art are perhaps notable exceptions, but the character and force of their opposition to and penetration of their sources have still not been analyzed, at least to my satisfaction.) In other words, art has increasingly lost its critical spirit or rather, as we will see, that spirit has degenerated into irony—which is perhaps all it was in the first place, and all it can be. It is because of this weakening of the critical spirit—modern art's increasing failure of nerve—that art criticism must increasingly serve the ends of the critical spirit in general rather than of the critical spirit in art, or art with or without the critical spirit. If it does not do so, it will lose the only source of sanity there is in the modern world, for if there is anything that modern thought and modern art have made clear since *Rameau's Nephew,* it is that critical—dialectical—consciousness is the only method of sanity in a world of increasing contradiction, of seemingly limitless alternatives, both in the realm of possibility and actuality. It is perhaps because of such insurmountable contradiction that art is overwhelmed, loses its nerve, plods along respectably, with no significant opposition inspiring it, its irony wearing thin, becoming an anemic ardor. As Greenberg once said, "modern art is able...to reconcile the most violent contrasts, something that politics, philosophy, and religion have been incapable of doing lately."[2] It may be that modern art has finally come to the point where it also is unable to reconcile such intense, unremitting contrasts, whose violence then overwhelms the art, not overtly, but by forcing it back on itself—perhaps this is the origin of art for art's sake—inhibiting it until it no longer even knows what it means to face up to contradiction, let alone to risk self-contradiction. No longer challenging the world of violent contrasts, the art is no longer aesthetically, intellectually, or humanly challenging. Reluctant to operate in the spirit of opposition, the art itself is opposed by the critical spirit. Art tries to duck under the storm, to live calmly in the eye of the hurricane, rather than to master or ride or simply navigate it—to respond to it as the critical situation it is. It may be that neither aesthetic utopianism nor sincere protest have the critical import—the same viability—they once did, for the violent contrasts may have gotten completely out of hand, certainly too complex for the hands of art to grasp and control. In a world in which any sort of reconciliation seems impossible, art seems altogether out of place. In a world in which the dialectical process is stalemated in violence, the critical spirit must look out for itself, find ways of putting itself across, with or without art.

But art seems no longer able to see the critical spirit through, not only because of external conditions but because of internal generic ones. For one thing, art is dependent upon a limited, material embodiment, notwithstanding some of the ambitions of conceptual and informational art which have not yet proven, even with the aid of Duchamp, that intention can exist independently as art. For another thing, this necessary material objectification makes art subject to dogmatization (worshipful collection), historicization (temporal siting) and acculturation (ideological usage). Art's necessary objectification undermines its critical intentions—makes them seem unnecessary. The consciousness "behind" the art comes to be understood as a ritual reaffirming of material rather than a symbolization and critique of a state of affairs. The art thus loses its consequentiality for the world and becomes a primordial phenomenon. It is simply "there," initially in an explosive way, later, when the shock of its coming has worn off, in an elegant way. And criticism is understood as an examination of its fallout. The critic keeps account of its radioactivity, always handling it with kid gloves, as though it were dangerous material from the moon, a mysterious boon to a poorly comprehending earth. Become precious, the work of art is humanly useless, as well as no longer clearly of use to itself. It is exhibited for blind adoration, and regarded as ultimately impenetrable and ineffable—too dumb to speak. No matter how much artists intend the public to become involved with their work, to treat it familiarly—walk on it, play with it—it becomes, as exhibited, no more than a playful object. And indeed art has—as though that redeems it—been connected, by Schiller among others, with the spirit of play. But we want to connect it with the critical spirit of which the spirit of play is only one aspect—and not inevitably a necessary one. It is only when the public experiences the work in critical opposition to it that the work will make its point. It is better that works be attacked—be physically violated—by an angry, offended public than that they be preserved intact and uninfluential in a museum. If this is the only way its critical power can be acknowledged and honored, so be it. That is the risk it takes when it transgresses the status quo.

Walter Benjamin affords us insight into the conditions for the contemporary failure of critical nerve in art, one in which it is no longer even possible for the art to state the contradictions which cause it to lose its nerve, an articulation which would amount to a minimum act of the critical spirit. But to fully understand Benjamin's remarks we must understand the critical spirit in which modern art originated in the first place—the spirit of the avant-garde, the spirit of protest. Renato Poggioli, among others, has pointed out that originally there were "two avant-gardes," and for a time, in 19th-century France, their meaning was fused in one art.[3] "The avant-garde image originally remained subordinate ... to the ideals of a radicalism which was not cultural but political." It was "only a few years after 1870," when a number of social crises seemed to be overcome (Poggioli does not talk about the quality of this overcoming, and the quality of its results), that "avant-garde" began "to designate separately the cultural-artistic avant-garde while still designating ... the sociopolitical avant-garde." Poggioli thinks this was "because for an instant the two avant-gardes appeared to march allied or united." He neglects the idea that the radicalism which applied itself to social change failed to effect significant change, and reapplied itself to cultural-artistic change, to greater effect. It was easier to make changes in ideology than in real social conditions. The barricades of established art and culture were easier to storm than those of the bourgeois. One could undermine the art of the bourgeois, but not destroy his economic power—one could undermine his art and hope to weaken his will, weaken him from within.

Now if the transfer of energy from the social and political to the artistic and cultural was in fact born out of frustration, rather than out of a transient sense of new possibilities in both realms—and I doubt Poggioli's interpretation, because in France radicalism achieved more significant results in art than in society, produced an important new aesthetic, not an important new society—then Linda Nochlin's understanding of the original "character of protest," the original critical spirit in modern art, is more to the point of an investigation of modern art's current failure of critical nerve than might be imagined.[4] For the failure was there from the beginning—implicit in the original, self-defeating character of the modern critical spirit, as it appeared in art. The radically critical spirit which first appeared in the sociopolitical realm carried the frustration it experienced into the cultural-artistic realm, where the transformations it effected were all based on this frustration—permeated by it. Nochlin's characterization of the radical critical spirit, as it appeared in Manet, as a form of wit, makes this clear. Nochlin observes that "such outright affronts to public sensibility as *Déjeuner sur l'Herbe* or *Olympia*" have "the character of . . . monumental and ironic put-ons, *blagues,* favorite form of destructive wit of the period, inflated to gigantic dimensions—pictorial versions of those endemic pranks which threatened to destroy all serious values, to profane and vulgarize the most sacred verities of the times." The nihilism of such wit is the translation into art of frustrated political radicalism. It is the theatricalization of aborted radicalism—a twisted radicalism tainting the rest of the world with its own sense of failure. It is the critical spirit still getting its innings in, if no longer winning the game, and no longer expecting to. The passive revolution of irony—quasi-radical because it never sees change through, and even stops suggesting change—replaces the active revolution of political involvement. An indirect, self-defeating artistic revolution replaces direct action for social revolution. The artistic avant-garde is born from the ruins of the political avant-garde, but it is a lame phoenix, with one wing lost to the flames—with strong memories of the way it was burned in another life. Thus, as Nochlin says, "Manet's works can hardly be considered direct statements of a specific viewpoint or position"—this is part of their nihilism. "Quite often they seem more like embodiments of his own essential feeling of alienation from the society of his times, a dandyish coolness toward immediate experience, mitigated either by art or by irony, or his own inimitable combination of both." Nochlin continues in a way that is directly to the point of my interpretation of the social frustration that is at the root of and feeds the artistic avant-garde. "The most authentic statement of Manet's sense of his situation as a man and as an artist may well be his two versions, painted in 1881, of *The Escape of Rochefort,* in my opinion unconscious or disguised self-images, where the equivocal radical leader, hardly an outright hero by any standards, is represented in complete isolation from nature and his fellow men: he is, in fact, not even recognizably present in either of the paintings of his escape from New Caledonia." "Equivocal radical leaders," isolated from their fellow men—who don't seem to want to be led by their self-proclaimed leaders—are what the artistic avant-garde produces, and necessarily so. As Nochlin concludes, "It is just upon such bad faith and alienation and the marvelously inventive, destructive and self-destructive ways of making art about them that the modern avant-garde has built ever since."

Now such "bad faith and alienation...destructive and self-destructive ways" are not the most viable, effective manifestations of the critical spirit, which opposes in good faith and out of commitment to the welfare of the social whole, and which is constructive and self-constructive. The original corruption of modern artistic criticality is compensated for by overwhelming creativity— relentless productivity. Possessed by the drive to work creatively, to be creative at all costs—which it mistakenly takes to mean to be radical, in effect to uproot, to expose the roots of society, humanity, nature, and art itself—modern art, with its mythification of creative work, only forges the chains of its slavery—its social alienation—even more tightly. Benjamin was one of the first critical thinkers to observe this—and it is the central condition for the failure of critical nerve in modern art, for it begins to work nervelessly, pointlessly, blindly, simply making art for the sake of making art (Picasso is a good example of this), much as capitalism must make commodities for the sake of making commodities, generating human need and greed to get them consumed. Art for art's sake, creativity for creativity's sake, alienation for alienation's sake inevitably lead to bankruptcy, and tighten the chains of slavery the critical spirit attempted to cut. As Benjamin says, talking about "the overtaxing of the productive person in the name of a principle, the principle of 'creativity'":

> This overtaxing is all the more dangerous because as it flatters the self-esteem of the productive process, it effectively guards the interests of a social order that is hostile to him. The life-style of the bohemian has contributed to creating a superstition about creativeness which Marx has countered with an observation that applies equally to intellectual and to manual labour. To the opening sentence of the draft of the Gotha programme, "Labour is the source of all wealth and all culture," he appends this critical note: "The bourgeois have very good reasons for imputing supernatural creative power to labour, since it follows precisely from the fact that labour depends on nature, that a man who has no other property than his labour must be in all societies and civilizations the slave of other people who have become proprietors of the material working conditions."[5]

The bourgeois remains the proprietor for the modern avant-garde artist who sells his product on the market like any commodity—a commodity whose novelty presumably enhances its saleability, and so its value. Also, the avant-garde artist's labor—his artistic radicalism—does not give him ownership of the material working conditions, nor does it significantly change them—change them for all workers. The avant-garde artist's mythification of creativity compensates for the failure of his radicalism to effect revolutionary, wide-ranging social change. At the same time, compulsive creativity plays directly into the hands of the bourgeois proprietors, for it gives them more products than they know what to do with, except sell for profit. The artist, also, makes his profit—fame, as it were, honorary ownership of his own work—a profit doubly enslaving, for not only does it lead him to tax his creativity with greater burdens but to forget its original critical point. A critical spirit, we must remember, which was frustrated from the start, and in its frustration turned itself inside out into alienation. Uncritical creativity is another form of bad faith. The overproduction it leads to does nothing to ease the artist's isolation in the life-world. He is famous, but without influence on—and so eventually self-defensively indifferent to—its historical course. Finally, the obsession with creativity for its own sake leads directly to its standardization, and *tedium vitae;* the latter, it seems to me, severely afflicts the current art world, for all its productivity.

Another reason for modern art's failure of critical nerve is its reliance on taste; the art of ironic protest quickly becomes an art of taste, which makes it into a form in its own right, and so assures its survival, independent of events, including those it was protesting. This initially awkward, indecorous, disreputable, and inconclusive art of protest becomes the emblem of a new elegance, allowing for its fashionable assimilation. Losing its frailty and aura of futility, it becomes a fixture, *de rigeur* in any art that would be recognized as avant-garde, or at least novel. But there is a more important if less evident reason for the radical artist's eager turn to taste. As his *raison d'être* becomes increasingly artistic—more and more a matter of art for art's sake than of art for life's sake—and so less and less critical, even self-critical, shifts in taste become a disguise for lack of essential change. Emphasis changes, not the mode of emphasis, the larger context of form, and what it symbolizes, which remains static and seemingly eternal. In addition, concern for good taste masks the artist's increasing ignorance of everything but his art. To have taste acknowledges the mystery of art, but it is a kind of ostrich hole in which one hides one's ignorance of everything else. Does taste at least tell the aritist—and the critic, and the rest of us—the complex nature and value of his art? No, for to see the art in terms of taste is usually to see it without its power of reference or communication—of symbolizing and clarifying. Viewed by taste, art becomes exclusive, but also inarticulate. It is as though struck dumb—but not even oracular—and so a weakened presence. This obviously becomes a further irony, confirming the alienation of the frustrated radical artist—and perhaps making his irony a little bitter and more obscure. Benjamin has set the stage for these thoughts:

> In a speech about trademarks Chaptal said on 17 July 1824: "Do not tell me that in the final analysis a shopper will know about the different qualities of a material. No, gentlemen, a consumer is no judge of them; he will go only by the appearance of the commodity. But are

looking and touching enough to determine the permanence of colours, the fineness of a material, or the quality and nature of its finish?" In the same measure as the expertness of a customer declines, the importance of his taste increases—both for him and for the manufacturer. For the consumer it has the value of a more or less elaborate masking of his lack of expertness. Its value to the manufacturer is a fresh stimulus to consumption which in some cases is satisfied at the expense of other requirements of consumption the manufacturer would find more costly to meet.

   It is precisely this development which literature reflects in *l'art pour l'art*. This doctrine and its corresponding practice for the first time give taste a dominant position in poetry ... In *l'art pour l'art* the poet for the first time faces a language the way the buyer faces the commodity on the open market. He has lost his familiarity with the process of production to a particularly high degree. The poets of *l'art pour l'art* are the last about whom it can be said that they come "from the people." They have nothing to formulate with such urgency that it could determine the *coining* of their words. Rather, they have to choose their words ... The poet of *l'art pour l'art* wanted to bring to language above all himself—with all the idiosyncrasies, nuances, and imponderables of his nature. These elements are reflected in taste. The poet's taste guides him in his choice of words. But the choice is made only among words which have not already been coined by the *object* itself—that is, which have not been included in its process of production.[6]

Missing from Benjamin's analysis is Nochlin's observation of the reason the artist wants above all to bring himself to art: it becomes the only "support" of his alienation, while at the same time giving it a chance to become fashionable or tasteful. This taste does not deny the frustration inherent in alienation—the frustration which leads to radical artistic "choice." Nonetheless, it does redeem that "suffering," as well as the radicality it leads to, for society.

   What is also important in Benjamin's analysis of the connection between taste and art for art's sake is his implicit conception of the critic of taste—and of the artist as critic of taste. In his hands, criticism, like art, is less a protest than an endorsement, however devious and ironical; it loses its spirit of opposition and becomes apologetic. Criticism is no longer an investigation into the "critical" meaning of artistic production, whether that has to do with a critical relationship to nature or society or art itself, but an examination of the art's tastefulness—ultimately, an effort to put the imprimatur of good taste on the art. This means a "critique" of materials and techniques, which are understood only in terms of their "inner necessity," and not at all in terms of their consequences for communication, their relationship to the natural and their effect on the social order, and on consciousness in general. The artist of taste puts less use and more surplus—seemingly so—value in his art, appealing to sensibility rather than respect for function. The critic of taste does not even look for use value—it would interfere with efforts of taste to take its profits, would skim the surplus aesthetic value from the work of art—and so in effect he represses it, as well as, without realizing it, the art as a whole, eventually leading it to sterility and redundancy. Taste produces an art which, as Benjamin suggests, lacks a value which would be too dear for the artist to put in, for it would question the very foundations of his art—bring it into severe conflict with itself—and undermine his taste.

To avoid facing the question of the use value of his art, the artist of taste turns increasingly to novelty—to novel choices of material and means. As Benjamin writes, "abstracted from the social being man," the art of taste "is forced to make novelty its highest value," and in the process "begins to have doubts about its function, and ceases to be *'inséparable de l'utilité'* (Baudelaire)."[7] The critic becomes the *"arbiter novarum rerum,"* as Benjamin says, "becomes the snob." The artist also becomes the snob. The transformation of the frustrated and failed radical who is a social outcast into the reputable and prominent snob who is a social insider and arbiter, and contributes to capitalist consumption by selecting the commodities that are to be valued and even produced (repressing production that cannot be arbitrated by taste), is the avant-garde success story. Indeed, the avant-garde critic, with his apologetic criticism and unqualified support of an art of taste, whether or not it meets the standards of the highest taste, is the hero of late capitalism. Without his sense of the ideal it would probably function with more difficulty than it already does, for he effects a happy union between producer and consumer, making the one feel that he is giving, and the other that he is getting, value. The tasteful critic cues both producer and consumer, mating the two in a perfect fit, as though they were primordially made for each other. Their perfection of unity and mutuality of sensibility implies the absence, the seeming lack of need for, a "critical" relationship between the two. In the best of all possible artistic worlds, effected by taste, there is no need for criticism. Unfortunately, the social reality which taste abstracts from to create its art takes its revenge by making this art meaningless to the majority.

Finally, the failure of critical nerve in modern art has to do with, as Benjamin says, "the disintegration of the aura (of art) in the experience of shock,"[8] where "aura" is understood as "the associations which, at home in the *mémoire involontaire,* tend to cluster around the object of a perception."[9] The point is that the experience of the modern world, with its violent contrasts—their violence seems to testify to their irreconcilability—disrupts the formation of both the aura of the perceived work of art and the *mémoire involontaire.* There is simply too much shock in the world—of art and life—for them to function properly, without self-dissolving self-contradiction. This dysfunction of the aura and the *mémoire involontaire* manifests itself in the phenomenon of seemingly random, arbitrary associations which seem to adhere to the perceived work of art, but not convincingly, so that they disrupt perception itself. They make a tangent to the work of art, but that is not enough to give it an atmosphere in which to breathe, an aura in which to shine. It is as though the radical work of art releases uncontrollable meanings into an already turbulent, uncertain climate of opinion, making it all the more explosive. The radical work of art seems to uproot associations from the *mémoire involontaire,* thereby eroding it. Radical art, like the radically self-contradictory art world and life-world, seems to "dis-organize," disjunct, fragment, altogether mocking the original radical dream of a powerful, ideal harmony of all human worlds. We have already indicated some of the reasons why the art and the "modern" world created by capitalism are shocking, unstable, explosive: insistence on blind productivity and creative novelty, "screened" by taste. But taste loses control of the situation when productivity conflicts with unsatisfied social needs—when, in general, there is a discrepancy between the claims made for productivity and the real lives of people. As reality becomes radically shocking, so does its analogue, the radical work of art, which eventually finds it must return to the tastelessness with which it began if it is at all to try to master the shock, or at least survive in the face of it. It becomes bumpy and uneven again, possessed by involuntary memories of an unchosen world, and as such with some aura, however partial and illegible. The aura of shock, too, as in the art of Francis Bacon—where it has become smoothed, and itself soothing—and in that of Leon Golub, is after all an aura, even if it communicates disintegration, and resistance to disintegration.

Arbitrary idea: there is an unspoken, hardly realized conspiracy behind the creation of the artistic avant-garde and the radical work of art, namely, to draw off all really dangerous criticism of the social status quo—to give the critical spirit an object, but an irrelevant one. The radical work of art is used as a target for the revolutionary energies in the world. Let it be loved and hated, admired and despised, so that nothing that matters will be. The work of art gets its authority simply because it is set up as an object of general criticism—everybody feels free to take a "shot" at it, to gamble with it, as they would not with the structure of our social relations and the character of our system of production and distribution. Modern art, and perhaps all art, at least as it is used today, is perhaps one big distraction, perpetrated by the upper classes in 19th-century France (note Manet's membership in the upper classes) and supported ever since, if not always openly, by the higher classes. Let the art be open to question—let us enervate ourselves trying to determine whether it is "higher" or not—so that we will not question the position, and the power it has by virtue of that position, of the higher classes. Let us try to educate ourselves to the art so as to vicariously join the higher classes, without really educating ourselves to their ways—which we really can't do because we don't have their position, and power. It may be that modern art is the cake the higher classes feed themselves—a shockingly fresh taste and stimulus for a weary palate—in lieu of giving any bread to the lower classes. In any case, at least one thing is not arbitrary: modern art is not a classless, universal art, telling us about the human condition and consciousness in general, but the product of a class that is frustrated for reasons of its own making. Nochlin does not go far enough in analyzing the reasons for Manet's artistic radicalism and that of the avant-garde in general. The alienation and isolation, reflected in yet transcended by wit, Manet experienced have to do with the psychology of his class—they are an unexpected consequence of its position and power—not with residual, atrophied social protest, a muted yet determined desire for social justice. At best, Manet was a rebel against his own class; he may have felt stifled in it. A study of Manet's life-world can tell us whether or not this is so—whether or not his "dandyish coolness toward immediate experience" had to do with the character of his immediate surroundings and of the internal relations in his class. Rebelling against it or not, Manet's "essential feeling of alienation from the society of his times" is a psychological component of his upper-classness. It reflects the unhappy consciousness—the bad conscience—of being upper class in the France of the 1848 Revolution and the 1870 Commune. Being isolated at the top of an unstable social heap—and Manet constantly tried to break that isolation, and at least in spirit come down from the top—had its psychological disadvantages, whatever social advantages it conferred. Manet, whose art can be read as a protest against privilege, nonetheless was stuck with the malaise privilege sometimes confers.

Social radicalism pursued authentic social unity and humanhood and failed to achieve it. Artistic radicalism not only accepts disunity, however unhappily, but makes a cult of it, and encourages alienation as an ironical, pseudo source of individuality. The isolation of the individual that results, felt by Manet, is an ironic testimony to his heroism—a mock heroism—in the situation of disunity. The isolation is really a form of insulation from the disunity as well as an expression of it. The health of the critical spirit demands a reinterpretation of the alienation and isolation of the avant-garde—refuses to accept them at face value—much as it insists on the class-consciousness of the avant-garde. It sees them as the symptoms of an illness of the critical spirit, as well as the consequence of its functioning in a world of violent contrasts. And the health of the critical spirit is more important than the health of art—or rather, is today responsible for the health of art.

Notes

1. Theodor W. Adorno,"Wozu noch Philosophie," *Eingriffe: Neun kritische Modelle* (Frankfurt am Main, 1963), p. 15.

2. Clement Greenberg, "Art," *Nation,* 158 (Jan. 22, 1944), p. 109.

3. Renato Poggioli, *The Theory of the Avant-Garde* (New York, 1971; Icon Editions), pp, 8-10.

4. Linda Nochlin, "The Invention of the Avant Garde: France, 1830-80," *Avant-Garde Art,* Thomas B. Hess and John Ashbery, eds. (New York, 1967; Collier Books), pp. 19-23.

5. Walter Benjamin, *Charles Baudelaire: A Lyric Poet in the Era of High Capitalism* (London, 1973), p. 71.

6. Ibid., pp. 105-6.

7. Ibid., p. 172.

8. Ibid., p. 154.

9. Ibid., p. 145.

The Necessary Dialectical Critic

If thought willingly emerges from its critical element to become a mere means at the disposal
of an existing order, then despite itself it tends to convert the positive it elected to defend into
something negative and destructive.

—Max Horkheimer and Theodor W. Adorno,
Dialectic of Enlightenment

To be worthy of the name today—even to be necessary to the art scene, as its
salvation—there must be a consciously new way to be a critic, a way which seems
self-contradictory, and yet is the only straight way: it is the way of dialectic, which
leads the critic to question his own will to believe in art, and his own tendentious
pursuit of the esthetic. There was once—not even so long ago—a different
necessity to criticism, a less devious meaning. The critic was once more
"positive": he documented the work as a fact, he judged it as a value that could be
clearly fixed, and, true master of the work, he illuminated the esthetic in it for
general contemplation, holding up to the masses like a priest at a ritual the sacred
substance, the divine principle that made the work what it truly was. He was
decisive enough to know the absolute in the work, and to exhibit it in an
unhesitating, resolute way that the work in itself could not accomplish, with its
admixture of charm and personality, the dross of signs that reveal the artist's
presence behind it. What the artist strove for was there for the critic's asking, as
though the artist was simply getting the work in position for the critic to see its
true import.

Those sanguine days are gone forever: neither artist nor critic are so lucky.
For the kind of mastery of the work the critic could have in the past would defeat
both the purpose of the critic today and the purpose of the work—to escape its
own administration, with the critic the means of that escape as much as, if not
more than, the artist, for he must finally leave well enough alone and display
what he has determined, but for the responsible critic display and determination
are never over. Today a positive approach to art would only sell it down the
river—administer it for those who do not want it to have any more dignity than
that of a slave on the auction block, sold to toil in the fields of commerce. To even
offer to contemplate the work today—to inspect it for the esthetic as if to inspect
a corpse for gold teeth—is to put it at the disposal of the existing order of

commerce and culture. The collusion of dealer and historian today—historical criticism is no longer what Oscar Wilde knew it as, "part of that complex working towards freedom which may be described as the revolt against authority,... the resultant of forces essentially revolutionary"[1]—makes a travesty of contemplation, turns the exhibition of art into a near Ecce Homo situation (a responsibility and martyrdom the art itself may not be equal to). To even offer to "master" the work today is to defeat it by offering it as a sacrifice on the altar of Mammon or by imprisoning it in the tower of Babel which cultural consciousness of it has become.

There is a necessity for a new type of criticism, already emerging in areas other than art—a new type of thought about art, which accepts both its own self-contradictoriness and that of art (systematic in the one case, less so in the other), as the only way of successfully locating the art without terminating it in its location. However eccentric the coordinates, they are not the deliberate dishabille of the bohemian poseur intellectual—as if that were the only way to escape academic respectability, with its pseudo-mastery—but the only possible poise in a situation which wants not for information and its academic codification, but for alternative concepts that offer a way out of the beaten track that leads art to the unhappy consciousness of being both cultural and a commodity: a cultural commodity. Only the dislocations of dialectic—even deliberately fabricated dislocations, which nonetheless carry with them their own curious intransigence, their own power of determination, and feel firm underfoot—can rescue art from the inevitability of its situation today, and rescue the critic from involuntary submission to both that situation and to that art that voluntarily submits to it. Like all true criticism, dialectical criticism avoids victimizing both critic and art in the name of the ideal and the absolute, and thus becomes a devious sanity in a situation in which it seems impossible not to be both victim and victimizer, administered and administrator, totalized and totalizer. To avoid collusion, even the collusion of neutrality, one must be dialectical—even more deviously dialectical, more cunningly self-contradictory, than traditional dialectic, which has already become a system, and so another way of administration, of subjection to inescapable categories. To unwittingly be the victim of a system is the kind of loss of innocence—an invisible rape—never to be wished for.

To be dialectical today is the only way to restore the critical element in thought about art. Dialectical criticism becomes the detotalizing of art history, the dismemberment of its conventions and patterns of possibility, for the sake of a new openness—which itself never becomes a totality or ideal—which is the only meaning of freedom that is not yet bankrupt, however much it has diminished in value. It may be that in the end dialectical criticism is powerless in the face of administered history and culture, but nonetheless, as Horkheimer and Adorno assert, "today critical thought... demands support for the residues of freedom, and for tendencies toward true humanism, even if these seem powerless in regard to the main course of history."[2] Art was once thought of as a residue of freedom, and dialectical criticism of it is the only test that can determine whether it still is, even if that freedôm means no more than a blindly willed, seemingly gratuitous and arbitrary gesture of resistance to administration, however unsystematic and of whatever kind—an administration which seems to be a non-administration, like dialectical criticism itself, which claims to administer the unadministrable and leave it intact as such, truly respecting its innocence. The openness of dialectical criticism is the only test for the openness of art, even if both must appear closed in the test.

Let us, then, go unsystematically through the systems the dialectical art critic must confront: first the system the positive approach to art imposes (the positivist fallacy), then the system the will to believe imposes (the partisan fallacy), and finally the system the transcendence of the esthetic imposes (the estheticist fallacy). These systems, with their moment of transcendence which becomes a refusal of experience, will be known through their critiques—through their alternatives.

(1) Why does dialectical method alone make sense? Because it alone acknowledges that nothing can be firmly posited about art without negating it as art—because today art itself does not wish to be firmly posited. To be positive about art, to take it as something positive—as something matter of factly there that must be made esthetically there, i.e., even more positively there, absolutely there—ignores the fact that it cannot be positively known as art. This is the meaning of the resistance to modern art—claims of its so-called obscurity or unintelligibility, and downright perverseness—that has been with it from the beginning. The public expected art to be positively identified as art. This was not simply a matter of living up to past expectations, but of positing an esthetic ambition. Yet this ambition, even in the neo-Mediterranean tradition of modern French art, was never unequivocally argued, never urged as the precipitate of all else, but seemed always to be a backdrop of something more insistent—of an intention oblique to the strictly esthetic intention, an intention having to do with the emerging recognition that art itself is a revolution in intention, and that the estheticist intention inhibits the profounder intention. The revolution in esthetics is simply a byproduct of the larger revolution in intention, which involves not simply new ways of codifying the world and a new consciousness of it, but a refusal of any final code, consciousness, or esthetic—of any ultimate style, and safe, durable (administrable) form.

In this situation, criticism cannot become an aid to the absolute esthetic, the final style, whether of art or consciousness. It cannot help make art or mind positive, as traditional description and judgment did. Instead, it must locate the work against its own grain—buoy it between the poles of what it does positively assert and what, within it, will disintegrate it, make it unadministrable, negative. Dialectical criticism views the work as not conforming to itself, and so not accommodating to the world by being graspable (even if unreadily). This puts it in a self-destruct position, as a self, and thus world, opposition. It mediates itself to its own detriment, and even when it mediates itself so as to conform to itself and to accommodate to the world, seeking survival in history and commerce— seeking power as fame or as unique product—it negates itself, for it loses its self-contradictoriness, becoming self-same. Whichever way it moves—to retain itself as an illusion and symbol of freedom or to make itself self-same like every other administered being (to find its place in the system, or in the fragment of system assigned to it)—it self-negates, perhaps pointlessly, perhaps for the sake of a future, perhaps as power and authority, but always with a loss of that self-identity which was itself non-self-identity. Dialectical criticism grasps this self-contradictoriness and manages it, preserves it, not as an artifact making an arabesque in history, an ornament of a historical moment, but as the core of that which alone is positive in the art, that which alone makes sense beyond its own coming and going, beyond its affinity with other art and its cultivation by culture and commerce. To show the preciousness of this self-contradictoriness becomes the whole point of dialectical criticism—to make of it something positive, and yet not to be possessive of it. Dialectical criticism here falls in with the best intentions in modern art itself—the intention to make art a revolution of intention, to introduce a note of self-contradiction in public intention (from which unexpected possibility can emerge), rather than confirm known intention and value. Indeed, the best traditional art looked like art because it transcended its contradictions, mediated unity and transcendental harmony, which, however out of empirical reach, was still accessible through clear consciousness of the art. The best modern art looks like art because it transcends its unity, its proposed transcendental harmony, toward a self-contradictoriness which itself never becomes transcendental because it is empirically accessible.

Dialectical criticism, insofar as it helps make this self-contradictoriness empirically accessible—without revelling in it as a rhapsody—becomes what Bertholt Brecht called "eingreifendes Denken," thought which intervenes: "the dialectic as that classification, ordering, and way of considering the world which, by showing up its revolutionary contradictions, makes intervention possible."[3] From this point of view, criticism itself is intervention in the exhibition of art—a necessary intervention, to show up the art's contradictions, which are the source of its revolutionary potential, i.e., its significance for freedom, for anti-authoritarianism. Without criticism's interference in the very presence of the art that presence has no revolutionary carrying power, is no opening toward the horizon of thought and action. It has only the carrying power that it is given by being culturally and commercially administered, a carrying power that, by its very nature, contradicts the idea that the work is self-contradictory or has any meaning or freedom, i.e., any revolutionary meaning. (All revolution creates new possibility.) Dialectical criticism, insofar as it works against administered criticism and the very notion of art as having any authority beyond what it can reveal of world historical contradiction, works against culture and commerce—

passes between that Scylla and Charybdis with the art, rescuing it for further sailing on the seas of meaning and intention. Above all, dialectical criticism, as an instrument against cultural appropriation and commercial authority, links up with the grand tradition of critical thought: the pursuit of that enlightenment which denies any authority, for authority imposes a reconciliation where there is none—makes relations "positive"—and does not recognize the self-contradiction on which it is based, the opposition on which its own absolute power, giving it the power of absolution, is premised. There is no absolution from contradiction and self-contradiction, except in ontological tyranny, in an over-reification of existence into cultural-historical heroic moments or other "authoritative" value absolutes. The lionization of art, by whatever means, forfeits it as a clue to contradiction—as contradiction written large enough to be, if not self-evident, nonetheless obvious enough to be worked with. The only privilege art has is that it makes enough of a fetish about unity to reveal contradiction, or enough of a fetish about contradiction to propose unity. It is the one place where the irresoluteness of the dialectic becomes transparent—where no sociopolitical, experientially concrete solutions are at stake, or even thought about, whether as utopian proposals or as realistic reforms. Where, in other words, there is nothing forced about the relation between the opposites (and can never be between unity and contradiction, reconciliation and opposition)—so that the relation can be recognized in its generality, as an alternative to the narcissistic system's insistence that, whether a system of contradictions or of harmony, the administered system is the best of all possible worlds, i.e., that there is no alternative world or fragment of a world—no freedom, mythical or otherwise.

Dialectical criticism rejects this positivist "myth of things as they actually are,"[4] in art and elsewhere. It does not respect what Coomaraswamy calls the "esthetic surface" of art things, which keeps them what they actually are, like the skin the taxidermist uses to preserve "history." What Gideon calls the "eternal present" of art and Robert Morris its "presentness" ignore—deny—its self-contradictoriness (only self-contradictoriness is unadministrered self-identity) and its contradiction of the administered world historical, including its own administered art historical world. They are easy formulas for self-sameness, making art self-administering—they are the utmost esthetic positivism, the most simplistic reconciliation with art imaginable, doing it the disservice of giving it a readily serviceable identity. Under the guise of neo-transcendentalism, these formulas further art's historicist tendencies, which lead it to want to usurp the present, be the positive in the present, and so relegate the negative to the future, making it a utopian negative.

Dialectical criticism, then, is not a positivistic search for information about art nor is it an historical or transcendental apotheosis of it, i.e., the reduction of art to the permanently positive, whether arrived at by contemplation or consensus. It is the reluctance to accept any identity for art which denies it a possible loss of identity as art and a role within the self-contradictions of the world. Art is not simply a question of estheticizing what Sartre called the practico-inert, but of deestheticizing the "beautifully" administered practico-inert. Art is not simply a question of transcendentalizing the historically memorable but of de-transcendentalizing the already transcendental history of dominance, that goes in the guise of the necessarily memorable. Art is not simply a question of separating the necessary from the contingent and disposing of the latter as the shell around the kernel, as the accident or occasion accompanying the essence or principle. It is rather a recognition that the necessary would not be what it is unless it stood in opposition to the contingent, that there would be no essence or principle unless there was an accident or occasion, and that art is a matter of denying the authority and administrability of both—the authority of one over the other, the administration of the one by the other. Art, at its best itself dialectical criticism, finally involves one simple fact-concept: that we are in a situation of dichotomous determination, and if this contradictoriness is repressed in a false consciousness then living death results—such living death as positive culture and commerce cultivate, wittingly or unwittingly. They eventually break down into their opposites—culture and commerce collapse or suffer setbacks (and carry much art with them)—or become negative, devaluing what they originally valued, negating what they originally posited, because they ignored the negative in the first place, the death that their life gave.

(2)Traditional positivist criticism assumes that criticism is necessarily partisan—and it is assumed that this is sometimes enough to make it sufficient. Partisan taste—and what else can taste be?—necessarily involves, in William James's words, "passional decisions" leading to a "voluntarily adopted faith."[5] Art becomes an article of faith, something to which one is converted—in the privacy of one's intuition or on the open road to another art—and something which always exists under the duress of becoming as radically profane as it was once regarded as radically sacred. Questions of criticism become questions of faith, for both involve being moved to the depths of our "passional nature" by a mystery that is always on the verge of becoming intimate and transparent—and that our passional nature can help "resolve" into clear and distinct being, by making it a part of that nature's own becoming. Indeed, passional nature exists to "establish" our becoming, to direct it toward positive being—to ground it positively, even if that means seemingly irrationally.

> Our passional nature not only lawfully may, but must decide an option between propositions, whenever it is a genuine option that cannot by its nature be decided on intellectual grounds; for to say, under such circumstances, "Do not decide, but leave the question open," is itself a passional decision—just like deciding yes or not—and is attendant with the same risk of losing the truth.[6]

When, in the course of criticism, it becomes impossible to decide on the value of an art on objective grounds—after intellectual analysis, with its references to history and publicity (of which commerce is the logical extension)—then our passional nature is necessarily called into play, and, however hardpressed, is forced to a decision. Indeed, it is just the amount of duress, the agony of decision, that guarantees the truth of the decision—the decision's power to penetrate art and determine its value, its artistic "truth," its esthetic significance. Only through the passional decision can the esthetic experience of the art be had, and thereby its value realized. Without the passional decision one is always in bad faith with the art, however well one has historically located it—which amounts to an intellectual compromise of it. The "openness"—agnosticism—which resists passional "judgment" risks the very nature of art, suspends belief in the very existence of value.

This conception of the partisan position, which "rationalizes" partisanship into the leap of faith and art into the object of faith—and it is the only significant justification of the partisan position—has as its ulterior motive an effort to generate a momentum of meaning about art which it might not otherwise have, a strong sensation of its necessity which might otherwise be lacking. There is seemingly no existential reason why we should have a passion about art, whether for better or worse—for ourselves and for the art. The partisan argument insists that the passion for art does not displace or sublimate other more primordial passions, as Freud thought, but is itself a primordial passion—so that art must be taken seriously, at least as seriously as Plato took it when he banned it from the Republic. The partisan argument becomes all the more acute in modern times, when the necessity of art is not self-evident—when it does not seem to be integral to life, whether as a convention or as a sublime goal. To regard it as unnecessary is one devious way of administering it—of making it ask forgiveness for its intractability, its seeming wildness of purpose, and humbly petition for admission to the system, humbly ask not to be mistaken as an "outsider," the sin of sins for the administering system, as Horkheimer and Adorno note.[7] Also, the partisan position shows the system of administration in extremis reaching out with all its being to surmount what seemed unsurmountable, to subsume what seemed unsubsumable, to grasp what seemed ungraspable. In this kind of final agony of administration the system does indeed administer, ruthlessly, repressively, absolutely—at its most ideal. Its faith in art means that at last art will have faith in it; its passionate commitment to art expects reciprocity. Art acquires necessity, i.e., a secure place in the system, by being believed in. Belief becomes the ultimate instrument of administration, belief in art once and for all appropriating or locating it, absolutizing its nature for the convenience of administration. Belief becomes the final fixing of being for the convenience of the administering consciousness.

Dialectical criticism dispenses with belief in art—with the will to believe in general. It wants to leave the question of value open, not in expectation of some answer to it, but because the look of the art under the pressure of this irresolution becomes a clue to its self-contradiction, to its defeat of its own self-identity, to its proposal of possibility, to the extent of its willingness to risk negativity. Dialectical criticism sees the passional nature as itself dialectical—concerned to overcome the possibility of its own negativity by being firm or positive about the work of art, whatever the specific character of its decision. Dialectical criticism is itself more clearly passional than partisan criticism, for it does not want to direct passion toward the goal of truth—to push it to use its power of decision—but rather wants passion to explore the situation of non-truth, of indifference to the positive truth (about art or anything else), which surrounds the truth, and permits a discovery of it as only one among many optional modes of relationship to art or any other reality. The issue is not one of faith or lack of faith, belief or disbelief, but of the necessity that compels toward one or the other, and that necessity is the compulsion to administer reality, to overpower it in the system of consciousness, and then in the *Realpolitik* of the world (for art, the politics of commerce). To resist the will to believe is to resist the will to administer, and to resist the will to administer is to keep possibility open—to allow art to remain a residue of freedom. Admittedly, a "residue" as much as a "freedom," and so perhaps dispensable to administered history—finally lost to history—but nonetheless viable as a way out of the positiveness of the present, even if this means positing a negative future. Only by suspending the will to believe— disengaging from all belief systems, personal or social—can the intention of the art be examined, can it be tested for its revolutionary potential. Belief in the art precludes such a test, for it sees the art in terms of esthetic value, which masks its value for intention. Esthetic value is a positive value, while intention, in a situation of positiveness—of false consciousness, of meaningless reconcilia- tion—is inevitably negative, if it is to be of any revolutionary value. Esthetic value is simply the dumb shadow of art's negative intention. The authenticity of the work of art resides in its negative intention not in its esthetic positiveness, which is all that the will to believe can discover.

In substitution for the will to believe one approaches the work of art with the will to negate it, which has nothing to do with disbelieving in it, but rather with refusing to administer it—to give it the intellectual-cultural and commercial succor it eagerly wants, the fixed art historical and social meaning that would give it destiny and security. No, it must remain undestined and insecure. It must not be known through any of the usual categories (these may be a starting point but not a positive ending), but through deviously self-contradictory, unstable categories that capture yet do not capture, that let the fish slip away, or rather slip it from net to net without finally putting a hook in it—to test its survival power, its ability to negate its own administration. One gives the art a chance to negate its own administration by not catching it on its own desire to be believed in. James's psychological update of the Pascalian wager, which is the ultimate situation of partisanship, is replaced by a more profound wager, which asks the work to show itself as a sign of freedom—and realizes it can only do so if it is not administered by belief. This perhaps is the ultimate question about art: does one want it for its negativity, as a sign of freedom, or does one want it for its positiveness, as a sign of the divine, i.e., the ultimate administrator, the authority on systematic administration.

(3)Talk about the esthetic quality of a work of art administers it with an iron fist; it is the velvet glove on the firmly administering hand of the authoritarian critic. Talk about the esthetic has a way of closing down the horizons of discourse about art. Hemmed in by esthetic demands, both critic and art succumb to authoritarian narcissism—the dreamless sleep of the well-administered reality, the reality that does not even know it is administered, and so thinks it is "naturally" self-same. The esthetic is the most facile belief system about the work of art. Belief in the esthetic value of art is the climax of partisan commitment in the search for art's truth, for what makes it positive, what makes it art— positively art. Estheticism, with all its alluring deviances—for it too claims to be an existential matter of faith—must be resisted, if one is even to begin to fathom the negativity of art, its refusal of positiveness (any kind of "imitation," of following) in the midst of positiveness (in the very act of imitating, of acknowledging and positing). Estheticism precludes making such a distinction, for it renders art's "imitation" of the given, of whatever kind, a technique for drawing out the best in the given, for affirming its "ideal" or "beautiful" nature, its harmony with itself and everything else. Estheticism ultimately issues in an epiphany of harmony—the most exquisite false consciousness which all beauty is—which, in its wake, reduces all negativity to a dross, a metaphysical illusion. It is the recovery of the negativity that permitted positive beauty that is the task of dialectical criticism. And it begins this recovery by seeing the unity of beauty, the esthetic itself—the very in-itselfness of the art it posits—as a lie designed to recruit art as an authority capable of administering art, or more simply, recruit art as a standard of administration.

The esthetic, with its insistence on positive exhibition, must be resisted, so that what the work negates in its exhibition can be acknowledged. The esthetic, which is itself the absolute administrator of art, must be shown to be anti-esthetic, i.e., to be self-negating. For the collapse of the negative—in effect the life-world—which is the aftermath of esthetic epiphany is momentary and illusory. The negated resurrects with all the force with which it was negated, with the secret repressive force of the esthetic itself, and overwhelms the work of art, sucks it into the world, absorbs it both in the most trivial way—as a commodity— into the system of the world's values, and in the most sophisticated way, as a symbol of cultural value. Both strip the esthetic work of its power of affirming beauty. They make its false consciousness of harmony simply one more ornament on the world's sordid reality, i.e., reduce all its efforts to raise consciousness to a transcendental level to nothing (the transcendental simply becomes the protective camouflage of the real). Worse yet, commerce and culture subtly rob—expropriate—the repressive power of the esthetic, its ability to push the world aside, to repress awareness of the negative, of conflict. This power is turned on the esthetic itself, revealing it to be the naively negative, or rather the naively positive in its negativity, for the truly positive are culture and commerce in that, open-eyed, they give us the world as it is, but as still of value—of cultural and commercial value. Their realism contrasts sharply with esthetic idealism, which claims to be a realism about the work of art, and the realism of culture and commerce shows itself as the only realism about the work of art. But this still leaves esthetic idealism with its own negativity—its power of negating the world. This, while it is no longer effective in cultural and commercial terms—in the world of commodities they jointly create—is still of use to dialectical criticism, to spotlight the world negated, to disclose the world in a new, negative light. To do so is the very raw beginning of authentic critical enlightenment.

The esthetic, which aimed to extend the charisma of art into a universal possibility of transcendence, ends involuntarily de-transcendentalizing art into a new kind of realism, a recovery of the negative aura of reality. Charisma, which is simply the absolutization of the presentness of the work of art under the auspices of the clear and distinct category, becomes thwarted with the recognition that it too is mediated. Charismatic art's repression of its mediation is entirely a function of its exemplariness in the universal system. The esthetic, which meant to bespeak the charismatic, almost as the aura of the aura, becomes its undoing, its negation. Appropriated by commerce and culture, the esthetic is recognized simply as the most conventional of all means of mediating the work of art. Without the esthetic effect to give it transcendental meaning the charismatic is reduced to a means at the disposal of the existing order: it is the charismatic that commerce and culture take advantage of, make a commodity of, package into the positive. This leaves esthetic beauty where it was in the first place—an overly abstract presentation of the negative. The esthetic can finally be pressed into the service of dialectical criticism, as the pure negative in search of reification. To convert transcendental esthetic into the revolutionarily possible is the task of dialectical criticism.

Perhaps the most momentous factor determining the role of art in the world today is awareness of it—voluntary and involuntary awareness—as a form of capital, or at least a mechanism for the creation of capital. The individual work has the possibility of becoming the most durable material capital created, and style has come to be thought of as perhaps the most durable psychic capital created—the very principle of consciousness, which gives it its form and capacity. An artistic object is understood to stand to an ordinary object as consciousness of a style stands to consciousness of a fact. There is a surplus value in artistic objects and a style that ordinary objects and ordinary consciousness can never hope to mediate. It is this sharing of surplus value that is responsible for the reciprocity of art and capitalism. Today it is assumed that they, and they alone, are sources of surplus value. Both mean to benefit from this power—in effect, the power to produce transcendence. Both mean to show that they are as transcendent as the trancendence they produce—as valuable as the value they confer. This is demonstrated when the reciprocity between art and capitalism is fully operational, when capitalism expropriates the aura of style from art to "explicate" the meaning of surplus value, and when art expropriates the meaning of surplus value from capitalism to "explicate" the meaning of style. Surplus value is then revealed to be the happiness of the legendary "promise of happiness" art offers, style's refinement of reality bespeaking that promise. Surplus value keeps the promise that style made, materializes the happiness that utopian style proposes. And in so doing it brings style down to earth, as the first intuition of the positive that the actual can be. In high capitalism the aura of style continues to be valued for its positive content, so that the possession of style becomes the final confirmation of happiness under capitalism. Style is not only the surplus value of the best commodities, but itself the best commodity, and, like art in general today, "renounces its own autonomy and proudly takes its place among consumption goods," as Horkeimer and Adorno say. What this means is that style renounces its utopianism. It is no longer the promise but the fulfillment of the promise, no longer the possibility of happiness but its actuality—its most intimate content. Capitalism comes to advocate style, as the truly positive in existence. And to consume style becomes a sign that one harbors no unhappy feelings—no negative intention—about the actuality created by capitalism. Art and capitalism bolster each other's self-regard by bolstering each other's positive view of what is really the case. Each becomes the catalyst of the other's self-approval, and, as such, the grand obsession of the other. Each wishes to be secretly possessed by the other, and is, openly, in the markets where valuable meanings are determined.

Positivist cultural history, which guarantees a positive approach to art—an approach which reduces it to a cast of stereotypes which seem to fulfill every individuality, which makes of it a happy progression of styles, each with its own nuance of happiness—is possible only in a world in which art and capitalism have married, in a world which finds their divorce and antagonism inconceivable. Art is capitalist booty, and positivist cultural history conquers world art, separating it from its utopian dream of its society, and presenting it simply as the fulfilled promise of beauty, there for the asking. But, more insidiously, cultural positivism is a mechanism for the capitalist transformation of the world into a positive commodity, a transformation whose first step occurs when, as Adorno and Horkheimer write, "the whole world is made to pass through the filter of the culture industry."[8] This determines the world as a stereotype, and to know something as a stereotype is to be prepared to consume it as a commodity. It is to possess it as something already assumed to be collectivized and standardized. The cultural positivist, whether historian or critic, who thinks he can demonstrate an art that will not pass through the filter—that is so unique as not to be susceptible to standardization, and so to consumption—is absurd, since the very activity of "positing" such an art extends the administration of the filter, bringing the unheard of under control. Despite his protests to the contrary, the cultural positivist does not preserve the integrity of the art entrusted to him, but creates a universal system of administration which absorbs it into the rigorous logic of the sterotype. It is the stereotype which creates the aura of the eternal present—of the settled status and meaning of art. It is the stereotype which affords relief from all further pressures of experience and meaning. It is the stereotype that is the ideal—the transcendent style—the individual always seems an inadequate instance of.

> The art historians and guardians of culture who complain of the extinction in the West of a basic style-determining power are wrong. The stereotyped appropriation of everything, even the inchoate, for the purposes of mechanical reproduction surpasses the rigor and general currency of any "real style," in the sense in which cultural *cognoscenti* celebrate the organic pre-capitalist past. No Palestrina could be more of a purist in eliminating every unprepared and unresolved discord than the jazz arranger in suppressing any development which does not conform to the jargon.[9]

The critical problem today is how to avoid conforming to the jargon—how to undermine the purity of the inescapable jargon. Horkheimer and Adorno write that "with the progress of enlightenment, only authentic works of art were able to avoid the mere imitation of that which already is."[10] It can be assumed that there are no longer any authentic works of art today—works of art which, in whatever way, avoid the mere imitation of that which already is, which generate critical resistance to it. Abstraction, once the most significant way of avoiding or resisting what was positively the case, has become a jargon—a source of stylistic stereotypes. Simply by being committed to its own history it has become critically obsolete. And so-called realism, whether it be a return to landscape, portrait, and still life, or an ironic reminiscence of the pseudo-detachment of the photograph, is a meek commitment to what is already the case. Behind the self-effacement of current realism is a refusal to see the treachery of the real, which generates its own resistance—exactly what we find in the realism of Goya and Courbet, who deny the pedestrianism of reality (which we find even in Impressionism) by disclosing it as "critical." Critical realism, under whatever stylistic auspices, hardly exists today, for the contradiction in reality itself is not available in the eternal present—hardly dares disclose itself in the face of the transcendence of art and capital. Today art plays the sycophant to the supposed nature of things in a way that would honor the most ingratiating courtier. The problem of authenticity is no longer a problem for art. Works of art today no longer even have the option of being authentic. That option, and its burden, exists only for criticism.

Accepting the view that in today's overdetermined, well-administered cultural world an authentic work of art can never emerge, the question remains as to whether the terms or categories of such administration can be made authentic, i.e., can be made to avoid the mere imitation of that which already is decreed to be cultural. Can they be made to resist that which they themselves have posited?

Can they be made to underdetermine what they have overdetermined, so as to restore to it the possibility of authenticity? Can the culture they have made inauthentic be made authentic again, with the understanding that all authenticity is the responsibility of—in the care of—critical mediation? Can cultural credibility be replaced by critical credibility? Is that any advantage, if critical credibility only means to confirm what is the case in a new way, as part of a "counter-culture" which is nonetheless an administered culture? Is it possible to forego the establishment of the normative, a renunciation crucial to critical authenticity? One is asking criticism not simply to become the systematically unsystematic, the affirmatively negative, but to become as evasively transcendental as authentic art under capitalism once supposed itself to be. One is asking criticism to imply but not offer a significance beyond immediate significance, an experience beyond immediate experience—to suggest the staying power of such transcendental significance and experience without fully defining it. One is willing to let criticism be arbitrarily contradictory, but not let its contradictoriness simply become the case. However hard it is to be authentic today—even to fathom the meaning of authenticity—only criticism has the opportunity of being authentic, of even positing the possibility of being authentic. Only criticism can change the terms of the discourse; art simply "interprets" them, necessarily conforms to them, in however "original" a way. Criticism thus offers a limited, residual freedom, which it indirectly offers the work of art—and which the work of art often rejects, to retain cultural approval. In general, one finds the residue of freedom in criticism, not art, which seems to be a residue of freedom only by reason of the way it is freed from culture by criticism. Horkheimer and Adorno write:

> The work of art still has something in common with enchantment: it posits its own, self-enclosed area, which is withdrawn from the context of profane existence, and in which special laws apply. Just as in the ceremony the magician first of all marked out the limits of the area where the sacred powers were to come into play, so every work of art describes its own circumference which closes it off from actuality. This very renunciation of influence, which distinguishes art from magical sympathy, retains the magic heritage all the more surely. It places the pure image in contrast to animate existence, the elements of which it absorbs. It is in the nature of the work of art, or aesthetic semblance, to be what the new, terrifying occurrence became in the primitive's magic: the appearance of the whole in the particular. In the work of art that duplication still occurs by which the thing appeared as spiritual, as the expression of *mana*. This constitutes its aura. As an expression of totality art lays claim to the dignity of the absolute.[11]

But what is art when the totality is in the administering cultural system? Simply the reflex action of the system. All enchantment is now in the system; it is the system which is magical. The work of art is merely the particular charged with the magic of the system, the thing spiritualized by the totalizing categories—stereotypes—of the system. All dignity is in the cultural system, not in the work of art, which becomes dispensable once it no longer seems to reflect the magic of the system. And the particular work of art does become dispensable quickly, for the system will never commit itself completely to any one of its particulars, since it retains much of its magic by implying that none can adequately exemplify it, and reveal the totality of its influence—have the same power to enchant that it has. No work of art can become exemplary in a well-managed cultural system, since the system itself is exemplary, i.e., retains all rights to influential power, to magical or charismatic domination. Thus, it is the system itself that is self-contradictory—uses its power to negate as well as affirm—and so appears authentic, adding to its charisma.

The dialectical critic does not naively confront this charisma with its own methods of mediation, but extends the system's power of negation to *reductio ad absurdum* by turning it against the system's claim to absolute power of determination. He makes the cultural system look undignified or unsystematic by creating alternative critical terms which de-totalize rather than totalize, disenchant rather than enchant—terms which withdraw totality from the work before the system decides the work does not conform to the mythical totality of culture. These alternative terms measure art by its conformity or non-conformity to actuality, and view style as a mediation of this conformity or non-conformity rather than as a transcendental epiphenomenon bespeaking the self-identity of the work. Thus, the dialectical critic does not put the work in its place in the totality, but presents it as always in some shaky, even preposterous and absurd, relationship to the totality. This makes it even historically indeterminate: it is historical determinacy that the cultural system gives to whatever filters through it—that neutral, minimal historicity which amounts to no more than putting in an appearance and being "positively" identified. The dialectical critic opens the work to actuality, giving it a kind of negative magic: the work is shown to be a ceremony of containment of actuality, enclosing it in intention. It is the actual that acquires a circumference or limit through the power of intention of art, making it sacred—sealing it into significance. Art becomes the open horizon of the actual, and the actual becomes a sacred realm of significance posited by art, a realm brought out of chaos into clarity and ready for fresh, unprejudiced exploration—exploration not predisposed by stereotypes and so able to discover the contradictory which can never be mastered by presuppositions and expectations. Dialectical criticism functions like dialectical phenomenology. It suspends any preconception of objective (cultural-historical) structure to concentrate on the critic's intention toward a complex of art, working through that intention toward concepts which can articulate the intention of the art, without then administering that intention for the cultural-historical system, i.e., stereotyping the intention as a fixed category of consciousness.[12] It can never be guaranteed that the intention will never be stereotyped, although its source in the free self-questioning of the critic—his questioning of his own intention to the art—suggests this.

It is taken for granted that no critic can avoid categories of the cultural-historical system. But it must also be assumed that the dialectical critic will question such categories—put himself in a negative or contradictory relationship to them—as soon as they emerge in his consciousness. The point is to establish the possibility of an alternative to the illusion of the "daily life" of art the system establishes—to break down the illusion of cultural and historical business as usual. Nonetheless, the dialectical critic must, in working out critical alternatives, not succumb to what art itself has submitted to in its desire to be easily administered by the system: namely, "the constant pressure to produce new effects (which must conform to the old pattern)" and serves "merely as another rule to increase the power of the conventions."[13] The dialectical critic does not want to be a victim of what might be called the "Orson Welles effect":

> Whenever Orson Welles offends against the tricks of the trade, he is forgiven because his departures from the norm are regarded as calculated mutations which serve all the more strongly to confirm the validity of the system.[14]

The dialectical critic must avoid the fate of the artist, who became "completely fettered" by "the pressure (and the accompanying drastic threats), always to fit into business life as an aesthetic expert."[15] While critics once "signed their letters 'Your most humble and obedient servant,' and undermined the foundations of throne and altar," today the critic is more likely to be "accused of incompetence" if he does not conform, or else, like Orson Welles, be tolerated as the official outsider. But this accusation and toleration alone make the dialectical critic a risk to the system, for, to the extent he finds concepts that contradict the system's positive categories, it becomes negligible if not directly disputable, i.e., the system reduces to a set of passive conventions rather than active categories. It is taken for granted—a fate worse than death for the system, which wants active loyalty, enthusiastic devotion. The system wants a hold on those it administers, for without that hold they are potentially free—in a state of what might be called lazy or unrealized freedom, a freedom on a par with and intimidated only by the ordinariness of the system, i.e., the ordinariness it possesses when it is taken for granted. Thus the cultural-historical system has more to gain from the acceptance, however reluctant, of the dialectical critic. For while such acceptance does not bring him under control—truly administer him—it puts the system itself in a situation of potential greatness, in the same way the work of art once did, viz., by "exposing itself to this failure in which the style of the great work of art has always achieved self-negation."[16] The dialectical critic is the system's exposure to possible failure, its achievement of self-negation and self-transcendence, the sign of its greatness. The dialectical critic acts out the system's own fear of failure. His mistrust of its style is its own submission "to the logic of the matter" it subsumes—its complete reversal of order, in expectation of unexpected possibilities, a fresh hold on the "matter" of art. This makes the dialectical critic either the ironic apotheosis of the system or the obscure fly buzzing around its dead face, no longer able to be a gadfly.

Finally, we might note that for the dialectical critic to intervene in the cultural historical system with his persistently perverse concepts and intentions—apparently misapplied to positive art—is for him to resist the system's reduction of art to amusement, and so, paradoxically, to save the system from itself, making it once again responsible to esthetic transcendence. "Amusement, if released from every restraint, would not only be the antithesis of art but its extreme role."[17] "The fusion of culture and entertainment that is taking place today leads not only to the deprivation of culture, but inevitably to an intellectualization of amusement."[18] "The culture industry can pride itself on having energetically executed the previously clumsy transposition of art into the sphere of consumption, on making this a principle, on divesting amusement of its obtrusive naivetes and improving the type of commodities."[19] The culture industry reconciles "the irreconcilable elements of culture, art and distraction." How does the dialectical critic intervene in a situation in which amusement has become as enchanting as art, and art has become as much of a distraction from actuality as amusement? How does one disenchant what seems to be inherently enchanting, distract from what seems to be inherently distracting? By, in fact, being amused by amusing art—amused to the point of laughing at it, laughing at one's own distraction by it and at its power of distracting. Dialectical conversion again frees one from dialectical inversion. The dialectic presents itself as the laughter that apocalyptically arises from the amusing: dialectic becomes a kind of dada. "Resounding laughter has served to denounce civilization in every age. 'The most destructive lava which the crater of the human mouth spews out is hilarity,' says Victor Hugo"[20]—exactly the hilarity that Duchamp spoke of and that is an eternal possibility of art, and a necessity in modern art.[21] Amusing, distracting art self-destructs by generating laughter, restoring dialectic to what seemed an unqualifiedly positive situation of art, in which it did nothing but make the actual amusing and so all the more imitable, i.e., something all the more desirable. Dialectic inevitably develops comically—seems comic—in the face of amusing culture, in response to art's intention to entertain. Dialectical criticism expropriates the comic from the distracting and amusing, using it for its own clowning purposes. Dialectical criticism becomes a kind of clowning about art: criticism for criticism's sake, dancing around art for the sheer joy of dancing around art—a fool about art fooling about art. And so, hopefully, restoring it to utopian significance, when it offers negative rather than positive satisfaction, the laughter at—resistance to—the world which is the expression of the unhappy consciousness hidden in art for art's sake.

Notes

1. Oscar Wilde, "The Rise of Historical Criticism," *Works* (London, 1948), p. 1044.

2. Max Horkheimer and Theodor W. Adorno, *Dialectic of Enlightenment* (New York, 1977), pp. ix-x.

3. Quoted by Jeremy J. Shapiro, "One-Dimensionality: The Universal Semiotic of Technological Experience," *Critical Interruptions* (New York, 1972), p. 186.

4. Horkheimer and Adorno, p. x.

5. William James, "The Will To Believe," *Pragmatism and Other Essays* (New York, 1963), p. 193.

6. Ibid., p. 200.

7. Horkheimer and Adorno, pp. 133, 150.

8. Ibid., p. 126.

9. Ibid., p. 127.

10. Ibid., p. 18.

11. Ibid., p. 19.

12. Shierry M. Weber, "Individuation as Praxis," *Critical Interruptions* (New York, 1972), p. 44.

13. Horkheimer and Adorno, p. 128.

14. Ibid., p. 129.

15. Ibid., p. 133.

16. Ibid., p. 131.

17. Ibid., p. 142.

18. Ibid., p. 143.

19. Ibid., p. 135.

20. Ibid., pp. 112-13.

21. See Donald B. Kuspit, "Comic Modern," *Decade,* 1 (Oct. 1978), pp. 8-12.

Part II

8

Utopian Protest in Early Abstract Art

This paper is mostly about Kandinsky, but it is meant to be valid for other early 20th century abstract artists, especially Malevich and Mondrian.[1] Utopian protest, by which I mean objection not to social and political particulars but to general conditions of existence and the values which sustain them, is one of the major motivating forces behind Kandinsky's early production. The concept is derived from Engels' account of utopian socialists, who "do not claim to emancipate a particular class to begin with, but all humanity at once."[2] For utopians,

> If pure reason and justice have not hitherto ruled the world, this has been the case only because men have not rightly understood them. What was wanted was the individual man of genius, who has now arisen and who understands the truth.[3]

Implicit in this are two ingredients, important for an understanding of Kandinsky: (1) a critique of contemporary values in the name of eternal values; and (2) a visionary overtone, tied up with apocalyptic and messianic tendencies, but also preaching the personal power of the individual to reach the absolute. Engels accuses the utopian socialists of being historically naive and thus ineffective; but what is historically naive may be aesthetically sophisticated, what is inadequately aware of the given world may be a sufficient condition for a new art.

Few art historians have cogently explored the social and political conditions of the development of abstract art. Apart from Meyer Schapiro, who regards abstract art as "a rebellion against the 'materialism' of modern society,"[4] abstract art is generally understood as part of the pursuit of a new formal style in response to the presumed exhaustion of the traditional "Renaissance" manner, now become conventional and banal. But Schapiro sees abstract artists, at least the revolutionaries of the movement, as concerned with "spiritual" and social issues as well as stylistic matters. In Kandinsky's case, the attack on materialism—in the name of revitalized spiritualism—includes a critique, however inarticulate, of "science and the socialist movement."[5] In Schapiro's view, Kandinsky aimed to supersede if not transcend materialism through a subjectivism aiming to "depict" mood in painting. In effect, Kandinsky did not so much reject representation of the material world, as become self-reflexively preoccupied with the mood in which he perceived and which was presumably evoked by the material subject. His consciousness of this mood became so overwhelming as to call for its own articulation, to the misfortune of matter, which lost both its "representativeness" in the human world, i.e., its import for human experience, and its "clarity and distinctness" as represented or reproduced in the art medium. Unfortunately, Schapiro's account of Kandinsky's protest against materialism is shortcircuited by the author's interest in the ramifications of Kandinsky's subjectivism, so that for all purposes of understanding the content of Kandinsky's protest is trivialized. Presumably it is Kandinsky's art that matters, not his opinions—the two can be separated—and in the end it is to this position that Schapiro returns, however much he intended the opposite.

In fact, Kandinsky is not so much protesting science, but science's pretension to conclusiveness—to its general presupposition that there was a universal order sustained by eternal principles, reducing science's task to the disclosing of this fixed order. His shock at the splitting of the atom[6] registers recognition of the destruction of this absolute order, which is suddenly revealed not to be a truth of reality but a presupposition of science; such presuppositions are discovered to be far from "final." Kandinsky's shock was by no means naive nor isolated, and was shared by such figures as Whitehead.[7] Just as it led Whitehead to an epistemological revolution, so it was instrumental in Kandinsky's re-orientation to the elements of painting. No longer could there be an absolute order to the total composition; at the most there was to be a chorus of components, structuralized by an underlying presupposition—which had more the character of the dominant key of a musical composition than of a principle— yet never finalized into a "statement."[8]

As for Kandinsky's presumed anti-socialism, it must be subsumed in the larger discussion of his protest against self-proclaimed absolute social orders. Such a discussion has as its ultimate ambition the demonstration that his attack on totalitarian social order is directly correlated with his refusal to allow any totalitarian form in his painting. Kandinsky's main objection to totalitarian society is that it hinders if not outrightly destroys individual spontaneity.[9] Spontaneity for Kandinsky means the possibility of exploring new aspects of experience. Strictly speaking, in the context of art, it does not mean a revolution in form, the development of new forms or orders of composition. There is no necessity that the exploration issue in form, in a new determinateness. He has a very personal yet professional reason for this stricture. For him, the idolization of form is the symbol of tradition's control on the creativity or spontaneity of the living artist. This control is effected by instilling the belief that all art is a search for ultimate form, that there is an absolute principle of form which sustains the best art much as antediluvian—before the splitting of the atom—scientists believed there were ultimate principles which sustained the universe's order.

Thus, for Kandinsky, "form" is the symbol of the effort to impose an absolute order or style of art. This effort ignores and threatens the artist's spontaneity as irrelevant to the achievement of a "final statement," but for him the solution is not the alternative of making an "informal statement." It is rather the abandonment of any attempt to make any statement, and with this the giving up of the presupposition of any absolute style for art. Instead, possibilities are explored, spontaneity is followed out, as a kind of Ariadne's thread both into and out of the labyrinth of composition, and no form issues because no total form is needed to achieve a painting of aesthetic value. What is important for understanding Kandinsky's attitude is less an emphasis on his "experimentalism" than on his abandoning the presupposition that anything like form is needed for fulsome, total aesthetic effect.

The connection between what has been said above about Kandinsky's criticism of the traditional approach to art and his anti-totalitarianism can be demonstrated by a sequence of passages in his *Reminiscences*.[10] Kandinsky writes that when he was a student he tried in vain "to capture on the canvas" the *"full power"* of what he calls a "color chorus...which, bursting out of nature, forced itself into my very soul."[11] He juxtaposes with this account of his artistic upheaval a long discussion of "other, purely human upheavals" which "constantly kept [his soul] in turmoil."[12] These upheavals were the student revolutions in Russian and western universities. He remarks, largely ignoring the particular issues, that he was especially struck by "the development of spontaneity on the part of the students,"[13] adding that, in the end, "politics" did not "ensnare" him.[14] Instead, he writes, he turned to "practice in 'abstract' thinking, in learning to penetrate to fundamental questions,"[15] especially in his study of law.

What most struck Kandinsky about laws was that they inhibited spontaneity. Their rigidity and quasi-absoluteness were inhuman. His abstract thinking about the law, his penetration of the fundamental question of law, was an attempt to re-establish the law on a basis which would allow for the free expression of spontaneity, which would recognize the human and be flexible in its working. He actually found such ideal law operational in Russian peasant law.[16] Like Kandinsky in his art, it passed "external phenomena without noticing them,"[17] seeing instead the inner and spontaneous. Kandinsky could be his spontaneous self and rise to the occasion of the bursting of color choruses out of nature, could see beyond nature and external phenomena to color choruses, much as Russian peasant law could ignore the "rigidity" of the external deed of the criminal and rise to seeing him as a soul. The analogy between art and law brings into focus Kandinsky's protest against any rigid approach to experience as destructive of its subjective side. Thus, he becomes sufficiently flexible to meet nature half way, so to speak; his spontaneity links up with its spontaneity, i.e., its color choruses, much as in Russian peasant law the community meets the guilty individual half way, treats him flexibly rather than according to general rule. At first sight, then, Kandinsky begins his art with a protest against the institutional inhibition of individual spontaneity, against the presumably "legal" restriction of human intensity and individuality. More acutely, his protest is against all social forms which hold man back from his abstract relation with his fundamental nature and from his fundamental relationship with abstract nature. It is a protest against the superficial view of man as a being determined by social rules and political orders rather than by ontological spontaneity, i.e., the spiritual in nature. This is the gist of his so-called "spiritualism."

That Kandinsky's appreciation of Russian peasant law, with its flexible attitude towards the human agent, is crucial for his conception of painting, is demonstrated by the fact that his *Reminscences* begin and end with footnotes on this subject. Art, in fact, should emulate Russian peasant law, in its respect for the spontaneity of the living artist rather than the formal modes of traditional art. Kandinsky, before he could paint, had to identify and establish a new kind of artist, much as Russian peasant law, before it could judge, had to identify the individuality and humanity of the criminal and thus establish him as spiritual. The first footnote runs as follows:

> After the "emancipation" of the serfs in Russia, the regime gave them a system of economic self-government, which, unexpectedly for many, made the peasants politically mature, and their own tribunals where, within certain limits, judges chosen by the peasants could settle disputes and also punish criminal "offenses." And here the people found the most human principle, to punish minor guilt severely and major guilt lightly or not at all. The peasant's expression for this is: "According to the man." There was thus no development of rigid law (as for example in Roman law—especially *jus strictum!*), but an extremely flexible and free form which was *not* decided *by appearance* but *solely by the spirit.*[18]

Certainly one can apply these last words to Kandinsky's painting. Moreover, this footnote is preceded by and juxtaposed with a footnote on spontaneity. The sequence is so close that in effect the footnote on spontaneity can be taken as the statement of the theory of which the footnote on Russian peasant law is the practice. The footnote on spontaneity runs as follows:

> This spontaneity or personal initiative is one of the happiest (unfortunately far too little cultivated) sides of a life that has been pressed into rigid forms. Every individual (corporate or personal) step is full of consequences because it shakes the rigidness of life—whether it aims at "practical results" or not. It creates an atmosphere critical of customary appearances, which through dull habit constantly deaden the soul and make it immovable. Thence the dullness of the masses about which freer spirits have always had reason for bitter complaint. Corporative organizations should be so constituted that they have the most open form possible and incline more to adapt to new phenomena and to adhere less to "precedent," than has hitherto been the case. Each organization should be conceived only as a transition to freedom, as a necessary bond which is, however, as loose as possible and does not hinder great strides toward a higher evolution.[19]

The footnote on Russian peasant law towards the end of the *Reminiscences* emphasizes the human gains of spontaneity, flexibility, and anti-absolutism.

In this sense Russian peasant law, mentioned previously, is also Christian and should be contrasted to heathen Roman law. The inner qualification can be thus explained by bold logic: this deed is not a crime when committed by this person, though in general it would be considered a crime when committed by other people. Therefore, in this case a crime is not a crime. And further: absolute crime does not exist. (What a contrast to *nulla poena sine lege!*) Still further: not the act (real) but its root (abstract) constitutes the evil (and good). And finally: every act is ambivalent. It balances on the edge. The will gives it the push—it falls to right or left. The external flexibility and inner precision are highly developed in this case in the Russian people, and I do not believe I exaggerate when I recognize a strong capacity for this type of development in general in the Russians. It is also no surprise that peoples who have developed under the often valuable principles of the Roman spirit, formal, externally very precise (one need only think of the *jus strictum* of an *earlier* period) react either with a shake of the head or with scornful condemnation to Russian life. Superficial observation especially allows one to see in this life, so curious to the foreign eye, only the softness and external flexibility, which is taken for unruliness, because the inner precision lies at a depth. And this has the result that free-thinking Russians show much more tolerance of other peoples than is shown to them. And that this tolerance in many cases turns into admiration.[20]

I have presented these extensive footnotes to emphasize that they help make sense of Kandinsky's abstract art. They demonstrate, in effect, a dialectic of abstract art, beginning (1) with a spontaneity which negates customary appearances, (2) developing or concretizing into a flexible lawfulness or free order, so to speak, which decisively reveals the spiritual in man, and finally (3) returning to the original initiative of spontaneity to show it transformed, apotheosized, as it were, into an inner precision fully able to cope with, fully adequate to if revolutionary in the outer real world. Spontaneity initially destroys appearances, upsets the order of the real world; doing this in the name of the spirit, it ultimately discloses a new, spirtual, inner way of dealing with reality which proves to be more adequate than the old, rigid, formal way, more adequate because it is more respectful of the human. Perhaps the most startling thing about Kandinsky's spontaneity, as a vehicle of aesthetic perception, is that unlike the kind of perception which representationalism implies, spontaneity is not concerned to overpower its object. Insofar as there is an object of perception, his spontaneous perception aims at revealing its inwardness or spirit, treats it with a flexibility which lets it reveal itself. Whereas traditional perception forces the perceived object into a general, presupposed order of vision, thus distancing the perceiver from the perceived: putting between their respective spirits an impersonal, impartial formal order which obviates any possibility of their mutuality. The ultimate aim of Kandinsky's abstract art is a root connection, a oneness of being or unity, through the spirit, between perceiver and perceived. Whereas the ultimate ambition of traditional representationalism is the demonstration that both perceiver and perceived conform to a universal form of perception, are the standard ingredients of an eternal perception, so to speak. For traditional representationalism there is one ultimate law of style, correlate with the unchanging order of perception; for Kandinsky's abstract art there is no law of style nor ultimate perception, only a spirit of unity with the intensity of other beings, other objects. Moreover, in representationalism being and object conform equally to the impersonal, absolute law of style; both man and thing have equal status as objects of perception. For Kandinsky's abstract art the human spirit—the sense of inner precision—has priority over the representation of things or the treatment of men as things, the reduction of them to, literally, "still life" status; what objects there are in the "image" share in the human spirit that perceived them. But strictly speaking for Kandinsky, there is no image, for that is merely customary appearance, formally convenient for perception. Perception, rather, is conditioned by the spontaneous grasp of spirit, prior to perception, and by the demands of inward precision. In this sense, perception becomes abstract, i.e., it dismisses the idea of the absoluteness of the image, it has no concern to formalize appearances, it does not believe in a total style which absorbs all appearances and to which spontaneity must conform.

What must be emphasized is that it is not simply that he wants inner reality in preference to outer appearance, but that he is protesting the legalistic aesthetics which treats any reality and appearance as necessarily taking its place in a total order. Composition is no longer total for Kandinsky, nor is it merely spontaneous, informal treatment of conventional components. Rather, it is the re-presenting, in an alien medium, of the free human spirit. Spontaneity is in a sense no more than the "instrument" for the exploration of this spirit; what is discovered is what this spirit grasps with its inner precision, and what it grasps is the possibility of the higher man. Whether specific paintings by Kandinsky live up to this program can only be known if it is understood that the "higher man" is not specifically emergent or evolved by the painting's composition itself, but that the aesthetic effect of the painting, the consciousness, as it were, which it induces, inspires the spectator with a new attitude towards man. Where traditional representationalism usually wants the spectator to recognize a given man or type of man, abstract art wants to make the spectator aware of the possibility of a new kind of spirit of man. Representationalism deals with established actualities, long sedimented in consciousness. He remains, in his *Reminiscences* for example, preoccupied with law because he is aware that society is the field of actualization of the new possibility of man. Painting can, at the most, revolutionize attitudes through novel aesthetics; the past's aesthetics precluded a new attitude towards man, it simply confirmed a familiar kind of man—it gave him his right to exist. All the kings and saints were confirmed in their royalty and holiness by being re-presented, and eventually ordinary men and ordinary things were validated in their ordinariness. The "problem" of Kandinsky's abstract art is: how to validate an attitude, especially one concerned not to confirm social rank or eternal verities or daily existence but to revolutionize human existence in general?

More specifically, the dialectic of development from spontaneity to spirit to a new kind of social existence, works itself out in the early Kandinsky in terms of his attitude towards color choruses. Initially, in his effort to grasp these color choruses emergent from nature, Kandinsky felt inhibited. He realized that the source of his inhibition was traditional social and aesthetic attitues towards conventional, customary, rightful appearances, which were treated as laws unto themselves, to which one must be strictly obedient as an artist. The second step in Kandinsky's development was a change in attitude towards these external appearances which destroyed their rightfulness, which in fact dissolved them entirely.[21] This step involves the development of uninhibited color perception, and of the spontaneous involvement of his total existence in this perception. It is at this stage that Kandinsky uses the language of jubilant, articulate emotion to the full—much more than naive enthusiasm for his own loss of inhibition. It is important to make clear at this point that Meyer Schapiro's use of the word "mood" falsifies this emotion. The subjective connotations of "mood," implying some personal psychological history, overlook the "purity" of the emotion, i.e., its strict correspondence with the perception of color. It is thus abstract emotion rather than personal emotion that Kandinsky experiences—the stage of protest is superseded by the state of purity, the personal overcoming is superseded by transcendent experience. Much as the color chorus transcends the conventional experience of nature, so the pure joy he experiences transcends his particular personality. Kandinsky in effect recognizes this when he writes of its independent "organic" presence in him, prior to the development of his mature personality.[22] The transcendent quality of the emotion is conveyed by his acknowledgement that it alone could lift him "beyond time and space."[23] It is only when this occurs that one can truly speak of the inception of abstract or non-objective art, for it is the moment when real objects—time- and space-bound—are forfeited, are left behind. It is noteworthy, I think, that the moment of the inception of, so to speak, pure art, is the same for Malevich, whose "pure feeling," as he terms it, corresponds to Kandinsky's pure emotion in the sense that it is a transcendental response to a transcendental phenomenon of pure perception; and for whom, like Kandinsky, color, the object of pure perception, becomes symbolic of the quality of spirit."[24] It is at this moment that, as Kandinsky says, one solves the problem of art exclusively on the basis of internal necessity, which was capable of overthrowing all known rules and limitations at any moment.[25] The overthrowal of representationalism or objective art is simply one side of this revolution against rules, this protest against rigid limits, monumentalized in critically acclaimed "perfect" forms. Thus, protest appears again in Kandinsky, on this new level: what was initially social protest becomes transformed into aesthetic protest. In the deepest sense, this aesthetic protest is less the negation of conventional rules than the affirmation of "internal necessity"—which alone, in a sense, is lacking in representationalism or objective or external art, in that in this art inner precision is subject and secondary to outer form. Thus, Kandinsky's protest once again shows its utopian character, for again it is less concerned to remedy particular rules or to acknowledge partial success, in the best representational works, in grasping internal necessity, i.e., he is less concerned to reform or to compromise than to revolutionize the total character of art. It is because of the utopian overtones of aesthetic internal necessity that, at this stage, "the realm of art" and "the realm of nature" "drew farther and farther apart" for Kandinsky.[26] Where the color chorus was initially embedded in nature for Kandinsky and in this sense one with it, at the second stage nature is negated, the color chorus affirmed and disinterred from it, and held up as something other than nature and at least on equal footing with it, for like nature the color chorus—practical symbol of art for Kandinsky—has a "law" of its own,[27] that in fact art like

> nature, science, political forms, etc., [is] a realm unto itself, is governed by its own laws proper to it alone, and which together with the other realms ultimately forms that great realm which we can only dimly divine.[28]

There is something dubious about this independence of art—it is an assertion of glory which mutes the modest, practical, almost positivistic experience with color choruses with which Kandinsky began in his aesthetic experience, and it is a glory which in effect corrupts the notion of internal necessity in composition by trying to sustain the notion in the old context of absolutist thinking. For it is just because nature, science, and political forms were realms unto themselves that they could apply their rules so rigidly. In fact, the assertion of the independence of art from other forms of human activity betrays his overriding concern for spontaneity and spirit in all human affairs. Indeed, the idea that art is a realm unto itself has degenerated into a *pro forma* a truth of the abstract movement, and perhaps has been responsible for the triviality or at least awkward pretentiousness of much abstract art, at least in its verbal claims for its accomplishments. Be that as it may, at the second stage Kandinsky's claim for the independence of art is not justified, but merely asserted, and remains incomplete if not generally inadequate. It makes sense only in transfigured form at the third and final stage of his early development.

At this stage, the ideological content of the second stage is fused with the first stage's concern for spontaneity, and the transcendent experiences of the second stage become the means of penetrating the unified realms of art, science, nature, and society, i.e., transcendent aesthetic experience becomes the means of grasping what is essential in the human spirit. At this stage the concern is no longer with the independence of the realm of art but with "the interrelationships of these individual realms."[29] These will be grasped by "revelations" "as by a flash of lightning."[30] Again a new barrier of inhibition—against interrelationship this time, rather than against independence—must be broken through, and now a transcendent, in effect divine spontaneity can do the job. Indeed, Kandinsky says that "art is like religion in many respects," for it develops by such spiritual revelations as his perception of color choruses.[31] The spontaneity of the first stage purifies art, raises it up into its own realm; the spontaneity of the third stage purifies the human spirit itself, showing it to be universal. The second stage is transitional and has the static quality of an ideal, yet one luring to a fuller revelation than art's. At the level of the third stage protest is more general. It is against those who would isolate men and their variety of projects from one another. It is an attack on those who would deny the mutuality of human enterprises. At this third stage art, which was an end in itself at the second stage, becomes no more than a vehicle for the revelation of a profounder, more general spirit. The utopianism of the final stage is extreme, and in a sense critical protest is dissolved in its religious rapture. Kandinsky the protesting prophet of a new art becomes Kandinsky the saint lost in a beatific revelation of the universality of the human spirit, almost lost in ecstasy with the spirit *per se.*

Indeed, Kandinsky's imagery becomes explicitly religious, and he in effect sees himself as the messiah of a new religion. The final revelation is at hand; the Old Testament revealed the Father, the New Testament revealed the Son, and a Third Testament would reveal the Holy Spirit—pure spontaneity of spirit, free of any incarnations, i.e., of any representations or objectifications, but direct, simple, rapturous.[32] This imagery is meant to convey that abstract art heralds and anticipates the direct revelation of pure spirit. Abstract art is, so to speak, the liquid from the cup that runneth over, the first outpouring of the full spirit. It is meant to be a testimony to the increasing spiritualization of art. In more strictly art historical terms, it is an attack on the entire Roman spirit of western art— from ancient Rome to Baroque Rome—as not sufficiently spiritual, not sufficiently concerned with the human spirit but merely with its formal appropriateness in limited contexts and the formal appropriation of some of its manifestations in an obvious style. Abstract art, at its inception, was a protest against the grand tradition of western art as inadequate to the human spirit, not simply in its expression but in its progress—nowhere did this art help spirit's development, but always only confirmed a past development, achieved by a non-artistic source. Kandinsky in effect is calling for a new role for art, and the pathetic character of his utopian call and perhaps, of his hopes for abstract art in general, is demonstrated by the fact that abstract art has itself degenerated into another spiritless convention, full of technical bravado, but ultimately one more formality with rigid, academically approved, laws of its own. In becoming the new academic art abstract art not only betrayed its revolutionariness, but demonstrated the justice of Engels' attack on the utopians as naive and unable to effect their own noble goals.

Kandinsky's third stage is a fulfillment of the first stage's protest against the inflexibility of form, for he conceives of spirit as pure flexibility. Ultimately, this is unrealistic and heretical, for the spirit needs its incarnations as much as it needs its purity, otherwise it becomes obscure however forceful, and rote however reckless. However, that Kandinsky claims for the internal necessity of abstract art "objectivity,"[33] shows that early abstract art, in addition to its spiritual claims, also insists upon its scientific or philosophical quality. This does not necessarily imply purity of purpose or concern with structures and patterns or a greater reflectiveness in contrast to impressionism's pursuit of immediacies, but a concern with criticality—with a recognition of the critical character of objectivity which brings to mind again his shock at the splitting of the atom. In fact, a case can be made for locating Kandinsky in the Kantian tradition of critical philosophy. Kandinsky in effect introduces the Copernican Revolution into painting, i.e., the insistence that the object conform to the subject, rather than vice versa, as was traditionally the case.[34] He brings art to where Kant brought philosophy and science more than a century earlier, with the difference that the object of experience is suspended for a deeper penetration of the subject. The parallels are awkward, perhaps even spurious in their particulars and forced in general, but what remains clear is that Kandinsky took a critical, intellectual approach to an art that had become conventional in its sensuousness, formally rigid in its style, and matter-of-factly rational. He did not try to give a new style to the old art, but to overcome critically the entire ground of the old art and plant the seeds of a new art. The old art was encrusted with many styles; what Kandinsky did was criticize the presuppositions of the old art, not its styles, and showed these presuppositions to be invalid, so that the styles could be easily dismissed rather than struggled through to come to a new style. Protest means criticism in the context of his *Reminiscences,* and that the criticism is utopian does less to invalidate it than to imply that it was thorough. In this sense Engels' critique of the utopians does not apply to Kandinsky, for Kandinsky was realistic in terms of art. He knew that unless his protest was against the very ground of art on which the old styles stood he would be misunderstood as offering simply another style which, however new, was based on the same old art.

In sum, Kandinsky makes a penetrating protest against the idea of absolute art. He shows that abstract art is in a sense art's self-criticism: its rejection of its own previous claims of being able to offer an eternal art, its recognition of the illusion of absolute form. His general concern for social spontaneity is directly correlate with this, for art can only criticize itself totally in terms of its interrelation with other human enterprises; it is of a piece with them in its general spirituality. In this sense, the spontaneous artist is the self-critical man, purified of all obedience to absolutes. Malevich is more explicit than Kandinsky about the social character of these absolutes, deriving them from bourgeois business mentality and labelling them in general "utilitarianism."[35] Mondrian, on the other hand, emphasized their effect, the misery they caused, and his insistence that abstract art is a contemplative refuge from this misery, in effect a private liberation from it, parallels, in a quieter statement, Kandinsky's transcendentalism.[36]

Alfred Barr's view of abstract art as one more stylistic development,[37] a view which Schapiro demolishes, is still the prevailing one. It strips abstract art of its full revolutionariness, *viz.,* its transcendence. In the same vein, other views, also tenaciously art historical, insist that abstract art is nothing new, and trace its ancestry to such styles as Greek Geometric. Other views, more anthropological, note the strong abstract character of the art of primitive societies, and trace the raprochement of primitive and modern style and outlook. Still other views, oriented to the future rather than the past, to the contemporary world rather than the primitive world, to criticism rather than history, regard abstract art as in effect the new western style, fated to have a development much as Roman style had in the past.[38] All this is part of the institutionalization of abstract art. It ignores the basic issues which led to the production of abstract art, and which are still latent in its interests. It tends to encourage the reduction of abstract art to pure aestheticism, e.g., in the works of Morris Louis, Helen Frankenthaler, Kenneth Noland. It thus ignores the intention of non-objectivity to protest against rigidification of the concept and meaning of art and against academic codification of style, in a word, against totalitarianism in art. It is just this totalitarianism which tends to overlook the relation of art to society, in which art alone makes full sense. Without the context of this relation, quality itself cannot be determined, let alone conceived. In effect, the stripping of abstract art's philosophy of civilization can only lead to abstract art's devaluation. In this sense, Kandinsky, Malevich, and Mondrian are more important for the comprehension of abstract art as new art rather than a new style than the late Monet, or Frankenthaler and Louis.[30] In a sense, the latter are its premature decadence, its despiritualization; without spiritualization abstract art becomes regressive imagistic art, forfeiting the intensity of its internal necessity for the sake of an adjustment to the old principle of art as power over nature. Current abstractionists have power over color, and so, unlike Kandinsky, cannot orchestrate its spirit, cannot unite with its intensity but simply, like lion tamers, make it jump through a technical hoop. Today's abstractionists have lost the core of abstract art.

Notes

1. The main sources are Malevich's essay on "Suprematism" in *Modern Artists on art,* edited by Robert L. Herbert (Englewood Cliffs, N.J., 1965) and the various essays by Mondrian in the appendix to H.L.C. Jaffé, *De Stijl 1917-31* (London, no date).

2. Friedrich Engels, *Socialism: Utopian And Scientific* in *Marx And Engels, Basic Writings on Politics And Philosophy,* edited by Lewis S. Feuer, p. 71. Garden City, N.Y., 1959.

3. Ibid.

4. Meyer Schapiro, "Nature Of Abstract Art" in *The Marxist Quarterly,* 1937, Vol. 1, p. 92.

5. Ibid.

6. Wassily Kandinsky, *Reminiscences* in *Modern Artists On Art,* edited by Robert L. Herbert, p. 27: "The crumbling of the atom was to my soul like the crumbling of the whole world." (Hereafter *Reminiscences.*) Kandinsky also remarks: "In one moment the mighty pillars of science lay in ruins before me. All things became transparent, without power or certainty." Quoted in Werner Haftmann. *Painting In The Twentieth Century,* Vol. I, p. 139. New York,

1961. See also *Concerning The Spiritual In Art and Painting In particular.",* pp. 31-32 (New York, 1947): "Still higher, we no longer find bewilderment. There work is going on which boldly criticizes the pillars men have set up. There we find other professional men of learning who test matter again and again, who tremble before no problem, and who finally cast doubt on that very matter which was yesterday the foundation of everything, so that the whole universe rocks." Kandinsky goes on to mention "the theory of the electrons ... designed to replace matter completely ..." (p. 32). (Hereafter *Spiritual In Art.*) In general, *Concerning The Spiritual In Art* is correlate with the *Reminiscences,* with the difference that the former is more didactic, the latter obviously personal, and both self-consciously messianic.

7. Whitehead remarks on the shock of the splitting of the atom and his "decision" never again to be misled by science's absolutes in the essay on "Process And Reality" in *Essays In Science And Philosophy* (New York, 1947). *In Science And The Modern World,* p. 104 (New York, 1948) Whitehead notes that "the atom is transforming itself into an organism."

8. See *Reminiscences,* p. 26, for Kandinsky's experience of Wagner's *Lohengrin,* one of the "two experiences which stamped my entire life and which shook me to the marrow." He remarks that "painting can develop just as much power as music possesses." Haftmann, Werner, *op. cit.,* Vol. I, p. 137, remarks that for Kandinsky "Colours lost their materiality and became tones, conjuring up musical associations.

9

Delaunay's Rationale for *Peinture Pure,* 1909-1915

As in the case of the nonobjective painting of Kandinsky, Malevich, and Mondrian, there is a transcendental purpose to Delaunay's *peinture pure,* where transcendental is understood not only in the sense of freedom from the conventional constraint of subject matter, but as the sign of a new understanding of the universe. That is, *peinture pure* embodies positive as well as negative freedom, the lyrical expression of what Delaunay called the infinite as well as the defeat of familiar form in a renewal of sensibility for pure color. Delaunay was not only conscious of the complexity of purpose implied by *peinture pure,* of its intermingling of artistic and philosophical motivation, but he ultimately intended the philosophical rather than the artistic. His regression to the artistic, under the auspices of a return to symbolism, brings into focus the difficulties of *peinture pure,* i.e., an art without an explicit content, an art in which there is, literally, next to nothing to see. It was Delaunay's implicit awareness of the conflict between the perceptual and the conceptual in nonobjective art, and his uncertain reconciliation of the two—he tended to heighten their conflict—that led him to abandon *peinture pure,* or rather to reduce it to a mèans of revitalizing subject matter, i.e., to take it as another style, one more novel determination of visual form. In the end, behind this regression, is an implicit return to inescapable nature and the suspicion that the sense of the infinite that emerged in *peinture pure* was only a sublime effect of perception of nature. However, there was a moment of spiritual ecstasy which led Delaunay to trust the infinite, and to try to make it visible to the naked eye.

Peinture pure, represented in Delaunay's oeuvre by the *Windows* and especially the *Sun Discs* or *Circular Forms* series, both of 1912, is sandwiched between two major representational styles. The first is manifest in the series of works devoted to *St. Severin* (1909-10), the *Spire of Notre Dame* (1909), and the *Eiffel Tower* (1911?), and the second in such works as the *Cardiff Team* (1913), *Homage to Bleriot* (1914), *Paris With Rainbow* (1914), and *Nude Reading* (1915). *Peinture pure* is basically an interlude between a style preoccupied with structural considerations and a style striving for allegorical import. When it is revived in the '20s—in such works as *The Merry-Go-Round With Pigs* (1912), *Propeller* (1923), and later versions of the *Eiffel Tower* (1922, 1926) and in the *Rhythms* of the '30s (1933-34), it is essentially technical and mechanical, lacking the spiritual import of the 1912 works. Delaunay, in describing his *Towers* series, notes its existence "between the destructive and the constructive," its tendency towards "the collapse of traditional perspective" and, simultaneously, its "transition towards constructive color."[1] Delaunay's second representational style is as preoccupied with the figure as his first is preoccupied with the tower and amounts to an attempt to integrate the two into *peinture pure's* "orchestrated arrangements" of color.[2] In neither style does stylistic exploration destroy the legibility of the subject matter. Instead, the two are intermingled: the expressive potential of the subject matter is realized through stylistic innovation, and the novelty of the style seems the consequence of a distinctive attitude to the subject matter.

Douglas Cooper has argued that Delaunay's "reaction in color, just at the height of Cubist evolution"[3] is a veneer disguising his more decided interest in subject matter. This is part of Cooper's general contention that the early Cubist style of Picasso and Braque, which constituted a "new pictorial language," was taken up without understanding by the Cubist school as an expressive overlay on the "realistic modernism of (their) subject matter."[4] It seems to me an exaggeration, at least in Delaunay's case, to dismiss his stylistic innovations as subsidiary to his interest in a novel subject matter. Such a view fetishizes the early analytic style of Cubism, allowing it a purity of purpose it did not in fact have, for its commitment was not so exclusive. As with the Cubist school, subject matter was pertinent, if not in the conventional manner. Still life, transfigured from a perceived reality into a conceived durability, from an externally given into a temporally formed, remains the constant theme of early Cubism, whether its ostensible subject matter be a figure, a building, a landscape, or the objects of a domestic, if slightly bohemian, world. In Delaunay's pre-*peinture pure* and post-*peinture pure* work there is a similar transformation of subject matter by style, a similar implication of style as a philsophical method converting the given into the conceptually significant. Such transformation achieves its climax in *peinture pure,* when the import of the subject matter is altogether abstracted and separated from its naive givenness in perception, as distinct from its simply being differentiated but not detached from it, as in Delaunay's representational styles. No doubt whatever equilibrium exists between style and subject matter is helped by the sense of the modern character of both, but such modernism exists less to compensate for the inability to create a significant pictorial language, as Cooper thinks, than to enhance the immediacy of sensation, and to suggest new possibilities of visual sensation. More decisively, to be modern was for Delaunay to evoke unexpected possibilities, to be exhilarated by a new vision of reality.[5]

Thus, however strong the presence in Delaunay of themes of "communal significance,"[6] specifically sport and flight, there is an equally strong nonobjective presence in no way explained by an interest in such subject matter, and generally not explained by anything superficially modern, including the assumption that Delaunay was deliberately competitive with the avant-garde, trying to be more original and inventive than the original Cubist inventors.[7] Instead, *peinture pure* is Delaunay's attempt to embody a familiar, even age-old, yet individually difficult to sustain, experience of the numinous and cosmic.[8] Delaunay's interest in modernist subject matter is his attempt to retrieve what is almost irretrievable, i.e., to find suitable symbols to express his profound, vitalizing experience of the infinite, to create the lingering effect of its joyous presence, and to remind us through nostalgia of its eternal possibility.[9] It is the ordinariness of these symbols that matters for Delaunay than their modernity, for by their commonplace concreteness they simplify our transcendence.

In *peinture pure* the balance tilts towards pure style because Delaunay trusts himself to the waters of an "oceanic experience," rather than because of any deliberate attempt to abandon subject matter. Nor is *peinture pure* simply the result of a sustained effort at "expressive control"[10] over visual forms, i.e., the consequence of purely stylistic considerations. The change from *Windows,* works which Delaunay said still involve "a remembrance of concrete reality," specifically of the city, to *Circular Forms,* works which have "their roots neither in any exterior representation, nor allusion to things, nor geometric forms or objects as in Cubism," is essentially a change from experience of the finite to the infinite.[11] This is made explicit by the fact that the *Circular Forms* are usually subtitled "sun" or "moon" or both, a reference to the cosmic bodies most familiar to human beings. On the border of infinite space, they imply the finite in transition to the infinite, their own finitude in the process of dissolution.

Windows and *Circular Forms* are basically similar in kind, the former tied for Delaunay to the cosmos of the city, i.e., the image of urban spaciousness and the scene of human activity, the latter to the impersonal spaciousness of the extended cosmos, the scene of "abstract" planetary and sidereal activity. These works communicate before all else the sensation of cosmos, i.e., of containment, a fundamental concept in the definition of reality for Whitehead.[12] Such containment is conditioned and in a sense defined by the activity it limits insofar as such activity is also conceived abstractly, viz., as pure movement free of any particular purpose. Thus, the *Windows* do not open on the ordinary city, nor do the *Circular Forms* describe ordinary objects—they do not even exist with geometrical accuracy. Instead, both communicate a determinateness beyond any determinate concretion, and establish it as a purely rhythmic presence, the consequence of rhythmic process, i.e., definite matter becomes the effect of indefinite movement. Delaunay's rhythms simultaneously convey expanding space and informal containment, an accessible yet evasive infinite, an enclosed cosmos of indecisive yet vigorous content—a cosmos of forces rather than of forms, of potential rather than actual being. *Windows* and *Circular Forms* are even more intimately united in that they stand to one another as micro- or macro-cosm, sharing the same lack of directionality and obscure demarcation of space—Delaunay remarked that *peinture pure* destroyed horizontality and verticality, the coordinates of space[13]—and strong rhythmic presence, only on different scales. Delaunay's "interpretation," if it may be called that, of analytic Cubist ambiguity of space and direction puts it on a new and superior plane: instead of becoming an exercise in construction, it becomes the sign of cosmic consciousness, transcendence to a *sub specie aeternitatis* point of reference. For Delaunay, the city and the cosmos, abstractly generalized, are realms defined by rhythms, regular patterns of movement, rather than by the matter that seems to be their inhabitant from the ordinary human point of view.[14] Seen *sub specie aeternitatis,* the rhythm of life in the city is conveyed by simultaneous contrasts of colors, and the rhythm of vital movement in the cosmos by a structured continuity of colors.[15] In each case color becomes the ground of differentiated movement as well as, in the purity of its presence, the sign of a "poetic" point of view of reality, a "sublime" outlook.[16] In essence, the city exists in relatively percussive rhythms, to contradict the containment of the window—the picture frame—through which it is seen, which threatens it with limits, while the cosmos at large, limitless to the human eye, is held together by the smoother, calmer rhythm of the circle (in which all color accents harmonize however much they contrast) which symbolizes its unity of being. The circle makes the infinite accessible in a finite form although Delaunay often leaves it incomplete, to keep the implication of infinity clear while the simultaneous color contrasts make the city vibrantly alive if indefinite in the nature of its life.[17] This interplay between the visually definite and indefinite keynotes *peinture pure*. The two are one in rhythm, understood by Delaunay as the fundamental fact of cosmic existence, that which alone stops him from leaving the canvas empty—for what image can do true justice to the sensation of the infinite?—in the equivalent of Mallarmé's blank page.

The cosmic note sounded by *peinture pure* is already present in the very first image (1909?) of the *Eiffel Tower* series, carrying the inscription "The tower addresses the universe—profound movement."[18] It is also in evidence in the arch of St. Severin and the spire of Notre Dame, the redundant vertical reaching its climax and greatest determination in the Eiffel Tower, implying a striving to surmount the world, to climb free of its constraints. It was only in the sense of rhythmic cosmic movement that Delaunay felt fully free of what he called "the horror of constraint" that finitude implies.[19] As he wrote, he felt himself in a state of "poetic purity" and in contact with "the eternal" in experiencing such rhythmic movement, a perceiver of and participant in the "universal drama." *Peinture pure* was for Delaunay the imaginative rendering of cosmic consciousness, "pure" to the extent it was free of ordinary consciousness of objects, and "poetic" in its insistence on transcendence. It seems the visual incarnation of the *"Infini libérateur"* Marinetti wrote of in his poem *A mon Pégasse (A L'Automobile de course)* (1905), in which the sensation of the infinite becomes the abiding end of art, the poem's implication being that, much as Pegasus once transported the poet to an infinite realm, so also will the modern racing car, new symbol of inspiration. It is its speed Delaunay is trying to generate in *peinture pure.*[20]

Marinetti's poem, and certain ambiguities inherent in *peinture pure,* prepare us to understand Delaunay's creation of the second representational style. Where the first heralded *peinture pure,* the second attempted to communicate it in more convenient, social form. This is made possible by the fact that in *peinture pure* objective reality is present by implication, is alluded to, however opaquely. How this is so in the *Windows* is self-evident, the window implying a view of the world, confirmed by the architectonic of colors—what Delaunay called the "phrasing of colors"—suggesting architectural structures.[21] In the *Circular Forms,* the forms themselves, as previously noted, can be taken as symbols of heavenly bodies as well as abstract representations of synchronous movement. The world, in other words, exists as an implication of stylistic method, rather than as an explicit form—exists as a possibility rather than an actuality, a phantom presence rather than a deliberate existence.

This allusive and evasive presence of the world is typical of symbolist art. It is not enough merely to note, as Cooper does, the symbolist tendencies of many members of the Cubist school, including Delaunay,[22] but also to understand the interplay between the symbolist method and *peinture pure.* It is not simply that the symbolist is trying to find a symbol for his sensation in a straightforward substitution of one "idea" for another, a substitution which will presumably allow an immediate translation of the symbol back into the sensation, the depicted object back into its subjective meaning. Rather, the symbolist attempts to indicate, by calling attention to his style, that his depiction is not meant to be taken on face value, e.g., as an imitation of nature, but that it is to be understood as a kind of mirror of the artist himself. The issue of the exactness of the equivalence of sensation and symbol becomes secondary to the question of the role of style, which is inherently ambiguous because of the conflict between its duties to depiction and to the artist. Symbolist art explores this familiar problem of style, its existence as a *double entendre,* in a unique way. For not only does it insist that style owes its existence to the artist before it must pay its debt to depiction, but the depiction itself is made to suggest the artist's subjectivity, so that all pretense to objectivity is lost, and the role of perceived nature destroyed and that of perception per se revolutionized. Totally nonobjective—purely subjective—art was bound to emerge from symbolist art (it is already present in Moreau), and eventually bound to return to a symbolist method to sustain, or simply retain, the special truths it discovered. *Peinture pure* would again seek dependence on the vestige of depiction in symbolism, if only to sustain itself as art, i.e., to give its audience something to see, and because it knows that the spectator's conventional expectation is that objects, however disguised, serve as the vehicle of meaning. That its meaning not become obscured by its method, nonobjective art becomes symbolist, as in the 1960s school of Abstract Imagists.[23] Delaunay was the first French artist to push symbolism into significant nonobjectivity, and the first to return to symbolism for succor—to use the visible and finite to sustain his sense of the invisible and infinite. However, for Delaunay there is a new twist to the symbolist approach: style—synchronous movement—controls the depiction not only on a visual but an ideological level. Thus, in the *Cardiff Team* an analogy is established between the soccer game, the ferris wheel, the Eiffel Tower, and the airplane that is as important as—and in contradiction to—the realism of their depiction. It is because they metaphorically imply the infinite while stylistically they remain deliberately finite and almost naively given that they take on iconic value, become votive offerings to a larger vision of reality. Perception of them is no discovery of objects, but worship before a final limit.

The subject matter of Delaunay's post-*peinture pure* style, e.g., the soccer game, ferris wheel, and airplane, are admirably attuned to the infinite, for they convey, respectively, energy, rhythmic ascent, and the destruction of limits. The return to directionality in this style—the renewed emphasis on verticality—assumes the spectator is no longer in pure possession of infinity, but must assert himself deliberately to grasp it. He must "ride high," and the carnival connotations of the signs in the *Cardiff Team* convey the exhilaration of his effort. More subtly, Delaunay's symbolist works, by depicting scenes of leisure life, a democratic *la vie jolie* in which there is a freer play of emotions and fantasy, permit him to make explicit the profound emotional impact of the sensation of the infinite, which Delaunay compared to the "primary musical emotion provided by Bach" in the fugue,[24] the *Circular Forms,* in fact, existing in a kind of fuguelike, if less strict, arrangement.

In general, Delaunay regularly recapitulated his accomplishments in the signpost of a single, monumental work. Thus, as the *City of Paris* (1911-12) recapitulated the *Eiffel Tower* series, so the *Cardiff Team* and the *Nude Reading* recapitulated the *Circular Forms,* applied them as an unconventional theory might be applied to conventional subject matter. A comparison between the *City of Paris* and *Nude Reading* is particularly instructive, because it shows how indifferent Delaunay is in essence to the modernism of his subject matter. What matters is not that the three graces are a more traditional motif—the nude is not a particularly modernist subject matter—but that the *Nude Reading* is resolved, if not entirely, into dynamic, circular forms, i.e., her flesh is infinitized, its form made into force, its matter into movement. Her being is, as it were, made to speed up. It is only stylistically that she has value, and indeed, the shape of the female body easily implies rhythmic movement. Thus, even in his symbolist works, Delaunay escapes from the ordinary definiteness of things, indicating, in true symbolist fashion, that it is his sensation that matters more than any subject matter. It remains the case that only in *peinture pure* is Delaunay speaking directly about that sensation. In his symbolist works he is showing its possibility for other human beings, the implicit presence of the infinite in the erotic, at moments of play, in the triumphs of technology, wherever there is a reliance on rhythmic, energized movement.

Notes

1. Robert Delaunay. *Du cubisme a l'art abstrait*. Paris, 1957, p. 62.

2. Ibid., p. 67.

3. Douglas Cooper. *The Cubist Epoch*, London, 1970, p. 84.

4. Ibid. p. 99.

5. Ibid., p. 79. While the "new reality" is explicitly associated with *peinture pure* in contrast to traditional painting (Delaunay, p. 83). Delaunay also regards it as the antithesis of "la réalité extérieure" (Delaunay, p. 226). The works which depict it have "une force beaucoup plus efficace" than those which depict nature (Delaunay, p. 68).

6. Cooper, p. 72.

7. Cooper, pp. 69, 104, seems to suggest as much in his discussion of splinter groups within the Cubist movement. Also, his distinction between the "true cubists" (p. 96), like Picasso, Braque, and Léger, whose subject matter "is always static," and Delaunay, the Futurists, and Duchamp, who "wanted to represent movement continuing on evolving in space," seems to suggest the superiority of the hypostatizers to the dynamicists.

8. Francois Gilles de la Tourette. *Robert Delaunay*, Paris, 1950, pp. 45, 50, 54, makes this dimension of *peinture pure* most explicit, without examining it in depth. As late as 1965, as in Bernard Dorival's introduction to the catalogue of an exhibition of the works of Robert and Sonia Delaunay in The National Gallery of Canada, it was argued that the transcendental dimension to Delaunay's abstract works was an extrapolation from his naturalism, in the sense that the pure color which conveyed it was but a symbol of "the inexhaustable life... of nature and the cosmos," and so distinct in kind from Kandinsky's "need to exalt color" with its theosophical overtones. However, this completely contradicts Delaunay's expressed affinity with Kandinsky in a letter to Kandinsky (Delaunay, pp. 178-80) as well as his general observations on, and attitude towards, color.

9. Cooper, p. 108. Cooper's contempt for the symbolists seems evident in his contention that, as in the case of Le Fauconnier, they "simply disguised a conventional allegorical subject by giving it a superficially Cubist look" (p. 71). In Delaunay's case, however, the allegorical subject is unconventional and the "Cubist look" is distinctly his own.

10. As Delaunay, p. 61 argues, at least insofar as *peinture pure* contrasts with more obviously "objective" painting.

11. Delaunay, p. 88.

12. Alfred North Whitehead, *Adventure of Ideas*, New York, 1955, p. 274.

13. Delaunay, p. 61.

14. Delaunay, p. 87 connects urbanism and rhythm. His perhaps most succinct statement of the "tautologous" relationship between color and circular rhythm is as follows (p. 97): "color is used in the sense of a gyration; the form develops in the circular dynamic rhythm of the color." In a more extreme statement in a previously "unpublished autobiography" in the exhibition catalog of the 1965 exhibition of his and his wife's work at the National Gallery of Canada, Delaunay

writes (no page): "It is the colour itself in *purely coloured* painting which through its play of light, sensitivity, rhythms and contrasts, forms the basic structure of rhythmic development and not the collaboration with old means such as geometry." The circle is such an "old means"; its appearance in *peinture pure* ultimately has less to do with its formal and symbolic—traditional—significance, than with its strictly organizational potential. Its contours eventually become contrasts within the color scheme rather than an independently affirmed form.

15.   Delaunay's contrast between line and color (p. 110) makes this point even more tellingly. On p. 111 he insists that "colour-construction" is the "key" of *peinture pure,* in the same way in which a piece of music is written in a given key.

16.   Delaunay, pp. 148, 150 speaks explicitly of his sublime intentions—the sublimity of his art.

17.   For a comprehensive discussion of "simultanisme" see Delaunay, pp. 106-15.

18.   The complete inscription reads "Exposition Universelle 1889. La Tour à l'univers s'adresse—mouvement profondeur 1909 France-Russie."

19.   Delaunay, pp. 141, 147. For Delaunay, the horror of constraint can be overcome only by the sublime—the active pursuit of the infinite.

20.   For Delaunay's ambiguous relationship to the futurists see Delaunay, pp. 135-43.

21.   Delaunay (p. 69) makes clear his awareness of the "architectural" implications of his color constructions.

22.   Cooper, p. 108.

23.   See H.H. Arnason, *Abstract Imagists,* New York, 1963, the catalog of an exhibition held at the Guggenheim Museum.

24.   Delaunay, p. 63. See also Delaunay, p. 67, where Delaunay compares his work to "bon jazz," and p. 97, where he compares his color rhythms to musical rhythms.

10

Malevich's Quest for Unconditioned Creativity

The principal phases of Malevich's art from 1910-1920 are: (1) colorism; (2) depiction of the eternal peasant; (3) estheticism; (4) simple Suprematism; (5) constructive Suprematism; (6) monumental Suprematism; and (7) depiction of the cross form. Simple Suprematism might also be called axiomatic Suprematism, in that it presents the terms of Malevich's Suprematist statement, or more precisely, argument, viz., the geometrical figure and neutral field, in a conflict which initially takes the tame dialectical form of juxtaposition. The Suprematist relationship between figure and field becomes strongly dialectical in the brief but pointed phase of monumental Suprematism, in which figure and field tend to, but never do fuse. The perpetual possibility of their unity gives their conflict a poignant, subtly dynamic edge, telling of Suprematism's ultimate goal—the communication of pure feeling. Thus, there is continuity between the Suprematist phases, but nonetheless a conflict of motivation, for while simple Suprematism aims to communicate pure feeling, constructive Suprematism with its obvious complication of figural forms aims to communicate pictorial-plastic feeling. Simple Suprematism uncovers the subliminal world of human feeling, making sensuously explicit what is emotionally implicit, while constructive Suprematism uncovers the subliminal world of pictorial forms, which interrelate to ground the sense of plastic movement. Such forms are usually disguised by the world-signifying content of the picture, much as, for Malevich, private emotions are usually hidden by public actions. In the last analysis Malevich's ambition, in his manifestoes as well as his art, is to communicate as directly as possible the fundamentality of feeling, rather than of action or intellect.

Monumental Suprematism is a successful, if momentary, attempt to unite simple and constructive Suprematism. It rids simple Suprematism of its intense contrast of form and field, giving form a power dependent on its "community" with field—indicated by their shared whiteness—rather than their geometry (e.g., *White on White*). The field converts, from the backdrop or setting of the form, explicitly into its ground. No longer simply the site of the form, it is the field that gives the figure decisive presence, rather than the innate geometrical nature of the form itself. That is, what the form acquires from the field becomes more decisive for its existence than what it is in itself. That the field openly becomes the ground and locates—if not exclusively—within the closed form, exemplifies Malevich's belief that pure feeling is formed in and echoes an existential situation of void. Monumental Suprematism rids constructive Suprematism of its almost anarchic, certainly arbitrary, abundance of forms: it regresses to the simplicity of the first Suprematist phase, retaining the perceptual ambiguities generated by constructive Suprematism. These irresolvable ambiguities make explicit that neither geometrical form nor neutral void can ever overcome each other in the tense conflict between them.

Malevich's depiction of the eternal peasant reveals that figural forms are bound by a "higher" necessity than nature, yet implied by nature. Suprematism treats this necessity—it cannot unqualifiedly be called artistic—as a phenomenon in itself, abstracting it entirely from the context of nature, and presenting it as an implication of forms grounded geometrically. In general, phases one and seven are "conventional," dominated by stereotype forms and ideas, presented unambiguously. Phases two and three are "stylistic," in the sense that their major ambition is to manufacture works of art that, whatever else they may imply, are meant to be modern, i.e., au courant and on a par with the advanced style of the day, in Malevich's case, cubo-futurism. Finally, the Suprematist phases are primarily "creative," i.e., decidedly unconventional and not so much concerned to participate in the modern revolution in art as to communicate existential feeling.

1. *Colorism.* The following works are typical of this phase: *Province*, 1910 (1); *Chiropodist at the Baths*, 1910 (3); *Greenhouses (Carrying Earth)*, 1910 (4); *Village* (5) and (6); *The Bather*, 1910 (8); *On the Boulevard*, 1910 (9); and *Argentine Polka*, 1911 (10).[1] In *Man with Sack*, 1911 (11) the eternal peasant makes his first appearance, and in *Peasant Women at Church*, 1911 (25) the type is treated, if not completely, in colorist terms. Beginning with *Peasant Woman with Buckets*, 1912 (27) color is largely contained by form, and the relationship between colors regularized. This new stability of color correlates with Malevich's change from gouache and paper to oil and canvas. In general, Malevich's handling, while loose, tends to confine colors in patterns of contrast within an ever more disciplined picture. In a sense, Malevich's painting can be understood as a successful attempt to bring coloristic effect under the control of objective order, to rid the perception of color from Dionysian implication by bringing it under the control of Apollonian form. In Suprematism, form so completely constrains and sublimates color that it no longer creates the "delirium" Malevich originally meant it to effect. Instead, particularly in axiomatic Suprematism, color becomes meditative, defining the form it marks as a place of entry into clear consciousness of feeling. Only in monumental Suprematism does Malevich dispense with color as a catalyst, realizing it is not essential to the communication of pure feeling.

Malevich's coloristic pictures, while expressionistically motivated, are less intense than Kandinsky's almost contemporary Murnau pictures. Malevich never discovers expressionistic antagonism against content—color as an enemy of the conventionally visible world—as Kandinsky does. Nor does he attempt, as Kandinsky does, to bring his pictures under the control of "inner necessity," to extinguish nature's apprearance into a spiritual pictorial pattern. In fact, at this stage, Malevich lacks a decisive artistic direction, not to speak of an artistic destiny. It will be shown that Malevich later comes to these not through art—through a struggle for his own style—but rather through his attempt to master content, in particular to penetrate to the meaning of the peasant. The eternal truth the peasant symbolizes is secularized by Malevich's cubo-futurization of him—a treatment which has the effect of removing him from nature—and is nonnaturally or abstractly articulated in Suprematism. The "message" of the eternal peasant remains in Suprematism, but purified of natural connotation and conventional depiction.

Expressionism confronts natural destiny with artistic destiny. It struggles against the self-evidence of nature to make art's power evident and to ground it independently of nature. Man is fated by nature; expressionism is one more, if violent attempt to show that art is part of man's fate, a weapon in the war against natural fate. But Malevich's colorism offers no alternative to natural appearance, for it neither consistently reduces it to essentials nor does it spiritually transform nature by imbuing it with esthetic purpose. Instead, Malevich simplistically identified with nature, naively translating its obvious vitality in color This is perhaps evident in *Chiropodist at the Baths,* 1910 (3), where the pail and the foot on the stool are green and brown, appropriating the colors of the earth they rest on. In a later (1916) rationalization of his extravagant use of color to vitalize natural presence, Malevich makes clear the completeness of his identification with nature and color. Nature is "a living picture" of which we are "the living heart," and color "lies within our organism," for our nervous system is colored and our brain "burns" with earth colors. "Color was oppressed by common-sense, was enslaved by it," its "spirit...weakened and died out"[2]—until Malevich's uncommon-sensical pictures freed and revived it. However, Malevich's words speak louder and stronger than his pictures' colors, although, admittedly, axiomatic and constructive Suprematism refine colors, particularly blue and yellow, into radical nonnaturalness and powerful concentration.

2. *Depiction of the eternal peasant.* However vital its implications, the color of Malevich's first formative phase wears thin because he is ultimately interested less in nature's vitality than in its eternality, exemplified particularly by the stoical peasants directly dependent on and in communion with nature. Fatalistically, they accept its givenness, their stolid substance and expressionless features corresponding to nature's own inert durability. They endure its seasons with indifferent bodies, as in *Morning in the Village after Snowfall,* 1912 (32). Their only activity is whatever is necessary for survival, such as hauling water, as

in *Peasant Woman with Buckets,* 1912 (27; coloristic version) (34; cubo-futuristic version); harvesting grain, as in *Reaping Woman* (26) and *Taking in the Rye,* 1912 (28); chopping wood, as in *The Woodcutter,* 1912 (29); and keeping necessary instruments in working condition, as in *The Knife-Grinder,* 1912 (37). The peasant manifests nature by his survival in it. The primitive simplicity of his life indicates the elementary level on which he endures, and emphasizes his closeness to nature. His plodding character mimics its eternality, duplicates its innocent inevitability. The peasant's fatalism—sign of his belief that nature is his fate—becomes evident in his face (18–20, 30) and leads to religious resignation, as in *The Orthodox* (31). Malevich's peasant ultimately becomes as durable as stone, a dead object in nature rather than a living person in the world, as in the climactic *Head of a Peasant Girl,* 1912 (33). In this picture the human is decisively objectified into the impassively immortal, its individuality destroyed in the name of its eternality.

In general, Malevich's peasant is heavy in body, mood, and manner, a case study of a possible effect of the eternal on man, particularly as manifest through nature: it makes him inert, its "gravity" binds him to the earth and makes him inflexible. He endures, but less as a vital self than as a heavy, almost inorganic form. His style of being demonstrates the law of fate determining man's narrow lot, and the restricted mobility, mental as well as physical, which is its consequence. Thus, there is no play of expression on the face of Malevich's peasant, his body's movements seem clumsy and contrived, as those of a tree uprooting itself. To walk, Malevich's peasant must rip his root-foot from the earth; as it returns, it spontaneously reroots, and must again be uprooted for the next step. In general, Malevich's treatment of peasant feet, as in *Man with Sack,* 1911 (11), *The Gardener,* 1911 (12), *Floor Polishers,* 1911 (13), *Peasant Woman with Buckets,* 1912 (27), and *Taking in the Rye,* 1912 (28), symbolizes the peasant's closeness to the earth, taking the intention of Van Gogh's depiction of peasant shoes a step further. In a sense, Malevich's poor depiction of movement epitomizes his view of eternal nature, which immobilizes man while giving him its strength. Antaeus-like, he is so rooted in nature he cannot adventure from it. The pictures in which Malevich depicts the eternal peasant are pervaded by the stillness of a being, perhaps best represented by the monumental *Washing Woman,* 1911 (17), that is sure of itself but forever bound by an unchanging—and so ultimate—situation.

Malevich's attitude to the peasant can be succinctly shown by comparing, in general terms, his treatment with Bruegel's. Breugel's peasant also labors anonymously in nature, but with a fuller life than Malevich's. Breugel's peasant reflects the power as well as grandeur of nature, which gives him vigor as well as dignity. But Malevich's nature overwhelms the peasant's humanity, denying the peasant the heroic intensity and at times ironical relationship with nature that Breugel allows him. Malevich's peasants labor under a burden and are themselves deadweights. Breugel's peasants are energized by the nature they are submerged in, and are as likely to be violently and spontaneously erotic as plodding and stoic. Breugel's peasants are alive with natural instinct, but Malevich's peasants, inherently dead, are enlivened by the planar disruptions of cubo-futurist style.

The peasant's totemic integrity remains intact even under these disruptions, which, in fact, articulate his inertia more pointedly. Although Malevich reduces the peasant's body to planes it retains, Léger-like, its bulk and stockiness. Its relationship with surrounding space is thus never as ambiguous as it would be in the customary cubo-futurist work. Moreover, Malevich's planes tend to be closed rather than open, as in more typical Cubist works, and as in Malevich's own estheticist phase. The weight and insularity of Malevich's planes stabilize the peasant figure they constitute, inhibiting the familiar cubo-futurist spatial dynamics. Ultimately, such figural stability reciprocates Malevich's traditional use of the canvas as a receptacle, particularly his reluctance, in this formative phase, of reconceiving it as a field. For most of its development Malevich's canvas remains a receptacle into which content is placed, rather than a surface flattening into a field which tends to absorb content—figuratively into the mind which is aware of it. However flat—depthless, spaceless—Malevich's canvas becomes, it generally preserves a residue of recognizable if ill-defined—peripheral and perspectiveless—space, functionally often no more than a minimal margin, or an incompletely determinate frame for the figural forms. The best Cubist works tend to absorb this margin, or else bring it under strict control by articulating it explicitly, as in the use of the oval, an artist- rather than spectator-imposed frame. But Malevich leaves the margin intact and legible as a suggestion of natural space. The eternal peasant pictures can thus be read discursively—traditionally—however much their content is presented in modern style. This discrepancy continues into the Suprematist pictures, where it is not always clear whether the canvas is a field or a receptacle, since it often functions simultaneously as both. However, in Suprematism the discrepancy—in which the geometrical forms seem to fit into the space of the canvas as well as partake of its flatness—is used to advantage to effect a psychic rather than strictly visible content, to evoke the world of pure feeling rather than simply to register the shapes from which perception, when it becomes a picture, is composed. But in his eternal peasant phase Malevich remains committed to a conventional kind of perception, despite his protestations to the contrary—despite his insistence that it is necessary to have a novel kind of consciousness to grasp his works.

The question, then, is why Malevich turned from colorism to cubo-futurism in his depiction of the eternal peasant. Was he updating his style, or was there a reason, inherent to the content, that turned him into a cubo-futurist? The latter is the case, for cubo-futurism is used unconventionally by Malevich. In the depiction of the eternal peasant it is less a means to mobilize immobile matter and to force vision to become spontaneous—to make connections itself, rather than to await them from the picture—than it is a way of emphasizing the passivity of the eternal peasant by reducing his being and world to a residue of inert planes. Cubo-futurism is not used naively to modernize Malevich's style, but analytically to create unitary, static, elementary planes, making the eternality of the peasant a visible constant. It is given its first formal appearance, in contrast to its informal manner of presence through colorism. In a sense, cubo-futurism phenomenologically reduces perception of the eternal peasant, thus more clearly revealing his meaning. He is no longer seen in his natural existence, but as eternally formed—constituted by universal geometrical shapes—and so as self-evidently eternal.

From another point of view, Malevich's eternal peasant begins as a plodding beast, as in *The Bather,* 1910 (8) and *Man with Sack,* 1911 (11), and ends as a primitive machine, as in *Peasant Woman with Buckets,* 1912 (34) and *The Knife-Grinder,* 1912 (37). In cubo-futurism Malevich is already implicitly the Cartesian he will explicitly become in Suprematism, for the cubo-futurized peasant can be conceived as the body-machine of Descartes' *Passions of the Soul.* In Suprematism the picture itself can be spoken of as a machine, its physiognomic implications simply the illusion of its "physiology." Malevich's cubo-futurist peasant is still physiognomically legible, but only because his planar organs hold together in a body. The question of Suprematism is whether an organization of mechanical forms to create the body of a picture—a "nonhumanistic" holding together of abstract forms—has physiognomic implications. Or is it legible only as an anatomizing of the picture, its forms analytically displayed in one of an infinite number of ways? Is the abstract picture in general and the Suprematist picture in particular an anatomy lesson of art or the revelation of pure, structured form as innately rich with physiognomic implications more profound than any communicated by the familiar surfaces of appearance? Is the Suprematist picture a "kind of qualitative combinatorics"[3] of abstract forms or an existential revelation?

3. *Estheticism.* Typical of this phase are: *Musical Instrumental/Lamp,* 1913 (39); *The Guardsman,* 1913 (40); *Desk and Room,* 1913 (41); *Woman at the Tram Stop,* 1913 (42); *An Englishman in Moscow,* 1913-14 (43); *Woman at Poster Column,* 1914 (44); and *Warrior of the First Division,* 1914 (45). A regressive interlude, these works show Malevich preoccupied with style and self-consciously modern. Dully successful, they hold their own with similar Cubist school products, and like them include a certain amount of obvious content, in Malevich's case more nativist. However, Malevich's estheticist works do not have the Cubist school's tendency to become poster art.[4] Instead, their content is not so much advertised by their style as disruptive of it. Content intrudes through style, and is incompletely assimilated by it. Subject matter is almost anarchistically woven through the estheticist picture, violently contradicting its conventional Cubist synthetic style. For example, in *An Englishman in Moscow,* 1913-14 (43) content decisively "transcends" estheticist form—the fish is not caught by its net—and is thus revealed as startlingly real. Its presence disrupts

the organic unity of the work in a way the usual appearance/reality dialectic of Cubism does not.

In general, there is no subtlety in the way reality breaks through the stylistic facade of Malevich's estheticist works, almost redeeming them. It is a blustering, blunt invasion of Russian reality into Francophiliac style, suggesting that Malevich's first priority remains the revelation of reality rather than the creation of his own style. Many of the estheticist works, particularly those of 1914, have a patriotic impetus, having to do with Russia's involvement in World War I and the resulting awareness of a larger world. But the main "creative" point is the refusal of reality to submit to art, even modern beauty's inability to overcome reality's coarse givenness. In Malevich's estheticist works reality is as much an untransformed content as a pictorial constituent. This ambiguity is in the end resolved by a leap beyond it and all estheticism to a Suprematist sense of reality as feeling—rather than object-oriented—and into a Suprematist sense of style as directly mediating reality rather than unwittingly obscuring it by beautifying it.

4. *Simple or axiomatic Suprematism.* Typical are: *Suprematist Painting, Black and Red Square,* 1915 (46); *Suprematist Painting, Eight Red Rectangles,* 1915 (47); *Aeroplane Flying,* 1915 (49); *Football Match,* 1915 (51); *Suprematism, Eighteenth Construction,* 1915 (52); *Suprematist Painting,* 1915 (53); and *Suprematist Painting, Black Rectangle, Blue Triangle,* 1915 (54). From one point of view these works are a radical clarification of Cubism, in the Purist vein, but one reductionist step further. However, where Purism restores cognizable conventional content, Suprematism cuts the Gordian knot that ties the recognizable to the habitually objective. Unlike Cubism, Suprematism is concerned neither with the painting's objecthood nor the vestige or phantom of reality remembered in it, but rather, a primordial objective content—geometrical forms—meant to imply primordial subjectivity. In Suprematism there is no echo of familiar reality. The integrity the work wins over the world is a Pyrrhic victory if it does not lead to a new sense of ultimate subjective reality. The question of Suprematism is whether indeed the world of feeling it is meant to imply is in fact evoked by its works.

Simple Suprematism primitively deploys universal forms to construct a purely visual world. It is a trial run in launching a world of appearances altogether free of the world of customary appearances, however much the titles of the works refer to that world. Such a nonnatural or abstract world is postulated on the assumption that it in some sense corresponds to, or is a privileged means of evoking, a more essential world than is ordinarily apparent. In a sense, it is this more essential world that is the true content of the Suprematist picture, for the possibility of revealing it is the only justification—apart from the myth of or a priori belief in pure art—for transcending the world of ordinary perception. Either the Suprematist picture is an empty image, a purification of forms in the name of a tautologous—hermetic and narcissistic—art, or it is a depth experience of a more meaningful world than the immediately given one.

That the Suprematist work is the latter rather than the former is apparent only after its physical forms have been forcefully asked to disclose their meaning. To presume this meaning—the implication of primordial feeling—from the beginning is to short-circuit its full effect, to trivialize its presence. The Suprematist picture is an anvil on which the spectator hammers his consciousness into an instrument for perceiving its subtleties. In the course of refining his awareness of the work he comes to make demands on it which it cannot satisfy. These demands are neither excessive nor inappropriate. They show consciousness its need for meaning, and work to the advantage of the Suprematist picture, giving its seemingly mechanical forms a depth of possible meaning. Because consciousness expects the Suprematist work to have meaning, its forms become revolutionized in significance. Consciousness, strained by the Suprematist work by being disrupted in its relations with—in effect being ripped away from—the world of ordinary perception, demands such significance. The world becomes invisible in the simple Suprematist picture, and in compensation for its sacrifice consciousness must be given entry into a world of extraordinary significance. Unless the sacrifice of the world of ordinary perception is made in the name of a higher purpose it becomes a meaningless gesture of pure art. The result is not so much high abstract art as a new estheticism.

In general, in the perception of the Suprematist work consciousness itself becomes revolutionized. Its response to the Suprematist picture's radical simplicity—to the picture's mechanical forms and seeming emptiness—leads consciousness to discover its need for meaning, to become aware of its orginal motivation. Self-conscious, it affirms the integrity of its own existence over against the world's. It is neither the mirror of the world nor the picture, as the abstract picture is no longer the mirror of ordinary consciousness or of other pictures. Thus the abstract picture is the catalyst for pure or self-reflective consciousness—consciousness aware of its implicit purpose—and such consciousness, purified by perception of the abstract picture, becomes aware of its existence as primordial feeling, or the feeling of creative potential. Thus, deviously, Suprematism realizes its purpose—the revelation of the world of pure feeling, the disclosure of the innate nature of consciousness.

How and in what specific terms does the depth experience of the Suprematist picture operate? Reduced to two essential terms, form and field, the picture shocks perception. The shock of reduction, contradicting the conventional expectation that a picture mirror a given world, is sufficient to make the spectator self-conscious. Today no longer shocking, such reduction has become matter-of-fact. The original contempt, outrage, skepticism—all attempts to keep the status quo of consciousness—with which it was countered have dissipated, and abstraction has become a convention. Yet it was the original negative response to abstraction that created the possibility of a depth experience of it. To deal with his defensive doubt and bafflement and to overcome the Suprematist pictue, the shocked, skeptical spectator must examine the intention of the work and conceptually reconstitute it. He can, of course, naively dismiss it, but he cannot remain in the precarious state of contemptuously perceiving it. Committing himself to examining the work, he changes his consciousness, putting it on the path to self-discovery. But he can satisfy his hunger for understanding only after he denies the dumb, mechanical character the picture had to contemptuous perception, and allows it a dialectical character, experiences it as a conflict between form and field. The Suprematist picture becomes the tension between value- (color-) charged form and neutral (uncharged) field. The picture becomes—and Suprematism is the unfolding of—the paradoxical relation between the two. The picture becomes a contradiction between the forms it thrusts at the spectator and the field that falls back to its own foundation. It wavers between colored forms which project it beyond itself and flat forms which are reabsorbed by the field from which they emerged.

The tension heightens as, in the course of perception, the field seems overly neutral, overly white. It comes to seem almost monstrous when it is realized that its total emptiness—consummate nothingness—makes it a poor foundation for the forms. Thus, in simple Suprematism, the field is neither easily characterized in itself nor necessarily linked to forms. It is essentially an absence that is in fundamental contradiction to the forms' presence, neither grounding nor opposing them, but simply altogether other than what they are. As such, it creates an uncertainty which undermines the forms' certainty. The field is an invisibility that becomes a possible alternative to the forms' visibility, an indeterminate constituent that is as essential to the picture as its forms determinate character. The simple integrity of the forms seems to resist the field's barrenness. Because the Suprematist picture was meant to exist on a philosophical plane, as Malevich implied when he asserted that "The square=feeling, the white field=the void beyond this feeling,"[5] the conflict between form and field becomes an ontic expression of the ontological tension between primordial something or "thereness" and primordial nothing (nonbeing). This tension, which existentially cannot be lessened because of the presence of death, lets us view Suprematism as an endless ontological debate about the very possibility of being.

This fundamental level is not always sustained, and in the second Suprematist phase seems altogether lost. In that "constructive" phase Malevich's pictorial-plastic instinct—his wish to make art objects—interferes. His desire to relate forms rhythmically mutes awareness of the field. One suspects, in view of the succeeding phase of monumental Suprematism, which achieves a final solution to the problem of the relationship of form and field, that Malevich's desire to create a rhythm of forms—to give them organic power—is compensatory for the field's complete lack of plasticity. It also amounts to an attempt to ignore the form-field distinction, emphasizing instead the interrelation of forms. This is indicative of a desire to abandon the ontological implications of Suprematism—perhaps because they are difficult to sustain—

and simply create a "dynamic" picture, muting all existential appeal and restoring the picture to ordinary perception.

An incidental character of the Suprematist picture is its lack of value for survival, which might seem irrelevant were it not for the fact that an important purpose of the traditional picture is to orient the spectator to a familiar world. This lack of survival value unconsciously adds to abstraction's shock value. It leaves the spectator in the lurch, for it does not confirm familiar beliefs about the world as representational art usually does. Like the new mathematically grounded science the new abstractionism in art created an apparently unbridgeable gap between the reality it "described"—to the ordinary mind, arbitrarily created—and experienced reality. And like the new science neither the truth-value nor the human use of the new abstractionism were self-evident. Only after Malevich began to "engineer" his forms did Suprematism seem to have implications for the human world, for it acquired architectural implications and became a playful lesson in making art. But this heralded the collapse of Suprematism's deeper human purpose, the revelation of primordial consciousness, which Malevich eventually codified in the religious form—and cliché—of the cross.

5. *Constructive Suprematism.* Typical works are: *Suprematist Painting,* 1915 (48, 55), 1915-16 (57, 58), 1916 (60), and 1917 (61); and *Supremus No. 50,* 1915 (56). Constructive Suprematism establishes Suprematism as a full-blown artistic phenomenon, no longer fragile and perishable, but full of modern bravado about a new destiny for art. The import of this phase is in its turbulence, geometry and color becoming increasingly various and complicated, as if to imply the infinite possibilities of their interaction. In general, constructive Suprematism is a tour de force of artistic creation, reasserted as a phenomenon *sui generis,* and more physical than psychic in its effect.

However, one might argue that the informational bits—the facts of form— exist as suspended particles in "Brownian movement." The field in this phase is more a continuum than an absence. Forms are suspended in it, tentatively moving in an overall pattern approximating a message. In a sense, constructive Suprematism creates an abstract picturesque world from bits and pieces of forms. The continuum gives it life, and deemphasizes the primordial character of the forms by giving them momentum. A world of its own inhabited by intelligible forms, the constructive Suprematist picture foreshadows Malevich's regressive and didactic attempt to conceive the abstract picture as a reconstructed natural world. It foreshadows the attempt to reduce abstraction to a novel source of dynamic effect, giving it a fixed role in art, and to establish a relationship between ordinary perception and transcendental consciousness by fiat.

6. *Monumental Suprematism.* Only a few works exemplify Suprematism's climax: *Suprematist Painting* 1917 (63), 1917-18 (64, 65), and after 1920 (70); and *White Square on White,* 1918 (66). Monumental Suprematism fulfills the promise of axiomatic Suprematism, creating an even more consummate

simplicity. The reciprocity of form and field is definitively asserted: they are shown to be distinct but not separate, in effect rooted in one another. Fewer forms are used than in axiomatic Suprematism, and their color is neutralized in all but one of the works (65). Even it implies, by reason of the fact that one of the edges of its form is open, the bleeding or fading away of colorful form into the neutral field.

Form and field differentiate yet fuse, unify yet declare themselves antithetical to one another. By reason of its constituents, the monumental Suprematist picture becomes subtly and vibrantly self-contradictory, and thus freshly charged. Abstract form reduces to an essential minimum, as if to generate a maximum effect—as if, in compensation for its own superficiality, it must deepen consciousness. Despite its monumentality, the form loses in forcefulness because it blends into the field however much its outline makes it distinct. Analogously, consciousness of the picture becomes equivocal, for while one is aware of the iconic power of the singular form its integrity is undermined by the field, and loses clear meaning. Thus, the conflict between form and field begun in the first Suprematist phase is more intense than ever. The ontological import is more subtle, and the monumental Suprematist picture acquires the clarity and distinctness of an idea, as if to transcend its own facticity.

The negative nature of the field and the positive nature of the form are affirmed through one another, showing polarity—the ultimate source of plasticity—necessary to constitute a picture. This is less evident in axiomatic Suprematism, where form and field are exaggeratedly independent of one another, each challenging the other with its own autonomy. But in monumental Suprematism the abstract form seems a consequence of the self-differentiation or individuation of the field. The picture as a whole becomes a kind of transcendental illusion, or evokes what is called "Maya." The feeling of nothingness symbolized by the field and the sensation of being symbolized by the minimal form exist simultaneously, the one spontaneously evoking the other, because neither can exist without the other. The ontological import of Suprematism acquires new depth, for it is created by a union of ultimate opposites. Malevich criticizes Cubism by giving it, although in a different form, the "philosophical freedom" Duchamp thought it needed. Through Suprematism as well as Dadaism art acquires the philosophical dimension without which it is nothing but a matter of style.

7. *Depiction of the cross form.* Examples are: *Suprematist Painting,* after 1920 (68, 69, 71-73); and *Suprematist Cross Painting,* 1920 (67). The Suprematist picture declines in significance when it unites the horizontal and vertical in a conventional cross form, restoring a naive frame of mind. The typical sense of tilting in the simple Suprematist picture reduces to cheap magic, becoming an ornamental backdrop (67, 72, 73) for the cross. When the cross itself tilts a naively picturesque effect results (68). This picturesqueness helps convey the cross's Christian message, for by the use of the circle (72) or oval (73)

frame the cross becomes conventionally orthodox (Celtic). Malevich's cross works are a shortcut to a sense of eternality. They trivialize his intentions and dogmatize his philosophy, not to speak of his art.

The cross works lack Suprematist constructive power or impacted monumentality. They are a false climax, attempting to usurp the power of monumental Suprematism, from which they are a decline. They give an answer where other Suprematist works raise a question. In them Suprematism's metaphysical ambitions collapse, and end in the old faith. Following the first three Suprematist phases they seem inexcusably reactionary, and antithetical to philosophical freedom, which is replaced by religious faith. Suprematism, which was a heroically inadequate art, has now become a trivially adequate art offering no subtle uncertainty to explore. The Suprematist cross appears less as an unexpected revelation, conveying miraculous meaning, than as the relic of an alien world. It is a regression to ordinary representation and conventional meaning, signifying that apprehension of content has again become riskless for content has again become obvious. Malevich's consciousness becomes so completely one with the cross as to be not only its mirror but the grave it marks. The Suprematist cross is the sign of Malevich's weariness with primordiality, and of a retreat from it into a conventional consciousness of ultimacy.

Notes

1. The numbers in parentheses are those used by T. Andersen in his *Malevich* catalogue (Amsterdam, 1970) to chronologically order the works.

2. Quoted by Andersen, p. 51-52.

3. James K. Feibleman, *Inside the Great Mirror,* The Hague, 1958, p. 61.

4. Douglas Cooper, *The Cubist Epoch,* London, 1970, p. 84. Malevich repeatedly denies estheticist intention (see Andersen,pp. 51-52) but his disclaimers offer a dogmatic religious alternative. In general, he tries to avoid discussion of the concrete character of his work by attributing cosmic implications to it. Thus, he remarks: "Neither color nor form are elements with which it would be possible to reveal or give shape to various sensations, since each sensation is an element of the whole sum of the forces of the universe" (quoted in Andersen, p. 53). This 1930 statement retrospectively articulates the paradox that is at the heart of Suprematism; namely, the more precisely one "devalues" sensation the more cosmic it seems to become in its implications. However, it devalues the physical constituents of pictorial form in the name of inflated claims for its psychic effect.

5. Kasimir Malevich, "Suprematism," *Modern Artists on Art,* ed. Robert L. Herbert, Englewood Cliffs, New Jersey, 1964, p. 96.

11

To Interpret or Not to Interpret Jackson Pollock

In place of hermeneutics we need an erotics of art.
—Susan Sontag, "Against Interpretation"

Since the time of the German romantics...the task of hermeneutics has been defined as avoiding misunderstanding.
—Hans-Georg Gadamer, "Aesthetics and Hermeneutics"

The meaning of Jackson Pollock's paintings, particularly the all-over pictures, has always been in question. But the real question is whether we want them to have a meaning, or more precisely, whether they need a meaning to make sense. In 1947 Clement Greenberg insisted that Pollock's work had, in their "very abstractness and absence of assignable definition, a more reverberating meaning." Even earlier, in 1944, Robert Motherwell wrote that Pollock's "principal problem is to discover what his true *subject* is. And since painting is his thought's medium, the resolution must grow out of the process of painting itself." But the resolution does not seem to have emerged, at least with any clarity, from the process. The true subject seems uncertain, although, as Thomas Hess wrote in 1964, it has to be a "Big Subject." And yet this, too, may be a false subject, for as long as any subject remains uncertain there is no way we can be sure of its quality. The sense that something important is happening in Pollock's paintings does not tell us that they are about important things.

In 1962, Greenberg attacked the problem more directly. Rather than trying to impose still another interpretation on Pollock's paintings, he argued that their only possible meaning grew out of the fact that they were made as art. Any approach which ignored their meaning as art gave Pollock's paintings a cultural determination which interfered with our aesthetic experience of them. The point was to see their power and importance as art, and not locate them culturally, for to do so neutralized them aesthetically. Thus, noting that Harold Rosenberg's conception of "Action Painting" originated "late in the same year as Pollock's Paris show," Greenberg writes:

Transposing some notions from Heidegger's and Sartre's Existentialism, Mr. Rosenberg explained that these painters (Abstract Expressionists) were not really seeking to arrive at art, but rather to discover their own identities through the unpremeditated and more or less uncontrolled acts by which they put paint to canvas.... The covered canvas was left over as the unmeaning aftermath of an "event," the solipsistic record of purely personal "gestures," and belonged therefore to the same reality that breathing and thumbprints, love affairs and war belonged to, but not works of art.[1]

Susan Sontag, in 1964, picked up and in fact dogmatized this idea. The point is to "reveal the sensuous surface of art without mucking about in it." What is needed, writes Sontag, are "acts of criticism" which "would supply a real accurate, sharp, loving description of the appearance of a work of art." Such acts would witness "*transparence*...the highest, most liberating value in art.... Transparence means experiencing the luminousness of the thing in itself, of things being what they are." Any art and its criticism should show "a directness that entirely frees us from the itch to interpret." "The sensory experience of the work of art cannot be taken for granted, now," and since interpretation takes it for granted, "and proceeds from there," it overlooks the essential nature of the work of art, i.e., its living presence in immediate experience.[2] We must "experience more immediately what we have," but interpretation, because of its insistence on abstract schemes of meaning as mediators for what we have, undoes the notion of immediate experience. For Sontag, "to interpret is to impoverish, to deplete the world—in order to set up a shadow world of 'meanings'."[3]

In her attack on interpretation Sontag insists that she doesn't "mean interpretation in the broadest sense, the sense in which Nietzsche (rightly) says, 'There are no facts, only interpretations.' By interpretation, I mean here a conscious act of the mind which illustrates a certain code, certain 'rules' of interpretation."[4] In other words, she is against interpretation which reduces art, or the world, to an example of the general principle, the case in point which "proves" an idea. But she is in fact more absolutely against interpretation than she admits, for she regards it as "the revenge of the intellect upon the world" and art. Interpretation does more than force experience into a Procrustes bed of consciousness. Interpretation analytically dismembers experience so that it cannot be reconstituted as a whole. It permanently reduces to a number of themes, sometimes logically, sometimes illogically related, but never recovers the original intense unity of the experience. This reduction is epitomized in the idea that there is a content to experience, separable from its form. Aesthetic experience is particularly susceptible to such nihilistic reduction to content, which becomes a convenient way of showing, as Greenberg puts it, that works of art belong "to the same reality" as other things. As Sontag says, "the habit of approaching works of art in order to *interpret* them...sustains the fancy that there really is such a thing as the content of a work of art." For her, "the idea of content is today mainly a hindrance, a nuisance, a subtle or not so subtle philistinism," which distracts from "what is needed, first," i.e., "more attention to form in art." Only form can convey "the naked power of . . . art": can show whether the art is "real" enough "to make us nervous," as all truly "real" art does. Thus, interpretation of art, revealing "a wish to replace it by something else," in effect represses its power and form, the source of that power. Interpretation, by emphasizing content, makes the art comfortable rather than nerve-racking. Interpretation, by eliminating the art in art, pulls out its sting. In her 1965 essay "On Style," a follow-up on her essay "Against Interpretation," Sontag defines content as "the pretext, the goal, the lure which engages consciousness in essentially *formal* processes of transformation."[5] It is not the theme we discover after the work of art is complete, but the catalyst that triggers its existence. But by this explanation content reduces to "metaphysical" nonsense, to a tautological affirmation of the work's formal power, which is exactly where Sontag wants it to be.

Now Pollock's all-over pictures seem eminently suitable to be the subject of an erotics of art. With their painterly directness, they seem unqualifiedly immediate in impact—ungraspable by any instruments of mediation. All the interpretations of them, which range from the art historical to psychoanalytic and autobiographical, seem to leave the works untouched. They remain as fresh as ever, their immediacy unchallenged, their directness unmitigated, their sensuous reality unsullied by ratiocinative machinations. They seem to be made to be lovingly described. Yet one wonders whether loving description will do justice to their freshness, bring out their apparent transparence and luminosity. A general consideration emerges in the course of description: does it not fail— blur—the work as much as interpretation? With more irremediable damage? Description, because it does not expect to lose contact with the work, because it does not doubt its sense of the work's immediacy—because it does not suspect itself—misleads more than interpretation. Worse yet, because it is unaware of the inherent inadequacy of language to its task, description cannot prepare us for misunderstanding—a misunderstanding it cannot avoid because it is so sure of its object and so unself-conscious about its methods.

A hermeneutics of art begins self-consciously and uncertainly. It is acutely aware of the contingency of its results and gambits—acutely aware of possible misunderstanding at the finish as well as start of its investigations. And so it is cautious and self-critical in a way unimaginable to the "erotic"—loving—formal approach to art. In its effort to transcribe, even embrace the work of art in its direct presence, formalist erotics falls back on the ineffable, after it has worn itself out with terms which reduce the work to matter-of-factness. After a futile effort at freshness, the formalist is left with the facticity of both his words and the work. One might say that description, forced back on naive indication (excited pointing) after using naive language (denotative clichés), banalizes or over-objectifies itself as well as the work of art. Both reduce to a simple, facile objectivity, to a barren terrain of purposeless fact, and so to an inertia which is altogether antithetical to any sense of immediacy, any freshness. Formalist erotics reduces to description which is neither spirited nor philosophic.

Description, then, can as little render the freshness and immediacy of the work of art as interpretation. These are apparent only under certain subjective conditions of consciousness, which neither description nor interpretation can create, at least with any completeness and guarantee that they will endure. But interpretation, because it is more aware than description of the difficulty and deviousness of establishing, however tenuously, a sense of the work's immediacy and freshness—and such qualities are always tenuous and fragile, idiosyncratic and unstable—is in a better position than description for gaining access to the work. Interpretation expects nothing from it; above all, it does not assume that it is necessarily experiencing the work directly. This in itself generates a certain freshness, a certain sense of immediacy. Moreover, interpretation recognizes the indirectness of its language—of any language, including that of description. This gives it a certain advantage over description, since it can avoid that straining for effect that reduces so much description to concrete poetry—that intense effort to evoke the work which all too often becomes a form of self-parody. Description, in fact, just when it thinks it is most in touch with the work, and so almost poetry, tends to be most prosaic.

Formalism, then, is not only indifferent to the misunderstanding it arouses with its myth of immediacy, but seems to court misunderstanding. Above all, it thinks that because words will ultimately fail us, because, as Sontag says, the most elementary "translation" of the work of art will ultimately prove inadequate, distort the work grotesquely, words must be used simply and directly, as markers—as directly as the work of art presents itself to us. Yet such linguistic directness is impossible, and fraught with misunderstanding; the pragmatics of language alone should tell us that. Interpretation is willing to acknowledge the difficulty of language, its inability to pin the work down—the very absurdity of the enterprise, and what that "down" implies for our sense of the work—and deal with that difficulty, by using language dialectically. Interpretation does something more like cornering the work—or else show that it can dance, with a step even surprising to itself, over an unexpected terrain—than pinning it down, than marking it with milestone words. Whatever the failings of its efforts, interpretation does not succumb to the futility about the work of art embodied in the notion of its supposed ineffability, which implies its permanent evasiveness. This notion, which is supposed to acknowledge the "eternal present" of the work, the undying freshness of its presence, is in fact description's compensation for its inability to pin the work down decisively, to be exact enough about it to hold it fast for contemplation. The work is never made completely clear and distinct—let alone fresh and immediate—by description, which is why it is reduced to insisting upon the work's ineffability. The supposed charm of its evasiveness only masks the inadequacy of the methods used to grasp it.

Much formalist description, when it is not secretly celebrating the ineffability of the work of art, articulates the clichés of some doctrine about art—or rather, turns its ideas into clichés. Just when it thinks it is most precise and objective, it is in fact most propagandistic. Thus Michael Fried's use of Greenberg's idea of Pollock. Fried's description of Pollock's *Number One,*[6] with its emphasis on Pollock's "opticality," is more concerned to articulate, in as nuanced a way as possible, a general criterion of modernist criticism than to give full play and weight to the values evoked by the picture. These cry out for mediation—however difficult they may be to mediate—but they will be ignored because they are presumably not immediate in the art, i.e., not art values. Fried does not risk articulating them because his method is unable to, and because he is concerned to establish that method's exclusive claim on the picture, as though, as its conquistador, it had the first right to the best pickings. A limited perspective on the picture is made into an irrefutable fact about it, as though now that the picture was firmly in one kind of focus all its richness was disclosed. In fact, that richness goes unmined. There is no reason why *Number One*'s "new kind of space . . . in which conditions of seeing prevail" should preclude exploration of all that we are conscious of when we subject ourselves to these conditions.

We can get at the problem more generally, as well as in relation to Pollock, through a quotation from A.N. Whitehead. Discussing how "language is always relapsing into the generality of this intermediate stage between animal habit and learned precision," Whitehead notes that:

> Coleridge, in his *Biographia Literaria,* objects to a party of tourists who gazed at a torrent and ejaculated "How pretty!" as a vague characterization of an awe-inspiring spectacle. Undoubtedly, in this instance, the degenerate phrase "How pretty!" lets down the whole vividness of the scene. And yet there is a real difficulty in the way of verbal expression. Words, in general, indicate useful particularities. How can they be employed to evoke a sense of that general character on which all importance depends?[7]

Whitehead's reference to the "general character on which all importance depends" goes to the heart of the critic's problem. How can one articulate that general character? If one doesn't do so, one doesn't know the importance of what one is describing; one can't even begin to describe it with any cogency. One's sense of the work of art's power depends upon one's sense of its importance, and that depends upon one's sense of its general character. The work's "immediacy," sensuous "directness," "freshness"—the urgency of its presence—qualify its power and are perceived through our conception of its importance. The language with which we describe the work gets its power through its ability to evoke the general character of the work. Is "opticality" much better than "prettiness" when it comes to evoking general character? Can this evocation ever be a matter of such simple-minded verbal ejaculation, in which a monolithic word is supposed to do the whole work and carry the full weight of understanding?

Sontag has no cognizance of any of this. Or if she does, like all formalists, she buries it in her incapacity to deal adequately with the general. There are two errors in her formalism, which show just how facile it is. First, her emphasis on the immediate preempts the general character of the important. By insisting that the critic simply describe what is immediately given, she assumes that all description will be self-evidently verifiable and coherent, when in fact its verifiability and coherence depend upon a general understanding that transcends the art's givenness. Second and more important, Sontag's separation of description and interpretation as irreconcilable opposites at cross-purposes repeats a pattern of bifurcation, serving reductionist purpose, that can be traced back at least to Descartes. Where in Descartes cognitive experience was given priority to sense or visceral experience, in Sontag the priorities are reversed, but with the same resulting hierarchization, and above all, with the same devaluation of the lower to the higher—the same effort to bring the lower under control of the higher. The disintegration of experience that results from this approach makes it easier to argue for the absoluteness of one or the other of its factors. Thus Sontag's insistence on formalist description of the work of art impoverishes our experience of it, as much as any attempt to make it exclusively the illustration of a certain code. Her version of description is as inadequate to the work of art as her version of interpretation. Missing in both accounts is a sense of the importance that determines description or interpretation. This sense of importance is, as Whitehead says, an "expression" or "instrument" of "some large generality of understanding" characteristic of the way "civilized beings ... survey the world."[8] Clearly, Sontag's "generality of understanding" is not "large, adequate." For Whitehead, "one characteristic of the primary mode of conscious experience is its fusion of a large generality with an insistent particularity."[9] For Sontag, insistent particularity is sufficient, which is why her experience of art cannot be said to be fully conscious. Her presumption, at one point, in evoking the Kantian "thing in itself," as though it was accessible through sense experience, shows her naiveté. She gives sense experience a power it never had for Kant, and rarely has for any thinker. She does not seem to think error is possible in sensing, and so she accepts it without qualification. The hermeticism of her formalist empiricism altogether belies the power of the work of art. Reduced to its insistent particularity—its sheer facticity—it does not so much make us nervous as bore us. The ennui that overtakes us in experiencing without generality of understanding testifies to the absurdity of pure fact. As Whitehead says, "A single fact in isolation is the primary myth required for finite thought, that is to say, for thought unable to embrace totality." Sontag reduces the work of art to a single fact in isolation, altogether unable to evoke totality—the large absence which surrounds and qualifies its small presence, giving it a good deal of its character and importance.

What is the significance of this line of thinking for Pollock's art, especially his all-over paintings? First, it must be recognized that the reason for the importance of Pollock's all-over paintings has not yet been firmly established, for their general character has not yet been made clear. Neither the art historical nor psychoanalytic approaches are sufficiently general. Whitehead has said that "perspective is gradation of relevance,"[10] and it may be that, because they are fact-obsessed and not sufficiently general, neither the art historical nor psychoanalytic perspectives can measure Pollock's relevance. They do not reach for Pollock's generality, and perhaps never can, given their character. For the visual generality of the all-over paintings seems to vehemently transcend their material factuality, however much the generality originates in the factuality. The properly general perspective can emerge only from an adequate account of what Pollock's art does for consciousness—what horizon the art suggests to it. This would be a true, phenomenological hermeneutics—a true aesthetic hermeneutics. No doubt it would begin by recurring to the "original definition of hermeuneutics," which, in Hans-Georg Gadamer's words, is "the art of clarifying and mediating by our own effort of interpretation what is said by persons we encounter in tradition."[11] Thus, we would examine the art historical and psychoanalytic approaches to Pollock, but with an eye for the kinds of meaning they find in his art rather than with trust in their description of its particularity. In effect, the fact that such description tends to become poetically tongue-tied or aborts in simplistic, stereotypical references to the materiality of the art, or the person of the artist, becomes another kind of meaning—one which will ultimately open us to the generality it empowers.

Indeed, the power of Pollock's all-over pictures is that they embrace generality, evoke totality. Their transcendence of the finite perspectives on them testifies to this, shows that they exist in the direction of totality, as the first inkling of its horizon, as it were. The ease with which they can be characterized by such Whiteheadean categories as "creative flux" and "creative impulsiveness" also shows their direct grasp of generality. They have concretized totality by overcoming traditional pictorial dichotomies. Fried says as much when he says that Pollock's "all-over line does not give rise to positive and negative areas," that "there is no inside or outside to Pollock's line or to the space through which it moves."[12] What is missing in Fried is the acknowledgment that this transcendence of finite contrasts gives rise not simply to the optical illusion of infinity but to a sense of the "concrete universal," the literal presence of generality, a graspable totality. In Gadamer's words, the all-over paintings transcend both their sources and vestiges, to "follow an old definition from Droysen's hermeneutics":

> Vestiges are fragments of a past world that have survived and assist us in the intellectual reconstruction of the world of which they are a remnant. Sources, on the other hand, constitute a linguistic tradition, and they thus serve our understanding of a linguistically interpreted world.[13]

Thus, Pollock's all-over paintings transcend not only the "purely personal 'gestures'" they solipsistically record—even the artist's self-referencing image of his own hand in some of his works—but also their art historical location, the conventions of Impressionism and automatism with which, among others, they have been identified. And even the conventions of perception, as Fried has shown. Personal and public history—handmark and trademark—become excrescences on the work, denying its transcendence to totality, its general role for consciousness.

Does this mean that Pollock's art can never be adequately described, that the conventions of language, which depend on finite distinctions, fail it? Are the all-over paintings at last truly ineffable art—pure painting picturing nothing, inaccessible to formal analysis as well as interpretative codification? Gadamer has said that "being that can be understood is language," and Pollock's art, since it can be understood as generality and totality, is language. To identify being and language is, for Gadamer, not a "metaphysical assertion," but "describes, from the medium of understanding, the unrestricted scope possessed by the hermeneutical perspective." "In the last analysis, Goethe's statement "Everything is a symbol" is the most comprehensive formulation of the hermeneutical idea. It means that everything points to another thing."[14] What other thing does Pollock's all-over painting point to? What is it a symbol of? The transcendence toward totality and generality is self-transcendence. Pollock's art reminds us that all art, all being tends to transcend itself—*must* transcend itself, if it is to be. This is perhaps why art that is really art makes us nervous, as Sontag says. It reminds us that we must change ourselves. Pollock's art epitomizes the hermeneutical idea that everything must point to another thing to be. Pollock's art, in its generality, seems to point to everything else, and so exists powerfully. As Gadamer says:

> For the distinctive mark of the language of art is that the individual art work gathers into itself and expresses the symbolic character that, hermeneutically regarded, belongs to all beings. In comparison with all other linguistic and nonlinguistic tradition, the work of art is the absolute present for each particular present, and at the same time holds its word in readiness for every future. The intimacy with which the work of art touches us is at the same time, in enigmatic fashion, a shattering and a demolition of the familiar. It is not only the "This art thou!" disclosed in a joyous and frightening shock; it also says to us, "Thou must alter thy life!"[15]

So immersed has Sontag been in the absolute present—abbreviated into material immediacy—the work of art implies, that she ignores the ready future it wills. Clearly, to interpret means to transcend all the descriptions that bog the work down in the present, that deny it future life. Pollock's art, perhaps more than any other in recent times, restores us to this future—restores the generality which conditions all finite perspectives that give importance, the totality which embraces possibility, and so permits us, as well as itself, to have a future, to alter.

Notes

1.   Clement Greenberg, "How Art Writing Earns Its Bad Name," *Encounter,* 17 (December 1962): 67.

2.   Susan Sontag, "Against Interpretation," *Against Interpretation* (New York, 1967), p. 13.

3.   Ibid., p. 7.

4.   Ibid., p. 5.

5.   Susan Sontag, "On Style," *Against Interpretation* (New York, 1967), p. 25.

6.   Michael Fried, *Three American Painters* (Cambridge, Mass., 1965), p. 5.

7.   Alfred North Whitehead, *Modes of Thought* (Cambridge, England, 1955), p. 7.

8.   Ibid., p. 5.

9.   Ibid.

10.   Ibid., p. 13.

11.   Hans-Georg Gadamer, "Aesthetics and Hermeneutics," *Philosophical Hermeneutics* (Berkeley, 1977), p. 98.

12.   Michael Fried, *Morris Louis* (New York, 1971), p. 18.

13.   Gadamer, p. 99.

14.   Ibid., p. 103.

15.   Ibid., p. 104.

Abstract Expressionism: The Social Contract

This essay is in response to an article by Peter Fuller in which he launches an attack on modern American art as a whole and Abstract Expressionism in particular.[1] While the grounds for this attack are not always clear, it does manage to raise fundamental questions about Abstract Expressionism. Despite the air of an arbitrary diatribe verging on the preposterous—confirmed by Fuller's gross ignorance of the American scene, his possession of the worst of clichés about it—Fuller does restore an earlier sense of Abstract Expressionism as a controversial art. This is valuable, for it puts the art sufficiently in doubt for us to feel compelled to renew our faith in it. Perhaps more is at stake than had been previously assumed, in a dimension previously unexplored yet signaled by the art. Beyond all his facile generalizations, anti-Americanism and anti-capitalism—verging almost on the order of mechanical reflexes—Fuller manages to restore a traditional criterion of artistic value, namely, the way an art reflects the society in which it appears. The psychological significance of Abstract Expressionism has been readily taken for granted—it has been assumed that its speaking in gestural tongues has profoundly personalistic implications—but the way it demonstrates the social contract has hardly begun to be articulated. The authenticity of Abstract Expressionism has never been measured by this criterion and, whatever else Fuller is telling us, he seems to be shouting that it is time that this be done. There is no way we can refuse him an answer without undermining the credibility of Abstract Expressionism.

What Fuller in effect does is locate Abstract Expressionism within a cultural logic which has previously not been thought to impinge on it, making us realize that this logic forces us to reconceive the subjective logic that Abstract Expressionism has been consistently thought to exemplify. The core of Fuller's argument is presented through an examination of the intentionality of Pollock's art. "Pollock," writes Fuller, "is symptomatic of the courageousness of what the Abstract Expressionists tried to do and of the enormity of their failure. He was a highly-skilled professional Fine Artist who sought to realize a historical vision through his painting." Carrying this line of thought forward into a general discussion of the Abstract Expressionists, Fuller asserts:

They were acutely aware of the difficulties involved in attempting through painting to make imaginative, empirical representations of, and to relate meaningfully to, the world. It was just these difficulties that they sought to transcend. They were looking for a route back to reality, much as an analysand does, through an exploration of their subjectivity. They sought to create visual equivalents not just for dreams, or immediate perceptions, but also for a wide range of experiences including anguish, hope, alienation, physical sensations, suffering, unconscious imagery, passion and historical sentiments. They had little in common except their diverse and desperate desire to seize hold of this new subject matter.

Returning to Pollock, Fuller argues that:

...the moment of history in which he lives was such that he could not avail himself of the visionary consolations of the "avant garde." In his personal life, he was increasingly subsumed by alcoholism and depression. In the 1950s, he went through long periods in which he did not paint at all, and expressed doubts as to whether he was saying *anything* through his art. When he did paint, he seemed to be struggling desperately to regain some way—any way—of meaningfully representing his perceptions and experiences through his painting. But he was unable to do so. He died at the vortex of a ferocious despair which he could never satisfactorily depict.

At the center of this argument—which reduces personal failure to a symptom of social failure—is the assumption that Abstract Expressionism, particularly as it is exemplified by its most exemplary figure, was unable to realize any kind of historical vision because the primary historical vision of avant-garde art, the vision of a utopian world, was no longer available, and if it was, it would no longer be viable. It had been refuted by history itself, by the reality of 20th century socio-political experience. No other social vision was available, although Fuller seems to be calling for an apocalyptic vision of capitalist social failure, in effect hoping that the Abstract Expressionists would have created such a vision, on the assumption that historically they were in a position to do so. That is, they were located in the capitalistically most advanced country in the world, and were possessed of a visionary talent which should have seen through the veneer of well-being with which American society masked its exploitive, strictly contractual, basis. They should have apocalyptically punctured the veneer, not retreated in the face of it to their subjective lucubrations, although such a retreat is in effect an acknowledgment of the hollowness of the capitalist promise, if not a turning of capitalist materialism back on itself. For Fuller, the alternative subjectivity, an update on an old-fashioned transcendental spiritualism, never has the strength to actively confront, whether materially or idealistically—i.e., whether revolutionarily or prophetically—the sheer qualitative and quantitative weight of capitalism. Instead of threatening capitalist control and methodology, the Abstract Expressionists retreated to a world of private methods and a seeming loss of control which became the emblem of an inner freedom, which, simply because it was inner rather than outer, was an absurd illusion. In other words, for Fuller, the Abstract

Expressionists retreated to a dubious fantasy world of ineffectual feeling because they could not develop a sufficiently strong reality principle. Unable to face up to the reality of the world they lived in and indirectly acknowledged in their personal suffering, they created a world of their own which for all its artistic novelty was not able to free them from their suffering—was not able to heal the wound inflicted by a life in capitalist society. The alternate world of art no longer existed as a utopian reproach to the real world of life, but as a cesspool draining negative feelings about society, which, backed up, became negative feelings about oneself—a questioning of one's own character as a social being. For this reason, Fuller argues, Abstract Expressionism ultimately became, to use his word, "kenotic" or self-emptying: this in effect is Fuller's unacknowledged understanding of automatism.

In any case, Abstract Expressionism shares in the general American development of what Fuller, in perhaps his best formulation, called "the mega-visual." That is, for all its seemingly transcendental subjectivity—its universality—Abstract Expressionism is sufficiently American to think big. While never spelling out what he means by the mega-visual—although by giving Hollywood a monopoly on it he seems to suggest that it is solely a matter of quantity—it seems fairly clear, from his wide-ranging use of the term, that he means it to be a matter of quality as well. The mega-visual means not simply the big picture—the expansive new grandeur emblematic of America's megalomaniac sense of significance—but the heroically entertaining image. Art as the grandest entertainment—this is the idea at the core of the mega-visual, and like all entertainment the mega-visual functions in one of two ways, which often unite. The entertaining is simultaneously a distraction from reality—Fuller says that the mega-visual develops in disassociation "from the material conditions of life"—and a false consciousness which blurs real conflicts in the haze of a teleologically presupposed harmony. For Fuller, the modernist emphasis on painting for the sake of painting, on the exploration of "pictorial conventions" for their own sake, is at once the instrument and final form of false consciousness artistically mediated. In assuming the possibility of an ultimate pictorial harmony, however abstract and "critical," modernism creates a false consciousness of painting. That is, it assumes a facile "higher" reconciliation of art and reality symbolized by art's reconciliation with its own reality, and at the same time it dismisses the possibility of conceiving art as a significant reaching out to or reflection of social reality. The supposedly higher reconciliation with reality is at once an illusion and the putting off of the very possibility of realistic reconciliation, whether in the most simplistic or dialectically complex way. Thus, one might say that the mega-visual is an authoritarian articulation of the modernist pretension to artistic transcendence, which in itself is an authoritarian version of the idea of art's autonomy.

While Fuller does acknowledge that "Motherwell was exploring a new way of expressing an individual response to history," and grants the Abstract

Expressionists their "occasional 'moments of becoming,'" on the whole he believes that "history had deprived them of representational conventions valid even for a single class view; although they tried, they could not transcend their own subjectivity," and as a result "splintered into a myriad of cul-de-sacs at the end of each of which was a solipsistic cell." The problem here is Fuller's expectation of *representational* conventions, as though they alone were capable of mediating a social outlook. He implicitly denies abstract conventions and abstraction's power of communicating sociality. He assumes only one method of communication; all others are mute and ultimately incomprehensible for him. Thus it is that he can quote his adopted mentor, John Berger, another facile, overgeneralizing Marxist: describing Pollock's 1947-50 all-over drip paintings, Berger asserts that "these gestures might be passionate and frenzied but to us they could mean no more than the tragic spectacle of a deaf mute trying to talk."[2] Pollock, continues Berger, "finally in desperation...made his theme the impossibility of finding a theme." There is, admittedly, a groping for meaning— but not for theme—in Pollock. It is possible to conceive the paint itself, refusing us any ready images and making those we extract suspect, as the theme, without making a modernist analysis of it, but instead noting that it relates to conventions of handling. Such connotations imply the objectification of an attitude—extravagantly subjective insofar as it seems to dismiss reality while rendering it or, to put it another way, the articulation of a dialectical moment, in which subjective and objective inextricably condition one another. The moment we understand the unresolved quality of Pollock's all-over drip paintings to be indicative of a dialectical intentionality, we can begin to understand the superiority of the abstract conventions he taps into to the representational conventions accessible to him—particularly those of the social realists. For such conventions either force us toward the objective, in a premature determination of it, or else lead toward, if not entirely effect, a facile bifurcation into objective and subjective, i.e., content and style. Such bifurcation, with its automatic assumption of content being an objective matter and style a realm of subjective implications, is another, more perverse species of false consciousness. Thus, Fuller mechanically assumes that Pollock's style is necessarily subjective. Not being able to conceive subjectivity as an objective content, or rather a content with implications for the nature of objectification, because it does not satisfy his canon of objectivity, which implies direct referentiality or easy mediation, Fuller dismisses Pollock's all-over paintings as without any social objectivity. Marxist though he may be—and I find his Marxism too superficial and specious to be worth the name—he is not a dialectician, subtle or unsubtle. His dogmatism precludes a dialectically subtle awareness. In all fairness, this may be in part because he assumes, unconsciously, that in a capitalist society subject and object bifurcate and are irreconcilable—the individual's world separates into private and public realms, with only the most distinct and certainly unclarified relationship between them. But this idea goes contrary to dialectical expectation, which assumes a steady if unstable connection between subject and object—their indissoluble reciprocity. Not truly respecting this reciprocity, Fuller is not truly a Marxist, or else he is a vulgar Marxist, allowing, when its suits him, for cultural superstructures which reflect no social reality but are privately accessible, as though privacy, and the notion of person it co-implies, were not social constructs.

Is there anything in the literature surrounding Pollock that might give us a clue to a social reading of his art? C.L. Wysuph, in his introduction to the psychoanalytic drawings of Pollock, repeats what is common knowledge about Pollock but which has been given little attention.

> At 16, Pollock enrolled in Manual Arts High School in Los Angeles, and before the year's end was expelled for having taken part in the publishing and distribution of two broadsides attacking the faculty and the school's overemphasis on sports. He returned to the school in 1929, but within the first month was in trouble again with the Physical Education department. From his letters, we learn that Jackson had come "to blows" with the head of the department, had attended Communist Party meetings during his expulsion, had showed an interest in Oriental philosophy, and had stated that people "frightened and bored" him.[3]

Perhaps in typical adolescent fashion, Pollock seemed to have difficulty accepting authority. He particularly felt compelled to challenge the most conventional American authority, that presumably epitomized the American way of competitive fair play and worship of winning—the authority that insisted that life was a game, not to be taken seriously yet energetically played. One was to be a sport—sporting in one's attitudes, sporting in one's commitments—shallow yet game, lively within the limited system of rules and conventions. Resentment of physical education requirements is not new, nor is the adolescent pursuit of social and personal revolution. Indeed, one might argue that Pollock was already facing the most crucial choice of his art, as Fuller might conceive it: should the art move in a social direction or in a personal direction? Should it be objective or subjective? The question assumes the lack of reconciliation of the directions, and even the necessity for this lack of reconciliation, as though in a decadent capitalist society one is forced either to play the game wholeheartedly or withdraw from it completely to the subjective sidelines. And yet the objective and subjective possibilities clearly arise out of common ground: both are premised on rebellion against and rejection of social authority, which insists that one cannot take a serious, questioning stand about either social or personal matters—which assumes them to be settled matters. This shallow attitude, which inevitably arises when there is no questioning, was altogether inimical to the attitude of aggressive doubt which led Pollock into the depths, an aggressive doubt which took its start from a disbelief in authority, which simply asked of one that one played the game with no questions asked about its nature. Even those who see Pollock choosing the subjective side, and gaining authority in subjective matters, and who in no way could conceive of such matters as on the sidelines of social life—who see Pollock as a Hercules at the crossroads choosing the virtuous path (sometimes this choice is presented as that between abstract and representational art, or between mytho-poetic and social realist art)—miss the point that Pollock's subjective orientation is rooted in rejection of social authority, with its superficial demands and sense of life. If this is correct, what it means is that in taking the subjective turn, Pollock was also being socially revolutionary—directly not simply indirectly. For the key element in Pollock's subjective turn, its starting point, is the complete rejection of social authority. This remains the touchstone of Pollock's subjective revolution whatever the sense of the subjectivity achieved, i.e., whether it be said that Pollock's art bespeaks Jungian ideas or is, more generally, psycho-mythic. The either/or postulation, which sees Pollock's art as becoming either social or representational or personal and abstract, misses the dialectical connection of the two.

This is a surprise in Fuller's case, for we expect a Marxist to be a dialectician, not simply a materialist. It is less of a surprise in those who see Pollock plunging the psychological depths, for they neither want to imagine a return from such depths—so happy are they to find an artist swimming underwater in the unconscious who can hold his breath for an unexpectedly long time—nor do they believe the surface of life is as interesting and important as its depths. They want an art of extreme situations, of a constant emergency situation, as though that alone is redemptive in a boring world—better to be frightened than bored, to know one's anxiety than to will it away into disillusionment with the world. Yet it is only the dialectical recognition of Pollock's subjective side that prevents us from misreading it as rank subjectivism, as a decadent pursuit of rare subjective sensation, as Fuller seems to imply. Moreover, dialectical recognition is the only kind that permits us to understand how Pollock, for all his defiance of authority, assimilates it—makes it part of his art's own authority.

Thus, from a dialectical point of view, not only does a psychological reading of Pollock's art imply its socially revolutionary meaning, but the famous pure physicality of Pollock's painting—a physicality seemingly developed in the most casual way yet ultimately, more than any cultural considerations, the source of his paintings' commanding presence—can be said to be the result of an *Aufhebung* of the physical that Pollock encountered in his adolescence. This is suggested by his sense of the picture as an arena in which the artist physically, even gymnastically, performs. Think of the famous film of Pollock painting, where the physical act of painting counts as much as the painting itself. Certainly these images of Pollock "educating" us to his own lived body as well as the lived body of the painting is one of the sources of body art. And certainly the physical act of painting, so determined to be as energetic as the painting itself, reflects a sporting attitude to painting as well as produces a sporting painting. Moreover, the authority the artist thereby acquires, over against the authority of works, makes him seem significant beyond any of his manifestations in his works, so that he becomes a kind of social force as well as an artistic presence. From this point of view, Pollock was struggling to enter the social arena by making painting a vigorous revolutionary gesture, whose sheer physicality was enough to disrupt the social order, with its superficially harmonious surface. Harold Rosenberg's description of Pollock's paintings as a kind of performance in the social arena—an intervention in social events—is far from wrong, if not altogether right in that it misses the fact that Pollock means to intervene with his physical person as well as his gesturing art. One thinks of Joyce's description, in *Portrait of the Artist as a Young Man,* of the revolutionary gesture that Stephen Daedalus inadvertently made in conversation with his girlfriend, and of the surrealist sense of the ultimate surrealist act as a terrorist gesture of arbitrary murder in the densely packed arena of a crowd. To this one adds Pollock's sense of painting as a disruptive social performance, an argument, as it were, not so much for a painting as for a revolutionary artistic presence in the world, where the artistic is the revolutionary, in however impacted a form. And Pollock means to free the impacted revolutionary in the artist—an intention which he means to be more than utopian, if less than socially constructive.

What I am arguing for, then, is a change in the by now standard conception of Pollock as a martyr to his own psychology—as a kind of Laocoön caught in the coils of his own suffering, and of his art as a kind of subjective Gordian knot which no objective sword can cut. I use these metaphors to suggest that the interpretation which views Pollock's art strictly in terms of its psychodynamics has become, in Kant's sense, rhapsodic. It is time to interpret Pollock's art in terms of its social dynamics, however dialectically disguised these may be. The Communist Party side is as active in Pollock's art as the Oriental philosophy side. Indeed, there is the same abstract messianic urgency—the same sense of forcing necessity, social and artistic—in Pollock's art as in early Communist ideology. There is the same abstract sense of the need for a revolution, and the same abstract sense of its possibility. The visionary need for a new kind of social and artistic authority necessarily formulates itself in abstract terms, for it involves a modal logic, not simply the logic of the given. The abstract is the necessary vehicle of the apocalyptic, which carries with it a new sense of necessity and possibility and the abandonment of an old actuality. The apocalyptic represents the overthrowal of the shallow surface of life by the depths of possibility, struggling for a wide vision than can be contained on the surface and so unsettling and finally disrupting it altogether. Whether the apocalyptic vision can ever realize itself does not matter; and in fact it was never meant to be realized. It displays itself as the fullness and energy that is in the depths, periodically announcing to life and society and art the necessity for and possibility of their own renewal, a renewal never completely actualized. The apocalypse, in other words, is a lure into the future, a revitalization of the future, a renewal of its meaning as fullness rather than emptiness—as owned by life rather than death. Apocalyptic art always proposes more than it can offer, and in

Pollock we have apocalyptic art par excellence, the exemplary apocalyptic art of the modern period, bringing to fruition the seed that Kandinsky planted. Indeed, it is Kandinsky—and the debt Abstract Expressionism owes him has been acknowledged only in the most half-hearted way—because of the repression the modernist conception of art has instigated, as epitomized by Clement Greenberg's essay on Kandinsky and William Rubin's account of the influences on Pollock and Abstract Expressionism, an account which goes against the testimony of such artists as Gorky, who first, in the modern period, saw the artist as an active social force by reason of his spiritual energy.

What Kandinsky showed us was that abstraction need not be merely surface decoration, but the artistic unconvention that could imply depth of meaning with a rawness and directness that no representational art, whatever its methods, could begin to fathom. Abstraction meant to enter the depth that representationalism could only suggest, as a nuance of the surface of objects. As such, abstraction worked against the charisma of surface by disrupting the order which created it and which it reflected, particularly the hierarchical ordering of space and the objects in them. In Pollock, with the realization of the all-over picture—presaged in Kandinsky—we find the collapse of hierarchical values synonymous with the sense of immersion in the depths. At the same time, for all its disorder, a surface is created and held together, but one which, because it is differentiated according to no single principle, does not achieve singularity as surface, and so always suggests the loss of surface and the plunge into the depth. This is true of Pollock's *The Depth,* and of most of his other paintings, after 1947, whether the figurative implications or not. One might say that in Pollock the dialectic between shallowness and depth—between a surface that is constantly betraying itself and a depth that is emerging or else submerged like a lost Atlantis, i.e., a depth that is archaeologically trying to restore itself—creates a sense of apocalypse, a sense of apocalypse which dominates the paintings and which can be interpreted socially. For it is to be understood in the same sense in which Gottlieb and Rothko proposed an art of the timeless and tragic—not in and for itself, but in defiance of American society, which was all too concerned with things temporal and banal. The problem is how to get out of the mode of everydayness into the mode of authenticity—this is an apocalyptic shift, and in art this shift is represented by the turn to a dynamic abstraction. That Pollock offers us the most dynamic abstraction since Kandinsky shows us just how thoroughly apocalyptic his art was, how desperate he was to escape from American ordinariness, its lure of banality. Calling the apocalyptic attitude elitist does not change its meaning, for the fact is that American society does not answer the need for meaning, for a sense of the profundity of life.

Ever since Gauguin asked the questions *Whence Come We? Where Are We Going? Who Are We?* the best modern art has been symbolist in intention, in the sense of trying to find depth of meaning in an increasingly secular and banal world. In Pollock we have a kind of ultimate symbolist statement: the meaning is not in the lost totems blurred in the mists of paint nor in the world never explicitly depicted, but in the very energy that seeks meaning. Both old and new totems—Pop art in a sense showed us the new ones, those of a self-banalizing secularity—suffer an apocalypse in Pollock, who abides only by the implication of depth of meaning that comes from the actuality of sustained energy. Pollock struggled to sustain his energy—hence his performances—in order to sustain the feel of possible meaning that goes by the name of depth. As long as the energy seems absolute and consistent, the depth will seem possible if inconsistently present, uncertainly there. The authority of the energy gives the depth the authority of authentic possibility, giving the art more social implication— making it a contract with the future of the life-world—than it would ever have if it presented us, with whatever grandeur or pessimism, an image of the known world.

Just as Rothko's early, pre-field paintings show strong signs of the apocalyptic, so Pollock's work "after" Benton, Siqueiros, and Rivera—including the psychoanalytic drawings—shows strong signs of an apocalyptic mentality, of a social contract with a future world and, simultaneously, a falling one. The field paintings make this mentality explicit. The de-centering, even dis-locating effect of the field bespeaks the raw, apocalyptic sensation of being thrown into existence, in the Heideggerean sense. The sense of being in an apocalyptic situation permits this metaphysical experience of raw thrownness (reflected in the handling of the paint). At the same time, the field also bespeaks the falling world that makes the sensation of thrownness—falling—possible. But the very lack of firm footing in the field of existence and the world becomes the opportunity for an energetic reworking of necessity into possibility. That is, the sense of fate accompanying the apocalyptic experience generates an energy which seems capable of counteracting the authority of fate itself as well as articulating the apocalyptic experience. We are all fated to have a surface, and fate makes a mockery of the center(s) and locations we construct on that surface, but the energy with which surface is given implies enough of a contradiction of surface to suggest, if not to give, depth. The self-contradiction converts the manifest into the latent, and it is important to see that this conversion, in and of itself, is socio-politically charged, for it denies the imposed, "fated" order that is one way of saving surface from itself. When energy, not order, emerges from surface—when the sense of the whole is contermanded by the energy that makes it possible—fate (necessity) seems overcome, and with it the authority that sustains surface, i.e., that "socializes" it.

The field paintings are at once regression in the service of the ego and the negation in which the negation of the negation is prepared. Thus, when Wysuph asserts that "rather than the overt political and social statements of Benton, Siqueiros and Rivera, he [Pollock] must have felt the need to express a more interior reality,"[5] he misreads the meaning of Pollock's shift to all-over abstraction, as well as the meaning of interior reality as such, which he absolutizes and conceives in disjunction from exterior reality. He in fact even seems to think of interior reality as a repression of exterior reality, much as exterior reality is conventionally conceived as the repression of interior reality. Pollock rejects the conventional conceptions of exterior and interior reality by means of his abstraction which is simultaneously both. (One might even describe it, on a theoretical level, as a new kind of subjective Cubism, creating an ambiguity of subjective and objective which decodes the conventional conceptions of both, and mocks the conventional conception of their bifurcation.) Pollock's abstraction moves beyond any shallow ideology which means to predetermine exterior or interior reality, and thereby convey the whole of reality's meaning, presumably making reality itself "whole," i.e., wholly exterior or interior. Pollock rejected the art of Benton, Siqueiros, and Rivera because he realized that their ideological orientations, however heroic and grand, were nonetheless premised on the unquestioned conventional secular assumption of the ultimate banality—and therewith non-apocalyptic character—of the world. Such an assumption takes the form of a pseudo-apocalyptic hierarchization of the world into the separate exterior and interior realms: the everyday stability of the world depends on the absolutization of this hierarchical assumption. Benton, Siqueiros, and Rivera, from this point of view, never successfully fused the subjective-mythic and socio-political aspects of their art, as Pollock did. In general, the apocalyptic vision of reality assumes the non-hierarchical if unstable unity of exterior and interior realities, to the point at which they seem undifferentiated. This unity—essentially that of the profane and sacred (one might say the struggle for sanctification in the face of being inevitably overwhelmed by the ordinary, including the ordinariness of paint)—is demonstrated as a *fait accompli* in Pollock's abstractions.

Pollock's mature paintings, then, are jeremiads against the prevailing shallowness—the shallowness which denies dialectical unity, and which must be resisted in the name of a possible depth of implication. His works express an apocalyptic intention which insists on the open reconciliation of the social and personal, and refutes any effort to set up separate realms of being in dubious communication with one another. The insistence on unity of being is in and of itself a political act, for it interferes with the functioning of advanced society, which depends upon the separation and hierarchization of the social and personal, establishing a scheme of priorities which seems to allow the autonomous functioning of each but in fact cripples the whole of being. The conventional demand for non-dialectical "positiveness" is exactly what leads to the bifurcation of America into a realm of shallow everydayness and a realm of such flagrantly expressive, hyperventilating art as Pollock at first glance seems to offer, a realm of expression so exaggeratedly free it seems to verge on the arbitrary. Pollock, then, does offer a utopian vision, but one quite different from either what Fuller expected or what was offered earlier in this century's art. The only reason I can see for not accepting the apocalyptic character of Pollock's paintings is that one has been taken in by the political appropriation of Abstract Expressionism for American imperialist purposes so well described by Eva Cockcroft in her article on "Abstract Expressionism, Weapon of the Cold War."[6] The assumption that the marginal freedom articulated by Abstract Expressionism has anything to do with the mainstream of conventional life in America can only issue from absolute naiveté or a cunning desire to whitewash American dailiness.

Notes

1.   Peter Fuller, "American Painting Since the Last War," *Art Monthly* (May-June 1979), pp. 6-13; (July-August 1979), p. 6-12.

2.   Quoted by Fuller, *Art Monthly,* May-June 1979, p. 8.

3.   C.L. Wysuph, *Jackson Pollock: Psychoanalytic Drawings* (New York, 1970), p. 12.

4.   Rubin has, incidentally, written about the Gorky-Kandinsky connection, but not the Pollock-Kandinsky connection. The Kandinsky connection—perhaps only an affinity—has not gone unacknowledged, but it has not been sufficiently analyzed on a theoretical as well as visual level. While the term "Abstract Expressionism" was originally used (by Alfred Barr) to describe Kandinsky's art, the use of it to describe the American Abstract Expressionists remains unclarified in import. Neither a convergence with Kandinsky's imagery nor expectations from art are implied, and yet it is such a convergence which would give full weight to the term. Moreover, Kandinsky remains defamed by Greenberg because he did not pass through the alembic of French Cubism on his way to non-objectivity—as though the Abstract Expressionists passed through the French Cubist filter and it "purified" them.

5.   Wysuph, p. 12.

6.   Eva Cockcroft, "Abstract Expressionism, Weapon of the Cold War," *Artforum,* June 1974.

13

Clyfford Still: The Ethics of Art

That thing is called free which exists from the necessity of its own nature alone and is determined to action by itself alone.

—Benedict de Spinoza, *Ethics*

And I will shew wonders in the heavens and in the earth, blood, and fire, and pillars of smoke.
—Joel 2:30

Begin by taking Clyfford Still at his word. The key to his art: the idea of freedom. He calls his paintings "fragments [s] of a means to freedom," and dedicates them "to all who would know the meaning and the responsibilities of freedom."[1] Still hopes to "restore to man the freedom lost in twenty centuries of apology and devices for subjugation," hopes "to create a free place or area of life where an idea can transcend politics, ambition and commerce."[2]

Run this freedom to the ground, first by understanding what it is freedom from, then by understanding what it is freedom for—how, after it clears the ground, it enables us to stand on it. (Then see how the painting is equal to its ethical task and how it accomplishes it, if it does.) Still helps us on both counts. First, he wants freedom from "all cultural opiates, past and present," "the combined and sterile conclusions of Western European decadence," found in the ideas of "Hegel, Kierkegaard, Cézanne, Freud, Picasso, Kandinsky, Plato, Marx, Aquinas, Spengler, Einstein, Bell, Croce, Monet."[3] Quite a list—if one were a decadent European thinker one would not want to be excluded. Still wants freedom from history and tradition, dogma and authority. He feels tradition is burdensome and totalitarian. It dominates us with its obsolete myths, which become alibis for our own inertia. Its decadence, then, is both passive and active—consoling, but hiding from us our impotence; narcotic, and robbing us of our free will and consciousness of our condition. Still reminds us of Marx in his stridency against the opiate of the masses which, for Still, is the religion of the European past—the religion rugged Protestant Americans have classically rebelled against, both for its cosmopolitanism and its effete spirtualism.[4]

This provincial spirit of rebellion in Still goes so far as to insist that "demands for communication are both presumptuous and irrelevant," for they put one in a position of subjugation to dogma, authority, tradition.

Communication inhibits the consciousness necessary for freedom, for it is historically determined and so interferes with self-determination. Art should not communicate, it should vitalize. Still's nihilistic refusal to have any historical obligations, whether of style or belief, exists in the name of a radical vitality, a freshness beyond all conventional causes and uses of art—a fresh wind which at times seems no more than the wake of an apocalyptic one. Thus, Still asserts that his paintings explicitly deny the foundations of our science and commerce, and would lose their vitality if they were made to conform to it.

Still's noncomformity, articulated as a passion for freedom—the myth of new beginnings, inseparable from that of self-creation—translates concretely into the freeing of the medium, taking artistic license to its limits. Still finds that

> To be stopped by a frame's edge was intolerable; a Euclidean prison had to be annihilated, its authoritarian implications repudiated without dissolving one's individual integrity and idea in material and mannerism.[5]

Not only was the frame a symbol of false necessity, of lost freedom, but so were "signs or symbols of literary allusions," which are "just crutches for illustrators and politicians desperate for an audience." Any focusing device for form, any cue to content, are anathema for Still, for they close one into a finite world of limited implications which altogether precludes even the possibility of the idea of freedom. There must be a lurking infinity about the image, an indefiniteness—incompleteness—which lures us to the idea of freedom, which shows us its possibility because it reminds us that there is much to be formed, to be made definite. Still takes limits, with their implication of a finished world of "vision"—literal and spiritual—and of completed content, very personally. For they seem so indisputable and inevitable in art—in any enterprise—that their repudiation takes the utmost conviction. Still is aware that to deny limits altogether, to assume that one can permanently escape from them, opens him to "the charge of affectation." Transcendence of the forming frame and context-creating allusions or associations is epitomized by Still in his deliberate omission of titles, because they would mislead the viewer and limit the works' meanings and implications. Still does not want to assist the spectator with allusions. In viewing Still's work, the observer shows what he is made of. But, we have a right to ask, will this tell us what the works are made of? Still makes Promethean claims for his art, but he does not tell us what kind of gift its visible fire is, although he insists that it can be used for good or ill.[6]

Still regards his act of painting as at odds with any system of associations and evaluations. To preserve the purity of this act—to make clear that it is the act that counts, not what can conventionally be made of it—Still insists on exhibiting his paintings as a set or in continuity, presumably because one will then be overwhelmed by their sheer presence, which will in and of itself suffice. The viewer will not search for crutches to make sense of the works, which will stand forth as a pure revelation of paint. The paintings must affect us, in Valéry's words, "as *unique presences* anterior to everything in the way of arrangement, summary, short cut, and instantaneous substitution." Valéry describes the meaning of these presences for the painter:

> Just as the thinker tries to defend himself from the platitudes and set phrases which protect the mind from surprise at everything, and make practical living possible, so the painter can try, by studying formlessness, or rather *singularity* of form, to rediscover his own singularity, and with it the original and primitive state of co-ordination between hand and eye, subject and will.[7]

For Still, the spectator can begin to make this rediscovery only when he deliberately strips away whatever might give the paintings form, whatever interferes with the effect and workings of their formlessness on him. The "crutches" of association—the natural tendency to associate a specific meaning with a random sensation of form, which gives definite form to what is not and was never meant to be finalized as such—particularly interferes. Still takes great pains to repudiate, often violently, the associations conveniently aroused by his works, associations which convert them from paintings to pictures, which make them "scenic." These associations are of two sorts: those which relate the paintings to the American prairie in particular or nature in general,[8] and those which relate them to the New York school of surrealistically derived or oriented "Myth-Makers" active in the early and mid-40's.[9] The paintings became disguised images of landscape or inner life (inner landscape)—vistas on nature or the self. Still, in shrugging off such associations, falls into a state of contradiction, from which he seems not to want to rescue himself. He does not want to "delimit the meanings and implications" latent in his works, but he doesn't like any meaning made manifest, any implication detected, any association that becomes explicit. For such meanings and implications would make his work "illustrative," give it "traditional, authoritarian, or public" meaning. Indeed, Still intends to "fight...any tendency to accept a fixed, sensuously appealing, recognizable style," not only because it is delimiting in and of itself, but because it easily becomes the vehicle of such public meanings.[10] "I am always trying to paint my way out of and beyond a facile, doctrinaire idiom," and especially to "disembarrass color from all conventional, familiar associations and responses; that is, from the pleasant, luminous, and symbolic." This has made his art appear to be "technically 'bad' painting...in keeping with my anti-elegant attitude."[11]

Still, then, sacrifices much in the name of his sacred freedom, whose self-proclaimed primitivism begins to seem absurd even in the context of 20th-century primitivism. His dismissal and slander of all styles and contexts comes in the end to seem a species of nihilistic nonsense. One can understand the desire of "genius" to remain uncategorized, unclassifiable—unappropriated and mysterious—in the name of his creativity, but to present his products as permanently incomprehensible is to insult the public they are made for. To be consistent, Still ought not to exhibit his paintings, with or without titles, together or individually—yet of course he does want to reach or create a public. If Still did not make such an ethical issue of his art, one would be tempted to interpret his attitude as simply another avant-garde strategy, the nihilistic moment, as Pogioli has described it, in avant-garde self-invention and radicality.

As it is, there is one association Still is willing to let stick to his art—the sublime—but the term is tautological as he uses it. It is simply a reiteration of his desire for an associationless art.

> The sublime? A paramount consideration in my studies and work from my earliest student days. In essence it is most elusive of capture or definition—only surely found least in the lives and works of those who babble of it the most. The dictator types have made a cliché of "sublime" conceits throughout the centuries to impress or subjugate the innocent or desperate.[12]

Thus, Still's sublime brings with it the whole baggage of his art's mysterious freedom, and the usual accompanying insults against the unfree. One is tempted to ask whether the genius types haven't also made a cliché of the sublime, and whether Still isn't an American version of the dictatorial or authoritarian type of modern artist, using the myth of primitivism—in its American version, of the perpetual new start and self-start, of permanent revolution—to impress or subjugate—blind—the consciousness of his spectators. He in effect asks them to scuttle their minds by believing in his self-righteously radical sublime primitivism, in the frontier wisdom of his art, yet doesn't allow them to crystallize any sensations or ideas about it. He subjects them to a stifling paradox, and invites them to a nihilistic adventure, in which the works become hidden reefs waiting to gash holes in the spectator's consciousness.

Still commits many atrocities in the name of freedom; he is a savage scalper of everything from past art to past history to past thought, and by his own admission his art does not accumulate much toward a future. What does this grand primitivist negation,[13] this grand return to origins,[14] exist in the name of? Does it finally affirm anything? Yes; Still affirms the "act," which quickly becomes the "Act," a communication made for its own sake, with no attempt to create history, with no authority beyond its own immediacy. The painting of the Act is the "free place or arena of life where an idea"—that of freedom—"can transcend politics, ambition and commerce." Still is quick to insist that this does not make him "an action painter." While "each painting is an act, the result of action and the fulfillment of action,"[15] it is also "intrinsic and absolute"—autonomous—rather than an act concerned to generate experiential associations beyond itself, as Still conceives Abstract Expressionist action painting to do.

At most, for Still, the painting is "the bearer of passion,"[16] "an extension of the man, of his blood, a confrontation with himself,"[17] i.e., a timeless, strenuous assertion of the artist's own identity in its self-encounter and self-reliance. To be "comprehended" it must be confronted much as to be created the artist had to confront himself and articulate this confrontation in "an unqualified act." For Still, this is an act of self-commitment, one in which the self is assumed as an absolute being, independent of its vicissitudes. Still believes that in unqualifiedly committing himself to his paintings the spectator comes to confront and create—the two are inseparable for Still—his own mythical, free self. He experiences a "fresh start," a "liberation of the spirit," not only from "that contemporary Moloch, the Culture State," but from "the density of being"—his own and the world's—in which he lives.[18] Still's art permits him, through its radical negation, to encounter his radical freedom as a real phenomenon rather than utopian phantom, as a concrete escape from all contingent orders. In other words, for Still art is a way of making freedom concrete—perhaps the only way— and is concerned ultimately with intrinsic rather than extrinsic values, i.e., with what is indispensable to existence, with enduring depth rather than changing surface. Art tries to suggest enduring depth through changing surface rather than to create a stable *look,* a false order. It is an "extension" of "mind and heart and hand," not simply, a dogmatization—validation—of known forms and thoughts.[19] Still means his paintings to be invitations to, and emblems of, an open horizon rather than signs of a closed consciousness, possessed by clichés of communication and affirming dogma, authority, tradition. Art is to rescue our freedom, not police our limits.

Still squarely asks: what is the broad human effect of art? The very assumption that it has such an effect, rather than simply an esthetic effect, shows that Still believes art has an ethical dimension. His question is: what is art's ethical role in human affairs? He answers: art does not originate any ideas or ideologies, it is not the invention of a system of thought or belief or the articulation of any fragment thereof, but rather it puts us in a position from which we can evaluate the claims of any notion, determine how it impinges on existence and whether we want to suffer that impingement. For Still the act of art is critical and disengaging rather than confirming and psychically coercive. Art no longer confirms and helps convince us of what is already given, whether it be nature or a religion—it is no longer an act of imitation—but suspends our relations with the given so that we can determine its meaning and freely decide our commitment to it. Still carries to an extreme abstraction's implicit disengagement from the given, not simply to assert the autonomous forms of art or to clarify the character of the given, but to insist on the free consciousness necessary for its true comprehension and assessment. Still means to make this freedom an active value rather than a theoretical goal.

In general, throughout his writings, Still thinks of art as value-laden rather than fact-oriented. He constantly alludes to the life-values implicit in art other than his own, and invites us to make value judgments on all art. The values at stake are not those of taste and sensibility, for these, while looking for refinements in the given, accept it as such. Rather, Still believes that all art deals, wittingly or unwittingly, with moral values, those which shape existence at the root. Taste takes an external approach to art, seeing not the values inherent in its creation, but only those having to do with its appearance. Thus, the recognition of the inherent values in his art is not part of the tradition of taste and form, and he categorically rejects any effort to "debase" the ideas originating in his works into esthetic or property values and educational aids.

"Except as a created revelation, a new experience," his works "are without value." For Still, "a single stroke of paint" can restore man's lost "freedom"[20]— by which he means that a single stroke of paint, applied to reveal values rather than to fix facts, can indicate the freedom to choose whatever values one will, which freedom is *the* value of existence. For Still, a stroke must become a value-sensation rather than a fact-sensation—must be "freely" applied, i.e., with no presupposition about its esthetic or historical point. Still means to present an autonomous, free "image," which is inaccessible to taste, and which liberates us inwardly from the conventions of our existence. Like a biblical prophet, Still reminds us of the vanity of taste and the art which appeals to it, and of our values and our unthinking acceptance of them.

Still in effect asks art to repent of its ways, for the attention to taste masks a deeper corruption. He is quite specific about both the art and the nature of the corruption. The "dialectical perversions" of Cubism and Expressionism "only reflected the attitudes of power or spiritual debasement of the individual."[21] More sweepingly:

> The manifestoes and gestures of the Cubists, the Fauves, the Dadaists, Surrealists, Futurists or Expressionists were only evidence that the Black Mass was but a pathetic homage to that which it often presumed to mock. And the Bauhaus herded them briskly into a cool, universal Buchenwald. All the devices were at hand, and all the devices had failed to emancipate.[22]

This is strong language, a violent accusation, and the question at this point is not whether it is true or false, but whether it suggests an appropriate mode for the evaluation of art. For Still, this is clearly not a farfetched approach. He views art as having significant effect on human existence, not simply a transient effect on sensibility. For Still, most modern art, knowingly or unknowingly, enslaved life, perhaps just because it sought to emancipate sensibility rather than life as a whole.

Still's paintings show their ethical purpose through the same combination of negation and affirmation one finds in his writings. Negation of dogmatic tradition, and all it implies, and affirmation of a new painting, offering new things to see and a new way to see. In general, traditional art is passive, except in certain ornamental aspects. It is a passive window on a world to be passively contemplated, no matter how active in itself. It is an art of control. Still's art is act-ive. The focus is never fixed or finalized. Its scene is composed of forces rather than forms, and it is to be consciously confronted rather than passively accepted. Only "engaged" will its full effect be felt, its full point disclosed.

The vehicle of traditional passivity in art, generating a sense of the foreknown—a fixed point and frame of reference—is the figure, however "serpentine" it may become, however ghostly it may appear. Still's art is also influenced by the seemingly inescapable figure, but radically transformed, beyond even a vestigial "presence." Still goes, as it were, underground—to the figure's underworld, its consciousness. Thus Still's art, which is figural in origin, negates the figure after a final totemic apotheosis of it, replacing it with, in Clement Greenberg's words, the "pregnant, activated emptiness" of the field.[23] The painting's field, however, can be interpreted as the field of consciousness. On the way to doing so, one must note that the key point in Still's Copernican Revolution is not that the field, in its vertical structure, retains an implication of figuration, but that the emphasis has been shifted from one of the fundamental terms of an image's organization to the other—away from the figure, with its objectification of forms, to the field which subjectively dissolves them. Still has thus, in effect, undermined the way figure and field traditionally relate, where figure dominates—stands out from and is set off by—field. In Still field dominates and absorbs figuration, which becomes its emanation, a sign that it is energized. This is in itself—climaxing in the mature works of the '50s, which seem to show the field's exclusive existence—disruptive or unbalancing of perception. It unsettles the spectator's expectations, "refuting" his familiar way of knowing the picture—of making it a world. That is, the monism of Still's field is not only provocative in itself, but also because it sabotages our innate tendency to know by duality, by contrast. The field's impact, whether perceptual or conceptual, is only a secondary source of shock. Indeed, since the "description" of the field inevitably gives rise to associations, the shock of an image which seems pure ground is muted, for such associations "people" it—add figuration to its topography. This comes to exist, for most observers, figuratively as well as literally, so that its radicality is lost. (Still fights this loss, in an effort to recover radicality by denying the possibility of any association.) But primordially—radically—experienced, the field's monistic unity, its demand that it be perceived as a whole which is more than the sum of its parts (for these cannot be clearly differentiated), undermines the "dialectical perversion" of our usual way of knowing (in the image, the tendency to divide it into figure and ground or space).

Unity—the unity of the field—is all for Still, and it is experienced as liberating.

> By 1941, space and the figure in my canvases had been resolved into a total psychic entity, freeing me from the limitations of each yet fusing into an instrument bounded only by the limits of my energy and intuition. My feeling of freedom was now absolute and infinitely exhilarating.[24]

In such a "resolution" "imagination...became as one with Vision" for Still.[25] Not only did the pictorial fusion of space and figure free him from the dialectical perversity of their traditional relationship and the dogmatism of their individuality, but this was experienced as liberation from a false, limited view of things. However, Still was implicitly forced to admit—and his development demonstrates—that unity cannot be forced; to do so leads to chaos or awkwardness. Unity may be ultimately real, but the extraordinary sense of integrity it conveys cannot be easily communicated intellectually or emotionally, let alone visually. The experience of unity is a developed achievement, which can as easily fail as succeed, for it is not entirely predictable. It requires special tension to succeed, and when it fails it produces a dismal sense of disintegration.

Still, indeed, comes close to failure many times, but in a sense it is his development which means more to him than any one success, as his emphasis on the continuity between his works makes clear. His development of pictorial unity—as an analogue of psychic unity—does not proceed mechanically but, necessarily, organically. He in effect "stifles" the figure with the space, slowly but surely. He turns a solid into a liquid into a gas, increasingly diffusing the figure in space, until it is totally absorbed. In 1941, for all his excitement at its prospect, Still had only intimated this development. It was not until the mid-'50s that, through painterly osmosis, the figure was implicated in the space, and their unity—the dissolution of both, the famous "spaceless space"—could be spoken of. However, the reciprocity between opposites can never be said to have come to rest in Still's pictures, for that would only be to falsify its functioning on consciousness.

In the '40s Still stripped the figure to bare bones or even intestinal coils— bones of being, coils of consciousness. This "nakedness" is evident as early as *1938-N*. It continues through *1934-J* and *1944-A,* among other works. The flattening or thinning out of the figure while it spreads in space is part of its diffusion. By *1944-G* and *1944-N* figuration reduces to a single tight coil; it is epitomized, as in *Self-Portrait* (1945). In a sense, this last picture marks Still's farewell to self-evident figuration, with its assumption of self-evident selfhood. Neither the figure nor its identity will be taken for granted or exist clearly. They will be submerged in the functioning of the picture—subliminally experienced, not obviously represented. By *1954-S, 1955-D,* and *1955-K-No. 1* figural diffusion is as complete as it will ever be, and the painting comes to exist entirely in terms of surface flow, with figuration—and the various grounds, literal as well as figurative depths, it implies—simply an aspect of its self-differentiation. Still has transformed the bone of being into the grain of being.

Not that Still develops consistently, or without pitfalls. The flow exists in a lame version as early as *1941-P,* together with nondescript figural forms. Sometimes the bony figures become dense and ominous *(1944-A),* sometimes dynamic *(1934-M).* It is hard to separate them from totemic import, with all its mythical implications. They seem a brittle, attenuated variant of the nightmare figure Pollack was painting at the time. Worst of all, the figural coil sometimes seems to function as purely formal device with no spiritual implications *(1945-R)*, a gestural innovation heralding Newman's gritty stripe, but without its open horizon. And sometimes figure and space do not seem so much to cross-fertilize as to crisscross ambiguously *(1946-C, 1946-T)*. It is not clear whether this is deliberate brinkmanship or confusion. One cannot determine whether novel unity or subtle disunity has been achieved. But the counterpoint of such images can also operate with glacial calm, singular unity *(1946-E, 1946-H)*. Also, the painterly osmosis is inconsistent: self-evident in *1947-F* and *1947-G*, less so in *1947-H-No. 1* and *1947-Y*. Such "flaws" are inevitable in any process, although they seem precluded by Still's visionary confidence. At the same time, seen within the continuity of his development, they punctuate certain decisions, some works seeming to function like exclamation points, others like dashes.

In the 1947 works contour seems more crucial than surface process, however much it may be part of it. Greenberg asserts that Still makes a shape's edges less cutting and conspicuous "by narrowing the value contrast that its color made with the colors adjacent to it."[26] But this is not true. Greenberg is interested in the process of color, its orchestration into understated harmony, rather than in the tension of the edges that keeps color intense. Neither saturation nor hue means that much to Still in the last analysis. The edges, with their incipient turmoil rippling through the color, do. Even in the mid-'40s, when Greenberg wrote about Still, edges were consequential for him, however simplified they seem in terms of the total configuration. The basic function of Still's edge becomes clear in the mid-'40s. It is not simply vestigial figuration, but boniness inside out, a spreading marrow which eventually becomes a clear field. Still's edges register the rhythm of the field, contract and expand—pulsate—according to the pressures in it.

The edges carry the burden of the painting's meaning. They can be described not simply as informal figuration but as operational inchoateness, a becoming which is prophetic of new being. Within the field, the figure, become "edgy," functions as a prophetic flow of blood, fire, a pilar of smoke, pointing the way to the promised land of freedom. If there is any symbolism in Still, it hangs on the organic vitality of the edge which, in its struggle to signal the integrity of what seems disintegrating, is as much a rebirth as a dying of form. Like the guiding cloud of Numbers 9:21, the edge can spread over the "scene" of the painting; or it can distill into a discrete unit, a pillar of smoke, to make its purposiveness clear. Such an interpretation of Still's edges connects him with such American "primitives" as Ryder and Burchfield—also edge-obsessed—absorbed by the interplay of elemental life-and-death forces, and the American abstract primitives—Still's "Myth-Makers"—who transcendentalized these forces. Still differs from both in that he is concerned with neither nature nor transcendence, but consciousness. He sees the life and death forces as neither immanent in nature nor as playing out their power on a cosmic stage, but as confronting one another in consciousness.

He is neither a naturalist *manqué* nor a disguised transcendentalist—he repudiates both possibilities—but a prophetic existentialist, aware of the life values at stake in the uncertain battle against living death. He tries, as it were, to ride the expressive waves of the force of this struggle. Mastering them gives a certain autonomy—a sense of self-creation, of simultaneously generating and witnessing the generation of one's own being, with both its lost possibilities and found actuality, and its continuous viability. This vision of self-determination through self-confrontation—confrontation of the life and death forces in oneself—is provincial romanticism, like much existentialism, but it becomes the ground of a creative response to what seems inevitable. In art, it is a way out of the fatalism of tradition, a kind of autonomy, and so authenticity, within the determinations of history. It at least permits Still to make new artistic decisions, to reach a kind of tense decisiveness in a world which tends to set looks—and outlooks—and reworked forms.

Still's edges, like those in Pollock's *The Deep* (1953), are the visible vector result of the conflict between implicit forces. They have a momentary look of autonomy and self-determination, but their rugged shape shows, like pines perpetually subject to the wind's force, that they are the product of violent invisible forces. Their wizened refinement, their virile cragginess—their mix of flexibility and power—shows they are survivors of forces beyond their control, which they have learned to master but not dominate. Tension and autonomy are simultaneous for Still. The apparent autonomy of the edges is the sign of some "staying" of forces. The edge's autonomous form seems idiosyncratic from the point of view of familiar form, but expressive from the point of view of invisible forces which seek a visible outlook. The edge articulates the inarticulate; it is rich with instinct, almost bloodlets it. The edge gives Still's best works their special character; a sense of involuntary, nervous, unresolved agitation—of a unity achieved in and through this agitation. There is a sense of both climax and anti-climax about them—of what Whitehead calls the subject-superejection of force. Its expression is simultaneously its formation, i.e. its organization or consolidation into an autonomous entity. For Whitehead, this is the duration of the process of becoming concrete; Still seems to have frozen that process, stopped it in its path at some irrational moment when its forcefulness is still experienced and the entities it conceives still unstable. Unlike Mondrian, who rationalizes the process itself—I have in mind his works transitional from naturalism to abstraction—Still allows both process and its resultant irrationality.

The edges, then, emerge as "themes" within the larger process of the field, seemingly self-determined yet radically incomplete and expressive of something other than themselves. Within the "total psychic entity" Still conceives the picture to be, the edges articulate intention. They are the themes through which the field of consciousness makes itself manifest as active. As Aron Gurwitsch notes, "the *appearance of a theme* must be described as *emergence from a field.*"[27] The theme—the visual motif—is in effect a melody within the larger music of the image. Indeed, Still's paintings can be understood as a refinement of Greenberg's polyphonic paintings, in which every element is "different but equivalent... in accent and emphasis." Where the surface of the all-over picture as originally conceived was "knit together of... closely similar elements which repeat themselves without marked variation,"[28] Still introduces a marked variation but without destroying the monotonic character of the whole, i.e., without undermining its function as a field. This marked variation—in the edges—restores the musical image to the symbolist context from which it emerged without, however (in the best symbolist spirit), specifying what the edges symbolize. They simply function poetically, as a sign of alert consciousness. In Jules Laforgue's words, they function as "a melodic phrase (a subject), the design of which would reappear from time to time" in the "inextricable symphony" which the poem-picture is.[29] The edges communicate this sense of emergence-appearance and reappearance, conveying the purposiveness of the field (of consciousness) which is crucial to establishing the picture's unity. Still exhibits his works as a group or continuity to sustain this sense of emergence, of purposive process within the pressures of the field. The tension of the process of emergence continues beyond the immediate image floating on the surface of the field, and beyond the frame of any one picture. It is as though the surface is in perpetual, restless labor, about to bring forth something divine or monstrous but unknowable as either.

To understand the intentional character of Still's edge it is useful to regard it as a "fringe," in two—reciprocal—senses of the term. One is William James's, where it means "psychic overtones," "suffusions" of "relations and objects but dimly perceived." It seems possible to understand the fringe as the implicit subject matter of modern art since Impressionism—more particularly since Cézanne, who was preoccupied with the psychic overtones of dimly perceived relations, which he articulated in "sensations" or suffusions. The fringe vibrates because it is "a particular class of transitive state" which conveys a "sense of affinity," which is "one of the most interesting features of the subjective stream."[30] The sense of affinity determines sensations of difference and of likeness—the fundamental, if constantly shifting, sensations of consciousness. The fringe conveys these shifting, transitive states of sensation: Still's paintings are pervaded by subtle resemblances and discrepancies between its elements, a kind of jarring unity of painful affinities. Such sensations appear, disappear, and reappear within the subjective stream or field of perception, which in Still's paintings exists with no one focus, but as a moving margin. The fringe can be characterized in this way as an affinity elision or a psychic ellipsis—as the abstract energy which establishes affinity, whether through likeness or difference, throughout the painting. It is the circuit which both connects and disconnects, unites and differentiates.

Still's paintings—like James's subjective stream or field of consciousness— never have a clear and distinct organization, a fundamental, and so final, form. Any such organization is "bestowed and superimposed on it from without"[31]— by the spectator. This is what Still means when he asserts that his works tell the spectator about himself, about his disposition and predisposition—about his "position." The field painting is not itself a position, nor does it establish one, but it creates the possibility of spectator positioning. Viewing it, the spectator is forced to position himself in terms of his sensations of difference and likeness. He finds himself coming into focus between these cross-hairs, experiencing a variety of affinities, and thus discovering his own consciousness and its purposiveness. He finds himself in a flux of emergent sensations which are analogues for the fringes of his consciousness. The painterly fringes activate the psychic fringes, so that the spectator can experience the freedom of unity through his subjective sense of affinity.

The second meaning of fringe—edge, theme—expands the first. It has to do with the fringe's "pertinence to the broader context" of the field, already noted. This pertinence is "an invariant of consciousness." At the same time, as Gurwitsch notes in words that can be applied *pari passu* to Still's field painting, "the *thematic field* does not coincide with the total field."[32] For the material contents of the two are not the same. Still's field is constituted by colors as well as fringes. Without this material difference the sense of affinity could not function to create its "unity by relevance." Perception or *per-cipere* is *ex-cipere:* it functions through the process of "standing out." The fluid unity of Still's pictures is achieved through the standing out—the "exception"—of fringes which seem thematically relevant to one another. Still's achievement is to make all "parts" of the picture seem to have affinity with one another, so that the picture as a whole seems the differentiation of a unified field. The fringes are differentiations or "exceptional" nuances which momentarily stabilize the field of perception to intimate unity without turning it into permanent organization. Still's "forms" always remain transitive, fugitive, fringelike, so that they can generate the sense of affinity which communicates unity without forfeiting freedom—without making it seem predetermined, but rather the result of autonomous perception. This is possible only because the fringe does not coincide with the field, but rather activates its emptiness.

Despite this, the sublime is not evoked by Still's paintings. They do not fade into the monotony of the infinite, but are infinitely renewable. This is not the same as an evocation of infinity, because in such an evocation the sense of affinity is de-activated. The sense of infinity depends on perception having nothing more to feed on—a forced asceticism. But Still's field, no matter how thin, remains active, offering fresh sensations, a fresh sense of relevance. Its infinity is not the banal distance or the exaggerated dynamics the sublime demands, but rather, in

Whitehead's words, "the infinite background" which "always remains as the unanalyzed reason why that finite perspective of that entity has the special character it does have."[33] Still's fields try to articulate the "infinite background," out of which finite forms arise. That is, he articulates the entire creative process, not only its products.

Such articulation gives Still's paintings a more ethical than esthetic import. Esthetic perception is concerned with grasping the final unity and form of the painting. It has no patience with the process of perception itself, with the choices or alternatives within the process. Taste does not accept a situation of permanent choice, of absolute tentativeness, of an autonomy which leads to and functions through "indecisiveness."

> Morality of outlook is inseparably conjoined with generality of outlook. The antithesis between the general outlook and the individual interest can be abolished only when the individual is such that its interest is the general good, thus exemplifying the loss of minor intensities in order to find them again with finer composition in a wider sweep of interest.[34]

Still attempts to reconcile and integrate the general ground of being with a specific kind of being in a new painterly becoming, creating a new sense of purposiveness beyond that communicated by either of them alone. This process of creative becoming is inherently moral, almost in a Hindu sense, for it recognizes that what will be newly created will depend on the action of what was previously created. Still revives an ancient truth, which the factualization of existence tends to obscure: existence is moral at its root, the "artistic" process of becoming is a moral process of which the "esthetic" result is the accompanying shell of form. The esthetic is the outside view of the inside process. One's morality—one's way of reconciling oneself with the world without sacrificing oneself to it yet acknowledging its formative influence—determines the "essence" of one's being. It is an essence which is only partially in one's control because the terms with which it works were not established by it. Like existence itself, the existence of Still's fields depends upon the moral relationship between general and individual, infinite and finite, abstract and concrete, as these are actually operational. The sensations of taste, the appropriation of the painting as property, its reduction to a formula–each ignores this moral relationship, or misreads its operation, seeing its end detached from its process.

Finally, Still's paintings can be regarded as religious as well as ethical, in the sense in which the religious is the ultimate expression of ethical process. Again in Whitehead's words, the sense of religion involves "an ultimate craving to infuse into the insistent particularity of emotion that non-temporal generality which primarily belongs to conceptual thought alone," thereby "stretching individual interest beyond its self-defeating particularity."[35] Still's paintings are visual metaphors stretching particularity. Recall his impatience with frames and the "Euclidean" order of the traditional picture—with any reliance on predetermined organization which creates particular form. Continuity within the painting, and between paintings, negates both the particularity of any painting and of any frame of reference which might be used to focus it—to make it stand out or be exceptional—and creates a non-temporal generality. Recall his passion for freedom and his sense of the self-defeat inherent in using any particular formal "idiom," since that degenerates into a minor intensity while creating minor esthetic intensities for taste. Finally, recall Still's refusal of particular associations—in itself a kind of non-temporal generality—for they would give his work a false individuality, reflecting the spectator's individual interest. Such associations miss the whole point: that the ethics of art involves the recognition that esthetic decisions are based on moral decisions, so that any esthetic perception or situation is subsumed by an ethical one. For Still, esthetic decisions suggest ways in which one is united with one's world, and so reflect the morality of one's outlook. Still wants to take us to the point where this becomes clear, where we recognize the free choice that created our kind of unity with the world, and then leave us to our ruminating devices.

Notes

1. Clyfford Still, "A Statement by the Artist," *Clyfford Still: Thirty-three Paintings in the Albright-Knox Art Gallery,* Buffalo, 1966, p. 18. Still's ethical orientation in particular, and philosophical approach in general, are noted by Henry Hopkins in "Clyfford Still," *Currant,* Dec. 1975-Jan. 1976, pp. 18-25. Still's reflections on his art can be found in his letters to Betty Parsons in the Parsons papers at the Archives of American Art..

2. Clyfford Still, "An Open Letter to an Art Critic," *Artforum,* Dec. 1963, p. 32. Still, incidentally, in his repudiation of these materialistic factors in human life, echoes the idealism, only more self-righteously, of such first-generation abstractionists as Kandinsky, Malevich, and Mondrian.

3. Clyfford Still, Letter to Gordon Smith, Jan. 1, 1959, published in *Paintings by Clyfford Still,* exhibition catalog, Albright Art Gallery; Buffalo, 1959, n.p. The presence of Cézanne in this list implies a re-evaluation of him, for in 1935 Still received an MFA from the State College of Washington for a thesis entitled "Cézanne, A Study in Evaluation." In this thesis Still clearly identifies with Cézanne, using him, in a general way, as a personal and artistic model. He seems to approve of the fact that Cézanne "pursued the lonely and isolated way" (p. 5), becoming in the process "the most unique paradox in the entire history of art" (p. 1). He notes that Cézanne's "lifelong ideal to subdue this emotional side of his temperament was never completely accomplished" (p. 12). Most important, he sees Cézanne as pursuing "effective unity" (p. 21), Still's own ideal. However, he notes that Cézanne understood this unity in strictly esthetic terms (pp. 18, 22), even subordinating his emotion for things to the ideal of esthetic unity. By 1959—certainly earlier—Still cannot accept the ideal of unity as purely esthetic in its implications, for he understands pictorial unity to have, inextricably, emotional and ethical implications, which are obscured by attention to the esthetic ones. Finally, one might note that Still accepts, and carries to abstract extremes, two of Cézannes ideas: (1) the reduction of line to "fragments of the edges of form or the intersection of planes" (pp. 23-24); and (2) the belief that "nothing was sufficiently stable in its nature," so that the picture could never be predicted or concluded.

4. E.g., see Ralph Waldo Emerson, "The American Scholar," *Selections from Ralph Waldo Emerson,* Boston, 1957, p. 79.

5. Ti-Grace Sharpless, "Freedom . . . Absolute and Infinitely Exhilarating," *Art News,* Nov. 1963, p. 37.

6. Ad Reinhardt, in "The Artist in Search of a Code of Ethics," *Partisan Review,* vol. 42, 1975, p. 284, mocks Still's assertion, not recognizing its derivation from the story of Prometheus, and above all, refusing the idea of the ethical importance of the abstract image. Reinhardt writes: "It is not right for the artist to make his bag of tricks a matter of life and death. Artists who send chills, however delicious, up curators spines with warnings like, 'Let no man undervalue the implication of this work or its power for life, or for death, if it is misused,' should be charged with arson and false alarm."

7. Paul Valéry, "The Ground and the Formless," *Degas Manet Morisot,* New York, 1960, p. 45.

8. See Benjamin J. Townsend, "An Interview with Clyfford Still," *Gallery Notes,* Albright-Knox Gallery, Summer 1961, p. 11.

9. Still, Letter to Gordon Smith, n.p. See Townsend, p. 11 for Still's approval of Hamlet's mocking rejoinder to Polonius, who sees, under Hamlet's ironical direction, a variety of shapes in a cloud—a camel, a weasel, and a whale. All are Polonius' self-projection—himself in a metaphor.

10. Townsend, p. 10.

11. Townsend, pp. 10, 13.

12. Sharpless, pp. 37, 60.

13. For the conception of Still as a primitive see "Thomas H. Hess, "The Outsider," *Art News,* Dec. 1969, pp. 34-37, 67-69.

14. For the conception of Still as a kind of creator ex nihilo see E.C. Goosen, "Painting as Confrontation: Clyfford Still," *Art International,* Jan. 1960, pp. 39-42.

15. Townsend, p. 14. Also, Sharpless, p. 60.

16. Still, Letter to Gordon Smith, n.p.

17. Sharpless, p. 37.

18. Still, A Statement by the Artist, p. 18.

19. Still, A Statement by the Artist, p. 16.

20. Still, An Open Letter to an Art Critic, p. 32.

21. Sharpless, p. 37.

22. Still, A Statement by the Artist, p. 16.

23. Clement Greenberg, "'American-Type' Painting," *Art and Culture,* Boston, 1961, p. 225.

24. Sharpless, p. 37.

25. Still, Letter to Gordon Smith, n.p.

26. Greenberg, p. 227.

27. Aron Gurwitsch, *The Field of Consciousness,* Pittsburgh, 1964, p. 319.

28. Clement Greenberg, "The Crisis of the Easel Picture," *Art and Culture,* Boston, 1961, pp. 155-56.

29.   Quoted by Kenneth Cornell, *The Symbolist Movement,* New Haven, 1951, p. 39.

30.   Gurwitsch, p. 309.

31.   Gurwitsch, p. 25.

32.   Gurwitsch, p. 320.

33.   Alfred North Whitehead, "Immortality," *The Philosophy of Alfred North Whitehead,* New York, 1951, p. 682.

34.   Alfred North Whitehead, *Process and Reality,* New York, 1955, p. 23.

35.   Ibid.

14

Symbolic Pregnance in Mark Rothko and Clyfford Still

By symbolic pregnance we mean the way in which a perception as a sensory experience contains at the same time a certain nonintuitive meaning which it immediately and concretely represents....It is the perception itself which by virtue of its own immanent organization, takes on a kind of spiritual articulation—which, being ordered in itself, also belongs to a determinate order of meaning....It is this ideal interwovenness, this relatedness of the single perceptive phenomenon, given here and now, to a characteristic total meaning that the term "pregnance" is meant to designate.

Can we continue to ask how signification, a meaning, issues from the mere raw material of sensation, considered as something fundamentally alien to meaning, once we have seen that this "unmeaningness" is itself a fiction?

—Ernst Cassirer, *The Philosophy of Symbolic Forms*

Yes, we can continue to ask, for it is the core epistemological question about abstract art, sharply and freshly raised by the works of Rothko and Still, which generate intense sensations and unpredictable meanings and the question of their interrelation. As Michel Conil-Lacoste wrote of the late Rothko, there are "two readings of Rothko: not only the technician of color, but also the engaged heart of mysticism."[1] The technician of color supplies the raw material of sensation, and the mystic communicates ideal meanings. But how much can the two be said to interweave, when the sensory experience of color is so intense it is almost indescribable and meaning so indeterminate it is porous? How, in the perception of color, can one discover spiritual meaning, when the perception is so much a private response and the meaning no more than suggested, erratically and ambiguously? Rothko and Still seem to carry to an extreme Redon's belief in:

an expressive, suggestive, and indeterminate art. Suggestive art is the irradiation of sublime plastic elements, drawn together and combined with the purpose of evoking visions which it illuminates and exalts, meanwhile inciting thought.[2]

The abstract irradiations of Rothko and Still evoke but do not name visions, incite but do not clarify thought, and illuminate and exalt but to no clear purpose. Rothko and Still produce pictures which are kinds of palimpsests, with layer upon layer of implication but with no firm, final layer of sense. Perceiving them, one experiences deeper and deeper sensations, profounder and profounder meanings, but one erases the other, and none reaches bottom, where all are rooted and connect. In the end, the pictures imprint no absolute sensation, no one meaning. Sensing comes to seem a hardly adequate response to them, and pursuit of meaning a game of blindman's buff.

The possibility of their collapse into meaninglessness suggests the "unreliability" and even groundlessness of their form and content. Unless color is understood as what Kandinsky thought it must be—"purposive playing upon the human soul"[3]—there is no way one can assume that the pictures imply the "tragic and timeless."[4] There is no way one can assume that the "immanent organization" of the pictures has a "spiritual articulation" unless one presupposes that form and color have spiritual import. Art supplies the abstract elements and culture the abstract meanings, but their transcendental unity is a wish—a matter of intention and belief, of a mystique of intention. It may be that such transcendental unity is not the true issue of abstraction. As Greenberg wrote:

> Abstract art is effective on the same basis as all previous art, and can convey a content equally important or equally unimportant; there is no difference in principle. On the other hand, it is possible to assert...that the great masters of the past achieved their art by virtue of combinations of pigment whose real effectiveness was "abstract," and that their greatness is not owed to the spirituality with which they conceived the things they illustrated so much as it is to the success with which they ennobled raw matter to the point where it could function as art.[5]

But Greenberg himself is confused about the role of content in abstract art, for he celebrates its hidden presence while being unwilling—or unable—to name it. Writing about David Smith's sculpture, he remarks:

> I am not able to talk about the content of Smith's art because I am no more able to find words for it than for the ultimate content of Quercia's or Rodin's art. But I can see that Smith's felicities are won from a wealth of content, of things to say; and this is the hardest, and most lasting, way in which they can be won. The burden of content is what keeps an artist going....[6]

The burden of content in Rothko and Still is conveyed by their intention that their works be spiritual or transcendental—communicate, in Greenberg's words, "metaphysical pretensions." "Pictures must be miraculous" wrote Rothko, "revelations," "unexpected and unprecedented resolutions,"[7] while Still thought he was presenting the "Vision" through the "Act."[8] But because the relation between form and meaning in their works "oscillates," to use Schiller's term, they do not show the transcendental as belonging to a "determinate order of meaning." It may be that the imprecision that arises because, as Schiller says, form and content are "contradictory impulses" is itself the transcendental, which shows itself as the perpetual disjunction between particular and universal. But if this is what the transcendental is, then the pictures have no chance at all for symbolic pregnance, which insists upon the synthesis of specific sensation and determinate meaning as its source. In fact, the Rothko-Still metamorphosis of form into configurative color obscures rather than illuminates spiritual meaning, for it establishes an infinite regress of sensation: meaning becomes completely indeterminate as one is overwhelmed and swept along by a continuum of sensation. Reflection on meaning becomes, on the one hand, a response to color consciousness, which can give no determinate meaning. On the other hand, it becomes a mediation on the artist's intention to be profound, but can find no profundity itself—which is why I speak of the mystique of intention sustaining and animating the works, rather than of unintended meanings realized through their intended sensations.

Thus, the art of Rothko and Still is susceptible to what has been called "metaphysical pathos," especially the "pathos of sheer obscurity, the loveliness of the incomprehensible," and, akin to it, the "pathos of the esoteric."[9] From its origin in the artist's intention to its perception and the attempt to determine its meaning, their art is inevitably subject to mythologization, which simultaneously preordains its greatness but hides the reasons for it.[10] While the pathos and myths must be cleared away before the pictures can be comprehended, they correspond to something in their condition. For, as noted, neither reading of Rothko-Still actively supports the other—decisively relates to the other. In fact, each seems to interfere with the other, because to be entirely absorbed in color sensations leaves no room for spiritual meanings, and to insist on such meanings is to be distracted from one's sensations. In Rothko-Still sensation and meaning are both, in a sense, abstract: neither is concretely grounded in nor firmly associated with the other. Thus, the pictures are "pathetic" not only because form and meaning in them seem mutually exclusive, but because this affords the opportunity to mythologize them as simultaneously physical and metaphysical. Their physical intensity is self-evident, their meaning mysterious—and so presumably metaphysical. They evoke the metaphysical without substantiating it because one expects them to be meaningful without knowing what they might mean. Thus, the pictures become arrogant: they dismember into esoteric sensations—sensations with a source but without a purpose—and farfetched but unmentionable meanings. They perfectly exemplify, in Neumeyer's language, abstract art's uncertainty of meaning and ineffability.[11] Since they do not refer to a familiar reality, they presumably refer to a higher reality, but what that reality might be, and whether it is knowable or unknowable, is never hinted at. Rothko-Still pictures are thus colossal promises based on exaggerated expectations—demanding that one believe in them, but not rewarding one's belief. Their physicality calls strong attention to them, but their ambiguous metaphysicality seems a poor, even illusory object for the attention they raise to a high pitch. The pictures, then, arouse faith in themselves, and it has been said that faith is a willing suspension of disbelief, but the rewards of such suspension are highly uncertain, and the ultimate object of faith so invisible it seems nonexistent. The pathos of the true believer's position is mirrored back to him by the art's supposed metaphysicality, but that is no more than a tautological hypostatization of his suspended disbelief.

The sensation of suspension—of indeterminate hovering—generates the momentum of Rothko-Still pictures, and is the source of their lovely incomprehensibility and esoteric implications. It is created by the "forthright verticality" Greenberg finds in Still, and the "scumbled over colors" he finds in Rothko, and is responsible for the "activated, pregnant 'emptiness'" he finds in both.[12] (This "emptiness," activated and made pregnant by color sensation, is the ambiguous sign of the transcendental spirituality of the pictures—"ambiguous" because it may be nothing but the physical effect of large shape filled with color, and so an indication of the absence rather than presence of spirituality.) More crucially, the sensation of suspension is created by "Still's slack, willful silhouettes"—Rothko's are as slack but not as willful and less "arbitrary in contour"—and above all by Still's "great insight . . . that the edges of a shape could be made less conspicuous, therefore less cutting, by narrowing the value contrast that its color made with the colors adjacent to it." This permits "the artist to draw and design with greater freedom in the absence of a sufficient illusion of depth," sparing the surface "the sudden jars and shocks that might result from 'complicatedness' of contour." This insight, accepted and adapted by the "less aggressive" Rothko to his less complicated, more convenient contours, is for Greenberg the gist of "field" painting. It is not simply, in Rothko's words, the creation of the meta-easel "large shape" that "has the impact of the unequivocal,"[13] but the projection of a subtly differential "flatness that breathes and pulsates."

Such an extensive, nuanced surface—Greenberg first experienced it as "utterly uncontrolled"—functioning as an environment for the viewer, is not without precedent. It originates not simply with Monet, but is recidivist romantic naturalism, as Greenberg implicitly acknowledges when he connects Still with Whitman and writes of the "fray-leaf and spread-hide contours that wander across his canvas like souvenirs of the great American outdoors." Greenberg, in fact, has argued that:

> The best modern painting, though it is mostly abstract painting, remains naturalistic to its core, despite all appearances to the contrary. It refers to the structure of the given world both outside and inside human beings.[14]

One can regard Rothko-Still pictures, with their rejection of the classicist "craving for clear lines of demarcation,"[15] as visionary English gardens—"dream landscapes," Greenberg once called Rothko's early pictures—and both artists can be viewed as belated, decadent, 19th-century romantics, abstracting romantic intention and attitude to an ultimate. Romanticism can "be described as a conviction that the world is an *englischer Garten* on a grand scale":

The God of Romanticism was one in whose universe things grew wild and without trimming and in all the rich diversity of their natural shapes. The preference for irregularity, the aversion from that which is wholly intellectualized, the yearning for échappées into misty distances....[16]

The irregularity of Still's images, Rothko's escapes into misty distance, the untrimmed quality of general configurations and particular shapes—making it hard to give them an intellectual import and intelligible meaning, but making them seem to drift in a netherworld of latent emotion—attest to a romantic yearning for a wild cosmos symbolic of a full, complex, difficult spirit. Rothko and Still are not *esprits simplistes* but "sensible of the general complexity of things,"[17] and as such find any straightforward image anathema and a betrayal of the complexity of art, as well as of nature and consciousness.

Yet they do not offer a full cosmos, only the activated, pregnant emptiness Greenberg encountered—really too loosely structured to be called a cosmos, and too uneventful to be called full. Nor does it make sense, in the last analysis, to regard their pictures as alluding, in however disguised a manner, to nature. While, in Ehrenzweig's words, Rothko's "use of the weakest possible forms, such as insubstantial quadrangles insecurely suspended against a more solid ground,"[18] conveys distance, it is not clear that the distance belongs to a landscape sky. As Friedländer wrote, "a low horizon is always and everywhere a sign of advanced contemplation of nature,"[19] and there is rarely anything that can be consistently called a low horizon in Rothko and Still, and so their pictures cannot be understood as advanced or abstract contemplations of nature. Even when the "lucid film-like transparency of the colour bands...thickened into almost solid cloud banks several miles deep," as in Rothko's black paintings (among others), it is not clear that because the distance now appears to be definite and measurable it is cosmic. This thickening, the consequence of what Ehrenzweig calls a "secondary solidification process," which also involves verticalization (powerfully evident in Rothko, Still, and Newman),[20] is not concerned to "naturalize" abstraction by showing it to deal in very dense, "figurative" matter. Rather, the conversion of "mobile pictorial space" (such as Pollock's) "into precise almost measurable illusions" aims to discreetly differentiate a potential chaos and thereby bring it under some control.

This chaos is a purely creative one—it, or transcendental unity of matter and meaning, can be the outcome of the creative process. Rothko and Still forestall the chaos by means of solidification and verticalization. At the same time, as noted, these do not necessarily produce the transcendental, but only suspension—between potential chaos and potential transcendence. The false perspective—self-evident in Rothko, implicit in Still (and Newman)—evoked by the solidification and verticalization processes does not promise transcendence because it does not point beyond itself. Rather, the space implied by the hypothetical perspective is static—almost stagnant in Rothko, and festering in Still—and directionless. It is because of these qualities that the space of their pictures is usually ignored: the works in fact are spoken of as spaceless, which really means, as Greenberg put it, that they are "almost altogether devoid of decipherable references" to Cubist space. However, it is not so much that there is no space in Rothko-Still pictures, but that it does not live up to our expectations of what space should do: contain something, in some orientation to it, and be a medium for movement. But Rothko-Still space seems constitutionally incapable of containing anything, and congenitally unmoved. It is these factors that are responsible for the sense of the emptiness of the pictures, and their impacted immediacy.

This unyielding, barren space seems to push the work in a transcendental direction, as well as keep it from sinking back into an inchoate state. Yet to say one knows what it does is to presuppose one knows what emptiness is about. It is this hovering emptiness, a negative of space, that one recurs to in considering Rothko-Still pictures—a saturated emptiness, an impure absence, which seems fraught with implications. Now it is noteworthy that Rothko describes the transcendental as though it were absent—in purely negative terms an unnamable alternative to the familiar.[21] And Still, while he shouts about it, also does not know how to name it. For both, in the last analysis, it remains a gray eminence, and their pictures are its runic remains. Both in fact are more certain of what they are doing when they deny the claims of those they regard as pretenders to the throne of the transcendental, than they are when they themselves pretend to it.[22] They are obsessed with separating the profane from the sacred, but this does not in itself assure them of their own priesthood, or even guarantee that what they wish to worship exists. They are *manqué* religious men, for whom the transcendental can never be self-evident, and thus whose aspiration remains peculiarly muted. This cannot be attributed to their being enamoured of the *deus absconditus*. Rather, it has to do with a hovering between scepticism and faith, and doubt of both. Magician-priests, they create pictures, in a genre familiar from Morris Louis, that are like temple veils or stage curtains— Rothko's has rents in it, Still's is in a tattered, fiery state. The Rothko-Still picture means to be, in Breton's words, "an intellectual event, or a landmark in the direction of mystery and fire." We are tempted to believe—and they themselves want to believe—there is something significant behind the curtain. But it is never lifted, the veil is never parted, the god remains invisibile or invented, a hope or a deception. The pictures strongly intend the transcendental, but leave it literally a matter of the artist's sleight of hand. In viewing them, we do not know whether we are in the temple or theater. They seem to call for ritual, but the script to accompany them has not yet been written. Rothko-Still pictures are either magical incantations or pious frauds, or perhaps both, for they traffic in the magic of belief as well as the belief in magic.

Yet viewers believe the pictures touch them with spiritual power, and are able to find "that lever of consciousness which will change a blank painted fabric into a glow perpetuating itself into the memory," as Kozloff puts it.[23] The glow, because it is inwardly as well as outwardly revealed, acquires spiritual significance. What is the nature of the "lever of consciousness" that converts glowing emptiness into pregnant perception—that needs no other confirmation than its own activity to find emptiness articulate? Spontaneous and self-justifying, its results stand in no need of clarification, because its force stands behind them. Ehrenzweig finds this consciousness implicit in the spacelessness of the pictures—the source of their emptiness. But more than being implied by the spacelessness, the spacelessness is the exemplification of the abstract consciousness:

> The lack of spatial depth suggested a mystic-oceanic feeling, of individual existence lost in the universe. The annihilation of space indicated a dreamlike level of experience where our commonsense concepts of space and time have no meaning.

The first sentence offers a conventional interpretation of the unusual experience of abstraction—the suspension of commonsense concepts of space and time—the second sentence reports. Ehrenzweig, like Rothko and Still, filters this experience of abstraction through a familiar concept—the mystic-oceanic feeling, the transcendental—to make sense of it. All three predetermine the meaning of abstract consciousness—the transcendental particularly puts it in a straitjacket—rather than accept it on its own, perhaps frightening terms: the suspension of active relations with everyday reality, allowing consciousness to show itself as a generalized state of feeling. The transcendental—the super-meaningful—is announced to fill the vacuum of meaning created by the removal of the commonsensical, as if to obviate the experience of death by the prediction of immortality. But the experience of abstraction is not one of mortification of matter and *contemptu mundi,* but rather of the revelation of consciousness as a phenomenon in itself, not one which will outlast matter but which dynamically charges it with purposive meaning. Abstraction, in other words, is the discovery of consciousness as the power of intention. To call abstraction transcendental is to call attention to it not only as a sign of the disengagement of consciousness from the commonsense world—rather than its engagement with the uncommonsensical world of the divine—but as a manifestation of consciousness in and for itself. The hovering emptiness of Rothko-Still pictures suggests both the disengagement and concentration of consciousness as reciprocal events. The hovering intends something, but nothing in particular; it is simply the muscle of consciousness. Ideally, abstract consciousness would like to mirror itself, as it seemingly does in the pictures; realistically, it can re-present the world as meaningful, as it would seem to want to do in the pictures, but they present no world for it to re-work. The purity of abstraction in Rothko and Still—for it can hardly be said to be significantly naturalistic or geometrical in derivation—is another sign that their pictures are about consciousness in a state of suspended animation or abstract suspension, full of intention toward the world but free of it ("oceanic"). The pictures are thus uncommonsensical, being essentially spaceless and timeless—non-worldly—and purely "sensible." The pictures show consciousness withdrawing into itself, and at the same time projecting the possibility of a meaningful cosmos, without saying anything about the actual shape or sense of such a cosmos. Rothko and Still carry the condensation and displacement of abstraction to an extreme in which consciousness itself seems to be revealed, with no commitment to either the reality of nature (space) or the self (time), the conditions of the world.

Consciousness at its root, as pure intention ("feeling"), abstractly reduced to its own activity, seems, as Ehrenzweig notes, to lack differentiation, and thereby to be able to "accommodate a wide range of incompatible forms," i.e., to suggest a world but not necessarily to give or commit itself exclusively to one. To reach the root level of consciousness, in which it seems vivid but indefinite, "suppression of form" rather than "precise articulation" is necessary. Rothko and Still show suppression of form in process. It is particularly evident in Rothko's development, where an early preoccupation with the "organic life" of abstract figuration is replaced by, in Hegel's words, the "principle of totality" which is responsible for all beauty. Still has always seemed midway between these extremes. His interest in both the organic and the beautiful seems tenuous and tentative. He has been concerned to accommodate a wide range of incompatible forms, which are not so much alive or beautiful as deviously disembodied, like fire was for Plotinus. Rothko also seems to achieve a Plotinean disembodiment, but he shows it to be charming—as Greenberg wrote, after 1955 he "produced far more gorgeous than achieved paintings."[24] This not only nullifies their "glow," making it less significant as abstraction and less the resolute step of consciousness coming to itself, but makes it seem hollow—exactly why Rothko's works seem less pregnant than Still's. The transcendental ego Rothko's works are pregnant with aborts. Nonetheless, the surface tension in both Rothko and Still signifies a state of crystallization so advanced that it can be conceived as an articulation of disembodiment rather than an abstraction from embodiment.

Ehrenzweig takes "the plastic quality of pictorial space in painting...as a conscious signal of a vast unconscious substructure." This substructure was self-evident in Rothko's early mythological works (mid-Forties), where it was directly connected with the idea of myth as an attempt to give body and voice to the ineffable.[25] Since then, Rothko's canvases grew increasingly empty, while Still's, despite similar mythologizing tendencies, also involving the use of a latent figuration, stayed more or less as they were in principle, i.e., in their indifference to the organic and the beautiful. Ironically, although Rothko's pictures became emptier than Still's, they never achieved the same pure concentration, because they were concerned to organicize and beautify—vitalize and aestheticize—the transcendental, rather than evoke the fitful play of consciousness, as Still's art does. Still's works risk more because they are less beautiful, and achieve more because they are less openly transcendental. They thus seem more able to evoke a vast unconscious substructure, without mythologizing or explicitly "figuring" it. That is, they are more personal—less universal—than Rothko's pictures. Still has an implicitly more individual content—and consciousness—than Rothko. Rothko's pictures have always been more easily labeled—mythological, beautiful, transcendental—than Still's because they run a culturally prescribed course. Still's, because they do not do so, can more easily signal the unconscious, without making it conscious. Their suspension exists to greater effect.

An understandable mistake in the interpretation of the work of Rothko and Still is to characterize this suspension as sublime, and to pay undue attention to the environmental scale and impact of the work.[26] This is to predetermine its meaning and formal effect. It is not transparently clear that the infinite is suggested by the apparently unscalable openness of the form, nor that its grandeur is all-encompassing. The big pictures are not blindly boundless but have both the circumference and center, only, in Nicholas Cusanus' words, the "center coincides with the circumference." That is, one's perceptual location in them always depends upon one's conceptual realization of them, a sense of their closure as forms of consciousness. Also, the pictures seem less a surrounding environment than a suppurating flatness—an irresistibly swelling flatness pushing one away rather than engulfing one, signaling one to keep one's distance rather than drawing one in. Engulfment occurs only if one abstractly attends to the flatness, rather than to the fact that it is a colored flatness—a flatness made pushy by color. As Ehrenzweig remarks, "The battle for the flat picture plane has been lost over and over again in the history of art." Color is another way of losing it, of achieving what one might call reverse or projecting depth—a space that pushes out at the spectator rather than into the picture. If this battle had not been lost—if the picture was perceived as nothing but pure plane—one would long ago have become indifferent to it, and the picture would have become nothing, i.e., another indifferent object. The Rothko-Still picture is empty but not nothing; its flatness is activated and its emptiness pregnant. It is because of the intensity and implications of the picture's surface that we cannot enter it as we would an environment. It is too forbidding, too swollen with its own self-absorption and self-esteem, to permit easy penetration of its surface. Its openness is a mirage; it is really an abstract wall. This alien abstract surface gives no clues to any content that might make us feel at home on it. It is sheer border, implying a vast unconscious substructure but not divulging it, implying a conscious world but not implementing it. The abstract surface gives the sensation of a boundary about to burst and impinging on and implying what is beyond itself, but this beyond is too absolutely beyond to be appropriated by vision, to be enjoyed as even an imaginary environment.

Kozloff has recognized this "brinksmanship" in Rothko, in which "mists are kept from becoming too introspective or nebulous by the austerity of the format."[27] Rothko's "combination of puritanic restrictions and lavish self-indulgence produces a drama." Rothko himself thought of his pictures as dramas,[28] and his preoccupation with the dramatic is an inevitable result of his brinksmanship. What he said of Milton Avery's pictures can apply to his own: they communciate at once "a gripping lyricism" and "the permanence and monumentality of Egypt."[29] But what is most important about the dramatic in both Rothko and Still is that it is the source of their art's symbolic pregnance, reconceived as indifferent to the question of referencing, with which it was so involved for Cassirer. In fact, true symbolic pregnance involves a deliberate refusal to reference particular meanings, an insistence on the indeterminate situation of meaning. To conceive, as Cassirer did, of symbolic pregnance in the first place as involving determinate meanings means to conceive of sensation as necessarily representational of reality. But sensation's role is different, once we recognize its subjective as well as objective origins. It invokes, even provokes possible meaning, like a gadfly; it does not fix or confirm actual meaning. All sensations are conditioned by our general sense of reality, bringing its indeterminacy to bear on particular situations, crystallizing the indeterminacy into a sense of living possibility. Sensations "dramatize" the indeterminate yet vital sense of possible meaning reality might have if it were subject to our intentionality, and the symbol resulting from any constellation of sensations articulates such a possible meaning. This dramatic character of sensations is evident in the unceasing drama of the Rothko-Still picture, and its correlate indeterminacy and unresolvable yet "felt" meaning. The drama in a Pollock or de Kooning has the same indeterminacy, but with less sense that it is the expression of strong intention toward reality. The Rothko-Still use of an open field makes clear that such indeterminate intention is not arbitrary, as the congestion in a Pollock or de Kooning might lead us to believe. At the same time, the openness or abstractness of the field makes it clear that the "reality" intended is uncommon.

In general, the best Abstract-Expressionist painting never resolves itself, never conveys a final meaning let alone a finished surface. The gestures that constitute that surface may be decisive in themselves, but their relation to other gestures is indecisive—"open." Moreover, Abstract Expressionism is not simply dramatic action between specific formal protagonists—e.g., color and format— but between the inherent possibilities of form and meaning. It is a search for, and setting in conflict of, all such possibilities, so that they apocalyptically cancel one another out in expectation of still more profound possibilities—of the final saving possibilities, which will make all come closer. These, of course, never arrive. Abstract Expressionism epitomizes the eschatological brinkmanship inherent in all art—that risking of chaos and meaninglessness (dogmatized uncertainty) to achieve a pregnance beyond ordinary, artless appearances. As such, it epitomizes the fundamental conflict between intended form and given content inherent in all art, a conflict whose resolution is always tentative, incomplete, and inevitably forced. The equilibrium that results is momentary, a truce but not a peace.

In Rothko and Still, the uncertain outcome of the battle or drama creates the effect of symbolic pregnance. It sets loose a totally abstract and completely arbitrary power of suggestion which holds full sway over the work. It is a dangerous, permanent undertow in the work, pulling one away from the safe shores of clear perception and known meaning into a sea in which one can drown in obscurity—which reads as profundity—of form and meaning. Such absolutely arbitrary power of suggestion, let loose by dramatic brinkmanship, undermines the effort to find anything innate to the art. Form and meaning become nominal, and the paintings of Rothko and Still cannot even be securely established as pictures, whether of an inner or outer world. In Kozloff's words, it is possible to read them as no more than "pigmented containers of emptiness," as forms of resolute absence. Their work shows that all absolutes of form and universals of meaning are illusions—perhaps possibilities, but magical ones. Their works leave us with a sense of uncategorizable form and makeshift meaning. A picture is produced in which everything seems possible but nothing is ever actual, leaving one in a state of perpetual turmoil of expectation, a kind of psychic randomness—a state of incipient chaos, a kind of nervous breakdown. One clings to the subtle surface differentiations, the formal possibilities, but these quickly slip out of one's grasp and become informal. One clings to a variety of attempted meanings, the most ultimate and the most banal, but none can be decisively articulated. The work perpetually surprises and perpetually stymies: it is infinitely rich with possibilities yet emptily finite.

In the midst of this arbitrariness, what then can the work of Rothko and Still be said to give, apart from doubts—apart from the temptation to end the willing suspension of disbelief and indulge in the pure suspension of scepticism? It gives the promise and pregnance of the life-world, its abounding with new possibilities, none of which seem to be interfered with by old actualities. The arbitrariness—the blank check on the power of suggestion—eliminates, as encrusting excess, given forms and meanings, well-known "truths" of statement (including Rothko's "stated" rectilinear forms, which in the "course" of his work slowly became "unstated"). It leaves a tabula rasa of creative intention, what Emerson called "heroic passion" using "matter as symbols of it(self)."[30] It generates pure abstrct passion, creating the illusion of being charged with absolute passion. To feel charged with such passion is to feel charged with inexhaustible, limitless potentiality. Their art is thus quintessentially romantic: it is an art of quintessential desire. The dramatic art of Rothko and Still creates the illusion of existing in a presuppositionless state of consciousness in which one's being is an undifferentiated continuum of potentialities, all of which seem realizable and none of which are specifiable, and which will never be put to the test—which will never have to stand up to reality, which has been dismissed by the same abstraction that generated the sense of potentiality. The art communicates a sense of inward plenitude, which one need not, in Ehrenzweig's Freudian fashion, identify with mystic-oceanic feeling, but recognize as a utopian source of fruition. In Rothko and Still emptiness turns inside out and reveals itself as disguised fullness, if the emptiness is approached in the proper spirit. As Rothko wrote, the picture can only show itself for what it might be when there is "a consummated experience" between it and the viewer. "The appreciation of art is a true marriage of minds. And in art, as in marriage, lack of consummation is ground for annulment."[31] This romantic, participation mystique conception of the relationship to art echoes Hegel's assertion that "The work of art has not such a naive self-centered being, but is essentially a question, an address to the responsive heart, an appeal to affections and to minds."[32] Sufficiently appealing, the question can be answered, the heart responds to the emptiness of the image with its own fullness, the involved mind gives the emptiness its own center—its own intention.

In a sense, Rothko and Still show a horror vacui in an abstract, ironical way. The abstract sensation of potentiality they supply is a product of the creative belief they stimulate. It is color that is the source of this belief for it creates a sense of inner movement, of inner timing that triggers expectations, which must be realized if only in fantasy. What Husserl calls inner time consciousness is involved in the perception of their color—a sense of an irrational color flux harboring potentiality. The abstract flux implicit in color generates the sense of potentiality which "fills" the vacuum of the large, open picture, the vacuum generated by its immensity of scale relative to the human body. (While Alloway has shown the figural implications of their work, the emptiness of the work, and the irrationality it introduces into the sense of scale, nullifies such implications, or throws them off.) It is the color flux that keeps the vacuum from being a total void, and, as long as it is perceived, that prevents the picture from losing its symbolic pregnance—its significance. It is the color flux that keeps the suspension dynamic—prevents the verticality from becoming either static or inspirational, but remaining ambiguously hovering. The color flux, which is so generative, is also responsible for the overall sense of off-symmetry in Still and anti-gravity in Rothko. The solidification of the color flux (Ehrenzweig) brings the matter which symbolizes the heroic passion of creative intention into being. As long as the color is in flux, the sense of potentiality is sustained, and the life-world will not abort its futurity to become empty facticity: the picture will not lose its blinding suggestiveness and become, in Ehrenzweig's words, mere form, academic and decadent. It is the color which sustains the myth of primordial creativity the picture means to establish.

The art of Rothko and Still thus presents such fluidity and interpenetration of percepts and concepts, such a fecundity of possibilities of sensation and meaning, that one cannot help but speak of it as "spiritual," for as has been remarked the realm of spirit seems not only to permit but to necessitate contradiction.[33] The Plotinean emanations of their pictures, leading to all kinds of discordant forms and meanings, and discordant relations between form and meaning—which Plotinus saw as inevitable in spiritual creativity, and as a sign of its fullness and diversity[34]—shows, in Rothko's words, "an insatiable appetite for ubiquitous experience in face of the fact of mortality."[35] This speaks not only for the artist's mortality, but for that of the work—not of its possible destruction or loss to history, but the way, during perception of it, it seems simultaneously consequential and inconsequential, becoming now another aesthetic appearance, now what Plotinus called the "self-intent" of consciousness. Abstraction, in Rothko and Still, has been stetched to a limit at which it almost breaks—becomes senseless. It has become so concentrated—so completely metamorphosized concrete being into pure intensity—that one can only respond to it silently. At the same time, while Rothko said that "silence is so accurate," it is often also purblind and close to indifference. The pictures may suffer from the same self-appointed or self-stylized greatness—self-prejudiced superiority—Rothko and Still were contemptuous of in intellectuals, critics, and historians.[36]

At one time I thought of their pictures in terms of Heidegger's conception of the ecstasy or standing-out of futurity, but I have come to see that the suspension implies no particular time-direction—certainly not memory and the past—and there is not a sufficient momentariness about it to convey the singular present. Then I thought they showed a concern for "symbolic immortality," in Lifton's definition "a compelling urge to maintain an inner sense of continuity, over time and space, with the various elements of life,"[37] but I do not see the elements of life in the pictures. I have thought of Rothko's pictures as "partaking" of the atomic bomb burst,[38] with its fusion of light and matter, surface and form in hovering smoke—a totalitarian synthesizing of all beings, an ironical unity. The glow of Rothko and Still seemed to me a sublime revenge against all matter. The pictures seem so much a matter of the world of color, which, as Goethe said, represents "the acts and sufferings of light," that they dissolve the seeming opposition between matter and energy. Yet because their matter is color it seems insubstantial, and because the light is not present as an independent phenomenon it seems consequential and energetic, more impacted, so that the co-implication of matter and energy in the works seems undermined by the ambiguously significant charge of each. Finally, I thought the spacelessness of Still's pictures was an ideal way of directly forcing time into the open, since it could no longer hide in space as its symbol (Bergson): but without the symbol the phenomenon did not seem to exist. The weakness of the works of Rothko and Still, if one can call it that, is that they give no determinate symbols, which can evetually lead us to become oblivious of them. The strength of the works is that they show us how belief generates symbols—how important the "lever of consciousness" is in the discovery of any kind of determinateness in art. I see the abstractions of Rothko and Still as a deliberate intaglio of consciousness, a visible relief of consciousness whose features are, if not invisible, forever changing—faster than Proteus—because they are not legible, but only felt as spontaneously on the move. Rothko and Still show Leonardo's blank wall overgrown with possibilities, pregnant with creative intention but not creative presentation.

Notes

1.   Michel Conil-Lacoste, "La transcendence de Rothko," *Le Monde des Arts,* March 29, 1972, p. 13. The scepticism of my article arose out of an experience of discrepancy between the two readings of Rothko and Still, i.e., my perceptual awareness of their art did not coincide with the conceptualization of it as transcendental. They themselves tried to force a transcendental or spiritual meaning upon their works: this straining for transcendental effect showed that it was not self-evident in the sensations aroused by the work. Shaped color is not in and of itself transcendentally convincing; expected meanings do not necessarily come into existence in experience. In a sense, the question of this article is whether the pictures of Rothko and Still are visual molehills whose interpretation has made them into transcendental mountains, or transcendental mountains that are inherently difficult to climb. To assume both—to accept both readings as a matter of course—is to be intellectually dishonest as well as false to one's experience. It is to evade the logic of the situation of the art as much as it is to accept an unstructured plurality of meanings. It is to ignore the fact that a picture by Rothko or Still is an incomplete symbol. Their art seems to stretch the limits of symbolism, perhaps beyond the breaking point.

2.   Odilon Redon, "Introduction to a Catalogue," *Theories of Modern Art,* Herschel B. Chipp, ed. (Berkeley, 1968), p. 120.

3.   Wassily Kandinsky, *Concerning the Spiritual in Art,* Chipp, p. 155.

4.   Adolph Gottlieb and Mark Rothko, "Statement," Chipp, p. 545. For Gottlieb and Rothko, the tragic and timeless are the only "valid" subject matter, so that the experience of their pictures in purely phenomenal terms—as nothing but a source of unique sensations—misses their point. Yet if the tragic and timeless are not directly experienced, but are read into the works—with the prompting of the artist—their meaning is falsified. The ambiguity of the works is that they sometimes seem tragic and timeless, but at other times purely immediate and without any connotations of value.

5.   Clement Greenberg, "Art Chronicle: Irrelevance Versus Irresponsibility," *Partisan Review,* 15 (1948), p. 577.

6.   Clement Greenberg, "David Smith's New Sculpture," *Art International,* 8 (1964), p. 37. Greenberg argues in effect that all content is implicit in the work; any content that is explicit has not been assimilated by its style. However, this does not mean the content cannot be articulated—is "ineffable"—only that in speaking of it one must also discuss its transformation by style and the point of this transformation. That is, style must be understood as an interpretation of content—a way of qualifying it.

7.   Mark Rothko, "The Romantics Were Prompted," Chipp, p. 549. Correlate with his desperate desire to produce visionary pictures was Rothko's sense of "the urgency for transcendent experience," but uncertainty of his ability to achieve and sustain such experience.

8.   Clyfford Still, "Statement," Chipp, p. 576. Both Still and Rothko suffer from a sense of histrionic self-presentation, which cannot abide any questioning of motives and results. Such hubris masks their uncertainty about the success of their great ambition.

9.   Arthur O. Lovejoy, *The Great Chain of Being* (Harper Torchbook, New York, 1960), p. 11. All quotations from Lovejoy are from this source.

10.   Still is particularly guilty of the attempt to absolutize his art. Its workings, according to Still, are mysterious, and its implications horrendous. Not only is the artist a kind of god—the update of this Renaissance idea is that he is now a *deus absconditus* rather than, as in the Renaissance, openly divine (Still's sense of the artist's "obscure" position thus represents a retreat from the

Renaissance artist's sense of his position)—but his work is also charged with divine power. It is to be regarded with awe and handled with the care that sanctifies. Thus, Still could assert, "Let no man undervalue the implications of this work or its power for life;—or for death, if it is misused" (Chipp, p. 576). (One might replace "misused" with "not properly respected and unquestionably worshipped.")

11.   Alfred Neumeyer, *The Search for Meaning in Modern Art* (Englewood Cliffs, N.J., 1964), pp. 88-90. Neumeyer's exploration of the uncertainty and ineffability of abstract art is based on the assumption that "Whatever insights we may gain, they come to us neither through nature nor as literary content . . . but solely through associations evoked by sense impressions which cannot be rationally checked." This does not preclude an implicit or hidden content; at the same time, it implies that this content can never be completely verified—our sense of its reality is not binding—but exists as one among many possible interpretations of the work.

12.   Clement Greenberg, " 'American-Type' Painting," *Art and Culture* (Boston, 1961), p. 225. All subsequent quotations from Greenberg are from this source unless otherwise noted.

13.   Gottlieb and Rothko, p. 545. Correlate with the large shape is the use of "flat forms because they destroy illusion and reveal truth." It is interesting that for Greenberg flatness is simply an essential property of the medium of painting, while for Gottlieb and Rothko it has transcendental significance, and becomes a way of achieving "the simple expression of the complex thought."

14.   Clement Greenberg, "The Role of Nature in Modern Painting," *Partisan Review*, 16 (1949), p. 81. The question, however, is not whether abstract art is naturalistic in origin and end, but why it presents outer and inner nature in abstract—"non-objective" or subjective—form. It is hard to believe that the reasons are purely stylistic, i.e., art historical origin, and without any general spiritual purpose. The shift to abstraction, in other words, involves inner as well as historical (outer) necessity.

15.   Lovejoy, p. 56.

16.   Lovejoy, p. 16.

17.   Lovejoy, p. 7.

18.   Anton Ehrenzweig, *The Hidden Order of Art* (Berkeley, 1971), p. 159. All quotations from Ehrenzweig are from this source.

19.   Max J. Friedländer, *Landscape, Portrait, Still-Life* (New York, 1963), p. 55.

20.   In Still the verticality is already apparent in a number of realistic works painted in the 1930s, such as the American scene picture *Grain Elevators* (1937) in the National Portrait Gallery, Washington, D.C. The uprightness of Rothko's pictures seems to imply the centrality of a wingless altarpiece, and Newman's verticality seems a romantic reminiscence of an obelisk. Thus, Still's verticality seems naturalistic, Rothko's religious, and Newman's nostaglic-historicist (a disguised quotation) in origin. In general, the verticality is meant to be the sign of a permanent transcendence—man, as it were, transcending the ground by standing upright on it, and no longer able to return to his prone relation to it. This uprightness is in effect the beginning of his spirituality, its first sign, for it gives him a look beyond his finite state and immediate situation and seems to free him from the material condition of being earthbound. See Erwin Straus, "The Upright Posture," *Phenomenological Psychology* (New York, 1966), pp. 137-65.
       Still and Newman tend to make the verticality more telling by placing it in a relatively horizontal format, as though in conflict with this context, and seeking to aspire or reach beyond—and dominate—it. Rothko's works, because they don't truly do so, convey a seemingly more self-assured, more recognizable spirituality or transcendence, but thereby a more static,

unmoving one. His verticality is fixed into and so an echo of his format, thereby losing the energy implicit in the transcendental "direction." Rothko's sense of transcendence is more charming and mechanical, and so less significant than that of Still and Newman.

21.   Rothko, p. 549. Rothko sees only a negative way to the transcendental, through the "pulverization" of "the familiar identity of things" in order to destroy their "finite associations." However much he argues that "not everything strange or unfamiliar is transcendental," the transcendental for him is experienced as strange or unfamiliar, i.e., as not fully possessed or known and as such not completely real.

22.   For Still (p. 574), particularly to be denied are "self-appointed spokesmen and self-styled intellectuals with the lust of immaturity for leadership." His contempt for them is the catalyst for his own higher purpose, but does not insure its success.

23.   Max Kozloff, "Mark Rothko," *Renderings* (New York, 1969), p. 152. All quotations from Kozloff are from this source.

24.   Clement Greenberg, "ROSC '71," *Art International,* 16 (1972), p. 62.

25.   Rothko's early works make a dogmatic assumption of mythological meaning amounting to the adoption of an ideology of mythology. Andrea Caffi's article "On Mythology" in fact follows Rothko's "The Romantics Were Prompted" in its original publication in *Possibilities,* 1 (Winter 1947-48), and is illustrated by Rothko's mythological pictures from 1946-47.

26.   The most convincing argument for the sublime character of the works of Rothko and Still was made by Lawrence Alloway, "Residual Sign Systems in Abstract Expressionism," *Artforum,* 12 (1973), pp. 36-42. Alloway's argument is that their paintings are disguised traditional pictures with traditional meaning. However, insofar as their abstraction is taken seriously, as something important in itself and not simply as a device for heightening (by hiding) well-known meanings, it transcends the sublime. Modern abstract art is interested neither in the beautiful nor the sublime, but the moment when "art"—with all its paradoxical, multi-level implications—seems to come into existence out of worked-over matter. It is concerned with the tension between non-art and art, the moment when one seems to become the other and vice versa. (On the most elementary level, this is the tension between material and the expressive use to which it may be put—and the way this expressive use does not always seem to be achieved, so that the art seems to reduce to an awkwardly "handled" material.) For a work to be recognized as beautiful or sublime one must already take for granted the fact that it is a work of art. Modern abstract art does not take its own artisticness for granted, but is always—at its best—in the position of demonstrating that it is art, not simply ordinary appearance. It is interested in the moment of imaginative transformation of non-art appearances into artistic appearances, not the aesthetic qualities that might result from this transformation.

27.   What Kozloff treats purely formally, Gottlieb and Rothko (p. 545) see as a "poetic expression" which has "the impact of elemental truth." Kozloff does not see the tension between subjective and objective tendencies in Rothko's work as related to subject matter, but reduces it to a matter of composition.

28.   Rothko (p. 548) asserts that he thinks of his "pictures as dramas; the shapes in the pictures are performers." He also remarks that "The presentation of this drama in the familiar world was never possible, unless everyday acts belonged to a ritual accepted as referring to a transcendent realm." Clement Greenberg, "The crisis of the Easel Painting," *Partisan Review,* 15 (1948), p. 482, remarks on the "dramatic imbalance" of forms in Rothko.

29.   Mark Rothko, *Milton Avery: Prints and Drawings, 1930-1964* (Exhibition Catalog, Brooklyn Museum, 1966), p. 16.

30. Ralph Waldo Emerson, "Nature," *Selections from Ralph Waldo Emerson* (Boston, 1957), p. 44.

31. Gottlieb and Rothko, p. 545.

32. Quoted by Bernard Bosanquet, *A History of Aesthetic* (New York, 1957), p. 472.

33. Lovejoy, p. 83.

34. Quoted by Lovejoy, pp. 65-66.

35. Rothko, p. 549.

36. Still, p. 547.

37. Robert Jay Lifton, *Boundaries* (New York, 1969), p. 22.

38. Willem de Kooning, "What Abstract Art Means to Me," Chipp, p. 560, remarks that "Today, some people think that the light of the atom bomb will change the concept of painting once and for all." It is possible to argue that the light that led Rothko away from his mythological paintings was that of the atomic bomb, and that in fact in a number of Rothko works one has disguised reminiscences of the famous mushroom shape of the atomic cloud. The cloud—made up of mists—can be interpreted as a libidinous discharge, helping explain Rothko's exploitation of the libidinous or erotic character of color. Also, the grand sensation it affords becomes the scaffolding for Rothko's attempt to create a grand manner of color.

15

Cosmetic Transcendentalism: Surface-Light in John Torreano, Rodney Ripps, and Lynda Benglis

The work of John Torreano, Rodney Ripps, and Lynda Benglis, especially certain "sparkling" objects which present rather than represent light and use it to dazzle our eyes rather than to reflect a surface, seem to me a new species of "luxury painting." Clement Greenberg once applied this term to French painting in the period between the World Wars. Its sweep included masters as different as Braque and Matisse. They all came together in a pursuit of sensation for its own sake, a luxurious handling of means with a near indifference to subject matter, or at most the acceptance of a convention of subject matter. For Greenberg, the problem with luxury painting was that it had lost all "truth to feeling." It did not bespeak the pessimism—later, after World War II, an existential pessimism—of the postwar years, but continued to cling to the mood of "optimistic materialism," as Greenberg called it, on which modernism came into being. By forcing this mood through an attention to surface, conceived as a rich material rather than a critical resource, luxury painting comes dangerously close to kitsch: Greenberg took any forcing of feeling to carry with it the threat of kitsch, i.e., of an art working more with received than achieved values, an art which did not question the conditions of its own givenness but accepted them as inevitable. If artistic conditions served to carry content to new heights of meaning, their own viability was never at stake. The difference between kitsch and modernism—and the luxury painting which almost makes modernism itself kitsch—is the difference between unselfconscious and self-conscious art, where the generation of consciousness of the conditions of art becomes art itself, and the goal of art.

Now in Torreano, Ripps, and Benglis what we have is a new luxury art that comes close to being kitsch by reason of its "sensational" handling of material. But that is not the end of their art. What redeems it for what I have before called Existential Formalism is their self-consciousness about its sensationalism, about its kitschy aspects. Torreano's use of cut glass, Ripps's swashbuckling, pasty-paint rosettes, and the Benglis's razzle-dazzle, shine-in-the-dark phosphorescence—all of this not only verges on an outright materialistic kitsch, but reminds us of the kitsch culture that we all, willy-nilly, inhabit. Torreano's cut glass has its affinities with artificial gems of all kinds; Ripps's rosettes seem like enlarged artificial flowers, at once as mushy as real flowers and nightmarishly giganticized, as in some Magritte dream gone soft; and Benglis's knots have that look-at-me, I'm-in-the-spotlight, don't-I-shine look of an abstract Liza Minelli strutting her stuff. The objects of Torreano, Ripps, and Benglis both borrow and enter, as art has been doing since Pop art, the realm of kitsch culture, and as such become a demonstration of what has been called the fine arts/ popular culture continuum.

But the point is not their demonstration of the continued viability of the continuum; it is these artists' self-conscious use of "luxurious" materials from the kitsch culture—or what passes for luxury, "big time"—to produce an art which mocks its own kitsch dimension and, in so mocking, transcends it, presenting a new decorative ideal—in fact, a kind of decorative transcendentalism, i.e., a self-mocking, gaudy, tinsel-and-stage-paint transcendentalism. In essence, this is a transcendentalism that knows its own cosmetic character, and which is an expression of a theatrical ambition. What Adorno deplored, the convergence of entertainment and art, and what Michael Fried insisted upon, the radical separation of theatre and high art, is, in the work of Torreano, Ripps, and Benglis, mocked and used as a new source for self-conscious transcendental effect, a grand effect which, in the very process of being achieved, shows the cheap stuff of which it is made. Torreano, Ripps, and Benglis accept the fact that in today's world art and entertainment are one, that modernist self-criticality and theatricality converge, and that the attempt of either side to repress the other only leads to the decisive infiltration of the one by the other.[1] The critical point is to explore the way each does in fact infiltrate the other, dialectically convert into one another. The new luxury art makes it clear that the distinction between high art and entertainment is obliterated today.

In Torreano, Ripps, and Benglis the major mechanism of this convergence is the use of light, that material which does not seem to have to demonstrate its transcendental nature, yet which seems so matter-of-fact. Torreano's shields, with their elusive incandescence, Ripps's efflorescing, almost blowsy flowers, with their faint fluorescence, and Benglis's knots, as archly naive in their projection as Ripps's quasi-callow flowers, all fill with a garish luminescence— all raise a barrier of light around their material. This flashy luminosity at once confirms the material's luxurious character and the "sensational" way it is handled. The light functions as a kind of anointing material and, at the same time, separates us from the object, so that it seems to shine in its own detached world as a kind of beacon that we might be foolishly lured toward, a kind of siren song full of unexpected rocks that we might crack up on. That is, the light seems at once organically of the object and an emanation from beyond it, cloaking it in mystery. It is the same kind of mystery as that generated by an externally applied cosmetic: it is meant at once to bring out the natural, organic color of the face it decorates and to demonstrate its existence in a realm beyond the ordinary, beyond the one its viewer inhabits.

The mystery generates an illusion of transcendence, and while we know that the illusion is manufactured, entirely a matter of artifice, we would like to believe the transcendence is inherent to the material it adorns: the shields, the rosettes, the knots all shine with a transcendental light, which is at once responsible for their "organic" character and their luxurious look. Transcendence is the true luxury, the true trick in a world recognized as being strictly material, and it is their ability to generate the illusion of transcendence while being self-evidently, even grossly, material, that gives the works of Torreano, Ripps, and Benglis their significance. Purely materially, these works seem corruptible, and even quaint in this corruptibility; and yet, at the same time, they emanate from the very heart of their garishness an incorruptible material, a light that absolves them of their vaudevillian traits. Despite themselves, these works become shamanistic, their puerile pursuit of the cosmetic revealing itself as a loyalty to the absolute—which today has to be invented anew out of its vulgar opposite.

We have come a long way from the idea of the transcendental as tragic and timeless; it is now theatrical and timely. Its whole point is to make the art object seem timely, smart. It belongs to its world as a necessary luxury, reminding us that nothing is raw and innocent these days—neither the illusion of transcendence nor the matter out of which it is made. Instead of that early inexperience in abstraction which led to a naive belief in its transcendental impact and implications, we are overexperienced in abstraction, and know the cosmetic character of its transcendence—the cosmetic value of transcendence for all matter in our world, giving it at last that luxurious character which will outlast its innocence, and make us aware that our use of it is not innocent.

Note

1.   I first pointed this out in "Authoritarian Abstraction," *Journal of Aesthetics and Art Criticism,* 26 (Fall 1977), pp. 25-38.

16

Lichtenstein and the Collective Unconscious of Style

"Pure psychic automatism" is the way André Breton defined Surrealism—the direct expression of the unconscious, "in the absence of all control exercised by the reason and outside all esthetic or moral preoccupations." Breton also said, "Surrealism rests in the belief... in the omnipotence of the dream and in the disinterested play of thought."[1] What, then, is Roy Lichtenstein, known for his literal, impersonal transcription of his popular sources—his unemotional use of a consciously chosen subject matter—doing with a Surrealist style? What is the master of the cooled image and the stereotyped format doing with Surrealism's radically personal, emotionally overripe imagery?

Lichtenstein has for some time been catching in the dragnet of his "comic," public style a variety of high and formerly highly personal styles, and reducing them to bold "looks"—popularizing them into appealing tokens. Under Lichtenstein's treatment, they become at once quaintly anecdotal moments in a picaresque narrative of modern art, communal forms rather than idiosyncratic inventions—friendly and fashionable rather than esoteric. It is as though Lichtenstein is saying, let these high styles survive in the glare of the spotlight— become show business—or disappear, with the mysteries supposedly in their care, into oblivion. Only that which makes it into the public realm means anything; only that which has a public identity can have a private meaning. Lichtenstein's historicism has become in some sense a matter of ordering priorities to a public logic.

With his assimilation of Surrealism, Lichtenstein has made something like a clean sweep of modern styles. Previously he had subjected Cubist- and Expressionist-derived imagery, and the styles of artists as diverse as Matisse and Mondrian, to the general law of his own style—itself borrowed. Now Surrealism too is flattered by being used as a subject matter—aped (which is one way of being apotheosized) and thereby demythologized. Read as a preconceived code, even reduced to a kind of stencil, Surrealism, like Cubism and Expressionism, degenerates in impact, however much, like all clichés it exerts a pull on consciousness.

The Surrealist image is reduced to a kind of slang, even slogan—a stylistic shorthand in which it seems stripped of its burden of implicit meaning and made entirely explicit, so that it can function efficiently in the lingua franca which constitutes the collective consciousness of modern art. Under Lichtenstein's treatment, Surrealism becomes at once a quickly circulating currency and a highly quotable motto, no longer enjoying the privileges of its original status. It loses its avant-garde character and "creative" meaning and becomes instead a matter-of-fact form, bespeaking its commonplace potentialities.

Yet something new is clearly afoot in Lichtenstein's handling of Surrealism. These new works make us look back afresh on Lichtenstein's earlier assimilations, and even on Pop Art as a whole. They raise the question as to whether Pop was not always subliminally Surrealist—whether the hypnotic effect of its popular imagery did not imply the existence of a kind of collective unconscious, and whether Pop Art was not a kind of exploration of the powerful workings of that unconscious and of the way it became personalized. Indeed, the welcome Duchamp gave to Pop Art by reason of its use of found objects—continued in Lichtenstein's use of found styles—should make us aware that more is involved than the appropriation and recycling of public signs. As Lichtenstein's Surrealist imagery makes clear to us, Pop was an examination of the subjective import of public signs—the way they are *felt* and thereby influence the formation of personal values.

In Lichtenstein's new works, there is hardly any direct quotation or inventory of known Surrealist imagery—no Miró or Dali, Max Ernst or Yves Tanguy. Lichtenstein's other historicist paintings have customarily functioned not simply as acknowledgments of once radical, now familiar styles whose shock and obscurity have worn off, but also as "catalogues" listing, as it were, the most transparent traits of the style they salute. But in Lichtenstein's Surrealist paintings, the sources have been transcended, or more precisely, transvalued. What Surrealist specifics there are can be traced mostly to Picasso—recalling Breton's praise of Picasso as the artist who "carried the spirit, no longer of contradiction, but of evasion, to its furthest point."[2] We will find a similar evasion in Lichtenstein, which bespeaks a similar toying with unconscious import—a similar disguising of personal meaning.

In Lichtenstein, the banalization of supposedly profound styles masks a profound personal involvement with and redefinition of subject matter. Picasso—as, earlier in Lichtenstein's career, Mondrian or Pollock or Monet, and even earlier, comic strip characters—is used Surrealistically, i.e., metaphorically, to express a personal content. In fact, in these explicitly Surrealist paintings, Lichtenstein himself makes his most personal appearance to date. He no longer hides behind well-known, preconceived content—or, rather, this content can now be read in personal as well as public terms. It has generally been held that the artist-as-subject is *persona non grata* in Pop imagery; yet Lichtenstein's appearance, however devious and phantom-like, in his Surrealist paintings should make us reconsider this belief.

Pop Art may well be as personal an expression as Abstract Expressionism. Expressionist energy should not invariably be read as personal. And in Lichtenstein's Surrealist paintings we will see that the personal can be spelled out relatively precisely as a dialectical structure—a situation of conflict, treated with a kind of sophisticated humor, sometimes tending to the black.

Lichtenstein's Surrealist paintings, then, are Surrealist to the extent that they propose a subjective enigma through objective means. Recall Breton's insistence on the "transmutation of those two seemingly contradictory states, dream and reality, into a sort of absolute reality, a surreality"—it is this transmutation that Lichtenstein gives us. Recall, also, Breton's rejection of "the slippery-floored halls of museums," where the only thing he found of value were "a few marvelous glances received from women," which led him to confess that "the enchantments that the street outside had to offer me were a thousand times more real" than the artifacts inside.[3]

In Lichtenstein, we find museum pieces—museum styles—put on the street, where they acquire a new kind of enchantment, and we find, also, an obsession with woman, as the high road to one's own subjective awareness: woman, in the Surrealist paintings, now no longer the weepy and romantically tortured ingenue of comic-strip love affairs, but a seductive, breasty, fleshy bathing beauty—the emblem, in her blondeness, of the bitch goddess of success that William James noted Americans so busily worshipping.

Lichtenstein in fact appears to be wrestling with the experience of success—this is one of the things his Surrealist paintings are about. So that while he makes Picasso a street person, and Picasso's metamorphic, seemingly endless freeform female a beach girl—as she also is, often more gratingly, in Picasso's own work—Lichtenstein still means to come to terms with the success of both, and with both as consummate symbols of success. At issue, actually, are not only success and sex, and the sexiness of success, but also the problem of influence—the pathos of subsuming and transcending one's awareness of other artists, which Picasso also suffered from and struggled with.

Personal content in these new works is signaled by an almost compulsive repetition of a certain kind of subject matter. The female figure comes back over and over again, in all her Picassoid flamboyance. While subjected to seemingly endless transformation, she always retains certain characteristic features: the perversely amoebic body; the shock of blond hair, like a kind of ornamental scroll signaling consistency of purpose in the midst of changing shape; the brazen red lips, wielded like a kind of branding iron; and the blue eyes, deceptive in their seeming innocence. All of this in primary colors, along with a male presence who, by contrast, is brooding and dark—even when he's borrowed from Léger, who shares with Lichtenstein a search for communal theme and a communicative art, without sacrificing estheticist considerations.

The male presence in these paintings takes many forms, often almost abstract, although never quite as freely abstract as the goddess. The male apparition changes form more completely than the female apparition, who keeps her generalized, clichéd aura of perpetual transformability. The male figure, whatever it becomes, becomes it stably: thus, however multiple his incarnations—the Léger gent, the wood-grain construction, the dark T-shirt or the shirt-and-tie "hieroglyph"—the man epitomizes stability, the woman instability. They exist in social proximity, but are psychologically apart.

This seems one aspect of Lichtenstein's message: the myth of the war of the sexes, or especially of its truce—its stalemate. Lichtenstein's passionate handling of forms—there is in certain passages a contrast that is almost violent between the formal constituents of male and female figures—bespeaks the passionate, yet impacted, love-hate relationship between male and female. And this becomes even more complicated when the female figure can be read as both the bitch goddess of success and the all-American love goddess, and the male figure as artist-lover-devotee who wants at once to possess her, to keep her at a distance as a muse, and to study her as a phenomenon in herself. In other words, the artist wants personal gratification from her, while treating her as an allegorical personification of his own artistic ambition which includes mastery of the American social environment he inhabits—and also the art he competitively means to and needs to master. (One should note in these works reprises of Lichtenstein's own brushstroke and mirror pictures, and other fragments of his past work. Proving he can develop beyond himself, Lichtenstein hangs on the walls of his Surrealist world not only the pelts of other styles, but the pelts of his own pictures. It is a typical self-critical gesture of the self-transcending, and so freshly developing, artist.)

In general, in his earlier phases Lichtenstein is preoccupied with the emotionally charged, potentially explosive moment, in effect the orgasmic moment—the moment when the tearful girl feels helpless and hopeless, or when the hot-shot pilot is pouring it into the enemy (both are evidenced in 1963 paintings). In such works, he deals with the stereotype of the woman's sphere as well as that of aggressive masculinity or competitive machismo, searching out the climactic moment in both. His abstraction of his war explosions into metal relief structures as well as his miltant Art-Deco Depression frieze also testify to this. His most successful earlier works are those in which dynamic formal values conspire with dramatic iconographical themes to convey a sense of violent emotion—the moment at which unconscious energies, the powers of instinct, break through the social facade of events and at the same time articulate their full significance.

There is enormous tension generated between Lichtenstein's apparently impersonal style and his depiction of a subjectively explicit moment. Moreover, in Lichtenstein's historical paintings, there is a tension between historical source—the style "found" in history—and the artist's use of it, which generates an unconscious resonance and implication. For—and this is the real irony—the Pop-pictured style represents the style as it exists in the collective unconscious rather than in personal awareness, and this collectively felt style becomes the starting point for any unconscious ruminations ("feelings") about it. That is, the style is evocative, now, only in its collective unconscious—i.e. "found"—form.

Lichtenstein's '60s imagery can be directly related to Max Ernst's remark in his 1936 essay titled "What is the Mechanism of Collage?" about his transformation, in his art, of the "banal pages of advertising" into "revealing dramas" of his "most secret desires."[4] Lichtenstein, also, has rummaged through the advertising images and meanings of our day to create personally as well as socially revealing dramas—to objectivy, among other things, his desire for an all-American success and personal sexual gratification. This objectification permits a certain detached amusement, the kind with which Duchamp claimed he looked upon the world and himself.

Psychologically, what has been at stake in Lichtenstein's paintings all along is the so-called "promise of happiness" that art is classically supposed to offer—a utopian promise that a proto-Symbolist poet like Baudelaire saw, and that a Marxist thinker like Marcuse sees. In Lichtenstein's Surrealist paintings, this theme of happiness becomes as explicit as it probably ever will be in his art. The vision involves the conventions of a peaceful, benign environment of plenty; a sense of strength in harmony, vigor yet order; and above all, satisfaction in love. Indeed, his Surrealist paintings can be viewed, thematically, in terms of the Mediterranean ideal of the good life—beach scenes feature prominently.

Self-love is also involved, or simply self-esteem, as in the 1978 *Self-Portrait,* where both narcissism in general and the artist's role as narcissistic imitator of reality are confirmed by the substitution of mirror for face. (One thinks of the Surrealist observation that the artist is a mirror. Lichtenstein has literalized the metaphor—illustrated as well as illuminated it here.)

Of course, as important for happiness as self-love, and the artist's love for the look of his world, is love of a fellow being—that completes and confirms happiness in a calm, paradisiac world. But one of the problems Lichtenstein seems to pose is whether woman is in fact man's fellow being. His images of women in these works epitomize otherness, from a clearly male point of view. The dark and pensive male figures project a generally melancholy presence that haunts the lively, "light" female. The wood-grained or business-suited male seems intrusive in the sphere of the billowy odalisque—an unlikely companion on the beaches of Cythera. In some cases, the male is Lichtenstein himself, in faintly ominous, T-shirted symbolic form; or he may be a bit of comic strip head (*La La La,* 1977); or a Léger character (*Stepping Out,* 1978); or, again in sharp contrast with the female, an abstract constructed form radically different from her own curvilinearity (*Figures,* 1977). The contrast between dark male and light female is perhaps most explicit in *Cosmology* (1978), where, as Minoan profile busts, they face each other from opposite sides of the canvas.

These works are clearly tragicomic allegories, almost vaudevillian in method, yet pointed in their tension, in the unresolved dialectic of relationship they bespeak—whether it be between man and woman or artist and world. Aspiration ends in polarization, the fight a draw. But the world the "partners" inhabit is kept pleasant by reason of their mutual need for one another. The dialectic between man and woman is emblematic of the dialectic between art and life.

These works take their place in the grand tradition of allegorical representations of the relationship between man and woman that appears in works as different as Titian's *Venus with the Lute Player* and Picasso's various renderings of the artist/model relationship. Lichtenstein's stylistic idiom is different, yet mythical in its own right, using modern mythical materials. Lichtenstein's art in general can be understood as dealing, as essentially as Surrealism, with problems of creativity, the myth of the artist's transformation of raw, worldly material into a subjectively expressive image which articulates reality. Lichtenstein's Surrealist paintings make explicit what his art has always been about: the infusion of subliminal meaning into blatantly given form and content. Only now the secret is more evident.

Notes

1. André Breton, "What Is Surrealism?" in Herschel B. Chipp, ed., *Theories of Modern Art* (Berkeley, 1968), p. 412.

2. André Breton, "Surrealism and Painting," Chipp, p. 407.

3. Breton, "Surrealism and Painting," p. 405.

4. Max Ernst, "What is the Mechanism of Collage?" Chipp, p. 427.

17

The Unhappy Consciousness of Modernism

Modernism—which I understand as that point of view which sees art as the mastery of purity—involves not so much a loss of tradition as a willing suspension of tradition. It is not so much that tradition is impossible from the perspective of the present, but that the very meaning of historicity—its implications of smooth continuity, of the easy inevitability that seems to make events flow into one another—has been bankrupted by a new sense of what it means to be the present. To be modern, as Jung says, means to be "fully conscious of the present," and that full consciousness is not possible from the point of view of traditionalism, which sees all presents as *petites perceptions* of an infinite continuum of events with no particular *telos,* but then also with no particular dead ends. There is simply the passage of events into one another, in an all-embracing temporality. To be modern is to discover raw possibility, giving the present an enormous presence, making it seem the totality of being, the very essence of being. As Jung says, man "is completely modern only when he has come to the very edge of the world, leaving behind him all that has been discarded and outgrown, and acknowledging that he stands before a void out of which all things may grow."[1] I understand modernism in art as a way of commanding the presence of the present from the perspective of modernity—a way of being responsible for the enormous charge of possibility that is concentrated in the pure present, for the sense of complete openness that gives the present its purity, an openness out of which new worlds are likely to emerge. Yet this openness remains bound by presentness, and so remains an abstract charge making the concrete presence of the artwork more "pregnant," to use Clement Greenberg's word, than it would ordinarily be. And in that tension between abstract charge and concrete presence we catch our first glimpse of the unhappy consciousness of modernism, or presentism, as it should properly be called. For the relationship between the abstract charge of possibility, or the aura of openness, and the actuality of material presence—the "closed" factuality of what is given to us in the present—is unresolved, and remains unresolved so long as the art is understood to be purely immediate, i.e., completely taken up by its presentness.

Presentness is self-defeating, for by consuming all openness—by allowing openness to exist only as a utopian aura to material presence—it depreciates, and with that material presence itself must be depreciated. The aura of openness degenerates into a felt void, and material presence fades into matter-of-fact givenness. The work of art becomes an "interesting fact," the dull shadow of a once-substantial present, and an echo of its own dream. Modernism collapses; full consciousness of the "basic" present becomes consciousness of the banally given. Any return to traditionism is precluded by the recognition that no amount of historical consciousness can restore the dream that was lost, can compensate for the abandonment of the sense of an infinite creative potential, which proved to be the mask of nihilism. The modernist work of art shrinks to an unresonant finitude.

But there is a more immediate formulation that helps us understand the unhappy predicament that modernism embodies. It has to do with the modernist sense of what is proper to art. Modernism understands the immanence of art in terms which deny it self-transcendence, or rather, which subsume its self-transcendence in its immanence. The givenness of a work should be its only effect; that is what it means to speak of the work as pure. Thus, when Greenberg acknowledges that the "unconscious or preconscious effect" of the modernist work of art is as constitutive of its quality as its "literal order of effects," yet never demonstrates how this is so, he implicitly assumes that such an unconscious or preconscious effect is sufficiently unspecifiable as to seem illusory or else is too negligible in its influence on quality to merit serious consideration. Paying attention to the modernist work of art's unconscious or preconscious effect distracts from the "proper experience" of the modernist work, the experience "which has to do with the making of art itself." It is that experience which is responsible for the "increasingly literal order of effects" in the modernist work. The modernist outlook views art entirely in terms of its making and the literal results of that making. In fact, the modernist outlook carries the Aristotelian sense of art-as-making to an extreme. Modernism represents the absurd argument for an exclusively materialist conception of art, which not only sees the work literally but reduces its "effectiveness" to its literalness, so that all it "communicates" is its own givenness. In Greenberg's thought, there is a quasi-Marxist aspect to this reduction, with unconscious or preconscious effect seen as a dispensable superstructure or ideological superimposition on the materially literal work of art. Such literalness is indisputable, and becomes the basis for "common sense" agreement about the nature of the work of art, the referent for unequivocal communication about it.

But communication exists in name only, for the materially abstracted work is addressed to no one in particular, and those who find themselves addressed by it are neither transformed by nor have any transformative effect on it. Their consciousness of it does not help constitute it, nor does their consciousness of the modernist ("presentist") work significantly constitute them. Communciation, then, is not assumed by the manifestness or literalness of the modernist work, which requires only that its addressee—who is never more than arbitrarily conceived, and is certainly not to be socially rooted, apart from having the leisure to contemplate art—conform to its visible character, acknowledge its givenness. Clearly this is a reversal of the Copernican Revolution that Kant effected, in which the object had to conform to the subject rather than vice versa. It is an unacknowledged if sophisticated return to a traditional conception of perception. The sophistication comes in with the concept of literalness, and above all with its effect on the subject, who is forced back on his own literalness, subtly cut off from his own history, the fluidity of his own experience. Pure or modernist art thus seems to succeed, where even religion never completely did, in liberating us from the limits of our own experience—by limiting us to our literalness.

The question, of course, is what it means for both the work and its serious contemplator to seem unencumbered by any other meaning than that of their own being—which hardly seems a meaning at all, since it is not a horizon by which either is framed. Self-framing, without context, both the modernist work and the modernist contemplator appear absolute by virtue of their literalness. But is not such absolute literalness an illusion—as much of an illusion from the point of view of unconscious or preconscious effects as they are from the point of view of literalness? Is not the impulse to purity, however cultivated and elevated, the sign of a general attitude, and as such fraught with social meaning? The reduction to the literal implies a search for the unchangeable in a field of rapidly changing historical experience, for the secular equivalent of the sacred in an unredeemably profane field of experience. The literal is seen as the holy grail, the unequivocally and divinely "communicable," in a world of highly equivocal, changeable communication—a world full of misunderstandings, in which the ground of communication seems like quicksand, and even seems to call itself into question. From another closely related point of view, giving allegiance to literalness, limiting art to literalness, is a way—like that of the ostrich who buries his head in the sand—of precluding, or at least seeming to escape, the expanded consciousness of reality in the modern world. The rhetoric of literalness that modernism asserts—fanatically advocates—not only seems a kind of know-nothingness in the face of an expanded knowledge of reality, but the articulation of an unself-contradictory knowledge in a situation in which knowledge inevitably becomes self-contradictory, in an expanded, one might say Faustian, field of experience which seems to demand self-contradiction if it is even minimally to be mastered.

In analyzing the concept of modernism, we begin to realize that purity is defined as much by what it negates as by what it affirms, and that its self-certainty or affirmative character rests on a foundation of uncertainty, a shaky negation. The concretely felt is always haunted by the vaguely known; the explicit experience of art is always hemmed in by the implicit experience of the historical world; our sense of the literalness of art must always struggle against our sense of its metaphoric relation with life. Our sense of the effectiveness of art must always struggle with our sense of our effect on it, with what we read into it to make it effective in our lives. Oscar Wilde summarizes the situation brilliantly in his account of "the highest kind of criticism," the criticism which "treats the work of art simply as a starting point for a new creation" and "does not confine itself . . . to discovering the real intention of the artist and accepting that as final." As Wilde says:

> the meaning of any beautiful created thing is, at least, as much in the soul of him who looks at it, as it was in his soul who wrought it. Nay, it is rather the beholder who lends to the beautiful thing its myriad meanings, and makes it marvellous for us, and sets it in some new relation to the age, so that it becomes a vital portion of our lives, and a symbol of what we pray for, or perhaps of what, having prayed for, we fear that we may receive.[2]

Clearly, the modernist does not want the kind of imaginative intimacy with the work of art which would give it an identity beyond itself, an existence beyond its pure or literal presence, and which would make it seem, as a whole, communicative of anything beyond the sum of its material parts. And yet modernism is unhappy with being merely literal, and is haunted by the desire to communicate beyond itself, to have effect that is more than itself. It knows, though, it can never communicate an effective whole of meaning, for it is too self-conscious of the conditions of communication. This self-consciousness is forced upon it by the state of communication today. For to be modern or fully conscious of the present, to take the present as the only perspective, means to acknowledge the bankruptcy not only of historicity, but of communicativeness. The easy inevitability of neither can be assumed today, and the dissection of the language of art which modernism implies—and which goes hand in hand with the rejection of historicity—carries with it an implicit acknowledgment of the difficulty of communication. This difficulty is ironically confirmed by our impatient expectation of achieving full communication—of the great possibilities of communication which an understanding of the mechanisms of communication seems to offer, but only in a utopian way, as an unrealized creative potential. Wilde is again a help to our understanding of modernist unhappy consciousness, the consciousness that is divided between a sense of the language of art and an awareness of its uselessness for communication. Speaking of the *Mona Lisa*, Wilde writes:

> Do you ask me what Leonardo would have said had anyone told him of this picture that "all the thoughts and experience of the world had etched and moulded therein that which they had of power to refine and make expressive the outward form, the animalism of Greece, the lust of Rome, the reverie of the Middle Age with its spiritual ambition and imaginative loves, the return of the Pagan world, the sins of the Borgias?" He would probably have answered that he had contemplated none of these things, but had concerned himself simply with certain arrangements of lines and masses, and with new and curious colour-harmonies of blue and green.

Modernism is caught between these two points of view. And even though modernism means to take the artist's side in the dichotomy, and has only a shrunken sense of the meaning that a work of art might have in even the most active imagination, it is driven to do so not only by its own desire for purity but also in part by its effort to escape the situation of meaning that art, and all understanding, finds itself in by being modern.

The modernist predicament is epitomized, although without awareness that it is a predicament, in Greenberg's assertion that:

Only by reducing themselves to the means by which they attain virtuality as art, to the literal essence of their medium, and only by avoiding as much as possible explicit reference to any form of experience not given immediately through their mediums, can the arts communicate that sense of concretely felt, irreducible experience in which our sensibility finds its fundamental certainty.[3]

Greenberg puts this even more strongly and particularly:

It follows that a modernist work of art must try, in principle, to avoid communication with any order of experience not inherent in the most literally and essentially construed nature of its medium. Among other things, this means renouncing illusion and explicit subject matter. The arts are to achieve concreteness, "purity" by dealing solely with their respective selves—that is, by becoming "abstract" or nonfigurative. Of course, "purity" is an unattainable ideal. Outside music, no attempt at a "pure" work of art has ever succeeded in being more than an approximation and compromise (least of all in literature). But this does not diminish the crucial importance of "purity" or concrete "abstractness" as an orientation and aim.[4]

The allusion to music brings to mind, not inappropriately, Valéry's sense of music "appreciation," which in fact Greenberg quotes with approval: "I conclude that the real connoisseur in this art is necessarily he to whom it suggests nothing."[5] Greenberg generalizes from this point of view: art as such suggests nothing, but rather presents itself. There are no hidden connotations within its denotation of its own making. In Kantian language, there is no synthesis of the work of art beyond the unity of its own making, its suggestive aura around it being nothing but the illusion—we would say projection—of our own needs. That the making of the work of art might have something to do with the satisfaction of our needs is of course not considered by the modernist, who rejects the notion that there is any higher purpose to art, any "spiritual" point to its production. That there might be a lower purpose—and that even the spiritual might have something to do with this lower purpose—escapes him, despite his obsessive, if inconclusive, interest in the emotional density of the modernist work of art. In all of this there is a refusal to consider the work of art as anything more than the material and work that went into it, with little interest in why the effect should be made, and in fact with a strong interest in beating back any such interest, as detrimental to an understanding of the immediate presence of the work.

From the modernist point of view, the aura of allusion that surrounds the work can never synthesize into a coherent consciousness of the work. It remains unavoidably incoherent and stammering, because the work speaks clearly only when it speaks literally, i.e., as a particular presence that can never be generalized by any emotional or spiritual use. Its stubborn particularity resists appropriation even by the aura of meaning it seems to adduce, for that aura finally seems to be no more than a sign of our own insecurity with meaning in general—with what anything might finally mean, might finally communciate, beyond its own being. Indeed, modernism seems to tell us that acceptance of the work of art as indifferent to and so in a sense beyond questions of meaning and the communication of meaning is a way of securing oneself against the general chanciness of communication and uncertainty of meaning that become apparent the moment one begins to question the conventions of both. Part of what modernism tells us is that one inevitably does begin to question those conventions, in even the most ordinary circumstances, because, from the perspective of the present, conventions always seem to be arbitrary and to interfere with creative potential, the expanded sense of possibility that comes with trying to be totally present. The presentness of the modernist work of art is one important—presumably unique—way of being secure in the present. And yet taking the point of view of the present exclusively was what made one insecure in the first place. The pure presence of the work of art seems to be an antidote to the poison that pure existential presentness let loose; yet it seems also to be another, more insidious, version of that poison.

There is, then, in the Greenberg quotations, the pseudo-dialectical structure typical of the unhappy consciousness. The structure is "pseudo" in part because it is unconscious of itself, unaware that the positive artistic presence it proposes is premised on a negative sense of artistic presence as failed communication. The structure is also "pseudo" because it implies that an unwillingness, almost an inability, to communicate is the hidden condition of art's purity, suggesting a division within the very structure of art that cannot be reconciled. For modernism, the reconciliation of art with itself—the happiness of art—can be imagined only in terms which put all the weight of reconciliation on the one changeless—pure—term in art, i.e., only in terms of a false consciousness of art. Thus there is pure or literally given art, whose integrity—the easy integrity that literalness gives—is conceived as entirely independent of its communicative potential. Such "renunciation" of communication is, implicitly, the first line of defense against the flux of historical experience and the relativity of meaning and communication that comes with that flux. Giving attention to literalness seems to stop the flux of relativity, or at least functions like a kind of breakwater that keeps it under control. Yet the weight of literalness as such is important in the pseudo-dialectical structure that means to reconcile art to itself, for any use to which literalness can be put implies the divided, "communciative" nature of art, and as such shows its unhappiness. However, Greenberg himself implies that modernism, with its emphasis on literalness for the sake of literalness, cannot help but reveal an unhappy consciousness when, in his notion of "art-adoration," he suggests that the pursuit of purity implies a pathological sense of experience. Attention to literalness for its own sake can indicate "moral or intellectual failing" in the face of experience, even an incapacity for experience, which implies a disorder of the will, a collapse or degeneration of being.

Yet what Greenberg calls "aesthetic transposition"—the starting point for the pursuit of purity—is an extricable part of historical experience. Whatever the esthetic might seem to be in itself, it is a transposition of experience, i.e., it seems to offer a perspective on experience. The problem with the esthetic perspective on experience is that it remains bound to the most immanent, untransposable aspect of experience—sense experience—which seems almost impossible to get a perspective on. Esthetic transposition fearlessly presents what is perhaps the central epistemological paradox. Modernism, without realizing it, falls into the trap of this paradox, this double bind, and suffers the unhappy consciousness that is implied by the paradox. The need to have a perspective on experience, to transpose it into the control of some form of clarity, implies the cancelling of the impact of its presentness or literalness. But it seems that the need can only be satisfied, perspective can only be gained, after plunging the depths of presentness. Indeed, gaining a perspective on experience as a whole sometimes seems to be the direct consequence of immersion in presentness, complete abandonment to sensory literalness. The esthetic perspective, esthetic clarity about experience, seems inseparable from perpetual bondage to the most intimate and uncontrollable experience, the sense-certainty of presentness. Indeed, the esthetic perspective may be a way of loosening the bonds of involuntary submission to sensory literalness, of making the sense-certainty of presentness more devious, without denying it. The paradox of the esthetic is that it seems to carry us deep into one kind of experience while promising to deliver us from all experience. The esthetic, in fact, seems the most difficult perspective to sustain, if the easiest to come by. Deeply dependent on the presentness of experience—it implies that experience will always be "modern"—the esthetic becomes the most tentative transposition of experience, the weakest demonstration of the inevitable generation of a perspective on experience, from experience. "High art"—esthetically pure art—offers a perspective on experience that refuses to function as one. Instead, in the act of monumentalizing presentness, it monumentalizes itself, thereby in effect self-destructing, and showing its uselessness as a perspective on experience. High art epitomizes the paradox of the esthetic, which implies the inadequacy of the esthetic to the experience. In modernist high art we see this inadequacy at its most acute. We see how the search for the unchangeable, which Hegel notes is characteristic of the unhappy consciousness, leads to the dead end of presentness. This is accompanied by a dead end conception of present experience as excruciatingly literal. This is also typical of the unhappy consciousness, which, according to

Hegel, finds the unchangeable in the literally particular, so that the unchangeable has no general credibility, and the search for it reveals itself to be a regressive form of understanding.

Communication demands and imposes perspective, but to offer presentness as the ground of certainty of communication—as the ultimate perspective—is to play a bad joke on communicative potential. Presentness is so narrow a ground of experience as such that when it is conceived as the ground of communication it becomes absurd beyond the usual reduction to absurdity. And the communication about presentness inherent in the esthetic, particularly in the modernist esthetic, adds to the absurdity. Presentness is so insecure a footing that it begins to seem a delusion. The "esthetic" narrowing of experience that presentness and communication about presentness imply does not so much intensify experience as cancel it into a fictional finality. The hypostatized present or pure presence is the most null concept of experience imaginable. And while superficially it is the most communicable experience, it stands outside experience, as a myth of what experience ought to be. But then we must ask, why should experience become esthetically present, why might it be expected to be pure?

We can begin to answer this question by examining modernism's obsession with the ineffability of art, which is an acknowledgment that art stands outside communication. We immediately find that such an examination immerses us in the larger cultural issues at stake in modernism, particularly the struggle between conformity and nonconformity. These are the terms in which the unhappy consciousness of modern society works, the terms in which, in Hegel's words, the modern "Alienated Soul" reveals its "divided nature," its "doubled and merely contradictory being." The myth of pure presence, of an absolute experience of presentness, originates in an effort to impose unity on this contradictory being, or rather, to present the higher unity of pure presence as the secret goal of alienation. It is presumably the goal in the name of which inner nature divides itself and suffers self-division, advocates and patiently endures a form of self-loss. The Soul is to reconstitute itself in the light of pure presence—to achieve and become such presence. But its doubleness is more evident, even seems primordial. This is nowhere more evident than in art, and in just that art which means to be pure, to be sublimely modern.

Valéry and Barthes give us clues as to how this doubleness works, why it should be so necessary as to seem primordial.

> Just as the thinker tries to defend himself from the platitudes and set phrases which protect the mind from surprise at everything, and make practical living possible, so the painter can try, by studying formlessness, or rather *singularity* of form, to rediscover his own singularity, and with it the original and primitive state of coordination between hand and eye, subject and will.[6]

There is a conformist language, largely practical in import and then the singular language of the wondering thinker, a language able to recover the freshness and surprise of being and so itself be fresh and surprising. The artist puts himself outside the form of vision to which all other eyes conform, and re-creates vision from the start, restores it to a kind of elemental state, in which it is full of surprises. The thinker makes a fresh start, the artist makes a fresh start. But the visionary pursuit of the mythical fresh start, with its sense of surprising being, generates a contradiction, even originates in a contradiction. For the fresh start implies the abandonment of the old history, which is far from mythical and more certain than the surprise of being. Clearly, the shift from familiar platitude to singular form, from a historical and conforming to an ahistorical and non-conforming language of vision—in effect, from an overly collective to a highly individual apprehension of being—implies the alienation of art from itself. The escape from what Valéry calls "the Nondescript" to surprise clearly implies the divided nature of experience itself, the shifting ground of response to being, which now seems stale, now fresh. Whether fresh language can induce fresh experience of being, or fresh experience of being generate fresh language, is beside the point. What is crucial is the inherent doubleness of experience, which makes language difficult, insecure, so ultimately uncertain as to demand platitudes and set phrases, as if to ballast experience—indeed, being itself. The nondescript is necessary to make surprise possible, and while the surprise, as Valéry writes, is not that of "shock which breaks with convention or habit," but rather a renewal of the "fresh look,"[7] it nonetheless presupposes convention or habit as the ground of the nondescript, the inert ground of history which paradoxically, is the catalyst of surprise. It seems that one does not need to break with convention or habit to generate the surprise of the fresh look, but, on the contrary, must embed oneself all the more deeply in convention and habit for the surprise of the fresh look to spring forth spontaneously. The more inert convention and habit are, then, the more inevitable and spontaneous the fresh look is, the more singular are the final results of understanding experience, the more intuitive is the relationship one has to being. By deliberately planting roots deep in convention and habit, by conforming willingly to tradition, the artist almost guarantees himself a fresh look, or guarantees that the forms he offers will look singular to the viewer who has lost the sense of the singularity of experience and comes to art to restore it, and finally to restore the sense of the uniqueness of being as such.

Now, the surprise of the fresh look, the unconventional and nonhabitual, of singular form, is ineffable, however much its point of departure is an all-too-obvious, all-too-historical and used, language. As Valéry writes, "We must not forget that a thing of great beauty leaves us *mute* with admiration." The thing of great beauty—the singular form—is mute because it is in no danger of becoming a platitude or set phrase, of being taken up by the collective historical language. That is why we are mute before it. We cannot use it, either for our practice of history or theory of being: our muteness before it is an implicit rejection of its usefulness, an explicit affirmation of its nonconformity. We admire its singularity, but we can have nothing to do with it until that singularity is assimilated into a set phrase, becomes familiar and even overfamiliar. Then it acquires collective historical value, and then—and this is perhaps the truly crucial point—it might catalyze a surprise, seem to encode a fresh look at experience, generate an intuitive grasp of being. As long as its singularity seems absolute, the artistic fresh look is beyond language, beyond communication, and seems to be surrounded by an "impenetrable neutral zone," to use the phrase by which Valéry characterized Mallarmé's "immensely refined politeness." This politeness was a sanctuary, within which Mallarmé retained the sanctity of his "notion of an absolute work of imagination," a work which at every turn was full of the kind of "indefinable yet powerful" surprises Valéry sought.[8] This "immensely refined politeness," this "impenetrable neutral zone," which initially terrorized Valéry, is the aura of the ineffable around the singular. It is the inarticulate existence of radically individual from, the languagelessness of absolutely literal, unique language, the artlessness of the all-too-artful. It is the zone of speechlessness that surrounds highly individual speech. Mallarmé's "immensely refined politeness" is the ornamental form of this sublime speechlessness, an attempt to socialize the ineffable. It is a kind of midway zone between absolute speechlessness and practical language, the unhappy meeting ground of the ineffable and the useful, the ultimately artistic and the ultimately inartistic. Ornamental, polite speech, while it is a matter of set phrases, is also, when refined or elaborated, unsettling, for then the way it verges on speechlessness becomes evident. Mallarmé's "immensely refined politeness" transformed the nondescript language of conformist sociality into singular form, making it ineffable, or at least an avoidance of practical communication. Mallarmé, in other words, made polite speech into a tentative art form so as to keep intact his dream of an absolute art form, one whose singularity was conceived from the start, i.e., one whose ahistorical nonconformity does not spring from historical, conformist language.

A retort to speechless singularity of form in general, whether such pure form be, as in Mallarmé's dream, parthenogenetically pure or, as is more common, pure by reason of nonconformity to some conformist mode of speech and being—comes from Barthes, who remarks the "opiate-like philosophies" by means of "which one gets rid of intellectuals by telling them to run along and get on with the emotions and the ineffable." This attitude implies, as Barthes says, a "reservation about culture," and thus "means a terrorist position."[9] Modernism, with its insistence on purity, and the ineffability of purity, and the correlation of this ineffability with what Gauguin called "transcendental emotivity," is a species of terrorism, and an opiate of the intellectuals. The proper experience of art, or the experience proper to art, as Greenberg calls it, is the means by which intellectuals distract themselves from the improper experiences the world inflicts on them, and the gross impropriety that depth analysis of the world and experience unavoidably becomes. The refinement of purity, the release from speech into ineffability, and the great relief this affords, is intended to be an antidote to, and a reprieve from, the crudeness of experience, and the indecency forced upon us by our analysis of experience. Pure form functions as an opiate dulling any sense of the extent and intensity of experience, interfering with even the most nominal analysis of experience, and pointedly giving us a new sense of the pristine decorousness and disinterestedness of art. Even more crucially, pure form precludes the clear emergence of any horizon of meaning, the frame of reference which alone makes the analysis of experience possible. Pure form makes all horizons of meaning seem negligible, collapses every perspective by which one might achieve an overview of the world of experience. All meaning and perspective are absorbed in the literalness of pure form. Every meaningful perspective is reduced to an evasive nuance of such form, or rather, dissipated by its pursuit. Meaningful perspective seems at once a possibility offered by pure form and an actuality dismissed by it. This self-contradictoriness is another expression of the paradox of the esthetic.

In any case, the critic of modernism must assume that pure form implies a world of experience, though it does so in the most inchoate way possible. He must try to reinstate the world of experience that pure form implies, taking pure form as a clue to a buried consciousness of experience, a lost horizon of meaning. From what Robert Pincus-Witten calls "signature material" the singularity of the world of experience—of which the singularity of the artist is only an instance—must be recovered. It is as though the pure presence of signature material were the dust of a world—the very fact that pure form can be regarded as signature material tells us that it must be—and, like a visionary, the critic of modernism must gain a perspective on the world of experience from its dust, from pure art. The criticism of modernism must in fact offer a vision of the world that can have a vision of purity.

The criticism of modernism completes itself, restores the implicit vision of the modern world that underlies the concept of modernist art, when it recognizes the dialectic of conformity and noncomformity that underlies that concept. Such a recognition restores an important sense of what it means to say the world is modern, but it does not give us any stable perspective on that modern world, for it cannot transcend the dialectic of conformity and nonconformity. But a fuller exploration of this dialectic, as it appears in art, gives us a kind of perverse perspective on modernity, on presentness itself, permitting us to transcend it without forfeiting it—to effect a standoff with it. Barthes offers us this avenue of exploration. The value of modernist works, he writes, is in "their duplicity," which means "that they always have two edges." They have an "obedient, conformist, plagiarizing edge"—Valéry's platitudes and set phrases—and a "subversive edge," "the place where the death of language is glimpsed."[10] This is the place of what Valéry calls formlessness, and the death of language is the source of what he calls surprise. In fact, the death of language is a positive resource—perhaps the only resource—for the sense of freshness of being and experience. The death of language is the source of singularity of form, and singularity of form generates the transcendent illusion of freshness of being, and the real feeling of freshness of experience—that restoration of subjectivity, that momentary sense of having an undivided nature.

Modernism assumes that language must necessarily die, that it can no longer be the ground of unity between speakers, but only, through its death, the ground for a possible unity of self, for a radical or singular sense of self. The singularity of form achieved through the subversion and death of language is emblematic of a radically individualized self. It is the form of the nonconformist self, the self that finds its unity in the dividedness of language, and that, in a sense, recovers its unity from the false, collective unity implied by historical, conformist language. In another sense, it recovers its authenticity from inauthentic language, using language against itself to break its hold on consciousness, and finally on being. Modernism not only comes to assume that language has died, that singularity of form is inevitable, that there is no need for plagiarizing conformity, that pure presence does not have to be achieved by the subversion of practical existence, but that it arises spontaneously from the very being of things, is innate to historical experience. Hence Duchamp's Readymades and Pincus-Witten's conception of signature material, and the credo of honesty to material that has dominated the production of much of modern art, and continues to be the ideology behind a good deal of contemporary abstract art. Carl Andre is perhaps the clearist representative of this ideology. (One might note that the reverse approach, which might be described as the romanticism—dandyism—of today, assumes that language, and by implication social "practice," can never die, or even appear to die, but has and will always exist in banal, nondescript, platitudinous form, which can be manipulated to bring certain obscured horizons of meaning to life. Robert Morris perhaps best exemplifies this atittude.)

Reaching this position, emphasizing pure presence as an absolute, modernism becomes unexpectedly paradoxical, in a self-destructive way. It contradicts itself, it becomes exactly the opposite of what it intends. It endures what Barthes calls the "novelistic instant"—in the case of modernism, the novelistic instant of communication. Despite all appearances to the contrary, despite the aura of ineffability that surrounds pure presence, it conveys the sense of inner communication with its viewer, who as it were hears what it has to say through an inner communion with it. It becomes like the demonic voice Socrates heard, compelling him to an unexpected sense of existence—a kind of sibylline voice speaking an unknown tongue and, just for that reason, a voice that is presumed to be saying something profound. Its message must be interpreted, its very sound has hieroglyphic connotations, i.e., the purity of its presence has meaning, however indeterminate. Felt meaning here is not simply the sign of a compulsive relationship to the pure work of art, but indicative of a belief that pure presence is divinely communicative, and communicates, like all divine beings, in a perverse way—by using our own being as its medium. Pure presence induces in us a sense of exalted communication—at once elevated and subliminal. Such exalted communication becomes evident through the sense of self-communication and self-possession that pure presence induces, catalyzes. This sense is reflected in Greenberg's notion of the 'sensation' of exalted cognitiveness—exalted because it transcends cognition as such," that taste affords. It is "as though," writes Greenberg, "for the instant, [one] were in command, by dint of transcendent knowing, of everything that could possibly affect [one's] consciousness, or even [one's] existence." In this "state of consciousness, not of a gain to consciousness . . . consciousness revels in the sense of itself (as God reveals in the sense of himself, according to some theologians)."[11] The "instant" described seems, on reflection, the "purely *novelistic* instant so relished by Sade's libertine when he manages to be hanged and then to cut the rope at the very moment of his orgasm, his bliss," in Barthes's words.[12] This moment is "the cut, the deflation, the *dissolve* which seizes the subject in the midst of bliss." In the midst of the bliss of pure presence, reaching that orgasm that only pure presence can give, one is deflated by a kind of coming to one's senses, a refusal of self-loss in pure presence, of the death that pure presence implies. This refusal takes the form of communication about oneself which seems to come from pure presence, and seems to enhance the bliss that one has in the presence of the pure work of art. But what is really discovered here is pure presence, for its silence is broken, its ineffability mocked, by attributing to it a communication of the fundamental nature of one's own existence. What is deflated in the novelistic instant that pure presence is unavoidably subjected to by consciousness is the ineffability, the quality of being beyond communication, of pure work of art. Pure presence is dissolved in the communication of consciousness with itself, which is the most primordial communication. While it looks as though pure presence triggered this communication, in fact this communication came to the fore of consciousness, because of the absence of communicative potential in the pure work of art. Consciousness came to itself to fill the void of literalness, to give it some magic, to make it meaningful, to get a perspective on it. The appeal to self-reference made by consciousness when it is faced with the pure work of art—the implicit appeal of consciousness to the higher self that its own self-awareness seems to generate—is a last-ditch attempt to fill a void, to end the emptiness of pure presence by giving it the seemingly global, though subliminal, fullness of self-consciousness. Self-consciousness is an underworld projected onto pure presence to give it a significance it does not otherwise have. The pure work of art is encoded in such a way that it becomes narcissistic, which is still to socialize it beyond all expectations. The sense of narcissistic communication that pure presence supposedly affords makes it collectively accessible, for it seems to echo the self-consciousness that is at the root of every consciousness. Each of us can know pure presence from within, where it seems to speak of that unity of being, that self-recognition, which otherwise evades us, in our usual state of self-contradiction.

Of course, the bliss of self-communion that is supposedly what pure presence communicates is another symptom of self-contradiction, is a transcendental illusion that seems to heal the relationship one has with oneself (which is unavoidably dialectical), and to put one in a "natural" relationship with others, i.e., demonstrate one's inclusion in a collectivity. But in fact this bliss of self-communion, this "communication" carried out by pure presence, confirms the Babel-like collapse of the conformist, collective language into singular forms that are mutually incomprehensible. It confirms, in other words, the death of language and effective society. The monad-like character of singular form reflects the atomization of society into a realm of hyperindividuals, answerable ultimately only to themselves. But the monadic hyperindividual, because his sense of self is premised on nonconformity, can hardly begin to know what it means to be fully answerable to himself, i.e., to have a self to conform to. The hyperindividual's purity of self is premised on the conformity of other selves and his own nonconformity, just as the pure presence of the modernist work of art is premised on the assumption of conformist communication within the world and its own nonconformist "communication." The nonconformist's only sense of responsibility is to nonconformity, to his own singularity of form. To sustain this singularity and remain nonconformist, he finally must become arbitrarily self-contradictory, i.e., root out any suspicion of self-conformity. Indeed, gratuitous nonconformity, a restless shifting of grounds of selfhood—becoming what Robert Jay Lifton calls the protean self—has become a fetish in our hyperindividualist society.

The production of modern art seems to depend on institutionalized nonconformity, a deliberate process of contradiction of or alienation from a collective style, regarded by Nicolas Calas as generating the tradition of the new. This institutionalized nonconformity is also the end-result, for selfhood, of the secularization of reality as pure fact. Modernism represents that secularization for art, i.e., the sense of the entirely matter-of-fact presence of the work of art, as being nothing but a material making. This seemingly demystifying emphasis on fact bogs down when it comes to dealing with individuality, and what finally emerges is a sense of the radical uniqueness of each individual fact. To sustain this idea of uniqueness, any one fact must be shown to be radically different from every other fact, to carry its own logic within itself, as it were—thus making it a monad. The literal becomes the individual—becomes, in the last analysis, a logic in itself. And thus we arrive, in Greenberg's words, at the literal order of effects as the only significant one, meaning the only order that will communicate the radical individuality of facts. But if literalness communicates singularity, and singularity becomes, in a completely secular world, the only substance of individuality and communication, then we are in a position that can only be described as narcissistic nonconformity. This is narcissism with a difference, the neo-narcissism prevalent in our world of exaggerated individuality. Modernism represents the narcissistic nonconformity in art, for it claims that the work of art's pure manner of presence, its self-possession, is a matter of its accepted nonconformity, a high tolerance for the individuality it achieves by abandoning any commitment to communication. It is quite possible that modernist art is admired just because it is able to mute itself in a world in which nothing is mute. It has out-individualized all those who achieve that individuality by communication, for out of the opposite it has created a new way of being individual, of nonconforming. This, too, is proving to be a collective nonconformity.

Notes

1.   C.G. Jung, *Modern Man in Search of a Soul* (New York, 1933), p. 197.

2.   Oscar Wilde, "The Critic As Artist, Part I," *Intentions* (New York, 1905), pp. 142-43.

3.   Clement Greenberg, "The New Sculpture," *Partisan Review,* June 1949, p. 637.

4.   Clement Greenberg, "Sculpture in Our Time," *Arts Magazine,* June 1958, p. 22.

5.   Clement Greenberg, *Irrelevance versus Irresponsibility,"* *Partisan Review,* May 1948, p. 574.

6.   Paul Valéry, "Degas, Dance, Drawing," *Degas Manet Morisot,* New York, 1960, p. 45.

7.   Valéry, p. 87.

8.   Valéry, pp. 28-29.

9.   Roland Barthes, *Mythologies,* New York, 1975, p. 35.

10.   Roland Barthes, *The Pleasure of the Text,* New York, 1975, pp. 6-7.

11.   Clement Greenberg, "Seminar One," *Arts Magazine,* November, 1973, p. 45.

12.   Roland Barthes, *The Pleasure of the Text,* p. 7.

18

Wittgensteinean Aspects of Minimal Art

John Perreault has remarked that Wittgenstein is "much in favor with the minimalists."[1] The question of this paper is why this is the case. It is merely circumstantial—Wittgensteinean analysis and minimalism being among the most radical enterprises of the 20th century in their respective fields—or is there a more profound affinity between the two?

The significance of Wittgenstein for philosophy lies in his studies of the nature of meaning or the logic of language, and especially in his use of the concept "language-game," the major means by which he explicates the distinction central to his thought, that between naming and describing:

> For, naming and describing do not stand on the same level: naming is a preparation for description. Naming is so far not a move in the language-game—any more than putting a piece in its place on the board is a move in chess.[2]

Or, in a quotation used by Barbara Rose,

> But what does it mean to say that we cannot define (that is, describe) these elements, but only name them? This might mean, for instance, that when in a limiting case a complex consists of only one square, its description is simply the name of the colored square.[3]

From this distinction a severe restriction in the philosophical use of language emerges: all conceptual abstraction must stand up to the test of concrete naming, and all systems of thought are understood to be played according to certain language-games.

The significance, for the history of art, of minimal art is due to the violent contrast of its "blank, neutral impersonality...with the romantic, biographical Abstract-Expressionist style which preceded it."[4] At their best, minimalist works.

> tend to be "wholistic" and unitary, stripped of incident, accident, or anything that might distract from the subtlety, the efficiency, or the clarity of the all-over effect.[5]

Between aesthetic unity and mechanical quality the majority of minimalist works convey an "empty, repetitious, uninflected" spirit, as if they were ordinary objects rather than art-objects, "big, blank, empty things" masking their "art-identity."[6] Behind this ambiguity, and apart from minimalism's existence, by reason of "its rational and conceptional method,"[7] as a criticism "of Abstract-Expressionist paint-handling"—the rejection of its "brushed record of gesture and drawing along with loose painterliness"[8]—minimalism represents a re-vitalized sense of integrity and purity in painting.

It is here that it coalesces and correlates with Wittgensteinean analysis. Both Wittgenstein and the minimalists suppose that self-integration can be realized only by self-criticism, that a discipline's consciousness of its own methods is the only way it has of restoring its sense of purpose. Barbara Rose has observed that

> If Jasper Johns' notebooks seem a parody of Wittgenstein, then Judd's and Morris's sculptures often look like illustrations of that philosopher's propositions.[9]

In effect, this amounts to the assertion that neither Wittgenstein nor the minimalists are concerned to create a system of thought or works of art, i.e., to tell the truth or create a style, but rather to grasp what it means to speak of a philosophy or of art. It is to be expected that such understanding is unavoidably critical of past philosophies and traditional works of art, if only because their self-declared purpose is no longer taken for granted. But what is most to the point is that Wittgensteinean analysis and minimalism radically re-orient their fields, a re-orientation which implicates the one in the other: art in philosophy, philosophy in art. Philosophies are seen to be composed much as works of art might be, according to the rules of a language-game, analogous to the rules of style. And art is seen to be not a matter of style or beauty but of consciousness, i.e., it is as much a matter of reflection on its purposes, articulation of its presuppositions, as of the construction of some art-object. Philosophy is as much a matter of form as art is a philosophical investigation into its own identity. These recognitions—this cross-fertilization—seem to devalue philosophy into a formal game, and to displace the weight of art from the art-object to the consciousness of the artist. In each case some seriousness seems to have been lost, philosophy apparently losing its power to create new concepts for the understanding of the world, and art offering the spectator little more than an opportunity for solipsistic reflection on its inherent nature. But such apparent loss seems secondary to the fact that Wittgensteinean analysis takes the mystery out of philosophical abstraction, showing it to be contingent on linguistic considerations, and minimalism takes the mystery out of non-objective art, showing it to be an exercise in the power of pure perception. The neutral quality and devaluating effect of Wittgensteinean analysis and minimalism are the consequence of their refusal to trust, in philosophy and art, whatever is not perceptually concrete or formally explicable.

They share what Greenberg calls "modernism" and seek "self-definition with a vengeance."[10] But however modern in origin the self-reflexive, self-analytic approach may be, it means to make claims for the activity per se. At stake is a re-definition of what philosophy and painting have always been about.

In painting, the reform has three axes to grind: (1) self-criticism as the be-all and end-all of art; (2) the creation of a logically perfect language of painting; (3) the criticism of transcendence in painting. At first glance, minimalism seems a refinement of modernism, art's rebuke to cultural attempts to assimilate it to other activities. Art insists on its value in its own right, on the ground of its mediation of an experience peculiar to it. Yet minimalism seems tempted by the possibility of becoming something other than art, despite disclaimers to the contrary, such as Ad Reinhardt's "Art-As-Art Dogma." Its springboard seems to be the distance that can be put between art and non-art. Thus Greenberg remarks:

> Modernism has found that these limiting conditions can be pushed back indefinitely before a picture stops being a picture and turns into an arbitrary object; but it has also found that the further back these limits are pushed the more explicitly they have to be observed.[11]

Yet minimalism lacks complete motivation without hyperconsciousness of the "arbitrary object." Distance may be put between the art object and the arbitrary object, but the alienation between them is so forced and studied—affected—that the defining conditions for the art object are never more than subtly—minimally—different from the defining condition for the arbitrary object. Modernism may be a high risk activity, but in minimalism finesse with fundamentals has become a game of brinkmanship. What originally was withdrawal from an explicitly art-alien world to an implicit experience which would increasingly be nothing but aesthetic, becomes curiosity about how the approximation to non-art can be a possible aesthetic experience. What originally was an involuntary experience of an abyss which was overcome by a new authenticity, becomes a willing exploration of the possibility of putting all art in jeopardy. Reinhardt, Newman, Stella, Lichtenstein, Morris, Caro are not Picasso, Braque, Mondrian, Miró, Kandinsky, Brancusi, who"derive their chief inspiration from the medium they work in."[12] Minimal art is inspired as much by working against as in the medium.

Much as Wittgenstein pushes philosophy back to "a queer use of words,"[13] so minimal art pushes painting back to a queer use of composition. As philosophy begins to collapse under the pressure of analysis, the experience it "symbolically proposes" becomes evident.[14] Analogously, as art begins to collapse under the pressure of minimalism, a picture-experience is precipitated. Transient but vital, the experience is a moment of pure perception, much as philosophy is seen to be "spiritual" experience of language.[15] The question is whether the picture does finally become something queer and arbitrary—as philosophy does—whatever it may be in moments of isolated perception.

I

Modernism, which began with uncertainty as to the ultimate significance of philosophy and art—true as much for Manet as Kant, the initiators for Greenberg—comes full circle to a new sense of certainty in minimal art. Self-criticism in the name of purity of the medium's purpose is apotheosized as *the* method of art, giving it new absoluteness and seriousness. In effect, the necessary condition of art—the medium—becomes its sufficient condition, i.e., the demonstration of its ground is its only end. While this makes for consistency, in part the consequence of the reduction of the number of variables out of which art might be made, and creates a kind of grandeur—perhaps simply monodimensionality mistaken for monumentality—art in its minimal form continues to remain uncertain of its cultural consequences, of the horizon it projects. In Kant, self-criticism had only a negative purpose, to prevent misunderstandings. With Wittgenstein, self-criticism becomes self-destruction—a demonstration of philosophy's impotence, its inability to say anything about "the sum total of reality" of the world. In Manet, the self-critique of painting still had about it art's "romance" with experience. Painting was still "attached to reality" by "reaching out to it," to use Wittgenstein's terms.[16] In minimalism, art is no longer attached to reality, no longer reaches out to it. Art becomes a tautology, preoccupied with self-identity.

There was never such narcissistic hyperbole in Kant or Manet. However much Kant criticized reason, he never doubted that it had its uses. Criticism was never for its own sake, but for the health of reason. However much Manet's pictures frankly declare their surfaces,[17] he never doubted that they depicted a world, made statements about reality, were images in part the consequence of an experience of life. Manet never disputed that his pictures existed as much for the sake of others as for the sake of his own conduct of art. Even pure "pictorial form" depended, for Wittgenstein, on "the possibility that things were related to one another in the same way as the elements of the picture."[18] Where Kant and Manet were critical, philosophical analysis and minimal art are reductionist. Where Kant studied abnormal ambitions of reason in the name of a sane use of understanding, Wittgenstein dismisses philosophical understanding as an illusion of the logic of language. Where Manet explored possibilities of new pictorial surface to render reality more subtly and faithfully, minimal artists are preoccupied with pictorial surface—the familiar flatness—as the most important reality of the picture in itself. Only Newman seems a last ditch attempt to give a picture some allusion to experience—of the sublime—but in the coolest minimal art all such allusions are pretenses and failings.

The continued effort at clarification of the medium ultimately leads to subtraction from its possibilities, diminishing returns. What began as self-criticism, and became self-refinement, ends as self-loss. In painting, minimalism is a mode which has been so reduced that it almost literally has become no more than an insubstantial veil of composition clinging to a flat surface. Tautness of surface, the quality the medium sought to achieve by self-criticism, reduces to momentary vibrancy of surface. So long as self-criticism did not hinder art's commitment beyond itself, as in the case of the first abstractionists, it remained quality- and value-charged. But when art gave up the question of the possibility of experience—Kant's original question of self-criticism—it passed beyond questions of quality to become a speculative enterprise. As determined to avoid ambiguities of ordinary perception as mathematical logic is to avoid ambiguities of ordinary language, minimalism creates a calculus of colors and shapes governed by rules. Colors are proposed as propositions are stated. Equivalent to a class of propositions, the shape of the canvas forces family likeness—vibrant interplay—on the stated colors, creating an effect of spatial unity. One can speak of the picture's system of logic, its determination by the formal relationship of color to shape and size of canvas. The picture as such exists only by reason of this relationship.

II

The minimal picture becomes a machine for seeing; as such, it aspires to be the logically perfect language of painting. The ambition is not new with minimalism. It dates to Kandinsky and the De Stijl movement, and to Seurat. What is new is the conception of the constituents of the language. While they are still "spaces, surfaces, shapes, colors, etc.," they are no longer conceived as limiting conditions but as tools. The shift in meaning is more than semantic, for its consequences are revolutionary. In modernism the limiting conditions of the medium are the subject matter of its works, but in minimalism preoccupation with instrumenting the picture indicates a new perfectionism. Wittgenstein in the *Tractatus Logico-Philosophicus* was also "concerned with the conditions which would have to be fulfilled by a logically perfect language,"[19] but in the *Philosophical Investigations* he became aware of "the multiplicity of the tools in language," "the multiplicity of language-games."[20] As languages go, a logically perfect language is primitive.[21] It is achieved by deliberately limiting the number of rules of the game, much as minimal art is achieved by deliberately limiting the number of rules in the art-game. The result is an exclusive language, spun for its own fine silk, rather than a language which is a "form of life."[22] For the later Wittgenstein, all language-games are life-forms, but for the minimalists, all painting-games are primitive perfections.

The search for a logically perfect language of art attempts to bring under control aesthetic experience. No longer a fluke of feeling, or subject to arbitrary presences, it becomes a carefully controlled effect caused by determinism of composition, what Fried calls "deductive structure." The artistic and aesthetic are closely tied together, their unity a consequence of perfected artistic techniques, with no interference from a subject matter, which might spark an inadvertent aesthetic response. Painting reduces to "a kind of qualitative combinatorics,"[23] the assembling of simples in a science of composition. Minimalism urges correctness in the use of pictorial tools, and assimilates the conception of the picture to its execution. It is misleading of Stella to assert that his pictures convince by reason of their "over-all effect" rather than because of their "technical niceties," or as Rubin asserts, what matters is "the importance of the *conception* of the picture as opposed to the refinements of its *execution*."[24] Neither is literally nor logically distinguishable from the other; Rubin in fact offers almost exclusively a technical analysis of the construction of Stella's pictures. Overall effect is simply another limiting condition constituting the meaning of picture as such, i.e., making the picture an art object rather than an arbitrary object. Over-all effect is the condition of pictorial self-containment. It is the most hypostatized of fundamentals in minimalism because without it there is no illusion of identifiable art. In Stella's pictures it is entirely the consequence of the shaped canvas and the deep stretcher, the repetition of shape on the raised canvas. Any normativeness achieved is the accident of persistent technique, much as the power of concrete or nonsense poetry is due to a consistent if absurd use of language. Even then, obedience to the rule becomes tedious outside its own universe because the rule has no inward necessity. It pictures no experience, other than what Hegel calls "sense-certainty." Basically its logic is what Hegel calls "Show," with understanding collapsed into sensibility but with sensibility trivial because it is empty.

The problem of conceiving of painting as a logical perfect language is that it is based on a logical absurdity. If, as Wittgenstein says, a picture has pictorial form in common with reality, and if pictorial form can be displayed but not depicted, then it is impossible to depict what is displayed. The attempt to do so is insoluble; the problem remains a permanent puzzle. If we accept Wittgenstein's teaching that insoluble problems vanish when their origin is discovered, then minimalism vanishes when its absurd conception of pictorial form is made evident.

Picasso was poignantly aware of the problem of pictorial form when he observed that abstraction in a picture was never complete. Traces of the object depicted were always visible behind the pictorial form displayed. The picture was never completely possessed by form, no matter how pure its determination, no matter how much it identified itself with its medium. If this is so, then the peculiar fact about art is that it is always non-art no matter how strictly it conditions itself to be nothing but art. However, this does not bring the art object closer to the arbitrary object, but reasserts its symbolic tie to reality. In essence, minimalism is an attempt to destroy this tie. By insisting on art's possible logical perfection, minimalism denies that art exists as an abstract analogue to concrete reality. Kandinsky's distinction between abstract and non-objective art does not negate Picasso's assertion, and is pre-minimal, for the non-objective conveys, if not the experience of objects, then consciousness of their life-world. For

Kandinsky, the non-objective is an analogue for a *Weltanschauung,* an intentionality. Thus, while there may be no "secret reality behind" a picture, it is experienced as more than a pictorial form. Its "content" may be obscure, but it is a vital spectre, a presence haunting the picture if not an existence revealed by it. The spectator implies consciousness of "forms of life."

III

The third ax is the sharpest. It is not another attack on the literary aspects of visual art, but a debunking of "metaphysical spectres and meaningless notions" in art, such as Rosenblum's abstract sublime and Kandinsky's spiritual. All such intellectual superstructures are dismantled. Much of the "coolness" of minimal art is the consequence of this rejection of—outright immunity to—"higher ideas." Such destruction is directly in line with the purposes of Wittgenstein's *Philosophical Investigations.* Self-criticism reduces philosophy to absurdity: "Philosophy may in no way interfere with the actual use of language."[25] Higher ideas are reduced to lower language. Analogously, the minimal credo seems to be that painting may in no way interfere with the actual experience of shape and color. Higher experience is reduced to pictorial form. In effect, painting is no longer an imaginative re-creation of the world, it is the disciplined perception of the visually objective. Imaginative inventions are inadvertent, and vanish once their origins are explained. Greenberg's account of past art is an exemplary instance of minimalism in operation. His discussion of anti-sculptural tendencies in painting achieves a minimalist apogee in his assertion that the past, while appreciating many masters "justly, often gave wrong or irrelevant reasons for doing so."[26] Their imaginative grasp of experience, which their pictorial form subserved, is no reason for valuing them. Only their contribution to the medium matters. But if this is so, it is no longer possible to say, as Greenberg does, that art is defensible on the ground that it mediates a unique experience. Uniqueness here is jargon, for the experience art mediates reduces to experience of the medium, of which there are a multiplicity, all equally unique.

Minimalism, however, strips art of more than its ideational allusions to experience. Attitudes are also to be stripped. There are to be no fixed expectations from art. One is to attend only to the immediate experience of pictorial form, with neither anticipation beforehand nor reflection afterwards. The pictorial experience is to be an immutable present of perception, the picture an intelligible immediacy, neither felt for nor intellectually compromised in a system of thought. In a sense, minimalism telescopes abstraction, moving from sensuous experience to contemplative experience of intelligible form in a single stroke, thereby muting the last vestige of subjective response that might taint the pictorial experience. The spectator almost always approaches the picture with a life-attitude, but the picture is to force him strictly into the behavior of perception. It seems to give an instant of intelligibility by contrast to pre-existent attitudes. It achieves this illusion of intelligibility—of eternal objectivity—not simply by pictorial form, but by negating the possibility of any attitude originating in the life-world assimilating it. Minimal art does not fit into any pre-structuring, pre-conscious attitude, not even, as has been noted, the approach to geometrical experience. This is perhaps its greatest achievement. Sublimely negative, its experience as nothing but a picture is foreordained. Before becoming an arbitrary object, the minimal picture is a momentary absolute. Much as philosophical propositions arise out of ordinary language, so minimal pictures emerge from ordinary visual language, before falling back into the sea of perception, as philosophical statements become familiar language.

IV

Minimalism began with indifference to the life-world, but made great claims for its contribution to art. As a hermetic enterprise minimalism is as irreproachable as any other absolute. All one can do is reproach it for the situation it puts us in once we have obeyed it. Thus, on the one hand, minimal art creates a new poverty of painting, much on the order of the new poverty of philosophy Marcuse accuses Wittgenstein of creating, and on the other hand, it is a defamation of alternative modes of painting which contradict the presumed perfection, established as tyrannical rule, of minimal methods.[27] This last resembles Marcuse's analysis of the implicit conformity to the status quo in the acceptance of ordinary language as the arbiter of thought. To find transcendent meanings in painting—meanings that transcend the necessities of composition—is to find what, from a technical point of view, is incomplete and imperfect. It is to find a piecemeal world, a partial experience, an oblique image of reality. It is to see the medium as a vehicle for a meaning beyond itself; it is to see pictorial form as possible experience; it is to see the picture as the agency of an attitude and an intelligence. It is to offer a way out of the conflict between schools of painting; Kant spoke of philosophy as the only intellectual enterprise smitten by a conflict between essential positions, but art must be added. It is to offer a legitimate alternative to an operational definition of art, assimilating all aesthetic experience to experience of the medium. It is to recognize that the therapeutic treatment of art by minimalism creates a new academic art, making the production of the tools of art an end in itself, manipulating perception through the control of conventional components. To restore transcendence to art is to restore sensibility to its role as a pilgrim on the path to life, offering a basic orientation to the life-world.

One might finally say, paraphrasing Gertrude Stein's remark to Hemingway that "remarks are not literature"—a retort given to Wittgenstein as well (remarks are not philosophy)—that Stella's *Protractor* or *Saskatchewan* series or Morris Louis's works are not art, but a species of comment on picture-making. One might say they are as original as Manet's works, i.e., a return to the origin of painting. But unless one specifies why they returned, and what they found when they returned, to call them original is to make an almost empty statement. Manet found a new closeness to experience—the open surface was appropriate to an experience of light, which discloses, in a sense substantializes, surface, with no help needed from shape. To depict this disclosing there was no need to depict more of substance than was given in a glance. Stella has found a less "fussy" abstractness—does that bring him to the origin of painting, or does it make another twist in the turning of the screw of technique?

The answer is uncertain, because the origins of painting as of philosophy, are inherently unclear. Each has an organic tie to experience; to sever that tie is to banish the activity to perpetual self-doubt, which in the end self-criticism becomes, or to illusory perfection, which in the end the imposition of arbitrary limits becomes.

Notes

1. John Perreault, "Minimal Abstracts," *Minimal Art,* ed. Gregory Battcock (New York, 1968), p. 262.

2. Ludwig Wittgenstein, *Philosophical Investigations* (New York, 1953), section 49.

3. Barbara Rose, "ABC Art," *Minimal Art,* ed. Gregory Battcock (New York, 1968), pp. 290-91.

4. Rose, pp. 274-75.

5. Perreault, p. 257.

6. Rose, pp. 281-82.

7. Perreault, p. 257.

8. Rose, p. 279.

9. Ibid., p. 291.

10. Clement Greenberg, "Modernist Painting," *The New Art,* ed. Gregory Battcock (New York, 1966), p. 102.

11. Ibid., p. 106.

12. Clement Greenberg, *Art and Culture* (Boston, 1961), p. 7.

13. Ludwig Wittgenstein, *Philosophical Investigations* (New York, 1953), p. 9. Hereafter *PI.*

14. *PI,* p. 85.

15. *PI,* p. 48. Also section 38 and *Tractatus Logico-Philosophicus,* 4.003 (hereafter *TLP.*)

16. Wittgenstein's picture theory of meaning is generally presented in *TLP,* the propositions beginning with the number two. This picture theory of meaning has been much debated. However, I have taken over the conception of picture which lurks in the theory, rather than the conception of meaning, for it is the former that affords a gambit into the minimalist conception of picture, while the latter has a strictly epistemological relevance.

17. Greenberg, "Modernist Painting," p. 103.

18. *TLP,* 2.14.

19.   Russell in the Introduction to *TLP* (London, 1922), p. 3.

20.   *PI,* 11.

21.   Ibid.

22.   Ibid.

23.   James K. Feibleman, *Inside The Great Mirror* (The Hague, 1958), p. 61.

24.   William S. Rubin, *Frank Stella* (New York, 1970), p. 32.

25.   *PI,* p. 103.

26.   Greenberg, "Modernist Painting," p. 110.

27.   Herbert Marcuse, *One-Dimensional Man* (London, 1964), p. 171.

Sol LeWitt the Wit

LeWitt's books are such poetic ABC-books, with each image in them a letter in an alphabet of elementary forms. It is an alphabet of hieroglyphs. Taken together, they seem to give us the power to speak some secret language of form. Running "them over in a continuous and uninterrupted act of thought," reflecting "upon their relations to one another," as Descartes suggested we do with any series of which we wish to become "much more certain," we not only "increase the power of our mind" over the known, as Descartes expected, but seem to give it the power to penetrate the unknown.[1] We seem to watch the secret life of simple form as it unfolds its multiple possibilities while retaining its unity, and even though these possibilities are limited and the unity finite, there is still a poetic evocation of infinity, generated simply by the filmic unfolding. However selfless and abstract the unfolding—however much it is a matter of procedural rule—a cadenced, even rhymed (especially with interior rhymes) poetry of self-transformation seems to be in process, with no limit to its reach, however limited its content. Even when it is exhausted, it is enigmatic, for the formal completeness of the series belies the informal relations we can spy between the individuals that constitute it. They never sink back into the generality of the series: there is always an asymmetry between its general rule and the particular details which gives the series its air of spontaneity. It is this illusion of spontaneity that suggests that the unfolding of any immediately given simple form into a complex continuum necessarily implies an alternative: a still more complex series, a still more differentiated continuum, a still more rigorous nuancing of the simple form. Our senses, searching for this alternative, contradict our reason, which tells us that there is none. It's out of this clash that the wit of the works is born.

Hauser, incidentally, tells us that this filmic unfolding, this stripping of form to its temporal duration—this use of spatial units to symbolize indefinite, open or transitive, temporal ones—has been characteristic of modern art since Cubism. LeWitt, particularly in his series of incomplete open cubes (1974), represents an ironical return to Cubism, following the letter of its textbook definition but in a different spirit. His filmic unfolding is not random, his transitive forms are not emblems of emotions, his "progression" is not organic or irreversible, and his forms are always true to type. LeWitt is the complete Cubist, but the incomplete Symbolist. He has made the cube itself the object, and by putting it through its paces has made it seem mysterious, but in a totally innocent, unsuggestive way.

Of course, by forcing the form through serialization, LeWitt puts its simplicity and unity at a distance. But not a great one, for they can always be inferred from any given instance of form. No matter how truncated such instances are, they always imply their own completeness—their "model"—for they are always intelligible, however sensuously novel. The rule which made them eccentric in appearance can always restore them to their original easy unity, to their boring self-sameness. But of course this self-sameness, because it is the "revelation" at the beginning and end of the series, is never boring, but, like Malevich's square, radiant against an imaginary infinite field—not even signaled in LeWitt by any ground, at least one that is decisively present. (In the wall drawings it is an ironic ground, since it belongs both to the drawings and the world of which the wall is a part.) Thus another poetic moment appears in the filmic unfolding of the ABCs of a form in LeWitt's books, one which makes the form, not its unfolding, a poem. LeWitt's work is as rich in numinously absent forms, often as charged with a subjective meaning as it is with obviously connected, varied serial forms, presented as a field of conceptual operations. The *Photo of Central Manhattan,* where he has blocked out the areas between the places he has lived, plays the same role as the subject matter in a Mallarmé poem. Its seeming autonomy ballasts the given words, keeping them from appearing altogether relative. The core of the poetry of LeWitt's series is, then, the give and take between its missing yet implied form and its explicitly given form, or between the simple rule which generated it and its complex variety. (When a form is present and complete LeWitt tends to isolate and fetishize, even apotheosize it. The modular cubes exhibited in Dag Hammarskjöld Plaza [1976] loomed like the totems of a self-proclaimed rational, and so indisputably modern, society.) The poetry is entirely paradoxical, as is shown by the fact that once we recognize the rule that generated the given series, its forms lose their spontaneous, illicit look—yet recover it in the looking. That the poetry itself seems to come and go, depending upon our recognition of the logic of the series, and that the logic itself should give rise to a series that is poetic in appearance, is itself part of the poetry—in fact, essential to its wit.

The wit is manneristic—the paradoxicality of the poetry already tells us that. In fact, one might say that LeWitt is a mannerist Constructivist. The self-contradictory use of Constructivist means, unwitting and inadvertent in Minimalism, becomes subtly explicit and self-conscious in LeWitt. Constructivist goals seem to be asserted, but by, as it were, de-constructed forms, or else by axiomatic forms in no need of construction. In either case what is given is so clearly given by rule—so intuitively clear in itself—that its actual construction seems an afterthought, a trivial realization of a transparent idea. Because the need of the construction is not self-evident, the idea of the structure stands at odds—in paradoxical relationship—to the material structure. Intelligibility per se—the source of structure—and sense experience, with its seeming unintelligibilities—in art signaled by the term "touch," or texture—seem to disjunct, to lose their expected necessity for one another. Abstraction and materialization, which came together in classical Constructivism, almost invisibly separate in manneristic Constructivism. Yet because they do not visibly disengage, whatever the efforts of Conceptual Art to force them apart, their relationship becomes witty if constantly threatened. The wit consists in surviving the constant threat while asserting it, in allowing both the precision of the idea and the imprecision of its materialization, without insisting on one or the other, or the superiority of one to the other. LeWitt's art asserts this self-contradictory situation as a logic in and for itself, without any solution. The Gordian knot is tightened, not cut. Thus, in LeWitt, Constructivism becomes ironic rather than utopian, quasi-apocalyptic rather than stabilizing, signals the seeming collapse of reason rather than its triumph, toys with disorder rather than confirms the ideal of order. LeWitt gives us, not a new version of the old idealistic Constructivism, but Constructivism for an age of doubt, an age saturated in and suspicious of reason—aware of the contradictions it gives rise to but unable to conceive of any alternative to it and its systems. LeWitt shows us the pointlessness, or as he terms it "uselessness," and perversity of these systems. It is as if, in glimpsing the irrational anomalies these superficially rational systems give rise to, one might glimpse some enigmatically "higher" or "deeper" principle than reason, or else recognize that reason itself is a species of poetry.

Indeed, LeWitt's works are comparable to anamorphoses, visually irrational—even fantastic—forms produced by rational means, with an intricacy of effect almost demonic in its implications. Meyer Schapiro remarks: "Such mathematically achieved deformation of the appearances of things could also become a vehicle of philosophic or religious ideas."[2] In LeWitt it is generally a cube, an elementary symbol of order, balance, harmony, and stability (in Plato's *Timaeus* it was the form of the earth corpuscle), that is given an irksome, irrational appearance, cutting into our consciousness of its primitive clarity, creating some doubt about the stability of its order, some hesitancy in our use of it as a symbolic form. It becomes "deranged," and if at all a symbol, not one of inner order—in Mondrian's words, a "manifestation of the unity... potential in our consciousness"—but one of inner disorder, of the chaos, the nonsense and malaise potential in our consciousness. It becomes the vehicle of the idea of the unreason within reason. The solemnly clipped wings of Newman's *Broken*

Obelisk barely foreshadow the zany, madcap, yet consistent, rigorous logic of LeWitt's incomplete open cubes. In Newman reason has just begun to crumble; in LeWitt it avalanches—systematically.

Whereas El Lissitsky told the *Story of the Two Squares* (1922) from outer space establishing harmony in a world of geometrical chaos, we might say that LeWitt tells the story of how a square from inner space sabotages a world of superficial geometrical harmony by showing its subtle disharmony. Disorder is always lurking behind the facade of order in LeWitt's work—a disorder which is integral to the order, and which grows out of it. The aura of disharmony emanates directly from the system of harmony in his art. This is another manneristic trait, and for me the most subtle and powerful example of the manneristic abstraction of the best Seventies art. It is the exemplary case of the turning of classical abstract forms, such as the Suprematist square, against themselves to witty effect. We see this in the asymmetries of Rockburne, Bochner, and especially Mangold in a similar though less insistent way. It is no longer the geometry that is supreme, but the rule that generates it. It is a rule that, cleverly used, can produce a witty geometry, i.e., one that is no longer consistently clear and distinct, yet still indisputable. It is a geometry that is empirically piquant because it never seems absolutely exact, exact as it seems. This is because conceptually the rule that generates it has somehow gotten out of hand, like the Sorcerer's apprentice. The rule doesn't stop ruling, so that the form becomes more and more "labored." The rule is overworked, and the form is worked over. This is an art in which the root rather than the bloom matters: its point is to trace the bloom back to the root. This is an art that wants to expose its roots, not hide them behind some facile look, although the brilliance of LeWitt is that his works seem to have this *facilità,* but it is only the sign of the rigor of the rule that creates them. The soil, of course, in which the rule is rooted is the general belief in scientific reason or logic that is the dominant ideology of our society. And the reason the bloom and the fruit no longer matter, and directly reflect and are reducible to the rule, is that we are disillusioned with the rule of reason, but we don't dare break any of its rules. We are afraid of living without rules, however useless they are to our welfare and however indifferent or irrational their results. We no longer trust these results, except as signs of the smooth functioning of the rule. But then why have the rule, if we find its results trivial or boring?

LeWitt's manneristic wit pointedly shows itself in his reversal or contradiction of the classical method of abstraction, epitomized in Descartes's *Rules for the Direction of the Mind* and *Discourse on the Method of Rightly Conducting the Reason.* The core of this method—and method, we must remember, is for Descartes reduction to simplicity and order—is the refusal to "accept as true" anything that was "not presented to my mind so clearly and distinctly that I could have no occasion to doubt it."[3] What LeWitt does is exploit, as it were, the subjective aspect of the accepting mind. The quest for certainty—

which it finds in the simple and orderly and so indisputable—is ridiculed by being reduced to a matter of obedience to trivial rule, suggesting not only an immaturity of mind but the sense of a desperate uncertainty, which is more willed away than truly overcome. LeWitt restores this uncertainty to its full rights by letting it seep into the structure of certainty. One method is to give the simple rules that create the simple structure a complex form, as in the wall drawings. The lines in the simple drawing can become like faults in a crystal. They imply uncertainty as much as certainty of form, because they seem overly different in kind from the rules that generated them. The rules seem incoherent because it is hard to follow them. The need for patience shows that the rule is neither simple nor intuitively self-evident. But the form and its location are. LeWitt's method is not characterized by intuitive certainty or self-evident simplicity at every stage. Certain densities—whether in the rule, or in the order that results from it—emerge that, while they can be read away, interfere with the smooth functioning of the method, and subtly undermine the intellectual ease and certainty it is meant to generate. Clarity is compromised by its own method of mediation.

LeWitt also shows that conceptual certainty is undermined by perceptual uncertainty, as in *Muybridge* (1964). (In general, Muybridge's work "had a great impact" on LeWitt's "thinking...and was the source of much of the serial work."[4]) Through a peephole we see an advancing nude who becomes clear and distinct as she approaches, but eventually loses her identity as a figure, and simply becomes flesh, and finally, as she is almost on top of us, alien matter. One is reminded of the various versions of Duchamp's *Nude Descending a Staircase,* and one suspects the same sort of emotional ambivalence about the female—the same temptation by and resistance to desire—as well as the same artistic urge to abolish the model, dependence upon nature, and work only from an inner model, a *disegno interno,* an idea. But in LeWitt there seems also a Swiftian imagination at work, as when Gulliver, perched on the breasts of a Brobdingnagian lady, becomes acutely aware of her pores, horrified at the prospect of falling into them, but even more horrified that the allure of his location has become lost in the reduction of his situation and his correspondingly reduced point of view. His point of view controls his intentions. In LeWitt's piece, the message seems to be that while the artist is a voyeur of form, the conditions of perception of form control one's conception of it—so perhaps it is better not to start with the perception of form but with its conception. (That LeWitt's spectator can begin with the concept rather than precept—where one usually begins—is another witty contradiction of expectation.) In fact, LeWitt seems to be constantly fidgeting with the controls that focus form, as in the tide of lines and overelaborated, mathematically archaistic descriptions of their location in his wall drawings. This fidgeting seems to cripple the focus in the very act of creating it; often there is no clear and distinct—intuitively singular—form in LeWitt's work. It is as though the very idea of the clear and distinct was on the verge of collapse, or else it is overdone, forced, as in the overblown modular cubes. In the very act of ardently constructing it, or pointing to it, he seems to obscure it, or at least raise questions about it. This is particularly the case in his page on "art" (1972)—it is clearly and distinctly marked, but it is conceptually unclear—and in his treatment of a text by Lucy Lippard.[5] Here LeWitt's systematic "fidgeting" violates or obscures the subject matter—a sentimental, narcissistic text, with references to himself—rather than illuminates or "secures" it. It is as though it has been capsized or placed in drydock; in any case, put out of commission. One might say that LeWitt's "highlighting" of certain of its abstract features, calling attention to the way it is constructed, lowlights its concrete meaning. LeWitt plays up its construction to play down its emotional meaning, in effect safeguarding his privacy, as well as mocking Lippard's over-expressivity. His Muybridgean treatment of Lippard's text devalues it. In another manneristic paradox, seriality does not reveal the inner dynamic, the power of movement, in static form, but confines its inertness. After LeWitt's "serialization" of it, Lippard's text lays dead on the page. It can be perceived neither as form nor content, like the advancing nude when she is flush against us; it is at that moment of ultimate closeness that she is most distant from us. LeWitt's serialization technique is, among other things, an effective means of distancing—creating psychic distance from—what is most familiar and close to us, while seeming to embrace it.

For LeWitt the two essentials of Cartesian reductionism—"intuitive apprehension" of the "intuitively simple" and serial deduction on its basis—are compromised or, as it were, contaminated from the start. They put us, in LeWitt's art, in just the situation of impulse and conjecture Cartesian method meant to preclude. While serial reduction is still the sign of mechanical inference, LeWitt's deductive chain as a whole has an impulsive look and makes us think it was created by conjecture, even when the rules for its creation are announced within or by the title of the work. This look and assumption are helped by the fact that there is generally no proportion between idea and image in LeWitt. We either have a very complex idea issuing in a simple image, or a simple idea issuing in a very complex image. Because of the disproportion between idea and image, a regress is set up which makes the ideas or rules seem groundless in themselves— however much they ground an image—and as such no longer unqualifiedly simple and self-evident. This reflects back on the image, and suddenly we realize that it guarantees nothing familiar—no sign of the artist, no beauty—only its own relation to the rule, to the idea or intention behind it. The creation of the work is left to assistants, and the creation of beauty is left to spectators. It is not only that LeWitt, who might be regarded as the John Donne of Minimalism, produces, in T.S. Eliot's words, "an eccentricity of imagery, the far-fetched association of the dissimilar, or the overelaboration of one metaphor or simile" (in LeWitt, modular form), but that he produces it gratuitously, with no higher spiritual purpose, with no secret beauty in mind. The eccentric, far-fetched, overelaborated character of his work is entirely a matter of the strict application of principle, not of any covert intention, which might unexpectedly show itself in the making or to the beholder. There is nothing that the artist knows that the assistant or spectator does not know. However, LeWitt initiated what they complete. But there is no need to mystify his intention because of this. He is simply the "idea man"; his assistants and the spectators are production men. LeWitt is the manager of his art, not its producer. There is an industrial model, a contemporary idea of division of labor, behind this. The value of this is that it gives LeWitt a kind of lyric freedom—or at least the illusion of such freedom, the abstract idea of it—to create his production rules. That freedom is immediately circumscribed by the fact that they must be "practical"—easily executed, easily perceived. There is a tension set up between LeWitt's possible freedom and his actual production—another mannerist paradox. It is on a par with LeWitt's assumption that one man's conceptual certainty is another man's perceptual uncertainty, and vice versa. LeWitt's art always mocks us with an imaginary freedom, the illusion of a margin of uncertainty—a will o' the wisp spontaneity—much as our society's rule by scientific reason promises us an imaginary emancipation, whose meaning we can no longer even guess at. That aura of intensity that transcends reason yet seems to emanate from it, that sign of the power of abstraction, is the myth that justifies its oppression. Reason is always in control, but it must give us the illusion of a spontaneity, a richness of being beyond control, so that we never question its control. We never question LeWitt's control because of the rich visual experience his art provides us, and yet we cannot help but wonder, once we are sated—and the task of criticism is to become as sated as possible at the banquet of art and still keep one's wits—why art must be so completely a matter of control, why only the instinct for control must be allowed to dominate. We are of course addressing the question to the society which LeWitt's art reflects, and assuming that his art is an ideological as well as intellectual construct. If we did not do so we would ignore LeWitt's political commitments, and his feeling that "American life is rapidly breaking down."[6] That breakdown reflects a loss of a reason for being while still existing for a seemingly fundamental reason. Like LeWitt's cubes, American society sometimes seems definitive and normative, sometimes broken down and abnormal. They exist by rule, yet seem demoralized, and as "decadent" and as "completely without any purpose" as American morality seems to LeWitt. LeWitt's rules have moral as well as mathematical meaning, for they imply a manner of being as well as inaugurate a world of abstract forms. It is impossible not to see his art as a critique of American society, for it is clearly an art of manipulative reason, reflecting that society's operational values. LeWitt's art mockingly mimics the operationalism of American society.

In one further reference to Descartes, we might note that LeWitt's demonstration, as it were, of the impulse and conjecture—"imagination"—serial deduction can set loose, undermines what was for Descartes one of its major uses, to symbolically generalize and bring order into the perception of what he called "sensible things," as well as to neutralize their expressive charge. They were made clear and distinct—intelligible—and thus completely objective. For Descartes, "the diversity existing between white, blue, and red, etc." could be reduced to "the difference between the following similar figures."[7] In general, "the infinitude of figures suffices to express all the differences in sensible things." But for LeWitt the infinitude of figures not only does not express all the differences in sensible things, but generates new ones. Because LeWitt takes the system of figures literally rather than symbolically, as sensible things in their own right rather than as an algebra of form, he sees them—particularly because he views them dynamically, in Muybridgean movement—as sensuously diverse, heavily nuanced by perception, during which they acquire all kinds of "accidental, secondary" traits. For LeWitt, the wall of a wall drawing is not a neutral ground for the figure but a visually rich environment on a par with the concept for the drawing. Similarly, in the corner grids, the apparently arbitrary play of light and shadow, and the new combinations of forms which seem to emerge from the piece as one shifts one's position in relation to it, are for LeWitt as essential to the piece as its structure. It is in such images as *Grid of Grids* (1976) that LeWitt's paradoxical fusion of systemic and sensuous elements—impersonal simple forms and complex personal surfaces, both vigorously asserted—seems most evident, although it has been apparent in LeWitt's art from his earliest work, the untitled pieces of the early Sixties. LeWitt's world is spattered with forms, like sudden epiphanies, and it is hard to separate their sensuous from their intellectual reality.

LeWitt's massacre of the innocents—of the innocence of Lucy Lippard, of a wall, of a simple cube, of art itself—is part of his mannerist wit, in the sense in which it is an attack on what seems self-evident, and secure in its self-evidence, with a barrage of seemingly selfless rules, seemingly purposeless formal strategies and instructions for their execution. All have as their ulterior motive the establishing of a tension with and within the self-evident, a tension exploding it into a paradox, in which the formal self that exists—whether it be that of a person, as in Lippard's case, or a geometrical shape, as with the cube—is denied the evidence for its self-sameness or unity of being, and so is dissipated, in the very act of being attended to or affirmed. It is stripped of all reason for being by being analyzed according to a system of rules tangential and ultimately alien to its apparent nature. What sense does Lippard's writing make when we pay attention only to the relationship between its vowels? What sense does a cube make when we present it in various stages of incompleteness and regard it as an open form? These are comic approaches to it—in LeWitt's words, they show a "weird humor"—altogether beside the point of its axiomatic definition, much as the vowels in Lippard's words are beside the point of her self-definition by her writing. LeWitt undermines—mocks—the seemingly *a priori* and absolute—

whatever seems to assert itself unconditionally and only in terms of its immanent logic—by putting it through arbitrary (for its self-definition) conceptual paces, which give it an unexpected look, make it an unexpected experience, and violate the convention which gives it meaning. LeWitt invades a given system of self-definition with an alternate system, which simultaneously trivializes the original self-definition and reconstitutes it with its "opposite," thereby "unnerving" it. Lippard writes personally; LeWitt shows that impersonal letters are part of that personal style, reminding us of Mallarmé's assertion that a poem is its words not its meanings. In LeWitt the poem is reduced even further, to its letters, as if it is harder today, in a world generating contradictory meanings, to get to their root— to the play of necessary forms that constitute them. Analogously, only moving in the opposite direction, the impersonal cube is personalized by being made incomplete—implicit rather than explicit. Lippard's very particular writing is treated in a general way, as so many letters, and the general form of the cube is treated in a particular way, reduced to a series of individuals. In both cases it is hard to tell which is fundamental, the general or the particular—another example of mannerist paradox. LeWitt uses reductive rules to move freely between particular and general, or vice versa, as the need may be—between type and individual, *a priori* and *a posteriori,* "rationally" converting one to the other. Neither has absolute authority and autonomy, but seem chance positions in a larger strategy. For LeWitt, it is the rules of the game of conversion that matters more than any particular conversion. LeWitt's wit consists in confronting the seemingly absolute and self-determined with its seemingly arbitrary opposite— and reducing it to this opposite, ironically, by axiomatically absolute, unconditionally applied rules.

The interplay that results can be regarded as a *discordia concors,* as Hauser notes, "the label often applied to mannerism."[8] For him, "the dialectical principle underlies the whole of the mannerist outlook," and issues in "piquancy—a playful or compulsive deviation from the normal, an affected, frisky quality." Such piquancy seems to me self-evident in LeWitt's art, in both its look and its methods. LeWitt's cunning, in effect his "coquettishness," to use the term Hauser applied to the "tricky game" of paradox—in effect the cunning or coquettishness of reason—leads him to produce an art "of irreducible tensions and mutually exclusive and yet inter-connected opposites." Hauser asserts, mannerism's

> paradoxical approach does not signify ... that each statement is the retraction of the last, but that truth inherently has two sides, that reality is Janus-faced, and that adherence to truth and reality involves the avoidance of all oversimplification and comprehending things in their complexity.

Moreover, what makes mannerism particularly remarkable "is not the simultaneous presence and proliferation of contradictions, but the frequent lack of differentiation between them, and their interchangeability." The difficulty of differentiation also seems to me self-evident in LeWitt. How are we to separararate the look of his "art" page or Lippard pages from the actual distribution of words and letters on it, a distribution that LeWitt had nothing to do with in the first place. Similarly, it is impossible to separate any series from the simple rule or form in which it originated and to which it constantly refers and "returns." It is hard to tell which is the thesis and which the antithesis in the dialectic, for a synthesis seems to have been there, at least implicitly, from the beginning—so that the "antithesis" was predictable. This logical predictability goes against all eccentricity of appearance. Yet experientially such a differentiation between the logical reality of the series and its eccentric appearance is possible, whatever their theoretical interchangeability. We can both oversimplify and overcomplicate what LeWitt has done, because the dialectical structure of his works is at once unresolved and resolved.

LeWitt has called his works "structures," and another way to understand the manneristic character of these structures is through George A. Kelly's theory of cognitive constructs. According to Kelly, the core of human personality is the "continual attempt to predict and control."[9] What can be predicted and controlled is the "truth," and has an air of "inexorable reality" about it. It becomes an essence of reality, an essential construct defining its nature. For Kelly, each such construct is conceived dichotomously, with its poles in hierarchical relationship, i.e., one is superordinate and the other subordinate. Now in LeWitt, who begins with seeming essences, with inexorably given formal realities, the dichotomous way of organizing them in a construct is, in the best irrational mannerist fashion, non-hierarchical. It is impossible to tell whether LeWitt's "manhandling" or working over of Lippard's pages is subordinate to the superordinate pages or vice versa. Similarly, it is impossible to tell whether the complete closed cube is superordinate to all the incomplete open cubes or vice versa. As Kelly says, "the construct is an idea or abstraction that has a dichotomous nature," but in LeWitt the idea has become irrational because it cannot organize itself hierarchically. Reason is inconclusive in LeWitt. It cannot decide between opposites, but endorses both in an unqualified way. Like the high mannerist he is, LeWitt "prefers reiterating and drawing attention to insoluble contradictions to screening or concealing them," even though they may secretly not be contradictions. He "emphasizes and intensifies them," rather than cut their Gordian knot by hierarchizing them. He is a priest marrying apparent opposites, in an effort to show their real unity, rather than a fanatical devotee of singular absolutes.

We may say, in summarizing the mannerist construct of LeWitt's wit, that it involves four questions: (1) that of the relationship of the rule to the image it generates; (2) that of the relationship of words to image (a subsidiary of the first question); (3) that of the energy level of the works; and (4) that of their cultural meaning. LeWitt responds to the first question in precise mannerist form when he says, in an unpublished interview with Ann Stubbs, that "logic is only a tool used to make anything, even irrational ideas," and "logical order equaling perceptual chaos." The belief that equality can be established between concept and percept is essentially mannerist—paradoxical. The classical rationalist Descartes, e.g., regarded the concept as superior to the percept. But the answer to the first question is necessarily qualified by the answer to the second one, which suggests how equality between concept and percept is established. They translate into one another through the intermediary of words. But such mediation is an equivocal business, and can lead, as LeWitt shows, to one's becoming tongue-tied. For words introduce another medium which is theoretically and experientially different from either concept or percept. The concept is intuitively simple while the words are discursively complex. And the percept, whether simple or complex in LeWitt, is intuitively apprehended, while the words must be reasoned out to be apprehended. Another discrepancy is introduced, the contradiction between the intuitive and discursive, the immediately apprehended and the reflectively understood. There are both continuities and discontinuities between idea, words, and image, on both psychic and physical levels. (LeWitt in general is interested in showing the interdependence between continuity and discontinuity, as in the *Four Color Drawing (Composite)* [1970].) The unity of idea, words, and image in any given work reveals it as a unity of a whole complex of opposites, and shows that LeWitt's structures are very intricate epigrams—visual conceits—like the best mannerist wit.

The epigram, as is well known, is a pyrotechnical display of opposites. Their unity is made possible by their concentration into a small format, which makes them succinct, as well as builds tension between them. They are in effect forced together. (One might also note the succinctness of LeWitt's writings, which have their own epigrammatic power.) Hence the overall simplicity of form, and its inner complexity. As Coleridge wrote, an epigram is "a dwarfish whole, its body brevity, and wit its soul." It is well known—Ernst Robert Curtius in his discussion of "brevity as an ideal of style" makes it clear[10]—that without brevity there is no "point" or wit to the epigram. In LeWitt the rule or the modular is a species of brevity, amounts to a concentrated format, within which the wit unfolds. Every one of LeWitt's images has its own succinctness, because of its unitary basis or inherent connection with the rule. Also, the brevity of the rule typically functions as the first part of a LeWitt epigram, arousing our interest or curiosity. The second part—technically called as well as experienced as a "point"—satisfies "our curiosity, often by some unexpected turn."[11] In LeWitt the irrational, complex, seemingly self-adumbrating image is the unexpected turn, the "point," satisfying our curiosity about what will result from the application of the simple rule. (The tension between the intuitively apprehended idea and the words in which it is stated is also an epigram. Still another epigrammatic structure is created by the tension between the words and image.) But in LeWitt the epigrammatic roles of the parts of the work are interchangeable. We can start from the image, curious about how it was derived—"deduced." As Lessing put it, which "particular object more or less held in suspense (in) our attention and curiosity" we start from does not matter. What matters is that our attention should "be gratified at a single stroke." In LeWitt, the leap between principle and application, or vice versa, or between mediums, gives us such gratification—so long as there is the sense of an unexpected move from one to the other, so long as there is the sense of the one being in surprising relationship to the other.

This question of epigrammatic tension in LeWitt's works takes us directly into the question of their energy level. Not only does the epigrammatic character imply an intense, if frozen, energy, but the sheer proliferation of forms and the suggested infinity of the series also do. At times we seem to be watching a dervish-like doodling to infinity, or perpetual motion within a closed system. Also, LeWitt's works demand our own intellectual energy to make manifest the latent content of their ambiguous unity. Finally, there is the energy which chose or intended the rule in the first place. This is the sheer power of command implicit in the works—LeWitt's creative energy lays down rules by fiat. This power of "first determination," as Hegel calls it, is seemingly compulsive, even obsessive, for it is applied to forms that are already determined. But to "intend" what is already intuitively given is to transform it from an inert idea into an "inspiring" force. It is to breathe new life into it, or rather, lend it the life of one's own consciousness—lend it one's self-consciousness. It unfolds its self-reflexivity as one's self-consciousness unfolds the logic of one's self. It also suggests a consciousness that is dissatisfied with given rules and forms but knows no other. It wants to make the discovery of its own limits a matter of self-expression. In a sense, the problem of LeWitt's art is how, without breaking its own rules—and realizing that in any case the rules are unbreakable, if one is to have an art—it can become heroically expressive: a paradox if ever there was one. Looking at the art from outside the intention, its expression seems eccentric, a distortion of primary structure however much an acknowledgment of it, an unnecessary exercise rather than a useful clarification. But this exercise shows a restless spirit, a typically mannerist spirit, which, as Hauser says, knows it can never be "completely expressed in material form." This spirit considers itself irreducible despite its reification. It hints at this irreducibility "by the distortion of form and the disruption of boundaries" in the material it uses, like borrowed clothing, to express itself. It bends the given to its will by putting it through a purposeless exercise, which, however much it makes the involuntary and eternal seem voluntary and temporal, adds to the world a series which can serve only to mark a private dynamic. The identity this dynamic expresses seems as obscure as the series seems unnecessary, however "consequent" in itself; neither seems an organic development. But, like the growth of a crystal, it is sometimes impossible to tell whether the growth of a LeWitt series is organic or inorganic. The distinction becomes blurred, because it is like a developing consciousness aware of its own unfolding, and energized—fueled—by this self-consciousness.

As to the cultural meaning of LeWitt's works, we have already connected them with an industrial-technocratic model of management and the general American belief in manipulative reason. To this we can add the fact that they have an anonymous, mass-produced look, which is perhaps inevitable for objects that are produced as part of a system. This look is paradoxical, because the structures are in fact handmade. They show signs of the vicissitudes natural to such a mode of production—some of the Museum of Modern Art wall drawings in pencil or chalk have smears—but the important thing is that these signs imply that the system never completely controls its content. LeWitt recalls "being disturbed by the inconsistency of the grain in the wood" in contrast to the structure built with the wood.[12] This frustration with inconsistency strikes me as singularly American. Rather than working with the grain in wood, as Gauguin and Max Ernst did in their different ways—the one trying to follow the organic structure it suggests, the other taking it as the inner texture of a visual idea— LeWitt imposes his structure and his own system upon it. But he continues to remain frustrated, because the grain won't disappear. He wants a mastery of nature and the identity of objects that it is impossible to have. And, paradoxically, he doesn't absolutely want it; he does and doesn't want the grain to disappear. He is perversely delighted by this natural eccentricity—by Nature's own weird humor, also no doubt the result of its lawfulness, some necessity or rule—and continues to use wood, as well as grainless metal. LeWitt, the thoroughgoing rationalist, the sustained reasoner, wants to eliminate "all the marks of the adventious, the improvised, and the provisional... from the formal structure," a typical ambition of the classical artist, as Hauser notes. But LeWitt the mannerist values these marks because they show up the supposed universality and absoluteness of the structures, symbol of the "System," showing that for all its hermeticism it is crawling—positively corrupt—with "alternatives," with nuances that make a crazy system of their own. He suggests that fantasy continues to exist in a closed system, as an implicit revolution against its explicit rules. At his best he tries to get the very closure of the system to generate a sense of fantasy. He seems to create a classical microcosm, but once one enters it, one finds oneself, as Hauser says, "using the well-known mannerist image," in a labyrinth, in which one can neither altogether lose one's way—one knows the rule that created it—nor from which one can altogether escape, for experientially there are all kinds of passages one's knowledge of the rule did not prepare one for. The experience of the labyrinth is quite different than its theory, all expectations to the contrary. The rule leads to a certain unruliness, as it were. In general, LeWitt's works are, theoretically, emblem-ornaments of the smoothly abstract formalist system governing in America today. Experientially, they are escape hatches from that system, even though they bail out on nothing. Especially do the wall drawings seem to me the witty ornament, the ironic decoration, for the witless surfaces of the slickly rational, slickly functional—or so we pretend it is—world we inhabit, making these surfaces witty and turning its own principle of reason against it.

LeWitt's art, then, is a parody of the rituals of reason—and of democracy—by which we suppose we live. The items of his series are so many steps in a high mass of reason, and through his books he mass distributes an elite, intellectual art—all to no avail. For we do not know if he has left us the sacred relics of reason, or a bureaucratized system of banal forms. Like Edgar Allan Poe, only more stoic, he is obssessed with reason and its inventions—his own work is one. And like Poe he uses de-individualizing reason to generate a sense of strange individuality. He thus shows that reason is another kind of misfit that can give rise to gothic effects.

Notes

1.   René Descartes, "Rules for the Direction of the Mind," *Philosophical Works* (New York, 1955), vol. 1, p. 33.

2.   Meyer Schapiro, "The Fantastic Eye," *Art News,* 55 (Dec. 1956), p. 51. Review of two books by Jurgis Baltrusaitis, *Le Moyen Age Fantastique* and *Anamorphoses ou Perspective Curieuses.*

3.   René Descartes, "Discourse on the Method of Rightly Conducting the Reason," *Philosophical Works,* vol. 1. p. 92.

4.   Alicia Legg, ed., *Sol LeWitt* (Exhibition Catalog, Museum of Modern Art, New York, 1977), p. 77.

5.   Lucy Lippard and Sol LeWitt, "Walls, Rooms, Lines," *Unmuzzled Ox,* 4 (1976), pp. 69-71.

6.   Sol LeWitt, "Statement," *Metro* (Venice), no. 14 (June 1968), p. 44.

7.   Descartes, "Rules for the Direction of the Mind," p. 37.

8.   Arnold Hauser, *Mannerism* (London, 1965), vol. 1, pp. 12-13, 24-25.

9.   S.R. Maddi, *Personality Theories: A Comparative Analysis* (London, 1972), pp. 148-50.

10.   Ernst Robert Curtius, *European Literature and the Latin Middle Ages* (New York, 1953), pp. 487-91.

11.   Edwin Post, *Selected Epigrams of Martial* (Boston, 1908), p. xxiv.

12.   Legg, p. 57. We might note that LeWitt's constant distinction between and effort to reconcile surface and structure—perceived surface and conceived structure—echo Noam Chomsky's distinction between the "surface" structure and "deep" structure of a sentence. (See *Cartesian Linguistics,* New York, 1966.) In LeWitt, the "grain" of the image—its surface—is ideally the result of the abstract or "deep" relations that determine its structure. And as in Chomsky, the operational rules that generate any given structure are limited in number, while the number of structures—whether of language or image—that can be generated is unlimited. And as for Chomsky, LeWitt's rules are "innate ideas." Both use Cartesian and mathematical models. But where LeWitt's problem is to make innate ideas seem intended, Chomsky attempts to see how they can "intend" what LeWitt takes for granted—an infinite variety of structures.

Part III

20

Nineteenth-Century Landscape: Poetry and Property

It has become customary to think of 19th-century American landscape paintings as communicating the "overwhelming natural energies" that generate the "emotion of the sublime," thereby confirming the transcendental ideality of nature. At the same time, it has been acknowledged that the sublime was part of "the rhetorical screen under which the aggressive conquest of the country" was carried out.[1] These paintings are as much practical as spiritual in orientation, showing a thoroughly material, exploitable nature, figuratively accessible or preliminarily explored by the pictures. They are, as it were, as much the result of Eastern ambition as of freshness of impression of a seemingly limitless Western wilderness. Nineteenth-century American landscape paintings are, in William James's distinction, complex combinations of tenderminded and toughminded attitudes—not simply to nature, but to a self that discovers itself by means of a raw, uninhabited nature—in the nature that is prehistory.

As Emerson wrote in his essay on "Nature," Americans wanted "an original relation to the universe," and thought they found it in contemplation of a nature which reflected their will. But this narcissistic idealism, in which the self realizes its unity with nature, was combined with a more "realistic" attitude, which viewed raw nature as a threat to survival while at the same time it seemed to promise abundance. Thus, the American's attitude to nature was a compound of the disinterested and the interested, a potentially explosive mixture of which the sublime is one expression. The sublime exists not for itself, but as the sign of tension between toughminded and tenderminded attitudes to nature, the one socializing it into a source of communal wealth, the other finding it esthetically and intellectually satisfying. In Emerson both attitudes existed side by side; for him, nature, "in its ministry to man," was simultaneously beautiful and a "commodity." The beauty of nature showed its value to man as "the symbol of spirit," and its commodity value showed its "discipline" for the hard-working will. Nature was both poetry and property; whatever difficulties Emerson had intellectually reconciling the two, he experienced no discrepancy emotionally. For the wilderness of nature was for him already half tame, since it had been the subject of much speculation and aspiration, both by him and by others; and his sense of solitude in it was always tempered by his desire to write about it for others—to bring it into a communal situation. But when this solitude is not forced (as it is in Emerson, who feels it necessary to self-consciously leave his study) but spontaneously confronts one with one's identity as part of nature itself, then the tension between the tenderminded and toughminded attitudes becomes explicit.

When nature is truly experienced as primordial, it generates a poetic feeling of loneliness, evocative of the deeper, instinctive aspects of the self; the view of nature as property—the deliberate effort to tame it, to make it of service to man—is a defense against and rejection of this primordiality—both nature's and the self's. Nineteenth-century American landscape painting begins, with early Cole, in a feeling of primordial loneliness; it develops, through the Luminists and other artists, towards an ideal of nature as a kind of communal property; and it returns, particularly in Homer, but also in Blakelock and Ryder, to a sense of the solitude of nature, romantically dynamicized. Throughout this development the concept of the sublime—a sense of the transcendental—is standard currency; but it is often a disguise for the transactions actually occurring between toughmindedness and tendermindedness. The sublime, in other words, has an ideological function, as Barbara Novak has suggested; but it is best ignored if one wishes to see the real complexities in changing attitudes of artists towards the American landscape.

The ideology of the sublime was a European import, superimposed, perhaps for reasons of sanity as well as of culture, on the primordial experience of American nature, which was difficult to face in its full intensity without any filtering device. It was as though the concept of the sublime prematurely made conscious (and so lost much of the import of) what was unconsciously felt about the original American wilderness. The original experience of the uninhabited American wilderness was one of fundamental loneliness—a sense of being thrown back on oneself, to the prehistory of oneself—to the self without other selves. Over and over again this note is struck in the literature on the America landscape, however blurred by accounts of its immensity, however moralized and rationalized. In his *Autobiography,* Worthington Whittredge writes,

> But how different was the scene before me from anything I had been looking at [in Europe] for many years! The forest was a mass of decaying logs and tangled brush wood, no peasants to pick up every vestige of fallen sticks to burn in their miserable huts, no well-ordered forests, nothing but the primitive woods with their solemn silence reigning everywhere.

The forest was raw with a terrible rawness, for it signified nothing human; and its silence forced Whittredge back upon himself, in a way he could hardly understand. He did not have the "emotion of the sublime" to control his response—to give him a measure of mastery of his loneliness by understanding it as a predictable consequence of confrontation with the infinite. Nor is it exactly an infinite that is there—rather a sense of absence—no peasants, no proper order to the forest. Two of the major trappings of society as he knew it—class and order—are missing, and with them society, human company.

This sense of absence of human company is also expressed by Cole in his *Essay on American Scenery* (1835, written one year before Emerson's "Nature"):

> He who stands on Mont Albano and looks down on ancient Rome, has his mind peopled with the gigantic associations of the storied past; but he who stands on the mounds of the West, the most venerable remains of American antiquity, *may* experience the emotion of the sublime, but it is the sublimity of a shoreless ocean un-islanded by the recorded deeds of man.

What is missed is personality and history—the presence of the individual and the race—and it is because of the lack of these in the American experience of nature that Cole hesitates to speak of the sublime. The European experience of the sublime was sustained, as Cole noted, by "historical and legendary associations," which American nature did not convey. For Cole, the sublime was not simply a response to a seemingly infinite space, but to the accretions of human meaning through historical time. The sublime was really a symbol of man's continuity—the assurance of his presence from the beginning of time—not of nature's infinity. To experience the sublime in the presence of the American nature, rather than in the Campagna, meant to read man into raw nature, and the only man that could be read in was oneself, the original viewer of original nature. Thus the emotion of the sublime was a projection of oneself rather than a discovery of the other selves. The American artist stood vertiginous before American nature as before an abyss of self-discovery.

Cole's recoil in mid-career to the transcendental, to steady himself with a familiar concept in the face of an unfamiliar feeling, also muted his self-revelation. The Cole who painted *The Course of Empire* series (1833-36) and the two *Voyage of Life* series (1839-40 and 1841-42), in which the supernatural more than the natural is involved, is not the same as the Cole who painted *Lake with Dead Trees (Catskill)* and the *High Falls of the Kaaterskill,* among other works which brought him fame in 1825. Although "such heroic cycles were the works dearest to Cole's heart," as Barbara Novak observes, the popular press of the day felt that they did not "have that originality and truth-telling force which his native pictures have."[2] This originality and truth-telling were premised on a sense of the primordial force of the American nature, not muted into an Arcadian scene of the imagination—as the press called his heroic cycles.

Not, that is, made sublime. Yet Cole could not resist the sublime, and if one asks why, the only answer is because he wanted to resist the full consequences—the full message—of primordiality. Since primordial American nature was a raw presence-at-hand (in Heidegger's words), it evoked one's own primordial, raw, instinctive nature. And it was this that Cole could not face, because it was essentially asocial and inhuman. American nature threatened to strip one of all acquired, conventional, cultural connections and meanings, reducing one to a kind of essential, instinctive level. On first experience this turned out to be almost like that of a stone. As D.H. Lawrence said, "*the* American soul" was "isolate, almost selfless, stoic, enduring." At the core of this primordial loneliness is the unconscious recognition that at some essential level the self is indifferent to the human community, for it knows it will die alone. The return to instinct—to primordial nature—has mingled in it awareness of death and isolation, an awareness which threatens to disrupt one's social self. In general, 19th-century American landscape can be understood as a struggle to tame and control the primordial experience of raw nature, or as a conflict between the instinctive power this experience releases and the cultural and social significance it is given.

Early Cole, as noted, represents the first stage of 19th-century American landscape painting. Cole avoided the extremes of classicizing and "everyday" landscape—both European in origin—which were dominant before him. Both extremes existed in Thomas Doughty (who was known as the American Claude Lorraine, and also produced works derived from the English picturesque school). Cole's original impulse, grounded on his acceptance of the primordiality and solitude of American nature, was to ignore alike the classical convention which reduced nature to a self-contained, static, measurable cosmos, and the picturesque convention that treated it as an accesssory to human activity, in particular enlivening tranquil domestic scenes. In other words, Cole offered a viable alternative to European idealistic landscape. However, later in his career his own idealism overtook him issuing not only in the pretentious mythological machines already mentioned, but in a number of genre scenes which almost fully blunted his initial primal power.

Cole's original force can be seen in *Kaaterskill Falls,* 1826, a view from the amphitheater behind the upper fall of the Kaaterskill, "then and now," as Howard S. Merritt notes, "one of the most curious and picturesque sites in the Catskills."[3] The amphitheater forms a panoramic span framing an abundance of natural detail, and creates a unity which prevents the proliferation of detail from becoming chaotic. But this framing device, and Cole's seemingly deliberate effort to present a kind of freak of nature—a natural shape seemingly made for a human purpose, and thus directly reflecting "Spirit"—are the least significant aspects of the picture. What matters is the way he almost splays the falls onto us, so close that we can't help but feel the water's force. We are as it were thrown back on ourselves by the drive of the water, which we recognize as indifferent to our presence and driven by a purpose of its own. The picture gives us a primordial experience of a primordial nature, stirring strong emotions and generating new energy in us. (The spirit of this work, incidentally, was not entirely unique to Cole, as is shown by Catlin's more crudely executed yet equally "instinctive" *View of Table Rock and Horseshoe Falls from Below,* painted one year after Cole's work.) The confrontational character of these works prepares us for Church's scenes of direct involvement, pictures before which, as David C. Huntington notes, "spectators imagined themselves in the very presence of nature. The artist had seemingly removed himself totally from the scene...."[4] But the important point is that the artist removes himself not simply to give an informational you-are-there immediacy to the work, but to put us in a situation of solitude in which we can experience nature's primordiality. The artist is less interested in his extraordinary ability to mimic nature than in eliminating any signs of human presence, including (or especially) his own. In looking at these confrontational pictures one is meant to enjoy the fiction that one is the first observer of the raw scene, and thereby to have a raw experience—personal sensations and novel associations—of one's own. Nature is meant to be shown as an essence unchanged by man, and thereby to throw one back to one's own unchangeable essence.

The full point of Cole's picture is made clear when one compares it with John Trumbull's inert, classicizing *View of Niagara from an Upper Bank, British Side,* 1806-8, and Alvan Fisher's everyday picturesque view of *Niagara Falls with Rainbow,* 1820. Trumbull and Fisher put their falls at a pleasant distance, so that they can be comfortably contemplated, not for any profound philosophical import, but for a generalized sensation of their grandeur. These pictures still seem to have a European way of looking at things, while Cole's and Catlin's works directly involve us in the American nature. Where Trumbull and Fisher are interested in a detached view of the grand form of the falls—in making its scale intelligible—Cole and Catlin are not in the end interested in the form and scale of the falls, but in its powerful movement. It is the curvilinear form in implicitly cyclical movement that matters to them, not the elegance of the falls' bow-like shape; even that form is more taut, charged with unspent energy, than in Trumbull and Fisher.

In their preoccupation with the water's intense "circulation," Cole and Catlin seem to link up with Emerson's conception of nature, in "The American Scholar," 1837, as without beginning and end, an "inexplicable continuity," or "circular power returning into itself." In his mythological and genre landscapes, however, Cole gives up his confrontational mode, locating his meaning now entirely in the picture, not in the spectator's imaginary experience of solitude with nature.

Durand not only ends the original isolation in and of nature in which the instinctive life of the will can be discovered, but he blurs the sense of nature's radicality as primordial presence-at-hand. Nature becomes peopled with *Kindred Spirits,* 1849, communing with it and each other. In Durand nature is an eternal companion encouraging companionship between mortal men—here Cole and the poet-philosopher William Cullen Bryant—seemingly lending their friendship its immortality. (The picture is in fact commemorative and nature is in effect their heaven.) In looking at the landscape, one responds to the prominent presence of the men—the work's title in fact signals them rather than the nature, although nature is implicitly "kin," too. This familiarity seems to me to mute one's relation to nature, which in any case, in Durand, is less dynamic and charged than in early Cole. Durand who after Cole's death became "dean of the Hudson River School," eventually painted an official *American Wilderness,* 1864, suiting his position as conventional philosopher and successful politician of art. As David Lawall remarks,

> As president of the National Academy of Design from 1845 to 1861, Durand held a position of social responsibility that precluded his surrender to the self-indulgence of pure Romantic lyricism. It was his task to promote a form of art that conforms the spectator to a salutary and humanizing order.[5]

Durand reduces Cole's instinctive energy to "Romantic lyricism"—and transcendental meaning has not been spared either. Durand whittles it down into tidy moralism, gentle do-goodism. He creates the American pastoral—the painting that exists more for its associations than for its primordial vision. (Cole foreshadowed Durand in his descriptions of what these "American associations" would be: they would have more to do with the present and the future than the past, and involve provincial, domestic scenes—pleasant knolls, secluded valleys, "enamelled meadows," grain, sunshine, inhabitants enjoying "peace, security, and happiness.")

Durand, as in *View in the Catskills,* 1844, and *Landscape with a Beech Tree,* 1844, is the first American vedutist (although that term is more properly applied to the Luminists). At the same time, he gives us his own version of the *paysage moralisé* (although his is without any choice between right and wrong, but rather leads us unequivocally into sterile goodness). We might say that Durand's moralized landscapes show us that virtue can be pleasurable. One doesn't have to climb for it; in America, it is spread at one's feet. In a sense, for Durand, America, which has the "manifest destiny" of becoming a garden of paradise,[6] is never at the crossroads; its virtue is inevitable, and reflected in its nature. While Durand does not signal the treatment of nature as "abstract fact" (which Clement Greenberg thinks Americans love more than anything else and which he finds overwhelming in the landscapes of the "irreligious materialist" Winslow Homer[7]), he does prepare us for its possibility. Durand does not reach the irreligious materialist landscape, but he introduces a heavy dosage of worldly concern, admittedly benign—not yet the interest of the American tradesman, concerned to win a profit from nature—but nonetheless indicating a leveling of the original primordial relation to the universe.

Durand's replacement of energetic immersion in nature by familial intimacy with it is signaled by an expanded interest in atmospheric and light effects—and this means a loss of proportion among the elements, which seemed to exist in balance in the early Cole. In Durand's *Kaaterskill Clove,* 1850, and *Vermont Scenery,* 1852, water and land lose weight in contrast to air and light. In these works pervasive air and light become means of, in Goethe's words, "attaining the general expression of the whole"; it is as though the artist had become "tired of using Nature's letters every time to spell after her"—and tired of going after every elemental word she writes. Durand wants a semblance of the whole with some salient detail integrated with it, rather than the entire individuality of each of its details. Goethe and Emerson regarded this loss of interest in the individuality of nature, whether taken as a whole or in its details, as an inevitable decline, and as the consequence of the search for a unifying principle—the result of a tendency to generalize. Durand's generalizing tendencies not only despiritualize nature, but deny what Emerson called our consanguinity—our instinctive, blood relations—with all its parts.

Both the final reduction of nature to ordinary proportions and the conventionalization of landscape so that it is more sky than land were accomplished by the Luminists. Durand can be viewed as a transition from Cole to the Luminists. He resembles Cole in his frequent use of a vertical format, retaining emphasis on mountains and trees, and in his spiritual import, however tepid and sentimentalized. At the same time, while lacking the Luminists' broad horizon and general horizontal emphasis, he shares their interest in atmosphere and light. As in John F. Kensett's *View from Cozzens' Hotel, near West Point,* 1863, and *Third Beach, Newport,* 1869, the Luminists turn their interest in atmosphere and light into the pursuit of special effects. Also in broadening the picture format (however small the picture) so that it loses its aspirational verticality, they altogether eliminate the primordial charge. Emphasizing the sea, they reduce the land to token significance. But even the sea exists in a generalized way, often for its shimmer—for the way it points up light and air, enhancing their effect. In a sense, the Luminists show nature to be a powerless place—a placid, picturesque accompaniment to human affairs. They take a conventional approach to nature—nature from the beach or settled shore, rather than wandering inland to its unexplored forest depths—and integrate its parts in a shallow, simplistic unity. They have untensed, even unstrung Cole's taut bow of nature.

It is accepted opinion that the Luminist landscape is spiritual in import, and implies a tranquil mysticism "that sets it in opposition to the earlier concept" of the dynamic, energetic sublime.[8] The "luminist atmosphere," as much crystal as air, with its "pure and constant light," guides the onlooker toward a lucid transcendentalism, in which the world is simultaneously concrete and dematerialized, so that the Luminist picture "becomes the monologue of transcendental unity."[9] While an internal reading of the Luminist picture does suggest a transcendental dimension, a closer reading shows that other, more prosaic, factors enter in, which permit us to argue that the transcendental appearance of nature in Luminism is a sign of nature's domestication, its subjection to human use. I am surprised that the horizon, one of its most prominent features, has not been more commented on in the literature, for it was "especially in the distant line of the horizon (that) man beholds somewhat as beautiful as his own nature" for Emerson and Schelling, the father of romantic transcendentalism. "The health of the eye seems to demand a horizon," wrote Emerson, but that horizon is the symbol of human ambition—material as well as spiritual. Thus, while, as Barbara Novak observes, "at the peak of Luminist development in the 1850s and 1860s, spiritualism in America was extremely widespread" and that Emerson conceived of light as the "reappearance of the original soul,"[10] it is also that the 1850s and '60s were a time of trade expansion. Lane, from 1848 to his death in 1865 lived in a house with a view of the harbor of Gloucester, Mass., making short trips to Maine, New York, Baltimore, and probably Puerto Rico. Does the fact that in all these places he painted the harbors with their ships—the instruments of the expanding trade—count for nothing? Is the subject matter so beside the point of its Luminist transformation? Is Luminism really "a realism that goes far beyond 'mere' realism," using a "magnified intensity that turns realism into a form of impersonal expressionism?"[11] Or is this super-realism the sign of a loss of intensity in response to nature? Lane usually depicts places like *New York Harbor,* 1850, in which ships are at anchor, but even when he depicts more remote, less commercially active harbors, such as *Off Mount Desert Island,* 1856, and at *Owl's Head, Penobscot Bay, Maine,* 1862, his nature is rustic and rural rather than primitive and unexplored. It is the ships, rather than the landscapes—including the sea—that generally are the active element in his pictures. Nature is subdued, even when it is about to storm, indicating that it is always a viable highway for the transport of goods. For Lane, the sea is in effect a kind of big ditch filled with water—a canal or trade-route for commercial activity, rather than a free, powerful element, as in Cole's early pictures of waterfalls. Lane's sea is simply an environment for human activity—nature no longer independent and isolate— and the luminescence that coats its surface is the symbol of its humbled state. This light itself is as unenergized (compare, for example, Turner's light) as the Luminist sea, and is in a sense no more than a sign of good conditions on the highway to progress. "Progress," as much as if not more than transcendence (which strikes me as a surface effect) is the secret message of Luminism. In a sense Luminist pictures are a kind of ideological justification of the atmosphere necessary for business, if also an exaggerated, idealistic rendering of this atmosphere.

Nor are Lane's boats ever (like those of Breugel) truly threatened by nature—thrown about by it. Lane's sea, for all its expanse—if it is anything more than the passive carrier of ships, it is simply picturesque, stagey scenery—has a certain hollow feel to it, obscured by the resonant light. (This is in part due to Luminist precision of execution, which ties it to the colonial limner tradition, but also shows, as does the depiction of ships, a preoccupation with "technology.") As in Martin J. Heade's *Lake George,* 1862, and *Salt Marshes, Newport, Rhode Island,* ca. 1863, the next step in the process of humanizing nature after moralizing it is to theatricalize it. Transcendentalism, in my opinion, is part of this theatricality. In general, Luminist theater occurs within a provincial context, where nature acquires provincial purpose. It becomes the amphitheater—Lane's safe harbor—for provincial activity, an ever-present milieu rather than an absolute power. One does not have to go far from home to encounter Luminist landscape, but the nature one encounters is thereby all the more uneventful. Luminist classicism, as it has been called, presents a finite world—its horizon is a limit rather than an invitation to the infinite beyond. Such a limited world is inevitably provincial; Clement Greenberg once wrote that the provinces are characterized by lack of variety, and if one examines the Luminist scene, one quickly realizes that it is peopled with very little—ships, anonymous people, some land, sea and sky and more sea and sky, all of this illuminated as though it were a permanent paradise, the 19th-century American dream of village life come true.

After the Civil War, the "subjective quotient"[12] of American landscape painting is again raised, particularly in Inness's landscapes, but the character of spirit has completely changed. The tainted tranquility of Inness's nature—its reduction to abstract fact, as in Luminism—continues Luminist passivity. The tranquility of American nature is in fact never doubted again until the landscapes of Blakelock, Ryder, and Homer. But what is important in Inness is that his tranquility shows the coloring of fact with mood, the giving of fact an emotional intonation. Inness, in other words, accepts and is completely at home in an objective nature, so much so that he can feel in and for it. For him, the emotion one feels in a landscape is as much a part of that landscape as anything else in it. He treats emotion in the same matter-of-fact, public way as the Luminists treat objects, and it is just as common.

Prior to Homer, one must backtrack to Church to find a special, if not exactly spiritual, charge. Church, Cole's only student, produced work as strong as Cole but different in quality, work which epitomizes the problems of 19th-century American landscape painting—as, without the same momentum, Bierstadt's work does. For in such works as *Niagara Falls,* 1857, *Twilight in the Wilderness,* 1860, and *Cotopaxi,* ca. 1863, Church shows himself poised between Cole's vision of nature as a source of instinctive power and a raw presence-at-hand and the Luminist vision of nature as illuminated fact, as an almost ornamental objectivity. Church can be understood as a highly ambitious visionary of the primordiality of nature, or as the greatest illuminator of its matter-of-fact objectivity. He is in fact a visionary of matter (much as the Cole of the mythological machines was a spiritual visionary and idealist). Church, in effect, shows nature to be cosmic property—matter that can be appropriated, yet that is as universal as spirit. Thus Church depicts the Andes Mountains, the Amazon basin, icebergs, observing matter in all kinds of states. He shows himself to be a "philosopher" of omnipotent, universal matter, and at the same time the first settler of nature, a trailblazer opening the way to its future exploitation. Church thus returns us with a vengeance to Emerson's sense of nature as an essence unchanged by man; but at the same time as he strips it of its sign of human presence, he makes it more accessible to the practical will, which sees everything in material terms. He is thus simultaneously the climax and destroyer of Cole's original relation to the universe. Church's nature is cold and specific, made up of particular places which are indifferent to man's spiritual aspirations but can be materially exploited. Church retains a sense of the original inhospitality and inhumanity of nature, but not of its impenetrability. Because it is indifferent to man it no longer contains his depths, and so it can be exploited by him without him violating himself.

The late seascapes of Winslow Homer make a fitting conclusion to 19th-century American landscape painting, because Homer restores in more fully realized form Cole's primordial nature yet does not forfeit the materialist's sense of its abstract facticity. He shows, in a sense, how the abstract became primordial, and vice versa. He neither spiritualizes nature nor renders it dully and bluntly, and for all the talk of his "reifying ephemerals" in his last sea pictures, of showing "the moment [that] yields up not its transience, but its quotient of eternity,"[13] the sense of eternity is more an illusion of Homer's emulation of the photographic ideal of capturing nature on the move[14] than of any religious feeling for the elements. The key to these pictures is indeed his handling of the sea as it gradually spreads all over the canvas, encroaching on and threatening to swamp all other reality, seemingly even the sky. These last sea pictures, I contend, are implicit prototypes for the all-over (abstract) American picture of recent years, and have the same depth-psychological implications as it does.

What is unusual about these late seascapes, from the point of view of traditional landscape, is that they do not have the "low horizon [that] is always and everywhere a sign of advanced contemplation of nature,"[15] and yet they clearly are advanced contemplations of nature. Not only does their horizon tend to be high, in contradistinction to Luminist landscapes, but it tends to be cragged and edgy—as though it was about to become a Clyfford Still contour—or at least interrupted by spray, which intrudes on it like raw nerve-endings suddenly erupting through the skin of the sea. Homer's sea is rarely at rest, is always charged with a mercurial violence indifferent to human presence. In these works, it is as though the sea were pushing away the human presence that forced itself on the rest of nature—that the sea was the one element that could not be tamed. Service on Homer's sea is hard, unlike in Luminist pictures, and those who observe it watch their own potential death by drowning. Thus intimacy with it, even the artist's, can never lead to a true marriage, nor even to the more immature love of narcissism, in which the sea mirrors back one's own undeveloped meaning. One can never move effortlessly through it to the horizon and the beyond, but is always caught up by its treacherous movement, which evokes one's own passion but rarely permits one to become tender—tranquil—with it. One can be as passionate about the sea as the sea itself is, but one can rarely take secure voyages on it. As in Hart Crane's poems, Homer's sea is a "sceptred terror of whose sessions rends/ As her demeanors motion well or ill." That is, it is a nature which refuses to be moralized, refuses to be rationalized, refuses to be spiritualized—refuses to be of human use, and yet demonstrates energy and strength which human beings can instinctively understand. It is this instinctive, aimless passion which is evoked by the confrontational mode of Homer's seascapes, in a much more intense way than Cole's and Catlin's confrontational pictures do, for they still have the restraint of relatively clear and traditional design.

In Homer's seascapes design becomes less and less significant, for the sea becomes more and more comprehensive and consuming—in many pictures it touches all four edges, as though it would do away with any frame, any containment. It is this fact that leads me to conceive them as "anticipations"—in that mealy-mouthed art-historical word which seems to imply historical inevitability, but is meant to suggest only a continuous modality as well as mode of conception and perception—of the Abstract-Expressionist "field" painting. In the all-over picture the sea as it were goes up and altogether over the horizon—swamps the picture's inner edge, much as it would like to obliterate its outer edges. One can argue in general that Homer's sea—not Lane's harbors or smooth shores—is abstract because, like the open sea itself, it has no apparent center. No one aspect of it is in stronger focus than any other—this, together with its encompassing if not unifying effect, indicates that all its parts can be read as of equal value. And as Greenberg points out, such "equivalence," in which no one part of the picture is more important than any other and yet no two parts are alike—this being nature's own "attitude" or perspective on things—is the outstanding trait of the all-over picture. The all-over picture is in effect a landscape in which all human value has been neutralized, all signs of human presence have been obliterated. It thus realizes, more perfectly than hitherto, the 19th-century ideal of removing any signs of the artist from the "scene," so that it will stand forth in all the primal clarity of first encounter.

At the same time, in one of those marvelous paradoxes possible only on the level of total abstraction, the sea, as Jung says, "is the favorite symbol for the unconscious, the mother of all that lives."[16] And in the unconscious everything is dissolved into elemental equivalence, insofar as it is subsumed under desire or passion. Greenberg has played down the depth-psychological aspect of Abstract-Expressionist painting, although he has acknowledged the implicit and explicit figuration in it—in Pollock's pictures, the "fabulous shadow only the sea [of paint] keeps," to again use Hart Crane's words. However, critics such as Harold Rosenberg have pointed it up, perhaps exaggeratedly, but nonetheless indisputably. In Homer the working of the sea is simultaneously abstract and has depth-psychological implications, the latter if for no other reason than that his depiction of it involves a refusal of consciousness of the everyday "humanized" world. We know that Homer's sea is deep and steep, not simply the shallow, broad surface presented by Luminism. Homer, late in life, retreated to the sea in Prout's Neck, Maine, a place he had known sporadically for the last third of his life, and committed himself to entirely in his last solitary decade. The sea is his leavetaking of the world. In his pictures it crashes in on the land, but always to recoil to itself; it is this recoil which is the subject matter of these grand late pictures. This leavetaking, when it is not death, must be to the unconscious—must imply an identification of the inner self with the sea's momentum, its "gestures." As the outer self seems about to be swamped, as in *Kissing the Moon,* 1904, the inner self seems immensely alive and alert, vividly signaling its existence—it is this moment between inner and outer that Homer seems to depict, the sea simultaneously a threat to the outer self that belongs to the world and a symbol of the expressive energies of the inner self. The specific threats of *Undertow,* 1866, and of sharks, as in *The Gulf Stream,* 1899, become generalized in the later works, as in *Driftwood,* 1909, where the human is reduced to a token presence, and the sea becomes almost all.

The sea, then, is the perfect "medium" for the abstract all-over look, as it increasingly verges on becoming in Homer, for its movement prevents any stagnation into monotony and is equally "valid" everywhere—spread "equivalently" throughout. The sea destroys the boundaries that inhibit the field and its flow, and in so doing—in the apparent obliteration of limits—seems to release us into the unconscious, and becomes itself emblematic of the dynamics of that unconscious. From the point of view of 19th-century American landscape as a whole, the key point of Homer's seascapes is that they strip away its spiritual utopianism while extracting a sense of its willpower. That is, Homer's seascapes increase simultaneously the objectivity and the subjectivity of 19th-century American landscape, realizing its potential for extreme statements of both. Even if Homer's works are interpreted, as has been done, in Darwinian context as narratives of survival against the elements (but the fittest are all too often anonymous and unheroic in late Homer, for all their muscularity), the main point of the pictures is their extreme objectification and neutrality in the face of the elementally expressive sea. Homer is the fulfillment not only of Cole's vision of a primordial nature but of an elemental self, both of which Cole tried to believe were sublime, but which Homer knew were simply what they were, materially real and blindly driven, with no higher *raison d'être.* Homer toughmindedly presents both nature and self without any religious or ideological fanfare, and thereby aggressively realizes both as absolute "values" in themselves, as worth encountering without expectation of experiencing anything other than what is given.

Notes

1.   Barbara Novak, "American Landscape: Changing Concepts of the Sublime," *American Art Journal,* vol. 4, pp. 37, 39.

2.   Barbara Novak, *American Painting of the Nineteenth Century,* New York, Praeger, 1969, pp. 68, 70.

3.   Howard S. Merritt, *Thomas Cole,* Rochester, University of Rochester, 1969, p. 22.

4.   David C. Huntington, *Art and the Excited Spirit,* Ann Arbor, University of Michigan, 1972, p. 24.

5.   David Lawall, *A.B. Durand,* Montclair, N.J., Montclair State Museum, 1971, p. 57.

6.   See Barbara Novak, "American Landscape: The Nationalist Garden and the Holy Book," *Art in America,* Jan-Feb. 1972, pp. 46-57.

7.   Clement Greenberg, "Art," *The Nation,* Oct. 28, 1944, p. 541.

8.   Novak, "American Landscape: Changing Concepts of the Sublime," p. 40.

9.   Barbara Novak, "Grand Opera and the Small Still Voice," *Art in America,* Mar.-Apr. 1971, p. 71.

10.   Novak, *American Painting of the Nineteenth Century,* pp. 122-23.

11.   Ibid., pp. 96-97.

12.   Matthew Baigell, *A History of American Painting,* New York, Praeger, 1971, p. 146.

13.   Novak, *American Painting of the Nineteenth Century,* p. 190.

14.   See Philip C. Beam, *Winslow Homer at Prout's Neck,* Boston, Little Brown & Co., pp. 104, 118, for photographs Homer took himself.

15.   Max J. Friedlander, *Landscape, Portrait, Still-Life,* New York, Schocken Books, 1964, p. 55.

16.   C.G. Jung, *The Archetypes and the Collective Unconscious,* London, Routledge and Kegan Paul, 1959, p. 177.

21

Regionalism Reconsidered

Regionalism has become an unfashionable word in America's cultural lexicon. It smacks of provincialism, and American artists supposedly banished that specter long ago. But regionalism may be sneaking back as more and more Americans seek their identity close to home. In this sense, a "region" becomes more than a physical locale—it becomes a psychic and spiritual locale.

—Jack Kroll, *Newsweek,* May 17, 1976

In such places—the Vancouvers, San Diegos, Portlands, Seattles and, yes, San Franciscos and Los Angeleses—can we hope for anything more than jazzed-up melding of New York styles or self-conscious lampoons that aspire to lift the curse of provincialism?

—Peter Plagens, *Sunshine Muse*

To answer Plagens by way of Kroll: yes, we can hope for something more, and in fact American art has always had it, off and on (latest on: in the 1960s, on Plagens's own West Coast turf and in Chicago)—a regionalism which is psychic and spiritual more than physical, although attention to *what* it is has been muted by attention to *where* it is. Geography has especially seemed important, with the development (not so very long ago, it must be remembered) of New York as a center-city for art, a city which seemed to draw to itself whatever significant psychic energy there was for the making and understanding of art. The question seemed to be, was there any significant spirit left outside the cosmopolis, in the regions?

The issue of regionalism in American art has been obscured by two related factors: (1) attention to the region as a literal place rather than a spiritual ideal or psychic home; and (2) the assumption that a regional style is necessarily derivative—an "inflection"—of cosmopolitan style(s). What is lacking is an attempt to define the provincial spirit, insofar as it is a constant, by way of an examination of pre-war and post-war regionalism. The provincial spirit did, of course, exist in American art prior to the 1930s, but before that it was not self-consciously provincial—it was provincial by default more than by intention. As for the second factor, it is a corollary of the first, and it can be dismissed if the idea of regionalism is extended beyond literal place. As we will see, the provincial spirit can flourish in or be transplanted to the cosmopolis. Certainly, eclecticism, wry wit, or expressionistic black humor, all of which are associated with out-of-New-York art, are not unique to the regions, and many New York styles are premised on one or the other of them.

In this essay I use the terms "regional" and "provincial" interchangeably; it should be clear that I am speaking of a provincial spirit that I see as a source of universal and constant possibilities and that is not bound to any particular place. Indeed, Harold Rosenberg makes clear the universal character of the provincial spirit when he describes its manifestation in Abstract Expressionism.[1] This spirit, as Rosenberg describes it, is improvisational, "anti-formal or transformal" (in that it is concerned more with "encounter" than style, and so has a "non-Look"), and implicitly originates in response to the "raw scene" of the American frontier. However, with use and refinement it becomes codified into a "Look," which makes it so accessible that it becomes an international style, in the process losing its "vitality and point." What I want is to recover the vitality and point of the provincial spirit, which had a kind of climax, or at least came forcefully into the open, in Abstract Expressionism. I want to understand this vitality and its point as it exists in other American expressionisms as well—both abstract and representational.

As Rosenberg suggests, the provincial spirit emphasizes content and its implications rather than form per se. It is concerned not with "how to manipulate a Look," but with "the tension of . . . singular experiences." Thus, provincialism reminds us that art is impure as well as pure. The regional spirit at its best reminds us, without forfeiting knowledge of style (only belief in its elite status), that there has always been an alternative dimension to art—that style never exists in and for itself but always as a symbolic physiognomy. The battle between cosmopolitanism and regionalism boils down to the conflict between the good look and the "moral" reference of art, where "moral" carries the burden of transcendence of the good look. For regionalism, the art intention is not autonomous, however much the work of art may have an autonomous look. At its deepest level, the question is whether art is "wrapped in life," in Huizinga's words, as it was in ancient and medieval art (regionalism), or whether esthetic self-consciousness is its first priority (cosmopolitanism).

The poles here established are of course theoretical; practice may fuse them, in varying degress. Also, while it is universally understood that style is always expressive of experience, the provincial attitude tends to see the two as disjunctive, or the one emphasized at the expense of the other. Cosmpolitanism, by contrast, tends to inbreed various styles, in a kind of hothouse atmosphere, and then go to nature for relief, for "raw" experience. The degree of disjunction between "content" and "form" fluctuates throughout the history of art, with the issue becoming crucial in contemporary art, where the autonomy of the art-intention becomes (upon occasion) absolute.

The conflict between regionalism and cosmopolitanism was already evident in the 1930s, even in New York where the polarities were an "urban regionalism" (e.g., Reginald Marsh, Kenneth Hayes Miller, even Isabel Bishop) and the rising abstraction based on the European avant-garde. However, regionalism, both urban and rural, generally swept the field. Regionalism or, more broadly, an accessible form of contemporary representationalism, was regarded as the manifestation of a consciously advocated American "art renaissance."[2]

Among other things, pre-war regionalism meant in principle that there were to be no privileged places in which art would be practiced. It was un-American to suppose that any American place would offer better conditions for the making of art than any other, especially when the American population was still as much rural as urban. All of America was "valid" as a homeland, so why should any part of it be more valid as a home for art? Similarly, in theory there were to be no privileged artists—no great individualists—for it was unconsciously supposed that they would pre-empt the potential, usurp the right, of others. While in fact there were highly individual regionalists, they did not think of themselves as such in an innovative or art-historical sense, but rather in terms of their own interpretation of the American experience. That is, they did not view themselves as creating unique styles but as using styles in a personally meaningful way, with the meaning coming from their sense of mission—"to paint a picture of America in its entirety," as Benton put it. (Many of the regionalist artists, like Benton, had negative experiences with modernism, drifting in and out of the latest advanced style, with no sense of anything "taking" that was relevant to their personal and social experience.)

In general, then, the regionalist ideal of the '30s was to raise the level of the Many, not to single out and exalt the One—reflecting a utopian social attitude prevalent at the time. The approach which sought out the One was regarded here as European: Europe represented hierarchical achievement and the dominance of a few supremely gifted, god-like "creators." It was only from ca. 1940 on in New York that "Europeanism" (in the above sense) could flourish—after many of Europe's great individual artists had immigrated to America under the duress of war.

Moral revulsion against Europeanism is an old American phenomenon, going back in articulate form at least to Emerson's *The American Scholar* (1837), where the problem—and the solution—is succinctly stated: "We have listened too long to the courtly muses of Europe. The spirit of the American freeman is already suspected to be timid, imitative, tame." How to show one is not "timid, imitative, tame," a client of the European muses? (The question is repeated later with respect to the New York muses.) Emerson's answer (and still, in different form and with different results, the American answer): let the young American "single man plant himself indomitably on his instincts, and there abide." Not only will this make "the huge world...come round to him," but give him his "own feet." Do-or-die self-reliance is the American answer to European courtly style. In America, Emerson seems to be saying, instinctive energy replaces civilized form, and the instinct-hungry American artist, with his energy straight from nature, is theoretically free to set his own standards, create his own norms.

Ironically, of course, Abstract Expressionism, New York's revolution of instinct, was not the pure product of the American freeman artist but was developed under European auspices—particularly the European idea of a style as a spiritual homeland, a home for instinct which one could take with one wherever one went, in an age of increasing physical restlessness and displacement. Abstract Expressionism resulted from a fusion of the American urge to articulate instinct with the modern European artist's idea of the abstract integrity of style. What I am claiming, then, is that Abstract Expressionism, not American-Scene art, made the crucial transition from a regionalism of physical locale to one of psychic and spiritual locale.

Pre-war regionalism was not generally successful as an expression of the provincial spirit—Benton among ruralists and Hopper among urbanists are major exceptions—because not only did it tend to reduce this spirit to a matter of local color and custom but it also compromised it by ideology. Nature, inner or outer, was rarely sought on its own terms. Instead, Benton, Wood, Curry and their lesser followers tried to image (however ironically at times) the idea of a stable, strong America—this during the Depression—and their expression had a propagandistic aura. The manic rhythm of Benton's figures, Curry's often violent nature indifferent to human existence, and Wood's twisted sardonicism, are all attempts to break the Depression's inertia and despair with defiant, compensatory energy that could, in terms of art, at least, "get America moving again"—revitalize it. But they offered artificial instinct, manufactured on the spot and in the service of institutional ideology rather than being spontaneously expressive.

In the post-war period, the provincial spirit is a much more complicated matter. In a sense, it goes underground in Abstract Expressionism. Pollock and Still were both accused of the "prairie look," and both denied it, but the point is well made: their best work has about it a raw look which implies instinct and at the same time abjures any recognizable European stylistic reference. Their works cannot, of course, be associated with any specific American region, only with an American spirit, which is the inner point the prairie association makes. Their ruggedness—instinct without ideology—was not achieved by pre-war regionalists however much they desired it. (Nevertheless the link between Benton and Pollock during the latter's student days is neither as fortuitous nor as short-lived as is often thought.)

At the time Abstract Expressionism was maturing, New York did not yet fully exist as a cosmopolitan art center. Today it does. Not only the production but also the distribution of art, including its communication, has expanded almost immeasurably, spilling across the country. The question today is how any artist, presuming he or she would want to, can remain authentically provincial—instinctive—in the face of such cosmopolitanism. Such an artist would presumably have to scrape away a tremendous amount of cultural encrustation before he or she could find any instinct on which to "stand indomitably." Indeed, cosmopolitanism seems so much to have swept the field that one hesitates to retain the regionalist/cosmopolitan dialectic.

Yet the post-war regional artists—especially in California and Chicago, where significant provincial art developed in the '60s—were never tempted to give up the dialectic, although they had to dig deeper and perform some strange involuted tricks, to recover instinct. (One might note that Pop art reacted in much the same way at the same time. But it is a very different case, lacking the provincial spirit in that it is not concerned with the articulation of instinct.) Regional artists had to react more intensely, even violently, against cosmopolitanism than pre-war regionalists had to react against Europeanism. They had to become expressionistically hysterical—their art can often be regarded as hysterical expressionism—to articulate their energy to any effect. They wanted, self-contradictorily—in the best provincial spirit—an image-smashing image. That is, they were subtly iconoclastic (it has been pointed out by Alan Gowans that iconoclasm is not directed against art in general, but against "fine art"—art which exists for its own sake, with no social or human function). Cosmopolitanism being implicitly equated with fine art, '60s provincials' affirmation of the innate was inseparable from negation of the acquired.

Sometimes they undermined wittily, as in H. C. Westermann, Jim Nutt and William Wiley; sometimes they demolished in moral outrage—partly as an expression of their suffering in the acquired culture—as in Edward Keinholz and Bruce Conner. And sometimes they splayed its forms ironically, as in much funk art—Harold Paris, William Geis, Robert Hudson, etc. By whatever means, they violated cosmopolitan—and so, presumably, the larger society's—norms, as well as conscious and unconscious codes of artistic behavior. They were in search of Wiley's inner "Wizdumb," in which art could be a pun or a kind of inspired foolishness, and the artist the wise fool. Their art was a new kind of praise of folly—that of being human rather than absolute.

Before examining the point of post-war regionalism more closely, it is necessary to make clear the gamble riding on the new provincial art. Above all, to make clear that it involves more than art, that it is caught up in a larger American social issue—pluralism.

Regionalism and cosmopolitanism exemplify a traditional American dialectic, what John Higham calls "the interplay between pluralism and opposing theories of assimilation."[3] Regionalism implies pluralism, cosmopolitanism represents the opposing theory of assimilation. The "cardinal assumption" of any pluralism is "that the persistence and solidarity of ethnic minorities is essential to democracy." If one reads "regional" for "ethnic" one sees the situation: if there is to be democracy—and this is the all-American issue—there must be regional art. The minority environment must recover its nerve—the provincial spirit must endure, whatever its expressionistic permutations.

But as Higham makes clear, pluralism is more complex:

> Thus pluralism posits a situation in which minorities retain their plurality and effectiveness; but it does not welcome all such situations. A pluralist wants to develop a mutually tolerable relationship between discrete groups and the social system in which they reside. Specifically, he seeks a relationship that will allow the individual groups both autonomy and unimpeded influence. He opposes assimilation on the one hand, because that threatens group survival; but he also opposes separatism, because that will exclude him from the larger society. Accordingly, pluralism addresses itself to the character and viability of an aggregate that has several components, and its special challenge arises from the attempt to define the aggregate in terms that none of its principal components need find unacceptable.

Higham also notes:

> The belief that a well ordered society should sustain the diversity of its component groups has, of course, deep roots in early American experience, but it became subordinated during the 19th century to the quest for unity.

Pre-war regionalism was a version of the quest for unity, as cosmopolitanism is, in a different way. Inevitably, pressure towards unity leads to a reactive pluralism—to an effort to regroup in a looser aggregate that is connected but not assimilated, discrete but related to the larger art system.

Now, in the '60s the provincial spirit tried to achieve this independence-interdependence by positing the decadence of the cosmopolis, which is a traditional romantic-provincial ploy. The cosmopolis is viewed as a center of secondary rather than primary function. The distribution and management—mediation—of art originate there, and whatever production originates there is seen as controlled by the mediation processes: this production in fact may even be seen as *self*-controlling, in that it gears itself to accepted norms. In conjunction with its mediating function in general, the cosmopolis is a showplace and marketplace for art; in particular, it is a center for criticism, which establishes and tends to enforce norms—if only in what it chooses to notice—not without flexibility, but always within certain limits. This dialectic (which Plagens makes so much of in *Sunshine Muse*) is, in the provincial view, more decadent than creative.

The best '60s regional art was a provincial response to this romantically imagined cosmopolitan decadence. Hysterical expressionism became the sign of authenticity and "human concern." Torment and laceration, funky cop-out, mockery or casualness, sardonic indifference and blatant anger, subtle and unsubtle distortion both of representation and of style, became deliberate provincial strategies. Sincerity stood against the cultural system, refusing mediation—and interpretation—a sincerity which, to prove that it was what it claimed to be, had to bend over backwards and contort. Extremes had to be experienced—one's works had to seem to bleed to know they were artistically alive in a seemingly overcontrolled artistic situation. Art had to become involuntary, a blind reflex, a stab in the dark, an uncontrollable pulse. Thus, instinct came to mean negation and even open damage, and finally—in a sense, the utmost damage to both itself and its participant/observer—unreadable in conventional esthetic terms.

So much of the literature on funk art, for example, remarks on the difficulty of describing, let alone interpreting and catching the nuances of, what is perceived and conceived. Harold Paris sums up the problem of such art:

> Funky art said that material was worthless, that only ideas were important (funky artists showed their art and then often threw it away) and that the value of the art was in its meaning. The intention was to get the idea down as quickly and freely as possible. The meaning of the art was not any way related to intrinsic worth of the materials. Funky artists were essentially assemblage people....
>
> Among funk artists there is little interchange of ideas, nor is there any great desire to talk about their work; they are afraid that to discuss their imagery would be to "reduce" it. When anyone asks what funk is, the answer is, "When you see it, you know it." And you do know it.
>
> However, to verbalize the "unverbalizable": funk is anti-camp, anti-intellectual, anti-formal, but its statements are paradoxical, primitive and universal; its imagery is profoundly moving; and the personal formality of the structural aspects in an individual piece is tremendous.[4]

For Paris, most crucially, "funk is concerned with man." But the "funk image of man is the final inversion: man actually turned inside out." For Paris this means a near-literal display of "the vital, sensitive organs" and "all the on-going decay" involving the "pulsations and metamorphoses" of life. But in the last analysis it means making explicit the in-dwelling force of life, the "personal formality"— once again instinct, but instinct which, in its situation of extreme duress generated by the pressures of cosmopolitan decadence, no longer trusts itself to be mediated by signs and symbols, or even, as Paris asserts, by matter and form. It wants an impossible directness. (Such directness is most obvious in assemblage, the pluralistic or aggregate and authentic, homemade, American work of art: the roughneck churlish assemblage, in which each component is a quantum of energy, with the aggregate indomitably raw.) This radical immediacy of communication, heart to heart, person to person, is supposedly altogether antithetical to cosmopolitan cultural mediation. It is an impossible ideal, to be realized through unrelenting negativism, which involves the investigative reporter's sense of spying on unholy, terrorizing situations—to which it responds with its own kind of angry terror.

The modern provincial spirit also attempts to restore the anthropological conception of art as a magical act using magical materials and having a magical effect. Many of the best provincial works of art resemble artifacts, and often are meant to bear a negative magic that sweeps away rather than affirms. The best California and Chicago art of the '60s is thus, in its monstrousness—in its tragi-comic grotesquerie—apocalyptic in stance.

In this, it is quite different from what is often understood as regional art but hasn't the real provincial spirit—for example, Andrew Wyeth's art. Wyeth reduces regionalism to a sentiment for dispirited folk artifacts. He treats even human figures as such artifacts, like decaying weathervanes that no longer move with the wind. He mistakes nostalgia for the crudity of authentic provincialism— even for its cruel indifference—and confuses long vistas with inward looks, and inward looks with latent instinctive energy. Wyeth is to authentic provincialism as a dray horse is to the wild horses imaged by the provincial Baldung-Grien. Similarly, the "spirit" of such Pacific Northwest artists as Mark Tobey and Morris Graves is not the naked negative instinct of the California and Chicago regionalists. The art of Toby and Graves is consciously "spiritualist," believing that spirit can be directly expressed, whether by technique (Tobey's white writing) or by traditional symbols revived and revised (Graves's birds). Such spiritualism is today a cliché which is a sign of assimilation, ameliorating all pluralistic differentiation.

The new provincial expressionism, then, verges on chaos, which is perhaps its only alternative. In part its chaos is an instinct for the jugular. Many provincial artists agree that the autonomy such chaos gives them is preferable to cultural assimilation, although they never entirely escape this. Of course these artists also have a tradition from which they draw. Their sources are Dadaistic and Surrealistic. But it is a Dadaism without social anarchy, a Surrealism without a connection to Freudian psychoanalysis. The paradox of their situation reminds us that art is a Gordian knot which can never be untied—a double-bind situation, in which all styles eventually deny their own intentions.

Notes

1.   Harold Rosenberg, "Parable of American Painting," *The Tradition of the New,* New York, McGraw-Hill, 1965, pp. 13-22.

2.   For a discussion of this see Matthew Baigell, "The Beginnings of the 'American Wave' and the Depression," *Art Journal,* Summer 1968, p. 389. See also H.W. Janson, "The International Aspects of Regionalism," *Art Journal,* May 1943, pp. 110-15, and by the same author, "Benton and Wood, Champions of Regionalism," *Magazine of Art,* May 1946, pp. 184-87, 197-98.

3.   John Higham, *Send These To Me,* New York, 1975, pp. 198-99.

4.   Harold Paris, "Sweet Land of Funk," *Art in America,* March-April 1967, p. 96.

22

Individual and Mass Identity in Urban Art: The New York Case

We all know that the point of New York "is to be modern, as modern as possible, not to be merely New, but ever-new, York," and that from the start of this self-consciously modern century artists "provided pictorial witness" to New York's "modernity and uniqueness," creating "a distinctively urban iconography."[1] But what is not altogether clear is how this iconography reflected the artist's own sense of identity in the city, or more simply, how much the artist accepted the city and took his identity from it, or how much he resisted it and saw it as a threat to his individuality. Since the city meant modernity, what we are really asking is how the experience of modernity affected the artist and his art.

Some artists, like Baudelaire, experienced the sensation of continuous novelty, such as Paris seemed to present in 1846, as an opportunity to be "heroic," to realize hitherto unheard of possibilities in the urban "atmosphere of the marvellous."[2] This atmosphere seemed to make anything "go." The seeming instability of the modern urban world is a sign of its immense fertility, its revolutionary creativity, and while we may understand it prosaically, as Baudelaire thought, it works upon us poetically. Unknown to ourselves, the city makes us fresh and originally individual, at least to the 19th-century artist— novel, whether or not we want to be.

Other artists did not enjoy this easy harmony with the city, or see it in an altogether benign light. Sadakichi Hartmann, celebrating the New York of 1903, admired its "exuberant, violent strength" and found "an infinitude of art and beauty" in it, but he also experienced it as "mad, useless, Materiality."[3] A note of melancholy creeps in with recognition of the city's violence, and develops into full-blown despair with awareness of the insane, empty materialism responsible for the violence.

Violence taints exuberance, and the strength which seems necessarily to spill over into violence must be corrupt at its source. In this view, the compulsion to be modern, symbolized by New York, is as dementing and draining as it is invigorating and exhilarating, and can lead to what Lewis Mumford calls "evolution by atrophy as well as by increasing complication," with "both processes...going on simultaneously and at varying rates."[4]

Equivocation about New York and modernity is evident in the earliest images of it, images which attempt to humanize it—and in that very attempt show resistance to it. Wanda M. Corn has shown that in the first decade of this century the city's artists, while implicitly recognizing New York as archetypally modern, treated it in a traditional, 19th-century manner as a poetic, picturesque spectacle. It was made moody—veiled, and so displaced—behind an atmosphere, whether gloomy or bright. Corn thinks this was done because the artists, stylistically unoriginal, were stuck with an earlier convention, and were not equal to the modernity of the city. But what must also be recognized is that this use of a traditional manner to treat an untraditional subject was as much a defense—or offense—against the subject as a sign of the artist's inadequacy to it. It suggests a resentment of modernity, a reluctance to accept its inevitability.

Such restraint in the presence of the modern, neutralizing its impact and assimilating it to known modes of experience, is evident in Stieglitz's 1903 photograph of the Flatiron Building.[5] Here the leading skyscraper of the day is measured by—and so visually reduced to the dimensions of—a tree, and shrouded by a snow storm. It becomes, in Ford Madox Ford's words, a "photographic shadow" in a "spectral mist." It is, in other words, made a part of nature. It is shown to be a manmade yet still somehow natural mountain. Its uniqueness as a human construction is destroyed. By theatrically enclosing, even rooting it in nature, Stieglitz humanizes the Flatiron Building, makes it an object of emotional experience—treats a public object in a private way by putting it in an intimate context. At the same time, there is a lurking malaise about the building. However much we "soften" it atmospherically, or subjectivize it by estheticizing it, we are still not at home with it. It looms in the background as an ominous presence, not at all subsumed by the scene of which it is a part, too unnatural to be an altogether acceptable part of it. A construction epitomizing the modernity of New York—and modernity expresses itself through novel constructions—is naturalized, and so neutralized as modern. We will see that the treating of modern constructions as natural organisms, or as organic parts of nature, becomes a standard way of feeling at home with them—but the very act of doing so implies that modernity is alien. Thus it is experienced from the beginning as a mode of self-estrangement as well as of self-expression.

The point is that from the beginning of the artistic recognition of New York's modernity—of the creation of the myth of ever-new New York, what Mumford calls "the myth of megalopolis,"[6]—there was a snake in the modern paradise. This snake is the tension—the dialectic—between individual and city. This tension is generated by the shifting appearance of the city, now benign and promising, a land of opportunity; and now malignant, an indifferent cancerous growth swamping the individual's life—nourished by rather than nourishing the individual. The whole dialectic—between individual existence and mass identity—has been brilliantly described by Georg Simmel in "The Metropolis and Mental Life."[7] This essay is the basis of my attempt to understand the mental life, and style, of metropolitan—New York—art from the start of this century to the present day. The key point is simple. For some artists New York was experienced, whether consciously or unconsciously, as a place where the individuality of their art could be brought to fruition, however intense the struggle to do so. However difficult New York was, it was a catalyst for individuality, a stimulus to self-realization. For other artists, whether knowingly or unknowingly, it was experienced as a place of living death, an inhuman, completely invented world antithetic to any kind of organic life—altogether unnatural, as its pervasive geometry makes clear. Abstract Expressionism, at its best an art of highly individuated gesture, superficially indeterminate and disintegrative yet ultimately in-formative and hermetic, is exemplary of a New York art of individuality, in a sense showing individuation in process. Precisionism, on the other hand, with its tightly closed, neutered planes, and sense of the object as a kind of inert machine, is typical of an art which works with the forms of the city, but sees them as anti-life and inimical to individuality. Franz Kline's *New York,* 1953, and *Wanamaker Block,* 1955, with their blunted geometry and lavish density, evoke the erratic organization of buildings on a New York block—and illustrate the Abstract-Expressionist mentality. Stefan Hirsch's *Manhattan,* ca. 1920, depicting the city as an industrial ghost town, a wasteland of mathematical forms, illustrates the Precisionist mentality.

In fact, I would like to argue—converting another useful distinction into another infamous dichotomy—that 20th-century New York imagery divides itself into an art of imprecision, suggesting a radically individualistic if ambiguous identity, sometimes signifying only its own atypicality; and an art of precision—a kind of constructivism—which whether utopian or empirically descriptive conveys, if only through the exaggerated clarity of its articulation, an estrangement from the reality it represents. The painterliness—in Stieglitz the atmospherics, in the Eight the pursuit of vibrant, fresh sensation—of the one and the architectonics of the other suggest the poles of formal response to modernity. Of course, I am using "precise" and "imprecise" relatively; I mean them more as forms of intentionality than as stylistic absolutes. Moreover, I mean them as often simultaneous in the same art, however much one mode is dominant over the other: Marin's work shows this simultaneity explicitly, and in Joseph Stella we see how these polarities can co-exist, and almost become interchangeable. His *The Port, New York Interpreted,* 1922, seems, in its highlighted architecture, a clarification—a making explicit—of the latent architecture in *Battle of Light, Coney Island,* 1913. Also, there is a latent architectonic, if not explicit architecture, in much Abstract Expressionism, and a repressed yet lurking painterliness in much Precisionism. The point, then, is to realize the snakiness of the dialectic—individual and mass identity intertwine, and however much the one seems to vanquish the other, it returns, if only as seemingly arbitrary background for its opposite.

Amy Goldin points out, somewhat scornfully, that "the Eight became a group by accident," that they "do not share a style," nor, for that matter, "a subject," and that in general

> they make a weird group by any artistic standards. You could just possibly find common ground among Henri, Luks, Shinn, Glackens and Sloan, but when you add Davies, Lawson and Prendergast, all generalizations fail.[8]

But that's just the point: they had an ideology of individuality, which was sustained by their sense of New York as a place of individuation. The first five artists, with their journalistic tendency, and the last three with their quasi-modernist interest in style for its own sake, all held together because of their common belief in individuality, and the city was the only place that "proved" this credo. New York validated individuality, and as such it was a community of individuals rather than a community to which individuals had to conform. The Eight represent a golden moment in New York art (and life), when individual and communal/mass-identity were synonymous. In their art, for all its overt differences, what Baudelaire called "the expression of the public soul," or what Henri called "the expression of ideas and emotions about the life of the time," was in harmony with "individuality of expression"—stylistic and esthetic individuality.

This religion of individuality, public and private, is thoroughly American, transcendentalist in origin, and ultimately derives from a romantic sense of nature as a realm of radical individuation. As William Homer points out, "these two doctrines of reliance on the compensations of Nature and of a self-respectful reliance on our own individuality" are Emersonian.[9] This derivation is important, for its makes clear that New York, however modern, was not experienced as alien to individuality—its modernity simply gave a new articulation to an earlier, romantic doctrine of individualism. Thus, when Goldin writes that "New York painted by the Eight was no city, but an innocent, overgrown village, governed by natural law," she neglects to note that it was an Emersonian village, cultivating individuality. We see this in the individuality of expression of George Bellows's *Cliff Dwellers,* 1913,[10] almost a compendium of visceral and facial expressive possibilities: even in the crowded tenements individuality was not lost, however antic it became. In fact, the congestion seemed to make the need for it self-evident. We see this also, if in an altogether different way, in the personal (to the point of eccentricity) style of Prendergast. Like Ryder, Prendergast generally lived in isolation in the city. The way the city allows isolation, as a choice—as a village would not, with its demands of communal participation and conformity—is also a confirmation, however ironic, of its belief in individuality. The much lamented loneliness of the city is as much a symbol of its opportunity as of its oppression.

What holds the Eight together, then, is their belief in the city as an uncommon place, affording the opportunity of individuality of observation and of expression. It was a place where one could see absolutely unique things, and have an absolutely unique style. This did not mean that the city had always to be one's subject matter, or that it had always to be depicted as a place of radical individualism. Henri's New York cityscapes, which hint at rather than fully realize the city's dramatic individuality, were produced only from 1900 to 1903.[11] Sloan, as in his *New York City Life* etchings, 1905-6, regarded it as a place where scenes of typical human interest were easily observed, because of congestion and forced closeness—because it was, in Mumford's words, "a multi-form non-segregated environment," where very different people from very different worlds rubbed shoulders and became more individual in the process.[12] The Eight, without always depicting the city at large or in detail, experienced it as an environment friendly to any form of uniqueness.

However, Corn argues that what the art of the Eight lacks is "the recognition that the new city experience demands an approach and style as progressive and unique as the experience itself." For her, this approach and style were offered by the Precisionists and American Futurists, particularly Marin and Stella. For Corn, the work of the Eight, and for that matter Stieglitz's early images of the city,

> have a basically static quality, like 'stills' taken from the pedestrian's earthbound perspective, providing, in the aggregate, a pictorial odyssey—often an eminently sensitive tour—of the city's highlights.

While after 1910 "this stationary, street-corner perspective became dated as modernist styles began to be adapted to the Manhattan scene," the fact of the matter is that the speed-up which these styles permitted, resulting from "an approach that synthesized many vantage points and many aspects of city experience within a single canvas," does less to "render the artist's peripatetic role obsolete" than to articulate relatively explicitly his subtle alienation from the city—his growing awareness of its monstrousness, outlandishness and massiveness. For Sloan as well as for Prendergast the city was a paradise of free expression. In general the Eight—migrants from Philadelphia—retained the immigrant's sense of naive wonder at the city, which went hand in hand with their sense of its uniqueness. In a sense, Baudelaire valued the modern, as exemplified by the city, because it aroused this fundamental wonder, as nature once did, gave the sensation of entering a lost paradise of feeling—hence, perhaps, the "naiveté" of the Eight. Indeed, there is an aura of waking dream, of somnambulist sensitivity, in Prendergast, and even in such works as Sloan's *The Wake of the Ferry*, 1907, *Backyards, Greenwich Village*, 1914 and *The City from Greenwich Village*, 1922.

In the Precisionists and American Futurists, this waking dream becomes a deliberately constructed, if profoundly felt, fantasy. This fantasy, while striving to sustain primordial wonder at modernity, involuntarily articulates alienation—particularly the new relationship to time it demands, and the new sense of transience it arouses. Where the Eight are aware of the city as a space for individual growth, the Precisionists and American Futurists, in their different ways, become aware of it as the embodiment of time. The city is no longer a place of individuals, but of objects whose individuality consists in the way they reify time. In such urban objects as Sheeler's *Church St. El,* 1920, Marin's *Woolworth Building,* and Stella's *Brooklyn Bridge,* we see time—accelerated, non-natural, non-seasonal time—in action. The modern appropriation of time, converting it into a kind of willed energy, seems to begin with the Cubist dismemberment of the object into ambiguously related planes. This attempt releases seemingly mechanical energy—an energy with a momentum independent of natural sources. New York, with its planarity and motion, was a seemingly perfect means for articulating, and symbolizing, this abstract energy. Max Weber's *New York at Night,* 1915, and *Rush Hour,* 1915, mean to convey it, as do Mark Tobey's Times Square and Broadway pictures of the 1930s. But the ripest statement of this abstract energy of time which modernity releases is in Marin, where time does more than cast long shadows as in Sheeler, but emerges from an intense angular interaction of planes which converts all space and matter into an abstract emblem of time. Time de-monumentalizes the skyscraper, and as it were reveals the abstract constructive will and energy which erected it. In Marin its singularity consists in this abstract energy, not in its steepness, much as for Delaunay the dramatic character of the Eiffel Tower had to do with the power that built it, not with its form per se. The wondrous power this energy—Marin offers a new visual definition of the power and motion, the feverish electricity Walt Whitman first found in the "democratic vista"[13]—is idolized, not the structure it raises.

But there is a negative as well as positive side to the new sense of time modernity generates. Hand in hand with the attitude which sees it as a new realm of possibility rather than as a finished actuality goes a heightened awareness of transience. Implicit in modernity is a sense of time as constructive fuel and as destructive transience. In the natural view of time transience is brought under the control of relatively predictable change—of the predictable transformation of nature. In the modern view time functions in a jerky, erratic rather than smooth way—transience is out of control. Since short-term novelty is demanded by modernity, long-term stability of time—a "tradition" of time—cannot be established. The cogency and durability of time resides in the moment, not in the season. Modern epochs epitomize inventive moments. In Marin's skyscraper we see a monument to the transient moment. The absence of permanence in these pictures—and in Stella it exists only as a half-measure, a pause in the headlong process of the city—works a destructive magic. There is a sense that structures can collapse. There is an apocalyptic as well as inspirational aura to them.

Precisionist planes convey an impacted, momentarily paralyzed energy. In Precisionism we see "eternal" geometry used simultaneously as a defense against transience and as an expression of modernity, much as in Stieglitz we saw "eternal" nature used as a defense against modern individuality and as a way of habituating it. Transience—modernity—is simultaneously an opportunity for radical individuality, and a threat to it. Thus a variety of traditional defenses is used to box it in, and in so doing gives it a familiar expressive embodiment. But these forms never quite work as expected, and in the end communicate, like Marin's skyscraper, the self-destructive, self-consuming quality of the modern as well as its constructive force. Marin, in fact, was as afraid of skyscrapers as he was attracted to them, the ambivalence of his attitude beautifully conveying the ambivalence of their meaning.[14]

For Mumford the skyscraper epitomizes the "aimless giantism" of the megalopolis, with its values inimical to individuality, which needs space, both literal and figurative—external and internal—to unfold in.[15] A sense of claustrophobia is conveyed by Marin's skyscraper—which seems to be having an apoplectic fit because of it—and Stella's Brooklyn Bridge, and by tightly integrated Precisionist planes in general. The Eight had a view from the street; the Precisionists and American Futurists often have a view from above. This difference itself conveys a displacement of the individual by the dynamic modernity of New York. Also, by engineering new "individuals," such as the skyscraper and bridge—mechanical individuals, which because of their grandeur seem to possess all the spirit there is to possess—modernity dispenses with the human individual. New York's destruction of human scale seems to imply the irrelevance of human identity, and its need to identify with a trans-human construction. The skyscraper stands out over the crowd, and the crowd is exhilarated—uplifted—by the skyscraper, but once the crowd dissipates the individuals who constituted it have no personal identity to go back to. Thus the absence of individuals in Marin, Stella and the Precisionists, thus the presence only of abstract space.

For Georgia O'Keeffe the skyscraper was not a symbol of abstract energy or the modern sense of time, but a kind of giant flower, an ornamental growth. Milton W. Brown remarks that "O'Keeffe has been more successful in her flower-pieces than in her representations of buildings."[16] He attributes this to her intrusive "prettiness of color" and "lack of strength" in the latter, and sees in *The Radiator Building—Night, New York*, 1929, "irrelevant embellishments," "decorative designs no more substantial than flower petals." But that's just the point: she is humanizing the building by naturalizing it, i.e., making it as accessible as a flower or tree. At its top the building becomes an inverted ornamental flower, its opening implicitly an entry into a world of natural mystery. The mass and scale of the building as a whole contrast with the "free" swirl of smoke to its side, smoke shaping itself into an open blossom. For O'Keeffe, the building ornamented is irrationally abstract. Assimilated, however partially, by natural forms, it comes within human reach, pluckable like a flower, and so becomes the symbolic source for personal identity. Admittedly, O'Keeffe's, like her husband Stieglitz's, organicizing of mechanical reality seems to miss the Constructivist point. But O'Keeffe's treatment of the skyscraper is nonetheless one solution—however 19th-century naturalist-transcendentalist— to making it a structure the human individual can dominate rather than be dominated by. Here O'Keeffe and Stieglitz join the Eight in their belief in individuality, and nature as a source of it.

In Abstract Expressionism the whole dialectic of individual and city comes to a head. Afterwards, in both Pop and Minimal-Systemic art, the ideal of individuality of expression seems to collapse. Urban materialism and deliberate lack of humanism become normative. The spirit of mass rather than individual identity presides, with individuality reducing to a nuance of mass form. Pop art is a conscious acknowledgement of two of the major forces of the megalopolis for Mumford, advertising and the media.[17] Their kind of control of and tendency to standardize individuality and history comes to dominate art, like everything else. From the 1960s on art seems to evolve by atrophy, as Mumford put it, i.e., by simplifying rather than complicating, or by making complication a mannerism of a fundamental materialistic simplicity. This is because the belief in the individual as a vehicle of complication falls away: "systems" evolve in a complicated way, not individuals. Individuals are no longer the vehicle for and expression of social evolution. Even in the '70s, the epoch of so-called post-movement art, where "individuals" seem to matter more than movements, the individual is not so much creatively expressive as operational within a system of predictable and well-known variables, manipulating them to make a mini-system.

Pop and Minimal-Systemic art lay to rest the issues of expressive-existential art, or open the way for it to become a theatrical matter.[18] It is no longer viable, either in art or society, as it once was. This is not to express nostalgia for it, in a "reactionary" manner. The power of clichés, visual and otherwise, cannot be ignored, as Pop and Minimal-Systemic art have made clear. But what is necessary is not the old Abstract-Expressionist sense of the triumph of individual identity in the face of mass form, but an art which raises the question of the meaning and scope of individuality within the context of the clichés, whether of form or meaning, we inhabit in the modern world. The irony that is supposed to be lurking in Pop art, and for some is lurking in the nuances of handling in Minimal-Systemic art, where it becomes intellectual irony, is for me not a convincing probing of the possibilities of individuation in the megalopolis-dominated world, but only the crudest scratching of the surface of the question. The same holds for most performance, body and/or narcissistic art.

Abstract Expressionism seems to me the last modern American art we have had which deals significantly with the question of individuation in the megalopolis of New York. It is no accident that it is known as "the New York School," even though it is claimed that New York is "a term not geographical but denoting a [stylistic] direction."[19] For the description of this direction makes clear that it has something to do with problems of individuation:

The works of its artists are...always lyrical, often anguished, brutal, austere, and
'unfinished'...; spontaneity and a lack of self-consciousness is emphasized;...the process of
painting them is conceived of as an adventure, without preconceived ideas....Fidelity to what
occurs between oneself and the canvas, no matter how unexpected, becomes central. The
specific appearance of these canvases depends not only on what the painters do, but on what
they refuse to do.

Harold Rosenberg, who recognized that the question of individuality was
uppermost in this art, unfortunately regarded that individuality as a
metaphysical achievement, in the face of all odds. However, he never quite
spelled out the odds, seeing them only in a general way. Abstract Expressionism,
for him, was only a new version of the old question of the relationship between
particular and general, a new working out of the indissoluble dialectic between
individual and world. But the world is New York—anonymous, absurd,
agonizing, a place generating, in D.H. Lawrence's distinction, loneliness not
aloneness.

There are remarks by Gorky and de Kooning and their friends about the
difficulty of living in New York in particular and the United States in general—
the feeling of the city's and country's indifference to their efforts at a highly
individual art. There is Pollock's remark that "living is keener, more demanding,
more intense and expansive in New York than in the West,"[20] and by
implication the rest of the country. But also, as Pollock experienced, more
debilitating. All of this suggests that Abstract Expressionism is an articulation of
a sense of radical artistic individuality in the face of an indifferent, mass world, in
theory the United States, in practice New York. The city, viewed in a positive
light by the Eight and more ambivalently by the Precisionists and American
Futurists, has an ever more ambivalent aura, tilting to the negative, in Abstract
Expressionism. In its so-called mythological phase Abstract Expressionism took
a self-conscious stance against American materialism in general—a materialism
best exemplified by New York—in a search for a generalized spirituality. But it is
when it becomes gestural that its true individuality—the individuality of its
spirit—is revealed. The Abstract-Expressionist gesture—for Rosenberg a
"signature"—is a seemingly chance, automatist expression, signifying inward,
"instinctive" activity. That is, it is a radically individual expression of radically
personal—almost incoherently personal—feeling.

But the Abstract-Expressionist gesture might be described very differently,
using Simmel's words from another context, "as a specifically metropolitan
extravagance of mannerism, caprice, and preciousness," whose meaning does
"not at all lie in its contents" but rather in it as a kind of "behavior" of "being
different," or "standing out in a striking manner and thereby attracting
attention"—a kind of behavior necessary in urban congestion, as if to prove to
oneself that one exists. This helps to explain why Abstract Expressionism is
more an art of gesture than of signs—an art of marks with no clear meaning
which simply "appear to the point," "appear concentrated and strikingly

characteristic," i.e., radically unique and radically unanalyzable, and so seemingly expressive of the unconscious. It is an art desperately stressing uniqueness in a congested, mass situation, a uniqueness which seems to raise to an ever higher pitch the convulsiveness generated by that congestion. One is reminded of Breton's idea, at the end of his novel *Nadja,* that beauty must be convulsive: the beauty of Abstract Expressionism is that of the convulsive energy of the congested megalopolis made unique.

Perhaps even more than Pollock's works, which seem to show this convulsiveness with an increasingly extravagant and abstract rawness, de Kooning's overly vitalized women seem to show it with a new individuality. Thomas Hess has shown how de Kooning "recognized and accepted the pinup as part of the anonymous American mid-century urban environment," and by "analyzing its hieratic pose" gave it a new artistic individuality—an identity beyond its mass meaning.[21] It is only a short step—leap of faith?—to recognize de Kooning's artistically refurbished female as an allegorical personification of the megalopolis, her alluring monstrousness exactly describing our ambivalent relationship with the super-modern city. Females have traditionally symbolized cities, as in the case of Venice, and de Kooning's female, her voluptuousness caught in and consisting of—constituted by—the transient blur epitomizing modernity, makes a perfect symbol of ever-new yet grossly present New York. (De Kooning's treatment of the pinup, incidentally, seems to show the way the modern artist can achieve individuality in a context of clichés—how by his art's sheer power of individuation he can convert mass identity into individual identity, simple cliché into complicated individual. De Kooning does not succumb to the tendency to evolve through simplification, but rather insists on—and his individuality creates—a complication where there does not seem to be one.)

The dialectic between individual and mass identity is, then, at its tautest in Abstract Expressionism (and snaps afterwards). Nowhere is this tension more the case than in the black-and-white paintings which for Barbara Rose "seem especially typical" of Abstract Expressionism, and whose "sooty black" she too literally equates "with the grime of downtown New York, and the white . . . with the white-washed walls of the studio lofts."[22] Around 1950 Kline, Motherwell, de Kooning, Pollock and Newman all were making black-and-white pictures, and New York is indeed a presence in them, as Alloway unwittingly suggests when he writes that they show a "jump from the autographic to the monumental."[23] However, New York is an abstract presence, not, as Rose suggests, quasi-literal in the works. It is an implicit rather than explicit presence—it haunts the works rather than is represented, however obliquely, by them. It is present the way the infinite is present in Malevich's Suprematism—as a theoretical presence, an imagined limitless ground for individual "figures" rebounding from it. The black in these works is, for me, an emblem of black humor—the irony of subtle individuation in the infinitely impersonal megalopolis. Individuality, indeed, becomes a gesture, half-empty, in such an over-full world—becomes a transient gesture, simultaneously confirming the modernity of that world, which can generate ever-novel gestures, and the hysterical, convulsive character of such gestures, as if to overcome the sense of the uselessness, in Hartmann's sense, of individuality in such a world. The black-and-white paintings show the pathos of individuation—always a finite, however vital, phenomenon—in the seemingly infinite, all-encompassing megalopolis. One sits up and takes notice of the individuality in the black-and-white paintings, but then they seem to dissolve into the shades of the city, and become the colors of cliché, of mass identity.

Notes

1.   See Wanda M. Corn, "The New New York," *Art in America,* July-Aug. 1973, pp. 59-65.

2.   Charles Baudelaire, "The Salon of 1846," *The Mirror of Art,* Garden City, N.Y., 1956, p. 130.

3.   Quoted by Corn, p. 64.

4.   Lewis Mumford, *The City in History,* New York, 1961, p. 451. The idea, developed by William Morton Wheeler, is essentially biological, but is used by Mumford to explain how mechanization can cause urban un-building, and generate a "here today and gone tomorrow" "image of human discontinuity" in the modern city.

5.   The Flatiron Building was a favorite subject in the first decade of this century because of the wind currents its design created. In ca. 1905 William Glackens depicted, in a cartoon, *Dust Storm, Flatiron Building.* One year later Sloan's *Dust Storm, Fifth Avenue,* shows the building, as in the Stieglitz photograph, as an ominous centerpiece, dwarfing the human world in disarray. This painting was considered "the first typically New York 'Sloan'," and won him critical acclaim when it was exhibited. See *John Sloan 1871-1951,* exhibition catalog, Washington, National Gallery of Art, 1971, p. 92.

6.   Mumford, pp. 525-67. Mumford describes the megalopolis as, among other things, "the bursting container." Marin's skyscraper is such a container, as is de Kooning's emblematic—of the megalopolis—female. The bursting apart of the megalopolitan container seems increasingly evident in 20th-century New York imagery, until, in some Abstract-Expressionist works, it seems to have altogether spilled its discontinuous contents.

7.   In *The Sociology of Georg Simmel,* New York, 1964, pp. 409-24.

8.   Amy Goldin, "The Eight's Laissez Faire Revolution," *Art in America,* July-Aug. 1973, p. 45.

9.   Quoted by William Innes Homer, *Robert Henri and His Circle,* Ithaca, 1969, p. 46. The statement is from Philip Gilbert Hamerton's *Human Intercourse,* which Henri considered "one of the best things I ever read." He copied the statement into his diary and mailed it to his parents, and it became, Homer believes, "the key note of Henri's philosophy."

10.   Bellows was not of the Eight, but associated with them, and is often regarded as the most journalistic of them. He was discovered by Henri, and brought to New York from Columbus, Ohio.

11.   Perhaps the most interesting of them is *Derricks on the North River,* 1902, which shows fascination with a skyscraper-like structure emblematic of modernity. Henri had previously (1898-1900) painted cityscapes of Paris, one of them (*La Neige,* 1899) being purchased by the French government. When he moved to New York he continued to paint cityscapes because, Homer suggests (p. 99), he had previously been successful in this vein.

12.   In 1949 Sloan remarked on "the peeper instinct" which could be fully satisfied in New York, where there was always, close at hand, something to see that did not think it was seen. *John Sloan 1871-1951,* p. 86. He also speaks (p. 109) of "night vigils at the back window" of his studio as being "rewarded by motifs."

13.   Walt Whitman, "Democratic Vistas," *Leaves of Grass and Selected Prose,* New York, 1949, p 497.

14.   Dorothy Norman, *The Selected Writings of John Marin,* New York, 1949, p. xi.

15.   Mumford, p. 531. Mumford (pp. 430-31) sees the skyscraper as a vertical "regimentation of congestion," in which the "sky is the limit" of controlled sprawl, much as "fast transportation" makes the horizon the limit in another direction. Apart from being "a status symbol of 'modernity,' " the skyscraper is for Mumford a capitalist way of "maximizing opportunities for profit," "in fact the principal motivating force" behind the "purely mechanical system of growth" which came to dominate the city and is responsible for it becoming the megalopolis.

16.   Milton W. Brown, *American Painting from the Armory Show to the Depression,* Princeton, 1955, p. 127.

17.   Mumford, pp. 537-38, thinks that all the media "work ... to give the stamp of authenticity and value to the style of life that emanates from the metropolis. They establish the national brand ... make every departure from the metropolitan pattern seem deplorably provincial, uncouth, and what is even more heinous, out-of-date," i.e., not modern.

18.   See my "Authoritarian Abstraction," *Journal of Aesthetics and Art Criticism,* Fall 1977, where I show how Minimal-Systemic art becomes theatrical.

19.   From the catalogue for an exhibition of *The School of New York* at the Frank Perls Gallery, Beverly Hills, California, 1951. Quoted in Maurice Tuchman, ed., *The New York School,* London, 1969, p. 38.

20.   Quoted by Tuchman, p. 115.

21.   Thomas B. Hess, "Pinup and Icon," *Woman as Sex Object,* eds. Thomas B. Hess and Linda Nochlin, New York, 1972, pp. 229-30.

22.   Barbara Rose, *American Art Since 1900,* second edition; New York, 1975, p. 175.

23.   Lawrence Alloway, "Sign and Surface: Notes on Black and White Painting in New York," *Quadrum,* 1960, no. 9, p. 53.

23

Richard Serra, Utopian Constructivist

Art is finished! It has no place in the human labor apparatus.
—Aleksei Gans, "From Speculative Activity of Art to
Socially Meaningful Artistic Labor" (1922)

Richard Serra is obsessed with the physical presence of his sculpture, but there is much more to it than that. In an interview in *Cover* magazine (January 1980), he himself asserts that while "art is useless and non-functional . . . it may have the capacity to fulfill many layers of meaning in one's life . . . but to ascertain what these meaningfulnesses could be is an assumption." But there is less presumed than might be imagined in the determination of the meaning of art. Art exists within a broader historical process than that of art history. This in itself does not guarantee art absolute meaningfulness nor automatically point the way to the contexts of meaning it does in fact inhabit. However, art's existence as part of a history other than its own makes it more historically representative than might be expected, or in the case of some art, wished. This does not mean that the art process is necessarily the microprocess of the world historical process, but rather that all the terms regarded as descriptive of the structure of the world historical process are useful for an understanding of the art process. It also means that all the terms that are regarded as applicable exclusively to art are insignificant in comparison to the terms applicable to both the art and the world historical processes. "Labor" is one of these terms, and is thus more useful for an understanding of art than "style," which is almost exclusively bound to an art process, or to a process interpreted as one. (The interpretation of the world historical process as productive of "styles" is about as useful for an understanding of it as the interpretation of an ostrich's hole as necessary for its survival is for an understanding of the ostrich's reasons for using it.)

One might also note that the artist can be unconscious of the world historical process—which does not mean that he escapes it. He may also suffer a failure of consciousness, despite efforts at it. If the artist is unconscious of what is central to the world historical process, however shifting that center may be, his art is likely to be incompletely realized, if not altogether beside the point. (Art, like history, has its interesting atavisms and startling anachronisms.) If the artist is conscious of the world historical process, his art is inevitably self-conscious, which permits him to structure its possibilities in a way which makes them seem to exemplify those of the world historical process itself. This is not simply a matter of a metaphoric reflection of the immanence of that process, but of an apparent intervention in the process. History becomes active in the art, rather than a burden it must passively endure.

Richard Serra is an artist whose sculpture shows all the signs of a powerful grasp of the world historical process, particularly of the situation of labor in it. His art takes a contradictory stance to labor, at once epitomizing the tension in its current condition, and, with a visionary accuracy, resolving that tension. The visionary is a dialectician, reconciling real opposites, with the utopianism of the reconciliation ultimately as real as the opposites. In modern labor leisure and work are unresolved, and the pressures for their resolution are greater than ever. It is these pressures that create a dialectical reversal that is crystallized by what occurs in the experience of Serra's sculpture.

The conflict between leisure and work that structures labor today involves much more than the status of labor itself, although that is an important part of the issue. The conflict also has to do with consciousness of time, as the popular conception of leisure as "free time" indicates. Smithson has pointed out, particularly in his articles on "Entropy and the New Monuments" and "Quasi-Infinities and the Waning of Space," that art in general, and particularly the sculpture of the Sixties premised on entropy, articulates "null time," the evasive present that binds infinitely remote pasts with infinitely remote futures. This temporal rather than spatial sublime stands on its head traditional metaphysical respect for the present as the one certainty of time—truly possessed time. Instead, the present becomes, to use a phrase from George Kubler that Smithson quotes, "the void between events," the neutered moment of transition that itself is "nothing." Energy-less, the present is authentic eternity, a null time precluding the historical, and with that, unavoidably, the anthropomorphic, and all the "expressivity" generated by the anthropomorphic. The present is a kind of zero-sum activity, the paradise of stationary being, ostracizing all becoming in the name of a purposeless completeness.

Now Serra's sculpture seems, at first glance, to indulge the eternalization of presentness by means of entropy that Smithson regards as the preeminent feature of art, particularly the Sixties sculpture of Judd, LeWitt, Flavin, and Morris, among others. For Smithson the entropic mode—entropic presentness—is not confined to art, but catastrophically visible almost everywhere in modern American society. Smithson picks his way through the ruined present of American society—the ruins, known as such in part by their "built-in obsolescence," that are built to constitute a present—towards the presentable ruins of American art, i.e., the objects that articulate the present as a void, a ruin of time. Both the society and the art are unequivocally identified by Smithson as the products of advanced industrialism, although Smithson does not attend to or is ignorant of the moral meaning of the socially produced entropy he identifies. He simply accepts its evidence of standardization as a sufficient and seemingly necessary "condition" of social and industrial (and artistic) advance—the social advance of labor. (One might note that this is a failure of dialectic typical when artistic production rather than social understanding is assumed to count for more in the final historical reckoning. Typically, the artist's desperate search for a new principle of artistic production shortcircuits his understanding of the social source and social force of that principle—exactly what makes it seem a "principle," i.e., a foundation and justification of production. The relevance the principle acquires artistically makes it irrelevant for a revolutionary understanding. The artist is more interested in the artistic consequences of his principle than its social consequences—in the artistic novelty it can produce rather than the social change it can implement.)

Serra's sculpture, then, seems to share the energyless, entropic, "negative" state of the sculpture of Judd, LeWitt, Flavin, and Morris, and the bland, neutered, redundant, mass-produced objects that proliferate on and constitute our social landscape. And yet there is no seriality in Serra, however much he may use planes of metal of the same size and substance. Serra is constructing, while the entropy sculptors are arranging. He is inventing a structure whereas they are filling predetermined—usually by seriality, i.e., by a readymade system—structure. The fact of construction—of deliberate structuring beyond preexistent systems and materially determined order, of the deliberate creation of coherence rather than the acceptance of received coherences—should immediately tell us that Serra's sculpture is not energyless, not neutered, not naively negative. His sculpture is not "fated"—predetermined by a seeming inevitability, a blind necessity, a dumb logic, whether social or intellectual. While it does not have the energy of Abstract Expressionism, neither does it have the deadness of entropy sculpture. Serra's sculpture involves a more considered energy than is actual in the one or possible in the other. It is the energy of work, at once a deliberate and spontaneous energy—an energy which bespeaks a new meaning for work as such, as well as artistic labor in particular. Serra's sculpture is about work struggling to be socially meaningful as well as artistically viable, work struggling to articulate a present but also to redeem a past and propose a future. Serra's sculptures are the projections of a utopian constructive energy of work, which means to recapture its primordial purpose from its inconsequential products, restore its originality in the face of its presentness.

Null time—that of the eternal present—implies null work, freedom from work, a product that seems unworked. Smithson implies as much in his analysis of Judd's "new approach to technique." It "has nothing to do with sentimental notions about 'labor.' There is no subjective craftsmanship. Judd is not a specialist in a certain kind of labor, but a whole artist engaged in a multiplicity of techniques." But what is at issue in entropy sculpture is not specialization in the kind of subjective craft labor traditionally regarded as artistic labor, but the status of labor as such. Entropy sculpture means to diminish work, to dismiss it as insignificant—presumably a sophisticated reflection born out of a Marxist understanding of the implication of high industrialization. It means, ultimately, to abolish work—to collapse work time into the free time or null time of the selfsame object, the entropic present of objective specificity. This involves a loss—and the loss is visible in the absence of energy in the self-identical object—of what work finally is all about: the making of history, the reconceiving of human relationship, the renewal of metaphoric meaning in a remade world. Entropy sculpture, with its implication of an end to work, implies an end to history—perhaps only of American history, but also of historicity as such. Entropy sculpture powerfully shakes off the metaphoric relationship which for Baudelaire was the cutting edge of the historical as well as artistic imagination, and insists only on the eternality of specificity, the transparency of presentness.

Now there is a perverse and unexpected irony in this, which throws us back to the problematic of labor in advanced industrial society. For entropy sculpture unwittingly exemplifies, with a vengeance, the popular conception of art as a leisure time activity. It is at once the "object" of free time and the object that seems to be produced not only in but by free time, i.e., the object that seems to be produced spontaneously, effortlessly, with no work, with no history before or after it, and as such it seems the completely free product. Insofar as art appears to be a freely produced product of free time it is outside of history, and embodies an ahistorical—eternal—perspective on life.

Entropy sculpture articulates this illusion more than any other I know, and in doing so, articulates a traditional utopian idea: that free time is more important and desirable than work time, that eternal leisure is superior to historical labor, and above all, that free time reinforces one's sense of being more than work, because free time is not only more conducive to the realization of one's potentialities than socially necessary work, but the necessary condition of such "self"-realization. That entropy sculpture satisfies one conventional conception of the appeal of art—its codification and embodiment of free time— is generally ignored, presumably because of the uncritical obsession with the supposed intellectual sophistication of entropy sculpture. Yet the recognition of entropy sculpture's realization of the traditional utopian conception of art's value highlights the untraditional utopian conception of art's value that Serra's sculpture implies, viz., the sense of art as a deliberate revelation of work and time, and, as a correlate, the almost deliberate destruction of timelessness or free time. For all the timeless look of Serra's sculpture, it is tense with temporal process. The work of time is visible in the rusting of its exterior, but, above all, in the precariousness of its balance, the possibility of its loss of balance—which would set time to work with a vengeance. (Entropy sculpture, incidentally, refuses rust, insisting on an immaculate, protected surface, one which, while not denying the natural material, neutralizes the effect of the wear and tear of time on the object.) In the rust, time is active, in the precarious balance it is passive, waiting its moment, its "chance."

Serra has structured his sculptures, particularly two New York pieces, so that the work in them *might* be released by time, and becomes identical with the potential work of time. The tension of Serra's New York sculptures is that of waiting for the work of time to manifest itself through the sculptures, and yet the sense that it need not be given its chance, at least not more than is minimally necessary, i.e., in the rust. To achieve this sense of abeyant yet expectant, covert yet catalytic time—which does not mean that it is a time even on the edge of timelessness—requires work, the creation of a tension in which energy is held back while seeming to press forward. Serra constructs this tension deliberately, as the latent power or untriggered spring within the structure decreed by the presentness of his material and its scale. (This tension is the personal element in his constructions. In general, it is the hardest thing to recognize the personal character of Serra's constructions, to see beyond their physical presence.) In setting up this tension, Serra recovers the primordial and intimate meaning of work as an articulation of energy at odds with time. Work is a precarious play with time, an awkward way of coming to grips with it, a Jacob wrestling it for a blessing. Work means to transpose the invisible power of time into visible energy, and use that energy constructively—to construct what is personally as well as socially meaningful, i.e., to construct a self as well as a society. Work exists in opposition to time, and the greatest dialectic achieves a synthesis of work and time—their unity in a "construction." In advanced industrial society, which has made selfhood, community, work, and time almost meaningless, the message of Serra's sculpture is simple: without the will to work there is no meaning. More precisely, Serra's sculpture asserts that without the primitive dialectic work and time there is no self and no community. One might say that the will to construction summarizes Serra's ethos and idealism in the face of contemporary nihilism. The brilliance of Serra's will to construction is that it is a phoenix arising from the flames of a dead, nihilistic industrialism—a bird whose very wings are of industrial materials, but which is the sign of something more primordial, the sign of the most elemental tension in being. Serra, then, has found a more effective way of dealing with time and work than entropy sculpture, which simply wants to blot out both with eternity—which substitutes the inertia of eternity for the process of time, fate for restlessness.

Constructive labor, while known as socially necessary, is no longer approached spontaneously and experienced personally. A spontaneous, personal relationship to work seems impossible—beyond even the reach of myth—in an industrial situation. But to become fully meaningful, such a relationship to labor must be achieved, however "received" the labor is. This once seemed an unnecessary achievement—making its impossibility beside the point—since spontaneous, personal relationships to time and one's own energy could be established in the play of leisure or free time. But in advanced industrial society free time and play have become as predetermined or standardized as work, with more disastrous effects on one's sense of self and one's sense of the energy at one's command. The sense of spontaneity that is the core of selfhood—the means of the recovery of one's sense of possibility—is betrayed by the hidden controls put on it, the hidden direction given to it, by a manipulative society. Indeed, in advanced industrial society it sometimes seems that criticism is not just the only way of decontrolling consciousness but the only form of personal spontaneity—it is easier to predetermine play or standardize spontaneity than work. Simply because free time is free it is more susceptible to manipulation and covert control than work time, which, because it is relatively set in its ways, does not even raise the issue of freedom. (Or if it does, as it finally must, it is through the issue of "artistic" work, "artistry" becoming the vehicle for a spontaneous and personal relationship to work.) The purification of the will to work—which in a sense is exactly what Serra has done in his early process and stacking pieces— becomes the way out of this double bind, in which both work and play, personally meaningless, become manipulated deadends. (This is exactly what Judd's boxes are—manipulated deadends of work and play. They have a less sublime, more deadly industrial meaning than Smithson thought, who while he recognized them as deadend, thought this was to their credit as emblems of eternity. Smithson did not realize that eternity is the sum total of deadends, and that Judd's boxes epitomize the manipulative mentality that characterizes advanced industrial society.)

Serra's sculpure, perhaps more than most, speaks to the condition of "will-less," depersonalized work and play. Conveying a sense of impacted spontaneity synergistically mutating into absolute will and presenting themselves as primitive persona, like monstrous robots caught in the act of becoming organically alive, Serra's constructions demonstrate the effect of undischarged spontaneity, suppressed desire for personal being. At the same time, they show how "artistry" can preserve spontaneity and personal being in relation to even the most resistant, indifferent, impersonal, unworkable material. (I experienced Serra's New York pieces the way Don Quixote experienced the windmills of La Mancha. They were giants in a desert—a vertical desert as well as a horizontal one—but to me more friendly than those Don Quixote experienced. The only battle I had with them was that necessary to know their meaning. They were oases in the urban desert, or the "delectable mountains" of Thomas Bunyan's *Pilgrim's Progress*. Indeed, criticism is a kind of pilgrim's progress to some unknown salvation, and it may be that the critic needs the vision of Don Quixote to do his job well.) Thus, the social dialectic that explicitly motivated Russian Constructivist art implicitly motivates Serra's sculpture, with the clear understanding that the terms of the dialectic have changed with the changed historical condition of labor. It is one thing to be a Constructivist artist in revolutionary Russia, with its minimum industrialization and its idealistic attitude to work. It is another thing to be a Constructivist artist in conservative America, in which maximum industrialization is a vital conception, in which there is acute awareness of industrialization as a mixed blessing, and in which there is an all too "realistic" sense of the banality of work. "Social construction" has quite a different meaning in these two societies, as does "artistic construction." In any case, Serra retains the dialectic, in its new form of the tension between labor and leisure, between the social meaningfulness and personal meaninglessness of productive labor, rather than, as in entropy sculpture, foreclosing on it with a premature and naive endorsement of free or null time as the "final solution" to the problem of labor.

The general Constructivist problematic or dialectic is epitomized in the quotation from Aleksei Gans that inaugurates this article: how to give art a place in the social labor process by which humanity defines and creates itself. The tension between artistic labor and what Viktor Pertsov calls "material labor—that labor in which the workers themselves are directly involved"—is of paramount importance in determining the shape of Constructivist dialectic. Artistic labor, insofar as it was craft labor, was assumed to be a kind of material work. But with the industrial liberation of labor its place in the social labor process became unclear. All kinds of questions arose: Could art industrialize itself? What would be the benefit to it and society from doing so? Did artistic labor have the limitless potential that industrial labor seemed to have? Artistic labor seemed to have been left behind—seemed quaint and socially meaningless—by the industrialization of labor. It seemed to be a form of pre-industrialized labor, and even if it could be industrialized while retaining the individualistic character it has had since the Renaissance, it was not clear that it would then become socially meaningful, except perhaps in a token way. And even to forfeit its hard-won individualism would not guarantee social meaningfulness, for there would still be the question of its social usefulness. Perhaps industrialized, individualistic artistic labor could become symbolic of the worker's personal stake in the social labor process, the emblematic reward of labor. But art's symbolic value cannot be conceived as essential to it, especially in a worker's paradise—a world of gratifying work. To symbolize the reward of labor is not to give or be the reward. Art was not the authentic pleasure that life was supposed to be about, but artificial, substitute pleasure—the fiction of pleasure in a workaday world, but still incompletely transformed by labor, still not full of the fruits of labor. Art is, as Serra says, "useless and non-functional"—and nobody knew this better than the worker with a place and investment in the social labor process.

Whatever the details of this argument, the industrialization of labor, with the bounty it promised, challenged art, and made artists self-conscious about artistic labor—about its methods and meaning. It was put in an apocalyptic position, in which it had to win self-respect, and finally the respect of society. Artists were also forced to question their social role. For industrialism brought with it the proletariat, a class which seemed to have no other identity than that conferred upon it by work, whose existence seemed ill-defined and empty when it was not at work. The effort to recover or revive the full humanity of this class which Marxism represents brought the artist's humanity into question. Was he a material worker or a spiritual bourgeois, taking his identity from received spirit in the form of property rather than achieved work in the form of a product? Wasn't the concept of a spiritual worker a contradiction in terms? Was his humanity revealed or concealed, enhanced or degraded by his work? Was his artistic labor an effort to humanize labor or was it a demonstration of his superiority to material labor, his being too good for it? Did his humanity follow from his work, or was his artistic work the gratuitous expression of his assumed spirituality? What exactly was *artistic* labor, as distinct from material labor? Under the impact of revolutionary industrialism and a revolutionary society or workers, artistic labor was in the process of being reabsorbed into material labor, into the social labor process, and had to justify itself, as did all individual—and individualistic—labor. It becomes crucial for the artist to identify himself as a worker if he is to survive this reabsorption, this resocialization of himself and his work.

Thus, the publicity pictures of Serra in front of his New York sculptures, *St. John's Rotary Arc* and *T.W.U.,* show him in working clothes. The sculptures were produced by industrial means, are of industrial material, and are on work sites owned by the city of New York. Serra identifies with the working class, much as Picasso did by wearing the blue overalls of the electrician, as Apollinaire reports. How seriously can we take this identification? We can neither dismiss it out of hand as specious—for that would be to assume that the modern artist has no place in the social labor process—nor can we automatically assent to it, for that would be to assume that art is self-evidently socially meaningful. There is no clear answer, only the sense of being trapped on the horns of a dilemma. For should we decide on the social meaninglessness of art in an industrial society we deny it meaning as work, but should we recognize its social meaningfulness we must show how it is meaningful as work.

Gans, while seemingly sceptical of art's role in the social labor process of industrial society—seeming to decide that art was socially meaningless and not even truly work—does wish "the masters of artistic labor" well. They are "confronted," he declares, "with the task of: Breaking with their speculative activity (of art) and of finding the paths to concrete action by employing their knowledge and skill for the sake of true living and purposeful labor." At the same time, Gans seems to think this almost impossible to do, for in the very next sentence he asserts: "Intellectual-material production establishes labor interrelations and a productional link with science and technology by arising in the place of art—art, which by its very nature cannot break with religion and philosophy and which is powerless to leap from the exclusive circle of abstract speculative activity." For Gans, "the more distinctly the motive forces of social reality confront our consciousness, the more saliently its socio-political forms take shape," the more art is confronted with the problem of changing itself from a kind of "abstract speculative activity" to a kind of "intellectual-material production." Gans is implicitly trying to deal with abstract art, which seems a socially meaningless production, and he is using the Marxist distinction between culture as an ideological superstructure and material reality as well as between religion and philosophy as one kind of thought and dialectical materialism as another, with all the value associations of those distinctions. But he does believe that art must change from the inside out as well as from the outside in if it is to survive—simply be accepted—in industrial, "labor-intensive" society. It must change its purpose as well as its material and means, putting its social character before its aesthetic character, with its ethical character determining its aesthetic character.

For the contemporary utopian constructivist, such as Serra, who has experienced enough of the modern social history of art to realize the difficulties of doing what Gans thinks is necessary, the demands made upon art by the industrialization of labor are not so clear. Industrialized capitalist society seems, paradoxically, to think that art is socially meaningful only as long as it is purely aesthetic, the social usefulness of art consisting in the decorative value of the aesthetic. As long as art is idle decor, passive display—which betrays both the ambition of art and of society—it is acceptable. To escape the dumbness of being decorative, art must become both abstract speculative activity and intellectual-material production simultaneously, forcing society to transcend its decorative expectations of art—forcing both society and art to think of each other in more meaningful terms. Serra's sculpture is one of the few arts that achieves this simultaneity, that is at once abstract speculative activity and intellectual-material production, and as such forcing society to a new sense of what is meaningful to it. Serra achieves a dialectically tragic sculpture, a sculpture perpetually contradicting itself, shifting meanings. It is the abstract speculative activity of free time and its correlate, free mind, achieving eternal presence, emptying us of history. It is also historically representative, urgent with the pressures of the industrial process, an intellectual-material production of the dialectic of labor and leisure, impersonal and personal work, spontaneous and calculating will.

From the start Serra's sculpture was directly conscious of and responsive to the work process. It took its entire identity and energy from specific work. I know of no sculpture that defines itself so insistently in terms of the work process as Serra's early sculpture, that takes such care to be nothing but its work. In this he outdoes Abstract Expressionism, which was always too bound to the search for symbols to take itself completely seriously as a work process. By being so exclusively—sublimely—a work process, Serra's sculpture achieves a social destiny, for it comes to codify the relentlessness of the labor process in industrial society, the sense of no alternatives to that process and so the sense of it as *the* work process. This leads to a sense of the work process as in and of itself the process of freedom. Work time is seen to be free time—the only time in which humanity is truly free, truly itself, for work time is the only time when it shows its power. For it involves, simultaneously, confrontation with natural reality and social reality, the dialectical transformation of both through the same work.

There is of course the usual complicating irony. Serra's sculpture, like all important art today, may be socially meaningful for an unexpected reason. It can be regarded as less of a dialectical transformation of objective than of subjective nature. It does more effective work on the reality of the spectator than on the reality of nature or society. Its significance lies less in its own process than in the self-process of the spectator. It is more a service industry than a "heavy" industry, more a matter of a secondary transformation of self than of the primordial transformation of material into a basic social product. Of course the personal service industry is fast becoming the most socially prominent and meaningful category of labor in contemporary capitalist society, and what was once regarded as a secondary form of social production is coming to be recognized as a primary form. This is correlate with the growing expectation that work and its products be personally as well as socially meaningful, and that personal meaningfulness is a major clue to social meaningfulness, rather than vice versa. The abstract speculative—pure or free—activity of art is recognized as personally meaningful because it revitalizes belief in the person as a realm of "abstract" possibilities that can be "speculatively" realized, i.e., that can be fertilized by speculative, "free" activity, by a "pure" approach to them. The self is an abstract speculative activity, and art is the realm of "self"-realization, i.e., it is by means of abstract speculative activity, undertaken as serious work, that we come to be ourselves. The synergistic effect of abstract speculative activity is crucial, particularly the synergistic effect on signs. In art their meanings seem to multiply infinitely; everything in art becomes a sign, an omen, multi-meaningful. The work of art becomes dense with meaning, charged with a crushing burden of significance, much of it unconscious and unreachable. It thus comes to possess a "self." The abstract speculative activity of art is a way of synergistically working matter until it seems a sign fraught with a multitude of possible meanings, meanings pressing in their possibility. As such, art "makes life meaningful." Making life meaningful is socially meaningful work, today perhaps *the* most socially meaningful work. Today labor looks to art as the model for an approach to life that makes it meaningful, and so justifiable. Art thus justifies itself: artistic labor is the ideal kind of labor to produce a self. Thus Serra's constructions, derivative from industrial, material labor, return "meaning" to the material labor process, converting it into a sign of self.

Serra's landscape pieces—works that result from his attempt, in his words, to "dissolve" "the discreet object . . . into the sculptural field, which is experienced in time"—directly incorporate "anticipation and reflection and walking and experiencing the time of the landscape," with the pieces "as barometers or viewing edges within the landscape." Clearly, the landscape pieces mean to generate abstract speculative activity in the participant spectator. Such activity is the spectator's way of metaphorically realizing his possibilities in time, or making time meaningful. One remembers that Aristotle's philosophy was called the peripatetic philosophy, by reason of Aristotle's habit of strolling while engaging in abstract speculative activity, a habit which he thought directly conducive to such activity. (One also thinks of Baudelaire's "rapid philosophical walk through the galleries" in the *Salon of 1859*. In Serra's landscape pieces this has become a philosophical walk—not always rapid, because of the terrain—through a single, "extended" work of art.) In a sense, the very ground of being was metaphorically explored by Aristotle. The very possibility of exploratory thought seemed to depend on being peripatetic, generating movement in a landscape which spontaneously turned into an intellectual landscape when it was moved through. The materially real landscape, by reason of the materially real work of walking through it guided by Serra's "artistic" treatment of it, became meaningful beyond itself. Serra has understood that passage through time is crucial for the generation of meaning, and by forcing us to take our time in a specific landscape he converts it into something more meaningful than in material fact it is. Serra is a new kind of "artist-engineer," to use Pertsov's term, one who "rationalizes artistic labor" in a new way, making constructions that are subtly meaningful rather than "obviously practical." Today's artist-engineer subtly generates abstract, speculative meanings in a world that, because it is determined so exclusively by material labor, is barren of them, or at least has them in short supply. In Serra's landscape pieces the peripatetic work, determined by the intellectual-material work of dissolving the sculptural object in the sculptural field, generates abstract, speculative meanings, giving the illusion of a kind of ultimate meaningfulness. Such a sense of ultimate meaningfulness, however indefinite, is an essential ingredient in our sense of "life's meaningfulness." Serra's constructions, then, not only satisfy our need for abstract, speculative meanings in a materialistic world, with a sense of such meanings as spontaneously generating in such a world. They also satisfy our desire for meaningfulness as such, some distillation of meaningfulness. At the least, Serra's sculpture opens the spectator's way to abstract, speculative activity, preparing him for its unexpectedly important results.

Serra's two New York sculptures show another aspect of his utopianism, its destructiveness. All utopianism is implicitly destructive of or aggressive toward the world in which it originates. It is a dialectical reaction to that world, branding it as worthless or as inadequate, at the least as human folly. Utopianism means decisive negation of the experienced world. Marie Louise Berneri, in her book *Journey Through Utopia,* observes that "authoritarian love of symmetry causes utopians to suppress mountains or rivers, and even to imagine perfectly round islands and perfectly straight rivers." Of course, such authoritarianism exists in the name of revolution—carries with it a passionate desire for radical, cleansing change. The city, as Berneri notes, with its sense of imposed order and thoroughly manmade character, was in origin utopian. The city, which has long outlived and completely betrayed its utopian heritage—and I know of no city which has done this more thoroughly than New York—has been the field of Serra's sculpture for the last few years. While his urban pieces do not so much dissolve as rebound and become super-concentrated in the field of the city, they still establish an immanent, primordial, and utopian relationship with the city. They exist to actively negate, or at the least to show up, their urban environment. Serra acknowledges as much when he remarks, describing *Terminal,* his 1977 Dokumenta piece now "placed in front of a train depot in the confines of the traffic" in Bochum, Germany, that it "reduces most of the architecture to its cardboard-model inventiveness." Serra's sculpture has been censured—campaigned against—by the CDU, a German political party representing the right, in my opinion in implicit recognition of its utopian destructiveness, its utopian challenge to the existing socio-political order and its representative architecture.

In the New York sculptures, Serra's sense of the pieces as "testing" the "tendency to overturn" confirms the destructive tendency that is a sign of their utopian intention. Serra's piece in Bellingham, Washington—the immediate predecessor of the New York pieces—initiates the current phase of Serra's long-term interest in achieving "gravitational balance" in the face of the tendency to lose balance, a dialectic inherent in all things. This dialectic is simultaneously destructive and constructive, and as such indicates the inherent utopianism of dialectic. In the Bellingham piece the dialectic of equilibrium is tested less decisively than in the New York pieces, perhaps because the Bellingham piece is in a natural rather than urban environment. Serra, modern rather than traditional utopian that he is, has more against society than nature. He does not want to suppress and correct nature with geometry, but propose to an unbalanced society that it balance itself—that it achieve at least a precarious balance. The precariousness of Serra's sculpture is a way of acknowledging and incorporating contingency, and potentially expanding the sculptural field to include all of the city. It is also a utopian way of being ironical. It says to the city, "I look unbalanced, but you really are."

Serra, then, like Mondrian, another utopian constructivist—who toward the end of his life (1943) remarked that "the destructive element is too much neglected in art"—means to achieve the "destructive natural appearance" while simultaneously achieving "construction through the continuous opposition of pure means." Serra constructs through such opposition, and destroys the natural appearance of the city. His sculpture holds its own against the natural chaos of appearance and perception in the city, and in effect overcomes the "natural attitude" to it. In this his New York sculptures are like utopian architecture, making a kind of clean sweep of the urban space they inhabit. (The industrial source of their material indicates just how socially outspoken Serra means to be.) Serra's *St. John's Rotary Arc* clarifies and cleanses the shabby trafficked space it inhabits, creating a sense of infinity in the forlorn finite space of the traffic circle outside the Holland Tunnel. It gives the driver exiting from the tunnel a sense of the amplitude of the urban space, a sense of the infinity of directions that constitute it—an amplitude and infinity in fact belied by the path his car must take. Serra's sculpture contradicts the fixed map of the traffic circle with its unfixed space. With its openness it contradicts the closure of the city; with its illusion of free movement it contradicts the constraint of the city. It frees and purifies the space it inhabits, and thus is more meaningful than the wretched, comparatively cloistered space of the city, with its vertical as well as horizontal closure. It thus achieves a utopian resonance—it is a utopian glove slapped in the face of the ugly city.

Similarly the abruptly shifting angularity of *T.W.U.*—abruptness of change ought to be a category for the formal understanding of modern art—and the way these angles interact with, more specifically argue against, the echoing angles in the surrounding architecture, dialectically negate this architecture and imply a potentially utopian architecture, as well as clear a space for it to inhabit. Serra's sculpture powerfully intervenes in its environment. It stands up to its environment, giving it the illusion of being more spacious than it in fact is— creating a spaciousness which is at once the hardest working and freeest, most negative space.

24

Francis Bacon: The Authority of Flesh

I. Introduction: The Problem of Realism

And the way I try to bring appearance about makes one question all the time what appearance is at all. The longer you work, the more the mystery deepens of what appearance is, or how can what is called appearance be made in another medium. And it needs a sort of moment of magic to coagulate color and form so that it gets the equivalent of appearance, the appearance that you see at any moment, because so-called appearance is only riveted for one moment as that appearance. In a second you may blink your eyes or turn your head slightly, and you look again and the appearance has changed. I mean, appearance is like a continuously floating thing. (Francis Bacon, Interview with David Sylvester, September 1974.)

Bacon's show at the Metropolitan consists of 36 paintings, largely portraits and self-portraits, all of which have been executed since 1968. The *Newsweek* critic Douglas Davis mentions, in the same breath and deliberately, this show and Brice Marden's concurrent Guggenheim exhibition, expressing discomfort with the former and ease with the latter.[1] Bacon is judged unfavorably when compared with modernist abstraction, triumphing anew in Marden. Bacon, himself, would have none of this because he repudiates the "willed, 'modern' image,"[2] i.e., the pure abstraction which claims transcendental pretensions but communciates histrionic decoration. Bacon remarks:

One of the reasons why I don't like abstract painting. . . . is that I think painting is a duality, and that abstract painting is an entirely aesthetic thing. It always remains on one level. It is only really interested in the beauty of its patterns or its shapes. We know that most people, especially artists, have large areas of undisciplined emotion, and I think that abstract artists believe that in these marks that they're making they are catching all these sorts of emotions.[3]

Again:

I believe that art is recording; I think it's reporting. And I think that in abstract art, as there's no report, there's nothing other than the aesthetic of the painter and his few sensations. There's never any tension in it. . . . I think it can convey very watered-down lyrical feelings, because I think any shapes can. But I don't think it can really convey feeling in the grand sense.

Bacon's abhorrence of abstraction, together with his determination to convey "feeling in the grand sense" yet as part of the process of recording-reporting—"what gives the feeling is that it is more factual"—recalls the efforts of another realist, Caravaggio, to charge fact with feeling. As with Bacon,

> most art critics and academicians condemned the "vulgarity" of Caravaggio's paintings, at times even with moral indignation....Being themselves committed to a standard of ideal beauty, they found his work no more than a base "imitation of nature" and charged him with having destroyed "good taste."[4]

Bacon's "imitation of nature" is in a sense even more "base"—more vulgar, i.e., more popular in origin—than Caravaggio's, for it begins with the base, unsatisfactory illusion of nature which the photograph is. What Plato thought about art in general is also true of Bacon's images, which are imitations of an illusion and so have nothing of the truth about them. They seem to be imbued with idiosyncratic commitment to the reporting of fact. Moreover, they show overeager ambition to express inchoate, inarticulate feelings. Bacon's pictures have about them an arbitrariness which defies any lasting intelligibility, however much they offer half-recognizable realities. It seems they use the photograph to move further away from rather than closer to "nature." They use it as a form of intensified sensation trailing in its wake inexplicable feelings that relate to the object photographed. The image created by Bacon's fluid, painterly stroke stands to the clarity of the photographic image the way, to use his own comparison, the image in a distorting mirror stands to the image in a normal mirror, recalling yet ruining it, focusing it yet making it incalculable. Bacon's transformation of photograph into painted image increases the distance from nature, however much it boomerangs back to the reality of feeling.

Thus, he can in no way be accused of creating ideal beauty, but rather, he destroys the shallow realism of the photograph with his fleshly, seemingly manic strokes. They testify to a disturbance, in itself sufficient to communciate feeling, to convey a sense of what Bacon calls "undisciplined emotion" and elsewhere "instinct." This instinct comes up against the photograph, the image of reality which is its discipline, as an obstacle to be overcome. The obscuring of the photograph underneath the seemingly vicious fluidity of Bacon's stroke both symbolically destroys the "discipline" of reality and releases emotion.

This release is never complete because it is masturbatory homage to reality. Bacon's art is about the vulgarity, the bad taste, of releasing feeling, and simultaneously the sense of restraint on that release. It treats the conflict between the undisciplined release of instinct and reality's restraints on and repression of instinct. Bacon's pictures deal with paranoia, which takes a form of self-enforced solitude accompanying release of passion. Bacon's solitary is no dreamer because he is too alert to the tension of the conflict with him. He takes to solitude to control the ambiguity generated in him by the conflict between passion and inhibition, between the authority of his instincts and that of reality.

For Bacon, realism is, ultimately, not simply a matter of charging fact with feeling, but of confronting fact with the fundamental feelings—the instinctive response. The very process of reporting reality becomes in effect the act of releasing emotion, and the more spontaneous—or as Bacon calls it, accidental— the report, whatever its precisions, the more instinctive and undisciplined the emotion released, i.e., the more horrific the expression of fact. Thus, the core of his problem of realism is expressionistic. It is the difficulty of eliciting feeling from a world whose surfaces are opaque.

Bacon's painterliness is a way of getting under the skin of things, of destroying their matter-of-fact surface appearance and revealing the flesh of feeling they are made of. Similarly, it can be argued that he puts his figures in solitary to take them out of the world's action, to make them passive so that the process of stripping their skin can begin. In a sense, solitude chloroforms them into stillness so that Bacon can begin operating on them.

The unlocking of the feeling in form, as Bacon calls it, does violence to the image. For Bacon, this violence is a way of forcefully referencing reality, as well as an emphatic statement of his assumption that reality in general is violent. John Russell connects Bacon's violence with the European experience of World War II, but the fact that it is sustained far beyond that existence indicates that it has deeper sources. As noted, it has to do with the character of instinct when it feels blocked by reality and the way, as a result, it experiences reality.

In a sense, Bacon is the perfect modern realist, for as the world has become more anonymous, feeling has had to become more acute to encompass it and find release within and through it. Bacon alludes to this anonymity through the everpresent photograph and newspaper, but overcomes it by the intensity of his feeling. (Both become increasingly abstract; solitude is a state of abstraction from the world, as are feelings which do not have the world as their object.) In sum, Bacon discovers the expressive potential in anonymous subject matter.

II. The Solitary Insomniac

Religion is what the individual does with his own solitariness.
Alfred North Whitehead, *Religion in the Making*

> Avaunt from sacred shrines,
> Nor bring pollution by your touch on all
> That nears you. Hence! and roam unshepherded—
> 'No god there is to tend such herd as you.'
Aeschylus, *The Eumenides,* Lines 197-200.

Bacon's figures are both insular and intimate, i.e., have the solitary alertness of self-aware subjects who choose silence. Yet they are subject to our witnessing glances, and at times (as in one of the *Three Studies from the Human Body,* 1970, and in one wing of *Triptych,* March 1974) to the more durable public witnessing of the camera eye. Thus, Bacon's images of himself and his friends are exposed to the anonymous glance of strangers and machines—are exposed indifferently on the rack of public appearance, although enclosed in the privacy of their own consciousness, symbolized by the privacy of the rooms they are in. One could regard these works as extensions of Degas's keyhole visions—images of anonymous figures performing intimate bodily acts under the assumption that they are unobserved—but for the fact that Bacon's figures are not anonymous but rather portraits.

Half-undressed, they are self-conscious in their privacy because they are haunted by the potential presence of the other as their witness, always sooner or later to appear on their private scene. So that the scene, self-contradictorily, is never truly private, but always potentially under view by some anonymous other. In fact, what Bacon calls the "armature" in which his figures are encased can be understood as a frame isolating the targeted figure.

Moreover, one comes to realize that the solitariness of Bacon's figures is entirely independent of their setting, as indicated by the *Portrait of a Man Walking Down Steps,* 1972, where the figure is outdoors, as is also the case in the beach scenes of *Triptych,* May-June 1974. Bacon's figure carries his solitariness with him wherever he goes. It is a habit of mind, an attitude of fixated self-awareness, a form of self-hypnotic narcissism. What Russell remarks as the sense of the presence of an eavesdropper in Bacon's pictures is as much the result of the figure's attempt to tune into his inner feelings as it is of his awareness of the unseen other. In general, Bacon's figure seems truculently self-absorbed, with his face usually turned aside so that his eyes do not meet those of the spectator, or, if face forward, with his eyes evading any encounter with the spectator's glance.

The eyes of Bacon's figure are often closed, as in *Three Studies for Self-Portrait,* 1974. And when not closed, then glazed, as in the self-portraits of 1971, 1972, and 1974. And when not glazed, then blurred—bleary-eyed—as in *Three Studies for Self-Portrait,* 1972, 1973. And finally, when not blurred, then glassily caught between defiance and indifference, as in *Three Portraits—Triptych,* 1973. It is as if he is acknowledging his vulnerability or helplessness before an alien gaze.

Bacon's figure sits, then, as if in detention, or as if, because he is often undressed, in a doctor's consulting room. Both these scenes will be dominated by a menacing figure. Yet he acts as if it will always exist, and can never be violated. This ambiguity symbolizes the simultaneity of the subject's solipsistic narcissism, its self-containment and closure to others; and its being haunted by the other, its involuntary openness to the other through the other's glance. The body's openness to the strange glance in part explains why Bacon acts so intensely on the body's flesh with his painterly stroke. This stroke is the equivalent to a harsh glance, violently caressing or raping. The body is manhandled, with no power to resist, by the other's objectifying consciousness, which twists it into sensate bits. All of Bacon's figures, with the exception of the 1973 self-portrait and Lucian Freud in *Three Portraits—Triptych,* 1973, sit crosslegged, sometimes jauntily so, as in the 1970 self-portrait. This conveys an ambiguous attitude: seemingly seated offguard, the figure is full of potential movement. He can spring to his feet in a moment, ready to act in relation to the other.

The solitude of these figures suggests paranoia. It involves fear of being taken by surprise. (One recalls Freud's theory of paranoia as fear of being buggered—taken from behind, a situation in which one always experiences incomplete awareness.) I should like to talk now about this paranoid consciousness. For it conditions the obscene handling of the flesh, creating its obscenic appearance.[5] (The flesh's obscenity in effect shows it being taken from behind, which puts it in a position to be turned inside out. This is done not simply to show, as has usually been said, its being subject to death and so putrescence, but also to indicate the completeness of its exposure to and possession by the absent but imagined other.)

The paranoid consciousness of Bacon's figure can be understood in three ways: (1) iconographically, as an expression of loneliness, with loneliness being a symptom of a "screened" attitude to the world; (2) psychologically, as an expression of insanity, i.e., unreason—for Bacon the release of undisciplined emotion or instinct in the face of the world; and (3) sociologically, as an expression of decadence, where solitariness is the acknowledgment of nihilism. Loneliness implies the loss of interpersonal values; insanity means the collapse of wholeness of being, and decadence implies the discovery of inertia as the major force and mode of being.

(1) Jedlicka observes that "The portraits and self-portraits of the twentieth century are in general manifestations of the solitary."[6] There is, then, at first glance, nothing unusual about Bacon's portraits and self-portraits. Typical of their times, they show the isolated, monadic creatures we are all to become—the unchosen independence we are all to achieve—in our anomic society. However, in examining the solitariness of Bacon's figure more closely, one discovers the atypical motivation behind it. Jedlicka argues that in Munch's portraits and self-portraits, solitariness exists with respect to nature, while in those of Beckmann it exists vis-à-vis society. For Jedlicka, Munch and Beckmann are linked as opposites, a polarization which continues in their handling of space: open, indefinite, and seemingly limitless in Munch, symbolizing the cosmic expansiveness of nature; and closed and cramped in Beckmann, symbolizing social constraint. Bacon's space is of an altogether different kind, and symbolizes an altogether different psychic state. It is a linear cage of self-control emanating from the solitary himself—as can be seen in the *Study for Self-Portrait*, November 1964, one of its most powerful manifestations—rather than an independent, surrounding space (whether infinite or finite) which conditions his solitude. It is a space self-created by the solitary, in line with the fact that his solitude has become so absolute that it no longer exists in relation to any world, whether that of nature or society. Rather, it is the sign of the absolute givenness

of the subject to himself, and so of radical subjectivity. The formal space with which he surrounds himself is simply the public announcement of his supposedly *sui generic* subjectivity.

The space cage is a kind of halo around the figure's solitariness, showing it to be sanctified by his self-awareness, as well as indicating that it is chosen. In a sense, it is the solitary's self-consciousness objectified, made "practical," i.e., become a world, however small, for him to inhabit. In other words, the space cage Bacon's figure inhabits is not a microcosm of the macrocosm of nature or society, but a private little cosmos with its own sanctity and laws—of feeling—if lack of "higher" purpose. Bacon remarks that "we nearly always live through screens—a screened existence." It is this screened state—a psychic state—that is physically manifested in the space cage. It is simultaneously transparent, to permit a view out, yet limiting, establishing the space of an inner world. It is also the stage on which the solitary's obscene flesh of feeling can be shown, the magic circle in which the solitary feels secure and "normal" while displaying himself. But the space cage is much more: its simplicity and order are meant to hide—in the sense of throwing off the scent—the asocial release of undisciplined emotion, the masturbatory relaxation of instinct. The space cage is social, as all space is, and a defense masking an asocial if not antisocial act. Bacon gives us the whole scene: the private place where feeling is expressed; the outer world (symbolized by the doorway present in many of the works), in which the observing other exists (sometimes he appears in the doorway on the threshold of the inner world); and the screen between the two, a pathetic—by reason of its transparency—creation of the solitary, mediating the relationship between the two worlds. It seems at times to exist more for his mental comfort than to perform satisfactorily the purpose for which it was made. It is as irrational and self-deceiving as the feeling it is meant to serve.

(2) The solitariness or asociality of Bacon's figure is a sign of insanity. The face is the particular bodily place where this insanity is most clearly revealed, and again the method of revelation is Bacon's "malerisch" technique. Bacon's fluid handling of the face's flesh desocializes it, i.e., makes it no longer manageable as social mask. The technique in effect unmasks and undermines the face by making it too vibrant, expressive, and resonant—too much a quivering piece of flesh to serve as a public mask. Becoming flesh—the part of the body one least expects this to happen to—the face loses almost all form. It is the case in point of the loss of self-control of Bacon's figure, which becomes too "sensational" to conform to conventions of social decorum (another reason it must be screened, or hidden away in a room like the portrait of Dorian Gray). It is too indecorous to belong to any reasonable order of things, too subjective and disorderly with its own instinctive energy to be brought under rational control. Foucault writes that

In the psychology of madness, the old idea of truth as "the conformity of thought to things" is transposed in the metaphor of a resonance, a kind of musical fidelity of the fibres to the sensations which make them vibrate.[7]

The flesh of Bacon's figure shows the mad music of uncontrolled or undisciplined sensation rebelling against any conformity to the outer order of things—symbolized by the mask of the face—and becoming a kind of idea in itself.

It is especially in the triptychs and couplings—wherever an attempt is made to bring figures together or wherever more than one figure exists in the same space—that the insanity of Bacon's isolated figure becomes evident. For no reciprocity—whether by sexual means or through conversation—is ever established between the figures. In the triptychs they exist side by side, unspeaking, in private cells. In the couplings there is an eternal return to the same ambiguously sexual act, to a union which never quite completes itself—the same mix of bitter struggle and sweet embrace. There is not the slightest sense of sociability, let alone friendliness—and of any reasonable relationship—in the participants of the triptychs or couplings. On the contrary, there are signs, as in *Two Figures with a Monkey*, 1973, that they unite only for purposes of vice (the monkey is its traditional symbol), and so only momentarily. There is no sense of any abiding, continuous relationship between them, only a half-lustful, half-aggressive attempt to possess each other, and that only in the least, however superficially fundamental way—through and in the form of flesh. In the couplings they wrestle each other, attempting to overpower one another, rather than harmoniously meet. There is no harmonious togetherness in Bacon's world, only conflict and self-conflict, and self-torture. Perhaps this is why the couplings never do depict anal intercourse, but only the inconclusiveness of their struggle. The one figure cannot really take the other from behind, nor do they confront one another. Their union is, literally, a stalemate and deadlock.

In the triptychs this lack of reciprocity—sexuality only proposes its possibility—is even more obvious, for the untouching contiguity of the figures suggests the parallel rather than interpenetrating lives the friends lead. They are more intimate with each other's photograph than each other's person. The triptych form originally brought together a central image with subordinate—often in form as well as content—side images. But for Bacon each image has the same individuality and validity, even when the artist himself is the central image, as in *Three Portraits—Triptych*, 1970. There is neither structural nor psychological necessity for the figures to be taken together. They neither constitute a rational unity nor even imply a system of irrational relations. They are essentially a sum rather than a whole. Togetherness, which requires reason to come into being, does not exist in Bacon's pictures; it is abortive in the couplings, or made a mockery of in the triptychs. How can, as Bacon calls them, futile, accidental beings come together for a purpose, or even take togetherness as purposive. Each has to play out, "by himself," the "game without reason" life is. For Bacon, togetherness is barely a hypothesis of experience. Even the couplings are images of private release of passion, each member an occasion for that release. Relationships in Bacon's art are so completely irrational they might as well not exist. In general, Bacon uses the triptych format, as in the May-June 1974 triptych, to create a series of staggered images, which interrelate as oblique duplicates. Each figure is in effect a Doppelgänger for the other—the death which the other is for the self. Or else, as in the May-June 1973 triptych, Bacon uses the format to trace the "progress" of a single figure—in this case George Dyer's movement toward death. (The image of Dyer on the toilet seat also occurs, incidentally, in the same left-hand panel of *Three Figures in a Room,* 1964.)

(3) In *The Will to Power* Nietzsche equates decadence with nihilism, and sees its appearance in physiological decline and the rise of pessimism and skepticism.[8] It is interesting that, in commenting on his respect for Baudelaire, Bacon claims that he particularly admires Baudelaire's poem "Les Petites Vieilles." This poem describes Baudelaire's "spying on odd, decrepit, charming creatures," "broken-down monsters, hunch-backed or bent double," whom he asks us to love "for they are still human souls." This sense of the decrepit and derelict, the misshapen and fallen—psychically—pervades Bacon's pictures, and can be regarded as the source of what has been called their charnel house atmosphere. Bacon's handling of the flesh is in effect a symptom of this psychic decadence—the decay of the mind into skepticism and pessimism and the correlate inertia, quasi-deadness or decline of the body, which seems as though it has begun to putrefy. Nietzsche does not regard decadence as limited to any particular period in the growth of a civilization but rather as a general accompaniment of "any increase and advance in life." In Bacon, the painterly handling of the living flesh can be interpreted as indicating a perverse— pessimistic and skeptical—attitude to life, an ironical accompaniment to the development of radical individuality.

Bacon's perverse painterly handling is essentially arbitrary, i.e., nihilistic in intention, because there is no clear reason for it in the depicted scene. Bacon's painterly interpretation of the flesh confirms the self-destructiveness of his solitary figures, premised on the meaninglessness of their existence, i.e, its lack of *raison d'être,* and its consequent solitariness. Perversely animated in their private voids, they have only their instincts to fall back on. They are in effect lepers—the deathlike blackness invading their bodies seems to testify to this— who keep to themselves because they see no strong reason for doing anything in particular. They are sick with death—not necessarily literal death, but rather the feeling of being nothing—and so diseased with the leprosy of loneliness, which fuses their individuality and instincts. Indirectly alluding to this blackness, Bacon says that he is haunted by

> a feeling of mortality all the time. Because, if life excites you, its opposite, like a shadow, death, must excite you. Perhaps not excite you, but you are aware of it in the same way as you are aware of life....

The sense of death-in-life is pervasive in many of the exhibition's so-called black paintings. But the point is that sustained, compulsive attention to the inevitability of death is a symptom of decadence, for eventually it leads to skepticism about—the deprecation and detriment of—life. Bacon, who has been called an existentialist—in our sense the most decadent contemporary philosophy—is simultaneously a decadent, in the sense of cultivating a nihilistic perception of and attitude to life. While he carries this cultivation to eloquent heights, making it the stance of a dandy, its nihilistic core remains articulate as more than a posture. There are moments in the current show when it seems theatrical, but they are lost in the general sense of oblivion Bacon communicates.

III. Self-Fulfilling Flesh

> All my life I have seen narrow-shouldered man, without exception, perform innumerable stupid actions, brutalize his fellows and poison minds by every conceivable means. The motivation of such behavior he calls, "Glory." Seeing these things I have desired to laugh with the others, but this strange imitation was impossible for me. I have taken a pocket-knife and severed the flesh at the spot where the lips come together. For a moment I thought to have accomplished my end. I looked into the mirror and inspected the mouth I had deliberately butchered. It was a mistake! The blood falling copiously from the two wounds made it impossible to distinguish whether this was really the laughter of other men. But after several minutes I could see clearly that my smile in no way resembled human laughter: in other words, I was not laughing. (Lautréamont, *Maldoror,* Canto 1, Stanza 5.)

> I've always wanted and never succeeded in painting the smile (Francis Bacon, Interview with David Sylvester, May 1966.)

> I did hope one day to make the best painting of the human cry. (Francis Bacon, Interview with David Sylvester, May 1966.)

Bacon has long been famous for his image of human flesh, which Russell sees as simultaneously marmoreal and pulpy, and which has been connected with Bacon's sense of the voluptuousness of male flesh—of "meat" on Michelangelesque backs. Bacon's treatment of flesh has been understood as alluding to the carcasses Bacon thinks we all are, a hint of our inevitable canceling by death. Bacon's flesh has also been understood as suggesting the fugitive, accidental nature of human existence, which, because it is essentially a gamble—a blind search for significance—has no fixed form, and is charged with violent, i.e., uncontrollable, energy and emotion. Bacon himself has said that he wants images which "would rise from a river of flesh," "pools of flesh" out of which beings arose, pictures of "figures arising out of their own flesh." He experiences such figures as particularly poignant—the only quality he wants his works to convey—because they convey "the shadow of life passing all the time," and bring the factual-figurative element in the painting "onto the nervous system more violently and poignantly." In a sense, Bacon's "poignant" treatment of flesh epitomizes his ideal of an image as "a kind of tightrope walk between what is called figurative painting and abstraction," an image which "goes right out from abstraction but will really have nothing to do with it." Bacon's flesh is such a poignant image, simultaneously factual and abstract, visceral and formal, illustrative and full of "glitter and color" like that which "comes from the mouth." He "always hoped ... to be able to paint the mouth like Monet painted a sunset," and one might add that he has the same ambiguous ambition with respect to the flesh in general, whether of the face or torso.

In general, Bacon's handling of flesh can be understood as the climactic act of his attempt to fuse fact and feeling, the conscious and unconscious, the critically controlled and accidentally instinctive, the illustrative and imaginative, the photo-slick technically reproducible and the singular texture of particular sensation. All the dichotomies come together in the flesh, which is simultaneously commonplace, and charged with rare personal feeling. In a sense, Bacon distorts flesh in the name of greater particularity or specificity of being, i.e., as a way of making anonymous being individual. But in another sense, touched flesh is simply the most obvious source of feeling. Feeling, particularly feeling which is instinctive in origin—for Bacon all feeling ultimately calls the instinctive into play—is inseparable from flesh, as such expressions as the "bowels of compassion" convey. In antiquity, feeling was located in a particular inner body organ, usually the liver or heart. In a sense, all Bacon's treatment of the flesh does is expose such inner organs, the sites of feeling.

The mouth, perhaps unexpectedly—for it is not altogether inner—is one such site, for it is the hole of flesh through which the feelings of the entirely inner organs escape, after writhing their way through the body. It summarizes flesh's openness and closedness. The mouth is thus emblematic of the body as a whole and of feeling in general, and in the smile and the cry or scream we have the antipodes of its modes of expression, the range of possibility of visceral feeling. Bacon is forever shut out of the smile; it is impossible for the solitary subject to smile, even to himself, for such a smile is a meditation on what is not the self, and thus breaks the fast of solitude. In general, the smile is an invitation to the other, a form of sociality, the potential establishment of reciprocity. Through the screaming mouth the body vomits its painful feelings like a volcano pours its lava; smiling, the mouth is only partially open—the face is at peace with, or at least accepts, the other, and the body has no need to exorcise its feelings in a cry. A smile is an exchange; a cry is an autistic event, the announcement of the subject in distress, opening wide to the outside, but with the traffic through it only one way, from within outward. The cry is open but one-directional; the smile is half-closed but two-way. In the cry Bacon shows the solitary vomiting his solitude into the world, making of it an object for others. The portraits and self-portraits establish painful autonomy; the cry hurls it into the world. The cry is an attempt to conceive the world as completely subjective, i.e., as charged with private feeling, which forces its way into the open. The cry is eschatological, a last thing of subjectivity, an ultimate assertion of the inner life of the self in the face of all otherness.

The mouth is the most mobile or least fixed facial feature, and is thus able to convey its expressiveness—its openness or closedness—all at once. Bacon notes that "you could draw...right across the face as though it was almost like the opening of the whole head, and yet it could be like the mouth." The mouth is "almost like the opening of the whole head" because it is capable of articulating any aspect of the face's entire range of expression. The cry—the Lamentation— is a traditional subject matter of religious art, but Bacon presents it not as a mourning response to a horrific outer event—the Crucifixion—but rather as the expression of the self-crucifixion by solitariness of the isolated figure. In a sense, Bacon's Popes scream because they know that, underneath their authority and power, they are solitary men—made even more solitary by this authority and power, which makes them other than themselves—with visceral feelings that must express themselves. Their worldly position has so repressed them that their feelings have lost all shape, and can issue only in the form of an instinctive agonized outcry.

The cry in Bacon's pictures is the interior monologue of his solitary figure turned inside out and become an exterior dialogue with his self-image. In a sense, the cry is the ultimate self-contemplation, in which the solipsist's power of creation brings his own being into painful birth in the world. The power of authority or "superego" lies in its ability to repress, in and of itself generating a feeling of perversity or abnormality, which finally articulates itself in a cry. In sum, the cry is the narcissistic, solipsistic, solitary subject's spontaneous way of escaping the claustrophobia of being himself by getting into the world, if in a highly indeterminate way. At the same time, the cry is the violent release of instinct which has been repressed by internalized social, rational authority. Instinct has come to feel strange to itself, and so must objectify itself to see itself for what it really is, viz., bodily feeling.

Bacon's great achievement with the screaming mouth is to turn it from being an abstract, formal device—an emblem of suffering—accompanying tragic scenes, as in Poussin's *Massacre of the Innocents* (which Bacon professes to admire), to a highly charged concrete space involuntarily ejaculating feeling into the world. Poussin's relatively standard scream stands no chance of carrying the emotion conveyed by Bacon's scream. Bacon's compulsive emotion would break Poussin's precious, porcelain mouth to pieces. Bacon is more truly interested in the wounded nurse's scream in Eisenstein's *Battleship Potemkin*, a scream in which feeling dominates fact, in which almost all formal control is released, and in which the sense of appropriate relationship between the cause of the scream and its effect is stretched to the breaking point. In the history of Western art there is only one screaming mouth that comes close to Bacon's in expressive power, viz., that of Caravaggio's *Medusa*, said to be a self-portrait. In a sense, the mouth is the major field on which the battle—between fact and feeling—of realism is fought out. For all the bodily parts, the mouth alone has the potential for spontaneously converting from a matter-of-fact local feature to a general area where the feeling of the whole body can be expressed.

In a sense Bacon's interest in the mouth, as the most expressive body site, links up with his treatment of sexuality. Because the mouth easily opens into a scream, it becomes the only place where the body attains full erotic release. In other words, the cry is sexual in connotation, confirmed by the fact that in Bacon the white teeth, not the fleshy tongue are articulate in it. What Freud in *The Interpretation of Dreams* calls the "dental stimulus" is a typical dream symbol of masturbation.[9] (Bacon's solitary figures are dream images, their distortion easily understood as typical dream distortion.) Masturbation, the solitary release of instinctive energy, is for Freud simultaneously a symbolic form of self-castration—in a sense, finalizing solitariness—and a confirmation of social isolation. The homosexual couplings Bacon depicts are not as satisfactory, from the point of view of achieving release of instinctive energy, as solitary masturbation is.

This sense that masturbatory release or onanistic self-creation is the key to whatever sexuality there is in Bacon's works, is confirmed by the presence, in a number of pictures, of what Bacon himself calls a "whip of white paint." The whip of white paint, falling to the picture ground like Onan's seed fell on earth, can be interpreted in a number of ways, which, taken together, summarize Bacon's *Weltanschauung*. It is the body's outcry, sign of its desperate release of instinct in the paranoid situation of its privacy. It is also symbol of the life-force of the man condemned to death, in a sense equivalent to the flaring loincloth on the dead body of the crucified Christ. It is the hanged man's last ejaculation of his instinctive energy, indistinguishable from his death throes—the involuntary fleeing of instinctive life from his body. The whip of white paint often exists in antithesis to the black picture ground, as well as in contrast to the paler manufactured light, with its noninstinctive even flow, of the lightbulb. It is the ghost that Bacon says fact leaves, the Holy Ghost of feeling that emerges from dead facts. It is also a kind of token of painterly technique, and in its isolation in the picture, epitomizes the figure's solitariness. It is, as it were, the figure making a sign of itself to itself, so that it will know it is alive. Masturbation is the solitary's way of pinching himself to prove to himself that he is alive—to wake up his feelings. It is a way of snapping out of the feelingless state that unstructured, undirected solitude induces, and is the psychic equivalent of death. Masturbation is also the supreme narcissistic satisfaction, the solipsist's way of proving that others do not exist. A neo-Cartesian, Bacon's solitary asserts "I masturbate, therefore I am." Masturbation is the perfect creation ex nihilo, for the masturbator's fantasy is that he gives birth to himself parthenogenetically out of his own seed.

But in the final analysis Bacon's tumultuous painterly flesh, epitomized by its own ejaculation of a whip of white paint, is not sexual in significance, nor a symbol of will power, but indicative of a deliberate choice of solitariness. In *Being and Nothingness* Sartre writes that

> human reality, far from being capable of being described as *libido* or will to power, is a *choice of being,* either directly or through appropriation of the world. And we have seen ... that each

thing is chosen, in the last analysis, not for its sexual potential but for the mode in which it renders being, depending on the manner in which being burgeons from its surface.[10]

Bacon's handling of flesh is the burgeoning of solitariness from the surface of his figure, a sign of the figure's refusal to choose any other being than itself, and so chooses its body. To be itself is to be nothing but its flesh—to possess its surfaces exclusively for itself. Masturbation is simply confirmation of this privilege. Solitariness is the condition for the burgeoning of the body's surfaces, and at the same time this burgeoning is proof of—a kind of response to—solitariness. The burgeoning of the surface of the solitary's being is his self-reflexivity in action: his own flesh becomes a burning bush, showing himself to himself as divine, and completing the solipsistic enterprise of self-creation.

Bacon's flesh, understood as the burgeoning surface of the subject's being, as the subject's call to and answer to itself, exists in sharp contrast to the nonburgeoning, neuter planar surface of the rooms in which he puts his figures. This contrast can be explicated through Bachelard's contrast between "exaggeration" and "reduction." Bacon's painterly handling of flesh is his way of "prolonging exaggeration," of trying "to avoid the habits of *reduction*." Why do so? In *The Poetics of Space* Bachelard writes that "The philosophies of anguish want principles that are less simplified,"[11] and insofar as Bacon offers us a philosophy of anguish he refuses the simple surface created by reduction and exaggerates the surface of his subject, in search of a more complicated and less conventional principle of subjective existence. Walls, however much they face us, have a side turned to the world. They are blank, feelingless surfaces, and Bacon profiles his exaggerated internalized figures against them. Bacon's flesh goes full circle, from the subject's exclusive possession to the other's possible possession. Flesh becomes self-flagellating at the approach of the other if only in the subject's fantasy. The anguish of Bacon's flesh—its exaggeration into uncommunicative tongues—is simultaneously a speaking to the self and for the other. Anguish is the emotion that compels the self and the other to intercept in an orgiastic moment of imagined unity. However prolonged, it cannot last, for the self collapses back upon itself, becoming dense and opaque; and the other becomes an anonymous stranger again.

IV. The Aphoristic Image

The symbolic reference leads to a transference of emotion, purpose, and belief, which cannot be justified by an intellectual comparison of the direct information derived from the two schemes and their elements of intersection. (Alfred North Whitehead, *Symbolism, Its Meaning and Effect*.)

I would like to characterize Bacon's pictures as aphoristic images, approximated by what Russell calls Bacon's pursuit of the single picture. By this I mean images concentrated into the sententiousness of the symbol, but which, because they can never be finally specified in meaning, effect a transformation of undisciplined emotion between themselves and the spectator. Moreover, I would like to claim that the homosexual aspect of Bacon's art and his attitude toward traditional old master art and modern photography contribute to the aphoristic character of his images. Three homosexual traits in particular, as articulated by Sartre, seem to be responsible for his attitude to the traditional masterpiece and the modern photograph, and to suggest the rationale behind his transformation of them into aphoristic images.

(1) The homosexual fake submission seems epitomized by Bacon's treatment of Velasquez's *Innocent X.* Bacon's destroys the image, and shows the Pope in an excruciating if not entirely specifiable subjective experience. Hence the modernization of the image, under the guise of rendering it more powerful and pointed. Fake submission also appears, in the passivity of Bacon's solitary figure, passivity which is that of a caged animal, ready to become violent if given a chance. The figure's sense of pent-up motion and emotion also creates a symbolic charge.

(2) Actively extending this fake submission, of which I have given a few details, is the homosexual's estheticism. In *Saint Genet, Actor and Martyr,* Sartre asserts:

> In the movement of heterosexual ecstasy, desire is projected outward, the male forgets himself, he is only the delicate light which envelops the silk of a foreign flesh and makes it glow. Genet, on the other hand, returns to himself, he loses himself in order to find himself. The *recognized* gesture sends him back to the world and the world back to himself; he remains "frightened at possessing the world and at knowing I possessed it." That is, he shelves the world: if he does "possess" the universe, it is not in the manner of emperors and captains of industry who boast of leaving their mark on it, but in that of a contemplative who discovers that "the world is its representation." And in this great body of *things perceived,* a gesture stands out, object of an aesthetic intuition, which reflects to Genet only what Genet has put into it: it is the appearance to which the Thief has assigned the function of delivering to him the totality of appearances.[12]

Old masterworks are, from the perspective of the present, so many shelved worlds. They offer particular appearances—"gestures"—which suggest a world they cannot deliver, but which nonetheless conditions their appearance. Thus, the old masterpiece no longer represents anything real. Its only value is as a symbol: it is charged with the feeling, a residue of the purposes and beliefs, of a lost world. Its existence is purely esthetic, and its value depends on the absence of any reference to reality. It is in effect a pure appearance charged with an abstract emotion.

Now Bacon finds purely esthetic-symbolic value in photographs as well as old masterpieces. They too hold emotion in suspension, so that it seems unconditioned and unconditional, and are no longer used for their reference to a particular world. Photographs and masterpieces become sources of symbolic reference for Bacon, and he uses them operatically, to create a highly charged atmosphere, in which the emotional effect is out of all proportion to the event that triggers it. In general, Bacon is not so much influenced by masterpieces and photographs—"influence" is a mnemonic device, and assumes continuity of context and meaning—as exploitive of their emotional possibilities. He finds in them not things he wants to remember, but gestures in what Sartre calls "the choreographic figuration of human transcendency," which for Bacon is nothing but the superiority of feeling to fact. Taking masterpieces and photographs as only incidentally referencing reality, he finds in them unique emotional opportunities. They become the armature on which he can hang pure feeling. The sense of oblivion of being in Bacon's pictures is due to the fact that they are meant to be nothing but appearances abstractly charged with emotion, rather than images of any reality—images with any kind of objectivity, which occurs in them only accidentally. What is normally accidental or momentary, the release of pure—undisciplined—emotion, is made absolute in Bacon, and what is normally all important to realism, the reference to reality, becomes casual and incidental.

One might note that influence takes place only within a tradition and within a world of uniform purpose and constant belief. Bacon, who believes that every artist today is "outside a tradition," asserts that all that is left for the artist is "to record one's own feelings about certain situations as closely to one's own nervous system as one possibly can." Because today there is no "valid myth where there was the distance between grandeur and its fall of the tragedies of Aeschylus and Shakespeare," all that remains is the emotional charge caused by such a fall without the framing myth to give it general significance or validity for others. This renders it seemingly unreal and exaggeratedly subjective, with purely esthetic and personal significance. Because of this, Bacon's emotional intensity makes us uncomfortable, since our emotions are aroused by real events. When his works do seem, whether retrospectively or immediately, to refer to real events, as his *Study for Portrait,* 1949, seems to allude to Eichmann on trial in his glass booth, and as the figure with the swastika armband in *Crucifixion,* 1965, alludes to the Nazis, our response is thrown off. We do not know whether to take the images for their world-historical implications or for their purely emotional implications. We are not helped by Bacon's perverse assertion that for him the swastika is simply an interesting shape in a red field. He regularly and maliciously insists on purely esthetic significance, e.g., in the case of the mouth, as if to throw the viewer off the scent of the worldly meaning of the work, to free him to respond to it purely emotionally. He wants the work to impress itself directly on the viewer's nervous system, rather than become something he associates with everyday reality and/or makes a moral judgment on. What is interesting is that we never think that the two—worldly meaning and emotional impact—can be present at the same time in Bacon's works, and the same is true for any other kind of public meaning, such as the religious. Thus, Bacon regards the crucifixion as today having purely esthetic and emotional significance. It is simply "a magnificent armature on which you can hang all types of feeling and sensation," and he doubts that even "the great Crucifixions... were painted by men who had religious beliefs." A religious belief is a proposed view of reality. On Bacon's terms, for an artist to have a religious belief would be for him to forfeit the emotional power he can generate by being purely esthetic. For him to have any belief about reality—about the facts—would be for him to become concerned to get the meaning straight, which would interfere with an instinctive response to appearances. The appearance of meaning is sufficient for Bacon, not its exact statement: the artist's meaning emerges from how convincingly he can charge his appearances. Bacon believes that, unlike himself, Velasquez and Rembrandt

> were still, whatever their attitude to life, slightly conditioned by certain types of religious possibilities (salvation), which man now, you could say, has had completely cancelled out of him. . . . You see, all art has now become completely a game by which man distracts himself; and you may say it has always been like that, but now it's entirely a game.[13]

For Bacon, art is a game of emotionally charging appearances rather than a question of presenting clear meanings, of whatever kind, and certainly not the political and religious, which are usually taken literally. In general, art exists for Bacon not to convince us of the truth about anything, to nail down reality by imitating it, but rather to use some of its appearances in a purely esthetic way and thereby to generate a radically subjective feeing. In a sense, art is proof that appearances transcend reality and that feelings transcend facts. By proper choreography, real facts can be made into strongly felt fictions. Masterpieces and photographs are storehouses of choreographed gestures which can be appropriated for purposes of conveying new kinds of feeling. Past art has the advantage of not being clearly connected with any firsthand experience reality, and photographs, especially when they are old and tattered from use, give us a secondhand reality, which with time seems a fantasy, and so can be emotionally exploited. The point, for Bacon, is to get distance from reality, so as to keep feeling pure and alert, charged with abstract power. This holds true for the reality of his own works, from which he tries to make the spectator keep his distance by framing them in gold and glass.

(3) Such framing is the major example of the homosexual's artificialism, which finalizes his estheticism. The way Bacon takes an appearance as "real" while knowing it is false is similar to Sartre's example of Genet's artificialism: the treatment of cut glass as a precious gem while knowing it is cut glass. Talking oneself into belief is crucial, to sustain the esthetic sensibility which is the foundation of emotional responsiveness in art. Bacon wants his framing methods—as though a precious setting would make us think the art precious, i.e., believe in it—to create "distance between what has been done and the onlooker" and serve to "shut (the work) away from the spectator." It is better that it remain a mysterious symbol than indicate a familiar reality, or itself become one. The full import of the glass framing is that it creates a quasi-old-master look, doubly removing the work, in space as well as concept. This removal—the added

distance—filters the feeling through with greater purity and power, as well as emphasizes that it is impossible for art to refer to anything beyond itself, i.e., that is not an appearance. Unwittingly, Bacon links up with modernism's self-reflexivity, but in terms of feeling rather than form. On the level of feeling as well as form art is *sui generic*.

In general, Bacon's art, to use Sartre's words, is "a compound of ceremonious politeness and aggressiveness."[14] These qualities are the vital ones of the aphorism, with its symbolic overtones and peculiar way of turning what is seen or known into an emblem of what is felt, i.e., into an esthetic intuition. Walter Kaufmann writes that "aphorisms reflect the experimentalist's determination to remain unprejudiced by any system," i.e., by any final, fixed view of reality.[15] The artist's insistence on appearance for appearance's sake, in Bacon's case correlated with an insistence on feeling for feeling's sake—a kind of final fling of romanticism—works through an aphoristic image which is a kind of experimentation for experimentation's sake.

Ironically, the sense of the aphoristic image as a mode of experimentation with intuitions serves the purposes of realism admirably. For in trying, at all costs—even those that lead to the distortions of expressionism—to avoid becoming bound by any fact or ideology realism must become an open-ended experimentation with appearances. It can never be satisfied that it has the final, certain, truthful appearance of reality. An experiment exists on the borderline between truth and falsehood. It is undertaken either to demonstrate some known truth or to test some suggested truth; in general, to confirm or disprove something doubtful. When sustained for itself, thereby becoming a mode of presentation in itself, the experiment—or aphoristic image—creates ambiguity about what is or is not the case and valid. Aphoristic experimentation thus becomes a way of penetrating reality without committing oneself to it. It is a way of charging appearances—apparent reality—without specifying the full import of the charge.

The aphoristic image thus has a highly irrational tone to it, regardless of the kind of emotion it does or does not express. Bacon's images are irrational not because they represent irrational emotions, but because in and of themselves, as experiments with appearance, they can say nothing substantial about reality yet they are intensely saying something. They are thus unfinished psychologically as well as perceptually. We cannot believe in them, although they communicate a sense of purpose to us. We can feel them, but we cannot say that what we feel is real. And that, ironically, is the state in which we exist in reality, testing and retesting our intuitions, but never finally certifying them as unconditionally objective, as definitively the case. Reality is never definitively what it seems to be, and for a realist to make this clear, as Bacon does, is a supreme achievement. Too much realistic imagery has tried to be definitive of reality, which has only caused it to dwindle into a document, i.e., another datum, rather than become an indication of the possible subject-object truth about reality.

Bacon's aphoristic approach shows us that reality is always in the process of being made into a symbol by the subject who perceives it. The subject persists in this process in order to release himself from reality's hold, and thereby uncover, in the abstract form of intuitions, the feelings it generates in him. This process of symbolization links up decisively with the homosexual aspect of Bacon's art: neither homosexual nor aphoristic penetration achieves ultimate possession of the object. Its reality is always discovered to be turned away from one, and wherever one has entered it, one finds that one is facing a behind. One always has an obscene, exaggerated, yet radically incomplete and inconclusive relationship with it, and one finds it degenerating into an appearance which cannot reference anything but itself. One finds one's relationship with it degenerating into an artificial game. One remains intact relating to it, but frustrated, because one has established no reciprocity with it, and so gotten nothing from it. One has only released oneself toward it, in its direction; a release which, because it has not found its mark, seems undisciplined.

Bacon's portraits, in the end, communicate no sense of character—of the basic reality of the other, the represented person. And they can never do so, because they are simply fantasy appearances of the other. I disagree with Russell's reading of the portraits of Isabel Rawsthorne as "an acknowledgment of all that is staunchest and most generous in human nature,"[16] which are much too determinate character traits to get out of a Bacon portrait. Russell is probably speaking from his own acquaintance with her. Basically, I disagree just for the reason Russell himself believes contemporary portraiture is difficult, and finally incapable of communicating any self-same self, any "owned" self:

> We disbelieve in the monolithic view of human nature; we are not awed—quite the contrary— by the trappings of power; we see human beings as flawed, variable, self-contradictory, subject to the fugitive and the contingent.[17]

When Bacon does try to convey inner character—to satisfy the ideas of traditional portraiture—as in *Study for Portrait III (After the Life-mask of William Blake)*, 1955, he becomes pompous and dull, affected and melodramatic. Generally, he offers us no sense of firm being in these portraits. He shows them as stereotypically frenzied, almost manic and raw beings.

Bacon, if anything, achieves his realism in the portraits by destroying the identity of his subjects. He blurs it until it seems insecure, leaving vestiges of its familiar daily appearance in the details of a few features, which seem typical only because they are repeated as we move from image to image of the same subject. But these features are no more than exterior appearances, and say nothing decisive whatsoever about the characters of the selves depicted. Instead, what Bacon does is create, through his painterly technique, a sense of involvement with and within them—a generalized kind of momentum in them which we share perceptually. Within this context of fluid, generalized surface, possible identities emerge but are not confirmed, are asserted but do not last—are purely momentary illusions of possibilities of appearance. All have more or less the same mood. In sum, Bacon's painterly technique is the core of the aphoristic intuition of subjectivity he offers, for it makes the figural image abstract. Out of this abstraction, identities emerge as experimental possibilities, but none is finally true or factually clear, although all are symbolically valid, i.e., valid as emotionally charged appearances, undisciplined releases of instinct, and dissipations of the raw possibility of being alive.

Notes

1.   *Newsweek,* March 31, 1975, p. 68.

2.   Quoted by John Russell, *Francis Bacon* (Greenwich, Conn., 1971), p. 87.

3.   David Sylvester, *Interview with Francis Bacon* (New York, 1975), pp. 58-59. All quotations from Bacon, unless otherwise noted, are from this book.

4.   Walter Friedlaender, *Caravaggio Studies* (New York, 1965), p. vii.

5.   Erling Eng, "Psyche in Longing, Mourning and Anger," *Facets of Eros, Phenomenological Essays* (The Hague, 1972), p. 76, notes that "the truth of eros has an intimate tie with the problem of the truth of theatre," as evidenced by the fact "that the root of 'obscene' is the Greek word *scene,* or 'stage,' the prefix 'ob-' having the value of 'against.'" Eng, p. 78 writes: "The obscene is to be understood from the scene as norm, as, in effect, a withering of the scene in its fullness, from virtual unity to breakdown into concreteness, from openness and depth to constriction and raised figures, from shared experience to one increasingly autistic." More particularly, the following "negations of the characters of a scene justify its being termed 'obscene': Instead of a scene that is shared, it becomes one that is private; rather than opening up it becomes constrained; rather than a vision of unity it tends towards the fragmentation, literally, of cannibalism." All of this can be applied directly to Bacon's pictures. What can also be applied, and what makes them lose their impact with familiarity—it is a risk Bacon himself provokes by dwelling on the same image—is that "what can be agreed on as being obscene becomes, to the extent that it is defined by consensus, already counter-obscene. Pornography is an instance of this." To the extent that Bacon's ob-scenes become pornographic in import, they degenerate into opera. Pornography orchestrates the parts of the body purely for effect—each becomes the cause for a disproportionate effect—and such orchestration can be undertaken for aggressive as well as sexual purposes.

6.   Gotthard Jedlicka, "Max Beckmann in seinen Selbstbildnissen," *Blick auf Beckmann* (Munich, 1962), p. 128.

7.   Michel Foucault, *Madness and Civilization* (New York, 1973), p. 127.

8.   Friedrich Nietzsche, *The Will to Power* (New York, 1968), pp. 25-27.

9.   Sigmund Freud, *The Interpretation of Dreams* (New York, 1965), p. 423.

10. Robert D. Cumming, ed., *The Philosophy of Jean-Paul Sartre* (New York, 1966), p. 337.

11. Gaston Bachelard, *The Poetics of Space* (Boston, 1969), p. 218-19.

12. Jean-Paul Sartre, *Saint Genet, Actor and Martyr* (London, 1964), p. 315.

13. Sylvester, p. 63.

14.   Sartre, p. 114.

15.   Walter Kaufmann, *Critique of Religion and Philosophy* (Garden City, N.Y., 1961), p. 14.

16.   Russell, p. 165.

17.   Russell, p. 136.

25

Leon Golub's Murals of Mercenaries: Aggression, "Ressentiment," and the Artist's Will to Power

One hardly dares speak any more of the will to power: it was different in Athens.
                                        —Friedrich Nietzsche, *Notes* (1880-81)

The vehement yearning for violence, so characteristic of some of the best modern or creative artists, thinkers, scholars, and craftsmen, is a natural reaction of those whom society has tried to cheat of their strength.
                                        —Hannah Arendt, *The Human Condition*

The figures are brute, raw, made of acidified, scraped paint. Light sinks into their harsh surface, confirming the density of their presence. They block our view, exhaust our seeing with their monstrousness. Even the field that sets them in relief is unrefined and unrelenting. Its redness has the scent of their blood, conveys the dynamic of their vulgarity, is essential to their *lumpen* aliveness. There is an antiaesthetic in operation here, a search for ugliness—for the nerve-grating, unassimilable surface—that is the exact opposite of the aesthetic that has implicitly dominated modernism: the search for a surface which, if not always soothing, is always refined, i.e., a finer surface than we could find in real life. This modernist surface was given mural potential by Jackson Pollock, and in what Greenberg called "American-type (field) painting" its potential seems to have been realized. Yet the ugliness and rawness of Clyfford Still—his explicit desire—seems simplistic and artificial next to Leon Golub's ugliness, and the heroic scale of Still's images seems less fully realized than Golub's truly mural, i.e., public, scale. Only Barnett Newman's *Vir Heroicus Sublimis* stands comparison with Golub's "Mercenaries" 1979-81, in public scale and, more to the point, in the rendering of what Martin Heidegger called the "public interpretation of reality."

And here we see the reversal of values that is the clue to Golub's muralism. The thrust of Newman's red seems subjective and idealistic, the articulation of an indwelling force given credibility by its grand scale, a scale which faces down the disbelieving public. By contrast, Golub's red and scale are outer rather than inner events—they thrust us all the more into our outwardness, reflect our trajectory in the world, rather than lure us from our being-in-the-world to a transcendental illusion of being completely in ourselves—absolutely self-defined and self-possessed. Golub's murals are militantly anti-transcendental. They articulate our being-in-time, our confinement by our material history, the smallness of our private affairs and perceptions and destinies. They are, in Karl Mannheim's distinction, ideological rather than utopian or ecstatic, and their aesthetic aspect depends entirely on the assumption of the world-historical as the first cause of art. The seared, worn, battered look of Golub's figures reflects their world-historical roles, not some preferred aesthetic; they are not another vision of art as atemporal or eternal.

The subject matter of Golub's imagery is aggression, potential (in the "Mercenaries") and actual (in the "Interrogations" 1980-81). Within his oeuvre, these images are more historically specific than the "Gigantomachies," 1965-68, yet less so than the "Assassins," 1972-74 which deal with Vietnam. They are less accusatory—less a matter of protest—than the latter, while potentially as mythological as the former. They mythologize war and institutionalized aggression in a free-floating fresco which, for all its anecdotal flavor, transcends narrative by reason of its starkness. The "Mercenaries" deal with the moments of dubious rest and recreation in the war zone; the "Interrogations" deal with the backrooms of modern violence, the rooms where the "big decisions" are made on the basis of extracted information. This generalized violence—this persistent modern expectation of violence—is compromised neither by the physiognomies of the actors, nor by the disturbed character of the emotional interchange between them, with its not quite manifest racism and latent sexuality. (The two intertwine in the glance of "Mercenaries" III, 1980.) On the contrary, their "personal" relations and "individuality" confirm their public identities, reflecting the inescapability of their social existence: they are completely determined by their social roles in the power structure. Everything about them reflects the modern habit of violence—an incendiary sense of everyday identity. While their might does not make them seem personally right, they never seem socially wrong.

This sense of them as "marked" men leads directly to the sense of them as mythologically and impersonally given. Their abstraction on a raw red ground confirms both their symbolic potential and inexorable actuality. Their violence is programmed by myth. They are puppets in a tableau that presents violent power as the ultimate principle of social activity and human expression. Physically and psychologically they are all mismatched, and an almost formulaic sense of off-balance is the structuring principle of the pictures. This is history painting which sees history as derangement rather than arrangement. The death wish rather than the pleasure principle drives these figures—Thanatos rather than Eros commands their lives—but this is less "willed" than might be supposed. The sense of them as involuntary figures in a drama not of their own making confirms their mythological nature, as do such tell-tale signs as the "flayed Marsyas" look to the naked figure in "Interrogation I" 1980-81 and the Roman realist character of the figures.

The mercenary role is as universal as that of the victim, the mercenary being to the world of political causes what the unattached intellectual—as identified by Max Weber and Karl Mannheim—is to the world of intellectual causes.

> Their own social position does not bind them to any cause.... By themselves they know nothing. But let them take up and identify themselves with someone else's interests—they will know them better, really better, than those for whom these interests are laid down by the nature of things, by their social condition.[1]

The mercenaries serve; they victimize in the name of causes they do not originate, but of which they are the indisputable master, to which they have the secret inner key—which they catalyze by their willingness to act: to go to war. And even when, as in some of these pictures, they turn smiling to their master— the "public" in whose name they fight (the spectator who blandly accepts them as "necessary")—they have already mastered him by their willingness to show him his own tendency to violence, his own desire for dominance and power. We are among them, not they among us. Their proximity to us—their "truncated" legs place them in our world—makes clear not only their matter-of-fact, daily involvement with us, but their position as signs of our intention. They are signs of ourselves, written large, made blatantly public—their blatancy disguising and dignifying their urgency, the nightmarish way they loom over us, dominating and possessing our spirits—in the way Plato said that myth functions. Myth is a nightmare from which we cannot awaken, for it is the very form of our psyche. Everything that makes these images outspokenly real for us makes them signs of what is ultimately real in our existence: in this case, the will to power.

In an unpublished interview Golub said that the "mercenaries point to the irregular use of power," and in general are "inflections of power." More particularly, "these kinds of figures in a strange way reflect American power and confidence." The question is, in what way do they point to, inflect, and reflect this will to power? What use do they make of power and to what end? We already know the "look" of these figures from photographs and films, some of which are Golub's sources. The very fact that Golub gives us an already known imagery, an imagery with an authority of its own—an imagery so powerful that we can control it only with our ennui, an imagery with which we collide and that makes us feel as helpless as the world historical events it embodies—should make it suspect. Such public imagery is never there entirely for its own sake, and however much the artist borrows its authority he means to establish his own over it. He reverses its public intention by putting it in the private space of his art. He takes a matter-of-fact public imagery, half-dead or dying because of its transience—yet sufficiently recurrent to become more than momentary in our minds—and makes it obsessive and intimate, transfiguring it for his own purpose. Such imagery becomes the instrument of his self-recognition, a recognition more crucial in the last analysis than public recognition. These pictures, I believe, are finally about private, heroic survival as an artist— allegorical investigations of the meaning of being an artist in the modern world—not gratuitous demonstrations of the artist's ability to "stretch" a canvas beyond expectations, to give us an oversized image catering to the public desire for "greatness."

Since Pop art, noninvented imagery—the Minimalist gestalt and grid are also noninvented images—has dominated American art, as if to verify Smithson's idea that art achieves its universality by being unoriginal and repetitive, and in confirmation of Lawrence Alloway's idea of the inescapability and highly fluid character of the fine art/popular culture continuum. (Repetition is the act that creates a sense of fiction—the dream state of eternal recurrence. The continuum helps us accept the fiction by assimilating it as a public event, if at a cultural pole opposite to its starting point.) Golub's imagery is popular in origin but unpopular or unentertaining in appearance and effect, reminding us that the popular realm is not always pleasant, does not always sugarcoat the look of things, but is sometimes raw and unrefined. (That was the trouble with television coverage of the Vietnam War: we did not really expect reality in a popular medium.) It is the unconcocted quality of the really noninvented image that appeals to Golub—and his imagery is, in origin, more truly noninvented than the comic strip and advertising imagery used by Pop artists. (They can be said to spice an old concoction with style.) It is this rawness in truly noninvented imagery—the power of unmediated reality—that makes it appeal to Golub's own will to power, his own will to be real as an artist. The rawness of reality invokes and provokes the artist's instinctive will to artistic power over it. (Such a "quality encounter" with reality is at the heart of "expressionism.") This will is unavoidably self-reflective: in dealing with raw reality the artist is inevitably questioning his own role in reality. In "engaging" raw reality, the artist is as much in search of his own unfiltered reality as he is desperate to prevent his art from becoming simply another filter, another glamorizing lens that gives a stylish look to things.

For Golub, the reality of the mercenaries is ultimately the social reality they represent. Their rawness reflects the rawness of life and of society itself. And the artist, as person and artist, can as little escape a raw social role—a raw deal—as any of us: he is simultaneously mercenary and victim in society. His will to power puts him in—and expresses itself through—a double bind. It is almost exemplary, because his product, not always being of clear use, is abused as much as used, which is the way it comes to be accepted by society. Two things should be noted here: 1) The recent insistence that art is "decorative," pure and simple, gives it a clear and obvious use, while signalling that it can be and dares be nothing else—that it is bankrupt as a critical instrument, as a "reflection" in an uncritically democratic society; 2) For all the current lull in the martyrdom complex of art, in part due to its finding commercial favor in a time of economic hardship, the "suffering" of art remains, because art is never valued for itself by more than the critically happy, Stendhalian few.

To the extent that Golub's art has always been a metaphor for the artist's situation in modern society it shares in the self-reflexive, self-critical center of modernism. We must remember that modernism is an extension of the old romantic myth of the heroic identity of the artist as a passionate member of the "resistance." Many avant-garde strategies are fresh, if convoluted and involuted, articulations of modernist resistance to society. This resistance often degenerates into an ironical stance, with modernist style at times seeming little more than an ironical gesture. (Does "punk" represent the latest ironical resistance, the latest desire to be used and abused by society, and to use and abuse in return? Martyrdom itself seems to have become a style.) In Golub's work, this increasingly tepid if superficially vivid irony has been replaced by a new, heroic relationship to modernist criticality—by an attempt to make criticality once again heroic rather than sneaky and stylish, a fangless snake in a fake paradise of art. Golub's criticality works with a directness that is not to the taste of the casuists of style who have reduced modernism to an "exciting look"—to the inconsequential criticality of relations between highly manipulable surfaces, the by now stale and traditional tension of the ambiguously positioned or ambiguously spaced.

All of Golub's figures can be read as self-images of the artist in "critical" condition, in danger of being facilely dismissed as "romantic." In the "Gigantomachines" the artist appears as an angry Titan, self-destructively at war with himself—his defiance spent on himself. In the "Assassins" the artist has cooled down to a guiltless criminal, guiltless because he is at one with the society he officially represents (itself implicitly criminal). In the "Mercenaries"—Golub's most sophisticated presentation of the artist's struggle with his will to power, his relentless effort to become powerful by representing and serving a powerful society—the artist has become a "hired hand" no longer at one with any society and so better able to represent the power at stake in every society. In each case the artist is depicted as socially entrapped and coerced: he is society's (half willing) instrument but also its "fool"—untrustworthy, disloyal, and suspect. Thus he is at once a blind tool and blind victim of society. James Joyce's credo of "non serviam" for the artist pales into naiveté beside Golub's Goyanesque analysis of the artist's complex involvement in society. In fact, Golub's "Mercenaries" are the contemporary equivalent of Goya's Quinta del Sordo murals, with their depiction of the nightmarishly sordid condition—mental as well as physical—of modern humanity. Golub is the last Goya of modern art, bringing it full circle back to its romantic origins—a rebellion that borrows its authority from the unspoken will of the people but takes an aristocratic, self-glorifying, self-exploratory form. The unconscious will, critical of the world, must backtrack to itself, becoming self-conscious, to launch an effective criticism of the world. In Golub's art, the pursuit of social criticism and self-knowledge are one and the same.

It should be clear that at the bottom of the modern artist's will to power is a subtle form of *ressentiment*—in Nietzsche's words, the "contradiction of natural values." An argument can be made for the general idea that the "alternatives" of artistic fiction (however much it reflects the world it turns away from) and of disinterested aesthetics (however much it represents the ultimate in contemplation) are expressions of a subtle *ressentiment* against nature and all that comes to be taken as "natural" in society. In Golub's art, *ressentiment* takes a paradoxical form, for the "natural value" he negates by means of his fictional, contemplative presentation of it, namely violent social power, superficially seems unnatural. And yet, of course, it is quite natural to modern society. It is quite natural in modern times that social power take violent form.

Nietzsche writes of "the counter-concepts of a *noble* morality and a morality of *ressentiment*—the latter born of the No to the former."[2] Golub's mercenaries are the horrific inversion of the noble, an ironical presentation of the "noble" as a No to human nature. Golub's mercenaries are the best that modern society can do by way of representing the noble. But then, in view of their pretense to nobility and our recognition of them as inhuman, we are forced to ask what the noble, a social concept, is. And we are forced to answer that it relates to social power, that it gives form to social power. Nobility is social power in harmony with individual strength, and thus social power with no need for violence to force a reconciliation between society and the individual. The jaunty, arrogant, pseudonobility of the mercenaries is the result of the collapse of the balance between social power and individual strength, leading to a falsification of human nature. It now becomes radically ugly—the ugliness which is the sign of the No to, in Nietzsche's words, "all that is noble, gay, high-minded on earth." Golub is in rebellion against this inescapable ugliness—resentful of but helpless before its presence, resentful of the vulgar beings who embody the modern will to power as an end in itself. Such power is violently destructive of strength, or else, when it has the look of strength, violently distorts it, as in the deranged—damaged—appearance of the mercenaries. The contrast between Golub's mercenaries, hardly honored for all their use, and Verrocchio's Bartolemmeo Colleoni, a mercenary who seems to epitomize nobility, shows us how far towards raw violence society has moved to maintain its power over the individual.

The artist's rebellion is made in the name of his own noble strength. Golub gives a new turn to the idea of the artist as rebel. The artist does not simply reject a society that rejects him with its indifference, but one that intends to destroy him and the ecstatic, critical awareness that is his strength. Golub offers us, in allegorical form, the struggle between social power and individual strength, between coercion and integrity. The mercenaries superficially reconcile the two in their person—serve society with all the strength of their being. But this is a submissive reconciliation with society that makes individual strength superfluous even while revealing it. The body—conscious as well as unconscious seat of strength—is the real subject of Golub's images, whether it be the mutilated, tortured body of the "Interrogations" or the uniformed, disciplibed body of the mercenaries and torturers. The contrast between nakedness and uniform, body and weapon, makes the point succinctly—it summarizes the dialectic of stength and power, the modern struggle between individual and society.

As Hannah Arendt points out, power is always social, "[it] springs up between men when they act together and vanishes the moment they disperse," whereas strength is "nature's gift to the individual which cannot be shared with others." Strength can cope with violence "either heroically, by consenting to fight and die, or stoically, by accepting suffering and challenging all affliction through self-sufficiency and withdrawal from the world; in either case, the integrity of the individual and his strengh remain intact." But, according to Arendt, power, as distinct from violence, can ruin strength, which is "always in danger from the combined force of the many. Power corrupts indeed when the weak band together in order to ruin the strong."[3] Central to Golub's "Interrogations" is the victimized strength of the naked figure, nature victimized by the violent use and abuse of social power. The "Interrogations" are the reality which stands behind and completes the revelation of reality begun by the "Mercenaries," the way flesh stands behind and submits to the uniform, and is revealed all the more realistically as one strips the uniform from it.

The predicament of Golub's murals is that we will never know whether the victim meets his fate heroically or stoically; we know only that he is ruined. We cannot read his response to the violence inflicted on him by power, although we can see that power in operation, the combined force of the many destroying the strength of the individual. Golub's *ressentiment* is against the "naturalness" of this situation, the difficulty of resisting violence that has come to be accepted as routine—unoriginally and thus unintimidating violence, repeated like a refrain as a possibility in every society. Golub's theme is the perpetual willingness of society to turn against individuals without giving them even the chance of self-explanation, but simply binding and gagging them, or reducing their voice to a scream, or to the silent agony of the hanging figure.

The tarnished noble torsos of Golub's victimized figures—hovering between nakedness and nudity—make clear their natural strength. They are classically based figures, more so than the mercenaries, who are deliberately de-idealized to imply their contemporaneity. The tortured torsos are timeless and seem autonomous, representing a lost world of antiquity when strength and power were one, when society was based on an attempt to be at one with rather than dominating nature. The partially idealized figures of the victims signal the suppression of natural nobility by arbitrarily used social power. It is a power which not only robs the individual of his strength, but makes it seem trivial in the social scheme of things, full of a rancorous yet disciplined violence that gains added power through its impersonality. The mercenaries themselves are its victims, corrupted as they are by their impersonal sense of power, signalled in part by their weapons, based on universal technology. Such technology is also an implicit theme of Golub's murals, permitting, as it does, the easy conversion of power into violence, the detached use of power as violence. The classical basis of Golub's tortured victims points to the presence of a potentially ennobling artistic element that is no match for the technological basis of his mercenaries, which points to the presence of a degrading, violent element in their social power.

The artist is the unmoved mover of the scene, which is not tragic because it does not deal with inherently flawed strength, and above all because it shows a flaw in society rather than in the individual. The artist renews the strength with which he makes art by recognizing the dominance of power over strength in the modern world. Such realism is the only source of art in a world where art can no longer ennoble strength. In a world in which being heroic or stoic no longer matters—in which the individual can no longer spiritually survive because the world has absolute violence at its command—the artist has only one means of self-preservation: the realistic appraisal of the overwhelming odds against any anonymous individual preserving strength in the face of society's power. The artist's will to power is embodied in his realism, which is his only alternative to helplessness.

Notes

1.   Karl Mannheim, "Conservative Thought," *Essays on Sociology and Social Thought* (London, 1953), p. 127.

2.   Friedrich Nietzsche, "The Antichrist," *The Portable Nietzsche,* ed. Walter Kaufmann (New York, 1954), p. 593.

3.   Hannah Arendt, *The Human Condition* (New York, 1959), pp. 179, 182.

26

Beuys: Fat, Felt, and Alchemy

Nothing has been created as *ultima materia*—in its final state. Everything is at first created in its *prima materia,* its original stuff; whereupon Vulcan comes, and by the art of alchemy develops it into its final substance. ... for alchemy means: to carry to its end something that has not yet been completed.

—Paracelsus

The essential feature here remains the ease of metamorphosis, the inability *not* to react (similar to certain hysterical types who also, upon any suggestion, enter into *any* role). It is impossible for the Dionysian type not to understand any suggestion; he does not overlook any sign of an affect; he possesses the instinct of understanding and guessing in the highest degree just as he commands the art of communication in the highest degree. He enters into any skin, into any affect; he constantly transforms himself.

—Friedrich Nietzsche, *Twilight of the Idols*

For at least the last decade and a half, Joseph Beuys has been the *Wunderkind* of contemporary German art, a hero at once of the avant-garde and the mass media. With his first American museum exhibition, a retrospective at the Guggenheim in November, 1979, Beuys showed himself as simultaneously *enfant terrible* and old master, or rather, showed the *enfant terrible* to be an old master and the old master to be an *enfant terrible.* All the familiar distinctions collapse with Beuys, whose works are bound at once by old European—specifically Germanic— ideology and modernist sensibility, involving at once respect for materials and a sense of limitless artistic possibilities.

Beuys achieved a certain notoriety with his lawsuits. The most recent was against the Leverkusen branch of the Social Democratic Party for the use of the *Bathtub* (1960) of his imaginary infancy as a beer cooler during a party at the local museum. The *Bathtub,* keynoting the autobiographical dimension to all his art—his sense of himself as a persona in the original sense of the term (mask) through which he became a spokesman-actor of universal ideas—earned him 180,000 DM ($94,000) in damages. More sensational was his dismissal from the Düsseldorf Art Academy in 1972, preceded by a 1968 accusation by nine other professors "of endangering the orderly working of the academy through political dilettantism, demogogic practice, intolerance, defamation and striving for power." The dismissal was followed by six years of lawsuits and demonstrations, generally in Beuys's favor, resulting in Beuys's victory. His terms for that victory were "retention of the title of professor in Düsseldorf"—while working as professor at the Vienna school of applied arts—"and of his room" in the academy, which is used as a branch of his Free International University (a spin-off of his involvement in the German student movement).

Beuys believes that art is simultaneously spiritual meaning and political action, suggesting a unity of the two which makes art a kind of ultimate activity, at once personal performance and social production—the scene for the evolution of selfhood and social revolution.

From the beginning Beuys's works were self-possessed and powerfully charged. Such early (1950s) works as his un-Christian (some might say insultingly barbaric, not simply self-consciously primitive) crosses, more or less coincidental with his first fat sculptures, are followed by a number of performances, with their residual artifacts. In general, his fat and felt works have an autobiographical dimension. Beuys, a pilot in World War II, was shot down during the winter in Russia. He claims his life was saved by Tartars, "who covered my body in fat to help it regenerate warmth, and wrapped it in felt as an insulator to keep the warmth in."

Among his more famous works are *Spade With Two Handles* (1965) from his Fluxus (Heraclitus: "All is flux") performance *24 Hours...And in Us...Under us...Landunder;* his attempt "to explain pictures to a dead hare" (1965), in which, anointed with honey and gold leaf, Beuys "silently mouthed to a mute animal what cannot be said to his fellow man"; his "constructed" felt sites (1967); his "Celtic" revival (1970); his 1971 "embrace" of the raw terrain of Northern Europe in *Bog* action (Beuys in general is obsessed with the European moors, literal *Urwelt* as well as symbolic *Urwelt* of spiritual consciousness); such "assemblages" as *Stag Hunt* (1971), "an infinity of materials"—including "newspapers as batteries of...ideas"—accumulated over the years on Beuys's shelves, his week-long "holiday" in 1974 living with a coyote in a New York art gallery (subtitled *I like America and America likes me*); his enormous, fiercely humming, foul-smelling machine, the *Honey Pump* (done for Documenta in Kassel, Germany, 1977); and his didactic lectures thoughout the 1970s, an effort to demonstrate "thinking as sculpting" and to liberate the spirit of his listeners.

In all of this, Beuys shows himself a multiform artist with the grand aspiration of being a preacher to all of humankind. Until about 1969—*The Pack* of that year seems a turning point—Beuys makes objects that are involved in a search for self-identity, including his social identity as a European. Thereafter, the social element is taken up with an almost missionary zeal, and seems to run away with the works, making them more a vehicle for social ideas—propaganda—than ends in themselves.

I had two thoughts on first experiencing the Beuys exhibition—or rather, two recollections, even though the texture of Beuys's objects is as far removed from that of Proust's madeleines as can be imagined. First, I recalled Clement Greenberg's warning against Germanic depth—*die Tiefe,* profundity—in art in general: the artist who promised such depths was a false prophet, full of false hope, and pretentious, for art could neither deliver the depths nor deliver one to them, for it did not deal in depth. For Greenberg, art was not "spiritual"; it had preconscious and unconscious effect, but what mattered most was its literal effect, its empirical reality. I recalled this caveat only to resist it, for I experienced Germanic depth in Beuys's art, and had no difficulties accepting that experience, even though the art itself at times seemed to make the depth all too easily accessible, as if one were dealing with a superficial conception of depth. But then I wondered if my sense of the superficiality of Beuys's depth was a measure of the extent to which I myself had unwittingly become infected with Greenbergian empiricism.

Second, I was reminded of my first experience of Beuys's objects, in their display cases in the Darmstadt Museum. I recall the high ceiling of the old-fashioned room, the palatial setting which seemed compromised by the plain cases, and the "melancholy lighting"[1] of the space, which gave it the spooky look of a mausoleum. Yet the cases, and the objects in them, did not so much dwindle in this aura, as seem restored to their primal—if not immediately nameable—significance, and so all the more primordial and charged. Under these conditions (not successfully duplicated in the Guggenheim Museum, whose processional interior structure outsmarted the art by seeming to propel one on past it), I had a strong sense of Beuys's works as not specifically art objects, but as belonging rather in a museum of natural history—more ethnographic than "high culture" in import. It was as if Beuys were deliberately reversing the direction early 20th-century art took: rather than beg, borrow or steal from "primitive" sources to achieve a modern look, Beuys precluded a modern look by making his things as materially raw—radically, one might even say prehistorically, unrefined—as possible, thereby saving the primitive from an artistic destiny.

I still experience Beuys's objects as resistant to codification as art—and yet as saying something about what art can be, and what it was when it was more integral to society, in some unspecified but long-past time. His works, albeit newly fabricated, hark back to an era when "art" objects were fetishes, functioning in a communal, magical way. After this sense of art, strongly evoked if not fully restored by Beuys's objects, I felt the triviality of most of the esthetically self-conscious objects of today. Being exclusively esthetic, they are stuck with themselves, limited in a way that Beuys's objects, with their "anthropological power," are not. Existing as relics of life, looking as though they were archeologically excavated from some strange site of experience, Beuys's objects seem at once familiar and unfamiliar, all too human yet from a world of foreign experience. As such, they exist not just esthetically, but with uncanny intimacy, for they seem at once the residue of and lure towards a possible experience of being.

Thus, Beuys's art seems to exist in a utopian way, as though offering us a substance and involving us in a process that might heal our wounds and renew our strength. As such, the works seem fragments of a titanic effort at social therapy—the afterbirth of a magical attempt at self- and world-renewal. Whatever the success or failure of Beuys's mission—and how can it help but be a failure in a world which has faith in art only insofar as it is esthetic—his effort and ambition are in themselves admirable.

Beuys's objects exist as much in terms of their projected human effort as in terms of their materiality. They are meant for a more comprehensive human audience than the esthete or connoisseur offers. Beuys does not want contemplative detachment—this is why he seems theatrical. For with detachment comes the separation of an object from its effect—from its "magic." The shamanistic pretensions of Beuys's performances can sometimes lead to a view of him as gratuitously theatrical. Indeed, shamanistic intentions inevitably seem pretentious from the estheticist perspective.

Beuys's art is a heuristic investigation into the human efficacy of art. As such, for all its anti-esthetic characteristics, it restores the original premise of avant-gardism—now lost with the voluntary assimilation of avant-gardism into commodity materialism—viz., that art is a spiritual transformation of life, leading consciousness to a new wakefulness about what is significant in life, and even leading life to a new identity.

The obscure and disturbing quality of original avant-garde art—and Beuys's art, for all his brilliant verbal elucidation of it, also has this quality—is only secondarily the result of its novelty. That novelty is itself no more than the external sign of the avant-garde call for a new consciousness of existence, a transvaluation of values. Beuys restores the anti-materialistic, visionary core of avant-garde art, continuing the idealistic tradition of such "Germanic" artists as Kandinsky and Mondrian. With them, he means to articulate the very substance of "modern," the belief in advance, whether by means of revolution or evolution, or, as Beuys puts it, by revolutionary evolution and evolutionary revolution.

His play on these terms, his emphasis on spiritual development, his explicit concern to free people for such development, links up with his belief in human self-transcendence through creativity. But creative power must be released from its bondage to its own materials, and for Beuys this magical release of creative power was heralded by alchemy, at once the truly modern and spiritually archetypal art.

Beuys's conception of art as spiritual alchemy, as a process of transmutation of material and personal beings—his performances mean to engender this process—was evidenced in the very structure of his New York exhibition, which was a performance in and of itself: the bays of the Guggenheim Museum were converted into a series of "stations," and labeled as such, not only on the way to an understanding of the development of Beuys's art and his personal Passion, but to the spectator's personal crisis of spiritual consciousness.

The alchemical conception of art is continuous with the Expressionist conception of art. Both make a Germanic medieval assumption of art's "religious" profundity, and imply that it is *the* means of directed transformation of being, a transformation effected by a primordial encounter with material being as such. The alchemical conception is the root of which the Expressionist conception is the fruit. One might even say that the Expressionist conception is the instrument of the alchemical idea. From this point of view, Beuys can be regarded as an Expressionist *in extremis,* and his work a heroically desperate, and perhaps final, efflorescence of the Expressionist idea—a revival of German Expressionism which goes to the alchemical root of the Expressionist idea, as if to keep it alive by showing that it can still flower.

For Beuys, that idea, despite its association, however tenuous, with Nazi ideology, is important for its revolutionary character. The very recognition of the alienness of Beuys's Expressionism in today's rationalist and materialist German context makes its political character clear—shows it to be, like the Expressionism of the Bridge and Blue Rider groups earlier in this century, a stand against bourgeois materialist attitudes.

Beuys's conception of the spiritual potential of material—of matter—is a direct rebellion against the commodity materialism pervasive in Germany today—a deliberate effort to use material, such as fat and felt, which in no way could be regarded as commodities, which have only negligible commercial value, yet seem almost exemplarily visceral. It is as though Beuys had searched far and wide for some substance(s) which could never be of much value to bourgeois society.

Beuys's "scandalous" approach to material links him directly to the heart of German Expressionism, which, as Walter Sokel has succinctly stated, "sought to be two things in one: a revolution of poetic form and vision and a reformation of life."[2]

The idea that art could reform life was as scandalous when the German Expressionists first proposed it as it is now: linking artistic revolution with social revolution—a linkage which initiated the idea of the avant-garde—seems, from the bourgeois point of view, as absurd now as it first did. For Sokel, "these two aims were hardly compatible." For Beuys, and myself, they are the only things worth making compatible in art. The effort to make them compatible is not only the major source of artistic advance but of the advance of ethical consciousness.

For Sokel, Expressionism, as a stylistic revolution, "was too difficult and *recherché* to serve its didactic and proselytizing ambitions." Beuys certainly shares these ambitions, but they are not, for him—and they never really were, for Expressionism—simply a matter of producing "the ideal of the 'new man,'" which would correlate with "the ideal of the 'new form'" (the latter as emblematic of the former). Rather, the Expressionist ambition was to create a style which would be an alembic for the creation of a new consciousness, one sensitive to the transformational power of nature—Expressionist style was to be a reminder that this force was universally accessible.

Viewed in the context of contemporary German society, Beuys's art is a penitential act reconstituting and reconsecrating the German mentality, restoring its umbilical connection with a romantic nature. It is as though Germany, materially restored after World War II—and Beuys's objects stand in ironical relationship to that material prosperity—must now spiritually renew itself by means of its traditional empathy with nature (an empathy most evident in Danube School landscape and Expressionist rendering of nature).

Clearly, in terms of Worringer's famous distinction between abstraction and empathy—and his book of that title was inspirational to the early Expressionists—Beuys rejects abstraction and is unequivocally on the side of empathy with organic being. This is why he was quick to deny the Minimalist derivation of one of his boxes,[3] and why he dismissed Duchamp's silence as overrated,[4] as if that silence epitomized abstraction. For him, it was a merely formal dead silence.

Abstraction has no alchemical dimension for Beuys: it exists formally rather than transformationally, coldly rather than empathetically. For Beuys, formalist abstraction is not authentically artistic, since it leads nowhere—sparks no human evolution or revolution—but to itself. The cleanness and clarity that emerge from formalistic reduction—and one can literally as well as figuratively dirty oneself touching many of Beuys's objects—are anathema to Beuys, even when buttressed by prosthetic theory (exemplarily the case with Duchamp and Minimalism). Formalist art is not an immersive or participatory experience, in the deepest, most serious sense, in which it can be said to transform its beholders, nor does it project an alchemical awareness of nature as a realm of forceful transformations.

The Expressionist, empathetic conception of art is manifested in the highest degree in Beuys—his sense of material as a realm of suggestions makes this clear. This is most apparent in the catalogue description of his sense of fat and felt, for him the archetypal *prima materia,* in the alchemical sense—the material to be transformed into *ultima materia,* yet for Beuys already complete in itself, for it reveals, in Paracelsus's words, the *quinta essentia* of "the life spirit" that can "cleanse a man's life";

> Fat infiltrates other materials, is gradually absorbed and brings about a process of INFILTRATION; felt absorbs anything with which it comes into contact—fat, dirt, dust, water or sound—and is therefore quickly integrated into its environment. Unlike the filter, it does not let things pass through it but soaks them up into its centre, becoming tighter and denser in the process, and therefore even more effective as an insulator:
> FAT expands and soaks into its surroundings.
> FELT attracts and absorbs what surrounds it.[5]

Fat and felt are clearly empathetic materials, involved with the existence around them. They demonstrate the interminglings, the "impure, informal" relationships which are the very stuff of existence. Beuys himself remarks that "it is the transformation of substance that is my concern in art, rather than the traditional aesthetic understanding of beautiful appearances."[6]

The transformation of substance starts the transformation of human beings: his *Fat Chair* (1964), Beuys notes, "started an almost chemical process among people."[7] This process is alchemically healing: Beuys describes fat as "a used and mineralized material with chaotic character"[8] (felt is "inert chaos"[9]), and insists that "chaos can have a healing character, coupled with the idea of open movement which channels the warmth of chaotic energy into order or form."[10]

The redemptive character of chaos becomes explicit when Beuys links it with socio-political events in German history, as in his Auschwitz display case. The furnace that converted human flesh (order) into soap fat (chaos)—a perverse Vulcanic furnace—is invoked not to acknowledge its monstrousness, but to suggest that its "magical" power of transformation of material can be for the good. *"Similia similibus curantur,"* writes Beuys, "heal like with like, that is the homeopathic healing process."[11]

Beuys's effort at dialectical conversion here is ultimately unsuccessful, for the attempt to regard the furnace of Auschwitz as Vulcan's furnace violates our sense of history, becoming a cheap irony. For how can Beuys's fat redeem Auschwitz's fat? Even more problematically, how can it finally justify Auschwitz's fat in the mind of the German public? Would we want it to? But is Beuys really trying to justify Auschwitz—justify evil—in some facile theodicy? If so, we have a fresh case of art obscuring rather than illuminating reality: there are some wounds which can never heal. If Beuys assumes that art can heal them, he deludes himself, and perpetrates a gross mystification.

Beuys's art is consistently haunted by the alchemical furnace of Vulcan. Vulcan, with his power of transformation, is the backdrop against which Beuys's objects must be understood. He is perhaps even the model for Beuys's own persona. Beuys's whole effort is to take a *prima materia* that reeks of death and make it a life-giving *ultima materia,* or to take a spiritual *ultima materia,* like honey (see *Honey Pump,* 1977) and release its healing power to make it universally accessible. The effort is clearly symbolic and utopian—as though he is looking for a panacea—and may be unsuccessful, but his obsession with the transformational process inherent to material is undeniable.

His obsession with self-transforming materials permits Beuys to assert that "the only decisive intervention [of the artist] is the choice of material and its size,"[12] with the clear understanding that this intervention initiates a shamanistic and/or therapeutic purpose, "a psychoanalytical action in which people could participate."[13] Thus, whatever the material—fat, felt, batteries, newspapers, Beuys's own person, thought as such (i.e., theory), words—the end is spiritual change:

> My intention is . . . to stress the idea of transformation and of substance. That is precisely what the shaman does in order to bring about change and development: his nature is therapeutic.
>
> Of course the shaman can operate genuinely only in a society that is still intact because it lies in an earlier stage of development. Our society is far from intact, but this too is a necessary stage. It's the point of crisis that sets in at every stage of history. . . . Once the intactness has gone, a kind of metamorphosis begins. So while shamanism marks a point in the past, it also indicates a possibility for historical development. It could be described as the deepest root of the idea of spiritual life. . . . When people say that shamanistic practice is atavistic and irrational, one might answer that the attitude of contemporary scientists is equally old-fashioned and atavistic, because we should by now be at another stage of development in our relationship to material.
>
> So when I appear as a kind of shamanistic figure, or allude to it, I do it to stress my belief in other priorities and the need to come up with a completely different plan for working with substances. For instance, in places like universities, where everyone speaks so rationally, it is necessary for a kind of enchanter to appear.[14]

Beuys here offers both an *apologia pro vita sua*—in effect responding to charges that he is a media opportunist, a sham rather than a shaman—and a working method for art in hard times, humanly and socially hard times. Beuys's theory of sculpture is the core of this method—of the attitude art should take in a hard world. "Based on the passage from chaotic movement to ordered form through sculptural movement," Beuys's theory of sculpture attempts to resolve primordial contradictions—chaos/order, undetermined/determined, organic/crystalline, warm/cold, expansion/contraction, and, implicitly, natural form/abstract form.[15] In his performances, Beuys means to live contradiction—to restate contradiction as a source of spiritual change, which alone can generate the power necessary for spiritual development. (Note Beuys's use of batteries, generators, energy sources.)

Living a contradiction generates a heightened sense of individuality, of personal potential; and living what is for Beuys the fundamental contradiction, between *prima materia* and *ultima materia,* the physical and the metaphysical, generates a sense of revolutionary individuality, of individuality able to evolve.

As Beuys notes, the "theme" of his "action" *The Chief* (1964) was "how to become a revolutionary,"

> a necessity for any evolutionary process. Transformation of the self must first take place in the potential of thought and mind. After this deep-rooted change, evolution can take place. There is no other possibility in my understanding, and this was perhaps too little considered by Marx, for instance. The idea of revolution coming from outer conditions, in the industrial field or the so-called reality of economic conditions, can never lead to a revolutionary step unless the transformation of soul, mind and will power has taken place.[16]

This idea of inner revolution as the necessary if not sufficient condition of outer revolution is the ultimate justification for the spiritual purpose of artistic alchemy.

Beuys explicitly acknowledges the alchemical, magical intention of his art,[17] and the generally "mystical" orientation of his position, which in large part is inspired by Rudolf Steiner's anthroposophy. (This reminds us of Kandinsky's and Mondrian's mystical idealism, the one in debt to Mme. Blavatsky's theosophy, the other to Schoenmaekers's nature mysticism.) Beuys quotes Steiner in his "Call for Alternatives" in the *Frankfurter Rundschau* of Dec. 23, 1978: "Freedom entails the individual impulse to carry out autonomous actions. However, autonomous action is not free unless it springs from 'insight into the conditions governing the life of the whole.' "[18] Beuys's commitment to socialism as a basis for spontaneous, spiritual individuality relates to Steiner's lectures "On Bees."[19] Beuys uses Steiner's conception of astral or aetheric levels to describe the ambition of his silent action *Drama 'Steeltable'/handaction (corner action)* (Jan. 23, 1969): the "silent sculptings of space through gestures" in that action "implied the 'extension of the human being into the astral or aetheric levels.' "[20]

One of the key points of Steiner's mysticism is the spiritual need for "going beyond"—transcending the senses and the material world they mediate. For Beuys, recognition of the expressive physiognomy of material is the first step of transformation, and its definition as spiritual. The whole aim of alchemy, as Paracelsus notes, is to articulate "the inherency of a thing, its nature, power, virtue, and curative efficacy, without any ... foreign admixture." Transformation as such is the spiritual revelation of substance, and alchemical art is, in Beuys's words, a "trans-mission" or transformation—transformation is the "spiritual-divine" element in the "earthly" material, and art is the demonstration of the spiritual-divine in the earthly, and the earthly form of the spiritual-divine. In Steiner's words, art "must realize that its task is to carry the spiritual-divine life into the earthly."[21] For Beuys, art, in Steiner's words, rediscovers materials as "intensities rather than extensions."[22] There is no unfaithfulness to nature in this, but an attempt to "purify seceded nature by artistic fashioning; then it will express the divine-spiritual."[23] "Thought lives in things," argues Steiner, and the effort to make this thought—crudely recognized as the expressive physiognomy of things—explicit, thereby making explicit the spiritual nature of things, is "the main impulse of ... all true art."[24]

Spiritual communicativeness or expressivity is an organic characteristic of things for both Beuys and Steiner. Being moves between what Steiner calls "the birth-pole" and "the death-pole."[25] Beuys's art means to embody the movement between these opposites explicitly. His art is full of images of fruition, epitomized by woman—Steiner regards "the upper gods" as female "because they transmitted fructifying forces"[26]—and images of decay, epitomized by fat and felt.

The chaos of death is perhaps most succinct and overt in his *Fat Felt Shoes* (1963), where the fat can "be read as the remains of a body, 'decay down to the base, leaving a residue of compost.'"[27] (Beuys's personal experience of regeneration by farm work, after his experience of degeneration as a pilot in World War II, is implied in this work, among others.) The sense of the unity of the opposites—the fundamental interrelation—of birth and death is crucial for alchemy, which takes the existential cycle of nature as the metaphor for its own essentializing activity.

"Decay is the beginning of all birth," writes Paracelsus, because "it transforms shape and essence, the forces and virtues of nature." "Decay," he continues, is "the midwife of very great things! It causes many things to rot, that a noble fruit may be born.... It brings about the birth and rebirth of forms a thousand times improved."

Beuys's conception of revolutionary evolution seems implicit in this view, although it has its dangers, even for Beuys: at times he seems to use it as justification for the holocaust, as though to deliberately create death is to ultimately improve things, which, indeed, is what the Nazis thought they were ultimately doing. Does it seem as if Beuys means to imply that an improved Germany emerged from World War II, with all its death—emerged from the dead Germany of that war? Alchemy, like Germanic depth, can become treacherous when it is abused.

The traditional Germanic image of Death and the Maiden, acknowledged by Beuys as a "key experience" for him—an artistic image for which he had "considerable feelings"—brings "figurative" death and emblematic fruition together, uniting what seems irreconcilable.[28] Beuys has been obsessed by this image in his own drawing, his way of "thinking form." The "hovering, almost mediumistic quality" of his drawing is "particularly accentuated when the subjects have to do with death, with natural, geological or skeletal structure, or with animals traditionally endowed with extraordinary power."[29] That is, Beuys's drawing becomes particularly thoughtful when it deals with structures which epitomize process and/or death, and when it deals with animals that "go beyond" death—for Beuys, the horse, the stag, the swan, and the hare. These animals bespeak immortal natural process because they, in Beuys's words, "pass freely from one level of existence to another . . . [and] represent the incarnation of the soul or the earthly form of spiritual beings with access to other regions."[30]

Beuys seems to conceive of himself as a kind of Germanic Knight accompanied, as in Dürer's famous print, by Death and the Devil, but also by his horse and faithful dog, perhaps the animal most clearly able to share in human experience, to empathetically participate in human spirituality. (It might be noted that Dürer has also depicted the stag and hare as spiritual beings.)

Beuys's art can be regarded as an exploration—one might say a deliberate evocation—of death, as if by letting loose the forces of decay he might effect a rebirth, purging material to make it quintessentially vital. This enterprise has an air of Northern Romanticism about it, the assumption that only the Germanic-Northern spirit (the two are synonymous for Beuys) is sufficiently death-obsessed to be life-renewing. One of the characteristic misunderstandings of Germanic-Northern Romanticism is that it is a potential source for Nazi ideology. While Beuys's work, which falls within the Northern Romantic tradition, does seem to risk serving such an ideology, with its assumption of an initiatory experience into the dark depths of life (blood and earth—i.e., primitive and primary materials), Beuys's alchemical motivation makes the transformation at once less ideological and more mystical, and more a matter of achieving individual than social identity. In the Nazi ideology such dark spiritual experience fuses one with the collective and involves a loss of personal identity. In Beuys it differentiates one, integrating one with one's own personal evolutionary powers.

Beuys does, it seems to me, redeem the ageless idea of spiritual death and rebirth—emerging with a sense of natural death and spiritual rebirth—but he does not entirely free it of the inhuman political uses to which it can be put. This idea can quickly translate into an excuse for active aggression—the sacrifice of others for one's *own* spiritual rebirth. As a self-process, then, Beuys's ideology makes sense; as a political process it makes less sense. And in recent years. Beuys's direction has become more and more explicitly political.

But there are even difficulties with the way Beuys understands the idea of spiritual development as a series of deaths and rebirths of the self, particularly when we look at Beuys's public persona. His performances and his proposed Free International University for Creativity and Interdisciplinary Research show Beuys viewing himself not only as a spiritually developing self, but as a kind of maximum leader. He may be setting himself up only as a mock *Führer,* but in the art world, as in the political world, the comical often has tragic consequences.

Beuys clearly views himself as giving rebirth, through his public persona, to the concept of leader, showing that the leader can be a spiritual force for the good, a creative power. Whether we accept this or not—whether we even think it is truly possible—we cannot deny "the density of material" in Beuys's art, the sense of a material that, in his own words, "had been worked over for so long" that "it worked like the accumulated charge of a battery."[31] We may not accept Beuys as the new creative leader, leading us to life after we have tasted death, but we cannot deny that death is the densest and most commonplace of materials, an everyday substance with an accumulated charge.

The question is whether Beuys's survival of his personal experience of death in a wartime airplane crash and the hope of survival he holds out to all of us is sufficient apology for the life lost to death, the death set loose by another German shaman. If we really have to accept, with whatever irony and belief in homeopathic magic, the idea that *The Greatest Contemporary Composer is the Thalidomide Child* (performed July 7, 1966), then our concept of humanity is flawed, for it is not clear that even rebirth can recreate it whole.

It may be that, in German society today, with its sustained *Wirtschaftswunder* (economic miracle) and renewed *Spiessbürgerlichkeit* (super-bourgeois mentality), only the twisted self can seem authentic. Only to twist beyond all twisting, to distort beyond all distorting—to endure what cannot be endured, to survive what cannot be survived—is to have a truly authentic individuality. Such a vestige of individuality, as a survivor but without the outcast's guilt, must perhaps be admired, however much it may be an evolutionary dead end. Beuys, in fact, when one forgets his spiritualist ideology, seems at times to show us art in an evolutionary dead end, and he may even show us that Nordic spiritualism is a dead end of thought.

Beuys's runaway spiritualism also seems to lead his art into a dead end: his pursuit of transformative communication at all costs finally seems to cost him his art. This becomes clear when we survey his development as a whole. From small, intimate objects, with an "anthropological"-magical aura, he moves to increasingly large scale pieces, often more grandiose than grand, and often bombastically charged with his own public persona as celebrity artist more than any other meaning.

The other meanings become absorbed in the cult of personality Beuys has made himself the willing victim of: even the shamanistic self comes to seem to exist for Beuys's cult of personality, his sense of himself as a public "phenomenon." Clement Greenberg once pointed out that when we take art as a phenomenon and trace it back to the phenomenon of the artist—as though he were some force of nature or history—we are no longer looking at art.

It may be that Beuys no longer wants to make art, so busy is he making himself: the production of art has for him become subsidiary to the production of personality. This is the consequence of what we might call the carnival atmosphere of his spiritualism. Beuys has become a barker for spiritualism, which doesn't do it much good, and doesn't do his art that means to bespeak spiritual ideals any good. With such pieces as the *Honey Pump* and *The Pack*, one has the sense of looking at Barnum & Bailey monsters, side show "characters" that claim center stage, so inflated are they by their own sense of importance.

While the spiritual ambition of these pieces and their physical reality imply a certain wit, a certain kind of melodramatic irony, one has a sense that Beuys is taking old, all-too-familiar, half-dead spiritual ideas and reviving them the way a taxidermist would. Beuys in effect stuffs and inflates the skin of spiritual ideas with scale. The ideas loom ominously and significantly, but we know they are only facades.

Beuys, in the name of what the linguists call pragmatics, is doing a difficult, indeed impossible thing: he is trying to address an audience that art as such has rarely addressed, that great indeterminate mass audience that Plato scornfully called the beast that swallows everything. Beuys needs a medieval world—a world of unified ideology—to be effective, and to avoid the self-idolization that is the punishment for being ineffective. He needs a universal ideology that would keep him from continually falling back upon himself as a dubious court of last resort. T.S. Eliot said that art was an effort to become selfless that could only really be attempted by those who were troubled by a powerful self. Beuys increasingly uses his art to bespeak a powerful self rather than to find an idea that can lead beyond that self. His marvelous early pieces, especially the "tool" pieces, in which personal self and spiritual belief are in balance, creating a sense of calm energy, have been replaced by lopsided works, overrun by a sense of self which mistakes self-belief for spiritual belief.

And yet Beuys remains a challenge to other artists, not because of the success he has had in creating a cult of personality, but in his sense of art's mission, which the cult of personality is a distortion of. Baudelaire once wrote that artists had to face the choice of "art for art's sake" or "art inseparable from social utility." Beuys, with his half-shamanistic, half-scapegoat stance, is trying to create a communally and personally useful art redemptive of communal and social possibilities.

This ambition (intention) leads directly to the difficulties Americans have with him. He represents an effort to come to terms with a range of experience— the holocaust—which is still a nearly taboo subject to many people who think there is no way of rationalizing it, even with the aid of the magic of art. It is a blunt fact of history, an intractable reality, which art can do nothing to "fictionalize," transform. This raw fact carries its own meaning within it, and no artist should be allowed to tamper with that meaning.

Beuys, then, takes a risk that perhaps only Germans—or at least not Americans, who have not had such a socially devastating experience—can understand. He attempts to come to terms with his country's—and his own— historical experience, so as not to repeat it. Santayana's idea that unless we know the past we are doomed to repeat it is at stake in Beuys. Beuys metaphorically repeats the past in order to avoid its literal repetition in some future, however remote.

Notes

1. Georg Jappe, quoted in Caroline Tisdall, *Joseph Beuys* (New York, The Solomon R. Guggenheim Museum, 1979), p. 162.

2. Walter Sokel, *The Writer in Extremis* (Stanford, 1959), p. 227.

3. The work in question is *Rubberized Box* (1957). Beuys remarks that "the rigid form of the box has nothing to do with minimalism." Quoted by Tisdall, p. 70.

4. On November 11, 1964, on the second channel of West Germany television, Beuys stated that "The silence of Marcel Duchamp is overrated." As Beuys remarks, the statement was in part a response to Duchamp's "very negative opinion of the Fluxus artists, claiming that they had no new ideas since he had anticipated it all." More generally, it was a condemnation of "Duchamp's Anti-art concept," which did nothing to counteract art's "retreat into over-specialist isolation." Quoted by Tisdall, p. 92.

5. Tisdall, p. 74.

6. Quoted by Tisdall, p. 10.

7. Quoted by Tisdall, p. 72.

8. Ibid.

9. Quoted by Tisdall, p. 162.

10. Quoted by Tisdall, p. 21.

11. Ibid.

12. Quoted by Tisdall, p. 162.

13. Quoted by Tisdall, p. 17.

14. Quoted by Tisdall, p. 23.

15. Quoted by Tisdall, p. 44.

16. Quoted by Tisdall, p. 95.

17. See Tisdall, pp. 83, 88, 273.

18. Quoted by Tisdall, p. 284.

19. Tisdall, p. 44.

20. Quoted by Tisdall, p. 175.

21. Rudolf Steiner, *The Arts and Their Mission* (New York, Anthroposophic Press, 1964), pp. 45-46.

22. Steiner, p. 23.

23. Steiner, p. 47.

24. Steiner, pp. 10, 47.

25. Steiner, p. 24.

26. Steiner, p. 39.

27. Quoted by Tisdall, p. 157.

28. Quoted by Tisdall, p. 50.

29. Quoted by Tisdall, pp. 20-21.

30. Ibid.

31. Quoted by Tisdall, p. 76.

Uncivil War

War is the father of all and the king of all.
—Heraclitus, Fragment 53

But Agamemnon, King and Lord, was not infallible. He was fallible. He had sacrificed
Iphigenia for the sake of glory in war, for the fulfillment of the superb idea of self, but on the
other hand he had made cruel dissension for the sake of the concubines captured in war. The
paternal flesh was fallible, ungodlike.
—D.H. Lawrence, "The Theatre," *Twilight in Italy*

The editors of Time-Life Books (those masters of the popular) inform us that
war, which a psychoanalyst tells us establishes "death as a criterion of truth,"[1] —
is one of the "great themes."[2] It embodies the basic issues of life, from love to
death, from power to selfhood. War is one of those recurrent, ugly, indisputable
facts of life that make overwhelming demands on us and threaten to take
command of our lives; it dominates and destroys our potential for freedom,
pushing our energies to an extreme from which there is no easy retreat, only
collapse. War summarizes what Freud almost euphemistically called "the
demands of reality," calling attention to itself whether by its presence or its
absence, and always by its real possibility. It is the latent content of the dream of
life, the hidden source of all the manifest forms of engagement. "Strife," as
Heraclitus stated, "is necessary to existence" (Fragment 80); he may have
thought "the tension of opposites" to be "merely a necessary phase in a great
cyclic process which goes on for ever," but it is the phase he dwells on most
emphatically and elaborately. War may finally be "the producer of harmony,
since the fairest harmony is made out of differing elements," but it is war rather
than harmony that Heraclitus emphasizes. It is war rather than "Peace, and
Stillness" that demonstrates the change or flux that is the root of being, that
makes it clear that "nothing, not even the most stable-seeming and solid
substance, is really at rest."[3] War, then, has both metaphysical and existential
meaning, and is the fundamental fact of cosmic as well as of human reality—the
grand arbiter of all being, the mechanism of all becoming. It is the motor that
drives the truth. It is on the field of battle, as the Bhagavad-Gita tells us, that the
god Krishna explained metempsychosis, and the morality of acceptance of the

world through lack of desire for it, to the Pandava prince Arjuna. Renunciation of attachment is an achievement taught by war; war is the scene that reveals the nothingness of it all—a very modern conception.

Is art adequate to the great theme of war? In that no means of communication can ever be adequate to the great, all-pervasive theme, there is an implicit negative judgment in the question. Let me then adjust it so that it is answerable. What are the artistic means by which war is "remembered, conventionalized, and mythologized"[4]—by which both deep and superficial experiences of it are idealized? What are the modes by which art makes the unpalatable truth a palatable fiction? This conversion is a particularly difficult problem in the visual arts, for as well as the obvious events of war, its invisible effects on human beings must be treated. It is hard to visually "civilize' an invisible, uncivilizing effect, hard to be critical about a trauma that cannot be adequately acknowledged, even symbolically. Art may of course be just another means of forgetfulness—Freud aligned it with intoxication as one of the means by which we endure life. This makes its task easier. The world of war is treated with the same comfortable mundaneness as that of peace; it is made picturesque rather than pressing, a fresh source of sensation rather than a call to anxious thought. Thus art, like society in general, shows itself as, in Freud's words, not "given to truthfulness," but concerned to maintain "a condition of cultural hypocrisy."[5] Like sex, war is treated hypocritically, and art, as a force for socialization—a "civilizing influence," as is said—is an instrument of hypocrisy.

The question of art's usefulness for an understanding of war—and with it the question of our respect for art—has become pressing. For with the apparent inability of society to create, as Thomas Hobbes put it, "a common power" to keep all human beings "in awe," we are increasingly discovered to be literally and continually "in that condition which is called war," a condition of "every man against every man." This is a matter of attitude as well as of event, a matter, as Hobbes says, of "the will to contend" as well as of "the act of fighting." It is a matter of the streets as well as of the trenches—of the streets becoming the trenches, the front existing everywhere, confirming Hobbes' assertion that in "a time of war . . . every man is enemy to every man," and that "the life of man" not only involves "continual fear, and danger of violent death," but is "solitary, poor, nasty, brutish, and short." In this state *"nothing can be unjust,"* because "where there is no common power, there is no law; where no law, no justice. Force and fraud are in war the two cardinal virtues."[6] Hobbes has described the condition of modern war rather than that of traditional "humanistic," just war, war made to uphold law. (The modern " 'totalitarian' system of warfare," as Arnold Toynbee reminds us,[7] is not a uniquely contemporary phenomenon, but involves a general attitude toward war and humanity. It will be treated as such in this article.) And it is the condition of modern war that we are experiencing in our society. We are in a situation of "endless war," which seems to have become "an inevitable condition of modern life."

To see if Modern art should be taken seriously, one would like to know its response to this state. The new eschatology of war is inescapable, our common fate, conditioning our intersubjectivity; can it be said that art, with its pursuit of stylistic novelty and its effete hedonism, has managed to escape it? Does Modern art, through its abstract pursuit of esthetic purity, offer us a Kantian promise of "perpetual peace," an almost unintelligible idea of peace, an absent ideal which today exists only as an archaeological relic or a hollow gesture? The idea of traditional, limited war implies the intrusion of a particular death in a general paradise; the idea of modern, total war implies the absence of the slightest hint of paradise—of pastoral retreat, of sanctuary—in a general wilderness of death. Modern art may seem to have built some sort of underground temple or shelter, but it no longer seems secure—in fact, seems altogether beside the point—in the face of nuclear radiation, which penetrates the very possibility and idea of earth. Is it time for the avant-garde—if it wants to remain "avant-garde"—to come above ground, out of the esthetic shelter, and deal with "the great themes"?

It is no accident that Modern art has systematically, almost programmatically failed to satisfactorily mediate the condition of modern war—has, it can be argued, deliberately repressed the thought of it. Behind Modern art's idea of its autonomous mission, its belief that it is the last standard-bearer for an almost defeated autonomy—that it is, in Clement Greenberg's hyperbolic words, "the only field of meaningful achievement left"[9]—is a basic indifference to the condition of war that dominates our personal and collective lives. (And I do not mean the kind of indifference that Krishna taught Arjuna.) While war may be kitsch, however, it also makes a mockery of art's self-styled autonomy. Art's limited autonomy is no more than a vestige of control in the face of events. It is bankrupt, an ostrich hole in which Modernism hides from reality. From Goya's picture of *Panic*, also called *The Colossus*, ca. 1808–12—for me the most profound embodiment of the disintegrative effects of total war, directly exemplifying Freud's analysis of panic (which he said is "best studied in military groups")[10]—to Picasso's *Massacre in Korea*, 1952, there has been an increasing if erratic degeneration in the treatment of modern war, because of an overcommitment to style. Picasso's picture, a hybrid unsuccessfully trying to fuse a traditional interest in the human effects of war with a rendering of modern total war, offers us more a reprise of such paintings as Goya's *The Third of May, 1808*, 1814, and Manet's *The Execution of the Emperor Maximilian*, 1867, than insight into the psychological state of the helpless victims or the social one of the shooting soldiers. This is in part why the Picasso work is a failure; it is also a failure because it is stylized to the point of absurdity. *Guernica*, 1937, stops short of this point, but though the terror it depicts is appropriate to modern war, it too affords little insight into that state. Picasso could not imagine modern war, so involved was he with a traditional conception of war as just or injust—which is why he took it personally, as an opportunity for symbolizing his own attitudes (to women) and conflicts (with women). He could not understand an indefinite state of undeclared war for which no one bore responsibility.

Images (such as those of Leon Golub) that try to deal with modern war, and that successfully fuse the traditional interest in the human effects of war with the modern sense of its total domination of the life-world—by showing how the condition of total war creates a modern man, carves in flesh a war physiognomy—are generally regarded as intrusive and beside the point of Modern art. What is that point? In a general way, it is novel style—the constant proof of our newness, of the freshness of our being. But there is a deeper point to Modernism, a point that penetrates despite all protests to the contrary: Modernism depends on the elimination—the forceful refusal—of the great themes. It is based on a skepticism about them which masks a helplessness before them, an inadequacy to them of which it makes a virtue. Modernism is viable only to the extent that it keeps every trace of a great theme out of it. Two quotations make the point succinctly. One is Greenberg's assertion that "we are through with the big words and what they advertise; their aesthetic credit, at least, is exhausted." The other is the famous opening sentence of Clarence Joseph Bulliet's book *Apples and Madonnas, Emotional Expression in Art:* "An apple by Paul Cézanne is of more consequence artistically than the head of a Madonna by Raphael." The next sentence is equally emphatic, equally self-righteous: "In the development we know as 'Modernism'—which is the reaffirmation and emphasizing of a strain that has been in art since the first caveman carved by the light of flaming faggots the reindeer and the mammoth of the hunt—it is the emotional power of the artist that counts, not the subject matter."[12]

This was written in 1930, when the value of Cézanne was still in doubt—when he was not recognized as the archetypal Modern artistic genius except among the elite cognoscenti. Bulliet was defending an art, an attitude, an idea. (What he was then defending as a minority position has now become gospel.) What matters is not his view of Cézanne as an expressionist—it has been recognized that Cézanne was as seminal for Expressionism as for Cubism—but his sense of the irrelevance of subject matter, of what Greenberg used to call "literature." Subject matter for Greenberg was not necessarily harmful, but it was not where the action was. Like Greenberg, Bulliet also rejects religion; not just because it is religion—there is no "enlightened" dismissal of it as an illusion, rather an absence of any stand toward it—but because it has nothing to do with art-making. It is a "great theme," a "big word," but art must find its own way of stating what Greenberg called "the truth about feeling"—the kind of feeling that religion codifies and institutionalizes (and war creates).[13] In Modernism the feeling is treated, not the theme. (But can the feeling then be treated adequately?)

One can defend both Cézanne and Raphael by arguing that their art cannot be discussed in the same breath; the comparison between them is false, artificial, unfair, and academic—a paradoxical move in an art-historical game. But this is to sidestep an issue implicit in artistic development: works of art do not exist on friendly terms in some grand, all-inclusive temple of art. Their harmony is not fore-ordained; they are at war with one another. They can even be said to exist to cancel each other out, to claim the whole field of art for themselves and to define it in their own terms.[14] This is the truth in the conceptualists' idea that each body of art defines art anew. Works do not fit together; they are not only visually and culturally differentiated, but incommensurate even to the extent of denying each other's right to exist. The development of a new esthetic, a new point of view on the possibilities of art, puts all existing works in jeopardy by subjecting them to fresh evaluation. Their value, even the understanding of their nature, is up for grabs and can radically change. A case in point: Dürer, from being seen as a humanist visionary—even a radical Lutheran fanatic—in his own day, was regarded in the Rococo period as a dry, dull technician. If such devaluation can happen to Dürer, it can happen to lesser figures.

The point is that the dismissal of any one artist's works, ideas, or attitudes by another is often the condition for the creation of new art. What one rejects determines as much as what one accepts. Bulliet's rejection of Raphael is a condition for his acceptance of Cézanne; his rejection of subject matter is a condition for his elevation of Modernism. While his understanding of Modernism may be problematic, he nonetheless cleared the field for it. Bulliet asserted that Raphael no longer told the truth about feeling; Cézanne, with his anxiety, did.

But does he still? I don't think so. To paint like Cézanne or any artist derivative of him—even his best heirs—today is to falsify him and art. It is to make what Greenberg called "luxury painting"—painting that has "lost faith in itself" and, in compensation, attempts "to emphasize the pleasure principle with a new explicitness."[15] It is to betray the mood of existential pessimism in which the work of Cézanne, and Modernism, originated. It is to confuse a late mood of cynicism with an early one of disillusionment. Above all, it is to insist that subject matter does not matter, when it might be that the problem of art now is to show that it is all that matters. Autonomy is no longer even a lucid myth, and the innovations and linguistic richness of Modernist art are betrayed by it. (The attempt to prop up the sagging fortunes of Modernism by regarding it as an exploration of absence, power, and desire—as an essentially apolitical, undialectical phenomenon—is another attempt to resensualize its language, which has become one of etiquette and politesse rather than of reflection and action. It is a language of manners rather than of morals.) The direct plunge into subject matter is demanded these days, rather than the finesses of form, which is all that Cézanne now means. His vein of golden anxiety has long been mined away; if there is anything about him that still resonates it is his refusal of formula—the lack of good breeding that made him reject the conventional rhetoric of naturalism to find in nature a subject matter which he thought disclosed his own salvation.

The absence of significant subject matter—the directly world-historical—in Modernism (with notable exceptions, such as those provided by some of the Dadaists and Surrealists and by some of the German New Realists) is compensated for by the abundance of it in photography. Here alone has modern war been adequately treated, "understood." It is appropriate that a seemingly impartial, mechanical means of perception, a technologically created instrument that seems to keep active cognition out of passive recognition, should be used to document modern war; for as Tyrone Slothrop, a character in Thomas Pynchon's *Gravity's Rainbow,* thought, modern war is "secretly"—blatantly, these days—"dictated...by the needs of technology."[16] Photography, with its "objectivity," is the ideal means of recording war; it makes it possible to voyeuristically relish it while keeping one's distance from it.

Toynbee has written that war can no longer be regarded as " 'the sport of kings' "; "the intrusion of two new social forces...the double 'drive' of Democracy and Industrialism [has] been keying up the scourge of War towards the pitch of enormity which it attained in the sixteenth and seventeenth centuries through the impetus of Ecclesiastical Fanaticism."[17] Photography is a democratic product of industrialism. It is involved either in a war of attrition with reality or else in an attempt to consummate a relationship with it in a single knockout blow, a unique moment of consummate disclosure. In this it mimics modern war, which, as Toynbee says, involves either "a war—or a series of wars—of attrition" or the search for a "knock-out blow' " that will give "decisive and definitive victory of one single Power through the annihilation of all the rest."[18] Again like modern war, photography ranges among "the civilian populations" at will—in contrast to the "eighteenth-century militarists" who "took pains to spare" them (who had a traditional, humanistic idea of war). Photography records their "wholesale annihilation,"[19] their inherent nothingness from the perspective of modern war; by its treatment of every subject matter, for all its hypothetical uniqueness, as a mass phenomenon, photography not only documents this nothingness but helps create it.

Photography summarizes the secularism of which modern war is more a symptom than a cause: the assumption that there is no binding arbitration of meaning in our world, no higher court of appeal that will tell us the "truth." The camera doesn't know the truth, is not interested in the idea of the truth. It wants only facts, whatever they may add up to. They may not add up to anything, may be just meaningless information; the camera is nihilistic. It is not responsible for what it records, just as modern war is not really responsible for what it does, since it just happens, forever. The camera is thus as comic as modern war—which is not at all tragic; as Friedrich Dürrenmatt wrote, "comedy alone is suitable for us" today, for "tragedy presupposes guilt, despair, moderation, lucidity, vision, a sense of responsibility," none of which exist in modern, total war. Modern war epitomizes the situation of the modern world, in which "things happen without anyone in particular being responsible for them...and everyone gets caught somewhere in the sweep of events."[20] This is a world in which one is possessed by a system and its fate; one can choose one's course as little as one can choose not to be photographed (that too, just happens to one). The message of photography and modern war is that the whole of contemporary life is a totalitarian system, and that it is this system that determines our lives, not we who determine it. Photography and modern war are among the instruments and exemplifications of this indifferent system, as well as being realms in which its tragicomic results become self-evident—for there is still a touch of tragedy involved in the overall comedy, since suffering individuals are involved. (Again, it should be noted that the "indifference" spoken of is not the ideal of the *Bhagavad-Gita*.)

It is clear, then, that there must be discussion of the photographic treatment of war. But there must also be discussion of Modern and traditional art. Using Baudelaire's definition of imagination as our touchstone, we must study the artist's use of "the raw materials" of war to reveal its effect on "the furthest depths of the soul." "A new world" of art and a "sensation of [the] newness" of the human is produced in the process.[21] In its imaginative treatment war becomes the scene of passion, *the* means by which desire is displayed—the "occupation" in which it is mastered and identity or selfhood achieved.

In amplified summary of what has been said so far, I propose the following alignment of analytic terms, which I think can be sustained more rather than less consistently. On the one hand there is a traditional, imaginative mode of picturing war, based on a traditional conception of war as a human event on a human scale, for all its cosmic implications and meaning. It is an event presented and understood in terms of its effect on the human—an event which, for all its terribleness, is still humanly controlled: consciously made by human beings for a conscious purpose. That purpose: the realization of identity or ego, specifically of male ego. Traditional war is the male mode of self-articulation, self-determination, self-definition. Gaining power is its incidental outcome; it is war's creation of selfhood that counts, from which power—control of natural strength and social force—follows. Traditional war is the method of turning the energy of instinct into the power of ego. Here, despite all appearances to the contrary, instinct is socialized or civilized; the instinct of aggression is used by the state, which, as Freud tells us, has monopolized it. Whatever irony there is in this is incidental to the way war imposes coherence upon instinct, shaping and "censoring" it until it has moral and rational, even esthetic—and so decisively social—form and meaning. This is the traditional value and end of traditional war.

On the other hand there is a documentary approach, generally applicable to and revelatory of the nature of modern war.[22] War is treated in the matter-of-fact way in which it itself treats people and the world, in a strictly surface, precise way, whose aim is that truthfulness we call accuracy. Photographic depiction becomes the model for this approach, and increasingly takes it over.

Photographic documentation—photographic realism—involves the renunciation of allegorical masks for war, whether they glorify it or fatalistically accept it, justify it or despair of it. It involves the renunciation of any imaginative, "humanistic" treatment through which war might be seen as the realm in which the tragedy of human existence is disclosed, in which the whole folly of the human condition becomes manifest. Artifice is substituted for art, strategy for re-creation, a dispassionate attitude for an impassioned one, objective tactics for subjective involvement.

However, under the surface of this dehumanizing approach to modern war (which corresponds to its own inhumanity—its indifference to the human and its preoccupation with systems and technology), the destructiveness of war is revealed as it rarely is in traditional imaginative treatment of it. Under the security blanket of the cool surface very hot events become self-evident. The violence of this self-evidence is almost as great as that of war. Under the cool photographic surface, a surface of voluntary objectivity, is the revelation of an involuntary, primordial destructiveness—a demonstration that total war means total disintegration. What Freud called the death instinct is unmistakable, grossly revealed in all its nakedness, made visible with a vengeance.

The cult of death that war reveals exists to suppress the sexual instincts, exists as the exact opposite and the enemy and violator of eros. And insofar as women are vehicles for the erotic, insofar as they epitomize and represent its veneration, war is about the renunciation, the contemptuous elimination, of women. Agamemnon makes his first step toward war, and thus toward manhood and selfhood, by sacrificing Iphigenia, and his last by turning all women left into concubines. The killing of other men confirms that first step, and could not occur without it.

War imagery is as noteworthy for the absence of women as for the presence of men. Women are at best elevated into symbols of war, when they lose their erotic character—and become as destructively aggressive as men, as in the case of Amazons and Valkyries. Or they seduce men to war, as in many miltary posters, embodying the subsumption of erotic to aggressive ends. Or they symbolize peace and plenty, as in works by Gerhard Marcks and Lovis Corinth. It is women, not men, who ask for an end to war, as in Käthe Kollwitz's Nie wieder Krieg! (Never again war!), 1924.[23] Generally war is about the destruction of the female principle, the eternal feminine, whether through the destruction of the sons of women, as in Franco Fornari's psychoanalytic conception of war as "deferred infanticide" and paranoid elaboration of loss,[24] or in Gaston Bouthoul's analysis of it as a way of regulating population.[25] War means death to woman. The homoeroticism that flourishes during it,[26] redirecting the erotic from the opposite to the same sex—so that the erotic is no longer a tension of opposites, a Heraclitan state of war—confirms this. What seems simply a convenient redirection of the erotic in a tense situation is in fact an unconscious dismantling and annihilation of its basic warlike structure in order to establish a state of peaceful sameness, a facile logic of oneness. In general, the destruction of the structure of the erotic is the metaphysical goal of war, inseparable from its origins. For the erotic, particularly as personified in the tense relationship between male and female, seems to contradict the idea of independent, self-sufficient male identity—whose symbol is the weapon of war. Modernism, with its sexless stance—it is the art of eunuchs, for all its macho pretensions to mastery of the physicality of the medium—can hardly begin to comprehend and compete with the concerns of the art of "the great theme," can hardly begin to realize the tensions implicit in war. The epicene hedonism of Modernism, passed off as "transcendence," is no match for an art that searches for the obscene meaning behind the great themes, the big words.

For me, the greatest imaginative treatment of traditional war is Velazquez's *Surrender of Breda (Las Lanzas)*, ca. 1638. Ostensibly dealing with the transfer of power from vanquished to victor (from Justin of Nassau to the Spanish commander, the Genoese general Ambrogio Spinola), this is in fact an extraordinary scene of chivalry and humanity. While the orderly row of Spanish lances and the calm, compact ranks of the victorious troops are in contrast with the disheveled, loosely knit group of Dutch soldiers, there is no loss of respect for the humanity of the defeated, no denial of their dignity and individuality. There is no sense of the unconditionally destructive intentions of modern war. Instead of the elimination of the human implicit in the latter—the experimental use of the human to demonstrate the power of weapons and thus of technology—there is on the contrary an insistence upon, even an elevation of, the humanity of all involved. The war is not going to be allowed to destroy that humanity; it is relegated to the distant background. The painting's central group is based upon a little-known 16th-century print (after Martin de Vos) of Abraham and Malchisedek;[27] Velazquez presumably implies that divine aid enabled the Spanish victory, identified with that of Abraham over Chedorlaomer, and called forth Christian charity and generosity to the defeated. This religious background to the work also suggests the power that Hobbes said created law. Justice must be done in the surrender because both victor and vanquished are under the rule of the common power represented by God—the power that prevents them from falling into a perpetual state of war, i.e., from becoming "modern."

This is the crucial difference between traditional and modern depictions of war. In the former it never becomes absolute or total, thus allowing for an imaginative treatment of the human beings involved—an imaginative recovery of their humanity from war, precluding its becoming the dominant, definitive situation of life. In the latter, war becomes total, implicitly an extermination of the very idea of being human, because there is no common power to insist on the humanity of the participants. Modernity means this absence of common power, of authority establishing justice for all—a justice on which dignity, self-respect, and respect in the eyes of others is premised. The *Surrender of Breda* is a far cry from the surrender photographs of modern war ("hands up!" rather than a handshake). Here "peace" does not mean the restoral of humanity to the warriors; there is no mercy or forgiveness in modern war, because there is no humanity to begin with.

There are numerous other images of "humanistic" war throughout the history of art—except in the Modern period. In the battle scene on the east pediment of the Temple of Aphaia at Aegina, ca. 490 B.C., the common power, in the person of Athena, is dominant and central—in fact the tallest, most upright figure present. The famous "fallen warrior" on the pediment retains his humanity even as he is dying, and no doubt even in death. Compare this to Robert Capa's famous 1945 photograph of one of the last soldiers to die in the Second World War—a mannequin out of commission that appears never to have had any humanity to begin with, was never more than a composite of costume (uniform) and weapon. Certainly the spilled blood must be ketchup. Similarly, Capa's photograph from 1936 of a soldier at the moment he is shot in the Spanish Civil War—perhaps the single best-known war photograph ever taken—or his photograph from the same year of a soldier fallen in that war, do not give their figures anything like the dignity that figures in similar positions have in Antonio Pollaiuolo's *Battle of Naked Men,* ca. 1465. For all the fierceness of these latter, for all their nakedness, they signal nobility, not just "body." If we compare Capa's fallen soldier to the Roman *Dying Gaul* of Pergamon, ca. 240 B.C., the point becomes transparent: Capa's figure hardly seems human to begin with. He was simply an instrument of war, which now had lost its usefulness; the Gaul is first and foremost a human being and only secondarily a soldier. His humanity has not been lost in his warrior role.

An interpersonal dimension always manages to intrude itself in traditional war scenes, the *Battle of Issus* in the House of the Faun at Pompeii, ca. 300 B.C., being an obvious case. Darius' brother receives a spear, presumably thrust by Alexander, meant for Darius. The consciousness of the event that crosses Darius' face, and which is echoed in an oblique way in Alexander's glance, lifts us out of the scene of war, reminding us of the fundamental "transcendent" humanness of the soldiers involved. Such consciousness is never present on the photographed faces of soldiers, in action or at rest in modern wars. They are only aware of the immediacy of the event—are completely absorbed in the action, and seem to have no ties with one another beyond those primitive cooperative relations called for by fighting. The modern war photograph does not fill out the consciousness of the people it depicts, as imaginative art can do.

There are other images that, in quite different ways, circle back to or force us to recall the humanity of the warrior. From Leonardo's *Battle of Anghiari,* ca. 1503-6 (copy by Peter Paul Rubens), and Michelangelo's *Battle of Casina,* 1504 (grisaille copy, 1542), to the various war-related pictures of David—*Oath of the Horatii,* 1784; *Lictors Bringing Back to Brutus the Bodies of His Sons,* 1789; *Battle of the Romans and Sabines, 1799; Leonidas at Thermopylae,* 1810-14— there is an enduring preoccupation with the humanity of the warriors, which is cherished even beyond its allegorical use. Delacroix's *Massacre at Chios,* 1824, and *Liberty Leading the People,* 1830, show this perhaps most tellingly; the insistence on the "human truth" almost breaks down the allegorical/historical narrative mode. Something similar happens in Rodin's *Burghers of Calais,* 1884–86; the dignity of the figures is never shaken by their desperation. Whether dealing with warrior or victim, the imaginative depiction of traditional war never allows the human figure to become mere cannon fodder—never allows war to become merely an "event," subsuming and devouring all who come in contact with it. Their human particularity, and their stature and status as examples of the human condition, are never lost. War is not yet all-consuming, imposing its will on all, brutality marking all it comes in contact with— disfiguring them until they are only a mocking reference to an ideal humanity.

It is perhaps in the image of the leader or warlord that human being and warrior are most fused together. A separate history of such imagery could be written, ranging from the equestrian statue of Marcus Aurelius, A.D. 161–81, through Paolo Uccello's *Sir John Hawkwood,* 1436, Andrea del Castagno's *Pippo Spano,* 1448, Andrea Verrocchio's *Bartolomeo Colleoni,* ca. 1479–88, and Charles Lebrun's *Alexander the Great Entering Babylon,* ca. 1660-68, to David's *Bonaparte on Mount St. Bernard,* 1800. Whatever the differences among such images, there is invariably a mix of majesty and might, personalized as much as publicized. These are images of achieved ego—of integrated, self-reliant, almost self-identified masculinity. However propagandistic and adulatory they may be, they make the point of war as a masculine proving ground, a scene of male self-realization and fulfillment. There is a kind of trickle-down effect that reaches even the lowest soldier, as Urs Graf's *Soldiers on the Road,* 1516, and Hendrik Goltzius' *Standard Bearer,* 1587, make clear. The figures here have the same masculine self-confidence, the same dandyish swagger as their leader. They carry aggression as if it were purely decorative, or rather, its decorative treatment masks their latent power, their casual readiness for action; in this aggressive yet beautified bearing they have a touch of their leader's grandeur and nobility. They have that peculiar haughtiness that is a synthesis of a taken-for-granted dignity and the pursuit of dominance.

For me the key image of total modern war is Goya's *Colossus.* (See also his *Disparate de miedo* [The folly of fear, 1815-24].) Max Klinger's *War,* from his second print cycle, "On Death," 1911, a work in the same allegorical vein as Goya's, is a possible second. War in these works is literally a monster, dominating the scene, filing the picture space—a freak of nature dwarfing human beings. The allegorical figure of war only adds to its psychological horror. The modern world at war is not a place to live; it is literally a place of death—or of living death, the living out of death. The "smallness" of human beings in a time of modern war bespeaks the meaninglessness of human life. This collapse, this nothingness, this sense of the utter irrelevance of humanity is conveyed most unremittingly and decisively in the many works of Bruegel the Elder dealing with total, mass war, especially the *Triumph of Death,* 1562. In the *Suicide of Saul,* 1562, and the quite different *Battle of the Money-Bags and Strong Boxes,* 1567, or *Battle between Carnival and Lent,* 1559, war is presented as a universal condition affecting all realms of human activity. It is an intimate matter—Saul is at war with himself; but his death becomes symbolic of that awaiting all soldiers. War is suicide, Bruegel seems to be saying; its folly is presented without comment, simply as a fact of human life set against an indifferent nature. War, indeed, confirms the triviality of human beings in the cosmic scheme of things. Bosch, in the center panel of *The Temptation of Saint Anthony,* ca. 1500-05, or in the "Hell" panel of *The Garden of Earthly Delights,* ca. 1505, and Albrecht Altdorfer, in *Battle of Issus,* 1529 (violently contrasting with the Hellenistic version), show this same cosmic indifference to the destructiveness of war; and the fatalistic acceptance involved symbolizes pessimism about human nature, a pessimism inseparable from the "human comedy."

The elevation of the victor at the expense of the vanquished in the *Victory Stele of Naram-Sin,* ca. 2300-2200 B.C., diminishes all of humanity, stereotypes it in a fixed position. Similarly, the downtrodden and destroyed in *Ashurnasirpal II at War,* ca. 875 B.C.), become more emblematic of humanity in general than the vigorously masculine king, who has achieved his identity at the expense of everyone else, including his own soldiers. He is unwittingly shown to be the exception rather than the rule of human life; his rule and lordliness paradoxically confirm the debased, enslaved state of humanity at large, which is confirmed by war. He is a perverse common power, signifying lawlessness and injustice—the demeaning of the human rather than its dignifying. He is, paradoxically, war as the common power. Similarly, in Jacques Callot's *Miseries of War,* 1621, no one wins, all are trivialized; it all comes to nothing. The sacrifice of one's enemies, as in the *Palette of Narmer,* ca. 3000 B.C., is a way of asserting one's dominance but of trivializing the state of being human in general; one can become a god through war—or a slave, as Heraclitus tells us (Fragment 53), neither of which are human states. War shows us that man's efforts at mastery come to nothing, for he cannot even master himself. He thinks he does so by mastering other men in war, but this coming into his own robs him of his larger humanity. He in effect falls out of sympathy with himself to become powerful.

The contrast between Goya's "Disasters of War," ca. 1814, and Georges Rouault's *Miserere,* 1917-27—both series of war prints—forcefully brings home the difference between the traditional and modern approaches to war. We are out of sympathy with the Rouault works today; they seem sentimental and bombastic. This is because they make the human factor, the human losses in war, excruciatingly plain. But the Goya works attract us because of their explicit, dramatic rendering of the annihilation of the human, showing to us our expectation of total inhumanity as natural to war. Rouault reminds us of our helplessness in the face of war, but implies the possibility of consolation for it; this is doubly disturbing, for it reminds us not only of our abjectness in the situation of war, but of the disappearance of any consoling common power in modern times. The Goya works, on the other hand, ruthlessly offer us nothing—and that we can accept, because we know that is our lot. Not only, as Hobbes says, is there neither justice nor law in a state of total war, but there is no faith, hope, or charity, since they too must be validated by a binding community, a society that holds together, whose members trust one another, as they never can in modern war. Goya shows us the falseness of solidarity in a society of masses, whether of victims in a mass grave or of soldiers in an anonymous army. Rouault shows us the heroism of suffering, of the victim; for Goya suffering, despite its physical concreteness, is quite abstract, for it neither redeems the sufferer nor forgives his victimizer.

Abstraction protects through its dehumanization, and at the same time gives voice to a larger impersonality; it gives the distance necessary to deal with the inescapable. It is modern in its dismissal of the human. It is a form of mithridatism; one consumes bits of it to avoid being consumed by the larger abstractness of our condition, to avoid overdosing on nihilism. When one looks at Modernist military images one sees them as displaying with no comment the abstract, "disinterested," disintegrative character of modern war. It speaks through the fragmented character of the picture; indeed, it can be argued that the Modern fragmentation of image bespeaks the disintegrative effect of the current endless state of war.

Otto Dix created some of the most unrelenting images of modern war I know of, holding their own with—and perhaps even greater than—those of Goya. He showed the stupendous, unassimilable nothingness of it all; death in his art has no magic face, but is all-consuming. This is a death with no resurrection, not even the hint of a promise of resurrection. And with it Dix announces, as does George Grosz, the hypocrisy and fradulence of our society, its total bankruptcy. His realism is a slashing, fearless indictment of the idealism our society pretends to. Dix's realistic apocalypse is unending; the decay of the bodies he depicts announces the decadence of our society as a whole. His images have the consummate holism of Leonardo's images of the deluge, and as with Goya, the technique of his prints embodies the violence they depict. War here is absence incarnate, desire abolished; aggression, for Freud the central problem of civilization, shows itself in war as desire inside out, desire determined to abolish itself.

The best Modernist war imagery, such as Gino Severini's *Armored Train,* 1915, and Max Ernst's *The Elephant Celebes,* 1921—the "beastly" war machine—utilize the insidiousness of abstractness to show us our entrapment by war. The Germans tend to be hectically obvious and insulting in their war imagery, as in Kollwitz's *Sharpening the Scythe,* 1905, from her series of prints on the Peasant's War, and in such works by Grosz as *Fit for Active Service,* 1916-

17, and *Civil War,* 1928 (not to speak of Rudolf Schlichter's use of a dummy of a German officer at the first international Dada exhibition, in 1920). This holds true even for Ernst Barlach's *War Monument* of 1927 in Güstrow Cathedral, supposedly showing a dying soul about to awaken to eternal life, as well as for his various warrior figures. The religiosity of these figures enhances—almost seems to engender—their sense of raw, rank power. The French, on the other hand, as in Roger de la Fresnaye's *Cuirassier,* 1910, and *Artillery,* 1911–12, and Jacques Villon's *Marching Soldiers,* 1913, tend to treat power decoratively; war is something to be dissipated, softened through decorative styling. One thinks of these artists as creating new coiffures out of old hair. The Italian Futurists, for all the bravado of Filippo Tommaso Marinetti's remarks—"we wish to exalt the aggressive movement," "no masterpiece without the stamp of aggressiveness," "we will glorify war—the only true hygiene of the world—militarism, patriotism, the destructive gesture of the anarchist"[28]—produced surprisingly few images dealing directly with war. And those, like Severini's *War,* 1915, and Umberto Boccioni's *Charge of Lancers,* 1915, seem—like Franz Marc's *Forms in Combat,* 1914, and Wassily Kandinsky's *Improvisation No. 30 (On a Warlike Theme),* 1913—to be more interested in an abstract dynamic than in concrete destructiveness. Unexpectedly, Marsden Hartley's emblematic *Portrait of a German Officer,* 1914, comes close to communicating that abstracted state of collective madness that modern war involves; but he, too, goes the way of all Modernism (at least in these World War I works), namely, toward dynamic geometricism. This demonstrates Barnett Newman's point that "the art of World War I" is based on "principles of geometry." His intention was to create "an art of no-geometry" as "a new beginning;" freeing himself from the "geometric trap," which he saw as a "death image," he was unconsciously freeing himself from the horrors of modern war.[29] What is interesting about his argument is its attention to geometric abstraction as death-predicated, and therefore indirectly as conveying modern war's mood of absolute, undialectical negativity.

American images of modern war may be naively celebratory, as are George Bellows' *Dawn of Peace* and George Luks' *Blue Devils Marching Down Fifth Avenue,* both 1916, or condemnatory, as is Bellows' series of 12 lithographs of "Huns," 1916. Otherwise they tend to be hysterically moralistic, as is David Smith's *Medal for Dishonor—War Exempt Sons of the Rich,* 1939-40. Both approaches are beside the point of either traditional or modern war. There is almost a tradition of lack of visual understanding of war in American art, reaching a kind of simplistic climax in Roy Lichtenstein's war pictures and in Claes Oldenburg's rocketlike *Lipstick on Caterpillar Tracks,* 1969. Both involve populist hyperbole masking moralistic condemnation—poking fun in order to both defang the snake of war and crush it underfoot. War is at once another deadly game and an empty threat by reason of the implicit invincibility of American might. Of course, Oldenburg is also showing the political significance of ordinary commodities, and the way they surrealistically connote military hardware. He creates a kind of twilight zone of amorality, in which immoral reality is evasively revealed. Lichtenstein and Oldenburg are really mocking a way of "interpreting" war, and self righteously warning against it in the process; but the warnings of both are ineffective, since neither really understands the nihilism of modern war. A kind of American inexperience of war, or refusal of that experience, is implicit in both.

And yet America experienced what has been regarded as the first modern war—the Civil War. Well-documented in photographs which reveal the radical nihilism of modern war, the Civil War prepares the way for the First World War, for some the true beginning of the modern mentality. The photographs that continue to document it all make, in their different ways, the same point: that there is no point to life. Modern war, which we think of as highly political, as fought for a radical cause, is really a metaphysical acknowedgment of the inevitable. It is the positivistic, mechanistic approach to life in action. Next to the devastating "empirical" photographs of modern war the imaginative treatment of it seems quaint and antiquated. It may have reached an inadvertent climax in the Douanier Rousseau's allegorical depiction of *War,* 1894; but then again, such works as Giorgio de Chirico's *The Philosopher's Conquest,* 1914, and René Magritte's *On the Threshold of Liberty,* 1930, with their cannons, and Max Ernst's *Europe After the Rain,* 1940-42, still tell us more about the insidious human effect of modern war than Duane Hanson's *Vietnam Scene,* 1969, with its television obviousness and casual carnage. For Hanson's figures lost their humanity before they put on uniform; they never had it to begin with. De Chirico, Magritte, and Ernst mourn for a humanity that is passing away into a machine, that is becoming a weapon against nature, a crime against nature. They remind us that war is a radical refusal to be in the world.

Notes

1.   Franco Fornari, *The Psychoanalysis of War,* Garden City, N.Y.: Anchor Press/Doubleday, 1974, p. 24.

2.   *The Great Themes by the Editors of Time-Life Books,* New York: Time-Life Books, 1970; Life Library of Photography, "War," pp. 207-40.

3.   Kathleen Freeman, *Companion to the Pre-Socratic Philosophers,* Oxford: Basil Blackwell, 1959, pp. 114-15.

4.   Paul Fussell, *The Great War and Modern Memory,* New York: Oxford University Press, 1977; paperback edition, p. ix. Fussell's book is a brilliant analysis of the literary treatment of World War I.

5.   Sigmund Freud, "The Resistances to Psychoanalysis" (1925), in *Character and Culture,* ed. Philip Rieff, New York: Collier Books, 1963, pp. 259-60. For Freud's "Reflections upon War and Death" (1915) and his famous essay "Why War?" (1932), see pp. 107-47.

6.   Thomas Hobbes, *Leviathan,* in *The English Philsophers from Bacon to Mill,* New York: Modern Library, 1939, pp. 161-62.

7.   Arnold J. Toynbee, *A Study of History,* vol. IV, New York: Oxford University Press, 1939, p. 151.

8.   Fussell, *The Great War and Modern Memory,* p. 74.

9.   Clement Greenberg, "The Art of Delacroix," *Nation,* 159 (Nov. 18, 1944): 617.

10. Sigmund Freud, *Group [Mass] Psychology and the Analysis of the Ego,* New York: 1961, pp. 45-46. Freud writes: "A hint to the same effect, that the essence of a group lies in the libidinal ties existing in it, is also to be found in the phenomenon of panic, which is best studied in military groups. A panic arises if a group of that kind becomes disintegrated. Its characteristics are that none of the orders given by superiors are any longer listened to, and that each individual is only solicitous on his own account, and without any consideration for the rest. The mutual ties have ceased to exist, and a gigantic and senseless dread *(Angst)* is set free. . . . The very question that needs explanation is why the dread has become so gigantic. The greatness of the danger cannot be responsible, for the same army which now falls a victim to panic may previously have faced equally great or greater danger with complete success; and it is of the very essence of panic that it bears no relation to the danger that threatens, and often breaks out upon the most trivial occasions. . . ."

11. Clement Greenberg, "Frontiers of Criticism," *Partisan Review* 13 (Spring 1946): 255. Review of *Les Sandales d'Empédocle* by Claude-Edmonde Magny.

12. Clarence Joseph Bulliet, *Apples and Madonnas, Emotional Expression in Art,* New York: Covici, Friede, Inc., 1930; 3rd edition, p. 3.

13. Clement Greenberg, "Art" (Adolph Gottlieb), *Nation,* 165 (Dec. 6, 1947):629.

14. This is, paradoxically, connected to an idea that art no longer wants—the avant-garde attempt to negate art through art. See Theodor W. Adorno, "Die Kunst und die Künste," *Ohne Leitbild; Parva Aesthetica,* Frankfurt am Main: Suhrkamp Verlag, 1967, p. 171.

15. Clement Greenberg, "The School of Paris: 1946," *Art and Culture* (Boston, Beacon Press, 1965; paperback edition), p. 120.

16. Quoted by Fussell, p. 187.

17. Toynbee, *A Study of History,* vol. IV, pp. 150, 151. See also Toynbee's brilliant account of "The Suicidalness of Militarism," pp. 465ff., especialy the section on "The Strong Man Armed," and also the "Annex" on "Militarism and The Military Virtues," pp. 640ff. Discussing "the blindness of the militarist," Toynbee notes his determination to prove, by keeping "the old barbaric dispensation," "that the sword is omnipotent." Toynbee, incidentally, regards the palette of Narmer, with its "royal conqueror" "swollen to a superhuman stature" and trampling "upon a fallen adversary" as articulating, in its gruesomeness, "the whole tragedy of Militarism" (p. 503).

18. Toynbee, pp. 153-54.

19. Toynbee, p. 154.

20. Quoted by Fussell, pp. 203-4.

21. Charles Baudelaire, "The Salon of 1859," *The Mirror of Art,* Garden City, N.Y.: Doubleday Anchor Books, 1956, pp. 234-35.

22. A brilliant, thorough examination of these two major types of war imagery is Siegmar Holsten, *Allegorische Darstellungen des Krieges 1870-1918,* Munich: Prestel Verlag, 1976.

23. It is worth noting that the only vote against American participation in World War I was cast by Jeannette Rankin (1883-1973). Rankin stated, "I felt at the time that the first woman [in Congress] should take the first stand, that the first time the first woman had a chance to say *no* to war, she should say it."

24. Fornari, p. 7, 12, and 13. Fornari remarks: "In other words war—while it makes men relive the primary psychic situations pertaining to the primary love and guilt needs in relation to their object of love and identification, threatened by destruction—betrays the love and guilt needs, elaborating them in the paranoid way." (p. 37.)

25. Gaston Bouthoul, *Les Guerres: Eléments de Polémologie,* Paris, 1951. Discussed by Fornari, pp. 7-21.

26. See Fussell's chapter on "Soldier Boys," pp. 270-309.

27. Carla Gottlieb, "An Emblematic Source for Velazquez' 'Surrender of Breda,'" *Gazette des Beaux-Arts,* 6th series, 64 (March 1966): 181-86. Gottlieb also regards Bernard Salomon's print of the same scene as a possible source for the Velazquez.

28. F.T. Marinetti, "The Foundation and Manifesto of Futurism" (1908), in *Theories of Modern Art,* ed. Herschel B. Chipp, Berkeley: University of California Press, 1968, p. 286.

29. Barnett Newman, "Statement," *The New American Painting,* New York Museum of Modern Art, 1959; exhibition catalogue, p. 60. Can it be that Modernist purity is an attempt to awaken from the nightmare of modern war? On May 15, 1919, writing in his notebook, László Moholy-Nagy observed: "During the war, but more strongly even now, I feel my responsibility toward society. My conscience asks incessantly: is it right to become a painter in times of social revolution? May I claim for myself the privilege of art when all men are needed to solve the problems of sheer survival?" He went on to note that "art and reality have had nothing in common during the last hundred years. The personal satisfaction of creating art has added nothing to the happiness of the masses." He did not see this as a proof of art's autonomy, but rather fell back on the old idea of the godlike artist as his justification for making art: "I can give life as a painter." His obsession with "light, color, form," especially with "Light, total Light," which "creates the total man" was clearly a reaction against the war-caused death he saw in his world. The question, of course is whether he was only sustaining his own life through his art or giving life to others. This paradigm was repeated in many of the early Modernists.

28

Betraying the Feminist Intention: The Case Against Feminist Decorative Art

There is a sentence in Max Horkheimer and Theodore W. Adorno's *Dialectic of Enlightenment* which seems to me to summarize the position of critical thought in any area: "If thought willingly emerges from its critical element to become a mere means at the disposal of an existing order, then despite itself it tends to convert the positive it elected to defend into something negative and destructive," i.e., into the authoritarian. To the extent that feminist thought willingly emerges from its critical element—the element which makes it, in the words of Horkheimer and Adorno, a "residue of freedom" and "tendency toward true humanism"—and attempts to bring a feminist order into positive existence—an order which is meant to confine all feminists as well as non-feminists—it betrays its own feminism. Such feminist thought replaces the critique of the existing order with idealism weighted with authoritarian overtones—an idealism which is meant to be a solution to all realistic problems, whether originating within feminism or within the existing masculine order. Such thought dispenses with the catalytic, revolutionary element within feminism—the critical element is the cutting edge of all revolutionary intention—to inaugurate a new tyranny. Feminist decorative art, more particularly but not exclusively pattern painting, is an example of feminist thought which has willingly emerged from its critical element, and as such signals the dawn of an era of authoritarian feminism, i.e., a feminism which means to entrench itself, to become as "corporate" and establishment as the masculine ideology it presumably means to overthrow. Wittingly or unwittingly, such authoritarian feminism strongly echoes the existing repressive order: however much it means to recast that order in feminist rather than masculinist terms, it also means to be as repressive—brutally dominant—as that order. Authoritarian feminism, of which feminist decorative art seems less the spearhead than the unfurled flag, bespeaks the mentality of the old regime while claiming to "realize," if only in an emblematic, utopian way, the new one. (It is well known that utopianism, after its initial critical impulse, degenerates into a messianic authoritarianism which means to impose itself as an absolute rather than offer itself as an alternative: it converts its critical ideas into absolute—totalizing—goals.)

What I am talking about is an art which calls itself feminist but is not, or, if it is feminist, can be said to have stood the feminist intention on its head, so that it is no longer the means of a new revelation of the life-world but an instrument foreclosing, seemingly deliberately, all fresh perception of it. Such presumptive and preemptive feminism does not arise simply from a misapprehension of the feminist intention: it is not an unwitting misstep or misreading of the cutting critical edge that is the vital determining factor in feminism. Rather, authoritarian feminist art arises from a willful exercise of power—an attempt to achieve dominance, or at least prominence, in the art work even if this means giving up the critical feminist attitude to the life-world. This is shown by the fact that authoritarian feminist art—feminist decorative art—originates in a compromise with those forces (essentially modernist) in modern art that stand for everything that the feminist intention in its critical prime rejects. For what the feminist intention as it operates in art urges is the ideological character of all art. The feminist intention in art is the most vital current expression of the general position which draws all art into the fray—which insists that no art can remain detached, neutral, non-interventionist, if it is to have any durability and vitality. From this viewpoint, all art is in dialogue with the life-world, however much this dialectic is at times hidden and subtle. This dialectic nourishes the art and determines its significance as well as its sense of significance.

Feminist decorative art, especially painting which relies on overt pattern—a preexisting order—as its major means of expression, means to be at once modernist and ideological. It is simultaneously purist—an articulation of material form for its own sake—and the self-styled product par excellence of feminine sensibility. Such self-contradictoriness gives pattern painting a superficial vitality, for it seems to echo the central conflict—equivocation—of modern art. This can be characterized as a tension between opposing tendencies. On the one hand there is the tendency towards an absolute abstraction which degenerates into a demonstration of pure means. On the other hand there is the tendency toward an art which, whether abstract or representational, critically resists the life-world in the very act of codifying it, thereby functioning as a kind of commentary on it—the loyal opposition to it. Such art, in the process of articulating the life-world, creates doubt about it. In contrast, transcendental abstraction ignores the reality of the life-world—or thinks it does—to achieve a larger ("cosmic") consciousness of a greater reality (the universal). However, its metaphysical pretensions come to seem belied by its all too physical character—the obviously fussy care with which it particularizes itself.

Feminist decorative art wants the best of both worlds of modern art. It claims to bespeak transcendental femininity, i.e., to articulate abstractly feminine spirit or sensibility as an indisputable absolute, given forthrightly in a cosmic artistic consciousness. It also claims to resist concretely the male-determined life-world which is indifferent to, or distorts for its own ends, this sublime and vital feminine spirit. Feminist decorative art means to intervene in the masculine world with pure femininity. However this might be denied, it is reflected in the tender loving care with which the medium is treated, in an effort to derive graceful, lyrical effects from it, as though such effects existed to set an example for the masculine world. Thus, feminist decorative art seems utopian in the best sense of the term. It does not mean to project, with naive optimism, a femininity that would be the cornerstone of a brave, new world. Rather, it assumes that consciousness of things feminine gives the masculine life-world a fresh topicality—makes it seem, under the pressure of the feminist alternative, to alternate or change.

This is theoretically well and good, but in practice feminist decorative art does not live up to its pretensions. For one thing, it is more easily read as a technical exercise than as a symbolic form of transcendental femininity: its use of the pattern makes its abstraction seem predestined, and as such undermines whatever aspirational aspect one might be tempted to read into it. Apart from that, sensibility always seems "transcendental," if not feminine, in the isolation to which modernist method banishes it in the effort to purify it—as if to imply that the only significant meaning art had was in its effect on sensibility. For another thing, the critical dimension of feminist decorative art seems to be non-existent. There is no critical point to the pattern: its revelation will not create any alternatives, for its alienation is passive rather than active. The pattern's unity does nothing to interfere with the world's variety, but seems to exist as a kind of static ornament within that variety—the lushness of the stasis of many of the patterns seems to imply this. On the whole, pattern painting's claim to be exemplarily feminist while having no clear critical dimension seems part of that general inflation of claims by which women who make art exploit what is topical by gratuitously declaring themselves to be "feminist," which makes the term arbitrary if not meaningless.

The most crucial reason that feminist decorative art's attempted synthesis of feminism and modernism is not convincing is that it represents a false consciousness, in particular, a false aestheticist consciousness. For what feminist decorative art means to do is to assimilate or subsume—and so neutralize—the aggressive feminist critical intention in a masculinist constructivist intention, with its self-righteous heroism. It is as if all criticality had to be made constructive rather than de-constructive (which is not the same as destructive), positive rather than negative, synthesizing rather than analytic in purpose. Pattern painting is self-righteous: it means to construct an exemplary pattern to which all must emotionally submit, as if hypnotized by the pattern. It means, like much constructivism—and pattern painting is a limp, remote reminder (the dregs) of the constructivist intention—to sweep us off our feet by its heroic implications, by its visionary promise. The pattern means to possess us to the point where we lose—never even generate—self-consciousness and general critical awareness: the generality of the pattern preempts all power of analytic generalization. Thus, the aesthetically elucidated pattern functions not simply with authority, but as an authoritarian repression of reflective thought. It is the positive declaration which means to preclude the negative thought, and as such it becomes thoroughly positivist, i.e., the dominating fact of art, and by implication, of life. This positivist dominance is confirmed by the fact that the pattern in feminist decorative art is always transparent, whatever its complexity of detail, even when that complexity is designed to mislead us about the easy unity of the basic pattern, as if to make that unity a more difficult achievement than it is. The complexity of detail is not the generative matrix of the pattern, but the ornamental elucidation of it, bejeweling it into a more attractive self-evidence than it might have unadorned—making it a "rich experience" rather than a bare shape. Also, the convenient reproducibility of the pattern, extending it in time as well as space, furthers its universality, making the obvious pretentious. All of this works to foster submission to a seemingly pure, yet rapturous and rhapsodic, construction. In general, uncritical submission is the secret message behind the heroic facade of constructivist art: one submits to the brave, new artistic world in preparation for submission to the brave, new real world. Metaphoric commitment quickly reinterprets itself as metaphoric submission in the context of an absolute order. Thus, the order of utopia and the order of style converge—both ruthlessly order life and art. Under the pressure of the intention to construct a pure, absolute order and in the resonant presence of this order, one foregoes all criticality—so trusting is one of any kind of pure intention, any kind of pure construction—and submits.

The sense of eternally existing order feminist decorative art conveys is incommensurate and irreconcilable with the critical mentality which freely questions any order, including an eternally given one. Even if one assumes that the critical dimension of the pattern exists in its power to connote feminine sensibility one must recognize that feminine sensibility itself is not a critical concept, and so is not feminist in import. Much as the pattern is given simply in the mode of what Whitehead calls "presentational immediacy," so the idea of feminine sensibility is naively assumed to be immediately given. Both pattern and idea offer themselves as ideal and finished things, easy constructions that articulate a self-evident absolute. Yet much as the idea of a pattern makes sense only in terms of the tensions it resolves, so the idea of feminine sensibility exists only in dialectical relationship with the idea of masculine sensibility. Without that dialectical relationship, there is neither the presence of the feminine nor of the masculine, but only the "intuitive" recognition of an order or pattern metaphysically regarded as feminine or masculine. But such intuition is inevitably an illusion: it is based on preconceptions, the sedimentations of obscured traditions of thought, thrown together into naive prejudices. In general, the trouble with the ideal of feminine sensibility—particularly as it is used by feminist decorative artists—is that it is a metaphysical rather than dialectical concept, and as such is hypostasized and hollow. In pattern painting the idea of the feminine rings hollow, for it is superimposed on the hypostasized pattern. Much as the pattern lacks dialectical tension to give it substance, so the idea of the feminine—as used in feminist decorative art—lacks the dialectical tension with the idea of the masculine necessary to give it a cutting edge.

Pattern painting, like all self-styled transcendental abstraction, quickly loses its transcendental look not only when the narrow modernist basis for this look is recognized, but when its mental function is acknowledged. The visionary, sublime look—the wiped clean, fresh start look, based on the absence of discernible, let alone comprehensible life-world meanings—is mentally necessary as well as the ornamental effect of modernism, and it is this mental necessity that feminist decorative art, perhaps more than any other modernist art, exploits. For the look of the absolute is the result of the natural tendency to read meaning into even the most meaningless material—a meaning which evaporates once the mechanism of its production is understood, but which never fully vanishes (however unconvincing it remains), and as such makes the world inhabitable, at least by consciousness. Transcendental sensibility, of which feminine sensibility is a derivative, is a transcendental illusion on the order of the illusion of the transcendental look—the look of the absolute. Transcendental sensibility articulates the narcissistic premise on which modernism is based, the transcendental look articulates the narcissistic premise on which consciousness is based, and feminine sensibility articulates the narcissistic premise on which authoritarian feminism is based. Feminist modernism, meaning to bespeak feminine sensibility, renders it as authoritarian as all narcissistic concepts are: this authoritarianism is exemplified in the rigid absolute pattern. Such rigidity suggests that feminist decorative art—feminist modernism—makes a mockery of the narcissism inherent in modernism in the process of carrying it to an extreme. Where in modernism (and consciousness in general) the narcissism is authentic because it is premised on self-criticism, in feminist modernism it is inauthentic because it is reified in a deliberately fixed—uncritically presented—pattern. There is no self-critical energy in the feminist decorative pattern, only the primitive unity of an empty gestalt. Feminist decorative art's pursuit of the sensation of essential if inert unity for its own sake makes it a species of what Clement Greenberg has called luxury painting. As such, it is very topical; luxury painting abounds. Luxury painting, as Greenberg defines it, involves the cultivation of a particular sensation for its own sake in an attempt not only to possess the sensation through the handling of its medium, but to cling to both to counteract the inability to face new life-world meanings that might inform art. Greenberg thought that luxury painting followed as the decadent if not entirely fallow aftermath of a particularly inventive period—he spoke of French luxury painting in the 1920s. It may be that feminist decorative art is also part of a decadent if fertile aftermath. In any case, the moment we recognize the luxurious character of feminist decorative art, we acknowledge its lack of success as an ideological, political expression of feminism

Yet it is a highly political art. For while feminist modernism has relinquished the critical purpose of de-totalizing the masculinist world—showing that such a world is not the whole story of the life-world—it means to totalize, to take complete possession of, the world of feminist art. Feminist modernism lays claim to an exclusive understanding of feminist intention, asserting that it is more feminist than any other feminist art and in general usurping, if not outrightly falsifying, the history of feminist art. (It is essential to distinguish between feminist art and women's art. The former is the avant-garde cutting edge of the latter, which includes all women making art, whether or not with a feminist intention—critical element—in it.) The implicit purpose of the pattern painters is to insist that they epitomize feminist intention, since they alone cogently reveal feminine sensibility. Yet, as indicated, feminine sensibility is in the last analysis an absurd concept, and any art that seeks its fortune in the revelation of such sensibility is misguided as well as uncritical. Indeed, to insist on the existence of feminine sensibility—one of the true triumphs of critical feminism is the reduction of this concept to antiquarian status—is to be reactionary.

The moment the reactionary character of the idea of feminine sensibility is recognized, one can begin to perceive its political usage. Feminine sensibility means to articulate all that is positive about being a woman—means to show that even what masculine sensibility finds negative about women is positive. This attitude means to posit a new order of womanhood, which claims as much positive authority as the old order of manhood: feminine sensibility means to assert an absolute, ideal womanliness on the order of absolute, ideal manliness. Such a brand of feminism becomes as authoritarian as traditional male machismo. In general, authoritarian feminism lays down the pattern of the eternal feminine—feminist modernism gives it a militant facelift.

Authoritarian feminism is aimed not only at authoritarian masculinism—a superweapon to match a superweapon—but at critical feminism. Authoritarian feminism in fact signals a split in the feminist camp. As the old critical, revolutionary intention seems to flag (yet it is still intact and vigorous in Nancy Spero's art), a new reactionary intention arises—perhaps expressive of the vanity of a successful movement (of a movement which expresses vanity to give itself the look of success)—with a vigor of its own (apparent in the belabored aestheticism of Miriam Schapiro and Joyce Kozloff). It is as if all the energy that once went into psychosocial criticality (witness Miriam Schapiro's *Woman House*) now goes into aesthetic transcendence, or rather, a facile version of it. The aesthetic has usurped, rather than combined with, the critical. The pretension of timelessness conveyed by the use of timeless patterns has robbed this feminism of all timeliness and topicality. This is perhaps most evident in Judy Chicago's *Dinner Pary,* where a seemingly timely setting—the sense of a table set and awaiting the arrival of guests—is reduced to a timeless pattern. Chicago's piece has the timeless look of a ghost ship. The meal about to be served is still hot, if rapidly cooling, and all hands are gone to an unknown destiny, never to appear again. As in all feminist decorative art, the only destiny in Chicago's work is in the pattern—the eternal form axiomatically given. Chicago means the female figures she evokes to be as axiomatically given—which they may be, but not because they fit into her pattern; rather, because of their critical achievements, which Chicago signals only mechanically.

Whatever the outcome of the conflict or polarization in feminist art, its existence indicates that the feminine task is profoundly unfinished. Only the critical feminists recognize this, and act on it. The authoritarian feminists are more concerned with their place in history—especially art history—than with making history. A paradox is evident here: an art which conceives of itself as an exclamation mark punctuating an important historical consciousness becomes merely decorative, while an art which is more concerned with world than art history makes its mark on both. The art which regards itself as directly influential becomes inconsequential; the art which regards itself as simply reflective of events helps change them. This is the irony that emerges from a contrast of authoritarian and critical feminism.

There is another irony: feminist modernism, which comes down decisively on the side of formalism, does not revitalize it, does not participate in what I have called Existential Formalism. There is no understanding of the self-criticality innate to formalism—the authoritarianism of feminist modernism or formalism precludes such understanding. In fact, art historically speaking, feminist formalism as evident in pattern painting is an overdetermination or exaggeration of formalism, reducing it to a familiar code, a clear and simple device—the pattern, uncritically used. However intense the pattern eventually becomes in feminist formalism, it remains the simplest instrument for the "creation"—most facile, naive articulation—of form. Indeed, to conceive of the pattern as conveying the essence of form is to completely misread form, implying an almost kitsch comprehension of it. It is reduced to something all too easily received rather than conceived and achieved with difficulty. In fact, form read as pattern is less conceived than preconceived. Thus, even art historically, pattern painting cannot be fully respected, particularly in view of the great formalist achievements of the last decades. Pattern painting reveals itself to be a minor, reactionary, decadent art, conservative by both art historical and critical feminist measures.

One should note that a conservative dimension was evident in feminist art from its start, only then it could be read as progressive. The first patterns appear in the so-called central or vaginal imagery of Miriam Schapiro and Judy Chicago and in the phallic imagery of Judith Bernstein. At the time of their first appearance, these strong, upfront—blatant—patterns seemed to function like the clenched fist of a rebellious military salute, i.e., as the aggressive visual slogan of a militant movement. Whether vaginal or phallic, the centrality and grand simplicity and directness of the image made it the monumental emblem of a proposed new mastery, a marching banner rallying the ranks, issuing military orders in a commanding way. Such imagery was emphatic about the new feminist sense of determination and self-determination. Its idealistic abstraction (even in Bernstein's case) perfectly suited feminism's sense of new expectation, new potentiality, new energy, and new clarity of purpose.

Now, retrospectively, the central image seems to have a different meaning. It seems to be an insignia on the order of a swastika-pattern. Swastika, vagina, and phallus are age-old symbols with a universal meaning that can be appropriated by a particular cause. Such appropriation is in and of itself phallic. In *Neurotic Styles,* David Shapiro writes, "The phase that can be described psychosexually as 'phallic' . . . may be generally described as characterized by the dominance of the intrusive mode, resulting in the establishment of an attitude of initiative." The initiative the intrusive—visually and psychically—central image represents, with its seemingly archetypal immanence in consciousness giving it a grand power of evocation, shows itself to be double-edged. For now one realizes that it signaled not only feminist initiative—critical intrusiveness—but a timeless pattern functioning metaphorically as a model self (the eternal feminine self in typical symbolic form).

For some feminists the formal authority of this timeless pattern comes to mean more than the radical initiative the critical use of feminist concepts instills. Formal authority repressed radical criticality, initiative gave way to the grand composure of the pattern. A new image of dominance emerged, based on a traditional sense of feminity—that was now to be dominant where it was once submissive, that was now to signal power where it had once signaled weakness. The pattern's reassuring hermetic completeness, emblematic of a closed system of femininity, made it seem an anchor in a sea of change, stable ground stopping the long fall critical feminism had initiated. The pattern gave a clear location in the midst of the bewildering dislocation inaugurated by feminist criticism—and all enlightened criticism dislocates, unbalances, reveals asymmetries and incoherences within superficially coherent orders. The pattern became the new *terra firma*—but in fact it offered a premature security, for the change initiated by radical feminism is not yet complete. The revolution is still in progress, and will not be done until it has thoroughly shaken up and dislocated every aspect of society. Because of the incompleteness of the feminist revolution, the feminist pattern becomes suggestive of an authoritarian leadership ambition. The collectivity the pattern implies seems forced—a mold rather than a freely developing form. The pattern's seeming self-sufficiency seems premised on an indifference to the complex needs of its constituents. The pattern, then, functions dogmatically and pompously, and seems a kind of convenient visual label masking a complex situation. The choice feminism currently faces is clear: either to win social acceptance through the cosmetic composure of the pattern, or to continue to risk subliminal social rejection in the name of continued critical relationship to the existing order. The pattern echoes the existing order's self-certainty, whereas the criticality that goes against society's grain reflects its uncertainty. Feminism's choice is between the pattern, new emblem of an old feminine conformity, or the risk of critical nonconformity and the dislocation of authentic autonomy.

29

Art in an Age of Mass Mediation

Democracy has ever been the form of decline in organizing power.
—Friedrich Nietzsche, *Twilight of the Idols*

How do we get to see and really experience art? It is certainly not by going to galleries and museums, in search of a direct relationship with original works. This is confirmatory, after the fact of the art we have known and come to love, a vindication and verification of it—the assurance that it exists, in however attenuated, objective form, i.e., as a specific, one might say terminal, object. To really see and experience art we look for it in its mass media image. We open an art publication, we look for a report of its existence, an account of its range of effect, its ability to refer beyond itself while remaining itself—this is its strength, its substantiveness. This seemingly secondary, derivative, imperceptibly yet undeniably "subjective" source, is in fact the primary source of the work of art. Indeed, it is only in its media filtered form that the work has any facticity, it is only by having its singularity passed through the mass media—in a rather undialectical or only naively dialectical way—that it acquires the aura of individuality, the tone of ultra-unique, hyper-individual inner life. Only publicized in the mass media does it seem to have a secret. Only when its finiteness is expanded by the infinity the mass media utopianly promises does it have a meaningful existence. Only when it has been infinitely extended by mass display, charged by the consciousness of a multitude, is it truly powerful, a reservoir of energy that can resist the entropy of its own objectivity, the degeneration brought on it by its own matter-of-fact givenness.

In the mass media, whether in the form of a text or an image, we see a reproduction of an original work of art, a mimetic rendering of its being subject to all the vicissitudes—particularly that of irony—of such a rendering. But this reproduction becomes the original in our consciousness, arouses in us all the frenzy and obsession of the engaged will, all the argumentative, loving energy of commitment. The really original work is all too neutral in its originality, all too uncritically given in its uniqueness. When its identity is made to hinge on its unique originality, it becomes an all too narrow, confining self-identity. Only the work of art that comes to us as the "emanation" of a mass media context sparks us into true wakefulness of its possible identity and the possibilities of our own. Only the mass mediated work of art, the work of art fattening into significance on the culture media of mass distribution, is truly disinterested, having the aesthetic value, almost erotic allure, of truly transcendental or ideal reality. In sum, the work is truly an aesthetic text when it comes to us in a mass media context. Its organic nature—our recognition of its creatureliness—is evident only when we see it as an occurrence within a mass media environment, which not only nourishes its growth, but makes it catalytic in the growth of other creatures.

We go to see the originally original work of art to free ourselves from the force of its flow into the world, to disengage ourselves from its context—to achieve an unpressured relationship to its reality, i.e., a mythical relationship to its immediacy. This relief we mistakenly call contemplation, which we assume leads us to the true transcendence of the work. But its true transcendence is its mass distribution, its essence is its mass identity. The originally original work of art is the residue of the mass distribution context, more precisely, its uniqueness is the dregs of that context, a kind of bland precipitate crystallized out of its dense solution. We store it in a museum, where it is on view like a corpse in a funeral parlor, as if to bring it into another realm of being, or rather as if we take it to signal the possibility of that realm, i.e., to promise us release from bondage to our own realm of being, finally from our own troublesome coming into being. In the museum we can never imagine that the work has its own becoming, which is why, momentarily, we can imagine it as redemptive. In the mass media we can never forget its becoming, the expansion of its identity as it is publicly appropriated. The work of art's dignity in its museum paradise seems trivial, a kind of negative definition of it, compared to its positively heroic character as a mass media celebrity. We finally come to prefer to see it as mass media produced, not simply reproduced, for we realize that its entire power of displacement, its whole effect on us, depends on the politics of its display. It is by taking its chances in the politics of display that it truly becomes a creative risk—critically forceful, socially effective, i.e., acquires a "moral" dimension (or perhaps only flavor) beyond its materiality and formality. We value the work of art only insofar as, through its mass distribution, it runs for office, makes an appearance in a campaign, submerges all its interests in its self-interest. Its desire to be "elect," to hold "office" (be official)—to legitimate its self-interest by its performance before the masses (whose imagined unity integrates the work in its own eyes)— frames and gives coherence to the issues of style and communication with which it is ostensibly occupied, and which superficially give it individuality and meaning. But in fact it finds its identity—its "authentic" style, its power of communication—through the politics of mass mediation. This not only determines its property value but its critical recognition. Indeed, its production through its distribution in the mass media is its critical recognition. The real critical feat of art is that it circulates through society—that it stays in the swim of society, whose currents not only give it its momentum but create that final magical effect which is finally what art is all about, viz., make it seem to live beyond its means, to have more means at its disposal than appears possible, make it seem to have a surplus of possibility that makes it seem actual and useful, and truly art. The magic of art is that it seems to be able to survive—to come into being—on next to nothing, a little flourish or flair of being, a little excess which is never used up. It is mass mediation that creates that magic—that is the art behind art, the real source of art's coming into being, the history behind its history.

This article is about the effect on art of mass mediation, an effect until relatively recently unconscious and now perhaps too obvious a fact of art's life. My basic contention, which I can demonstrate only in limited detail here—I am more interested in laying out the principles that determine the shape of the work of art which has mass mediation as its major horizon of expectation, its secret immanence—is that modernity begins with mass mediation, and modern art is art that incorporates or realizes mass mediation in its identity, that in effect lives only for mass mediation or has its existence only through mass mediation. This is more than acknowledging that the expectation of mass mediation—the simple assumption that the work of art exists for an audience—conditions its production. Such an assumption assumes the intervention of a commonly held ideology between the being of the work of art and the being of the audience. The shared ideology does the work of mediation, becomes the matrix of relationship between the work and its audience, the source of communion which nonetheless allows each its independence, the realm of discovery which permits for aesthetic perception and appreciation. This is the case in all traditional art—in the context I am trying to establish, the very definition of traditional art. But in modern art there is no ideology, only mass mediation—the belief in mass mediation as such is the ideology. In this sense, from Impressionism on, through Post-Impressionism and Cubism, and perhaps climactically in Dadaism, there is a progressive purging of ideology from art, even if it is ostensibly in the name of an alternate ideology, a new belief system, a more urgent dogma. This occurs even in the seemingly regressive—from the perspective of eliminating, whether by obviating or precluding, ideology—movements of Futurism and Surrealism, not to speak of the subtly regressive aspects of Constructivism, Suprematism, and De Stijl. By proposing an alternate ideology to the socially prevailing one— an ideology which can be realized only in art, not in social life—the very principle of ideology is undermined. That is, belief, while seemingly being redirected, is in fact neutralized, or at least subtly weakened or confused—put in conflict with itself, and so forced to defend itself. It loses legitimacy, particularly when it comes to operate only in the art context, finally becoming—after being drawn away from all socially real objects—a belief in nothing but art, thus subsumed in an art for art's sake credo. Undermined in its psychosocial specificity and simply reinforcing a finally naive or uninformed—unjustifiable, unself-justifying—belief in art, belief can bind itself to no ideology. Every ideology pales beside the fact of belief's commitment to art, which finally becomes nihilistic in effect if not in intention. Belief centered only in art is ultimately non-ideological, a blind commitment to an idol which, just because it offers a merely alternate, not truly binding ideology, seems to have clay feet. In this context, the open acceptance of art as non-ideological—perhaps most explicit in the anti-humanism of neo-peinture pure—prepares the way for its mass mediation, and the acceptance of its mass acceptance as the only source of its identity and power. Unadulterated—uncompromised, one might say—by ideology, by expectations of reasons to be believed in, i.e., by the assumption of ideology as the ground or via media of relationship to art, belief in art can become entirely a matter of its mass mediation. Works of art compete for space in the media, yearn for a collective identity—a fully publicized identity, a totality which is created by mass mediation—and in their very being assume a facility or efficiency of form that assures them mass mediation.

The question is how art's mimesis of mass mediation works, shows itself stylistically. What are the aspects of mass mediation that are appropriated by art? How does the work of art democratize its style sufficiently to be easily mass mediated? This is a pragmatic question—a question about the way the work's pragmatic end affects its semantics and syntactics. It is not a question of describing the work's fall from the grace of autonomy into false consciousness of itself—consciousness of itself as at home in the world, at one with itself because it has a place in the world. It is rather a question of instrumentation, ways in which the work of art achieves distributive efficiency, and as such fundamentally appears—makes a fundamental appearance, giving it the familiarity or habituality that makes it seem inevitable in its existence. This may also be a kind of false consciousness of it, but only if that inevitability is assumed to mask absoluteness of being.

What must be mimicked is the sublimity of the media—those aspects of the media that make it sublime, seemingly infinitely extensive, a truly mass mediation, i.e., creating a seemingly limitless "mass." These aspects are, simply, speed and spread, i.e., a sense of instantaneous access to limitless information, a sense of an eternal flow of information which can be dipped into at will, and given a momentary shape by the spontaneity of that will. The media give us a sense of easy access to an easy flow of information, the ease of access guaranteed by the ease with which information can be formulated—the ease with which reality can be reduced to information, which in part depends on the ease with which reality can be laid out, "flattened." Abstraction, which began as the difficult task of flattening a naturally "rounded" reality, in the name of its "inner truth," i.e., as a way of mediating its felt significance, has become a way of reducing reality to information—or of codifying reality—and quickly mediating information (not reality) in a formulation which is progressively streamlined into a formula. Ideally, this formulation includes the original sense of uncertainty that came with the reduction—the sense of something lost, of awkward absence accompanying the slick presence of abstract information. This uncertainty shows itself in a certain tentativeness, even fitfulness of layout, or else in a sense of the incompleteness of even the most seemingly complete form, the instability of the most seemingly stable format. The media are a mode of abstraction, flattening the reality of what it appropriates into a "fast" formulation—into fast information—that bespeaks a sense of abandoning reality—of leaving that sinking ship—as much as of firmly grasping it. This makes for the sublimity of the media formulation, the sense of its infinite malleability—endlessly manipulable information—yet steadiness, the sense of formulation as an eternally unfinished business and yet of a cleverly accomplished business, another demonstration of the cunning of reason.

In general, speed and spread are the desiderata of modernity, the instruments of its sublimity—the very roots of its necessity. Speed and spread are, in Kant's language, the dynamically sublime and the mathematically sublime respectively, shaping our sense of the modern social landscape as much as Kant saw them shaping our sense of nature's timeless landscape. Speed of movement of information is the modern form of the dynamically sublime—the qualitative experience of the modern sublime. The sense of an increasingly accelerated and increasingly unscannable flow of information—information that by the very momentum of its flow creates a sense of unstoppable power—is the source of the modern sense of absolute, ceaseless, and so finally infinite, energy. The sense that this limitless, fast flow of information can be given some kind of form, however limited and tentative—however much a manipulation or directing of that flow if not a complete control on it, and a manipulation that cannot even predict with certainty the effect it will achieve—gives us the quantitative experience of the modern sublime. The magnitude of the form seems to increase by reason of its perpetual need for reformulation, so that the form seems always just out of reach, and presents itself as a kind of absolute intelligibility mastering the absolute flow of information. But the absoluteness is speculative, the forms used seem tentative and inadequate and finally shabby and silly—trivial hypotheses rather than global theories—and what finally remains is a sense of the incomprehensible totality of information. The formulation of the information does not totalize it—as little as its flow can be stopped. The modern sublime issues form a sense of an infinite amount of information managed by a half-formulated—perpetually revised—code or form, serving more to more cue our response to the flow of information than to help us be fully informed.

In a sense, the explicit recognition of form as a code signalling an infinite abundance of information never to be encompassed and therefore only indirectly related to occurred with Minimalism. The boring nothingness or minimal nature of the finite gestalt is the "negative" of the infinite flow of information, the limit of its limitlessness, as it were. The infinity is not so much supposed by the gestalt as mediated through its finiteness, i.e., exists ideally as the aura of its

392   *Art in an Age of Mass Mediation*

simplicity. The importance of speed—of creating a fast image, an image in ever accelerating motion and thus seemingly disintegrating, becoming nothing but a matrix of forms—was already recognized by Cubism, if only implicitly—explicit in Futurism. But it was not really until Abstract Expressionism, particularly with Pollock, that the image was more or less left behind and the idea of instant and absolute and irreversible acceleration, making for an effect of spontaneous speed or instantaneous flow, was truly realized. Speed becomes an unspecifiable immediacy, immediately and freely transmitted energy. What image there is comes to us with such speed—speed of course is the final image—that we are left with a sense of unfathomable flux, a dynamic which exists only for itself and which finally cannot be managed even by a name. Now the minimalist gestalt— the minimal form—conveys the same sense of instantaneousness, only now through a namable form, which while it apparently has nothing to do with motion, implies the same untotalizable totality of information as Abstract Expressionist flux. In the Abstract Expressionist case speed has become so sublime it seems at a standstill, and in the Minimalist case form has become so sublime it seems facile, which makes each convey a transcendental illusion of totality. They are thus united as the optimum formulations of speed and spread respectively—as optimum fictionalizations of the infinite, in its manifestation as a flow and a form. Both have that immediacy of impact which is the ideal of mass mediation, and that comes only from the illusion of completely fluid information or completely managing form.

Neither Abstract Expressionism nor Minimalism are obviously media-determined movements. That they nonetheless reflect media methods and ideals shows the domination of mass mediation, as an ideal to be realized as well as a fully operational reality to be experienced. Pop art is explicitly media-oriented, and as such is more useful than Abstract Expressionism and Minimalism as a revelation of media ends. What it makes most explicit is the media's de-organicizing, if not explicit robotization, of reality. What the media do is encourage the conversion of everything organic into an abstract mechanism— information is a form of mechanism as well as flattened reality. Mechanism, as Karl Mannheim says, "denotes a system put together by a craftsman for some specific purpose, rather than a living being evolving spontaneously and seeking to maintain its internal balance."[1] The figures in Lichtenstein, Warhol, and Wesselman are mechanisms crafted as informational abstractions—systems of information in a formulation "individualized" by means of "art." Warhol in particular shows a strong tendency to reduce living beings to arty mechanisms, completely craft-determined (photography is the major source of determination of the mechanism of the figure for Warhol). Another artist—not explicitly Pop but also explicitly media-motivated—who shows the mechanistic effect of informational over-coding is Alex Katz. His figures—the portraits at the corner of 42nd Street and Seventh Avenue in New York City are most exemplary—are nothing more than a composite of cues crafted into a superficially totalizing mechanism, i.e., a mechanism which seems to have summed up all the "necessary" information about its organic (figural) source. But of course a sum is only a superficial specificity of instantaneous information, conveying the momentary exaltation of quickly achieved, facile abstraction.

This makes for a certain kind of hyper-visibility—Pop art achieves the same effect—which eliminates, in Oscar Wilde's words, all the wonder and mystery of the work of art, the effect of the belief that it is organic, and in some sense evolves spontaneously and works to maintain its equilibrium or wholeness. The residual organic quality of the work of art is dismissed by the hyper-obvious effect of the fully mechanized work. As a mechanism the work is democratically accessible—like a scientific experiment, it can presumably be duplicated by everyone—and a summary of collectively available information. The democratic accessibility achieved by the hyper-visible effect is perhaps the ultimate media effect. It is, of course, epistemologically, what photography aims at, which in part explains why already in the 19th century artists were turning to photography: not only as a mnemonic device but for its effect of hyper-visibility, or hyper-immediacy, as it might also be called. The Cubist use of collage by Braque and Picasso is also a way of achieving the hyper-visible, democratic effect that the manipulation of information into a mechanism can give. (Cubist paintings and sculptures are perhaps the first explicit mechanisms in art, i.e., the first works of art that want to be flat information rather than rounded reality—a new ideal of mimesis, or rather a pseudo-mimesis of reality, putting it in deliberately reduced or flattened and mechanical form.)

In general, mass mediation—easy and rapid accessibility—of information leads to the creation of a new public rhetoric—the rhetoric of information—that comes to dominate and finally empty of meaning the ideal and idea of personal, organic style, which becomes no more than an ability to manipulate information with the mechanism of art. While superficially replacing what Husserl called the natural attitude with the meaningful, sophisticated information that results from a phenomenological reduction of reality, the mass media approach to art oversocializes it into a mechanism, which in the end weakens its power. The power of art to effect a subtle identification between viewer and work of art is undermined by the increasing mechanization of art into a democratic system of information. The viewer can no longer turn to art to find his own spontaneity and equilibrium—to recover from the art context what may be hard to have in actual experience. And since in the end he can find all the information about reality he needs from reality, he turns less and less to art, even though it is more and more accessible. It has become accessible just so he will turn to it, not forget its existence. But he turns to art to resist information—to resist the informational reduction of reality—and to recover his sense of his own rounded reality, and the roundedness of reality (even if this has to be accomplished by "informational" strategies that do not seem reductive but rather integrative). Since art no longer resists being information, it is less and less useful in the attempt to recover the sense of oneself as a living being from the field of information—to recover from being a unit of information in someone else's reductive field. The fact that art no longer works against the reduction of reality to a flat information abstraction in the name of a return to roundedness—and once the use of reductive informational abstraction or the flattening of reality was a way of restoring the sense of its living roundedness or spontaneity and equilibrium (spontaneity issuing from equilibrium and never unbalancing life)—indicates just how much the media have become the model for art. Adorno's idea that the media administer or filter culture has to be superseded by the subtler idea that the media, by their creation of information, create the modern actuality of art. To serve our roundedness, or at least free us from our flatness, our existence as information for others, art must resist its media model. But how this is to be done remains unclear, for we are dominated and formed by the media.

Index